P9-AZX-878

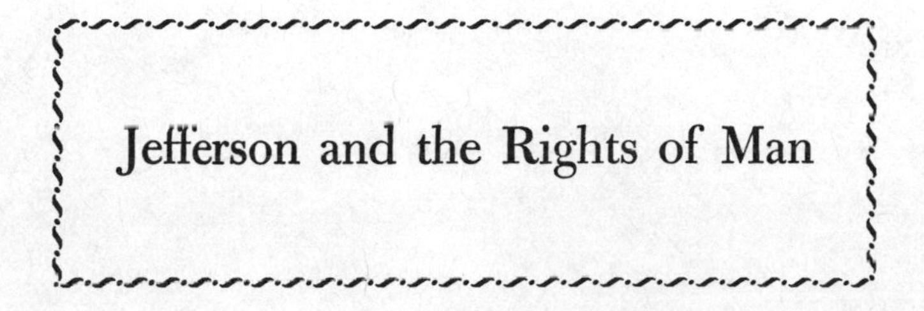
Jefferson and the Rights of Man

JEFFERSON AND HIS TIME

VOLUME TWO

Jefferson and the Rights of Man

BY DUMAS MALONE

LITTLE, BROWN AND COMPANY
BOSTON • TORONTO • LONDON

10

BP

Published simultaneously
in Canada by McClelland and Stewart Limited

PRINTED IN THE UNITED STATES OF AMERICA

This work as a whole is for

ELISABETH GIFFORD MALONE

This volume is for

PRINCETON UNIVERSITY

Home of the greatest edition of Jefferson's papers

and the Alma Mater of my son

Contents

THE STRUGGLE WITHIN THE GOVERNMENT

A FEUD BREAKS OUT

Introduction

THIS book, which is a unit in itself, is the second volume in the series I am writing under the general title, *Jefferson and His Time*, and a sequel to *Jefferson the Virginian* (1743–1784). That volume carried the story through the American Revolution and ended with Jefferson's departure for France. The present one (1784–1792) includes his European mission, which lasted through the opening months of the French Revolution, and all but the final year of his service in his own country as the first secretary of state under the new Constitution. In the perspective of history the winning of American independence was a cosmic event, and Jefferson, during the period of his life that we have already described, proclaimed and sought to implement a philosophy which he regarded as timeless and universal, but the setting of the previous volume was chiefly local. To me the Virginia of his youth and early manhood will ever be a charming scene, but Paris and Versailles in the time of Louis XVI, London in the reign of George III, and New York and Philadelphia in the presidency of George Washington provided a far richer and more colorful background than Monticello and Williamsburg; and Jefferson participated in far more complicated movements and events in this second period of his public life than in his first. Furthermore, as the bibliography shows more specifically, the materials for these years, while sometimes disappointing, are in general so extensive as to be positively embarrassing.

The complexity of the events and the vastness of the materials provide a sufficient explanation, I hope, for my inability to carry this volume as far in point of time as I formerly expected and indiscreetly predicted. When I wrote the introduction to the earlier book, assuming that four volumes would be all the publishers or public could be expected to stand for, I was planning to carry Jefferson to the presidency in the second. It became obvious, however, that this would be impossible if the scale of the first volume were maintained and the far more extensive materials were exploited to a comparable degree. Accordingly, with the generous concurrence of my publishers, I set out to find another logical terminal point.

Washington's unanimous re-election to the presidency at the end of the year 1792 provides a good one. This is a convenient date in the domestic story, for a new chapter in the history of American political parties began thereafter. The period of eight and a half years that is covered in the present volume has biographical unity, since Jefferson was concerned primarily with foreign affairs throughout the whole of it. There was a marked change in the international situation early in the next year. Great Britain was then drawn into the European war and Jefferson was faced with a new set of problems as secretary of state. Some loose ends of diplomacy, left dangling in the summer of 1792, will need to be tied up in the third volume of the series, but to all practical purposes it will start with the year 1793 and extend to the beginning of Jefferson's presidency in March, 1801. That volume will trace the rise of political parties which existed in only rudimentary form in 1792, and it will be set on a background of world war and revolutionary violence, while the present one largely falls within a period of general peace and relatively philosophical revolution. It is unwise to make precise predictions in advance, but I see no reason why the presidency cannot be kept within the limits of a fourth volume, and the years of retirement covered by a fifth, if the strength of the author and the patience of the publishers and the public will hold out that long.

Throughout the months since I wrote the introduction to *Jefferson the Virginian* I have kept in mind the purposes that I stated there for the work as a whole, namely, that it be comprehensive and relate the man to his times and be true to his own chronology. A work of historical biography like this, predominantly narrative in form, does not lend itself to ready summary, but I will make a few observations in the light of these avowed purposes.

The goal of comprehensiveness, that is, of showing the whole man and not merely certain segments of him, is difficult of attainment at all stages of Jefferson's career and is specially so during his years in France. He was a public official, engaged in diplomatic activities which seemed relatively unrewarding at the time but are of genuine historical importance since they foreshadowed later policies and attitudes. I trust that I have treated these with sufficient fullness. His time was far less absorbed by routine tasks, however, than it was after he became secretary of state at home, and the vaunted scene of Europe offered this man of vast energy and curious mind personal opportunities such as he had never had before and was never to have again. Despite his nostalgia and his sense of the futility of Parisian life, it seems that in France

Jefferson was better able to do the sort of things he wanted to do, and to be the sort of man he wanted to be, than he ever was afterward while in public office. Never again did he live so well or indulge his tastes so freely. Never again, until his final retirement from public life, could he be to such an extent and for so long a time a detached philosopher. He may have preferred the rural atmosphere of Monticello, as he always said he did, but this highly cultivated man became well oriented in France, and he lived there a life of extraordinary intellectual and spiritual elevation.

He was well aware of the dangers implicit in the political and economic situation, but for him this was the hour of the full flowering of the Enlightenment, and he never gave clearer proof of his undying belief that men and society can be saved by means of knowledge. This faith, coupled with a "zeal to promote the general good of mankind by an interchange of useful things," provides the clue to his manifold activities. It was not merely that he loved music, though he said it was the favorite passion of his soul; it was not only that he gazed rapturously on beautiful buildings like the Maison Carrée at Nîmes; it was not merely that he found in scientific inquiry a supreme delight. He was primarily concerned with the uses of all these things. His spirit, as I understand it, is best set forth, perhaps, in the chapter entitled "Minister of Enlightenment," though there are plenty of clues and examples elsewhere in this book. He believed that men could become free and happy if they came to know more about everything, and there was a utilitarian cast to all his thinking. Thus when he spread information in Europe about his own country, when he sent home books and architectural drawings, when he reported agricultural conditions in France and Italy and Germany, he was in the fullest sense a public servant.

At the same time, this was one of the richest periods of his life in private friendship. He had to argue with the officials of other countries in his efforts to open the channels of trade to his own country, but political controversy imposed no such barriers as it did afterwards at home and he was free to be what he liked to be – everybody's friend. He had contacts everywhere, though he set slight value on those with the world of fashion, and his most intimate associations, by and large, were with Americans. Without attempting the impossible task of describing all of his associations, I have tried to lay the emphasis where I believe he laid it: on his own domestic circle and the Americans who gathered round him as host, patron, and friend; on the little artistic group which included Maria Cosway, Angelica Church, and Madame de Corny; on Lafayette and liberal nobles like La Rochefoucauld and Condorcet, who were so close to him in political spirit; and on certain of the men of science and learning.

The most important single observation that should be made here about the relation of the man to his times is that he continued to view his age as an enlightened liberal. The best single clue to his political attitudes, as well as his intellectual activities, is to be found in his determination that men should be set free and kept free in order to move forward in the light of ever-expanding knowledge. Like other men of state he had secondary objectives, but he rarely if ever lost sight of his clear-purposed goal of human freedom and happiness or failed to reach his important judgments in the light of it. Among the statesmen of his time he was most notable for his high purposefulness and it would be a grave fault in a biographer to minimize it. On the other hand, as one sees him in thoughtful action day by day, he seems to have been in the best sense an opportunist with respect to immediate ends and particular means. He was neither a doctrinaire philosopher nor a self-seeking politician, but a statesman who effected a distinctive combination of idealism with common sense.

The two greatest events or series of events of this decade were the outbreak of the French Revolution and the establishment of a new government in the United States. One of these was a liberating movement which carried with it grave dangers of destructiveness. The other was constructive, but seemed to many people to be moving toward centralized power and away from human rights. To say that Jefferson approved both developments sounds more paradoxical than it is. Actually, he approved them both *with qualifications,* and judged them both in terms of human values.

Highly exaggerated statements about his personal part in the preliminaries and first stages of the French Revolution were afterwards made by his political foes. In reality this personal part was slight, though the influence of the American example was great. As an observer he was by no means uncritical, and he reported to America with extraordinary fullness the course of events through the summer of 1789. Insofar as he exerted a direct personal influence he did so primarily on Lafayette and a few other kindred spirits. The record leaves no possible doubt that it was a moderating influence. No one was more aware than he of the imperative need for drastic reformation in France, but, despite certain stock quotations which keep reappearing in the history books, what he advocated can be much better described as "reformation" than as "revolution." He favored the rule of reason, not the rule of force.

He had strongly supported the successful movement for the political independence of his own country, and, in the Declaration of Independence, he had justified this revolt against what he regarded as tyranny on philosophical grounds which he deemed universal. But this does not mean that he advocated the use of force to attain immediate economic and social ends. He was no prophet of class warfare. He opposed all forms of political, military, and intellectual tyranny; and he championed self-government, believing that, after this had been considerably attained, economic and social ills would be progressively corrected by the orderly processes of legislation. "Rebellion to tyrants is obedience to God"—this was his motto, and he steadfastly hoped that the spirit of resistance would never die. That is the real meaning of his famous saying that is so often misapplied: "The tree of liberty must be refreshed from time to time with the blood of patriots and tyrants." In the light of previous and subsequent history, this statement may be regarded as thoroughly realistic; but when viewed in its own setting of time and circumstance it was no invitation to bloodshed and certainly not to social revolution. As any reader of Chapter IX in this volume can see, this was a private remark which was related, not to the French Revolution, but to the Shays Rebellion in the United States and to the repressive spirit which had been excited there before the constitutional convention met. Jefferson feared harsh repression at home because he had seen the results of it abroad; and he believed that traditional American freedom, even though it occasionally manifested itself in violence, was infinitely preferable to European tyranny. Many months before there were revolutionary excesses in France, he had concluded that his own free country was actually more orderly than that state was under absolutist rule.

His hope for France was not that the monarchy would be overthrown all of a sudden, but that it would assume a modified form, and head in the right direction—that is, toward individual freedom and self-government. He rejoiced when the government became committed to the fundamental and to his mind universal principles that were embodied in the Declaration of the Rights of Man and the Citizen. Beyond that point, however, he was an opportunist, and his optimistic philosophy enabled him to be patient when progress seemed slow. He was always fearful lest the impatient reformers would move too fast and create a reaction which would cause them to lose their gains. Furthermore, he saw clearly that the politically unschooled people of France were not ready for such a degree of self-government as Americans enjoyed. The combination in him — passionate and unyielding devotion to fundamental principles, with patience in the actual working out of reforms — was a rare one, and in it, perhaps, lies the major secret of his political success. It may be commended to our own generation as an alternative to violent revolution on the one hand and blind and stupid reaction on the other.

The Revolution developed faster than he expected or desired, but, while he was in France, the ills were less than he had feared. There were grave dangers on the horizon, a number of which he pointed out, but he viewed the situation with deep satisfaction. He approved the Revolution on two main grounds. It marked the victory of reason over ignorance, superstition, and hereditary privilege. Furthermore, it represented the adoption by the French of principles which might be and often were called American. This was no triumph of a foreign ideology. It was a recognition of eternal truths which Americans had successfully proclaimed. The matter is summed up by a later saying of his which is so apt that I have used it more than once: "The appeal to the rights of man, which had been made in the United States, was taken up by France, first of the European nations."[1] He further summed up his own attitude as follows: "I considered a successful reformation of government in France, as ensuring a general reformation through Europe, and the resurrection, to a new life, of their people, now ground to dust by the abuses of the governing powers."[2] His main concern, during his last months in France, was not that this "reformation" should be complete, but that it should be successfully begun.

The French Revolution did not become a major issue in American politics during the rest of the period covered by this book. It still seemed to him a "philosophical" revolution in 1791, when he was unwittingly involved in a controversy with his old friend John Adams growing out of the American publication of the first part of Paine's *Rights of Man.* (This is described in Chapter XXI.) He continued to support the rights of man against hereditary privilege — but so did the vast majority of the American people, and the forces of political reaction in his own country could not make much capital of the French situation as yet. They did exploit it afterwards, but most of that story belongs in another volume. The great political struggle of this period in the United States was fought on domestic lines, and the feud between Jefferson and Hamilton would have arisen if there

[1] Ford, I, 147.
[2] Ford, I, 129.

never had been a French Revolution. It could hardly have arisen, however, if one of the contestants had not been a champion of the rights of man, in the spirit of the Declaration of Independence. He was always that, through revolution and reaction, and more than anything else this attitude is the basis of his abiding fame.

His relation with the new American government is the major theme of the latter half of this book, and I deal in Chapter IX with his attitude toward the Constitution while he was in France. His fundamental sympathy with the constructive spirit of his friend Madison and others in their efforts to create a more effective government, and with the larger national purposes of George Washington, may be safely assumed from the fact that he himself took office as secretary of state. The best answer to the charges of disloyalty to the Constitution and Washington that were afterwards made by Hamilton and the latter's partisans is provided by Jefferson's own contemporary words and actions. Without attempting to summarize these here, I can at least say that he proved to be a devoted public servant in America, just as he had been in France, that his respect for the first President throughout this period amounted to reverence, and that he was so busy trying to make this political experiment a success that he seemed for a time almost to have forgotten the "reformation" in France. Coupled with the constructive spirit of so many of the leaders of the era, however, were certain political tendencies which he regarded as reactionary and he was deeply disturbed by these from the moment that he became fully aware of them. He summed them up in the term "monarchical," and in view of the persistence of the republican form of government in the United States this now sounds exaggerated. What he meant was that certain American leaders, though not the people generally, wanted to turn back toward the system of hereditary privilege and oligarchic power from which the country had considerably escaped in 1776 and from which France was now struggling to emerge. He used the language of his day, not ours, opposing "monarchy" and "aristocracy," and he thought primarily in political terms, not economic.

In certain important respects the financial system which Hamilton was establishing was foreign to his thinking. Here the customary labels will not fit, for on financial questions Jefferson was characteristically conservative, while Hamilton, who was creating fluid capital by governmental act, was much more the innovator. The chapters that deal with the successive stages of Hamilton's financial policy and Jefferson's attitude toward it should leave no doubt that the sort of property the latter understood best and valued most was real property, not securities. This lover of the land did not like the sort of financial and industrial economy that the Secretary of the Treasury was promoting, but, characteristically, he objected to his colleague's policies first and most on moral and political grounds. He deplored the mania of speculation which accompanied them and the "corruption" of the legislature by financial interest, and he deeply feared the "system" which Hamilton was building up, regarding this as potentially if not actually despotic. Yet he co-operated with his colleague cordially at first, and throughout his life he maintained a considerable degree of flexibility in economic matters. To describe him as an agrarian is to employ an insufficient term and to rob him of part of his universality. The thread of consistency which runs through his entire career and unites him with lovers of liberty in all generations was not his attitude toward a specific economic system. It was his eternal faith in the right of men to rule themselves and his undying hostility to any sort of despotism. If we may use modern terms in this connection, he regarded the Hamiltonian system as tending toward totalitarianism.

This is the fundamental reason why he opposed it, but he first clashed with his historic rival over questions of foreign policy. The main lines of his own policy were worked out while he was in France on what he regarded as a realistic appraisal of the international situation, especially with respect to trade. Writers have often termed this policy pro-French, but it can be better described as anti-British and better still as pro-American. It antedated the French Revolution and was wholly independent of political ideology, since Jefferson distinctly preferred the British governmental system to the French at the time. Throughout his career his foreign policy was flexible – much more so than Hamilton's, I believe – and its consistency lay in his opposition, in varying degree, to those countries which, in his opinion, most threatened the security and prosperity of the United States. Throughout this period these were Great Britain and, to a lesser degree, Spain. The complications which arose from general European war belong chiefly in the next volume. The main points to be made here are that Jefferson as secretary of state carried on the policy he had adopted while in France, and that Hamilton's interference with this, for political and economic reasons that seemed good to him, was probably the first cause of the personal feud between them.

In my opinion, Hamilton was clearly the earlier and much the greater offender against official proprieties, though he and his partisans sought to create a very different impression. The antagonism between the two men was too deep-rooted to be explained primarily in terms of personality, but Jefferson's fears about his colleague's policies were unquestionably accentuated by his growing awareness of the powerful position which the Secretary of the Treasury had assumed in the new government and by the aggressiveness and imperiousness of the man himself.

In the effort to understand the clash within the government I have paid so much attention to the organization and operations of the executive departments that at times this work may read like the history of an administration. To me the study of the actual workings of the Washington government has been distinctly illuminating. In the footnotes and bibliography I have gratefully acknowledged some recent treatments of the subject, but scholars and writers have paid relatively little attention to it and I believe that I have corrected a number of continuing misapprehensions about the President's relations with the department heads and the actual formulation of policies. (This matter is dealt with in Chapter XV and elsewhere.) Jefferson performed services in the domestic sphere which deserve to be emphasized afresh, such as those connected with patents and the establishment of the new Federal City, and I have been impressed anew not only with the diversity of his talents but also with the closeness of his personal tie with George Washington. On the other hand, the Department of State was dwarfed by the Treasury as an administrative organization, and the procedure in these early years served to facilitate Hamilton's designs and to restrict Jefferson's influence in larger matters of policy to a degree which I did not realize before I began this book. Besides having no such access to Congress as the Secretary of the Treasury, the Secretary of State had no chance to pass on his colleague's legislative proposals before they were presented. Some of the implications of this situation, it seems to me, have been generally overlooked.

Besides seeking to understand governmental organization and procedure, I have tried to understand, not merely Jefferson, but Washington, Hamilton, and the other major actors on the scene. Others must judge whether or not there is any freshness in the interpretation of these men, but I can at least point out a few of the changes that this study has brought in my own mind. Washington, whom Jefferson and Madison admired so greatly and viewed so uncritically at this stage, emerges as an even more commanding and appealing figure than I had expected him to be. On the other hand, I am sorry to say, Hamilton comes out of my investigations worse than I had expected. No reader need accept any of my judgments, but they are based on the fairest reading that I could give the records of the time, including Hamilton's own writings. It has been said before now that he was his own worst enemy, and I believe that his own words, as cited in the last chapters of this book, clearly prove it. As I have lived through these events in spirit my wonderment has been, not that Jefferson resented the words and actions of his brilliant, egotistical, and overbearing colleague, but that he maintained so long an attitude of impersonality and was so slow to anger. I have tried to judge Hamilton's bold policies on their merits, but I cannot escape the conviction that he, more than any other major American statesman of his time, lusted for personal as well as national power. No doubt there was more personal charm in the man than appears in his writings. I may have missed something that I should have found, and it is partially for that reason that I am reproducing what I regard as the most charming of his portraits.

In this volume, as in the one that preceded it, I have tried to show the central figure as a living man and growing mind in a changing world, not as a statue in a niche or a portrait on the wall. Jefferson was never static, and in this period of his life he had to adjust himself to momentous changes in external circumstances. This part of the story of his mind is essentially one of adjustment. His years in France were a time of extraordinary inquisitiveness, acquisitiveness, and intellectual stimulation, but they served to confirm him in the fundamental philosophy he had already adopted, not to give him a new one. He sounded more democratic in France than he ever had before, but his most striking utterances were made *before* the revolution and were based on the contrast between European absolutism and American freedom and self-government. The main political lesson that pre-revolutionary France taught him was what Americans should avoid; but, as we have already said, he recoiled against the dangers of sudden change in an old society and urged his liberal-minded friends to make haste slowly. Thus one gains an impression of unusual consistency in his basic thinking, coupled with a rare ability to adapt himself to the circumstances and conditions of the moment.

The importance of keeping the study of such a man true to his own chronology will be obvious, I believe, to any reader who has the patience to follow him step by step through this narrative. I don't try to sum him up completely anywhere and will certainly not do so here. I will say something, however, about the degree of my success or failure in determining when and how he first became a politician, in the sense that we now commonly use the term. He certainly did not become one while in France, where he was an appointed official who rejoiced that he could serve his constituency, the American people, without being directly accountable to them or having to curry popular favor. He did not think of himself as a politician when he became secretary of state and was directly responsible to nobody but the President. Readers of this book may be surprised, as I myself was somewhat, to learn how little direct part he played in partisan politics at this stage. One reason is that the historic American parties had only begun to take form by the year 1792, when Washington was unanimously re-elected. Another is that, contrary to a very common tradition, Jefferson was extraordinarily scrupulous as an official and stuck closely to his own exacting business. By contrast, Hamilton was incessantly active in the elections of 1792, and if either of the two men should be described as a manipulator and intriguer, it was not Jefferson, but he. I am driven to the conclusion that the traditional picture of Jefferson the politician, which still lingers in the history books, is largely the creation of Hamilton and his partisans. As the latter chapters of this volume show, they also did much to establish him as a symbol of anti-Hamiltonianism, building him up as a popular figure by the ferocity of their personal attacks. These were largely unwarranted except on the ground that the two men and their philosophies were fundamentally antagonistic. By the end of the year 1792 Jefferson was the first name in the political group which called itself republican. (I deliberately refrain from capitalizing the word as yet.) This was not because of his personal political activities, but because of what he stood for and what he was. I shall have to wait to see whether or not the statement will still seem true at the end of another volume.

To say just how Jefferson himself emerges from my investigations for the present volume would amount to retelling most of the story, but I can say that he has withstood microscopic examination even better than I expected. This is not to claim that his judgment was always right, but no one can read his voluminous state papers without gaining increased respect for his ability, and, considering the enormous body of personal papers he left, they show amazingly few spots on his character. His chief weakness, and up to this point he has not shown it often, was a defect of his politeness and amiability which caused him to seem deceptive. (See Chapter XXI and the Freneau episode.) This was also a reflection of an extreme distaste for personal controversy. With the possible exception of Washington, he was the most sensitive of the major public men of his era, and he was far more disposed to battle for principles and policies than for his own interests. Perhaps that is the real secret of his eventual political success, as it assuredly is of his enduring fame. He was a true and pure symbol of the rights of man because, in his own mind, the cause was greater than himself.

Special acknowledgments for aid rendered me and kindnesses shown me in connection with this book are made elsewhere. At this point, therefore, I will content myself with expressing gratitude to Thomas Jefferson for the extraordinarily rich and incessantly useful life he lived and for the amazing records that he kept.

DUMAS MALONE

NEW YORK, *June 1, 1951*

Chronology

1784

July 5 TJ sails with his daughter Martha from Boston on the *Ceres*.
Aug. 6 TJ and his daughter arrive in Paris.
30 The commissioners (Franklin, Adams, and TJ) hold their first meeting at Passy.
Oct. 16 TJ rents a house on the Cul-de-sac Taitbout.
Nov. 11 The commissioners make their first report to Congress.
29 William Short arrives by this date.

1785

Jan. 26 Lafayette brings TJ news of the death of his youngest daughter in Virginia.
May 2 TJ receives notification of his election by Congress to succeed Franklin as the Minister to the French Court.
10 The first printing of the *Notes on Virginia* is completed.
23 The Adams family leave for London before this date.
July 15 Franklin leaves Passy on his way home to America.
Aug. 15 TJ proposes to Vergennes the abolition of the tobacco monopoly.
Sept. 24 William Short is invited to become TJ's private secretary.
Oct. 17 TJ moves to the Hôtel de Langeac, where he lives during the rest of his stay in France.

1786

Jan. 7 TJ has conversed with Buffon by this time.
Feb. 8 The French committee on American commerce has its first meeting.
Mar. 11 TJ arrives in London to join John Adams.
Apr. 26 TJ sets out from London for Paris.
June 13 TJ has started the model of the Virginia Capitol on its way.
Aug. 2 John Trumbull arrives in Paris and stays with TJ.
Sept. 18 TJ sprains his wrist about this time.
Oct. 12 TJ writes his "My Head and My Heart" letter to Maria Cosway.
22 Calonne writes TJ about the dispositions taken to favor American commerce.

1787

January The Shays Rebellion occurs in Massachusetts.
Feb. 13 Vergennes dies.

Feb. 22 TJ attends the opening of the Assembly of Notables.
28 TJ sets out from Paris for the south of France.
June 10 TJ returns to Paris after his trip.
July 15 Polly Jefferson joins her father and sister.
August TJ writes Jay, Adams, and others about the prospects of European war.
Sept. 5 TJ takes possession of his retreat at Mont Calvaire.
Oct. 12 TJ is elected as the Minister to France for three more years.
Nov. 13 TJ writes William S. Smith about supposed anarchy in America and the new Constitution.
Dec. 31 TJ learns that the substance of Calonne's letter of Oct. 22, 1786, has been incorporated in an *arrêt.*

1788

Mar. 4 TJ sets out from Paris to join John Adams in the Netherlands.
16 Adams and TJ complete financial negotiations in Amsterdam about this time.
30 TJ sets out from Amsterdam for a trip up the Rhine.
April 23 TJ returns to Paris and soon introduces the subject of a consular convention to Montmorin.
June 19 TJ sends travel notes to Shippen and Rutledge.
July 30 TJ informs Montmorin of the ratification of the American Constitution.
Nov. 14 TJ and Montmorin sign the Consular Convention.
19 TJ asks a leave of absence.

1789

Feb. 23 Gouverneur Morris is in Paris by this date.
Apr. 30 George Washington is inaugurated as President in New York.
May 5 TJ witnesses the opening of the Estates General.
June 3 TJ sends Lafayette a proposed charter for France.
July 4 TJ gives a dinner to Americans in Paris and receives a testimonial.
6 TJ considers Lafayette's Declaration of Rights.
14 TJ learns of the storming of the Bastille from M. de Corny.
Aug. 26 The French Declaration of Rights is adopted. Leaders of the Patriot party dine at TJ's house about this time.
27 TJ receives permission to return home on leave.
Sept. 11 Alexander Hamilton is commissioned as secretary of the treasury.
26 The nomination of TJ as secretary of state is approved by the Senate. TJ and his party leave Paris.
Oct. 22 The Jeffersons embark on the *Clermont.*
Nov. 23 The Jeffersons disembark at Norfolk.
Dec. 9 TJ is welcomed by the Virginia Assembly in Richmond.
12 At Eppington, TJ receives Washington's offer of the secretaryship of state.
23 The Jeffersons arrive at Monticello.

1790

Jan. 14 Hamilton communicates to Congress his first Report on the Public Credit.
Feb. 11 Madison speaks in Congress on the funding proposals.
14 TJ accepts the appointment as secretary of state.
23 Martha Jefferson is married to Thomas Mann Randolph, Jr.
Mar. 1 TJ leaves Monticello for Richmond.
21 TJ arrives in New York and reports to George Washington.
Apr. 10 The first Patent Act is approved.
12 The Assumption measure is defeated in the House.
May 1 TJ begins to have a headache which largely incapacitates him for a month.
15 Washington's life is despaired of about this time.
June 2 TJ removes to 57 Maiden Lane.
20 The Residence-Assumption "Bargain" is reached about this time.
July 12 TJ outlines a policy in case of war between Great Britain and Spain over the Nootka Sound affair.
13 George Beckwith arrives in New York as an informal British representative about this time.
TJ submits his Report on Coinage, Weights, and Measures.
Aug. 12 Congress recesses.
15 TJ leaves for Rhode Island with the presidential party.
28 TJ replies to Washington's queries about the possible movement of British troops through the United States.
Sept. 1 TJ leaves New York for Monticello, arriving Sept. 19.
Nov. 23 TJ arrives in Philadelphia to resume his duties, having left home Nov. 8.
Dec. 11 TJ begins to take possession of Thomas Leiper's house.
13 Hamilton presents his second Report on the Public Credit.
15 TJ reports to Washington on the mission of Gouverneur Morris to Great Britain.
16 The Virginia Assembly adopts resolutions against Assumption.

1791

Jan. 19 Washington submits to the Senate TJ's Report on French protests against the Tonnage Laws.
24 TJ writes his first letters to the Commissioners of the Federal District.
Feb. 4 TJ's Report on the cod and whale fisheries is submitted to Congress.
14 Washington reports to Congress on the Morris mission.
15 TJ gives Washington his opinion against the constitutionality of the United States Bank.
23 Hamilton gives Washington his opinion upholding the constitutionality of the Bank.
The movement for commercial discrimination against the British is checked in Congress.

Feb. *28* TJ offers a clerkship to Freneau, who declines it.
Mar. *3* The last session of the First Congress ends.
May *8* TJ explains to Washington his connection with the publication of Paine's *Rights of Man.*
17 TJ leaves Philadelphia to join Madison on a Northern trip.
June *8* The first of the PUBLICOLA letters of John Quincy Adams appears.
19 TJ returns to Philadelphia after his Northern trip.
July *17* TJ writes John Adams about the episode of *The Rights of Man.*
19 Petit, TJ's maître d'hôtel, rejoins him.
Aug. *12* Ternant, the new French Minister, is received by the President.
16 TJ appoints Freneau as translator.
30 TJ again writes John Adams.
Sept. *8* TJ and Madison attend a meeting of the Commissioners, at which the decision is reached to give the name Washington to the Federal City and Columbia to the District.
12 TJ arrives at Monticello.
Oct. 7 Hamilton has a conference with Ternant.
12 TJ leaves Monticello with his daughter Polly.
21 George Hammond, the first British Minister, arrives in Philadelphia.
22 TJ returns to Philadelphia.
24 The first session of the Second Congress begins.
31 The first number of Freneau's *National Gazette* appears.
Nov. *4* St. Clair is defeated in the Northwest.
Dec. *5* Hamilton's Report on Manufactures is communicated to the House.
15 TJ summarizes to Hammond the British actions contravening the peace treaty.
19 Hammond reports his first "long and confidential" conversation with Hamilton.
22 The nominations of Pinckney, Morris, and Short are submitted to the Senate.

1792

Jan. *11* TJ's Report on negotiations with Spain is submitted to the Senate, with the nominations of Carmichael and Short as commissioners.
15 TJ has decided to retire from office at the end of Washington's first term.
Feb. *27* TJ, acting for Washington, dismisses L'Enfant.
28 TJ and Washington talk about retirement.
Mar. *5* Hammond presents the British case with respect to the peace treaty.
8 Attack on Hamilton's special relations with Congress is narrowly defeated.
9 William Duer suspends payment, in a time of financial panic, and is soon arrested.
10 The House adopts resolutions regarding the new French Constitution.

Mar. 15 The *National Gazette* begins to attack Hamilton's policies more vigorously.

18 TJ drafts instructions for Carmichael and Short regarding their negotiations with Spain.

Apr. 4 TJ gives his opinion that the apportionment act is unconstitutional and Washington shortly vetoes it.

May 5 Washington consults Madison about a farewell address.

23 TJ writes Washington about the causes of public discontent and urges his continuance in office (letter received May 31).

26 Hamilton attacks TJ and Madison in a letter to Edward Carrington.

29 TJ replies to Hammond.

July 10 TJ talks with Washington about the causes of discontent.

13 TJ leaves Philadelphia for Monticello.

25 Hamilton launches a newspaper attack on Freneau and TJ.

Aug. 3 Hamilton receives Washington's letter of July 29, giving 21 objections to his "system" as reported by TJ.

18 Hamilton replies to the 21 objections.

23, 26 Washington writes TJ and Hamilton, deploring dissensions.

Sept. 8 First Aristides paper, defending TJ, appears.

9 TJ and Hamilton reply to Washington.

15 Hamilton publishes his first paper as Catullus.

22 First paper of TJ's "Vindication" (by Monroe and Madison) appears.

26 Madison publishes "A Candid State of Parties."

Oct. 5 TJ returns to Philadelphia.

31 Pamphlet against TJ, *Politicks and Views of a Certain Party*, is published by this time.

It is generally assumed by the leaders that Washington will accept re-election.

Nov. 16 By this date TJ is informed of republican gains in the congressional elections.

Dec. 9 TJ informs Leiper that he will give up his house after three months.

17 TJ makes a private note on the Reynolds affair.

19 TJ is sure of the re-election of Adams as vice president by now.

22 Hamilton's last paper as Catullus appears.

31 The last paper in TJ's "Vindication" appears.

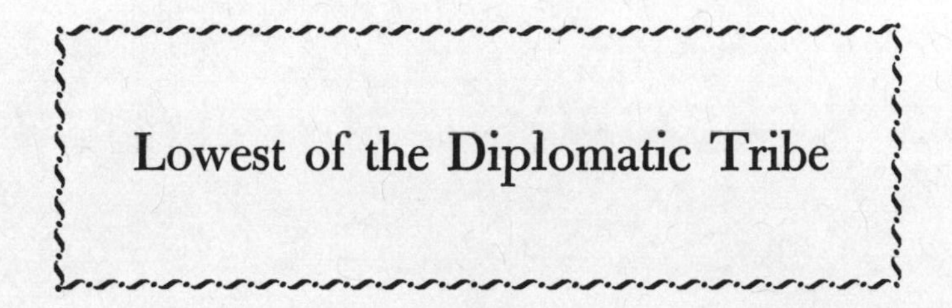

Lowest of the Diplomatic Tribe

[I]

Introduction to Paris

EARLY in August, 1784, Thomas Jefferson and his daughter Martha – familiarly known as Patsy – arrived in Paris. It took them a month to get there from Boston, whence they had sailed somewhat by accident, and five and a half years to get back to their home in Virginia, where his dearest memories lay buried with his wife. He did not anticipate that long a stay in France, for he went there on a special mission limited to two years, even though its objectives were as broad as the face of Europe. At this place, or any other that might seem appropriate, he and John Adams and Benjamin Franklin were to negotiate for the young American Republic as many treaties of amity and commerce as they could. The famous trio of the Declaration of Independence was reassembling in a far larger and more renowned city than Philadelphia.

The eldest commissioner, then much the most eminent of the three, had been serenely awaiting the coming of the others. The venerable Dr. Franklin was living in the village of Passy, west of the city and adjoining the Bois de Boulogne, and was fully entitled to rest on his bright laurels. Since he was seventy-eight years old, had "the stone" (in his bladder), and was pained by the jolting of a carriage, he remained as much as he could at Passy and let the world come to him. Jefferson promptly paid his respects to him after his own arrival, and when the commissioners began to hold formal sessions they did so at the old man's house. Franklin always liked his agreeable colleague from Virginia, and had wanted him to come to France with him eight years earlier; he was not at all displeased at the report already going the rounds that Jefferson would succeed him as minister to the Court of Versailles some day.[1]

[1] TJ's Account Book, Aug. 6, 10, 1784; Franklin to John Adams, July 4, 1784, in the latter's *Works,* VIII, 207.

NOTE. Explanation of the abbreviations used in the footnotes and further details concerning the works referred to may be found in "Symbols and Short Titles" and "Select Critical Biography" at the end of this book.

John Adams, who was also familiar with the French scene, was a week behind Jefferson in reaching the city. He had recently been in the United Netherlands with his son John Quincy, and had gone from there to London to meet his wife and daughter, whom he was hungry to see after more than four years' separation. Bringing his family with him to France, he took them to the village of Auteuil, beyond Passy and adjoining the Bois de Boulogne, where he loved to walk. It was here at Auteuil that he had recently recuperated after the peace negotiations which ended the American Revolution, and he regarded his house and garden, and his situation away from the "putrid streets" of Paris, as all that heart could wish. Jefferson liked both the place and the family and went there very often.[2]

The secretary of the commission, Colonel David Humphreys of Connecticut, completed the little official circle. Jefferson had hoped that he and this recent aide of Washington could sail together, but Humphreys left New York on the *Courier de l'Europe* ten days after the *Ceres* lifted anchor in Boston Harbor, and arrived in Paris just about that long after Jefferson. A rather pretentious young man and a budding poet, he described his voyage to the Old World and his own emotions in an epistle in verse addressed to his friend Timothy Dwight.[3]

Jefferson, who sailed on the *Ceres*, left a prosaic and more precise record of his first crossing. Every day at noon he recorded in his account book the latitude and longitude, the distance covered, the winds, the reading of the thermometer; and he made observations about whales, sharks, and other strange creatures as he saw them.[4] Also, with the help of a grammar and a copy of *Don Quixote*, he studied Spanish. Years later he remarked to John Quincy Adams that it was a very easy language since he had learned it in a voyage of nineteen days. "But," said the serious son of his old friend, "Mr. Jefferson tells large stories." [5] Both of the Jeffersons enjoyed the voyage. Having favorable winds, they made an unusually quick passage and they were blessed with sunshine and smooth seas nearly all the way. Though an indifferent sailor, the father was hardly sick at all. The passengers were few – six, Patsy said – but they were congenial. The owner of the practically new ship, Nathaniel Tracy of Newburyport, was on board, ready to talk with the Virginian about the state of commerce.

[2] John Adams, "Diary," Aug. 13, 17, 1784 (*Works*, III, 389).
[3] F. L. Humphreys, *Life and Times of David Humphreys* (1917), I, 307–309.
[4] Account Book, July 5–25, 1784.
[5] *Memoirs of J. Q. Adams*, I (1874), 317; Nov. 23, 1804.

At the time this was a discouraging subject, and they may have regarded it as a portent that they ran into thick weather as they neared the European coast.[6]

Jefferson had intended to transfer immediately to a vessel bound for France, without setting foot on England, but they fell in with none and at the end of the voyage Patsy was ill. They landed at West Cowes, and on her account they remained several days at Portsmouth, though her condition was not too serious to prevent her father from making a little trip inland and doing a bit of shopping. By the last day in July they were at Havre, after a brief but stormy passage of the Channel. The rain was violent and the cabin so small that they had to crawl into it. Patsy slept in her clothes on what she called a box, and in these cramped quarters her distinguished father must have regretted his long legs. They ran into further difficulties on landing at Havre, owing to their unfamiliarity with French as a spoken language and Jefferson's ignorance of the wiles of porters. One of the latter roundly cheated the gullible American, who kept his accounts carefully but never had any taste for haggling. As they followed the Seine to Paris during the first days of August, beggars surrounded their carriage wherever it stopped. They found this shocking, but both of them greatly admired the countryside. Patsy had never seen anything so beautiful; after the forests of Virginia it seemed a perfect garden. Jefferson himself reflected that no soil could be more fertile, better cultivated or more "elegantly" improved. It was not he but his daughter who wrote back to America about the fine churches and stained glass they saw on the way; he looked first at the land and pronounced it good. But he kept on regretting that they had not brought the bright skies of Virginia with them to France; it was more than a year before he could report a wholly cloudless day.[7] He liked neither Gothic arches nor shadows; he admired classic columns and loved the sun.

They lodged first at the Hôtel d'Orléans in the Rue de Richelieu, near the Palais-Royal, moving four days later to a hostelry of the same name on the Left Bank in the Rue des Petits Augustins. Desiring to fit Patsy out in the Parisian manner, the widower – before proceeding upon official business – summoned staymaker, milliner, and shoemaker, meanwhile buying a sword and belt, buckles, and lace ruffles

[6] The best accounts of the trip are in Jefferson's letter to Monroe, Nov. 11, 1784 (Ford, IV, 5), and in Martha's to Mrs. Elizabeth Trist, August, 1786 (Edgehill Randolph Papers, UVA). For all his travels, Edward Dumbauld, *Thomas Jefferson, American Tourist* (1946), referred to hereafter as Dumbauld, is invaluable.

[7] Oct. 16, 1785; daily chart of temperatures in Account Book.

for himself; and, before the first formal meeting of the commissioners, he got his young daughter placed in school. This was at the Abbaye Royale de Panthémont, a convent much patronized by English people and considered the most genteel in Paris. It is said that no pupil was admitted except on the recommendation of a lady of rank, and that a friend of the Marquis de Lafayette sponsored Martha.[8] After three years' observation of the convent Jefferson termed it the best house of education in France, and he assured his sister in Virginia that no word was ever spoken to the Protestants on the subject of religion.[9] There were fifty or sixty pensioners when Patsy arrived, including three princesses each of whom wore a blue ribbon over the shoulder. Her father visited her very frequently until she got oriented, and she fell into the life quickly and happily. She wore a crimson uniform, laced behind; she came to be known as "Jeffy" and soon could chatter like everybody else in French.

Her father said that he never became fluent in the language, though eventually he made himself understood; he even claimed that he could not write it, though there is plenty of record that he did.[10] His progress was naturally slow, since he was past forty and, his first associations being predominantly American, he rarely got beyond the sound of his native tongue. The Americans who happened to be this far from home sought each other out and constantly exchanged hospitalities; they comprised a close-knit group. Jefferson was one of the most honored members of this little band from the first, and after the departure of Adams and Franklin he became its acknowledged chief.

His closest personal relations during his early months in France were not with Franklin, who was nursing his gout and stone and already had as much social life as he could manage. The younger man heard a good many of the elder's bons mots and had the palate to relish them, and he picked up a number of stories about Franklin which have got into the biographies, but their meetings were chiefly official. Mutual cordiality marked their intercourse throughout life, but Jefferson was more intimate with John and Abigail Adams. They were much closer to him in age and less sought after by others, while their do-

[8] Account Book, Aug. 26, 1784; later story by Virginia Trist (Edgehill Randolph Papers, UVA). Lafayette was still in America at this time, but the tradition may be correct.

[9] To Mrs. Bolling, July 23, 1787 (*Domestic Life*, p. 130). Other comments chiefly from *Journal and Correspondence of Miss Adams* (1841), p. 27 (hereafter referred to as *Miss Adams*). See also Helen D. Bullock, *My Head and My Heart* (1945), pp. 5–6; and, for an account of the place, Thiéry, *Guide des Amateurs et des Étrangers* (Paris, 1787), II, 568–569.

[10] The best discussion of his use of French that I have seen is by J. M. Carrière, in *French Review*, XIX (May, 1946), 398–399.

mestic life was more to his taste than Franklin's less conventional ménage.

Jefferson's appointment had given John great pleasure. "He is an old friend, with whom I have often had occasion to labor at many a knotty problem, and in whose abilities and steadiness I always found great cause to confide," he said.[11] His associate, younger by seven and a half years and taller by six inches or more, had not wounded his vanity as yet. Adams, also a very domestic being, was more fortunate in that his wife and two of his children were with him. John Quincy was already impressively learned at seventeen. Abigail, wife of John, was more than a year younger than Jefferson, and the daughter of the same name was nineteen. The girl was known as "Abby" in the family, but everybody else called her "Miss Adams." In that formal age Patsy was referred to by her elders as "Miss Jefferson," though she was only twelve.

The two families met almost immediately as the dinner guests of Thomas Barclay, the American consul general, and were on the friendliest terms thereafter. At first Jefferson dined more often at Auteuil than the Adamses did with him in Paris, for he was at a disadvantage as a host until he got a house.[12] But he maintained the balance in other ways and was specially agreeable to the children. Thus, after a dinner at Dr. Franklin's, he took Abby and young John to a concert at the Château of the Tuileries, where they saw the brother of the King of Prussia; and at his invitation the family went a few days later to Patsy's convent to see two nuns take the veil. Miss Adams cried, like many others, but she was glad to learn from Miss Jefferson that ordinarily the place was not so sad. Most of these family memories were sweet and they survived the storms of controversy and ravages of time. Shortly before his son became the sixth President of the United States, aged John Adams wrote from Quincy to his somewhat less aged friend at Monticello: "I call him our John, because, when you were at the Cul de sac at Paris, he appeared to me to be almost as much your boy as mine." [13]

Colonel Humphreys, whose stiff manner greatly puzzled young Abigail at first, generally accompanied the more agreeable Jefferson to dinners. Then thirty-two, he was a dark man of military bearing who did not look the part of a poet. Like his friend John Trumbull of Connecticut, he recognized Jefferson as a man who combined literary

[11] Adams to James Warren, Aug. 27, 1784 (*Works*, IX, 524).

[12] Early dinners are described in *Miss Adams*, pp. 14, 16, and *Letters of Mrs. Adams* (1848 edn.), p. 194 (hereafter referred to as *Mrs. Adams*).

[13] Oct. 4, 14, 1784 (*Miss Adams*, pp. 20, 23–27); J. Adams to TJ, Jan. 22, 1825 (*Works*, X, 414).

merit with public virtues; he brought and presented to him with the author's compliments a copy of Trumbull's epic work, *McFingal.*[14] But the historic stature of the Secretary of the Commission is better reflected in his epitaph than in his own poetry:

> To sum all titles to respect, in one –
> There Humphreys rests – belov'd of Washington.[15]

He stood next to Washington when the General resigned his commission at Annapolis, but he was a sort of protégé of Jefferson in these Paris days, the first though not the most cherished of the young men who gathered about the generous Virginian and basked in the sunshine of his good will. Jefferson was only a little taller than this recent soldier, but he took him under his wing at once. He engaged lodgings for him in advance, immediately invited him to live with him, and made him a member of the family from the time that he himself acquired a house. About the middle of October Jefferson rented one on the Cul-de-sac Taitbout (now the Rue du Helder) near the Opéra. He kept it only a year, but this inveterate builder had two rooms remodeled while he was there. He assured Humphreys that he would really add nothing to the expense by moving in, and when William Short arrived late in the autumn said the same thing to him.[16]

Short was more than a protégé; to all practical purposes he was a son. A Virginian and twenty-five years old, he had attended William and Mary, where he was one of the earliest members of Phi Beta Kappa. His acquaintance with Jefferson probably arose from his relationship with the Skipwiths, with whom Jefferson was connected by marriage. The former Governor was one of Short's examiners when he was admitted to the bar – George Wythe being the other – and had guided him in his studies before that. But the young lawyer developed an insuperable aversion to practice, and was dissatisfied with the honorable position on the Virginia Council to which he was elected at an unusually early age. He wanted to go abroad with Jefferson – as his private secretary if he should have one, but to go with him in any case. For various reasons they were unable to go at the same time, but Short followed his patron after a few weeks and made headquarters with him from the first. For a time he went into a French household at Saint-Germain to improve himself in the lan-

[14] Trumbull to Jefferson, June 21, 1784 (MHS). Trumbull, the poet and jurist, is not to be confused with the painter of the same name who became an intimate friend of Jefferson's a little later.

[15] Humphreys, *Humphreys*, I, i.

[16] Humphreys to Washington, Nov. 6, 1784 (*ibid.*, I, 317).

guage, and not until summer could anything official be found for him to do. Soon after that, Jefferson made him his secretary; and if he did not already regard him as the greatest young man he knew, he soon came to. This slim Virginian had none of the stiffness or pomposity of the poetic Colonel; he had social grace and fell into the little American circle with ease. Miss Adams and her mother, who described him as modest and soft in manners, liked him from the start. Also, he formed intimate French connections – rather more intimate than his adopted father liked.[17]

Jefferson was a generous host from the beginning, as his nature and tradition required, but he was junior to both Franklin and Adams and regarded his official position as obscure. The specific task he had assumed was formidable enough. As Franklin said, if they were to make twenty treaties they were not likely to eat the bread of idleness.[18] Idleness was the last thing on earth the youngest of the commissioners wanted, but these representatives of a feeble Republic had to play a waiting game. They met at Passy every day at first, and they dispatched many letters, but during the autumn and winter they saw no concrete results. Jefferson's reception by Vergennes and other officials was as polite as he could wish, but the fact was that he found himself to be a person of no particular importance, on the outskirts of a formal Court deeply engrossed in its own affairs. The political scene in the Monarchy was somnolent; and in a few months he described himself and his fellow commissioners as "the lowest and most obscure of the whole diplomatic tribe." Except in physical stature he was the lowest of the three.

He soon realized that he was going to run into financial difficulties.[19] When Franklin and Adams came over, actual expenses were paid

[17] Short arrived by Nov. 29, 1784; Jefferson to Gov. Va., Jan. 12, 1785 (Ford, IV, 26). See also *Miss Adams*, Dec. 1, 1784, Jan. 27, 1785 (pp. 35, 45); *Mrs. Adams*, Dec. 3, 1784 (p. 207). He was born Sept. 30, 1759, the son of William Short and Elizabeth Skipwith (Family Chart in Short Papers, LC). The recommendation of Jefferson that he be admitted to the bar was on Sept. 30, 1781 (VSL, courtesy JP). Of several early letters from Short to Jefferson, those of May 8, 14, 1784, are most interesting (LC, 1689–1690, 1697–1699). See also O. M. Voorhees, *History of Phi Beta Kappa* (1945), ch. I; and A. B. Shepperson, *John Paradise and Lucy Ludwell* (1942), pp. 308–309. There is further information in the useful master's essay of G. G. Shackelford, "The Youth and Early Career of William Short" (UVA, 1948).

[18] Franklin to John Adams, Aug. 6, 1784; (Adams, *Works*, VIII, 208–209). Their official activities are described in the following chapter.

[19] To Monroe, Nov. 11, 1784 (Ford, IV, 11–13). Good later summary in letter to Madison, May 25, 1788 (*ibid.*, V, 12–16). See also TJ to Samuel Osgood, Oct. 5, 1785 (L. & B., V, 163–164).

by Congress, but the salary of a minister was afterwards fixed at 2500 guineas a year, and with Jefferson's appointment it was reduced to 2000. Franklin said that his American visitors would have to content themselves henceforth with plain beef and pudding; and in Jefferson's opinion, the reduction in the allowance was an important reason for the Doctor's insistence on a recall.[20] Franklin was less frugal in practice than in theory but he lived plainly, Jefferson said. Increased debt was inevitable on a reduced stipend and Poor Richard was averse to that. Adams was no little mortified that a fifth of his salary had been cut off at the very time when the arrival of his family had added to his expenses. He realized that he must be less hospitable, though the interest of the United States would be better served by his entertaining more.[21] Jefferson regarded his friend Abigail as a most excellent "economist," but in spite of her care and their modest life, he doubted if the Adamses could make both ends meet. The financial problems of American diplomats were distinctly embarrassing at the beginning of the Republic – as they continued to be for generations.

Jefferson was granted an advance of two quarters' salary, but no provision whatever was made for his outfit. Soon after he moved into his first Paris house he wrote James Monroe, as a friend and a member of Congress, that his furnishings and equipment cost him nearly 1000 guineas and he would have to stay in debt to Congress for them. He afterwards revised his figures upward until they exceeded a year's salary; and, besides being unable to refund the advance, he went deeply into debt to private creditors. He continued to insist that an allowance of one year's salary for furnishings and equipment was necessary and proper, but not until after he had returned to America and been for some time secretary of state did he make his point. Throughout his entire stay in France he was in the dark about the intentions of an indifferent and impecunious Congress in this crucial personal matter.[22]

The fundamental difficulty arose from no extravagance on his part; it grew out of the confusion of American finances and political affairs. He cannot be blamed for buying furniture rather than renting it at the exorbitant annual charge of 40 per cent. On the other hand, he was personally fastidious, adding to his financial difficulties by remodeling and redecorating houses in which he did not stay long,

[20] Franklin to Adams, Aug. 6, 1784 (Adams, *Works*, VIII, 208–209); TJ to Madison, May 25, 1788 (Ford, V, 14–15); Carl Van Doren, *Benjamin Franklin* (1945 edn.), pp. 636–637.

[21] Adams to James Warren, Aug. 27, 1784 (*Works*, IX, 525–526).

[22] For the final outcome, see pp. 204–205, this volume, esp. note 6.

and getting more and better furnishings than he needed.[23] During his first winter at Paris he told Monroe that he was living about as well as they did when they kept house together in Annapolis as members of Congress. He kept a hired carriage (buying one in the spring) and two horses, but at first he could not afford a riding horse. After he succeeded Franklin (in May, 1785) a better style of living was expected of him, he thought. "This rendered it constantly necessary to step neither to the right nor the left," he reported, and "called for an almost womanly attention to the details of the household." [24] From the beginning he had a full staff of servants, including a *valet de chambre*.[25] The well-known Petit came into his service in May, 1785, but left him after a time and did not become his maître d'hôtel until later. Humphreys and Short had servants of their own and paid them, but there were that many more mouths for Jefferson to feed. He could hardly have been happy in a small establishment; and his nature and habits demanded comfortable, agreeable, and hospitable living. He was probably the least thrifty of the three American ministers, and had the most expensive tastes; but by the standards of Versailles he was economy itself. In his first summer he wrote John Adams, then in London, that he could not follow the Court to Fontainebleau, though the season was a particularly good one for doing business with Vergennes. The rent of a house there for a month would have taken almost his entire salary, leaving him nothing to eat. He viewed without regret the departure of the beau monde from the city in summer. "We give and receive them you know in exchange for the swallows," he afterwards said.[26] Of his own longing for the country, however, there can be no doubt.

The first months of this transplanted Virginian in the French metropolis were relatively gloomy, partly because he was not well. Abigail Adams reported sympathetically in December that he had been confined to his house for six weeks and, though recovering, was still feeble.[27] His confinement actually extended through most of the winter. Such a "seasoning" was the common lot of strangers, he reflected, but

[23] Items for wallpaper, carpentering, plastering, etc., in Account Book, Dec. 20, 30, 1784 and Jan. 15, 1785. The rent itself was supposed to be paid by Congress. For his purchases, see Marie Kimball, *The Furnishings of Monticello* (1940), pp. 5–6.

[24] To Madison, May 25, 1788 (Ford, V, 15–16).

[25] The scale of his establishment from the beginning is suggested by the purchase on Oct. 22, 1784, of 6½ doz. plates and 3 doz. carafes (Account Book).

[26] TJ to John Adams, Aug. 10, 1785 (L. & B., V, 59); to Humphreys, Aug. 14, 1786 (*ibid.*, V, 401).

[27] Dec. 9, 1784 (*Mrs. Adams*, p. 216).

he believed that his experience was more severe than the average. He particularly regretted the unwholesomeness of the water and the dampness of the air. Others condemned the climate even more roundly than he. Baron de Grimm reports a poem in a single verse written in dispraise of the four seasons by a gentleman of the Court:

Rain and wind, and wind and rain.

"At least you will not find it too long," the gallant author said to a friend. The friend replied, "Pardon me it is too long by half. *Wind and rain* would have said all."[28] The sun was Jefferson's great physician and by spring he regarded himself as almost re-established by it; in the middle of March he was walking four or five miles a day.

His moods always varied with the seasons, but he was never again so gloomy as in that first grim winter, when, besides being ill, he had devastating news from home. Patsy was in Paris enjoying perfect health, but he had left two daughters with Francis and Elizabeth Eppes in Southside Virginia, knowing that the little girls were much too young to travel and could not be in better hands. But in January, through letters brought from America by Lafayette, he learned that whooping cough, "most horrible of all disorders," had attacked the children at Eppington and carried off his youngest daughter, Lucy Elizabeth, then two and a half years old, and one of her little cousins. Polly Jefferson, now six, had coughed violently with the others but was quite recovered. Under the burden of double tragedy Elizabeth Eppes regarded life as scarcely supportable. Jefferson wrote his brother-in-law, Francis Eppes, that since nothing could possibly describe his state of mind or bring any comfort, he would simply dismiss the deeply painful subject. To Dr. James Currie he wrote more freely, speaking morbidly of the "sun of happiness, clouded over, never again to brighten," and of "schemes of life shifted in one fatal moment." He was back in the mood of melancholy that had followed his wife's death, but his mind soon shifted to the future. Now having only two daughters, he was quite sure that he wanted both of them with him, and the effort to get Polly from Eppington to Paris became one of his major tasks from the time he knew that his own stay would be extended. The task required complicated planning, much persuasion, and some guile, and it consumed two more years. Not until the summer of 1787 was the circle of his little family completed, and not until then did the American Minister become fully reconciled to life in France.[29]

[28] *Historical and Literary Memoirs . . . from the Correspondence of Baron de Grimm*, II (London, 1814), 123–124.

[29] Francis Eppes to TJ, fall of 1784, and Elizabeth Eppes to TJ, Oct. 13, 1784

By the spring of his first year, however, life was quickened by both the season and the march of events. The state of his health, combined with his grief, had caused him to forswear dining out for four or five months, and he did not think proper to make an exception even of the Adamses, though they occasionally dined with him. Late in March, John spent the evening with him, and on that very evening the Queen was delivered of a son. Lafayette told John Quincy the next day she was so large that they really expected twins; Calonne, the Comptroller General, had prepared two blue ribbons in case two princes should be born. A few days later Jefferson and the Adamses, on invitation of Madame de Lafayette, went to Notre Dame to hear the Te Deum sung in thanks for the birth of a prince, the King himself assisting. All the polite world was there and Jefferson must have enjoyed the fine music. On the way he remarked to young Abigail – with a degree of exaggeration – that there were as many people on the streets as in the whole state of Massachusetts.[30]

Within another month Jefferson was officially informed that he was to succeed Franklin, while John Adams learned with great satisfaction that he was going to England, where he was sure that he could accomplish much. A round of hospitalities was in order, and Jefferson gave a dinner.[31] The Marquis de Lafayette and his lady were guests, along with a few other nobles. The Adamses headed the American delegation and John Paul Jones was there, being addressed as Commodore. Abigail had previously noted that the famous sailor was not stout and warlike but small and soft-spoken, and that he understood the etiquette of a lady's toilet as perfectly as he did the rigging of his ship. Jefferson followed foreign dinner customs which seemed strange to the American matron. Before dinner the men stood or walked about, shutting off the fire from the seated ladies, and there was no general conversation at the table or afterwards but only tête-a-tête. A stranger would think everybody was transacting private business. Abigail was distinctly impressed by French politeness, nevertheless, and greatly liked this host, especially when he visited them in a friendly, informal way. "One of the choice ones of the earth," she

(*Domestic Life*, pp. 101–102); Dr. James Currie to TJ, Nov. 20, 1784 (LC, 1864); TJ to Francis Eppes, Feb. 5, 1785 (Randall, III, 588); Currie to TJ, Aug. 5, 1785 (LC, 12331). Jefferson got the news on Jan. 26. The next day young Abigail Adams noted in her diary that he was "a man of great sensibility and parental affection," and that he and Martha were greatly affected by the tragedy (*Miss Adams*, p. 45). The story of Polly's arrival is told in this volume, ch. VIII.

[30] *Memoirs of J. Q. Adams*, Mar. 27, April 1, 1785 (I, 15–19); *Miss Adams*, April 1, 1785 (pp. 65–68).

[31] *Mrs. Adams*, May 7, 1785 (pp. 240–241; see also p. 208).

called him, and when she went to England, after a succession of dinners, she was even more loath to leave him than she was her garden. She thought of him particularly when she heard the "Messiah" at Westminster Abbey. It was sublime beyond description, she said, and would have gratified his "favorite passion" to the highest degree. She started a correspondence with him which he was delighted to continue, and in their hands even purchasing commissions assumed charm and grace.[32]

Shortly before the departure of the Adams family Jefferson went through certain ceremonies at Versailles. After communicating his appointment to Vergennes he delivered his letter of credence to the King in a private audience; then he had his first audience with Louis XVI, Marie Antoinette, and the Royal Family in his quality as minister plenipotentiary of the United States to the Court of His Most Christian Majesty.[33] He was not much impressed by these or any other ceremonies and he never admired this queen, but the numerous notes of congratulation he received – all phrased in formal but delightful terms of politeness – showed that he was now an official of established standing. He was entitled to attend the King's levee every Tuesday and dine with the whole diplomatic corps afterwards, but he was never so thrilled by this experience as was young David Humphreys, and he had no high opinion of the diplomats generally. Toward the end of his ministry he told Gouverneur Morris that they were really not worth knowing. He made a slight exception of the Baron de Grimm, the minister of Saxe Gotha, whom he found the most pleasant and communicative member of the entire corps. Rousseau's biting anecdotes about him (in the latter part of the *Confessions*) appeared in print after Jefferson left Paris, and Grimm's famous *Correspondance* was published after he had grown old. The American saw him as "a man of good fancy, acuteness, irony, cunning and egoism," with no heart and not much science, but with enough of everything to speak its language. This oracle of society in letters and the arts might easily have introduced Jefferson to Diderot had the Encyclopedist lived a few months longer. Diderot died the week before the Virginian reached Paris. Rousseau, with whom he would have had much less in common, had been dead some six years by then.[34]

[32] Mrs. Adams to TJ, June 6, 1785 (LC, 2136–2137); TJ to Mrs. Adams, June 21, 1785 (Ford, IV, 60–64). See also *Mrs. Adams*, p. 248.

[33] Account Book, May 17, 1785; documents, LC, 2082–2083.

[34] Humphreys to Washington, July 17, 1785 (Humphreys, I, 328); G. Morris, *Diary of the French Revolution* (1939), I, 135; comments on Grimm and the *philosophes* in letter of Apr. 8, 1816, to Adams (L. & B., XIV, 468–469). See also,

Jefferson already knew a member of the French Academy in the person of the Marquis de Chastellux, whom he had entertained at Monticello. Through John Adams, he became friends with the three abbés, Mably, Chalut, and Arnoux – though the eldest of these, Mably, a writer of some note, died that summer (1785). Lafayette opened many doors for Jefferson, including that of his aunt, Madame de Tessé, though the Marquis was not much in Paris until the autumn of 1785. Perhaps it was through him that Jefferson met the Duc de la Rochefoucauld, who was almost exactly his age and had a like passion for the physical sciences, along with a deep concern for the freedom and happiness of man. The "curious" Virginian could not have failed to admire the cabinet of minerals which the Duke kept on the second floor of the Hôtel de la Rochefoucauld and he must have seen there the Marquis de Condorcet, who of all the *philosophes* was probably the most like him in spirit and temperament. These friends – Lafayette, La Rochefoucauld, and Condorcet – constituted for him the triumvirate of liberal aristocrats throughout his stay in France. He and William Short soon began to visit the château of the Duke's mother, the old Duchess d'Anville: La Roche-Guyon, on the borders of Normandy, where the liberals and savants also assembled. Short kept his eyes mostly on the young Duchess, Alexandrine, familiarly known as Rosalie, who was the Duke's niece and incredibly young to be his wife, but Short's friendship with her was only in the bud as yet.[35]

Jefferson had various letters of introduction, whether he needed them or not, and Franklin was certainly a natural link between him and the world of letters and philosophy. The story of the latter's most spectacular meeting with Voltaire was still current; in 1778 the two men had embraced publicly in the French manner at the Academy of Sciences, kissing each other on both cheeks to the delight of the assembled savants. The recognized high priest of philosophy after the passing of Voltaire, Franklin might have been expected to introduce the apostle of enlightenment from Virginia into the innermost circles. Probably there was little opportunity to do this during Jefferson's first winter, when both of them were so much confined, but before Franklin finally left Passy in the summer of 1785, in a litter furnished by the King, he

---

Aug. 1, 1816 (*ibid.*, XV, 48); and Adams to TJ, Mar. 2, May 6, 1816 (*Works*, X, 213, 218). Jefferson met Grimm during his first winter in Paris.

[35] On La Rochefoucauld, see sketch in E. Jovy, *La Correspondance du Duc de La Rochefoucauld d'Enville et de Georges Louis Le Sage* (Paris, 1918). On his cabinet, see Thiéry, *Guide des Amateurs et des Étrangers* (1787), II, 487–489. On a visit to the château of the "Old Duchess," see Philip Mazzei, *Memoirs* (1942), p. 296, though Mazzei can never be trusted implicitly in regard to dates.

enlarged the circle of his successor by inducing him to go to Sannois to meet the Comtesse d'Houdetot and by introducing him to the salon of Madame Helvétius at Auteuil.

Madame d'Houdetot, mistress of Saint-Lambert and the adored heroine of the latter part of the *Confessions* of Rousseau, was an ardent admirer of American revolutionaries in general and of Franklin in particular. Jefferson visited her dutifully, and conscientiously relayed to her news of her departed American hero whenever any came. He found her an exceedingly kindly woman and shared her solicitude for the sons of Saint Jean de Crèvecoeur when their father left them in France later on. To him she was always the "good old Countess" – not a cabinet of antiquities, as she afterwards appeared to Gouverneur Morris – but he belonged with younger people and did not go to see her as often as she liked. She found him wise and humane, intelligent and amiable, but she gave no fête for him as she had for Franklin. He gained some literary acquaintance in her circle, but neither here nor elsewhere did he attempt to take Franklin's place.[36]

He made more valuable contacts at the salon of Madame Helvétius, which Franklin called "*l'Académie des Belles Letters d'Auteuil.*" As this intimate friend said, men of literature and learning attached themselves to Madame as straws to amber.[37] Abigail Adams described her as a decayed beauty and shameless creature; though she had declined to marry Franklin, she dined with him regularly and made great display of her adoration. Jefferson followed no such dining practice, but he afterwards said that Auteuil always seemed to him a delicious village, and Madame Helvétius's "the most delicious spot in it."[38] Here he found the Abbé Morellet and La Roche – who were in effect members of the family – along with Cabanis, whom Madame had adopted as a son. Here he could meet Volney and young De Stutt de Tracy. Morellet was admitted to the Academy in the summer of 1785; he was a friend of Chastellux, and after another year became the French translator of the *Notes on Virginia*, which Jefferson had printed privately in May. He spoke most respectfully of Franklin's successor, as everybody in this circle did, but he did not write a delightful drinking song about him as he did about "our Benjamin."[39]

[36] TJ to Abigail Adams, June 21, 1785 (Ford IV, 63); Gilbert Chinard, *Les Amitiés Américaines de Madame d'Houdetot* (1923), p. 30 and elsewhere.

[37] On Franklin's relations with Madame, see Van Doren, *Franklin*, pp. 646–653.

[38] To Cabanis, July 12, 1803; Chinard *Jefferson et les Idéologues* (1925), pp. 25–26. See also Antoine Guillois, *Le Salon de Madame Helvétius* (Paris, 1894), p. 45.

[39] Saying that the latter's real object in the Revolution was to give the Americans freedom to drink French wines instead of English tea and beer (*Mémoires de l'Abbé Morellet* (Paris, 1821, I, 287–289).

Nobody talked about "our Thomas," and although Jefferson's spirits lightened as his sojourn lengthened, he could not bring Franklin's gaiety into a salon. He was making contact with the *philosophes* and *literati*, and his predecessor could report in America that he had recovered his health and was much respected and esteemed.[40] He had survived his diplomatic novitiate and his physical "seasoning," and had begun to carve for himself a niche in France. It was always smaller than that of Franklin, but no other American of his century had one that was so large.

Never did the nostalgic note wholly disappear from Jefferson's personal letters, and it dominated the intimate ones at first. During his weeks of confinement he was vexed by the difficulties and delays attending transatlantic correspondence. The packet from New York to Havre came only once a month; letters committed to the post were almost certain to be opened and sometimes were not resealed; and his friends, he thought, were very slow in writing. Whenever possible he sent his own letters by the hand of some passenger, and he used a cipher when speaking of public persons to such intimates as James Madison and James Monroe. He sent off far more letters than he received, sometimes going a couple of months without getting anything at all from overseas. Official communications were slow enough – that was one of the greatest difficulties under which an American diplomat in Europe labored – but it was harder to learn of small things than great. "Tell me who dies, that I may meet these disagreeable events in detail, and not all at once when I return; who marry, who hang themselves because they cannot marry, etc.," he asked.[41] He longed for the sights and sounds of his native land, for the gossip of the countryside; and, taking a leaf out of his own experience, he painstakingly passed on to other displanted persons details of information which had come to him.[42] This restrained and highly intellectual wanderer was still a home-loving countryman, who liked nothing quite so much as to be with friends.

It was partly for this reason that he urged Monroe and Madison to come over and spend a summer with him, though he justified the invitation on other grounds. "I view the prospect of this society as inestimable," he said. The trip might cost 200 guineas but this would be a small price for the knowledge of another world.[43] That was

[40] Franklin to Jay, Sept. 19, 1785 (*Works*, Bigelow edn., IX, 251).
[41] To Mrs. Elizabeth Trist, Aug. 18, 1785 (L. & B., V, 81).
[42] For example, to William Carmichael in Spain.
[43] To Madison, Dec. 8, 1784 (Ford, IV, 18).

what he was getting, at the price of loneliness. The process was slower than he had expected but the harvest ripened as the months wore on.

Without pausing here to speak of the books he assiduously assembled from the start, the music he heard, and the "beautiful" inventions he began to report immediately, we can appropriately speak of the early impressions that French life made on him as a social being. The first balance sheets that he drew were unfavorable, but there were large items on the credit side. He immediately recognized that nowhere, not even in Virginia, had he met with such good manners. Here, "a man might pass a life without encountering a single rudeness"; the roughness of the human mind was so rubbed off that one might glide through a whole existence without a jostle.[44] Any new country like the United States was crude by comparison. A scrupulously courteous and deeply sensitive man himself, he envied these people the politeness which he perceived among high and low in France – and did not observe during his later brief visit to England. His comments on the "slanders" against his country and countrymen from which John Adams suffered in England were revealing. "I am fond of quiet," he wrote Abigail, "willing to do my duty, but irritable by slander and apt to be forced by it to abandon my post. These are weaknesses from which reason and your counsels will preserve Mr. Adams."[45] It contributed no little to his peace of mind that he was placed in a society where he was met everywhere with the outward forms of kindness.

He also commended the French for their temperance, regarding them as superior to Americans in this respect and much superior to the English. He himself was always temperate, but it was in this land that he learned to be a genuine connoisseur of food and wines. Again he made comparisons with the English, though he had been only briefly on their island. "I fancy it must be the quantity of animal food eaten by the English which renders their character insusceptible of civilization," he wrote Abigail. "I suspect it is in their kitchens and not in their churches that their reformation must be worked, and that missionaries of that description from hence would avail more than those who should endeavor to tame them by precepts of religion or philosophy." He was speaking lightly, but he regarded the French as far superior in cookery and in almost all the graces – as they were. He always valued their arts highly, especially their music, and as his health permitted he saw French and Italian comedy and attended *con-*

[44] To Charles Bellini, Sept. 30, 1785 (L. & B., V, 154); to Mrs. Elizabeth Trist, Aug. 18, 1785 (*ibid.*, V, 80).
[45] To Mrs. Adams, Sept. 23, 1785 (LC, 2547–2550).

certs spirituels. He found innumerable delights in this highly agreeable and cultivated society.

Nevertheless, in the beginning, before the fragments of his family were assembled and great things began to happen in the public world, life was spoiled for him by its emptiness. Personal circumstances accentuated the severity of his judgment, but he was not using idle words when he spoke of the "empty bustle" of Paris, and he never veered from his first impression that this was an impure and purposeless society.[46] The brilliance of the Court never dazzled him in the slightest, and although he himself was the product of what was regarded in America as an aristocratic society, he missed the bourgeois virtues without precisely saying so. He deplored the extravagance of life in France, but what appalled him most in the upper circles was the absence of conjugal love and domestic happiness such as he himself had experienced in full measure. If he was shocked, as Abigail Adams was at first, by dancing girls who sprang into the air and displayed their drawers and garters, he did not say so, but Short remembered that he sometimes blushed at suggestive stories.[47] He cracked marital jokes about pregnancy, but anecdotes about lovers and mistresses such as were current did not strike him as amusing, and one of the things he approved in Louis XVI was his faithfulness to his Queen, though he understood that she did not reciprocate. Intellectually, he was a kindred spirit to Franklin, but morally he was entirely at ease in the Adams household at Auteuil and later at Grosvenor Square. His friendship with Abigail was moral and domestic at base, however much he may have embroidered it with his lighter fancy, and he and she drew a contrast between the simple innocence of Americans and the wordly sophistication of Europeans which helped start a literary tradition. In later years the same theme was treated hilariously by Mark Twain and with infinite subtlety by Henry James.[48]

In spite of all his moralizing, however, Jefferson liked his own life to be rich, not plain, and as time went on he lived with considerable impressiveness. Not only did he powder his hair and acquire a maître d'hôtel; he also got a house of becoming dignity and pleasant setting. This was at the Grille de Chaillot, on the corner of the Champs-Élysées and the Rue Neuve de Berry. As he wrote Abigail, it suited him in

[46] Besides the letters already cited, see Jefferson to John Banister, Jr., Oct. 15, 1785 (L. & B., V, 185–188); and his well-known later letter to Mrs. William Bingham, Feb. 7, 1787 (*ibid.*, VI, 81–84). Her reply of June 1, 1787, is in *Domestic Life*, pp. 98–100.

[47] *Mrs. Adams*, p. 234; Randall, I, 421 *n.*

[48] See Philip Rahv, *Discovery of Europe: the Story of American Experience in the Old World* (Boston, 1947), pp. xiii, 52.

everything but the price, which was rather beyond his means. It was barely within the city, the grilles which marked the customs barrier being just beyond it, one across the Champs-Élysées and the other – a smaller one – across the Rue Neuve de Berry. It was known as the Hôtel de Langeac, and had been built for the mistress of one of the ministers of Louis XV by the architect Chalgrin, who afterwards designed the Arc de Triomphe. Jefferson moved into it in the autumn of 1785, but since he had to give six months' notice to his landlord on the Cul-de-sac Taitbout, he had to pay double rent that long; and in the new house as in the old he had alterations made to suit his personal convenience. For a widower whose daughter was away at school the house was capacious – it had a basement, ground floor, mezzanine, and first floor. One of the rooms, probably the oval one on the garden side, had a ceiling richly ornamented with a painting of the rising sun then regarded as remarkable. The extensive grounds, entered from the Neuve de Berry and separated by a dry moat from the Champs-Élysées, were treated in the informal "English style," then very fashionable in France.[49] The place was admirable for hospitality, the new tenant delighted in the garden, where among other things he eventually cultivated Indian corn for his table, and, being so near the Bois de Boulogne, he could easily go walking. Patsy was there with him on Sundays, as Short was all the time. Jefferson afterwards annexed the painter John Trumbull and through him gained a fresh group of musical and artistic friends. Life became rich, while remaining simple by the standards of the Court, and it appeared to the outward eye that a cultivated gentleman had made himself very much at home.

[49] Howard C. Rice, *L'Hôtel de Langeac, Jefferson's Paris Residence, 1785–1789* (1947) is a definitive account. See also Dumbauld, p. 63, and *Alumni Bulletin, Univ. of Va.*, 3 ser., XII, 217–253. The latter tells about the marking of the site in Jefferson's honor during the First World War.

[II]

The Rebuffs of a Commissioner

1784–1786

LIFE in Paris might not have seemed so empty at first if Jefferson's diplomatic activities had not been so futile. The only official reason for his presence in the pleasure-loving capital, during his first ten months there, was to share with his more experienced colleagues the task of negotiating commercial treaties with various European states, but they could hardly have accomplished less had he been absent. On the day that the Virginian was forty-two, and while he was beginning to recover from his first Paris winter, Adams wrote John Jay, the American Secretary for Foreign Affairs, that the commissioners had not accomplished the ends desired by Congress and could not be expected to. "I am very happy in my friend, Mr. Jefferson," he added, "and have nothing but my inutility to disgust me with a residence here."[1] They signed a treaty with Prussia after that, but in practically all other respects their mission was unsuccessful. The fault was not theirs; it was inherent in the situation.

When Jefferson went abroad the independent American Republic already had a few treaties, largely because of his two colleagues. In 1778 a treaty of amity and commerce had been made with France, along with the historic alliance, and it was then that the fame of Franklin came into fullest flower. John Adams had negotiated a treaty with the United Netherlands in 1782, and Franklin had signed one the next year with Sweden. Congress authorized the negotiation of supplementary treaties with these three countries, if feasible, but the main idea was to add to this short list. Congress assumed that in a world constantly threatened by war the neutral rights of a newcomer among the nations should be guaranteed by numerous bilateral agreements. Even more important was the need to break into the closed

[1] Adams to Jay, Apr. 13, 1785 (*D. C.*, I, 483).

economic systems of which the western world then consisted. Having cut loose from the closed British system the American states were confronted with commercial barriers everywhere. Under these circumstances, not unnaturally, they advanced the doctrine of freedom of trade, and hoped to penetrate if not to break down these barriers by means of agreements based on principles of commercial reciprocity.[2]

The question was not theoretical but severely practical. How were the surplus American products – fish, tobacco, rice, lumber, furs – to find markets? How were American ships, which had performed a legitimate function within the British system, now to be employed? Congress did not merely want commerce with Europe to be facilitated; the opening or reopening of trade with the possessions of European countries in the West Indies was even more important. It soon appeared, however, that the governments of the Old World set no store by special treaties with the United States, for two reasons: they believed that they could get what they needed from the country without modifying their customary policies; and they doubted if the feeble Republic could enforce any special agreements which might be made. Before Jefferson returned home in 1789 the American government had assumed new strength; but when he began his attack on monopolistic commercial systems he was feebly armed and was confronted with a task which would probably have been hopeless even if his arms had been stronger.

Beginning with their first meeting at Passy on August 30, 1784, the commissioners had many at the same place. By the middle of October they had made offers of negotiation to all the powers of Europe, according to their instructions, and on November 11 they sent back to Congress the first of their numerous reports.[3] They gave their secretary, David Humphreys, plenty of paper work to do. They sent circulars to the ambassadors or other resident ministers of a dozen countries, receiving replies from nearly all of them, generally quite polite. But Jefferson himself noted that the disposition to treat with the United States on "liberal principles" – which had "blazed out with enthusiasm" on the conclusion of the peace – now had considerably subsided. At

[2] V. G. Setser, *Commercial Reciprocity Policy of the U. S.* (1937), pp. 2–3; S. F. Bemis in *American Secretaries of State*, I (1927), 205–207. The specific instructions on which Jefferson acted were those of May 7, 1784 (Ford, III, 489–493). These were based on the earlier report of a committee of which he was chairman, and this itself went back to still earlier instructions, the existing treaties, and the so-called "Plan of 1776."

[3] Franklin to Chas. Thomson, Oct. 16, 1784 (*Works*, Bigelow edn., IX, 65–66); Report of Nov. 11, 1784 (*D. C.*, I, 534–540).

first he attributed this declining enthusiasm not to the realities of the international situation, which made the currying of American favor seem quite unnecessary, but to the unfavorable reports of American anarchy spread by British design.[4] Already convinced that the British would yield to nothing except a genuine threat of discrimination against their trade, he had no real hope of a treaty with them. Eventually the Duke of Dorset, their ambassador in Paris, made himself personally agreeable to the Americans, but he started out by wounding their *amour-propre*. Instructed by his Court, he assured the three commissioners that the British would consider proposals tending to establish "a system of mutual and permanent advantage" to the two countries, but he asked them to send a properly authorized person to London.[5] Not being authorized to say that the United States would send a resident minister to England, as to France, they referred that matter to Congress, but declared that they themselves had full powers and were willing to go to London if necessary, inconvenient as it would be. Jefferson supposed the British had no objections to the commissioners personally, and believed they only wanted to gain time to see how their "schemes" would work without a treaty.[6]

As the winter of his "seasoning" wore on, the commissioners hopefully sent drafts of treaties not only to Prussia (with which country negotiations had actually been begun before he arrived) but also to Portugal, Tuscany, and Denmark.[7] By this time he was fully aware of the difficulties attending his mission. "We do not find it easy to make commercial arrangements in Europe," he said. "There is a want of confidence in us." [8] A little later he wrote his friend Monroe in cipher: "Our business goes on very slowly. No answers from Spain or Britain. The backwardness of the latter is not new." [9] He continued: "The effecting treaties with the powers holding positions in the West Indies, I consider as the important part of our business. It is not of great consequence whether the others treat or not. Perhaps trade may go on with them well enough without. But Britain, Spain, Portugal, France are consequent, and Holland, Denmark, Sweden may

[4] TJ to Monroe, Nov. 11, 1784 (Ford, IV, 6–7).

[5] Duke of Dorset to commissioners, Nov. 24, 1784 (*D. C.*, I, 542–543).

[6] Commissioners to Duke of Dorset, Dec. 9, 1784 (*D. C.*, I, 543–544); Jefferson to Monroe, Dec. 10, 1784 (Ford, IV, 21). British policy is discussed more fully in ch. IV of the present work. It is admirably described for this period in G. S. Graham, *Sea Power and British North America* (1941), ch. I.

[7] 2nd and 3rd Reports of Commissioners, Dec. 15, 1784; Feb. 1785 (*D. C.*, I, 544–545, 551–552).

[8] TJ to Nathanael Greene, Jan. 12, 1785 (Ford, IV, 25).

[9] TJ to Monroe, Feb. 1785 (Ford, IV, 30, 31). See also Adams to Jay, Mar. 9, 1785 (*D. C.*, I, 475–477).

be of service too. We have hitherto waited for favorable circumstances to press matters with France. We are now about to do it though I cannot say the prospect is good. The merchants of this country are very clamorous against our admission into the West Indies and ministers are afraid for their places." Lafayette had returned by this time, however, and he soon proved a help.[10]

The basic weakness of the position of the American representatives was revealed by a letter from the Duke of Dorset in the spring. He inquired whether they were merely commissioned by Congress or had received separate powers from the respective states, and asked what engagements they could enter into which could not be rendered fruitless and ineffectual by any state.[11] Practically speaking, the question was still unanswerable, but to the mind of Jefferson the legal difficulties were overcome by the making of special treaties in the name of Congress, since the jurisdiction over the commerce of the states then sprang into existence. He wrote James Monroe: "You see that my primary object in the formation of treaties is to take the commerce of the states out of the hands of the states, and to place it under the superintendence of Congress, so far as the imperfect provisions of our constitution will admit, and until the states shall by new compact make them more perfect."[12]

Soon the commissioners were authorized to announce to the Duke of Dorset that a resident minister would proceed to England. Congress was regularizing the small diplomatic establishment and putting its inadequate house in better order. In December, 1784, John Jay at length assumed the office of secretary for foreign affairs, to which he had been elected months before and which he continued to fill until Jefferson came home.

The general sense of Congress had long been favorable to the appointment of a minister to London and they finally made the logical choice of John Adams. There never was any real doubt that Franklin's request to return home would be accepted or that Jefferson would be elected to succeed him as resident minister to France.[13] Lafayette and Marbois favored his appointment, and the general impression was

[10] Negotiations with France are discussed in the next chapter.

[11] Duke of Dorset to commissioners, Mar. 26, 1785 (*D. C.*, I, 574–575).

[12] To Monroe, June 17, 1785 (Ford, IV, 55).

[13] Monroe reported to Madison, Dec. 18, 1784, that Richard Henry Lee wanted Jefferson sent to Spain, in order to leave the Courts of Great Britain and France to himself and friends (S. M. Hamilton, I, 58). This intrigue proved vain, and the vote in Jefferson's favor on Mar. 10, 1785, was unanimous; Rufus King to Elbridge Gerry, Mar. 20, 1785 (Burnett, *Letters of Members of the Continental Congress*, VIII, 68).

that he was "peculiarly acceptable" to the Court of Versailles.[14] As we have already seen, Adams got his word toward the end of April, while Franklin and Jefferson got theirs about a week later, in early May.

Technically speaking, these events did not mark the end of the commission, for it continued in the persons of Adams and Jefferson for another year and they acted jointly in various matters after that. They treated with Portugal, for example, and dealt as best they could with the Barbary pirates. But they had no direct part in the important negotiations with Spain, which were transferred to America and conducted by Jay himself. Henceforth, Adams's main effort was to penetrate the armor of British complacency, while Jefferson devoted himself chiefly to France. Before the litter of the aging Franklin left in the summer, he signed the only treaty the three commissioners actually negotiated, the one with Prussia. Besides incorporating the principles of the previous treaties, it contained certain unusual provisions relating to the status of noncombatants and prisoners of war and to compensation for contraband. These have been generally credited to Franklin, though they were quite in accord with Jefferson's advanced humanitarianism. He signed the document some days after Franklin, and it was then sent to London to John Adams, who had really started these negotiations. William Short then carried it to The Hague, where Baron Thulemeier signed it for Prussia on September 10, 1785. It involved a great deal of trouble and was something to be thankful for, but it was hardly a rich fruitage for the labors of a year.[15]

After twelve months of diplomatic futility Jefferson still retained some hope that commercial treaties could be negotiated, and inevitably he continued to give major attention to matters of trade throughout his stay in France. He still thought agriculture the best way of life, and, as he wrote John Jay, if he were wholly free to decide the question he would want Americans to engage in farming as long as possible. Cultivators of the soil, in his opinion, were the best citizens. Those who followed the sea were the next best, while those engaged in manufacturing were the worst. His observations in Europe had created in him no desire to usher the industrial revolution into America. "I consider the class of artificers as the panders of vice and the

[14] Besides Monroe's letter of Dec. 18, 1784, see Lafayette to Washington, Dec. 21, 1784 (*Mémoires*, 1837, II, 111), David Howell to William Greene, Feb. 9, 1785 (Burnett, *Letters*, VIII, 25–26).

[15] Franklin signed July 9, Jefferson July 28, Adams Aug. 5 (8th Report of Commissioners, Aug. 14, 1785, and Report of Jay on this, in *D. C.*, I, 597–600). See also Jefferson to Adams, July 28, 1785 (L. & B., V, 39–43); Jefferson to Thulemeier, July 28, 1785 (*ibid.*, V, 43–44); Bemis, in *Am. Secs. State*, I, 207–208.

instruments by which the liberties of a country are generally overturned," he said. Even as a moralist he looked with relative favor on shipping, but he regarded the carrying trade as no matter of theory. It was a practical matter with which the people he represented were deeply concerned. "Our people are decided in the opinion that it is necessary for us to take a share in the occupation of the ocean," he said, "and their established habits induce them to require that the sea be kept open to them, and that that line of policy be pursued which will render the use of that element as great as possible to them. I think it a duty in those entrusted with the administration of their affairs to conform themselves to the decided choice of their constituents." [16] At this stage of his career he was specially intimate with New Englanders and there was no clash of local interests between him and John Adams or Nathaniel Tracy, owner of the *Ceres* on which he had sailed to France.

He afterwards described commerce as the handmaid of agriculture, and at this time he wished that it could be wholly free. In any treaty made by the United States with another country, he would have liked to prescribe that no duties should be paid by either party on the products of the other. He preferred Adam Smith to the mercantilists – partly because he sought the highest possible degree of individual liberty in all things, partly because free trade seemed both desirable and practicable for a country that was as unembarrassed by established systems as the United States. For European countries, however, he recognized that free trade was now quite impossible. "These establishments are fixed upon them," he said; "they are interwoven with the body of their laws and the organization of their government and they make a great part of their revenue; they cannot then get rid of them." [17] The only feasible alternative was that duties be paid on the basis of the most favored nation, as Congress had perceived, discrimination by European nations being countered by American threats against their trade. In America itself matters could not be left to the caprice of individual states, as Jefferson, Jay, Adams, Madison, Monroe, and practically every other leader who gave serious thought to international affairs fully recognized. Jefferson wrote Madison that only when the disposition to invest Congress with the regulation of commerce appeared to be growing was he able to discover "the smallest token of respect towards the United States in any part of Europe." [18]

If the inevitability of national regulation of external commerce was

[16] TJ to Jay, Aug. 23, 1785 (Ford, IV, 88).
[17] TJ to Monroe, June 17, 1785 (Ford, IV, 56).
[18] TJ to Madison, Sept. 1, 1785 (L. & B., V, 108). See Setser, pp. 74, 80–81.

recognized by this champion of local self-government, so was the probability of war perceived by one who was temperamentally a man of peace. Jefferson's chief grievance against commerce was that it bred wars. Despite the best intentions, it laid any country open to the danger of violations of property and insults to persons. The obvious safeguard was the development of naval strength. "I think it to our interest to punish the first insult," he wrote John Jay; "because an insult unpunished is the parent of many others. We are not at this moment in a condition to do it, but we should put ourselves into it as soon as possible. . . . Our vicinity to their West Indian possessions and to the fisheries is a bridle which a small naval force on our part would hold in the mouths of the most powerful of these countries." [19]

When speaking of loss of property and insults to persons, he was thinking less of the West Indies than of the Barbary states on the north coast of Africa, whose raiders terrorized the Mediterranean and penetrated the Atlantic. The profits of the piracy of Algiers, Morocco, Tunis, and Tripoli did not come merely from taking ships and cargoes, but even more from holding captives for ransom. Several hapless American vessels and crews were taken during Jefferson's first winter abroad, and he said that his mind was "absolutely suspended between indignation and impotence." [20] Among the maritime powers, the British generally managed such matters best, and they had provided relatively effectual protection to the commerce of their colonials before the Revolution, but they had no thought of protecting the shipping of the independent American States. Indeed, the depredations of the pirates on the commerce of rival countries were so advantageous to the British that there was point in the maxim Benjamin Franklin had heard in London, that if there were no Algiers, it would be worth England's while to build one.

The three American commissioners had explicit authority to make treaties with the Barbary powers, but, quite obviously, these would have to be paid for. Jefferson was convinced from the beginning that the cost of peace would be excessive, and that the wiser policy would be to win it by force of arms. He had been only a few months in France when he wrote Monroe: "We ought to begin a naval power, if we mean to carry on our own commerce. Can we begin it on a more honorable occasion, or with a weaker foe? I am of opinion Paul

[19] TJ to Jay, Aug. 23, 1785 (Ford, IV, 89–90).

[20] TJ to Nathanael Greene, Jan. 12, 1785 (Ford, IV, 25). On the subject generally see Bemis, *Secretaries of State*, I, 265–271, and R. W. Irwin, *Diplomatic Relations of the U. S. with the Barbary Powers* (1931).

Jones with half a dozen frigates would totally destroy their commerce . . . by constant cruising and cutting them to pieces by piecemeal." But it was the judgment of Congress which determined policy; and Congress did nothing for a navy, trusting to negotiations and offering a modest price.[21]

Late in the spring of 1785 the commissioners learned that a sum not to exceed 80,000 dollars would be available for this purpose, and that they might delegate the negotiations to a suitable agent. They availed themselves of this authority after Franklin had left. Congress sent them papers by Captain John Lamb, who had been engaged in the Barbary trade, and during the summer and early fall of 1785 Jefferson and Adams impatiently awaited his arrival. Before he got there they had decided to send Thomas Barclay, consul general in France, to Morocco, the outermost and most amenable of the Barbary states. They were not required to avail themselves of Lamb's services but both of them assumed they were expected to; and when he finally reached Paris in September Jefferson recommended and Adams immediately agreed that he be sent to Algiers, the strongest and most bellicose of these powers. By this time Jefferson had received a credible report that two more American ships and crews had been taken by the Algerines, and had heard the amusing rumor, spread by the British, that Franklin himself had been captured as he started home. Jefferson and Adams were forced to limit Lamb to a ransom of 200 dollars per captive, and they must have feared that the Dey would regard this as trivial. It turned out afterwards that the potentate wanted 6000 dollars for a master, 4000 for a mate, and 1500 for each sailor, and was not at all interested in a treaty. He had set the captives to carrying rocks and timber on their backs over great distances in sharp and mountainous country, and had put some of them in chains.[22]

While Lamb and Barclay were on their way to North Africa, John Adams in London began negotiations with the ambassador of Tripoli, who made advances to him, swearing by his beard that his intentions

[21] TJ to Monroe, Nov. 11, 1784 (Ford, IV, 10–11). For the later naval situation, see TJ to Demeunier, Jan. 24, 1786 (Ford, IV, 145).

[22] Adams to TJ, May 23, 1786 (*Works*, VIII, 393–394). For the arrangements as a whole, the more important documents are: Adams to Jay, May 30, 1785 (*Works*, VIII, 253); TJ to Adams, Aug. 6, 1785 (L. & B., V, 54–55); Adams to TJ, Aug. 18, Sept. 16, 1785 (*Works*, VIII, 300–301, 314–315); TJ to Adams, Sept. 24, 1785 (L. & B., V, 142–146); Adams to TJ, Oct. 2, 1785 (*Works*, VIII, 316–317); commissions and instructions to Barclay and Lamb (*D. C.*, I, 656–662). Jefferson left a chronological memorandum of the entire negotiations with the Barbary powers, 1785–1790 (LC, 41540–41541), but this is less reliable for dates than the letters. See also TJ to Franklin, Oct. 5, 1785 (L. & B., V, 159).

were peaceable and humane. It was partly because of this prospect that Jefferson made a visit of two months to London in the spring of 1786, but the conferences with the Tripolitan served chiefly to elicit financial information and to contribute to the education of the Virginian in the ways of pirates. He found that Tripoli wanted 30,000 guineas, while bespeaking a like sum for Tunis, and that from 200,000 to 300,000 guineas represented a fair estimate of the total cost of peace with all of the Barbary powers. In comparison with this, what he and Adams had to offer was but a drop in the bucket.[23] Adams and Jefferson thought that a large loan might be secured in Holland to ransom the American captives but Jay saw no prospect of more money from the States, and thought it unwise to obtain new loans until there was better prospect of paying the interest on the old ones.

After he got back to Paris, Jefferson learned that Lamb's mission to Algiers had failed utterly. This was partly because of the Captain's maladroitness, but chiefly because the pirates demanded far more than he had been authorized to offer. Fresh reference of the entire matter to Congress was necessary and the return of Lamb to America was urged, but he proved obstinate. Jefferson afterwards wrote Monroe: "I am persuaded that an angel sent on this business, and so much limited in his terms, could have done nothing. But should Congress propose to try the line of negotiation again, I think they will perceive that Lamb is not a proper agent." [24] Afterwards he was rather troubled in conscience that they had appointed Lamb, but Adams assured him that they were not censurable. "We found him ready appointed on our hands," he said. "I never saw him nor heard of him. He ever was and still is as indifferent to me as a Mohawk Indian. But as he came from Congress with their dispatches of such importance, I supposed it was expected we should appoint him." He thought no harm had been done. If Congress had sent its ablest member he could have done no better.[25]

It was under these deeply discouraging circumstances that these representatives of a weak government discussed in long letters the

[23] TJ to William Carmichael, May 5, 1786 (L. & B., V, 306–307). The beginnings of the negotiation are described in letters of Adams to Jay, Feb. 20, 22, 1786 (*Works*, VIII, 374–376, 377–380), and the results in a joint letter of the commissioners to Jay, Mar. 28, 1786 (*D. C.*, I, 604–605). Jay reported on this to Congress, May 29, 1786 (*D. C.*, I, 606–608).

Jefferson's visit to London as a whole is described in Chapter IV of this volume.

[24] TJ to Monroe, Aug. 11, 1786 (Ford, IV, 264). On Mar. 29, 1786, Lamb advised the abandonment of the mission (*D. C.*, I, 739–740). TJ reported the matter to Adams on May 11, 1786 (L. & B., V, 333); and they sent a joint letter to Lamb on June 29 (Adams, *Works*, VIII, 405–406).

[25] Adams to TJ, Jan. 25, 1787 (LC, 4741).

highly unpalatable alternatives of ransom and war. Adams still believed that it would be easier to buy peace than to induce the American people to go to war, and that the commercial gains would be sufficient to justify the great cost, but he thought the whole question academic until Congress could get more money and pay the interest on outstanding loans. "The moment this is done," he said, "we may borrow a sum adequate to all our necessities; if it is not done, in my opinion, you and I, as well as every other servant of the United States in Europe, ought to go home, give up all points, and let our exports and imports be done in European bottoms."[26]

Jefferson fully agreed that the commissioners were really helpless, and he thought his own private judgment inconsequential. But he stuck to his original opinion that, on grounds of honor and justice, war would be better than the purchase of a peace, and he disagreed with Adams that it would be more expensive. Oddly enough, he emphasized the importance of a navy more than Adams did, his estimate of the necessary strength being based on inquiries into the past experience of the French and British.[27] Uncertain as the outcome of war would be, he questioned the durability of a peace bought with money from such people as the Algerines, by a country like the United States without naval power to enforce it. Furthermore, he believed that it would not be necessary to fight alone; he thought that Naples and Portugal and possibly others would join the United States in this endeavor.

Besides his realistic comments on the necessity of a navy, Jefferson's chief constructive contribution to the solution of this problem consisted of a plan for concerted action against the pirates by the powers habitually suffering from their depredations, or by any two of them. This he embodied in a convention which called for constant cruising along the coast by a naval force provided on a quota system and directed by a council of ambassadors at some one court, such as Versailles. The aim was not temporary immunity but perpetual peace, without tribute. Lafayette liked the idea so much that he proposed himself to Jefferson as "a chief to the anti-piratical confederacy," and, according to the latter's own later story, a number of smaller powers

[26] Adams to TJ, June 6, 1786 (*Works,* VIII, 400); see also July 3, 1786 (VIII, 406–407).

[27] See Count d'Estaing to TJ, May 17, 1786 (*D. C.,* I, 752–754). He believed that the effects of bombardments were transitory – "like breaking glass windows with guineas" – but that even an imperfect blockade would be unendurable to the pirates in the long run. Several powers in co-operation could force them to become merchants in a few years. See also TJ to Adams, July 11, 1786 (L. & B. V, 364–368).

were favorably disposed to such an association – but feared the opposition of France. Jefferson sounded out Vergennes, and got him to say that the English would not be permitted to interfere. The presumption was that France would not; and Jefferson attributed the failure of the scheme not to European opposition or indifference, but to the financial impotence of the American Congress.[28] It is possible that concerted action such as Jefferson suggested would have removed the menace of the pirates, who gained their ends more by terror than by strength, but the idea was ahead of its time. In that age of unabashed economic warfare the very advantages gained by one country from the depredations on the commerce of another would have made co-operation of this sort difficult, and it would have been most surprising if anything had come of the proposal.

Something did come of the negotiations of Thomas Barclay. Luck was with him, and his mission to Morocco proved to be wholly successful. At the relative low cost of 30,000 dollars he got the captives released and negotiated a treaty which called for no annual tribute. Except for the treaty with Prussia, it was the only one which could be chalked up by Adams and Jefferson on the credit side of their mission, but actually it was chiefly due to the support of Spain, given for political reasons – in order that Spain herself might exact more favorable terms from the United States, especially in the matter of the navigation of the Mississippi.[29]

During the rest of his stay abroad Jefferson continued to be concerned about American captives of the other Barbary powers, and, despite his reluctance to enter upon a ransoming policy, tried to get the prisoners in Algiers released through the indirect employment of that means. Soon after the treaty with Morocco was negotiated he learned of a religious order, called the Mathurins, which made a business of begging alms for the release of captives and had representatives in all the piratical states. After interviewing the general of the order and receiving an offer of his services, Jefferson wrote John Adams and referred the matter to John Jay for the consideration of

[28] His proposals, along with his account of the circumstances, are in his autobiography (Ford, I, 91–94.) He had them translated into French and Italian (LC, 4472–4474; 6239–6242; 41539–41539a). For Lafayette's proposal, see Gilbert Chinard, *Letters of Lafayette and Jefferson* (1929), pp. 64, 101. The question came up in Congress July 27, 1787, when a motion along the line of Jefferson's recommendations was introduced. It was then moved that the matter be referred to the Secretary for Foreign Affairs to report (*Secret Journals of Congress*, 1821, IV, 372–374). There it died, for apparently Jay neither reported to Congress nor wrote Jefferson about it.

[29] Bemis, *Secretaries*, p. 268; Irwin, p. 33. The treaty was made in January 1787, and ratified in July.

Congress. Some nine months later (September 19, 1787), he received the necessary authorization, being told to offer ransom at a normal rate; but the funds were not made available to him until two years after that, when he was on the point of returning home. Meanwhile, the cost of ransom seemed to grow with every inquiry. He wanted this tricky business to be done as indirectly and unofficially as possible, and in the matter of price sought to avoid the establishment of an impossible precedent. For that reason, while he was waiting, he caused it to be believed in Algiers that the American government had withdrawn attention from the sixteen or seventeen captives there. The only perceptible effect of this maneuver was to distress the captives and cause them to blame him, but for their own sakes and for the sake of others who might come after them he believed that he must not correct this temporary and false impression of his own inhumanity.[30]

In the end, nothing came of these devious and long-continued negotiations. After he got back to his own country he found that new difficulties confronted the Mathurins and, despite the much more generous financial offers he could then make, all these efforts were of no avail. During the French Revolution the order itself was dissolved, and the problem of the Barbary pirates remained on his docket not only while he was the Secretary of State but also when he was the President of the United States.[31]

[30] TJ to Jay, May 4, 1788 (*D. C.*, II, 148).

[31] The Mathurin episode is treated in Irwin, *Diplomatic Relations of the U. S. and the Barbary Powers*, pp. 44–46. Jefferson's own activities in this connection while he was in France can be traced through his official letters: to Adams, Jan. 11, 1787 (*D. C.*, II, 25–26); to Jay, Feb. 1, 1787 (*ibid.*, II, 28); to Jay, Sept. 19, 1787 (*ibid.*, II, 86–87); to Jay, Aug. 11, 1788 (*ibid.*, II, 182); to the Commissioners of the Treasury, Sept. 6, 1788 (*ibid.*, II, 193); to Jay, Aug. 27, 1789 (*ibid.*, II, 319). For his reports of Dec. 28, 1790, when he was Secretary of State – on "Prisoners at Algiers and the Mediterranean Trade" – see *A.S.P.F.R*, I, 100–108. The memo. in his own papers (LC, 41540–41541), giving in outline a record of the negotiations with the Barbary powers, contains a few details, especially about prices, which do not seem to be in print.

[III]

At the Court of Versailles

1785–1787

LATE in his life Jefferson said that as Franklin's successor he found the Court of Louis XVI a school of humility. This remark, now well-known, was not an example of false modesty. The fame of his predecessor, as John Adams had said, was more universal than that of Leibnitz or Newton, Frederick the Great or Voltaire. He himself observed that the respect for Franklin was greater than that shown to any other person in France, foreign or native. Many admiring Frenchmen regarded the soberly dressed Philadelphian, with his invariable spectacles and unpowdered hair, as the first citizen of the world. Jefferson did not personify the cult of simplicity so ostentatiously, his scientific achievements had not been spectacular, and he had not learned to be any sort of a showman. Thus his proper reply to questioners was that he did not replace Franklin. He could not do that and nobody could. He merely succeeded him.

Franklin had not only drawn lightning from the skies. As Turgot's line put it, he had also wrested the scepter from the tyrant's hand. By any reckoning his political achievements had been momentous; and there is no need here to weigh with apothecary's scales his credit for the alliance, for aid to the United States, for the treaty of peace. The important fact is that general French opinion credited him with practically everything that had been accomplished. To the French he was not merely the embodiment of science and philosophy and simplicity; he was also the supreme symbol of the American Republic. They coupled Washington's name with his, to be sure, but the General was far distant, and if people did not see Franklin himself they saw his picture everywhere. He grew weary of sitting for artists and sculptors; he appeared on medallions, snuffboxes, and pocketknives – even, it is said, on a *vase de nuit*. But when Jefferson arrived in France he himself had not yet had a single portrait painted.

Unlike John Adams, Jefferson had no jealousy of Franklin – partly because of the circumstances of their association, partly because of age, partly because of temperament. Adams could not conceal his not unnatural resentment that his world-renowned colleague had gained nearly all the credit for public achievements in which other men, including himself, had shared. The New Englander, suspicious by nature, never overcame his distrust of the wily Doctor, regarding him as subservient to the French and wondering how such an invariably amiable man could possibly be sincere. Jefferson, on the other hand, believed that the French government was more under Franklin's influence than he under theirs, and that as a public man he stood head above all other Americans with the single exception of Washington. Several years later, when Secretary of State, he proposed that the executive department wear mourning for Franklin, but President Washington demurred, saying that he did not know where they would draw the line once they began that sort of ceremony. "I told him," said Jefferson, "the world had drawn so broad a line between himself and Dr. Franklin, on the one side, and the residue of mankind, on the other, that we might wear mourning for them, and the question still remain new and undecided as to all others."[1] If a distinction can be made between vanity and sensitiveness, Adams's weakness was the former and Jefferson's the latter. Franklin never wounded him, and the Virginian valued his predecessor at Versailles as a human being for just the reason that the New Englander suspected him – for his invariable and universal amiability. A major secret of Franklin's appeal, so he told his grandson, was that he never contradicted anybody. This did not seem a virtue to brusque John Adams.

It was easy for a man of Jefferson's catholicity and tolerance to like both of his fellow commissioners better than they liked each other. Persons whose general attitude he approved he nearly always accepted uncritically at first, and this often caused more suspicious people to think him gullible, as he sometimes was. Not until after Adams had advocated pomp and ceremony as Vice President in the new United States government did Jefferson quote Franklin's now-famous saying about him: "always an honest man, often a great one, but sometimes

[1] TJ to Benjamin Rush, Oct. 4, 1803 (Ford, VIII, 265). This opinion is in direct contrast to the one expressed by John Adams to William Tudor, late in life (June 15, 1817, in *A.H.R.*, XLVII, 807), when he declared that both Franklin and Washington shone by reflected luster.

absolutely mad."[2] He himself never had occasion to be critical of Franklin and he rightly deemed it an honor to succeed him.

The French were glad to get Jefferson if they could not keep Franklin. La Luzerne, the Minister to the United States, wrote Vergennes about him before he had even sailed from Boston. The comments were not wholly flattering, for La Luzerne said that as Governor of Virginia Jefferson had shown himself incapable of holding the helm in stormy weather. But the Frenchman referred to his reputation for enlightenment and integrity, to his passionate love for the arts and sciences, and said other things which were of even greater interest to a minister of foreign affairs:

> . . . He is full of honor and sincerity and loves his country greatly, but is too philosophic and tranquil to hate or love any other nation unless it is for the interest of the United States to do so. He has a principle that it is for the happiness and welfare of the United States to hold itself as much aloof from England as a peaceful state of affairs permits, that as a consequence of this system it becomes them to attach themselves particularly to France, even that Congress ought as quickly as possible to direct the affection of the people toward us in order to balance the penchant and numerous causes continually attracting them to England.

Marbois, the chargé d'affaires, whose questions led to the *Notes on Virginia*, was highly complimentary in his turn, saying: "Mr. Jefferson is an upright, just man, who belongs to no party, and his representations will have the greatest weight on the general Congress."[3]

Vergennes would not have welcomed John Adams or John Jay with such satisfaction. Both of these men had shown considerable suspicion of him during the late peace negotiations, and Jay's recent appointment as the Secretary for Foreign Affairs was not viewed with favor in France.

There is no reason whatever to impugn the loyal patriotism of any one of the three men. The question is altogether that of their respective judgments of the existing international situation. Jefferson started out with a presumption for the French and against the British because of what had happened in the past, and it was a matter of considerable

[2] TJ to Madison, July 29, 1789 (Ford, V, 104), wording slightly modified from a doubtful text.

[3] La Luzerne to Vergennes, May 17, 1784 (quoted by Bemis in *Secretaries*, II, 7, and in this work by permission of Alfred A. Knopf); Marbois to Rayneval, Aug. 24, 1784 (quoted by George Bancroft, *Hist. of the Formation of the Constitution*, 1882, I, 379).

weight with him from the beginning that the French officials were the more friendly.

He found Vergennes a most agreeable person to do business with, even though he believed that age had chilled that statesman's heart. Unlike many other members of the diplomatic corps and his own countryman John Adams, he did not regard the famous foreign minister as slippery. On the other hand, he had no illusions about the attitude of Vergennes toward republican institutions. He wrote Madison: "His devotion to the principles of pure despotism renders him unaffectionate to our governments. But his fear of England makes him value us as a make weight." Thus the American pierced to the heart of the Frenchman's correct, cordial, and calculated policy.[4]

Jefferson also commented on Rayneval and Hennin, whom he termed the "two eyes" of Vergennes, finding much duplicity in the former and genuine liberalism of philosophy in the latter. Unfortunately, the affairs of the United States fell in Rayneval's department. Also, he had frequent occasion to regret that certain decisions which vitally affected the United States were really made by the Comptroller General, Calonne, who, in Jefferson's opinion, was caught in the toils of the existing system to a greater degree than Vergennes. Another just grievance of Jefferson's against the French was the secrecy of their procedure, which was partly owing to deliberate policy, partly to the lack of co-ordination between the various bureaus of a lumbering and inefficient government. A highly important decree respecting the West Indian trade, issued about the time that he arrived and while Franklin was still minister, was quite unknown to the latter, as well as to Adams and Jefferson, and was learned about in America before any of them reported it. Another decree, when he was minister, he did not learn about until six weeks after it had been issued.[5] Any person dealing with the French bureaucracy had to learn to be patient.

The commissioners had soon concluded that no supplementary treaty with France was feasible. Jefferson tried to secure particular concessions by ordinary diplomatic procedure, and in his own later opinion he accomplished little that was important. The issues were certainly not as crucial as they had been in Franklin's day, but his modest statement was hardly just to his own assiduous attention to his duties or to his actual accomplishments.

The decree of August 30, 1784, for which he was not responsible and of which he was so long ignorant, was important because it ad-

[4] TJ to Madison, Jan. 30, 1787 (Ford, IV, 366). For an admirable statement see Setser, *Commercial Reciprocity Policy* (1937), pp. 81–83.

[5] TJ to Monroe, July 9, 1786 (Ford, IV, 248–249).

mitted American commerce to the French West Indies in considerable degree and thus served to offset the loss of the former commerce with the British Islands. The trouble was that the French merchants were furious about it and brought great pressure against it. Soon after he became minister Jefferson wrote Monroe: "The Ministry are disposed to be firm, but there is a point at which they will give way, that is, if the clamors should become such as to endanger their places. It is evident that nothing can be done by us at this time, if we may hope it hereafter." A few weeks later he wrote Adams that there seemed to be considerably more American vessels in the French West Indies than previously, and that he now had no fears that the decree would be revoked. By fall, however, American privileges had been reduced by other measures, and in December, when Jefferson conferred with Vergennes about the whole state of commerce, he did not press the question of the West Indian trade, despite his recognition of its great importance, for he then regarded efforts in favor of this as desperate.[6] In this area he thought his bargaining position weak. He doubted if further formal concessions by the French in the West Indies would be possible except on the promise of American aid in war, and he had neither the desire nor the authority to associate his country that unequivocally with France. The best of all arguments in favor of concessions in the West Indies was that illegitimate trade would go on without them. This consideration finally proved influential without Jefferson's being put to the embarrassment of advancing it, and at this stage he concerned himself chiefly with the improvement of commerce with continental France.

One obstacle which Vergennes continually alluded to and Jefferson himself clearly recognized was the American habit of trading with England, which the war had temporarily disrupted but had not fundamentally changed. It was but too true, Jefferson wrote Monroe, that that country furnished a market for three fourths of the exports of the eight northernmost American states.[7] He had several objections to the continuance of this course of trade. It galled him to think that the British still regarded their former colonials as economic dependents. Furthermore, while recognizing that commerce with the British West Indies was of prime importance, Jefferson believed that American trade with England was a losing business. It went there, not because that was the best market, but because England provided the readiest credit. Being a Virginian, he was fully aware of that. Finally, this was to a

[6] TJ to Monroe, June 17, 1785 (Ford, IV, 51–52); to Adams, Aug. 10, 1785 (L. & B., V, 58); Memo. of conference of Dec. 9, 1785 (Ford, IV, 129–130).

[7] TJ to Monroe, Aug. 28, 1785 (Ford, IV, 85).

considerable extent a luxury business. He would have preferred that the Americans learn to do without European luxuries and gewgaws in this time of stress, but at all events there were other places than England where these were to be had if only his countrymen could get acquainted with them. To certain correspondents at home he advocated a reformation in manners and commerce, but upon Vergennes he urged that the real difficulty lay in commercial arrangements. Americans could not buy in France unless they could sell there.

On his part the Count complained sharply about the commercial regulations of the various American states, saying that French merchants found these disgusting and that his government could not sufficiently depend on arrangements made with the Republic. However, he fully agreed with Jefferson's major contention that there could be no durable commerce without exchange of merchandise, and that it was natural for merchants to get their returns in the ports where they sold their cargoes. Jefferson had no doubt of the sympathy of the Foreign Minister with his desire to facilitate direct commerce between the United States and France.[8]

Jefferson summed up the possibilities as follows:

> . . . We can furnish to France (because we have heretofore furnished to England), of whale oil and spermaceti, of furs and peltry, of ships and naval stores, and of potash to the amount of fifteen millions of livres; and the quantities will admit of increase. Of our tobacco, France consumes the value of ten millions more. Twenty-five millions of livres, then, mark the extent of that commerce of exchange, which is, at present, practicable between us. We want, in return, productions and manufactures, not money. If the duties on our produce are light, and the sale free, we shall undoubtedly bring it here, and lay out the proceeds on the spot in the productions and manufactures we want. . . . The conclusion is, that there are commodities which form a basis of exchange to the extent of a million of guineas annually; it is for the wisdom of those in power to contrive that the exchange shall be made.[9]

In his diplomatic activity as a whole Jefferson maintained a nice balance between the American regions, representing all of them as effectively as he could. Through the good offices of Lafayette he

[8] The best statement of the whole situation as he viewed it during the Vergennes tenure of office is in his memorandum of their conference of Dec. 9, 1785; and his later reply to specific complaints, sent with his letter of Jan. 2, 1786 to Jay (Ford, IV, 117–130). See Jay's comments, June 16, 1786 (*D. C.*, I, 722–723). See also TJ's earlier letter of Nov. 20, 1785, to Vergennes (*D. C.*, I, 708–709).

[9] *Ford*, IV, 128.

gained his first success in concessions on the importation of fish oil, and the effort to find a larger market in France for South Carolina rice consumed days and weeks of his time later on.[10] The most interesting of his early efforts to facilitate commerce related to the staple product of his own region, but he concerned himself with the tobacco trade not merely because he was a Virginian. It was exceedingly important, and was shackled in France to notorious degree.

Very early in his stay in France his attention was called to the tobacco monopoly by James Monroe, who expressed the opinion that it was contrary to the spirit of the existing treaty. During his first winter, while he was still only a commissioner, Jefferson wrote his fellow Virginian: "The abolition of the monopoly of our tobacco in the hands of the Farmers General will be pushed by us with all our force. But it is so interwoven with the very foundations of their system of finance that it is of doubtful event." [11] The existing arrangement was part of the prevailing system of farming out to individuals or groups of individuals the right to collect indirect taxes. The Government granted for a lump sum the sole right to purchase tobacco, thus forcing individual sellers to deal wholly with the Tobacco Farm. From the American point of view the monopolistic system was bad enough in itself, and the difficulties were accentuated when the Farmers General made a contract with Robert Morris early in 1785. This meant, in effect, that all American tobacco must go to them through him, and it created a double monopoly.[12] This contract was made before Jefferson became minister to France and he appears to have known nothing of it at the time. It was approved by the Comptroller, Calonne, but seems not to have been submitted to Vergennes, who was much more interested in developing American trade.

Jefferson's personal activity in this matter began in the summer of 1785, soon after he became minister, and was stimulated by Lafayette. The Marquis had returned from America in January and he and Jefferson had renewed acquaintance at once though the circumstances were sad, since it was he who brought the letters about the death of

[10] Vergennes to TJ, Nov. 30, 1785, and Calonne to Lafayette, Nov. 17, 1785 (*D. C.*, I, 710–711), stating that until Jan. 1, 1787, Americans should pay no more duties than the Hanse towns. Hitherto payments had been as by all other nations *except* Hanse towns. The rice question will be referred to hereafter.

[11] TJ to Monroe, Dec. 10, 1784 (Ford, IV, 20); Monroe to TJ, May 25, July 20, 1784 (S. M. Hamilton, I, 30, 37).

[12] Contract signed by the farmers-general Jan. 11, 1785, by Morris April 10, 1785. It called for the delivery of 60,000 hhds. of tobacco, 1785–1787, at 36 livres the hundredweight, Morris receiving an advance of a million livres. Whole matter discussed by F. L. Nussbaum, "American Tobacco and French Politics," *Pol. Science Quart.*, XL, 497–516 (Dec. 1925).

little Lucy. Almost from the beginning of his ministry Jefferson found the ardent young nobleman the most valuable auxiliary he had. He had good reason to be grateful to the Marquis for military services in Virginia, and his friend Madison, who had had recent opportunity to observe Lafayette's political attitude, wrote most encouragingly about him. "I take him to be as amiable a man as can be imagined and as sincere an American as any Frenchman can be," he said.[13] During most of the summer of 1785, however, Lafayette was in Central Europe attending army maneuvers, and Jefferson viewed the tobacco situation with his own eyes.

"I am very sensible that no trade can be on a more desperate footing than that of tobacco, in this country," he wrote; "and that our merchants must abandon the French markets, if they are not permitted to sell the productions they bring, on such terms as will enable them to purchase reasonable returns in the manufactures of France."[14] He saw but one remedy for the situation – free sale – and in August he boldly proposed to Vergennes the abolition of the tobacco monopoly. Perhaps this was a breach of diplomatic etiquette, but there were a good many French critics of the monopolistic system, and the Foreign Minister himself did not like this aspect of it.[15]

Jefferson's major reason for making this frontal attack on the established system was his desire to improve the commerce between the United States and France. His approach to the problem was practical, not theoretical, but this contest revealed his growing sympathy with economic *laissez faire*. "It is contrary to the spirit of trade, and to the dispositions of merchants, to carry a commodity to any market where but one person is allowed to buy it, and where, of course, that person fixes the prices," he said.[16] He made it clear that he had no thought of diminishing the revenue of the King, and he was entirely correct in saying that the cost of collecting it in this case (the profit of the Farmers General) was excessive. The supression of the monopoly would be advantageous to France as well as the United States, he believed, for the Crown's revenue would be increased if translated into import duties, the impost on the people would be diminished, and the French would be able to pay for their tobacco in merchandise instead of coin. His opinion, as expressed here and elsewhere, was that the

[13] Madison to TJ, Oct. 17, 1784; Hunt, II, 86. On Lafayette's invaluable services see Louis Gottschalk, *Lafayette between the American Revolution and the French Revolution* (1950), ch. XV.

[14] TJ to Messrs. French and Nephew, July 13, 1785 (L. & B., V, 35).

[15] TJ to Vergennes, Aug. 15, 1785 (L. & B., V, 68–76). They had discussed the matter previously but Jefferson felt surer of himself in English.

[16] L. & B., V, 70.

annual consumption of tobacco in France did not exceed the amount of commodities which Americans could buy more advantageously in France than in England. Direct exchange to that extent at least was economically desirable, besides its advantages in cementing the friendship between the two countries.

His well-reasoned argument, and particularly the part of it relating to the advantages to the Crown itself of a change in the method of collecting the tobacco revenue, commended itself to Rayneval, of whom he was rather suspicious, and his somewhat presumptuous proposal was strongly supported by Vergennes, who submitted it to Calonne. A new contract or lease with the Farmers General was pending, and Jefferson's hope was that the article of tobacco might be withdrawn from it. His representations played a part in delaying the completion of this new lease, but by the end of 1785 it was thought too far advanced to be changed. Through the veil which covered the transaction Jefferson perceived the true obstacle. Calonne's position was too precarious for him to risk the hostility of the Farmers General, whatever the joint interests of France and the United States might require. Meanwhile, Jefferson found comfort in the thought that the idea of discontinuing the farming out of the tobacco revenue had been lodged in the mind of Vergennes. Rayneval observed to him "that it sometimes happened that useful propositions, though not practicable at one time, might become so at another." John Jay warmly commended Jefferson's efforts but reminded him that governments, like individuals, often become strongly attached by habit to things that do them harm. He continued: "So that we may apply to errors in politics, what was wisely remarked of errors in morals; it is hard for those who are *accustomed* to do evil to learn to do well." [17]

Meanwhile, Lafayette had strongly reinforced Jefferson. Returning from Berlin in the fall of 1785, the Marquis, zealous in all matters affecting the United States, brought his American friend into contact with several Frenchmen who were acquainted with commercial questions. These men recommended that he propose to Vergennes the appointment of a committee. Jefferson demurred at that and got Lafayette himself to do it. Vergennes befriended the proposal and by early February, 1786, a large committee was set up by Calonne. This was made up of members of the council, intendants of commerce, a merchant, farmers-general, and – what was most important to Jefferson – Du Pont de Nemours and Lafayette. The event was significant in Jefferson's own history, entirely apart from the diplomatic results, for

[17] TJ's memorandum (Ford, IV, 120); Jay to TJ, June 16, 1786 (*D. C.*, I, 722).

he thus began his long and fruitful friendship with one of these two men and deepened his friendship with the other.[18]

They used arguments and figures which he supplied, but he thought their views were somewhat different from his. They were less hopeful that the Tobacco Farm could be overthrown and more disposed to seek temporary palliatives, bringing their guns to bear chiefly on the existing contract of the Farmers General with Robert Morris, which Jefferson afterwards said he acknowledged as binding.[19] A renewed lease with the Farmers General was signed in March, 1786, when he was temporarily in England, and tobacco was included in it. The right of the Crown to withdraw this was recognized, but Vergennes made it clear in May that the right was not likely to be exercised; the financial situation was too hazardous to permit any interruption or temporary diminution of the revenue. The question of the Morris contract remained. This was considered at a meeting of the committee on May 24, 1786, at Berni, the seat of the Comptroller General, which Vergennes attended. It was then resolved that the Morris contract should not be annulled, but that no similar one should ever again be made. It was also agreed that the Farmers General be required to purchase a stipulated amount of additional tobacco from merchants bringing it in French or American vessels, prices being set at a definite figure. Jefferson thought this the least objectionable of the various palliatives proposed, but he correctly perceived that the arrangement contained the seeds of trouble – that the Farmers General would multiply difficulties and vexations, and that individual merchants would make continual complaints. He only hoped that there would be enough trouble to force the ministry to reopen the whole question of abolishing the monopoly.[20]

The previous effect of the Morris contract, as he reported in the summer of 1786, had been to throw the tobacco trade in agonies; but

[18] Lafayette to Lambert, Sept. 10, 1787, reviewing past events (text and translation in Chinard, *Letters of Lafayette & Jefferson*, pp. 114–122). TJ gives an account of the setting-up of the committee in his letter to Monroe, May 10, 1786 (Ford, IV, 223–225); and to Jay, May 27, 1786 (Ford, p. 233). Gottschalk lists the members of the committee and describes meetings in ch. XVI.

[19] Jefferson stated to Monroe on Dec. 18, 1786 (L. & B., VI, 15–16) that he never asked the abolition of the Morris contract but always assured Calonne that annulment would be unjust. He said the same thing later to Gouverneur Morris and convinced that interested gentleman of the truthfulness of his assertion (July 21, 1789, Morris, *Diary*, I, 159*n.*). However, he unquestionably spoke of the ill effects of the contract (to John Adams, July 9, 1786; Ford, IV, 252–253). He probably saw no escape on legal grounds, and he certainly thought the root of the trouble lay much deeper. Thus his position seems somewhat equivocal but is not inexplicable.

[20] Resultat of committee held at Berni, May 24, 1786. (LC, 3594–3595); comments to Jay, May 27, 1786 (Ford, IV, 232–236); Lafayette's "Resumé," ed. by Nussbaum in *Jour. Modern Hist.*, III (1931), 592–613, with notes and narrative.

he regarded the Decision of Berni as a minor American victory and believed that it would serve to stabilize prices at a higher level. The efforts of the American committee brought other favorable results. The duty on fish oils was reduced, for one thing, and Jefferson was hopefully considering the prospects of new trade in furs and rice.[21] The activities of the committee had broadened out so as to include the whole subject of American commerce, and Jefferson continued to arm Lafayette with facts and figures. The American gave his friend and willing helper an estimate of the exports and imports of the United States, based partly on such figures as had been made public, partly on information he himself had collected in many of the states – especially during his trip (1784) to the seaports of New England.[22] The net result of these continuing activities was a letter from Calonne to Jefferson, dated October 22, 1786, in which the various dispositions taken to favor American commerce were summed up.[23]

This letter did not embody all the recommendations of the committee, such as the entire removal of all duties on oils, but Jefferson described it as almost a verbal copy of one drafted by the committee. It repeated past promises about free ports and the reduction and simplification of port charges, reaffirmed the decision about tobacco, and granted for ten years the temporary privileges already given to whale oil, spermaceti, and other products of the sort, while removing entirely the heavy duty on fabrication. It removed the considerable duties on potash, beaver skins and raw leather, and on all woods used for shipbuilding, as it did on some other things which were of special interest to Jefferson – shrubs, trees, and seed, and all kinds of books and papers. He had no objection to the principle of importation in French or American vessels which was insisted on throughout, and no doubt regarded the exemption of the latter from the duty of 5 per cent on the purchase of foreign-built ships as a further encouragement to shipping interests in his own country.

Considering the times, the concessions were real, and he was warranted in viewing Calonne's letter as a visible proof of the disposition of the French ministers "to produce a more intimate intercourse between the two nations." He sent printed copies of it not only to America but also to the French ports, which he proposed to visit personally in the spring; he thanked Calonne, and he wanted Congress

[21] TJ to Jay, May 27, 1786; Ford, IV, 230–232, 236–237.

[22] Letter of July 17, 1786, and tables (Ford, IV, 255–259). Jefferson was apologetic because able to give only an approximation. See Gottschalk, ch. XVII, for a full discussion.

[23] Translation in *D. C.*, I, 827–829. See also TJ to Jay, Oct. 23, 1786 (L. & B., V, 450–454, wrongly dated Oct. 22).

to give special thanks to Lafayette. However, this was hardly an "ultimate settlement" of the conditions of American commerce with France, as he fondly hoped. In this over-governed and badly governed country ministerial words were not immediately translated into official practice, and gains once made could be preserved only by the exercise of eternal vigilance.

The mutual respect of Jefferson and Lafayette had now blossomed into enthusiastic mutual admiration. At the very beginning of the work of the committee, the latter wrote George Washington that words could not express his delight with the public conduct of the American Minister.[24] This highly favorable judgment was underlined in later letters to the General and to John Jay; the Marquis was very happy to be the aide-de-camp of one who transacted the affairs of America to perfection. On his part, Jefferson appreciated Lafayette from the outset, because of past services in Virginia. Already commissioned to have two busts of Lafayette made by Houdon, one to go to the capital of Virginia and the other to be presented to the City of Paris, he suggested early in 1786 that his native Commonwealth make the young Frenchman a gift of land. Even at this date he thought it not unlikely that Lafayette would need an asylum someday; he doubted if the impressions made on him by republican America would permit him ever to accommodate himself to monarchical principles, and thought that all his prudence, with that of his friends, would be required to keep him safe in France.[25]

The busts were delayed but, in late September, 1786, one of them was presented by the State of Virginia to the City of Paris. Then confined to his room with a dislocated wrist, resulting from an unhappy accident which we shall describe later, Jefferson was represented at the ceremonies by William Short, who bore a letter from him to the municipal officials. Thus he did not see the assembled dignitaries, nor hear the much-applauded speech of Éthis de Corny, an aide to Lafayette in the American Revolution and fellow member of the Society of the Cincinnati who was now described as "*Avocat et Procureur du Roi.*" He did not hear the military music which was played when the bust was placed in the great hall of the Hôtel de Ville, or see that many tears were shed. But the tribute to the Marquis in his letter has been described as the most sincere and striking ever paid to Lafayette.

[24] See particularly, Lafayette to Washington, Feb. 8, Oct. 26, 1786 (*Mémoires*, II, 141, 157); to Jay, Feb. 11, 1786 (*ibid.*, II, 146); to Washington, Jan. 7, 1787 (Chinard, *Lafayette and Jefferson*, p. 69).

[25] TJ to Madison, Feb. 8, 1786 (Ford, IV, 195–196).

To the proper thanks he gave the young nobleman for his military services, culminating in the victory at Yorktown, he added an important observation which he himself had made while Governor of Virginia. Throughout the military operations, he said, Lafayette paid implicit regard to the laws of the land. Jefferson liked not only what the gallant soldier had done; he liked even more the spirit in which he did it.[26]

His deep appreciation of past services was now increased by gratitude for Lafayette's vigorous efforts in behalf of American commerce, which seemed to him to warrant the special thanks of Congress. These thanks do not appear to have been given, but the inhabitants of the island of Nantucket thought of a way to indicate their appreciation of what Lafayette had done for whale oil. They agreed that each of them would give the milk of his cow for twenty-four hours in order that a cheese of 500 pounds could be made for the Marquis.[27] Jefferson's own best summary of his friend's services and character in this period was the private one he gave James Madison. Lafayette's zeal was unbounded, he said, and his influence great. Commerce had been an unknown field to him, but he quickly comprehended whatever was explained to him. In France there was nothing against him but "the suspicion of republican principles." As a man he had one weakness, "a canine appetite for popularity and fame," but he would get over it. The word "canine" was unpleasant, but Jefferson had correctly judged Lafayette's love for glory to be practically insatiable.[28]

Now regarded in his own country as the special guardian of American interests, Lafayette was credited by many people with the "liaisons" of commerce supposed to have been established. He basked in this mild glory, and in his own house he assumed American customs in a way that bordered on affectation. The place breathed with simplicity, even the children spoke English, and a costumed Indian served as courier.[29] But Jefferson had no doubt of Lafayette's sincere devotion to the "good cause," and gave little or no sign of personal jealousy of the showy and vainglorious young nobleman, though he was

[26] TJ to the *Prévôt des Marchands et Échevins*, Sept. 27, 1786 (L. & B., V, 428–429). The comment on the tribute is that of Chinard (*Lafayette and Jefferson*, p. 67). There is an account of the ceremonies of Sept. 28, 1786, in Thiéry, *Guide des amateurs et des étrangers*, II, 684–686. G. G. Schackelford, in his unpublished thesis on Short, quotes a letter to William Nelson, Oct. 25, 1786, giving details about the ceremonies and saying they created a sensation in France. The story of the reception of the bust is fully and well told by Gottschalk, *Lafayette between the American Revolution and the French Revolution*, pp. 250–252.

[27] Gottschalk, p. 254. This was in September, 1786.

[28] TJ to Madison, Jan. 30, 1787 (Ford, IV, 366).

[29] Étienne Charavay, *Le Général La Fayette* (Paris, 1898), pp. 137–138.

sometimes disturbed by indiscretions.[30] His contemporary comments were thoroughly consistent with those of later years. Nearly forty years after these events, at a dinner to Lafayette in Charlottesville, Virginia, he paid striking tribute to the services of his ancient auxiliary. "All doors of all departments were open to him at all times," he said; "to me only formally and at appointed times. In truth, I only held the nail, he drove it." [31]

He was in a grateful and optimistic mood in late 1786 and early 1787. He wrote Madison: "Nothing should be spared, on our part, to attach this country to us. It is the only one on which we can rely for support, under every event. Its inhabitants love us more, I think, than they do any other nation on earth. This is very much the effect of the good dispositions with which the French officers returned." [32] He did not change his opinion while he remained in France, but he soon found out that congratulations about the improvement of Franco-American commerce had been premature.

Calonne's letter was duly reported to the States and well received there, and Jefferson scattered copies of it in France, but no instructions seem to have been sent by the French authorities – because of bureaucratic stupidity, Lafayette thought.[33] American ships arrived, only to find that the supposed changes in regulations had not gone into effect, and they bore back to their own country the news that French promises had not been kept. Calonne promised that the unjustly collected duties would be repaid, but the chief financial minister of a government that was facing bankruptcy had more pressing problems on his hands. The Assembly of Notables abruptly terminated his tenure of office, and in the confusion of subsequent ministries nothing was done about the new American regulations. Meanwhile, the great Vergennes had died (Feb. 13, 1787) and been succeeded by Montmorin. Jefferson liked him and, after a bit, took up with him the tobacco question, but in the summer of 1787 he received intimations that the time was not suitable to press American commercial questions; the ministers had other problems which seemed far more crucial.

In the fall, however, when Lambert was in the Comptroller General's office, Jefferson and Lafayette brought matters to a head. They did not now seek changes of importance, except possibly in the tobacco

[30] See, for example, TJ to Lafayette, Aug. 24, 1786 (L. & B., V, 417) and Lafayette to TJ, Aug. 30, 1786 (Chinard, *Lafayette and Jefferson*, p. 106).

[31] *Portsmouth Journal*, Nov. 20, 1824, separate at UVA. The aged Jefferson was present but his speech was read by another.

[32] TJ to Madison, Jan. 30, 1787 (Ford, IV, 367).

[33] Good account of circumstances in letter of Lafayette to Lambert, Sept. 10, 1787 (Chinard, *Lafayette and Jefferson*, pp. 120–121).

trade. They wanted to regularize the promises already made and to get these incorporated, not in a letter which could be revoked by another letter, but in an official order. Lambert was insecure in office and Jefferson was fearful lest Necker should succeed him, but he stayed long enough to be very helpful, while Du Pont de Nemours in his lesser position did valuable service. Jefferson wrote to John Jay about the latter: "I have found him a man of great judgment and application, possessing good general principles on subjects of commerce, and friendly dispositions towards us." The net result, as reported by Jefferson the last day of 1787, was that the substance of Calonne's letter was incorporated in an *arrêt*, the continuance of the Order of Berni being merely promised in a letter.[34]

Jefferson had brought the same arguments to bear on Montmorin that he had used with Vergennes.[35] He sought precise information about the results of the Order of Berni, which had stipulated purchases of tobacco beyond the Morris contract and which, supposedly, had been in effect more than a year. His opinion was that the Farmers General had not complied with this, even though he could not prove it, and no evidence appears ever to have been adduced that they had.[36] But Jefferson was not chiefly concerned about such temporary relief as might have been afforded by this order.

> . . . The radical evil will still remain. . . . It is very much to be desired, that before the expiration of this order, some measure may be devised, which may bring this great article into free commerce between the two nations. Had this been practicable at the time it was put into Farm, that mode of collecting the revenue would probably never have been adopted; now that it has become practicable, it seems reasonable to discontinue this mode, and to substitute some of those practised on other imported articles, on which a revenue is levied, without absolutely suppressing them in commerce. . . . By prohibiting all his Majesty's subjects from dealing in tobacco, except with a single company, one third of the exports of the United States are rendered uncommerciable here. This production is so peculiarly theirs, that its shackles affect no other nation. A relief from these shackles, will form a memorable epoch in the commerce of the two nations. It will establish at once a great basis of exchange, serving like a point of union to draw to it other members of our commerce.[37]

[34] TJ to Jay, Nov. 3, 1787 (*D. C.*, II, 109), commenting on Du Pont; Dec. 31, 1787 (*D. C.*, II, 126–130) about the *arrêt*.

[35] See especially TJ to Montmorin, July 23, 1787 (L. & B., VI, 180–187), in which he also summarized past developments.

[36] TJ to Montmorin, Sept. 8, 1787 (L. & B., VI, 289–291).

[37] L. & B., VI, 184–186.

By failing to heed his wise counsel the nation which had expended so much treasure in helping establish American independence missed a great opportunity to recoup its fortunes by becoming the entrepôt for the European tobacco market. The Farmers General were denounced by Frenchmen themselves in the Assembly of Notables, but it took a revolution to dislodge them. Jefferson could not have been expected to breach that wall of vested privilege with the voice of reason. The best he was able to get out of the French government was an extension of the Order of Berni, without stipulation as to the price which should be paid for the tobacco purchased. The Morris contract ran out after its term of three years, and the net result, under the regulations, was that the Farmers General bought most of their tobacco from shippers bringing it directly from America in French or American bottoms. Jefferson could do little to free commerce from its ancient governmental shackles, but he believed that the tobacco trade, to the approximate amount of the French consumption, was diverted from England to France.[38]

Jefferson's liking for the French harmonized with his American patriotism because of his sincere belief that there was little natural rivalry of political interests between the two countries, despite the vast difference in their institutions, and that their commercial needs were to a large degree supplementary. "Each nation has exactly to spare," he said, "the articles which the other wants. . . . The governments have nothing to do but *not to hinder* their merchants from making the exchange." [39] His ideal was economic *laissez faire* but not on grounds of theory alone, for at this time it was clearly to the interest of the United States to break down commercial barriers. As John Jay warned him, on the basis of his own disillusioning experiences, the "spirit of monopoly and exclusion" had prevailed too long in Europe to disappear quickly; but when the Secretary learned of the commercial arrangements Jefferson had made with the French officials he expressed genuine pleasure over them. "They bear marks of wisdom and liberality," he said, "and cannot fail of being very acceptable." [40] The American representative had not done as well as he hoped with respect to whale oil any more than he had with tobacco, being unable to get all the duty removed despite extended arguments which endangered the whole agreement, but he probably had done better than

[38] TJ to James Maury, Nov. 13, 1787 (L. & B., VI, 374–375); to A. Donald, Feb. 7, 1788 (*ibid.*, VI, 425); Nussbaum, pp. 515–516. Further reasons for his anti-British attitude will appear in the next chapter.

[39] TJ to Montmorin, July 23, 1787 (L. & B., VI, 186).

[40] Jay to TJ, Apr. 24, 1788 (*D. C.*, II, 140), after receiving TJ's letter of Dec. 31, 1787.

Jay expected. Already he had been officially approved by Congress. It was largely because of his own insistence that the question of his re-election for three more years as minister to the Court of His Most Christian Majesty was brought up long before the expiration of his first term. There was no vote against him on October 12, 1787. One state, Connecticut, was opposed to having any ministries abroad, and Massachusetts was uncertain; but no one could doubt that this feeble Congress was fortunate in having a representative of such caliber and diligence.[41]

Until this time, there had been an American of comparable stature in England; but there now seemed no sufficient reason for him to stay there. John Adams had found the situation impossible, as Jefferson himself did on the brief, futile, and unforgettable visit he made to his friend and colleague.

[41] *Journals Cont. Cong.*, XXXIII, 665; Jay to TJ, Oct. 24, 1787, sending commission and other documents (*D. C.*, II, 81–83); Madison to TJ, Oct. 24, 1787 (Hunt, V, 37–38), telling about the vote. TJ's informal proposal that the American debt to France be transferred to Holland had been turned down shortly before this and the report on it may have been interpreted as a mild rebuke, but the general tone of the communications was distinctly favorable. The question of the debt will be discussed hereafter.

IV

Confronting John Bull

1786

THE American Minister to France had long contemplated a visit to England. In the spring of 1786 he made one, but he did not regard it as a pleasure trip. He went on official business, expecting to return to his comfortable quarters at the Hôtel de Langeac after three weeks and then to resume with Vergennes and Calonne his negotiations about tobacco.[1] Already he had probably imbibed from the French the idea that the English amused themselves sadly, and he had other reasons for not expecting to have much pleasure with the islanders. He stayed among them twice as long as he had intended and found the atmosphere even less agreeable than he had anticipated. The results of his trip were almost wholly disappointing, and the negative impression it left on him was indelible.

There never was any doubt about his receiving a warm welcome from his friends the Adamses. He and Abigail had been in constant communication ever since she left Paris, carrying on an animated correspondence in which mutual shopping commissions played an important part. Concerning these he engaged in much high-flown banter which she greatly enjoyed without quite admitting it. Thus, only a few months after she had gone to London, he wrote her:

> . . . I immediately ordered the shoes you desired, which will be ready tomorrow. . . . I have also procured for you three plateaux de dessert with a silvered balustrade round them, and four figures of Biscuit. . . . With respect to the figures I could only find three of those you named, matched in size. These were Minerva, Diana, and Apollo. I was obliged to add a fourth, unguided by

[1] The new lease with the Farmers General, including tobacco, was actually signed while he was away but his presence would have made no difference. The Order of Berni was issued after his return.

your choice. They offered me a fine Venus; but I thought it out of taste to have two at the table at the same time.[2]

He completed the quartet by sending her a calm, bold Mars. Obviously delighted, while claiming to be totally foiled in the matter of compliment, she responded by getting him the biggest tablecloth she could find in any shop. It was not as large as he had asked for, but she informed him that rarely in London were more than eighteen persons at the table and that he would have to be content with a cloth five yards long. Afterwards she found out that she herself had to be philosophical, for the gods and goddesses were dismembered on the road.[3]

Abigail had lamented the separation of her husband from the only man in Europe with whom he could talk unreservedly, and John Adams had now summoned Jefferson to join him before their joint commission to negotiate treaties of commerce would expire in May. They had carried on continuous correspondence about official matters but this was a poor substitute for conversation. Consultation between the ministers was desirable on many grounds, but the main idea was that they should treat in London with the ministers of Portugal and piratical Tripoli, both of whom were supposed now to have the necessary powers. The Americans also intended to make a final effort to get a treaty with Great Britain, Adams being somewhat more hopeful of this than his colleague.

Setting out in early March with Adams's messenger and future son-in-law, Colonel William S. Smith, former aide to Washington and now secretary of the legation in England, Jefferson arrived in London after six days of disagreeable weather. He was not a house guest of John and Abigail on Grosvenor Square but took lodgings, and he soon found out that the minister of Portugal had been taken ill. It was for this reason, chiefly, that he prolonged his stay. Eventually he and Adams were cordially received by the Chevalier de Pinto and they negotiated a treaty with him. This involved no special advantages to the United States, but promised to get rid of certain existing obstacles to American trade. It amounted to nothing, for it failed of acceptance in Portugal.[4]

As we have already seen, the meeting with the Tripolitan minister

[2] TJ to Mrs. Adams, Sept. 25, 1785 (LC, 2547). Ford's rendering of this passage (IV, 98–99) is inaccurate.

[3] Mrs. Adams to TJ, Oct. 7, 1785 (LC, 2611–2612); TJ to Mrs. Adams, Dec. 27, 1785 (LC, 2885–2886).

[4] TJ to Jay, Apr. 23, 1786 (*D. C.*, I, 725); Adams & TJ to Jay, Apr. 25, 1786 (*D. C.*, I, 602); TJ to Monroe, May 10, 1786, commenting on it briefly (Ford, IV, 220). A draft of a treaty with Portugal is in LC, 4606–4629.

was even more fruitless. That bearded, pipe-smoking emissary calmly asserted that it was the duty of his countrymen to make war on "sinners" and asked for much more peace money than they could pay.[5] Jefferson and Adams undoubtedly talked long hours about the pirates, American debts to Europe, and other official matters of deep concern to both of them. The most important consideration, however, was the improvement of American commercial relations with Great Britain, hopeless as their negotiations turned out to be.

What they wanted was a commercial treaty, based on grounds of "mutual advantage and convenience," such as Lord Shelburne had promised in 1782 before the fall of his ministry and William Pitt had proposed early in the next year. The suggestions made to them by the British minister in Paris, in 1784, seemed to bear out this hope. But other counsels had prevailed, and British policy had already assumed the form which it retained until the outbreak of war with France, when Jefferson himself was secretary of state. It was a contemptuous policy, based on the assumption of American weakness, and it represented a continuance of the historic navigation system, as affording the best support of sea power and strongest guarantee of national security.

Months before he reached London, Jefferson was convinced that nothing but fear of reprisals would cause England to treat American commerce more favorably. "It is a nation which nothing but views of interest can govern," he had written Madison, who fully agreed with him about the desirability of American discrimination against the British and thus foreshadowed his own later policy. John Adams had even more reason to be perturbed, for British policy wholly excluded American shipping from the West Indies, and New England was specially concerned with the carrying trade. Furthermore, not even in British ships could fish be imported from the United States into the West Indies. Adams retained his confidence in the power of negotiation somewhat longer than Jefferson, but his position was essentially the same. "We must not, my Friend, be the bubbles of our own liberal sentiments," he had written to his colleague. "If we cannot obtain reciprocal liberality we must adopt reciprocal prohibitions, exclusions, monopolies, and imposts." Both he and Jefferson were aware that the American market for British manufactures was important, and that the United States had products which the British needed and could get nowhere else. Adams no less than Jefferson favored giving the French the preference if the English would not meet them halfway, and at this time he was not averse to an offensive and defensive alliance with the former. Earlier he had said to another: "I never however was much

[5] Adams & TJ to Jay, Mar. 28, 1786 (*D. C.*, I, 604–605).

of John Bull. I was John Yankee and such I shall live and die." Neither was Jefferson much of Louis Capet, though he preferred him to George III.[6]

As an observant official Jefferson was convinced that the hostility of the British government to the independent American States had continued since the peace. Not only did they regard their former colonies as a wholly alien country; the "God-dem-mes" were contemptuous of the parvenu Republic. This was enough to take the bloom off his enthusiasm at visiting the Old World home of his ancestors. He was sure that the English were chiefly responsible for the reports of American anarchy and discontent which had flooded Europe. These stories were a blow to his pride as a citizen, and he did everything in his power as an official to counteract them. There can be no doubt that the British government was engaging in what we now call propaganda, designed to discredit further the weak American Confederation and at the same time to salve their own wounded pride. Many other Americans who were abroad noticed it, and if Jefferson presented too rosy a contrasting picture at times the fault can be easily condoned. He wrote to a German friend: "There are not, on the face of the earth, more tranquil governments than ours, nor a happier and more contented people. Their commerce has not as yet found the channels which their new relations with the world will offer to best advantage, and the old ones remain as yet unopened by new conventions. This occasions a stagnation in the sale of their produce, *the only truth among all the circumstances published about them.* Their hatred against Great Britain, having lately received from that nation new cause and new aliment, has taken a new spring."[7] His friend Charles Thomson, secretary of Congress, writing him while he was in England, was equally optimistic about the prospects of the American States, though recognizing one serious weakness. "It is true," said

[6] TJ to Madison, Sept. 1, 1785 (L. & B., V, 109); Adams to TJ, Sept. 4, Oct. 3, 1785 (LC, 2470, 2587); Adams to James Warren, Aug. 4, 1778, quoted in Koch & Peden, *Selected Writings of John and John Quincy Adams* (1946), p. vii. British policy during this period is admirably described in G. S. Graham, *Sea Power and British North America* (1941), ch. 1. By the Order-in-Council of July 2, 1783, which was periodically renewed until 1788, when its main provisions were embodied in an act of Parliament, American shipping was wholly excluded from the West Indies and certain staple products were excluded even if brought in English ships. On the other hand, certain American products could be imported into the West Indies in English ships, and the most important West Indian products could be brought to the United States in the same way. The British themselves thought of the policy as involving some concessions, and they counted on American acquiescence, as Lord Sheffield predicted. The point of major emphasis was the carrying trade.

[7] TJ to Baron Geismar, Sept. 6, 1785 (L. & B., V, 128). Italics mine.

Thomson, "that individual happiness is yet the general object, and the people are not yet sufficiently impressed with what they owe to their national character."[8] Jefferson himself was aware of this, but with foreigners it was not a good talking point.

It was while he was briefly in England that he felt the full brunt of the official arrogance he had already observed from a distance. Within a week of his colleague's arrival Adams asked the foreign minister, Lord Carmarthen, if he might present him. There is no record that the Marquis was positively insulting, but the Americans found him evasive and cold. They left a draft of a treaty with him but he did nothing about it. When they learned by accident that he thought it went too far, they sent one in modified form – and this he quite ignored. They had only one conference with him and he was unimpressed by the information that there was need for speedy action since their commissions would soon run out and one of them had to go back to Paris. Jefferson wrote him finally to ask if he could bear any messages for him, thus maintaining the forms of politeness on his own side at any rate. But, as he wrote John Jay, he found British silence invincible; and he never doubted that it demonstrated hostility and contempt.

"With this country nothing is done," he said; "and that nothing is intended to be done on their part admits not the smallest doubt. The nation is against any change of measures. The Ministers are against it, some from principle, others from subserviency, and the King more than all men is against it."[9] As in the Declaration of Independence he personified his charges rather too sharply, but his survey of the reign of George III had convinced him that, with the single exception of the treaty of peace, the British policy had been the policy of the King, and he noted that the treaty was followed by a change in the Ministry. He never ceased to regard this Monarch as a narrow-minded and mulish being, and he expected no change of policy during a reign which promised to be long.

His animus against George III had not been personal until this time, and the open discourtesy he suffered when he was formally presented may have been less due to his association with the Declaration of Independence than to the general attitude of the King toward the United States. Whatever the reasons, the atmosphere had thickened since the Adamses first came to Court, for they had been received more politely.

[8] Thomson to TJ, Apr. 6, 1786 (LC, 3404).

[9] TJ to Jay, Apr. 23, 1786 (*D. C.*, I, 725). He said practically the same thing in several other letters. Official letter of Adams and TJ, Apr. 25, 1786 (*D. C.*, I, 600–601).

Abigail had regarded the King as personable, though she did not like his white eyebrows and red face. Jefferson gave no details about his own reception the following year, but he did say that nothing could have been more ungracious than the notice given him and Adams by the royal pair. The story that came down in the Adams family is more specific – namely, that the King turned his back on both of the Americans and that the surrounding courtiers took full notice of what he did.[10]

Jefferson's low opinion of His Britannic Majesty cannot be attributed to this or any other single incident. It was too long-standing and well-reasoned for that. But this memory could hardly have failed to rankle in his mind. "They dare to displease," said Emerson of the English in the next century. "Of all nations on earth, they require to be treated with the most hauteur," said Jefferson the year after his disagreeable experience. "They require to be kicked into common good manners." [11]

George III was still the villain of Jefferson's international drama, and it may be assumed that his indictment of English manners was directed primarily against officialdom and the courtiers. He had slight chance to observe the county gentry and to compare them with the genial squires among whom he had grown up in Virginia. With the hauteur of the officials he met from time to time, and of the members of the ruling class he saw on his one brief visit, this highly sensitive man who set such store by politeness was ill-prepared to cope. Blunt-spoken John Adams was a better match for the "God-dem-mes," though his vanity was a weakness. His wife Abigail was now no more impressed by the manners of the upper classes than she was with the brilliancy of the Court, in comparison with the more splendid Court of France. "According to British ideas," she said, "good breeding consists in an undaunted air and a fearless, not to say bold, address and appearance." [12] She did not find that sort of breeding in her cherished friend Jefferson; he was a gentleman who was gentle and who liked to please – too much, if anything.

It is improbable that in 1786, in England, any patriotic American would have regarded any Englishman as "amiable" who did not show signs of generosity of spirit towards the United States. Abigail Adams liked to listen to the sermons of Dr. Richard Price and described him as "amiable." Jefferson and Price had already exchanged writings,

[10] TJ in autobiography (Ford, I, 89); C. F. Adams, in *Works* of John Adams, I, 420.

[11] Emerson, *English Traits* (1856), p. 106; TJ to W. S. Smith, Sept. 28, 1787 (L. & B., VI, 324).

[12] Mrs. Adams to Mrs. Cranch, May 21, 1786 (*Mrs. Adams*, p. 289).

and they dined together at least twice on this visit. There was always a special affinity between the prophet of religious freedom and liberal-minded clergymen, and in this one he found a kindred spirit. Not only did Price go with and beyond him in hostility to slavery; he had a strikingly similar vision of the future of the American Republic. Thus he had written the year before: "The eyes of the friends of liberty and humanity are now fixed on that country. The United States have an open field before them, and advantages for establishing a plan favorable to the improvement of the world which no people ever had in an equal degree." [13] He was one of the few prominent Englishmen who favored reciprocity of trade with the United States, though he had already predicted to Jefferson that this would not be brought about. The latter observed that, unfortunately, Price was in no position to influence public policy. There was no open opposition to governmental policy regarding America, nor was there any political group in England with whom Jefferson could feel at home, as he did with Lafayette and his coterie in France.[14] His fruitful personal contacts with Englishmen were and long continued to be almost wholly intellectual. In spirit he belonged with those who afterwards fostered the Dominions and made the British Commonwealth of Nations what it is today; but their time was far away.

The differences between Jefferson and the ruling class of that era were not confined to the realm of manners. The dominant Britishers did not share Dr. Price's vision of the mission and future of the United States. They had formally conceded American political independence, and Jefferson heard some of them say that they would not take the colonies back if they could get them, but many of them hoped that the loose American Confederation would break up. Very few thought that the Republic was a power to be seriously reckoned with – that it should be granted the treatment of a most-favored nation, either by necessity or as a right. They regarded themselves as "realistic," and in the immediate international situation probably they were, but to the far-seeing Jefferson they seemed blind in their arrogance and stupid in their selfishness.

Aware though he was of the weakness of the Confederation, Jefferson did not doubt that the American venture in self-government would be successful. An independent nation, such as he and Adams deemed theirs to be, had a right to respectful treatment and should not be discriminated against. But entirely apart from matters of right and

[13] Price to TJ, Mar. 21, 1785 (LC, 1991).
[14] TJ to R. H. Lee, Apr. 22, 1786 (Ford, IV, 206).

dignity, which were dear to the heart of a philosopher and gentleman, Jefferson as a realistic statesman believed that commercial reciprocity would be mutually advantageous to the two countries in the long run, and he regarded the denial of it by the British as irrational. It should be remembered that he hoped his own country would remain agricultural; he did not want it to become another England by developing industry. His Britannic Majesty and the Marquis of Carmarthen probably had no proper idea of the sort of a man and economic philosophy they were repelling, and the ministers were too engrossed in the affairs of the moment to take the longer view. If they had taken it, they would have frankly accepted American independence as an indisputable fact to be seriously reckoned with and might have adopted a generous commercial policy at the start.

The probable political results of such an attitude and such action would not have been wholly welcome to Jefferson. The tie between the United States and France would have been weakened, and the British might have gained a degree of support in the duel with their ancient rival which was presently resumed. Jefferson had no desire to nestle in the arms of Mother England, and soon after he returned to Paris he wrote a jocular letter to Abigail Adams in which he described King George as America's greatest benefactor. He was still driving them toward independence.

> He is truly the American Messias [Jefferson said], the most precious life that ever God gave. . . . Twenty long years has he been labouring to drive us to our good and he labours and will labour still for it if he can be spared. We shall have need of him for twenty more. . . . We become chained by our habits to the tails of those who hate & despise us. . . . He has not a friend on earth who would lament his loss as much and so long as I should.[15]

At a later time, in partisan hands, this passage might have been regarded as an expression of gratitude to the King for driving the United States into the arms of France. But, despite the fact that as a human being Jefferson liked the French better than the English, he based official policy on his observation of the situation, not on sentiment, and he would have been under no such necessity to develop Franco-American commerce had Anglo-American commerce been permitted on better terms. He was struggling for larger commercial freedom at a time when the dominant British statesmen were still mercantilists at heart. The views of Lord Sheffield were in the ascendant among them,

[15] TJ to Mrs. Adams, Aug. 9, 1786 (Ford, IV, 261).

not those of Adam Smith. They still believed in closed economic systems and saw no reason why they should admit the temporarily successful American rebels into theirs. "It is not that they think our commerce unimportant to them," Jefferson wrote John Jay. "I find that the merchants have set sufficient value on it; but that they are sure of keeping it on their own terms." At the time it seemed they could, whatever Jefferson or John Adams might say. Their policy had distinct short-range advantages in terms of the carrying trade and sea power, and, while Congress fumbled in impotence, they could see what they could see.[16]

Even so, their official rudeness was inexcusable and, in the light of history, exceedingly unwise. John Adams was even more firmly fixed in the role of John Yankee; at no time, not even during the French Revolution, could he view John Bull with the eyes of Alexander Hamilton or John Jay. Jefferson was confirmed in the personal predilection he already had for the French, and the enhanced reputation for arrogance which the British had gained with him they never wholly lost. They had nothing to gain and much to lose by affronting this accredited representative of the potential Giant of the West, even though they did not know how deeply sensitive he was and could not be expected to realize the vast influence he would one day wield. To the historian there is irony in the fact that he and his colleague now tower in stature above the men that snubbed them. Even though he had been already prepared in mind for what he met in England it is ironical that when Jefferson recrossed the Channel, after his only real visit to the land of his ancestors, he felt that he was leaving enemies and coming back to friends.

Jefferson did not anticipate Emerson in finding England "the best of actual nations." To him the United States was that. But he did perceive some of its advantages. The people were not as free-minded as most Americans supposed, he said, but they were less oppressed than in France. He had no doubt whatever that the British monarchy, as a form of government, was distinctly better than the French. His comments about the Britishers were less moralistic than the ones he

[16] TJ to Jay, Apr. 23, 1786 (*D. C.*, I, 726). The official letter of the commissioners to Jay, Apr. 25, 1786 (*D. C.*, I, 600–601) shows their clear recognition of the importance of the carrying trade in the British mind, whether or not Jefferson realized quite as fully as Adams the connection between this and ideas of national security. The latter wrote Governor James Bowdoin of Mass., May 9, 1786 (*Works*, VIII, 389): "Seamen, the navy, and power to strike an awful blow to their enemies at sea, on the first breaking out of a war, are the ideas that prevail over all others." Graham points out that even Adam Smith placed defense over opulence (*Sea Power and British North America*, p. 4).

made about the Parisians, and considerably less so than those of his friend Abigail – possibly because he did not stay so long among them. He was more accustomed to their kind of immorality, having observed in his youth in Virginia a rage for gambling. Intemperance in drink was also an American failing, though he found more of it in England. He said less about avarice than Mrs. Adams did, but observed that nobility, pomp, and wealth were the main objects of admiration. He thought the men of learning fewer, less learned, and much less emancipated than in the land of Louis XVI. Despite the shortness of his stay his comment has value, for he did not often overlook an important man of science or philosophy, wherever he was. In company with John Adams he met Sir John Sinclair, with whom in later years he exchanged agricultural information. Starting with the acquaintance made in London, he afterwards wrote about philosophical and mathematical instruments to Benjamin Vaughan, who, as Benjamin Rush had told him, was "a fellow worshipper in the temple of science." [17]

He had a high opinion of the instruments of the English, and at this time he gave them the palm in the fields of the mechanical arts and domestic gardening. He could have written volumes on their mechanical achievements, he said.[18] Being himself of an ingenious turn, he always had an eye for gadgets, but he was most impressed by the use of steam in grist mills and felt confident that it would be applied to boats in America. To a greater extent than in France he was observing the beginning of the industrial revolution. He was not one to miss the chance of shopping in such a market, though he did not buy as much as he had expected to. The main things he took back with him were instruments: thermometer, protractor, globe telescope, solar microscope, hydrometer, camp theodolite, and the like.[19] He had a model made of a portable copying press, picked up a sealing candlestick, and sent to Charles Thomson in America one of the newly invented lamps they had been writing about and which were better made in England than in France. On request he sent another to Richard Henry Lee. He had expected to buy a riding horse, but got one in France a little later. He ordered a carriage, which was several years in coming and called for vast correspondence, and he bought plated harness – not from love of the English, as he afterwards explained to Lafayette, but because the kind he wanted could not be obtained in France. He sent a trunk of clothing for the wife of his friend Nicholas Lewis and his

[17] Rush to TJ, Jan. 24, 1783 (Madison Papers, LC, 3:66).

[18] See especially TJ to Chas. Thomson, Apr. 22, 1786 (L. & B., V, 294–295), and Sept. 20, 1787 (Ford, IV, 449).

[19] Account Book, Mar. 21, 1786, and later.

sister Nancy in Albemarle, meanwhile reminding his friend to look after his grass and trees.[20] One of the most important of his orders, though he did not make it until he got back to Paris, was for a harpsichord. He had a low opinion of the architecture of London, but obviously he liked its shops.

Most of all he liked the English gardens. In the first half of April he made a tour of them with John Adams, separating that colleague from his wife for the first time since she had come abroad, though she saw some sights with them after they returned from the major trip. Of the two men the Virginian was the more practical. At Chiswick, Hampton Court, Stowe, Blenheim, and elsewhere he went over the grounds with a standard book on gardening in his hand, and he left prosaic notes on sixteen places.[21] "My inquiries were directed chiefly to such practical things as might enable me to estimate the expense of making and maintaining a garden in that style," he said. He was thinking of his own Monticello and what he might do there. As an observer he was cool and detached, referring incidentally to literary and historical associations but indulging in no rhapsodies. It was John Adams rather than he who commented on the significance of Edgehill and Worcester in the history of liberty, and who reminded the natives at the latter place that this was holy ground. Jefferson recorded in his account book that he paid a shilling at Stratford on Avon for seeing the house where Shakespeare was born, and another for seeing his tombstone, but Adams left a fuller record of their visit. According to the custom, they cut a chip off the wooden chair in the chimney corner where the poet used to sit. There could not have been as many visitors then as later, else the chair would have wholly disappeared.

The surviving comments of the two men suggest that Adams was more interested than Jefferson in Shakespeare, more conscious of the literary and historical traditions of the race, but that when it came to architecture and landscapes the Virginian had the keener eye. Adams found the various gentlemen's seats "superb," "elegant," or "beautiful," though he questioned the desirability of their existing at all. Jefferson termed Hampton Court "old-fashioned," said of Chiswick that the garden showed too much art, described the clumps of

[20] TJ to N. Lewis, Apr. 22, 1786 (LC, 3418); to Anna Scott Jefferson, Apr. 22, 1786 (*Domestic Life*, p. 81).

[21] Thomas Whately's *Observations on Modern Gardening* (1770). His memorandum, covering the period Apr. 2–14, 1786, is in L. & B., XVII, 236–244. See also Account Book for these dates; *Garden Book*, pp. 110–114; and Diary of Adams in the latter's *Works*, III, 394–397. An admirable recent account is that of Marie Kimball, in *Jefferson: The Scene of Europe* (1950), ch. VII, esp. pp. 142–156.

trees at Esher-Place as "a most lovely mixture of concave and convex," remarked on a beautiful Doric temple at Paynshill while describing the architecture of the house as incorrect. He commented on the useless appearance of the Corinthian arch at Stowe, and waxed most enthusiastic about the building at Moor Park. As his general plan of Monticello had shown, he liked the idea of connecting dependencies with the main structure. His liking for classic columns had already been manifested, and these comments show that he favored naturalistic rather than formal landscapes.

In almost everything he did in England Jefferson was associated with the Adamses. With them and a few others, he went to the annual ball at the French Embassy on St. James's Park, having dined beforehand at 28 Charles Street with John and Lucy Paradise.

Mrs. Paradise, a beautiful and highly temperamental woman of thirty-five, had been born a Ludwell of Virginia and had claims to confiscated lands there in connection with which she sought the assistance of her guest. This was one of the reasons, no doubt, why she made herself so agreeable to the tall Minister at this and later times, and the interest he took in her complicated affairs was an amply sufficient recompense. At the Embassy he probably danced the minuet with this accomplished partner, finding in her social chatter an antidote for the aloofness of the British guests which John Adams remarked. But Jefferson's interest in this couple was more owing to his instinctive liking for John Paradise, a gentle, scholarly man with whom he had many common tastes. Paradise, who had been born in Greece, delighted his new-found friend by offering to instruct him in the pronunciation of the modern Greeks – thus giving him a clue to the pronunciation of the ancient language which he had been wondering about since his school days. He did not have time to avail himself of this offer while in England, but after he went back to Paris he asked for written instructions. It was probably soon after this that he began reading Homer with Madame de Tott, whom he met at the home of Lafayette's aunt, Madame de Tessé.

For the "multiplied civilities and kindnesses" he received from the Paradises in London he was properly grateful, and even though he may have seen through Lucy immediately, he could hardly have objected to her reference to him as "the first character in our state. . . . the first in the Continent of North America." His immediate effort was to induce John, who was entirely impractical, to go to Virginia in person and straighten out the tangle about those lands. He gave a vast amount of time during the next few years to the confused affairs of the Paradises, thereby showing his characteristic kindness and solicitude to a very marked degree. John accompanied him part of the way when he returned to Paris, and directly aided him in connection with the harpsichord he ordered soon after he left.[22]

The Paradises were to remain his affectionate and often trying friends, but the strengthening of his already strong ties with the Adams family was the most important personal consequence of his brief trip. That family was enlarged shortly after he returned to Paris by the marriage of young Abigail to Colonel William S. Smith (June 12, 1786). By that time Jefferson, who had genius for friendship with young men, had strongly attached to himself the Secretary of the Legation. To Smith he gave his own friendship unreservedly, and in turn the younger man performed innumerable commissions for him. The Colonel was a constant correspondent, as the older Abigail said, telling Jefferson so much that there was really little left for her to say. She asked him to have Petit get for her in Paris four pairs of silk shoes, however, and gave him her parental impressions of the arrangement which her daughter and son-in-law had effected with the assistance of the Bishop of St. Asaph. It was true that she now had a new son of whom she thought highly, but she had three boys already and could ill afford to lose her one daughter. "Now I have been thinking of an exchange with you Sir," she said. "Suppose you give me Miss Jefferson, and in some future day take a son in lieu of her. I am for strengthening the federal union." So was the Minister to France, and he replied that he would be very glad to have her son. He could not give up his daughter, however, and he always expected to gain in his trading with the Adams family.[23] It would have been more correct to say that his personal commerce with them closely approximated the ideal of mutual benefit, and unquestionably the tie of federal union between the American ministries in London and Paris was already very strong.

There was soon a portrait of Jefferson on the wall of the Adams house – the one by Mather Brown, presumably the first of him ever to be painted. He sat for it in London, and afterwards he got the original while the Adamses kept a replica.[24] This first of his portraits

[22] On the association, see A. B. Shepperson, *John Paradise and Lucy Ludwell* (Richmond, 1942), pp. 203–211, and elsewhere. On the dinner, see Abigail Adams to Miss E. Cranch, Apr. 2, 1786 (*Mrs. Adams,* pp. 280–281). Letters specially worth citing are TJ to John Paradise, May 4, 1786 (LC, 3463); Lucy Paradise to TJ, May 5, 1786 (LC, 3468); TJ to John Paradise, May 25, 1786 (LC, 3610); TJ to Wythe, May 29, 1786 (LC, 3632); TJ to W. S. Smith, Aug. 9, 1786 (LC, 3966–3969).

[23] Mrs. Adams to TJ, July 23, 1786 (LC, 3901); TJ to Mrs. Adams, Aug. 9, 1786 (Ford, IV, 261).

[24] Abigail Adams mentions a portrait in her letter of July 23, 1786, and Jeffer-

is probably the most artificial, for, more than any other, it shows him as a man of fashion. He did not wear a wig and appears never to have done so, but the hair is powdered and rolled over the ears. The hand which emerges from the ruffles on his sleeve is slender, almost effeminate. The face is ruddy, the nose prominent, the mouth firmly set, but this might have been the picture of almost any wit or gallant. At this time more than any other in his life he was a courtier, and history should remember that he once played that role. But the portrait of him that John Trumbull did in Paris, showing unpowdered hair and a stronger face, is more in character. Toward the end of the summer Trumbull came visiting, and, as it happened, ushered him into an episode which was gallant while it lasted.

---

son paid Brown for one just before he left London. From later correspondence with Trumbull it appears that he did not get this until he neared the end of his stay in France. The Adams replica, which has survived and is still in possession of the family, was probably made about that time. The best description of it is in Fiske Kimball, "Life Portraits of Jefferson," *Procs. Am. Philos. Soc.*, vol. 88 (1944), 500–501.

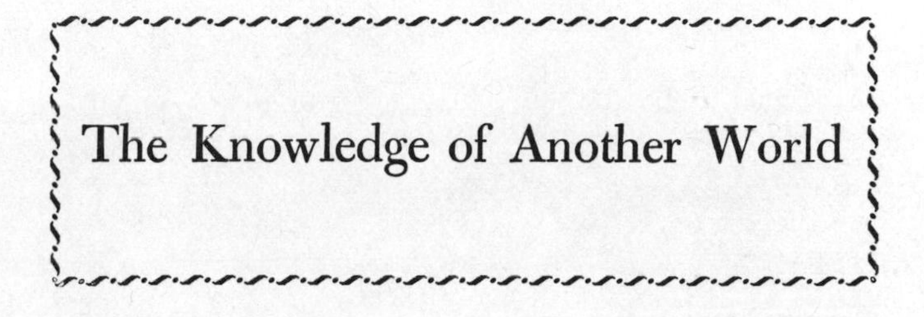
The Knowledge of Another World

V

Sentimental Adventure

1786

AS Jefferson passed through Calais on his way back to Paris, he paid a small gratuity to one whom he described as the successor of Laurence Sterne's monk, thus showing that he was still familiar with *A Sentimental Journey*.[1] He relished the whimsies of that little book of travels, chuckling over its amorous absurdities no doubt, but he was returning from a journey of his own which he regarded as largely utilitarian, and the widower appeared to be in a strictly practical state of mind when he got back to the Hôtel de Langeac and went over the household accounts for the two months he had been away. Apparently these were not to his liking, for he dismissed his head servant Marc a few weeks later and set Petit permanently in the top place.[2] He had returned to a society more congenial to the benevolence of his mind than that of England, as Abigail Adams thought; but there was no forewarning of any sort of personal adventure as he picked up the domestic and official threads that summer.

He was busily engaged in diplomatic correspondence – discussing the Barbary pirates with John Adams, writing John Jay and James Monroe about the contract with the farmers-general that had been signed in his absence and about his continuing struggle against the tobacco monopoly. Also, he was helping various people with pieces they were writing about America; he was buying books for friends, and corresponding with Virginians about the plans for their new state capitol; and he talked with intrepid John Ledyard about the exploration of uncharted continents.

Ledyard, a veteran of Captain Cook's last voyage who often dined with Jefferson – finding fifteen or twenty Americans at that hospitable table – now wanted to cross Siberia to Kamchatka, to pro-

[1] Account Book, Apr. 28, 1786.
[2] Account Book, May 1, June 26, 1786.

ceed thence to the western side of North America, and to go through the continent to the Atlantic Coast. Finding from the Baron de Grimm that the Russian Empress regarded the plan as chimerical, Jefferson hoped that an alternative expedition, westwardly from Kentucky to the South Seas, would prove feasible. But Ledyard, hoping to get to Kamchatka somehow, set out for London, and a little later wrote Jefferson from there, addressing him as "my friend, my brother, my father." Later still he made his way to St. Petersburg, determined to be the first circumambulator of the globe. This he did on his own responsibility, though he was originally encouraged by Jefferson in his ambition to be the greatest walker in the world.[3]

Besides exciting conversations with Ledyard, Jefferson carried on an animated and detailed correspondence with John Paradise and Dr. Charles Burney, father of the novelist Fanny Burney, about the harpsichord which was to be made for him in England by Kirkman. Since this was to go ultimately to Monticello, where there would be no skilled workmen to keep it in order, he wanted to avoid a complication of stops; but after careful investigation he insisted, against Kirkman's objection, that a "celestine apparatus" be put on it by Mr. Walker. The affixing of Walker's celestine stop served to delay the instrument considerably, and he did not actually receive it until more than a year had passed, but in the first weeks after his return to Paris he gave abundant evidence of his technical knowledge of musical instruments and of his intense interest in the details of their construction.[4]

This incessantly active man did not trifle away many of his precious hours that summer, but as the season wore on he seemed a little bored. "Nothing worth reading has come from the press, I think, since you left us," he wrote Benjamin Franklin in August. He envied Francis Hopkinson the latter's Wednesday-evening meetings with Franklin and David Rittenhouse in Philadelphia. "They would be more valued by me than the whole week in Paris," he said.[5] John Trumbull had reached the Hôtel de Langeac a little before this, and he found his tireless host ready to explore new fields.

Jefferson had met this son of a Governor of Connecticut in Lon-

[3] TJ to Ledyard, Aug. 16, 1786 (LC, 4016); to Ezra Stiles, Sept. 1, 1786 (Ford, IV, 298); to John Banister, Jr., June 19, 1787 (L. & B., VI, 130); to Charles Thomson, Sept. 20, 1787 (Ford, IV, 447–448). See also Helen Augur, *Passage to Glory: John Ledyard's America* (1946), esp. pp. 167–170, 173–177, 180–182; and Dumbauld, pp. 132–133.

[4] Entire episode admirably described in Shepperson, *Paradise and Ludwell*, ch. XI, where letters of TJ to Paradise, and to and from Dr. Burney in the months of May, June, and July are printed.

[5] TJ to Franklin, Aug. 14, 1786 (L. & B., V, 399); to Hopkinson, Aug. 14, 1786 (Ford, IV, 271).

don, and had warmly approved the young man's plan to paint the events of the American Revolution. With characteristic hospitality he had invited him to be his guest in Paris. Trumbull, then thirty years old, arrived in early August, bearing a full letter from Abigail Adams and bringing along a couple of his pictures to be engraved. The two Ministers had approved the subjects: "Death of General Warren at Bunker's Hill," and "Death of General Montgomery at Quebec." Much impressed by the collection of paintings at Versailles, Trumbull was persuaded by his host to linger in Paris longer than he had intended; for five or six weeks he remained a member of the household and he was numbered henceforth, along with Short and Smith, a member of Jefferson's devoted band of young men. On a later visit the Minister arranged for Rochambeau and Lafayette to sit for other historical paintings, and Trumbull began the composition of his "Declaration of Independence." Lafayette was out of town at this time, but Madame was in the vicinity and she and Madame de Tessé invited Jefferson and his guest to Chaville for dinner.[6]

Jefferson knew far less about art than architecture at this point, and never claimed to be a connoisseur, but he found that Trumbull's work was greatly admired by others – including Grimm, who was the "oracle of taste" in these matters – and to him himself in 1786 Trumbull's natural talents seemed "almost unparalleled." Until the end of his life he regarded him as superior to any historical painter of the period except the French artist David.[7] Besides embracing Trumbull as a friend he now made him a guide and, to some extent, a mentor. The two men often took jaunts together. One day at Suresnes, near St.-Cloud and about four miles from the house, they witnessed the ceremony of the crowning of the *Rosière* – that is, of the most amiable, virtuous, and industrious poor girl in the parish. They returned by the Pont de Neuilly, which they both admired. Jefferson afterwards described this stone bridge as the handsomest in the world when he was talking to Gouverneur Morris, who had not specially noticed it until then.[8]

[6] John Trumbull, *Autobiography, Reminiscences and Letters . . . 1756–1841* (1841), pp. 95–96. This work is not wholly reliable for dates, and more exact details can be determined from TJ's own correspondence, beginning with his letter to Thevenard, May 5, 1786 (Bixby, p. 18). He received Abigail Adams's letter of July 23, 1786, on Aug. 2; and Trumbull left on Sept. 10 (TJ to W. S. Smith, Sept. 13, 1786; LC, 4144). Charles Bulfinch was in Paris that summer, and bore to London TJ's letter of Aug. 9, 1786, to W. S. Smith. On the Lafayettes, see Chinard, *Lafayette and Jefferson*, pp. 103–104, 106.

[7] To Ezra Stiles, Sept. 1, 1786 (Ford, IV, 299); to James Barbour, Jan. 19, 1817 (L. & B., XIX, 242–243).

[8] Trumbull, *Autobiography*, p. 101; Morris, *Diary*, May 19, 1789 (I, 83).

Jefferson was on the most intimate terms with Trumbull until the very end of his stay in France, and he always associated him in memory with what he called "our charming coterie in Paris." This included Mrs. Maria Hadfield Cosway, an artist in her own right who visited Paris that fall with her artist husband, and Madame de Corny, who had a pretty house on the Rue Chausée d'Antin, not far from the Opéra and whom Jefferson had probably met before Trumbull arrived. Her husband, Louis-Dominique Ethis de Corny, was a liberal-minded friend of Lafayette and the American Republic, and there was sufficient reason for Jefferson to go to the house on the Rue Chausée d'Antin on his account. Madame was away when he went there in August with Trumbull, but many times afterward he took tea with her in surroundings which he found most charming.[9] She was not one of those futile ladies of fashion of whom he soon spoke so disrespectfully to beautiful Mrs. Bingham; she was a lovely, delicate, essentially domestic creature who enjoyed fussing over the tall Virginian and was much flattered by his friendship.

He liked women who were gentle and accomplished. He was rather fearful of the effects on his susceptible young countrymen of the voluptuous dress and arts of European women, and he warned them at times against "female intrigue." Of his own special women friends Maria Cosway was the most talented; he found modesty and softness of disposition in her – but no doubt he also found her the most coquettish of them all. For knowing her, he was directly indebted to Trumbull, who had encountered her and her husband Richard, a highly successful miniaturist, at the atelier of the painter David on this visit. Trumbull began to go with them everywhere; he kept talking to his host about them; and after a bit he contrived a meeting. Then began an adventure such as Jefferson had certainly not expected, in a late summer which was amazingly like spring.

To put it somewhat differently, a generally philosophical gentleman, hungrier for beauty and a woman than he realized, was quite swept off his supposedly well-planted feet.[10]

All this began at the Halle au Blés, whither Jefferson had gone

[9] Gilbert Chinard, *Trois Amitiés Françaises de Jefferson* (Paris, 1927), ch. IV. Jefferson wrote Maria Cosway that Madame de Corny did not get back until October 6.

[10] Trumbull, *Autobiography*, pp. 108, 117–119. Beginning Aug. 19, 1786, the diary fails for twenty days, unfortunately, but Trumbull remembered that Jefferson's acquaintance with Mrs. Cosway commenced during that time. His letter of Oct. 12, 1786 to her (Ford, IV, 311–323) remains the best source for events until that date. For the Cosways and later letters, see Helen D. Bullock, *My Head and My Heart* (1945). Marie Kimball treats this episode in *Jefferson: The Scene of Europe*, ch. VIII.

with Trumbull for purposes which seemed safely utilitarian. He wanted to get some ideas for a public market to be built in Richmond, and he would have liked to put on it a "noble dome" like that.[11] He thought this a superb piece of architecture until he was distracted by the sight of Maria Cosway and the soft music of her voice. Then twenty-seven years old, she had a slim figure and graceful carriage, and her small head was crowned with a mass of curly golden hair. Though of an English family she had been born in Italy, where she had studied art and music. She spoke a mélange of languages and liked Italian best. Such a battery of charms Jefferson was peculiarly unfitted to withstand. Feeling deliciously at home in such company, this normally punctilious man conspired with the others so that they might spend the rest of the day together, even though this involved the shattering of engagements on all hands. In this mad moment he sent a "lying messenger" to the old Duchesse de la Rochefoucauld d'Anville, saying that, just as he had started on his way to dine with her, important dispatches arrived requiring his immediate attention. Then he went surreptitiously to St.-Cloud for dinner, saw sights with his gay companions on the way back to Paris, and ended a memorable day with a visit to the harpist and composer Krumpholtz. By that time he must have learned that Maria sang, played the harp and pianoforte, composed music for songs.

In the month that followed he saw or heard something beautiful with her almost every day. It is impossible to determine from the surviving record how often they went alone. No doubt Trumbull accompanied them sometimes, before he left Paris. Richard Cosway, who was about Jefferson's age, had come from England partly for a holiday, but he had portraits to paint and clients to see and was willing to leave his young wife considerably to her own devices. Despite the fact that he enjoyed the high favor of the Prince of Wales and other prominent patrons, he was personally unpopular, and, "although a well-made little man, very like a monkey in the face."[12] Maria, coming to England from Italy after the death of her father and the decline of the family fortunes, had made a marriage of convenience with him five years before and had greatly embellished his establishment thereafter. At least she admired his art. He was rather jealous of hers, and tried to keep her in the professional background, though she exhibited to some degree. Jefferson himself never belittled Richard Cosway, and his manner towards him appears to have been scrupulously correct. While Maria fully appreciated the good things of life which

[11] Ford, IV, 313.
[12] Bullock, p. 15.

her absurd little husband provided, she was undoubtedly glad to get away from him to make expeditions with a distinguished man who was an enthusiast for the arts and who was obviously impressed with her graces, her beauty, and her charm.

In speaking of these experiences afterwards Jefferson invariably employed the language of friendship and sentiment, not passion. But, difficult as it is to get far beneath the surface of the record, there can be no doubt that he fell deeply in love during that golden September, and there is no reason to suppose that the lady was displeased. Her eyes are said to have been blue as violets; her mouth as she herself painted it was rather pouting, but any normal man would pronounce it kissable. Jefferson, who walked and rode so regularly, was still a vigorous man at forty-three. James Boswell, who addressed her as "serenissima Principessa," accused her of treating men like dogs. It is hard to see how she could have failed to be a flirt, and at one time and another stories were told about her. But she was a devout Catholic and had wanted to become a nun. If Jefferson thought of her as voluptuous he did not reveal it. He found her a lovely, talented, capricious creature – half woman and half child. Illicit love-making was generally condoned in that society, as he himself had noted. If he as a widower ever engaged in it, this was the time; but he gave no ready handle to later political foes and scandalmongers, and the Hamiltonians appear to have overlooked this adventure. Like other deep intimacies of his life, this one remains obscure and mysterious. Not the least significant aspect of it is the beauty with which he garbed the relationship in his own memory, and it would be both vain and cruel to attempt to draw aside the veil.

He left record of some places and things they saw together that September: "The Port de Reuilly, the hills along the Seine, the rainbows of the machine of Marly, the terrace of St. Germains [Saint-Germain-en-Laye], the châteaux, the gardens, the statues of Marly, the pavillon of Lucienne [Louveciennes]." She was with him, no doubt, when he saw the King's library and attended a *concert spirituel.*[13] She was not bookish as he was, but an important part of her charm to him was her love of music. He mentioned Madrid and Bagatelle – palaces in the Bois de Boulogne – and a place which he called "the Dessert," with characteristic indifference to spelling. Now identified as the Désert de Retz, it had extensive grounds and romantic prospects, and a house built rather fantastically but most ingeniously in the form of a ruined column, with a spiral staircase which Jefferson

[13] Ford, IV, 314; Account Book, Sept. 5, 8, 1786.

much admired.[14] Far more important than any list of things seen or done, however, is the record which this normally restrained man left of his emotions. The wheels of time moved faster than those of their carriage; nature was radiant; no scene could be dull or insipid in the presence of Maria.

The delicious expeditions ended abruptly and rather ingloriously when the middle-aged widower fell and dislocated his right wrist. The accident seems to have occurred on September 18, as a gossipy old neighbor of Franklin's at Passy reported to the latter's grandson; on that day the injured man paid fees to two surgeons, though they did not help him much. Until October 5 he had his secretary, William Short, write all his letters; then he wrote a very shaky one with his left hand to Maria. About two weeks after that he wrote to his young friend, William S. Smith: "How the right hand became disabled would be a long story for the left to tell. It was by one of those follies from which good cannot come, but ill may." [15]

So far as is known, he never told the long story, and thus we cannot be sure just what he thought his "folly" was. It may have consisted merely in his attempt, while promenading along the Seine, to make a jump which was beyond his physical powers; it may have lain in his delay in consulting the physicians, or in his venturing forth too soon. But the temptation is irresistible to associate it with Maria. Extreme reticence about purely personal matters was characteristic of him, and it was even more characteristic if a lady was involved. It is a good guess, therefore, that she was with him – whatever the precise place and circumstances – and that he connected the unlucky accident with her in his own mind.

She was uneasy about him but did not come to see him just as soon

[14] Identified and described by L. H. Butterfield and H. C. Rice, Jr., in their brief but important article, "Jefferson's Earliest Note to Maria Cosway with Some New Facts and Conjectures on His Broken Wrist," *W. & M.*, 3 ser., V, 31–32 (Jan. 1948).

[15] TJ to Smith, Oct. 22, 1786 (Ford, IV, 325). The letter of Oct. 5 to Maria was published for the first time in the article of Butterfield and Rice already cited. This article convincingly reconstructs the calendar of events, and supersedes all previous accounts of this mysterious accident. The date Sept. 18 for the accident is given in a letter of Le Veillard to W. T. Franklin, under date of Sept. 20. This was discovered by Mr. Butterfield in the Franklin Papers (Am. Philos. Soc.), after the publication of the article, and was made available through his kindness. The exact wording, as finally deciphered by Mr. Rice and his wife, is: *Mr. Jefferson s'est démis avant hier le poignet de la main droite en voulant sauter par dessus une barrière du petit cours, le poignet est bien remis mais il a beaucoup souffert et je ne vois pas qu'il puisse écrire d'ici à un mois.* Mr. Rice believes that Jefferson was promenading in the Cours la Reine, along the Seine from the Place de la Concorde, and tried to jump some little fence.

as she had intended, for reasons beyond her control. Shortly after his fall she wrote: "Oh I wish you was well enough to come to us tomorrow to dinner and stay the evening. . . . I would serve you, and help you at dinner, and divert your pain after with good musik." [16] But he did not join them until October 4, more than two weeks after the accident, and that proved to be too soon. He was confined at home until then, suffering greatly but attending to some necessary official business with the indispensable assistance of William Short.

It was under these circumstances that his secretary acted for him in the ceremonies honoring his friend and invaluable auxiliary Lafayette. After delays that had already excited adverse comment, the time came, in late September, for the presentation of Lafayette's bust to the City of Paris; but Jefferson had to send the resolutions of the State of Virginia by the hand of Short instead of bearing them himself. He also sent a handsome written tribute to Lafayette, and no doubt Éthis de Corny readily forgave him for not being present to hear his acceptance speech, but on both public and personal grounds the Minister himself should have been there.[17] Probably this was his chief embarrassment at the moment, but the accident also forced him to revise his own plans. He had been expecting to accompany the Court to Fontainebleau early in October, and, after a short stay there, to make a tour of six weeks in the south of France – which he regarded as more useful and more pleasant than lounging at Fontainebleau.[18] But it now looked as though he could not go anywhere.

When he did venture from his chamber, about a week after the bust of Lafayette was presented, his purposes were wholly personal and the results were bad. This was on October 4. The Cosways were expecting to leave next day, so he wanted to see them – one of them anyway. But the carriage rattled too freely over the pavement for his shattered wrist, which was badly set in the first place, and his highly indiscreet day was followed by an excessively painful and wholly sleepless night. Reluctantly concluding that he could not see his friends off if they were going as intended, he told Maria in a laborious little left-handed note that he would have to relinquish her charming companionship for that of the surgeon he had summoned.[19]

[16] MHS, undated but presumably soon after Sept. 18, 1786; letter printed with minor changes in *Domestic Life*, pp. 85–86.

[17] The ceremonies of Sept. 28, 1786, have already been referred to. See pp. 44–45.

[18] Stated in several letters in September, including one of the very last before the accident: TJ to W. S. Smith, Sept. 13, 1786 (LC, 4143). This, it may be noted, is in his normal handwriting.

[19] TJ to Maria Cosway, Oct. 5, 1786 (printed in Butterfield and Rice, pp. 26–27).

She replied immediately – probably by the same messenger – reporting that her capricious husband was in the notion to go that day, despite inadequate preparations, and saying how sorry she was that she was in any way responsible for the fresh suffering of her friend. "Why would you go? And why was I not more friendly to you and less to myself by preventing your giving me the pleasure of your company? You repeatedly said it would do you no harm. I felt interested and did not insist." Of course she would write him, as he had asked; it was impossible to fail a person who had been "so unusually obliging." She would remember with infinite pleasure the charming days they had spent together and would long for the spring, when she hoped to come again to Paris. Meanwhile, would he send her a line to Antwerp that she might know how he was?[20]

The note was too much for the suffering gentleman, who was not content to await the coming of the spring. Rating as an ignoramus the surgeon whom he had called and abandoning him for more delightful company, he got out of bed, accompanied the Cosways to the post house at Saint-Denis, provided refreshments for them there, and handed Madame into her carriage after the horses had been changed. Then, after the wheels had actually started rolling, he turned on his heel and walked, "more dead than alive," to the carriage he had hired and was taken home.

This he reported to her a week later in a very long letter which he urged her to read piecemeal – to take in half a dozen doses. Sending her at the same time a song from Sacchini's *Dardanus* which by its very title recalled their happy days, he put the letter under the cover of one to John Trumbull, who was to meet the Cosways in Antwerp, asking his young friend to deliver it personally. The painter, who was fully conscious of the lady's charms, did so with alacrity and some glee.[21] It contains the elaborate and rather well-known dialogue between Jefferson's Head and his Heart, and is the major source of information about his association with Maria Cosway until that time. Even in its physical form it is extraordinary. Originally it filled "three mortal sheets" of paper, and in small print it occupies a dozen printed pages, yet it was written wholly with the left hand while the right was useless. It was a feat of ambidexterity, and

[20] This undated letter from MHS (printed in *Domestic Life*, p. 86) is given this date and setting by Butterfield and Rice – properly, in my opinion.

[21] TJ to Mrs. Maria Cosway, Oct. 12, 13, 1786 (Ford, IV, 311–323, 323–324); to Trumbull, Oct. 13, 1786 (LC, 4249); from Trumbull, Nov. 3, 1786 (LC, 4397). For the reconstruction of events at Saint-Denis I am indebted to Howard C. Rice, following him in the belief that TJ went to the Village, rather than the Porte. For the song, see Bullock, p. 27.

if not a masterpiece of gallantry it is one of the most unusual tributes ever paid a pretty woman by a distinguished man.

Opinions differ about it as a piece of writing. One critic, who intensely disliked the author on political grounds, regarded the dialogue as absurd. Jefferson's labored efforts to be gay reminded him of the German who, to give himself the air of lightness, threw himself out of the window.[22] On the other hand, various admirers of the author's statecraft and philosophy have seen in this dialogue a reflection of his subtlety and discrimination, his tenderness and charm. To most moderns it will seem stilted in manner. The best of his letters to Abigail Adams, while they do not escape the artificialities of eighteenth-century gallantry, are more playful, less pretentious, less self-conscious. This one was a *tour de force.*

The recipient realized that it required hours for full understanding, but she violated instructions and read it all at once, hence she may be pardoned if she missed some points. She was much pleased by the many kind expressions in it, most grateful at having such a friend, and she sounded very young when she said so.[23] As a woman she could not help being flattered by the remarks about her delightful companionship which her admirer's Heart kept making; but almost any woman would also have been appalled when his Head kept asking if he really should have been with her at all. In the dialogue the Heart spoke the last word, but why all this labored argument to show at last how glad he was that he had known her? As a love letter this is full of vexing qualifications, and probably it should not be singled out on its own account as literature. But as the revelation of the mind of a great man it is notable, and for Thomas Jefferson it is unique.

He was not often that subjective, but he had thought through this distracting business with abnormally sharpened mind as he tossed on the bed of pain, and he summed things up quite as much for his own relief as for Maria's sake. If his fall did not shock him into a consciousness of folly her departure did, and the dialogue was his explanation of his conduct, his apologia. The dichotomy of nature which he now revealed and so elaborately described, the struggle which had been going on within his breast during these delightful and disturbing days, was not so simple as that between virtue and vice, between chastity and amorous temptation. This writing is marked by no consciousness of sin, no concern over any disregard of the

[22] H. Taine in *Nouveaux Essais de Critique et d'Histoire* (edn. 1909), p. 211.

[23] Undated letter, nearly all in Italian (MHS) which probably should be dated Oct. 30, 1786. Largely reprinted by Marie Kimball in *Va. Quart. Rev.*, IV, 408–409; Mrs. Bullock dates it in *My Head and My Heart*, p. 42, but quotes only a few sentences.

proprieties. He weighed the balance between intelligence and the emotions, between reasoned conduct and spontaneity. Himself a man of deeply serious purposes who generally pursued the even tenor of his way, he had been spontaneous to the point of rashness. He was aware of his deep infatuation, and well knew that no permanent satisfaction could ever come out of it. His conduct had been thoroughly irrational and the experience had been profoundly disturbing. He had let himself go, and later actions showed that he did not intend to do so again. Yet he gave no sign of regretting his delicious adventure in irrationality which ended with a broken wrist. The experience had been costly, but he did not blame Maria for either his physical pain or his psychological upheaval. The joy had been worth the price, and his "folly" had revealed to him anew the limitations of sheer intelligence. His very arguing of the case made him sound cold-blooded, but the most significant conclusion that emerges from the dialogue is that this highly intellectual man recognized in human life the superior claims of sentiment over reason.

His excellent mind told him that the world was not a place in which man should live at random. "Everything in this world is a matter of calculation," said the Head. "Advance then with caution, the balance in your hand. . . . The art of life is the art of avoiding pain: . . . The most effectual means of being secure against pain is to retire within ourselves, and to suffice for our own happiness. Those which depend on ourselves are the only pleasures a wise man will count on: . . . Hence the inestimable value of intellectual pleasures. Ever in our power, always leading us to something new, never cloying, we ride serene and sublime above the concerns of this mortal world, contemplating truth and nature, matter and motion, the laws which bind up their existence, and that eternal being who made and bound them up by those laws. Let this be our employ. . . . Friendship is but another name for an alliance with the follies and misfortunes of others."[24] Thus spoke the man of pure science, the sensitive sufferer from public criticism and personal tragedy who longed to be a philosopher in a cloister.

But the Heart had the last word in the dialogue as in life. "Let the gloomy monk, sequestered from the world, seek unsocial pleasures in the bottom of his cell! Let the sublimated philosopher grasp visionary happiness while pursuing phantoms dressed in the garb of truth! Their supreme happiness is supreme folly; and they mistake for happiness the mere absence of pain. Had they ever felt the solid pleasure of one generous spasm of the heart, they would exchange for

[24] Ford, IV, 317–318.

it all the frigid speculations of their lives. . . ." The Heart recalled the Head to the proper limits of his office: "When nature assigned us the same habitation, she gave us over it a divided empire. To you she allotted the field of science; to me that of morals. When the circle is to be squared, or the orbit of a comet to be traced; when the arch of greatest strength, or the solid of least resistance is to be investigated, take up the problem; it is yours; nature has given me no cognizance of it. In like manner, in denying to you the feelings of sympathy, of benevolence, of gratitude, of justice, of love, of friendship, she has excluded you from their control. To these she has adapted the mechanism of the heart. Morals were too essential to the happiness of man to be risked on the incertain combinations of the head. She laid their foundation therefore in sentiment, not in science."[25] Thus spoke an apostle of reason who clearly perceived reason's limitations. Thus spoke one who made a fine art of friendship and devoted most of his life, not to "sublimated philosophy," but to the useful arts and the public service.

Having greatly relieved himself by this vast utterance, Jefferson resumed as best he could his ordered and useful life, while the Cosways and Trumbull, after a brief spell of picture-buying in the Low Countries, returned to the clouds and smoke of London. He now believed that his wrist was well set, but it recovered slowly. Short wrote official letters for him in the meantime (there were important ones that fall), and in personal correspondence he continued to display to his astounded friends his skill in writing with his left hand. He termed it "an awkward scribe," and no doubt it was a slow one, but he wrote with amazing clearness. He kept saying that he must not waste words, but within a month he sent to M. Le Roy of the Académie des Sciences almost as long a letter as the one he wrote to Maria. It is even more extraordinary in that it contains well-executed diagrams.[26] Replying to an inquiry that he had received soon after his accident, he wrote elaborately of the Virginia winds, proceeded to discuss tropical winds and the Gulf Stream, and spoke of the possibility of cutting a canal at Panama. This would not be a difficult work, in his opinion; he believed that after a small opening had been made the tropical current would enter in and widen it – with remarkable consequences both in trade and climate. His fantastic conjectures were based on most

[25] Ford, IV, 319.

[26] Nov. 13, 1786 (LC, 4435–4441; printed in L. & B., V, 463–472). In spite of what he said in the beginning Jefferson may have done part of this with his right hand.

imperfect information about isthmian topography and ocean currents, but apparently his accident had done more than reveal his virtuosity. It or something else had stimulated his imagination.

In this crippled state he appears also to have been in a mood of some playfulness, which contrasts pleasantly with the stiff formality of his love letter. Thus, when writing William S. Smith about various commissions that obliging young man was performing for him in London (and which Trumbull was beginning to share), he sent his regards to the ladies of the Adams family. He hoped that Mrs. Adams was well, and that Mrs. Smith was or had been very sick. "Otherwise," he said, "I would observe to you that it is high time." [27] It will be recalled that Smith and the younger Abigail had been married since summer. This sort of banter he kept up with the young matron herself. Soon she wrote him in some embarrassment that she was much troubled by the nonarrival of some corsets she had ordered from Paris, and wanted him to have Petit inquire about them. Early in the new year he sent her two pairs, not knowing whether they would fit since she had sent no measure. If too small, he suggested that she lay them aside for a time. "There are ebbs as well as flows in this world," he said. "When the mountain refused to come to Mahomet, he went to the mountain." [28]

By that time he was writing normally. The "first homage" of his recovered right hand he owed and gave to Maria Cosway, he said, with slight and pardonable deception – he appears to have used it a few days earlier, on November 14, in a letter to George Washington. To her and others, however, he continued to talk of the pain, and toward the end of the year he told Abigail Adams that if his hand was now good for writing it was good for nothing else. "The swelling has remained obstinately the same for two months past," he said, "and the joint, tho' I believe well set, does not become more flexible." He had been advised to try the mineral waters at Aix-en-Provence, as he did a little later, and Abigail suggested British Oil, but nothing could be really efficacious since, as he found out afterwards, "the joint had never been replaced." More than two years after the accident he still had a withered hand with swelled and crooked fingers, and he believed that he had forever lost the use of it except for writing. He learned to do more with it than that, and it does not seem to have handicapped him much; but it stiffened seriously after he began to grow old, and

[27] Oct. 22, 1786 (LC, 4358–4359).

[28] From Mrs. Smith, Dec. 2, 1786 (MHS); to Mrs. Smith, Jan. 15, 1787 (MHS; extract in *Domestic Life*, p. 78). His anticipations were entirely correct. On May 26, 1787, he congratulated Smith on the birth of a son (MHS).

caused him pain. He mentioned it, not unnaturally, in almost the last letter he ever wrote to Maria Cosway.[29]

Because of his wrist and for other reasons, he did not write her as often as she would have liked before he set off in the spring of 1787 on his postponed southern trip. She was quite willing to take him in smaller and more frequent doses, she said, but she did not regard the lengthy dialogue as in any sense a dismissal. Indeed, it raised her hopes too high. Probably failing to perceive its subtle implications, she was enormously flattered by it and not unnaturally vexed when relatively few other letters came. Also, she must have noted that his tone became more restrained.

Henceforth it was she rather than he who displayed emotions; and, however reckless he may have seemed in October, he appeared much older after winter settled down. The gay, mad mood of his memorable adventure he could not or would not maintain. He had not become cold-blooded, for he could not be that with her, but henceforth his head was in control. His dialogue may have been partly intended to serve as a warning that it would be. Whatever passion he had felt for her had now given way to tenderness; his written words to her, he said, were the "breathings of a pure affection." He continued to think of her as wholly charming, and he was genuinely and affectionately her friend. He had begun to act middle-aged; and, not having reached such years yet, at first she did not understand.

He did not dismiss her as a disturbing and flirtatious creature; she had been disturbing, without a doubt, but she had taken herself away and she was more than a coquette. She continued to love the good things of life which her ridiculous but successful husband gave her, but the letters she wrote him in this period reveal her as no mere lady of fashion, no mere seeker of pleasure in the common sense. After she returned to the gloom of London, she reported that she painted by day and generally practised on the harp or harpsichord in the evening, and she sent him some of her own songs and duets with harp accompaniment. To him she was art and music and the embodiment of loveliness. She confessed to talking much feminine nonsense, but was also a moody creature – oppressed by the melancholy climate and tone of England, longing for the sunshine of Italy and the gaiety of France. She loved the sound of church bells, believed in prayer, and in her immature and unsystematic but endearing way was philosophical. Her mind had no such strength as that of Abigail Adams, but it was bright and sensitive, and she must have had exquisite taste.

[29] TJ to Mrs. Adams, Dec. 21, 1786 (LC, 4528); to Dr. George Gilmer, Dec. 16, 1788 (LC, 7714); to Mrs. Cosway, Dec. 27, 1820 (Bullock, p. 176).

Her middle-aged admirer was being gallant when he sighed for the cap of Fortunatus, in order that he might fly to her, and when he chided her for not keeping her promise to return to Paris in the spring. But he did not have much time for her that winter and that spring; and when, somewhat later, she did return he was even busier, even more a settled man. By then his second daughter, his own little Maria, had finally arrived from Virginia, and he had settled into a pattern of domesticity and official labors into which Maria Cosway did not quite fit. He did not embark upon another adventure with her, but he embarked on no romantic adventure with anybody else. She had to share his friendship with other women, but her position in his life and memory was unique, and in the more restrained and mature sense he loved her all the rest of life.[30]

[30] His relations with Mrs. Cosway on the occasion of her visit to Paris in 1787 will be referred to in a later chapter. The following letters, not previously cited, have been drawn on chiefly in this account: Maria Cosway to TJ, Nov. 17, 1786 (MHS; thus dated and largely reprinted in Bullock, pp. 51–53); TJ to Maria Cosway, Nov. 19, 1786 (Bullock, pp. 55–56, from UVA); Maria Cosway to TJ, Nov. 27, 1786 (MHS; Bullock, pp. 53–54); TJ to Maria Cosway, Dec. 24, 1786 (Bullock, pp. 60–61, from UVA); Maria Cosway to TJ, Jan. 1, 1787 (Bullock, pp. 62–64, and Marie Kimball in *Va. Quart. Rev.*, IV, 411–413); Maria Cosway to TJ, Feb. 15, 1787 (MHS); TJ to Trumbull, Feb. 23, 1787 (LC, 4868; partly in Bullock, p. 64). In *My Head and My Heart*, Helen Bullock gives numerous vivid details about the musical aspects of TJ's associations with Maria, which I have not overlooked but could not find space for here.

VI

Minister of Enlightenment

AS an amiable human being who was at the same time a lavish buyer, Jefferson delighted in performing commissions for his friends. The reciprocal services done for him in London by Colonel Smith, and later by John Trumbull, were so great that he probably gained on the whole by his exchange with England. This traffic flowed both ways; but he could expect no return from his distant friends in the States, for whom he bought things during the whole of his stay in France, wanting them to share the advantages of this enticing Old World market. A long, varied, and fascinating list of purchases for a large number of people could be easily compiled from his letters and accounts. No unusual interest attaches to the gown and ribbons he sent his sister Nancy from London, to the wines he kept ordering for his brother-in-law Francis Eppes, to the "*vinaigre à l'estragon*" he got for Francis Hopkinson, or even to the spectacles which he accidentally found that Charles Bellini needed and sent to that professor of modern languages in a box of books for George Wythe in Williamsburg.[1] Such thoughtful and generous actions were wholly in his character, but others were more distinctive.

He was not merely a friend of particular individuals. He had "zeal to promote the general good of mankind by an interchange of useful things."[2] That zeal was greatest in the field of agriculture; it was manifested more in architecture than in any other art because architecture was so useful; it extended to various instruments and devices, especially to mathematical instruments – which were tools of science – and to appliances that facilitated the operations of the mind and pen. He was always trying to find the latest thing in letterpresses. He had

[1] TJ to Hopkinson, May 8, 1788 (LC, 6669); to Bellini, July 25, 1788 (*W. & M.*, 2 ser., V, 9).

[2] TJ to Malesherbes, Mar. 11, 1789 (*Garden Book*, p. 143). He characterized himself in describing Malesherbes.

a model of a portable press made for him in London, afterward had copies made in Paris, and scattered these among friends and correspondents with generous but discriminating hand. There was something almost symbolic in his enthusiasm for "phosphoric matches," and for a newly-invented cylinder lamp, which burned olive oil and was said to give a light equal to that of half a dozen candles. He sent one of these lamps to Charles Thomson from London and wrote him about the matches. "They are a beautiful discovery," he said, "and very useful, especially to heads which like yours and mine cannot at all times be got to sleep." It was very convenient to light a candle without getting out of bed, to kindle fire without flint, to seal a letter without calling a servant.[3] He rejoiced in such inventions, not merely because his incessantly curious mind invariably delighted in scientific curiosities, but also because they served to dispel darkness and create light. He was pre-eminently a minister of enlightenment.

He has been aptly described as America's "scientific scout." He once said: "Science is more important in a republican than in any other government. And in an infant country like ours we must depend for improvement on the science of other countries, longer established, possessing better means, and more advanced than we are." His own emphasis was definitely utilitarian – just as Franklin's was. The science of his famous predecessor was justly esteemed, he thought, because Franklin always tried to direct it to something useful in private life.[4]

In this period he seems to have underestimated scientific progress in Europe rather than magnified it. Early in his stay in France he reported to a professor at William and Mary: "In science, the mass of the people are two centuries behind ours; their literati half a dozen years before us." Toward the end of his ministry he wrote to the President of that College: "As you seem willing to accept of the crumbs of science on which we are subsisting here, it is with pleasure I continue to hand them on to you, in proportion as they are dealt out." [5] His relatively unfavorable judgment on European science was owing in part to the many misconceptions he himself had discovered

[3] TJ to Thomson, Nov. 11, 1784 (Ford, IV, 14).

[4] R. H. True, "Thomas Jefferson in Relation to Botany," *Scientific Monthly*, Oct. 1916, p. 351; C. A. Browne, *Thomas Jefferson and the Scientific Trends of his Times* (1943), pp. 23, 59 (citing L. & B., XV, 339). The latter study appraises his scientific work and contains a collection of pertinent quotations, such as TJ to Thomas Cooper, July 10, 1812 (L. & B., XIII, 176), about Franklin's science.

[5] TJ to Charles Bellini, Sept. 30, 1785 (L. & B., V, 153); to Rev. James Madison, July 19, 1788 (*ibid.*, VII, 73).

in the fields he was most familiar with, and which he sought to correct in his *Notes on Virginia.* It may be partly attributed to the fact that there were some important current developments which he did not understand. This was specially true in the field of chemistry. A minor count in his indictment of Buffon was that the famous naturalist affected to consider chemistry as but cookery and he himself described this, afterwards, as a science that was "big with future discoveries for the utility and safety of the human race." But at this time, he was most impressed with its embryonic state, not realizing that modern chemistry was really being born before his eyes. The notable and successful attempt of Lavoisier to reform chemical nomenclature he regarded as premature.[6]

This universal reporter may be forgiven for not being a competent critic in all fields, and for following a conservative line when in doubt. Upon their face, however, some of his negative statements about scientific knowledge seem hard to reconcile with his philosophy and practice as a whole. In this period he said: "Ignorance is preferable to error: and he is less remote from the truth who believes nothing, than he who believes what is wrong."[7] He was issuing a warning against credulity, realizing that the road to knowledge begins with doubt. But he neither proclaimed nor followed the doctrine that men should devote their intellectual efforts to the avoidance of error rather than to the pursuit of truth. His scientific position cannot be described as that of a traditionalist, yet he was more cautious than has commonly been supposed. He was boldest when thoroughly informed. In life as he lived it there was no real inconsistency between his recognition of the necessity of scientific doubt and his deep faith in the power of scientific knowledge. He did more than serve as a channel of information to his compatriots. He issued a stirring challenge to present scientists—and, even more, to the coming generation. Thus he wrote to President Willard of Harvard toward the end of his stay in France:

> . . . What a field have we at our doors to signalize ourselves in! The Botany of America is far from being exhausted, its Mineralogy is untouched, and its Natural History or Zoology, totally mistaken and misrepresented. . . . It is for such institutions as that over which you preside so worthily, Sir, to do justice to our country, its productions and its genius. It is the work

[6] TJ to Rev. James Madison, July 19, 1788 (L. & B., VII, 76), discussed by Browne, pp. 10–11.

[7] In *Notes on Virginia* (Ford, III, 119*n*). He said almost the same thing to Rev. James Madison (L. & B., VII, 74).

> to which the young men, whom you are forming, should lay their hands. We have spent the prime of our lives in procurring them the precious blessing of liberty. Let them spend theirs in showing that it is the great parent of *science* and of virtue; and that a nation will be great in both, always in proportion as it is free.[8]

He was by no means done with the struggle for "the precious blessing of liberty" which, as he kept saying throughout life, deflected him from the delightful paths of science, but during his stay abroad he was not personally engaged in political conflict and was free to write about the progress of human knowledge to those of his compatriots who would most appreciate it, such as the presidents of the leading colleges. With his old school friend, the Reverend James Madison of William and Mary (not to be confused with the statesman of the same name), he naturally corresponded more regularly and extensively than with the presidents of Yale and Harvard, but he had established intellectual companionship with the Reverend Ezra Stiles on his stop in New Haven shortly before he sailed, and if he had not met the Reverend Joseph Willard when in Boston, that gentleman was sufficiently impressed with his achievements to confer on him an honorary degree. Another indication of his standing in the intellectual circles that centered in Boston was his election, during this period, as a fellow of the American Academy of Arts and Sciences.[9] An honorary degree was conferred on him by Yale at just the time that he was seeing the sights of Paris with Maria Cosway and shortly before he broke his wrist, and he acknowledged it – more briefly than he would have normally – soon after he resumed his right-handed writing. President Stiles spoke of the degree as a token of respect and honor "for one of our first literary characters in the Republic of Letters." [10]

Nobody then seemed to know just where letters began or science ended, but if we use the terms in their later sense, Jefferson conversed with these men chiefly about scientific and rarely about literary matters. His fellow members of the American Philosophical Society remained very close to him – especially Charles Thomson and David Rittenhouse, who exchanged information between themselves and passed it on to Franklin. To such men as these in Philadelphia and Williamsburg, Cambridge and New Haven, Jefferson reported interesting things he saw or heard about. He told about the tragic failure of a balloon to fly

[8] TJ to Joseph Willard, Mar. 24, 1789 (L. & B., VII, 328–329).
[9] Certificate dated May 29, 1787 (MHS).
[10] Stiles to TJ, Dec. 8, 1786 (LC, 4487–4488). Also, Stiles, *Literary Diary*, Sept. 13, 1786 (III, 239); Stiles to TJ, Sept. 14, 1786 (LC, 4177).

the Channel and described the propulsion of a vessel by a screw. This screw operated in the air, however, and he thought it would be more effectual beneath the water. When in England he described the use of steam to turn the stones of grist mills, and when he afterwards discussed these mills in France with their owner, "the famous Boulton," then visiting there, he reached the mathematical conclusion that the work of a horse in one day could thus be performed by a peck and a half of coal. Years afterwards, he said that of all the machines employed to aid human labor, he was least acquainted with the most powerful one, the steam engine.[11] He talked about it when he was in Europe, however, and if he did not keep himself fully informed afterwards about its numerous uses and modifications this was because farms interested him more than factories. It was on the subject of agriculture, probably, that he sent fullest information home. But he did this chiefly after he had made the most extended of his European journeys, which we are not ready to describe just yet.[12]

In his opinion, it did not take long for European advances in knowledge to find their way into books, and it was by means of these primarily that he sought to bring his American brethren up to date in their scientific information. Thus he sent Ezra Stiles and the Reverend James Madison a book containing an account of all recent improvements, along with a sheaf of almanacs, explaining that the latter contained some "precious things in astronomy."

He sent all sorts of works to a variety of people, but the bulk of the "literary cargo" which he started on its westward course consisted of the *Encyclopédie Méthodique*. The subscription lists were still open when he got to France, and about two fifths of the projected sixty volumes were ready. The total cost was to be thirty English guineas, as he told James Monroe, reporting that he was subscribing for him. He got the work for many friends, including both the Madisons (probably for the College of William and Mary in one case), Thomson, and Franklin (possibly for the College of Pennsylvania). These were not gifts, since they would have been beyond even his great generosity, but they called for some advances and a good many complicated records. It would be easy to find other instances of Jefferson's extensive and efficacious book buying, but in this connection he per-

[11] TJ to George Fleming, Dec. 29, 1815 (L. & B., XIV, 365). Earlier letters of special interest: TJ to Charles Thomson, June 21, 1785 (L. & B., V, 24-25); Sept. 20, 1787 (Ford, IV, 449).
[12] See the following chapter.

formed his greatest service to Madison, the person who used the expression "literary cargo." [13]

For Madison he bought nearly 200 books altogether. There was no financial problem, since he was somewhat in debt to this scholarly little friend and all these purchases could be charged against his account. Madison had pored over the catalogue of Jefferson's own library, which included items wanted but not yet bought, and they had undoubtedly talked enthusiastically about future acquisitions before Jefferson went to the best book market he had ever known. Madison afterwards summed up his desires in Jefferson's own apt phrase, asking that he procure books which were either "old and curious or new and useful." [14] As the shipments came along, the selection was so much to his liking that no further suggestions were needed. It was a wide and catholic selection, including books of natural science and works of Pascal, Voltaire, and Diderot, but its chief significance does not lie in any connection with the history of literature or manners or with the forward march of science. The supremely important thing about it was the great and immediate effect it had on Madison's constitutional studies.[15] On the strength of it he plunged into a study of ancient and modern confederacies, using and citing authorities which previously he had not had access to. Jefferson was abroad during the fateful period when the American Constitution was being framed and adopted, but by these indirect means he made a significant contribution to it and his friendly assistance to Madison is a striking example of the fruitful activities of his seminal mind.[16]

"You see I am an enthusiast on the subject of the arts," said Jefferson to this same friend when he had been abroad only a little more than a year. No less significant is the justification which he added: "But it is an enthusiasm of which I am not ashamed, as its object is to improve the taste of my countrymen, to increase their reputation, to reconcile to them the respect of the world, and to procure them its praise." [17] At the moment he was thinking of his fellow Virginians and speaking particularly of the plans he had sent them for the new state capitol. Except for agriculture, and possibly music, there was nothing in the civilization of the Old World that interested

[13] No attempt is made here to do more than suggest TJ's purchases on his own account. A fuller story of the formation of his library will be given in a later volume of this work.

[14] Madison to TJ, Apr. 27, 1785 (Hunt, II, 133).

[15] Brant, *Madison*, II, 410–411.

[16] See ch. IX, for the constitutional story.

[17] TJ to Madison, Sept. 20, 1785 (L. & B., V, 136–137).

him more than the buildings. A little later he said that he was so violently smitten with the Hôtel de Salm that he used to go to the Tuileries almost every day to see it, generally sitting on a parapet and twisting his head around until his neck got stiff.[18] Probably he would not have suffered so for any painting. His exploration of the arts in France constituted a part of his education and left a deep impress on him, but the desire to serve his countrymen played an important part in determining the precise direction which his artistic explorations took. One of the earliest of these led him to Houdon and sculpture, which he valued below architecture but above painting.

When William Short joined him that first winter he brought a commission from Virginia for a statue of George Washington. Franklin and he talked with the noted Houdon, who agreed to go to America and make a plaster model of the General to be rendered into marble in Paris afterwards. Houdon's departure was delayed until Franklin himself sailed during the next summer. By then it had been decided that a pedestrian statue should be made for Virginia, and the sculptor hoped also to make an equestrian one for Congress. Jefferson had looked at a good many statues in the meantime, especially the one of Louis XV which he thought probably the best in the world, and was now more convinced than ever that the General should be depicted so as to appear life-size. "A statue is not made, like a mountain, to be seen at a great distance," he said. Also, he gave his vote for modern dress, though he thought it superfluous since this was the sentiment of such authorities as West, Copley, Trumbull, and Mather Brown in London. Gladly noting Washington's approval, he wrote him: "I think a modern in an antique dress as just an object of ridicule as a Hercules or Marius with a periwig and a chapeau bras." [19] However, there was a difficulty about the inscription. Houdon, back in Paris in Jefferson's second winter, with "the necessary moulds and measures," objected that the proposed inscription was much too long. Jefferson, apparently not knowing that this was from the hand of Madison, suggested a shorter one without saying that he wrote it, only to find that the question could not be easily reopened since Madison's words were in the original legislative act.[20] Before the statue was done Gouverneur Morris had come to France, and at the request of the sculptor and Jefferson he had agreed to "stand" for the figure of the

[18] TJ to Madame de Tessé, Mar. 20, 1787 (L. & B., VI, 102). Built about this time by the architect Rousseau; after the Revolution it became the Palace of the Legion of Honor.

[19] TJ to Washington, Aug. 14, 1787 (L. & B., VI, 275).

[20] TJ to Madison, Feb. 8, 1786 (Ford, IV, 194–195); episode fully described and well commented on by Brant in *Madison*, II, 321–322.

General.[21] In the course of time Houdon made for Jefferson, besides the latter's own bust, a number of plaster busts of notable contemporaries – Washington and Lafayette, Franklin and Voltaire, Turgot and John Paul Jones. When picking a sculptor Jefferson chose well and he was moved by a double purpose: to commemorate the great men of his age, especially the Americans – as he also did by procuring portraits of Washington, Adams, Thomas Paine, and others – and to enrich his native civilization with the fruits of European art.

His services to architecture at home were much more notable. At one stroke he provided a monumental setting for the government of his own Commonwealth, brought the support of classic authority to American republicanism, and started the classic revival in the United States insofar as any single person could. All this he did by sending to Richmond the plans of a new state capitol.[22] This was modeled on the Maison Carrée at Nîmes (spelt Quarrée by Jefferson), generally regarded as "one of the most beautiful, if not the most beautiful and precious morsel of architecture left us by antiquity," and described by him as "noble beyond expression." [23] It was all that, no doubt, but when he first commended it with such enthusiasm he had seen it only in books. Perhaps Madame de Tessé, aunt of Lafayette, had talked with him about it, but not until later did he write her from Nîmes that he was gazing at it rapturously, like a lover at his mistress.[24]

This fascinating episode seems to involve a contradiction. Jefferson, like Janus, was looking in opposite directions: forward to the glorious future of republican society in America, backward to the architectural glories of the past. An eager and incessant champion of intellectual freedom, he seemed to be putting his own mind into the strait jacket of ancient rules and orders. Undoubtedly there was literalism and probably there was pedantry in Jefferson the architect. He was a self-taught draftsman without artistic training; he did not approach architecture from the side of art but from that of mathematics.[25] To him, Palladio had seemed almost like another Euclid, and when he set out

[21] June 4, 1789 (Morris, *Diary*, I, 106).

[22] Exhaustively and authoritatively discussed by Fiske Kimball in *Thomas Jefferson and the First Monument of the Classical Revival in America* (1915), where the documents are given *in extenso;* and in *Thomas Jefferson, Architect* (1916), pp. 40–43, where conclusions are summarized, and pp. 142–148, where the drawings are analyzed.

[23] TJ to Madison, Sept. 20, 1785 (L. & B., V, 135–137); to James Currie, Jan. 18, 1786 (Ford, IV, 133); later comments in Autobiography (Ford, I, 63–64). He also sent to Virginia plans for a prison, based on the idea of solitary confinement but the prison as later built was designed by Latrobe (Kimball, *Jefferson, Architect*, pp. 43–45).

[24] Mar. 20, 1787 (L. & B., VI, 102).

[25] Kimball, *Jefferson, Architect*, p. 143.

to copy an ancient building he did not think that its proportions should be trifled with. Later he became more eclectic, but one is most impressed by his purism at this stage. Whether he be termed "radical" or "conservative" depends on the point of reference: there was something very modern in his wanting to slough off excrescences and attain simplicity, and he was more in character as an austere patriot than he ever was as a man of fashion. If he was creative in this field it was in his adaptation of old things to modern uses. There can be no possible doubt of his supreme desire to be helpful. If he cared little for government as such, he was deeply concerned with attaching dignity to a pure government, that is, to American republicanism as he idealistically conceived it. In public buildings, therefore, he sought a monumental quality and forms with the "ring of eternity" in them.[26] Not quite the same thing was necessary in domestic structures, but the forms of public monuments should be magnificent and at the same time pure. It was little short of inevitable, therefore, that he should turn to Roman classicism.

The request from the directors of public buildings that he have the plans of certain public buildings drawn for them, especially a capitol, was received by Jefferson several months after he got the commission to procure a statue of George Washington. It will be recalled that Richmond had become the seat of the government in Virginia during his own administration and that no permanent public buildings had been erected. The young Commonwealth was practically unhoused, and Jefferson thought it in the infancy of good taste. To a later generation his strictures on Georgian architecture seem much too severe; and the twentieth century would probably not mind if such a structure as the Wren Building in Williamsburg or the State House in Philadelphia had been erected in Richmond. But, at best, this would have lacked the monumental quality he was seeking, and the rough and tentative plans the directors had sent to him called for a boxlike building with four porticoes and without distinction of any sort. They had not allowed him much time, and he was fearful lest they might start laying bricks before he could get a better plan to them — as actually they did. "But how is a taste in this beautiful art to be formed in our countrymen," he asked Madison, "unless we avail ourselves of every occasion when public buildings are to be erected, of presenting to them models for their study and imitation?"[27]

The model which Jefferson intended to present could have been seen by him at Monticello in *The Architecture of A. Palladio.* Naturally

[26] Karl Lehmann, *Thomas Jefferson, American Humanist* (1947), p. 161.
[27] TJ to Madison, Sept. 20, 1785 (L. & B., V, 136).

he had not brought that work along, but he bought another copy while in France. He undoubtedly saw the building in the *Monuments de Nîmes,* a copy of which he afterwards bought from the author himself, Clérisseau. The latter was the "architect" whom the Virginian consulted and asked to provide drawings on the scale of the proposed building, which was to be considerably larger than the Maison Carrée. That Roman temple had Corinthian columns, a deep portico, pilasters on the sides, and no windows. It was a "precious morsel" of architecture but it was not built for the purposes of executive, legislative, and judicial departments. It had the sort of exterior Jefferson wanted, and he began with that, but changes proved unavoidable and the final design was not a copy but an adaptation, for which Jefferson himself was more responsible than Clérisseau. Ionic columns were substituted for Corinthian because of the greater difficulty of the latter; the pilasters were removed from the sides; the depth of the portico was reduced from three columns to two; windows were inserted. Possibly the most interesting feature of the interior was a monumental hall, in which George Washington's statue was to stand. In this new temple a republican hero was to replace a Roman god, and Jefferson approved, knowing the sort of hero this one was. He not only sent plans for this structure, which he described as "simple and sublime," but also, after considerable delay, he sent a plaster model which finally reached Richmond in safety and has been preserved until this day. The Maison Carrée has considerably more grace and beauty than his adaptation of it, despite all his care about proportions. The old building is richer in ornament, and it has no windows to mar its lines. But he had provided an impressive symbol of the majesty of a republican state; and if the portico should be derided as nonfunctional, he thought of it as having a very important function to perform: it was to be "a frontispiece to all Virginia." [28] Thus did he introduce the temple form into his country, and from this beginning monumental classic forms came to dominate the public architecture of the United States.

His hopes for his native State were only partially realized. Work had already started on the capitol before his matured plan got there — not started on the basis of the "mere essay" originally sent by him, but on other ideas that were quite different.[29] The arrival of Jefferson's design caused considerable embarrassment. There was strong opposition to the new building among members from outlying districts, and to have pulled down the existing construction would have been to play into their hands. The problem was solved by using Jefferson's

[28] This expressive phrase is from Kimball, *Jefferson, Architect,* p. 41.
[29] Edmund Randolph to TJ, July 12, 1786 (LC, 3842).

plan except for the extension of the front, or so it was reported; these changes required only the removal of one side wall and a few partitions. "Our capitol rears its head, to the approbation of most people," wrote Governor Edmund Randolph to Jefferson a few months later; "but I tremble lest we should have committed some blunder in proportion." [30] When Jefferson saw it, still in an unfinished state, on his return from France in 1789, he thought some of the changes unfortunate. Nevertheless he wrote to William Short: "Our new capitol, when the corrections are made of which it is susceptible, will be an edifice of first rate dignity." Whenever it should be finished with the proper ornaments belonging to it (not in that age, he feared) it would be worthy of exhibition alongside "the most celebrated remains of antiquity." At the time he may have been more the patriot than the artist, for he also reported with satisfaction that one street in Richmond "would be considered as handsomely built in any city of Europe." But if his countrymen were not emerging very rapidly from their infancy in good taste, he was certainly doing everything in his power to help them grow.[31]

Jefferson's activities as a minister of information were also directed to the people among whom he was now living. Part of his task as a diplomatic representative was to correct erroneous reports and impressions of his country and to maintain and increase its prestige. There was no such desperate need to gain French favor as there had been during Franklin's wartime mission, but in certain respects the situation was less advantageous. During the period between the two revolutions the officials of the Monarchy saw no reason to emphasize American affairs; and, now that the war with Great Britain was over, the French naturally fell back into the easy way of getting news of the western world from English papers, which Jefferson regarded as a prejudiced and impure source. Wild rumors ran around and occasionally he could check one. Thus, when Franklin was sailing

[30] Randolph to TJ, Jan. 28, 1787 (MHS). The model, which seems to have lain in a warehouse at Havre for six months after TJ shipped it in June, 1786, had not yet arrived; TJ to Messrs. Buchanan & Hay, June 13, 1786 (L. & B., V, 346, misdated June 15); Dec. 26, 1786 (LC, 4544).

[31] TJ to Short Dec. 14, 1789 (Ford, V, 136–137). For a distinctly unfavorable impression of the capitol as late as 1796, see Isaac Weld, Jr., *Travels through the States of North America*, I (1799), 189–190. This observer, however, saw great merit in TJ's original plan.

TJ also sent to Virginia plans for a prison, which have not been found. He got these from an unidentified architect in Lyons and reduced the scale. The Virginia prison that was built later was designed by Latrobe (Kimball, *Jefferson, Architect*, pp. 43–45).

home, his successor heard someone at a dinner party express grave fears for the fate of the venerable Doctor, having been informed that he would be stoned by the people because of their dissatisfaction with the revolution and their anger against him for his part in it. Jefferson replied ironically that the American populace would probably salute Franklin with the very same stones they had thrown at Lafayette.[32] The Marquis and other returned French officers were the best evangels of good will, and Jefferson relied on them to correct gross false impressions. There was little he could really do about the newspapers, and for this reason at least it was fortunate that they were relatively unimportant at that time and place. Books exerted a far greater influence upon opinion, and literary journals, while theoretically subject to censorship, were actually much freer than the gazettes of France and her neighboring countries. During this period increased attention was paid American affairs in books, and through books, directly and indirectly, Jefferson brought his personal influence strongly to bear in behalf of his country.[33]

To regard him as a mere promoter of American interests, however, is to do much less than justice to the motives of one who was so eager "to promote the general good of mankind by an interchange of useful things." Just as he sought to make available to the New World the finest fruits of Old World civilization, he wanted Europe to benefit from the best products of the American mind and spirit. It was not patriotism merely, and certainly not pedantry, which made him so anxious that the French be correctly informed about the American scene, the institutions of the States, the history of the country, and the achievements of his countrymen. Convinced then and ever afterwards that the greatest of these achievements was political and intellectual freedom, far exceeding anything he had found in Europe, he emphasized this freedom whenever possible and tried to show that its results were good. He positively shrank from personal publicity, however, and was generally successful in keeping out of sight.

His most memorable personal contribution in the name of his country to the enlightenment of Europe consisted of his *Notes on Virginia*, but the book was printed in France somewhat by accident and was not originally expected by him to reach many people there. Besides this work, which increased in fame through the years as he did, he served the cause of history by aiding the writers of various books about the

[32] TJ to Monroe, Aug. 28, 1785 (Ford, IV, 87).

[33] For a good general characterization of the relative importance of books and periodicals in this period, see Bernard Faÿ, *Bibliographie Critique des Ouvrages Français Relatifs aux États-Unis* (Paris, 1925), pp. 60–70.

United States. The results of his labors for these men were generally disappointing at the time, but his activities reveal much about Jefferson himself, and taken in connection with his own book they form an episode of considerable importance in the history of international learning and understanding.

The printing of the *Notes on Virginia* was completed when the author had been in France about nine months. He could have taken a fresh copy to Louis XVI when he went to Versailles for his first audience with the King as minister to that Court, though such action would have been wholly wasteful. The work had been chiefly written four years earlier, during the summer following his retirement from the governorship of his state and after his fall from his horse.[34] He had prepared it in response to the queries of the Marquis de Barbé-Marbois, and this secretary of the French legation had received it in the spring of 1782, just about the time that the Marquis de Chastellux was visiting Monticello. Chastellux probably saw a copy of the answers before he returned to France the next year, as did Charles Thomson, the Secretary of Congress. Portions of it were read by others, especially the section devoted to natural history proper (replying to the sixth query of Marbois), and this section in particular was expanded to include additional information sent by obliging friends. Jefferson tried to get some printed copies struck off in Philadelphia as he passed through the city in 1784 shortly before he sailed for Europe, but he found the cost excessive and the time too short. So he brought his manuscript with him to Paris. It was considerably supplemented by then, though it was never drastically revised.

Sometime in that first autumn he found on Rue Saint-Jacques a printer in the person of Philippe-Denis Pierres, who had done important work for Franklin and was probably recommended by him.[35] The printing, which may not have started until the new year, was finished on May 10, 1785, and was paid for in August. Appended to the enlarged reply to Marbois was Jefferson's draft of a constitution for Virginia.[36] There were 200 copies.

Thus the first "edition" of Jefferson's only book was in reality a

[34] Circumstances of composition are described in *Jefferson the Virginian*, pp. 373–377, and notes.

[35] For printing details, see Alice H. Lerch, "Who was the Printer of Jefferson's Notes?" in *Bookmen's Holiday* (1943), pp. 44–56.

[36] See *Jefferson the Virginian*, pp. 379–382, 400–401; Ford, III, 320–333. For cancellations and appended material in later bindings, see Coolie Verner, *A Further Checklist of the Separate Editions of Jefferson's Notes on the State of Virginia* (1950), pp. 5–6.

small private printing. He was offering copies to a few friends and to "some estimable characters beyond that line," but he stated explicitly that he was "unwilling to expose these sheets to the public eye" and specifically enjoined his friends to guard them against all danger of publication.[37] In France at the outset he gave copies to Lafayette and Chastellux, and to Buffon through the latter, and he intended one for the naturalist Daubenton; he sent one to Dr. Richard Price in England by the hand of John Adams. The others were intended almost wholly for Americans. Franklin and John Adams, both of whom were in Paris at the moment the printing was completed, must have had copies, and certain lesser officials got them – like Barclay, the consul general, and William Carmichael, chargé in Madrid. The earliest recipients across the Atlantic were Jefferson's most intimate political friends in Virginia, James Madison and James Monroe, and members of the Philadelphia group who were so close to him in scientific spirit – Charles Thomson, David Rittenhouse, and Francis Hopkinson. The American list, like the European, was afterwards somewhat extended, but first the author consulted Madison about his major purpose, his doubts and fears.[38] If feasible, he wanted to put most of the books into the hands of the young men at the College of William and Mary, on account of both the political and scientific parts, but he was fearful lest his "strictures" on slavery and the constitution of Virginia would give offense and produce an irritation which would hinder rather than help the reformations he had in mind. He had not ceased being realistic and patient as a reformer, and his stay abroad had not diminished his distaste for political controversy. He was hoping that his *Notes* might set the young students of Virginia "into a useful train of thought," but in no event did he propose that they should go to the public at large.

While waiting for a reply from his wise friend Madison, he engaged in illuminating correspondence on the question of slavery with Dr. Richard Price. Thanking Jefferson for the account of Virginia, this liberal-minded Englishman said: "I have read it with singular pleasure and a warm admiration of your sentiments and character. How happy would the United States be were all of them under the direction of such wisdom and liberality as yours." But he had recently

[37] He so stated on the flyleaf of several presentation copies, such as that of Lafayette (now at UVA), as shown in Ford, III, 70. Ford's editorial notes (III, 68–71), though incorrect in minor points, are still invaluable, especially because of the letters and portions of letters he reprints. As in *Jefferson the Virginian*, I am citing Ford's text (III, 85–295) because of its availability.

[38] TJ to Madison, May II, 1785 (Ford, IV, 46–47). See also TJ to Chastellux, June 7, 1785 (Ford, III, 70–71).

heard from South Carolina that his own pamphlet on the American Revolution was attacked, because in it he recommended the gradual abolition of slavery. "Should such a disposition prevail in the United States," he said, "I shall have reason to fear that I have made myself ridiculous by speaking of the American Revolution in the manner I have done; it will appear that the people who have been struggling so earnestly to save themselves from slavery are very ready to enslave others; the friends of liberty and humanity in Europe will be mortified, and an event which had raised their hopes will prove only an introduction to a new sense of aristocratic tyranny and human debasement." [39]

This question went to the heart of a problem which Jefferson himself had clearly perceived, and it was answered by him as a realistic observer who was at the same time a true friend of liberty. His summary of American opinion on slavery, in the different states and regions, comes as near being an authoritative expression as any that a historian is likely to find, but it errs on the side of optimism in regard to Virginia. He expected the next attempt to redress the enormity of slavery to be made there, and was counting on the young men, who had sucked in the principles of liberty with their mother's milk. "Be not therefore discouraged," he wrote. "What you have written will do a great deal of good: and could you still trouble yourself with our welfare, no man is more able to give aid to the laboring side." He wished Price would address an eloquent exhortation to the young men to whom he wanted to send his own book. The clergyman was comforted but, as he said afterwards, he did not intend to write on public affairs again. He was going to devote himself to divinity and morals.[40]

Charles Thomson, whose mind ran in the same channel with that of Price and Jefferson in these social matters, tried to encourage the Virginian just as Jefferson had sought to reassure the English clergyman. Slavery was a cancer that must be got rid of, he said, a blot on the American character that must be wiped off, and he believed that philosophy was gaining ground on selfishness. "If this [slavery] can be rooted out," he added, "and our land filled with freemen, union preserved and the spirit of liberty maintained and cherished I think in 25 or 30 years we shall have nothing to fear from the rest of the world." [41] That was just what Jefferson was thinking.

[39] Richard Price to TJ, July 2, 1785 (LC, 2214).

[40] TJ to Price, Aug. 7, 1785 (Ford, IV, 82–84); Price to TJ, Oct. 24, 1785 (LC, 2676–2677).

[41] Thomson to TJ, Nov. 2, 1785 (LC, 2703).

But slavery was a far more ticklish subject south of Chesapeake Bay than north of it, and Madison's counsel had more immediate value. After reading the *Notes* and consulting judicious friends in confidence, he concluded that the freedom of the strictures on slavery and the state constitution would be displeasing to some, but that the work was too valuable not to be made known – at least to those for whom the author had intended it. Thus reassured, Jefferson said he would send over the remaining copies to be given to some of his friends and to "select subjects" in the College.[42] Consultation with other friends confirmed Madison in his original judgment. One of these was the other James Madison, president of the College, whose first view of the book convinced him that it would be highly profitable to youth. He wrote the author: "Such a work should not be kept in private. Let it have the broad light of an American sun." Later he reported that it was read with the greatest avidity by everyone who could get hold of it, and he was impatient because the copies for the College had not yet come. It is hard to say just when they did arrive, in those slow-moving times, but they inspired this enlightened clergyman with hope, not fear. More than three years after the book was printed he wrote: "I hope your notes judiciously distributed among our young men here will tend to excite the spirit of philosophical observation. Never was there a finer range for the exercise of such a spirit than this country presents, and . . . among the different sources of satisfaction, which you must experience from your patriotic exertions, it will not be the least that you have been foremost in exciting among your fellow citizens so laudable as well as so necessary a spirit."[43]

This man of science and learning was specially pleased with Jefferson's refutation of certain opinions derogatory of America. So was Joel Barlow, who informed him in 1787 that the *Notes* were getting into the newspapers in spite of his request that they should not be published. Said the poet: "We are flattered with the idea of being ourselves vindicated from those despicable aspersions which have long been thrown upon us and echoed from one ignorant scribbler to another in all the languages of Europe." Charles Thomson had already described the work as the equal and possibly the superior to the natural history of any country yet published, and David Ritten-

[42] Madison to TJ, Nov. 15, 1785 (Hunt, II, 214–215*n.*); TJ to Madison, Feb. 8, 1786 (Ford, IV, 193), crossing in the mail the letter from Madison, Jan. 22, 1786 (Hunt, II, 214–215), containing George Wythe's suggestion that distribution to the students be made at the discretion of the professors.

[43] Rev. James Madison to TJ, Mar. 27, 1786; Dec. 28, 1786; Feb. 10, 1789 (*W. & M.*, 2 ser., V, 84, 87, 89).

house found it "an inestimable treasure."[44] The author's scientific brethren always liked his work, and the immediate impression on them was that he was not so much a critic of his country as a defender of it.

If Jefferson feared that his *Notes* would excite political controversy in Virginia, he had little reason to believe that any storm of scientific controversy would be occasioned by the few copies of the first printing which he distributed in France. It is true that he criticized the work of noted French naturalists like Buffon and Daubenton, but his differences with them were not a public matter, and his personal attitude toward them could lay him open to no charge of discourtesy.[45] As though forewarned of Buffon's vanity, he paid him a mollifying compliment, calling him "the best informed of any naturalist who has ever written." He had no such respect for the Abbé Raynal, who had so offended his patriotism by asserting that the human species had degenerated in the New World. The sentimental and fantastic writings of Raynal still appealed to many people, but he did not run in the best scientific circles. Indeed, he had come into conflict with the political authorities and had had to run away.[46]

Jefferson prepared his natural history section in the first place as a description of the minerals, the flora and fauna of Virginia, but as friends kept sending him information he had expanded it until at last it covered at least a continent, and parts of it constituted a direct refutation of certain ill-founded theories of other writers.[47] Also, it provided incidental but important clues to his own spirit and procedure as a scientist. When discussing minerals, he considered the problem of fossil shells that had been found far from any seashore, and almost immediately after the first printing he altered the wording of one passage and rejected an explanation of Voltaire's which he had previously tolerated.[48] Churchmen in later years seized upon his

[44] Barlow to TJ, June 15, 1787 (MHS); Thomson to TJ, Mar. 6, 1785 (LC, 1977); Rittenhouse to TJ, Sept. 28, 1785 (LC, 2566).

[45] Nothing seems to have come of his authorization to Chastellux to publish extracts from the *Notes* in the *Journal de Physique;* TJ to Chastellux, June 7, 1785 (L. & B., V, 3).

[46] Raynal's *Histoire Philosophique et Politique des Etablissements et du Commerce des Europeéns dans les deux Indes,* first published in 1770, went through many editions. For a critical discussion, see Faÿ, *Bibliographie,* p. 43.

[47] Query VI; Ford, III, 111–176.

[48] Ford, III, 116–119, and 118–119*n.* Jefferson inquired into Voltaire's statement about shells unconnected with animal bodies, supposed to have been seen near Tours, when he himself was at Tours on June 8, 1787 (L. & B., XVII, 232–235). He regarded the alleged "facts" as not contrary to any law of nature, but as so little analogous to the normal processes as to seem extraordinary.

denial of the biblical story of the deluge, as an explanation, but scholars and philosophers today will be more struck by his intellectual honesty and scientific caution. At another place, but in the same spirit, he warmly commended one of Buffon's striking sentences: "I love a man who corrects me in an error as much as one who apprehends me of a truth, for in effect an error corrected is a truth." [49] This implies more modesty in Buffon and more negativeness in both men than is borne out by their total record, but it also shows that Jefferson viewed the intendant of the Jardin du Roi with no hostile eye.

It was quite obvious to him, nevertheless, that Buffon needed to be informed about certain American animals and that some of his generalizations were illogical and unsound. In the opinion of the Count the wild animals of the New World were smaller than those of the Old, and domestic animals transported from Europe to America degenerated there.[50] For this he assigned climatic reasons: America was colder than Europe and more moist. Jefferson, who was enormously interested in climate, doubted this, and questioned its significance if true. He thought it unproved that heat is friendly and moisture unfavorable to the production of large quadrupeds, and he did what he could to collect and present more facts. The tables he drew, with the most dependable weights obtainable, were proof of that.[51] One of his purposes was to make a zoological defense of the New World against the aspersions of the Old, even though the question of the relative stature of wild animals had no social significance. The effort to disprove these contentions of Buffon was a fascinating game into which he entered with vast enthusiasm. As a lover of tall tales he delighted in this contest over big animals.

He was unable to take a moose with him to France for purposes of exhibition, but before he sailed from the States he picked up an uncommonly large panther skin in a shop in Philadelphia, paying sixteen dollars for it. By this means he hoped to convince Buffon that this animal and the cougar were not identical, and he afterwards said he did. This minor triumph was long deferred, however, for the Count, who had a passion for work as well as glory, spent most of the year in his country retreat at Montbard where he could write with only slight disturbance. Perhaps Jefferson fired two barrels at once by having the Marquis de Chastellux deliver the skin and a copy of the

[49] Ford, III, 145. Compare with this Jefferson's own statement of his preference of ignorance to error (*ibid.*, III, 119*n.*).

[50] More fully and precisely stated in Jefferson's own words (Ford, III, 135–136). See also his letter to Chastellux, June 7, 1785 (L. & B., V, 3–7).

[51] Especially, Ford, III, 139–142.

Notes simultaneously. The elaborate argument in the latter, denying the identity of the mammoth and the elephant, left the old naturalist unruffled; he maintained his opinion that they were the same. But, acknowledging the gift of the skin on the last day of 1785, he invited the donor to come with Chastellux some convenient day and dine in the Garden.[52]

Jefferson availed himself of the invitation very quickly, and found Buffon agreeable and entertaining; but immediately afterwards he sought additional specimens from America. He had noted various gaps in the King's cabinet of natural history; these should be filled, and the curator should be further educated.[53] He told his doubting host about American deer with horns two feet long, and boasted that the American moose stood so tall that the reindeer could walk under his belly; but not until another year and a half had passed was he able to make a display that was really impressive. In the early autumn of 1787 he received from General John Sullivan of New Hampshire a large box containing the skin, horns, and skeleton of a moose, along with horns of the caribou, elk, deer, and spike horned buck. Buffon was then away from Paris, but Jefferson wrote him at some length and sent these precious acquisitions to him in care of Daubenton.[54] The moose was seven feet tall and good enough to be stuffed and exhibited, but Jefferson regretted that the creature had lost so much hair on the voyage. He also explained that the horns of some of the other animals were unusually small and that he was trying to get others. He was surprised by the cost (which may have reached £60 Sterling) until he learned from General Sullivan that the services of twenty men had been required on a difficult hunting expedition toward the White Mountains. He succeeded in convincing Buffon of some errors, or so he thought. The old naturalist promised to make some corrections in his next volume, but he died the next spring. Some months later, at the French Academy, he was lauded for his literary style and described as "the French Aristotle."[55] By that time Jeffer-

[52] Memorandum of Jefferson's conversation by Daniel Webster (1824) in Ford, X, 332*n.*, giving the most vivid details but lacking the authority of a contemporary document; TJ to Hogendorp, Oct. 13, 1785 (Ford, IV, 102); Buffon to TJ, Dec. 31, 1785, from the Jardin du Roi (LC, 2893).

[53] TJ to Francis Hopkinson, Jan. 3, 1786 (L. & B., V, 242); to Archibald Cary, Jan. 7, 1786 (L. & B., V, 244); to Archibald Stuart, Jan. 25, 1786 (Ford, IV, 189).

[54] Sullivan to TJ, Apr. 26, 1787 (LC, 4957, 4975, 4976); TJ to Sullivan, Oct. 5, 1787 (L. & B., VI, 328–330); TJ to Buffon, Oct. 1, 1787 (Ford, IV, 457–459); note of Oct. 1, 1787, to Daubenton, and acknowledgment from him Oct. 2 (LC, 5718, 5722); TJ to John Rutledge, Jr., Sept. 9, 1788 (LC, 7266).

[55] Grimm, *Memoirs,* II, 395–403. Buffon died Apr. 16, 1788, and was eulogized Dec. 11.

son may have concluded that the animal game he had been playing was really not worth the candle.

His reply to European allegations of the inferiority of the human species in America was another matter. Buffon had not lent the support of his glowing pen to the assertions of the Abbé Raynal that the European stock had degenerated in the New World, but he had painted an afflicting picture of the aborigines which seemed to Jefferson merely the creation of a vivid imagination. He was sure that the stories about the Indians of South America that circulated in Europe were no more trustworthy than the fables of Aesop. He himself had been seeing North American Indians since his boyhood in Albemarle and his college days in Williamsburg; he had smoked the pipe of peace with chiefs and had called them his brothers; he had supplemented his own knowledge of the natives with the comments of hunters and explorers who had seen them more often and knew them better. He recognized that fuller and more precise information was needed, and continued to seek it for many years, but he already knew enough to correct gross misapprehensions.

It was not merely in the name of scientific accuracy and simple justice that he spoke. He also defended the honor of human nature and challenged the doctrine of human inequality. He showed no such negativeness here as in matters of chemistry and zoology – where he thought doubt was wisdom and ignorance preferable to error – but appeared as a man of faith. He never denied human variations, but he always hoped that the causes of sharp differences between men and races would prove to be differences of circumstance, not nature. He was troubled about the black race, which he had seen so close at hand in servitude, and there is significance in the fact that he did not discuss the Negroes in his natural history section but in connection with the practical question of emancipation. Dubious of the natural equality of endowment of the blacks with their masters, he was keeping his mind open about them, but he already believed that the Indians were equal to white men in native powers of mind and body. Hence scientific observation and social philosophy converged in his defense of the aborigines.[56]

The passages relating to the Indians in the *Notes on Virginia* can be matched in fervor only by those glorifying religious and intellectual freedom and those denouncing dictatorship. Taking into full account the differences in the environment of whites and redskins, and recognizing that the latter were still barbarians, Jefferson warmly

[56] There is a stimulating treatment of this question in D. J. Boorstin, *The Lost World of Thomas Jefferson* (1948), ch. 2.

defended them against charges of deficiency in sexual ardor and lack of domestic affection, praised them for courage and fortitude, and attributed to them genuine capacity for friendship and a distinctive sense of honor. "The principles of their society forbidding all compulsion, they are to be led to duty and to enterprise by personal influence and persuasion," he said. "Hence eloquence in council, bravery and address in war, become the foundations of all consequence with them. To these acquirements all their faculties are directed." [57] He and his countrymen had had multiplied proof of their prowess in war, but they had had fewer examples of Indian eloquence since this was displayed chiefly in their own councils. For this reason he displayed one lustrous example – the touching speech of the Mingo Chief, Logan, addressed to white men after the murder of his family.[58] Since this seriously reflected on a white man, it was afterwards used as a political weapon against Jefferson in America, but the main thing it showed at the time was that he had retained his youthful enthusiasm for Indian eloquence. He was on the whole much more influenced by the rationalistic elements in eighteenth-century thought and literature than by the romantic, but this was one place where his sentiment overflowed.

The spirited defense of the Indians, chiefly directed against Buffon, was much longer than the reply to Raynal, who had belittled the achievements of white men in America.[59] The Abbé was astonished that America had not yet produced a great poet, an able mathematician, a man of genius in any art or science. Jefferson reminded him that the country was young and had a relatively small population. Judging from the centuries it took France and England to produce a great poet, he thought the United States might have to wait a considerable time for one; but, pointing out that the country had produced a Washington, a Franklin, and a Rittenhouse, he was entirely confident that it would continue to produce its quota of genius. He expected achievement to be varied but showed clearly what he valued most – not the minor kinds of "genius," which serve only to amuse man, but the nobler kinds, "which call him into action, which substantiate his freedom, and conduct him to happiness." [60] He himself was the best fulfillment of his own prophecy, for his active, useful, and purposeful genius was of just this sort.

* * *

[57] Ford, III, 155.
[58] See *Jefferson the Virginian*, pp. 385–387.
[59] Ford, III, 166–170.
[60] Ford, III, 169.

Even though relatively few copies of the first and private printing of the *Notes on Virginia* were distributed in France, the mere existence of the book helped establish the author in the minds of the savants who learned about it. If he needed any further commendation to the world of science and learning, the Marquis de Chastellux, who had introduced him to Buffon, provided it in the year 1786 by describing him in the account of his own travels in America. Chastellux, who was a member of the Academy and had been a major general in Rochambeau's army, had made an unforgettable visit to Monticello. In his *Voyages*, probably the most distinguished French book of the era relating to the western world, he availed himself of considerable information which had been supplied him by his inexhaustible host and described him in terms so laudatory as to be positively embarrassing. Here, under distinguished sponsorship, Jefferson appeared in his true light as a man of the most varied tastes and accomplishments, as a natural philosopher who loved the world only as he might serve and enlighten it.[61]

The esteem of his peers was always dear to Jefferson, but what he was most anxious to do was to spread correct ideas about America. For this reason, without any emphasis on his own authorship, he distributed some copies of the report of the revisers of the laws of Virginia and considerably more of the Act for Establishing Religious Freedom. These documents were sent him in 1785 and 1786 by Madison who, as a member of the Assembly, deserved the lion's share of credit for the success of such of these enlightened and humane measures as were enacted.[62] He responded with alacrity to the requests of various diplomatic representatives for copies of the act for freedom of religion to send to their sovereigns. It was translated into French and Italian, he reported, and he thought it would do good even in countries with despotic governments. He was largely responsible for the fact that it found its way into so many of the books about the United States.[63] He missed no good chance to point out that after so many years in which the human mind had been held in vassalage the standard

[61] See *Jefferson the Virginian*, pp. 391–393, for the visit of Chastellux to Monticello in 1782; TJ to Chastellux, Sept. 2, 1785 (Bixby, pp. 11–15), for comments on the proofsheets of the latter's book; Randall, I, 373–375, for the well-known description. The book itself, *Voyages de M. le Marquis de Chastellux dans l'Amérique Septentrionale*, was first published in 2 vols. (Paris, 1786); for critical comments on it, see Faÿ *Bibliographie*, pp. 62–63, 65.

[62] Madison to TJ, Jan. 9, 1785, and Jan. 22, 1786 (Hunt, II, 118, 216). On the measures themselves, see *Jefferson the Virginian*, chs. XIX–XX, and the admirable account of the struggle for religious freedom in Brant, *Madison*, II, ch. XXII.

[63] See especially his letters to Wythe, Aug. 13, 1786 (L. & B., V, 395–396), and Madison, Dec. 16, 1786 (Ford, IV, 334). He appended it to the first edn. of the *Notes on Virginia* in later bindings.

of reason had been erected in the forests of Virginia. When the Comte de Mirabeau stated in print that there was no place on earth, not even in America, where it was sufficient to practise the social virtues in order to participate in all the advantages of society, he hastened to send him the original and a translation of this act of "one of the legislatures of the American republics." This example of "emancipating human reason" by removing all religious disabilities was part of the general reformation of laws which had been going on in America, he said. He seized upon every proof that there was tranquillity there, not lawlessness – that society was ruled by reason, not force, as it should be everywhere.[64]

The translation of his *Notes* into French and their publication in Paris, under the title *Observations sur la Virginie*, were the result of unforeseen circumstances.[65] Despite his care and admonitions a copy got into the hands of a bookseller, who hired a translator and was about to publish the book in what the author regarded as a most injurious form. He was much relieved, therefore, when the Abbé Morellet, a member of the French Academy whom he had known for some months and to whom he had given a copy from the private printing, heard of this threat and offered to make a translation subject to his approval. Jefferson afterwards described this translation as bad, and he did not quite like certain rearrangements Morellet made in the order of sections and paragraphs, but he reconciled himself as best he could to the imperfections of this fortuitous French publication. However, he faced the danger of its later retranslation into English and its unauthorized publication in even more imperfect form; and it was in order to avoid this misfortune that he had the work published in Lon-

[64] TJ to Mirabeau, Aug. 20, 1786 (Ford, IV, 283).

[65] *Observations sur la Virginie*. Par M. J. xxx. *Traduites de l'Anglois* (Paris, Chez Barrois, l'aîné, 1786). Extracts from letters to C. W. F. Dumas, Madison, and Edward Bancroft, in February, 1786, explaining the circumstances and the arrangement with Morellet and the latter's preface, are in Ford, III, 72–76. TJ's own list of errors and corrections in Morellet's translation (Jan. 19, 1787) has been published by J. M. Carrière in *Papers of the Bibliographical Soc., Univ. Va.*, I (1948–1949), 4–24. The plate for the map, engraved in England by Samuel J. Neele on order of W. S. Smith, was not sent to Jefferson until Dec. 21, 1786, and it was being corrected as late as March 12, 1787, soon after which date 250 copies of the map were struck off for him; Neele to TJ, Dec. 21, 1786 (*Papers, M. H. S.*, pp. 24–25); Short to TJ, Mar. 12, 1787 (LC, 4897–4898). Those that were to be struck off for Morellet were delayed until after July 2, 1787, because of the dilatoriness of the printer Barrois (TJ to Morellet, July 2, 1787; Ford, III, 77–78); but the book was reviewed in the *Mercure de France*, June 2, 1787. On Morellet, see Antoine Guillois, *Le Salon de Madame Helvétius* (Paris, 1784), pp. 37–38, and *Mémoires de L'Abbé Morellet, . . . précédés de l'éloge . . . par M. Lémontez* (2 vols., Paris, 1821).

don in his own language. With both editions now appeared a map, based considerably on his father's but taking in more territory. This he himself prepared, though he did not put his name on it; he thought it "very particular" and much more valuable than the text. The making and correcting of the plate and the printing of the maps delayed the appearance of both editions. The French one has the date 1786 on it, but actually they both were issued in 1787. Thus at the age of forty-four Jefferson became for the first and last time the author of a full-fledged book.

The French edition of Barrois came out a few weeks earlier than the English edition of John Stockdale, but the latter really represented Jefferson's first offering of his work to the public. Stockdale suggested it in the first place, but the printing was the result of Jefferson's deliberate negotiations; the book bore his full name, not merely the initial "J" as the French edition did; it was based on a corrected text of the original which he supplied, not on a translation which he really did not like; it represented the workmanship of a printer whom he trusted to a fuller degree than he ever could the dilatory and negligent Barrois. This English edition contained as appendices, besides the notes of Charles Thomson which he valued so highly, the draft of his constitution for Virginia, and the Act for Establishing Religious Freedom which he prized more than almost anything else. He still regarded the body of the work as hasty and undigested, but he had gone to great pains to make it accurate in detail; he did not personally correct the proof but he urged the utmost care in this connection; and all later printings of the *Notes* in his lifetime followed this text. In his history as an author the appearance of this edition was a significant event.[66]

The less comprehensive and less authoritative French work had no such enduring literary importance, and its public reception at the time may have seemed disappointing. In France, Jefferson was not a public character in the dramatic sense that Franklin was, and a book of his was not exciting news. This one was filled with statistics and tables which would discourage frivolous minds in any age; it contained some fervid passages, but to a generation that had been fed on fantastical and sentimental accounts of the New World it must have seemed sedate and cool — as the author himself did to anyone viewing him superficially. It appealed most strongly to the small group of savants and political liberals who already knew the author or would

[66] For this reason, a fuller note than can be appropriately inserted here is given in the bibliography. Stockdale wrote Jefferson on Aug. 8, 1786 (MHS), and Jefferson's preface was dated Feb. 27, 1787. Printing was done soon thereafter but, because of delays connected with the map, he did not get bound copies until August.

naturally appreciate such a spirit and such a mind. Chastellux commended it in advance of publication, and Morellet not only praised it in his preface but did so again in the memoirs of his old age. In the first instance he said that the title was much too modest, and in the last he summed it up in words which were apt and just. "It is a useful book for the knowledge of the country," he said, "an interesting and varied book, enriched with philosophical observations full of accuracy and reason."[67] The anonymous writer of a long and favorable contemporary review must also have known and recognized the author as a kindred spirit. Likewise commenting on the modesty of the title, he described the *Observations sur la Virginie* as one of the small number of truly instructive books – full of facts and useful information, marked by simplicity and controlled eloquence while warmed by sentiment for the rights of man and zeal for truth.[68] Far from objecting to the criticism of Buffon's theory of the degeneration of animals in America, this reviewer found it "a model of good logic and excellent discussion," and he thought the reply to Raynal even better. He ranged Jefferson (and John Adams) with Washington, Franklin, and Rittenhouse as enlightened and virtuous men who had established in the New World "the empire of reason and the inestimable blessing of liberty." Thus, while the book gained no large French audience, it improved the author's standing in the little circle of men whose approval he valued most, establishing him more firmly in their eyes as a representative and spokesman of a free and reasonable society.

During the five years he was in France Jefferson spent far more time helping other people who were writing about the United States than would ordinarily have been expected of one in his position. Normal appeals for information were multiplied because he had participated actively in historic events and could give much firsthand information, and also because he was known to be a savant. The generosity of his response may be attributed to his sense of official responsibility, to his patriotic concern lest his country be thrown into unfavorable light by erroneous statements, and to his scholarly concern for accuracy and his zeal for the promulgation of truth. That he was able to provide so much detailed information when separated from his own library and records is proof that among other notable gifts he must have had an unusual memory, though it was not always impeccable.

[67] *Mémoires de L'Abbé Morellet* (1821), I, 286. See also Chastellux, *Voyages*, II, 303*n.*; Faÿ, *Bibliographie*, p. 67.
[68] *Mercure de France*, June 2, 9, 1787.

His comments and suggestions to authors are of value as representing his own contemporary judgments on the particular historical events and circumstances they were describing. These judgments are even more valuable in showing the workings of his own mind and revealing his spirit as a patriot, scholar, scientist, and philosopher. He was completely loyal to the country he represented, but he had no tolerance of what he regarded as historical or scientific error; he eschewed sheer sentimentalism; he was a passionate advocate of intellectual freedom and sought to spread light and reason.

The period of his residence in France was marked by the publication there of an impressive number of books about America. Some of these were hostile, many were sentimental, and most of them were inaccurate.[69] He did what he could to improve them, as can be shown by a few examples.

One writer who got his help in generous measure was Jean-Nicolas Démeunier, who was preparing articles on the United States and the various states for the *Encyclopédie Méthodique* and sent him a long list of questions. Thinking it important to set things straight in an important work of reference (which he himself was in the process of acquiring for his own library and his friends), he began to send detailed information in January, 1786; and he read the long article, "*États-Unis*," in proof. Finding this "a mass of errors and misconceptions," he made numerous corrections and suggestions, of which the author availed himself sufficiently to make it a fairly good account.[70] In Jefferson's opinion, it was the only thing in print which gave a just idea of the American constitutions, but he was much embarrassed by the author's effusive praise of him. "He has paid me for my trouble in the true coin of the country, most unmerciful compliment," he wrote John Adams.[71] When he got around to the article "*Virginie*," Démeunier followed Jefferson pretty closely, drawing heavily on the *Notes* and reprinting the statute for religious freedom of which its author was so proud.

The most interesting aspect of this entire episode, however, related to the Society of Cincinnati, which had been attacked by Mirabeau in a violent pamphlet and against which Démeunier had written what Jefferson termed "a mere Philippic" when he saw it in proof. At his suggestion Démeunier rewrote this section, following quite closely the historical account which Jefferson had sent him and which was

[69] Faÿ (*Bibliographie*, pp. 18–25, 61–71) lists and comments on these.

[70] For his answers of Jan. 24, 1786, and his comments of June 22, see Ford, IV, 138–185.

[71] TJ to Adams, Aug. 27, 1786 (Ford, IV, 297). See also TJ to Hogendorp, Aug. 25, 1786 (Ford, IV, 284–287).

much fairer than anything which had yet appeared in France. Jefferson was anxious that the original motives of the veterans, and particularly of Washington, should not be misunderstood, but in writing Washington himself about it he showed that his observations in France had definitely increased his fears of the Society and any sort of hereditary order, class, and privilege.[72] This episode serves better than almost any other to date the crystallization of his hostility to aristocracy, which he had long regarded as theoretically undesirable and against which he had directed preventive measures in his own State of Virginia. For a vivid illustration of the social evils of a hereditary system he had to come to France.

Jefferson astutely avoided involvement with writers he mistrusted, and, despite his incredible industry, he was not one to waste his time. His greatest activity in behalf of historical accuracy was in the year 1786; by the next year he had found the result of his efforts distinctly disappointing. His state of disillusionment is illustrated by an amusing letter he wrote to the editor of the *Journal de Paris*, protesting against the statement in a recent book that John Dickinson was solely responsible for the pronouncement of American independence, when actually he was unique in opposing it:

> . . . When young, I was passionately fond of reading books of history & travels [he said]. Since the commencement of the late revolution which separated us from Great Britain, our country too has been thought worthy to employ the pens of historians & travellers. I cannot paint to you, Sir, the agonies which these have cost me, in obliging me to renounce those favorite branches of reading and in discovering to me at length that my whole life has been employed in nourishing my mind with fables & falsehoods. For thus I reason. If the histories of d'Auberteuil & of Longchamps, and the travels of the Abbé Robin can be published in the face of the world, can be read and believed by those who are cotemporary [*sic*] with the events they pretend to relate, how may we expect future ages shall be better informed? [73]

He was seeking no credit for himself, for he did not mention his own name in connection with the Declaration of Independence; nor did he employ here such bitter tones as he did against falsehoods

[72] TJ to Washington, Nov. 14, 1786 (Ford, IV, 327–329). For earlier discussion see *Jefferson the Virginian*, pp. 414–415.

[73] TJ to the Editor of the *Journal de Paris*, Aug. 29, 1787 (Ford, IV, 439–442). On these writings see Faÿ, *Bibliographie*, pp. 16, 17, 19, 21. Hilliard d'Auberteuil was one of the writers Jefferson distrusted and avoided; see letters to him, Feb. 20, 1786, and Jan. 27, 1787 (L. & B., V, 283–284; VI, 62); and to M. Charles, Dec. 7, 1786 (*ibid.*, VI, 5).

emanating from the British. But, as he humorously bade adieu to history and travels, he seemed resigned to the indifference of his age to facts. The taste of that frivolous society was not for documents but for phantasy and theory.

As a promoter of accurate history he was most successful when helping fellow Americans. He regarded Dr. David Ramsay's *History of the Revolution of South Carolina* as authentic and reliable, and went to no little trouble having this work translated and published in France. The author sent him printed sheets month by month as they issued from the press in Trenton, New Jersey; and on his part Jefferson consulted with booksellers and the Marquis de Chastellux, made the necessary financial arrangements, and saw the whole project through.[74] He fully appreciated the importance of these special histories of the Revolution which must be written before a general history could be expected, but he anticipated no wide interest in this one and his judgment proved correct.

He gave help of another sort to Philip Mazzei, who described himself as a citizen of Virginia and was the same Florentine who had engaged in vine culture at Colle near Monticello. Mazzei arrived in Paris late in 1785 or early in 1786, in financial difficulties as usual, and began to prepare what turned out to be one of the largest and probably the most reliable of all the works of the period on the United States.[75] Much of the author's knowledge of American affairs had been gained from his former neighbor in the first place, and the historical value of his work was considerably if not primarily due to his reliance on this invaluable personal source. Literally, Mazzei was a headache to Jefferson, but that long-suffering gentleman commended him as a well-informed man, possessed of a "masculine understanding"; and he regarded the book as a good one, though he claimed no special credit for it.

In some sense it was a tie between him and Condorcet, whose *Lettres d'un Bourgeois de New Haven* were reprinted in it and who assisted in the translation. Mazzei wrote the book in Italian and the translation in the main was the work of an obscure young man, but the Marquis and Marchioness de Condorcet did some of it and may

[74] The American edition was in 1785, the French in 1787. For TJ's comments, see letters to the Count del Vermi, Aug. 15, 1786 (L. & B., VI, 283), and Dr. Gordon, July 16, 1788 (L. & B., VII, 66–67). The full story of this episode has been worked up by Miss E. Millicent Sowerby, and I hope it will soon be in print.

[75] *Recherches historiques et politiques sur les États-Unis* (4 vols., Paris, 1788). This was largely written in 1786, and the story of it will also be told by Miss Sowerby. See Mazzei's *Memoirs* (1942), p. 293; TJ's letter of Nov. 1785 (Ford, IV, 108–116) which he incorporated; and *Recherches*, III, 92–93).

have supervised the whole. It was also asserted by the Baron Grimm that Condorcet wrote the eulogistic review of it in the *Mercure de France* — which, incidentally, involved Jefferson unwittingly in religious controversy.[76]

One of Mazzei's major purposes, which he said Jefferson approved, was to refute the Abbé Raynal and the Abbé Mably; and his answer to the latter on the subject of freedom of the press and freedom of religion was given special attention and special praise in this review. The reviewer referred to the "famous" preamble of the Virginia statute for religious freedom (reprinted by Mazzei) and the "illustrious citizen" who drafted it, and he quoted with approval various expressions of Jefferson's which Mazzei had drawn from the *Notes on Virginia.* In these Jefferson went the whole way in his championship of intellectual freedom, denied the legitimate powers of government in all matters of opinion, and not only countenanced but actually approved varieties of belief. Even in their original context some of his expressions would have displeased almost any traditionalist or absolutist, and these sounded much more irreverent when torn from their setting — much more irreverent, actually, than Jefferson himself was. A champion of orthodoxy in another paper was astonished that anything "so harsh, so revolting, so absurd" should have been allowed to appear in the *Mercure de France.* This stanch defender of the established order was specially horrified by the statement that no man could harm another by saying that there were twenty gods, or none; and he was tempted to believe that the author of the extract [Jefferson] was "absolutely devoid of sense and philosophy." [77] Jefferson's fellow diplomat, the cynical Grimm, who was himself no friend of orthodoxy, said that the proprietor of the *Mercure* was threatened with the loss of the *privilège* of the paper as a result of this literary controversy.[78] Relaxation of the censorship was by no means uncommon in this period, however, and nobody seems to have been punished in this case.

Jefferson's unwitting involvement in the affair could not have failed to be unwelcome to him. Belief in the freedom of religion — which to him meant freedom of the mind — lay at the heart of his philosophy and he was always proud to be identified with it; but he was an accredited diplomat, a scrupulously polite man, and, unlike many of the *philosophes*, he was no atheist. Years afterward, when John Adams

[76] *Mercure de France*, Feb. 23, 1788.

[77] Entire letter, unsigned, in *L'Année littéraire*, 1788, II, 256–272 (Mar. 18, 1788).

[78] Grimm, *Correspondance*, XV, 251. Ch. J. Panoucke "*acquit le privilège*" of the *Mercure de France* in 1788. I have found no evidence that he lost it.

and he were writing each other from Quincy and Monticello about philosophical matters, this old companion inveighed against the atheists who had such vogue in eighteenth-century France. Replying gently to the outburst, Jefferson observed that criticism of the existing religious order tended to take the form of atheism in Catholic churches, and of deism in Protestant.[79] He himself was the product of a wholly Protestant society which, in the Virginia of his youth, had been relatively tolerant, and which he expected to become far more so now that the connection between Church and State had been severed. His own religious views, which he regarded as wholly private like his domestic affairs, tended toward deism. He believed in one God, not no God, not twenty gods; but he thought it much better for the human spirit if a country had twenty sects rather than only one. He was no Voltaire, no Thomas Paine. If he was ever drawn into an attack on any Church it was not because it was a religious organization but because it had assumed a political character, or because it limited, in one way or another, the freedom of the mind – on which, as he never ceased to believe, the progress of the human species toward happiness depends.

[79] TJ to Adams, Apr. 8, 1816 (L. & B., XIV, 468-471); cited and well discussed by Koch, *Philosophy of Thomas Jefferson*, pp. 95-96.

VII

Traveling with a Purpose

1787

IN the spring that he became forty-four, Jefferson made a trip which lasted more than three months and proved to be the longest of his life. His daughter Patsy, who was immured at Panthémont and did not get as many letters as she wanted while he was away, suspected that personal pleasure was a more important object than he admitted. Loving as he did "the precious remains of antiquity, loving architecture, gardening, a warm sun and a clear sky," it would have been strange indeed if he had not enormously enjoyed the monuments, the countryside, the delicious air of southern France and northern Italy after the wind and rain of Paris.[1] But he had been planning the trip for months, he believed that it was justifiable on official grounds alone, and he was not one to seek idle amusement.

Before he dislocated his wrist in the early autumn of 1786 he had expected to accompany the Court to Fontainebleau in October and to proceed, after a bit, on a trip of six weeks to the Mediterranean coast, the Canal of Languedoc, and the cities on the west coast—thinking that this would be more useful and agreeable than to lounge among the courtiers and diplomats.[2] His accident defeated this plan, though it eventually gave him another excuse for going south. His

[1] He applied this description to Madame de Tessé in his letter of Mar. 20, 1787, from Nîmes (L. & B., VI, 103). The whole trip is admirably described by Dumbauld, ch. V, on the basis of manuscript and printed sources, and he gives a full itinerary, pp. 233–235. Besides the letters of the period, Jefferson's travel notes in L. & B., XVII, 153–236 are the chief source.

[2] Among numerous letters, the following in particular may be cited in this connection: TJ to John Banister, Jr., Sept. 7, 1786 (LC, 4074, 4110); to W. S. Smith, Sept. 13, 1786 (LC, 4143–4144); to John Jay, Oct. 23, 1786 (L. & B., V, 452, wrongly dated Oct. 22); to Madison, Jan. 30, 1787 (Ford, IV, 367).

physicians advised that the slow recovery of his wrist might be hastened by the healing effects of mineral springs, and for this reason he altered his itinerary to include Aix-en-Provence, thus showing that there was some credulity in his nature. In the meantime he received the important letter from Calonne that summarized the arrangements about American commerce.[3] It now seemed safe to leave what Lafayette called "the busy center of public affairs," and desirable to view with his own eyes the situation in the seaport cities. By visiting the Canal of Languedoc he hoped to gain information of that "species of navigation" which might prove useful hereafter. Agricultural purposes actually bulked largest in his mind, however, and these caused him to extend his itinerary into northern Italy. This deviation he explained with some care to Secretary John Jay, whose interest in the culture of rice was not so keen: "The mass of our countrymen being interested in agriculture, I hope I do not err in supposing that in a time of profound peace as the present, to enable them to adapt their productions to the market, to point out markets for them, and endeavor to obtain favorable terms of reception, is within the line of my duty."[4]

These objects of public utility he dilated upon when explaining his plans to persons of political consequence at home, but he was abundantly warranted in seeking a change of air for his own sake. His head had not been injured by Maria Cosway, whatever she may have done to his heart, and he wrote some very important things soon after she went away – using one hand or the other. But he was keenly aware of the futility of social life in Paris during his third winter in the metropolis. "I am here burning the candle of life without present pleasure or future object," he wrote his warmhearted American friend, Mrs. Elizabeth Trist, with whom he had lodged so pleasantly in Philadelphia. "A dozen or twenty years ago this scene would have amused me, but I am past the age for changing habits." A few weeks later he wrote to beautiful Mrs. Bingham, who had been back in the States for about a year, reminding her of her promise to tell him if she had not found the simple domestic pleasures of America preferable to the empty bustle of Paris.[5]

He did not get out of this bustling emptiness until after Vergennes had died and he had had a reassuring conference with Montmorin, the great minister's successor. He did not go until after he had attended

[3] Oct. 22, 1786 (*D. C.*, I, 827–829).
[4] TJ to Jay, May 4, 1787 (Ford, IV, 378).
[5] TJ to Mrs. Trist, Dec. 15, 1786 (Ford IV, 330); to Mrs. Bingham, Feb. 7, 1787 (L. & B., VI, 81).

the opening session of the Assembly of Notables on February 22, 1787. His hopes for this meeting rose after he gained a little perspective, but the most notable immediate effect of it that he observed was a flood of witticisms, and it seemed to him that nothing important could really be expected from so frivolous a society. He wrote Abigail Adams, that "a good punster would disarm the whole nation were they ever so seriously disposed to revolt."[6] Praying that Heaven would send them good Kings, he himself sought reality away from the Court in the open country and among the people themselves. He set out on the last day of February and did not come back till June. For a supposedly crippled man he showed great energy and endurance, he picked up an amazing stock of information, and he renewed his spirits.

Speaking of the trip at the end of it, he said: "I was alone through the whole, and think one travels more usefully when alone, because he reflects more."[7] Certainly he wanted no casual acquaintance along, to fill the precious hours with idle chatter. He valued friendship next after domestic affection and he loved quiet. "But between the society of real friends, and the tranquility of solitude, the mind finds no middle ground," he said.[8] Periodically he felt impelled to withdraw from the meaningless clatter of the world, and he now sought the privacy of the road. From a dirty hostelry in Marseilles, he wrote:

> . . . A traveller sais [*sic*] I, retired at night to his chamber in an inn, all his effects contained in a single portmanteau, all his cares circumscribed by the walls of his apartment, unknown to all, unheeded and undisturbed, writes, reads, thinks, sleeps just in the moments when nature & the movements of his body & mind require. Charmed with this tranquility, he finds how few are our real wants, how cheap a thing is happiness, how expensive a one pride.[9]

On this journey he even hoped to escape the distractions caused by familiar servants. Leaving all his own at home, he expected to get a servant at the first principal city, to be attended by him there and on the road to the next city, and then to change him for another. But he found such a good man at Dijon, by name Petitjean, that he kept him for the rest of the journey, taking an additional *valet de place* wherever he stayed a day or two.[10] Obviously this fine gentleman was not going to deprive himself of accustomed personal services, but he was

[6] TJ to Mrs. Adams, Feb. 22, 1787 (Ford, IV, 370).
[7] TJ to John Banister, Jr., June 19, 1787 (L. & B., VI, 131).
[8] TJ to Madame de Tott, Apr. 5, 1787 (quoted from LC in Dumbauld, p. 97).
[9] Dumbauld, p. 96.
[10] TJ to Short, Mar. 15, 1787 (cited by Dumbauld, p. 87, from LC).

seeking fresh information and wanted quiet to think about it and write it down. He carried letters of introduction to some important people, but if good dinners and good company had been his objects he would have remained in Paris – or so he politely said to Chastellux. Through the Marquis and others he got into touch with various *abbés*, whom he found most useful acquaintances – "unembarrassed with families, uninvolved in form, . . . frequently learned and always obliging." [11] He also found that he gained highly satisfactory information from gardeners, vignerons, and persons of that class, and deliberately sought them out.[12] They were real people and they were representative, unlike the "hackneyed rascals of every country" most naturally seen by travelers – the tavern keepers, guides, and postilions.

His own policy and procedure as a traveler were afterwards summed up in the systematic advice he gave some young countrymen of his.[13] He began with a map of the country, and plans of all towns where they were procurable. Because of this trip he acquired large-scale plans of Lyons, Montpellier, Marseilles, Turin, Milan, Bordeaux, and Orléans.[14] He made it a policy to walk around the ramparts of a town when he first got there, or to go to the top of a steeple for a bird's-eye view. As a sight-seer he was diligent but discriminating, trying not to miss anything good since he was unlikely to come that way again, but not wanting to waste his time or clutter and fatigue his mind with the valueless details rattled off by guides. He generally did his duty by the sights the first thing, gulping them all down in a day. "On the other hand," as he wrote Lafayette, "I am never satiated with rambling through the fields and farms, examining the culture and cultivators, with a degree of curiosity which makes some take me to be a fool, and others to be much wiser than I am." [15]

He advised his young fellow Americans to give their attention first to agriculture and everything belonging to it, and he put gardens high on his list of important objects – because noble gardens could be made in America more easily than anywhere else. The traffic in seeds and plants that he engaged in was comparable to that in books. As in all commerce, he tried to promote a genuine exchange, and he had already sought for French friends magnolias from South Carolina,

[11] TJ to Chastellux, Apr. 4, 1787 (MHS).
[12] TJ to Philip Mazzei, Apr. 4, 1787 (LC, 4923).
[13] His travel notes for John Rutledge, Jr., and Thomas Lee Shippen are reprinted with valuable comment by Elizabeth Cometti in *Jour. Sou. Hist.*, XII, 89–106 (Feb. 1946), cited hereafter as Cometti; partially printed in L. & B., XVII, 290–293; comments by Dumbauld, pp. 140–141.
[14] TJ to L'Enfant, Apr. 10, 1791 (LC, 10867–10868).
[15] TJ to Lafayette, Apr. 11, 1787 (L. & B., VI, 106).

pecans from the western country, seedling oaks and other plants from his own Virginia.[16] At the country place of Lafayette's aunt, Madame de Tessé (Chaville, near Paris), he had carried on many delightful conversations about gardens and architecture, and no doubt she had made helpful suggestions about this journey. His good offices to her and other horticultural friends increased after it, but the information, the seeds and plants and trees he sent home to America constituted its most notable agricultural result.

Along with farms and orchards and vineyards and gardens, he thought that the mechanical arts should be specially observed by an American, though he was more interested in bridges, boats, and canal locks than in factories. He was influenced by his own preference, no doubt, when he said: "circumstances rendering it impossible that America should become a manufacturing country during the time of any man now living, it would be a waste of attention to examine these minutely."[17] The southern country was richer in architecture, anyway, and this seemed to him worth very great attention, because America must build so much and so often. Taste ought to be introduced into an art which was visible to so many eyes. On the other hand, painting and statuary were too expensive for Americans at present. "It would be useless therefore & preposterous for us to endeavor to make ourselves connoisseurs in those arts," he said. "They are worth seeing, but not studying."[18] He himself went into flights over a beautiful statue on this very trip, but he wanted to use his limited time, and wanted his countrymen to use theirs, to the utmost advantage.

He thought the courts of Europe worth looking at just as a menagerie was, and thought them just as cruel beneath their glittering surfaces and behind their imposing façades. In any country it was the relation of government to the happiness of the people that should be most carefully observed. His advice to American travelers was the same that he gave in other words to Lafayette and that he himself followed on this trip:

> . . . "Take every possible occasion of entering into the hovels of the labourers, & especially at the moment of their repast, see what they eat, how they are cloathed, whether they are obliged

[16] The best idea of his continuing interest in gardens, plants, and agricultural products generally can be gained from the Betts edn. of the *Garden Book*, where letters, lists, and account book entries are assembled under the appropriate year. For the years 1785–1789, see pp. 105–147.

[17] Cometti, p. 100.

[18] *Ibid.*

to labour too hard; whether the government or their landlord takes from them an unjust proportion of their labour; on what footing stands the property they call their own, their personal liberty &c." [19]

Except for a visit a year and a half earlier to Fontainebleau, he had hitherto seen common French life only in Paris and its environs. Now he could observe it in many provinces, and he was never so busy noting soil or crops or climate as to overlook the people living in that lovely and ill-governed land.

Before he got back to Paris he saw parts of France that Lafayette had never visited, and he left an informal record of his observations which a person with literary ambitions could easily have turned into a fascinating book. It is an objective record of things that he wanted to remember, of information that he wanted to use, but it contains wise social reflections and flashes of aesthetic judgment. He saw butterflies and heard nightingales; he was immersed in architectural antiquities and was enchanted by a château in the Italian Alps that seemed hanging to a cloud; he chuckled over the huge boots of the postilion. This deeply serious and unvaryingly systematic man was far from inhuman, but he was most uncommon, since nothing escaped his observing eye and everything interested his devouring mind.

As originally planned the trip was to be a circuit, with minor deviations, but, as we have said, Jefferson turned eastward from Marseilles and made an unanticipated journey into Northern Italy. If drawn on the map the latter journey appears as a loop, connected with the larger one by a string from Marseilles to Nice. This period of three months can be divided into three approximately equal parts:

1. From Paris to Aix-en-Provence and Marseilles, with a brief side trip to Nîmes.
2. From Marseilles into Northern Italy (Turin, Milan, Genoa) and back.
3. From Marseilles to the Canal de Languedoc, to the west coast and Brittany, and back through Touraine to Paris.

On the first stage of the journey, when passing through Burgundy – where he noted incidentally that the cattle were all white – he began a thorough investigation of wines and the wine business, which he continued in the third stage, especially in the Bordeaux region, and supplemented the following year when he added notes on champagne

[19] *Ibid.* Compare with letter of TJ to Lafayette, Apr. 11, 1787 (L. & B., VI, 109).

and Rhine wines on another journey.[20] He rambled through orchards, talked with vignerons and wine merchants, inquired into processes and costs, and acquired a total body of information on this subject which probably no other prominent American of his time could even approximate. The practical results were negative, since he declined to commend the culture of the vine to his countrymen, being convinced that it was not desirable on lands capable of producing anything else. To him the vine seemed the "parent of misery" – not because of drunkenness, for he was impressed with the lack of that in the wine-drinking countries, but because those who cultivated the vine were always poor.[21] The positive value of his observations lay in the contribution to gracious living which they enabled him to make. Increasingly he himself became a connoisseur and gourmet, and his knowledge and discrimination were of value to his countrymen throughout his years in public life. This was another field in which he sought to cultivate good taste.[22] However, he became aware of a chain of economic and social circumstances which a mere connoisseur would not have noted. "At Pommard and Voulenay [Volnay], I observed them eating good wheat bread; at Meursault, rye," he said. "I asked the reason of this difference. They told me that the white wines fail in quality much oftener than the red, and remain on hand. The farmer, therefore, cannot afford to feed his laborers so well. At Meursault, only white wines are made, because there is too much stone for the red. On such slight circumstances depends the condition of man!" [23]

He failed to get full details about the noted hermitage wine, for he afterwards asked friends to fill in some of them, but he went to the top of the hill where the hermitage itself stood, overlooking the Rhone valley, and viewed the sublime prospect from there.[24] In due course he wrote a full account of the wines of Bordeaux, both red and white, though he himself preferred the latter. To his countrymen, visiting France in later years, his comments would have been illuminating and the names themselves would have had a familiar ring.

[20] L. & B., XVII, 157–159, 222–226, 257–258, 264–269, 282–289. He was already informed about Madeira, which came to America in better quality than to France, and he sent back home for that.

[21] TJ to William Drayton, July 30, 1787 (L. & B., VI, 198); to George Wythe (L. & B., VI, 297).

[22] Of the Burgundy red wines he concluded that Chambertin was best, though Volnay, which sold for much less because it did not keep so well, was its equal in flavor and was often ordered for his own table while he was in France. Montrachet was the best of the white, he said.

[23] L. & B., XVII, 157.

[24] Cometti, pp. 103–104.

In Bordeaux itself, the white wines made in the canton of Graves were most esteemed, he said, while in Paris those most liked were Sauternes, Prignac, and Barsac. He ranked them in that order for pleasantness, and in the reverse for strength – all being stronger than Graves, he said.[25]

In Beaujolais, above Lyons, the richest country he ever saw, he passed some time at the Château de Laye-Epinaye, to which he had been introduced by the Abbés Chalut and Arnoux, and it was here that he fell in love with a morsel of sculpture – a "Diana and Endymion" by Michael Angelo Slodtz, done three years before he himself was born. This he reported to Madame de Tessé after he got to Nîmes. From Lyons onward he was "nourished with the remains of Roman grandeur," but the defacement of some monuments by recent barbarians aroused his indignation. The Praetorian Palace at Vienne had had Corinthian columns cut out to make way for Gothic windows; and at Orange, where he specially admired the triumphal arch, they were pulling down the circular wall of the amphitheater to make a road.

A little above Avignon he left the direct line to the waters of Aix in order to visit Nîmes, which he passed through again on the third leg of his journey. It was on his first visit that he saw for the first time the Maison Carrée, which he had already commended so highly to his fellow Virginians as a model for their capitol. But, as he told John Jay, seeing the antiquities was a pretext. The real reason for his turning off the road was to see a Brazilian who had written him the previous autumn and who might have something interesting to say about his country and the possibilities of revolution there. At the moment of his arrival at Le Petit Louvre, Jefferson wrote in French to the man whom he had come to talk with; during his four days' stay he conferred with him; and before he went back to Paris he reported the conversation to John Jay, giving him at the same time information that he had previously acquired about conditions in Mexico. He delayed or interrupted his architectural reveries long enough to give the Brazilian his private ideas: "that we were not in a condition to meddle nationally in any war; that we wished particularly to cultivate the friendship of Portugal, with whom we have an advantageous commerce. That yet a successful revolution could not be uninteresting to us." [26]

It was about this time that the American admirer of Roman remains

[25] L. & B., XVII, 222–226.

[26] TJ to Jay, May 4, 1787 (Ford, IV, 378–385, esp. p. 383); to Dr. Mayo Barbalho Vendek, Mar. 19, 1787 (Colonial Williamsburg, courtesy JP).

wrote to his fellow enthusiast, the Comtesse de Tessé, a letter which that lady read to Philip Mazzei as though it were from an apostle in the assembly of the first Christians. In this he said that from morning to night he was immersed in antiquities; and that if he were to attempt to give her news he would tell her stories a thousand years old, he would detail to her the intrigues of the courts of the Caesars.[27] It looked as though his left hand did not know what his right hand was doing. But his architectural enthusiasm was real even if it did not dominate him completely. For him unquestionably the empire of Rome now lived again in all its ancient splendor, and he feared the incursions of modern Goths and Visigoths, Ostrogoths and Vandals. He saw the amphitheater as well as the Maison Carrée, and strongly recommended them afterwards to his own countrymen as two of the most superb remains of antiquity that existed. He also reported that Le Petit Louvre was a good inn, that the *vin ordinaire* was excellent and cheap in Nîmes, and that this was an admirable place to buy silk stockings.[28]

Arriving at Aix on March 25 he stayed at a good hotel, found an excellent *valet de place*, and noted that the temperature of the waters was 90° Fahrenheit at the spout. After four days of ineffective douches he moved on to Marseilles. He had found Provence very beautiful, and he was so delighted with the softness of the language after Parisian speech that he regretted the historical circumstances which had caused French rather than Provençal to prevail. "Every letter is pronounced, the articulation is distinct, no nasal sounds disfigure it, and on the whole it stands close to Italian and Spanish in point of beauty," he wrote to Short. Hearing a celebrated actress from Marseilles, he concluded that she had a great advantage over her sisters in Paris "in being clear of that dreadful wheeze or rather whistle in respiration which resembles the agonizing struggles for breath in a dying person." [29]

To a representative of American commercial interests Marseilles was the main objective in this stage of the journey, and Jefferson spent a week there – going on excursions to the Château Borély and, by water, to the Château d'If, but mostly attending to business. The results of his inquiries about American commerce in American ships were almost wholly negative – largely because of the Algerine pirates, he thought. At all the seaports on this journey he tried to find out

[27] TJ to Madame de Tessé, Mar. 20, 1787 (L. & B., VI, 102–106, esp. p. 106). Her reply of Mar. 30 is in Chinard, *Trois Amitiés*, pp. 100–103.

[28] Advice to Rutledge and Shippen (Cometti, p. 105).

[29] TJ to Short, Mar. 27, 29, 1787 (LC, 4913, 4918).

precisely how many American vessels had come in during the four years since the peace, and he was most successful here, learning that there had been thirty-two.[30]

He did not ignore ships but he preferred farms, and, having given so much attention to tobacco, he now had his mind on rice. Some months earlier he had been elected an honorary member of the South Carolina Society for Promoting and Improving Agriculture,[31] and he had made extensive inquiries in Paris about the sources of the supply of rice in that important market. He had found that two varieties were sold there in approximately equal quantity: Carolina rice, superior in beauty and definitely preferred for serving *au lait;* and Piedmont rice, preferred for serving *au gras* – chiefly because the grains were less broken. The assumption was that a different machine was used for husking, and he hoped to find out about this Piedmont machine at Marseilles, a great emporium for rice. However, few people observed as accurately as he did, and he got a variety of descriptions here just as he had received confused reports from retailers in Paris. On one thing at least his informants were agreed – he could see a machine in Piedmont. This he determined to do, only to find later that Piedmont rice was actually raised in Lombardy. Thus it was in pursuit of a useful purpose that he crossed the Alps; he penetrated Italy as far as Milan, but it was in search of a husking machine, not a cathedral.

From Marseilles he went through Toulon, where he specially observed the capers; through Hyères, where he saw an orange grove; and to Nice, passing the largest olive and fig trees he had ever seen. He found the climate delicious and was enraptured by the unfolding scene. At Nice he passed a couple of days most agreeably in a fine English tavern, called on a local merchant with an Italian name to whom he had been recommended, and picked up from somebody the information that a thousand mules loaded with merchandise passed between Nice and Turin every week. Since there was then no highway along the Mediterranean from Nice to Genoa, this seemed the best way to Italy; so he now hired some of these useful mules to take him through the Col de Tende. The road seemed to him the greatest work of its kind ever executed, though it did not cost as much as a year's war. He seems to have gone by carriage part of the way, mounting a mule in only the steepest part.

He found this passage of the Alps curious and enchanting. He

[30] TJ to Jay, May 4, 1787 (Ford, IV, 377); June 21, 1787 (L. & B., VI, 138).
[31] Wm. Drayton to TJ, Nov. 23, 1785 (*Garden Book*, p. 107).

noted, on his own forty-fourth birthday, that on three successive mountains he lost the olive tree as he went up, only to recover it as he came down; and he formed in his mind a scale of plants from the tenderest to the hardiest in the order of their resistance to cold: caper, orange, palm, aloe, olive, pomegranate, walnut, fig, and almond.[32] His eye was by no means blind to picturesqueness and scenic grandeur. "Fall down and worship the site of the Chateau di Saorgio," he afterwards admonished other travelers; "you never saw, nor will see such another." He wrote down a description of this at the time and used it almost word for word a few weeks later in a letter to Maria Cosway:

> . . . Imagine to yourself, madam, a castle & village hanging to a cloud in front, on one hand a mountain cloven through to let pass a gurgling stream; on the other a river, over which is thrown a magnificent bridge; the whole formed into a bason, it's sides shagged with rocks, olive trees, vines, herds, &c. I insist on your painting it.[33]

Nor had he forgotten his ancient history. As he descended into Italy and saw the plains of the Po spread out before him, he thought of Hannibal, though he was most uncertain just where the Carthaginian had crossed. He noted that there were speckled trout all the way from Nice to Turin, and in the latter city drank a singular but pleasing red wine called Nebiule. "It is about as sweet as the silky Madeira, as astringent on the palate as Bordeaux, and as brisk as Champagne," he said.[34]

The ostensible object of his journey was to see rice and husking machines, and in Lombardy he did – at just about the time that he noted the first swallow. He was impressed with the insalubrity of the culture of wet rice, and for this reason sought samples of dry rice from the Orient when he got back to Marseilles. His more immediate concern, however, was to get samples of Piedmont rice that were suitable for planting, since he soon concluded that the husking machines used in Italy were like the ones Edward Rutledge had told him they used in South Carolina. Only an unusually exact memory of

[32] TJ to Drayton, July 30, 1787 (L. & B., VI, 204). He noted that the order of the fruit was somewhat different. For example, the caper was so easily protected that its fruit was among the most certain, while that of the almond was uncertain because of its forwardness.

[33] TJ to Mrs. Cosway, July 1, 1787 (quoted by Bullock, p. 68); entry of Apr. 14, 1787, in L. & B., XVII, 185; comment to Rutledge and Shippen in Cometti, p. 102.

[34] L. & B., XVII, 189.

mechanical details could have enabled him to make the comparison, but he was not quite sure of everything. For example, in some of the Italian machines the pestles were armed with an iron tooth, consisting of nine spikes hooked together; and, not remembering that these were similar to the ones in South Carolina, he had a tooth made and sent it to the agricultural society there. The export of Piedmont rice in rough form was under penalty of death, but he took this occasion to defy the law. He arranged with a muleteer to smuggle out a sack of rough rice, and, just to make sure, took out some more of it in his own pockets.

Jefferson rarely recorded the sort of information which could be easily obtained from guidebooks – which he always made a point of buying. He advised that visitors to Italy also buy the travels of Addison, who visited the country as a classical amateur.[35] By chance comments or deliberate recommendation to others he revealed some of his own choices as a sight-seer. In his items relating to Milan and vicinity he mentioned a fine excursion to Lake Como, another to hear the echo of Simonetta, and one from Rozzano to Pavia to "the celebrated church of the Chartreux, the richest thing I ever saw." The cathedral at Milan affected him differently. He described it as "a worthy object of philosophical contemplation, to be placed among the rarest instances of the misuse of money." With grim hyperbole he added: "On viewing the churches of Italy it is evident without calculation that the same expense would have sufficed to throw the Apennines into the Adriatic & thereby render it terra firma from Leghorn to Constantinople."[36] His own interest was reflected in the elaborate notes he made on the making of Parmesan cheese, after spending a day, from sunrise to sunset, in a dairy to observe the process.[37] Also, as he passed through Turin, Milan, and Genoa, he inquired into the practicality of introducing American whale oil, talking with merchants and seeking to win their good will; and he initiated efforts in encouragement of direct tobacco trade with the United States.

He spoke to other travelers of the pleasure of applying one's classical readings on the spot but he scarcely got into classical ground, as he reported somewhat apologetically to George Wythe. To Maria Cosway he said that he "took a peep only into Elysium." He wrote an Italian friend: "Milan was the spot at which I turned my back on Rome and Naples. It was a moment of conflict between duty which urged me to return, and inclination urging me forward."[38] But there was

[35] Cometti, p. 99.
[36] Cometti, p. 103.
[37] L. & B., XVII, 195–198; Memo. of Apr. 23, 1787, courtesy JP.
[38] TJ to Wythe, Sept. 16, 1787 (L. & B., VI, 297); to Mrs. Cosway, July 1, 1787 (Bullock, p. 68); to Gaudenzio Clerici, Aug. 15, 1787 (LC, 5516).

no sharp contrast between utility and beauty in his philosophy. The gardens of the Count Durazzo at Nervi, he said, "exhibit a very rare mixture of the *utile dulci,* and are therefore to be peculiarly attended to by an American." The only thing he had seen that was superior in this combination of the sweet and the useful was Woburn in England, where farm, pleasure garden, and kitchen garden were all mixed, "the pleasure garden being merely a highly-ornamented walk through and round the divisions of the farm and kitchen garden." [39] It was just such a journey amid things physical, practical, and human that his richly ornamented mind was taking all his life.

The return trip, from Genoa to Marseilles, was very fatiguing. At sea for two days and mortally sick, he covered forty miles. Then, forced to land at Noli because of change of wind, he climbed and rode muleback up the cliffs. He stayed at a miserable tavern at Noli and at an even worse one at Albenga, but at the latter place he took occasion to speculate about the causes of the apparent color of the sea and to soliloquize on the facilities afforded here for delightful solitude.

> . . . If any person wished to retire from his acquaintance, to live absolutely unknown, and yet in the midst of physical enjoyments, it should be in some of the little villages of this coast, where air, water and earth concur to offer what each has most precious.[40]

Concluding that the wind would not change, he hired mules; and a little later traveled by night as well as day. A superb road could be made along the sea to Nice, he said, anticipating a later development, but he went by a rough and tiring way. At Marseilles he wrote a letter to Patsy, chattering pleasantly enough but also including one of his characteristic paternal admonitions:

"Determine never to be idle," he said. "No person will have occasion to complain of the want of time who never loses any. It is wonderful how much may be done if we are always doing." [41]

Nobody could possibly say that his practice differed from his preaching.

The last stage of his journey was less exciting than the second, and parts of it were less beautiful than the first. At Avignon he saw the tomb of Petrarch's Laura and made a charming excursion to the

[39] Cometti, p. 101; L. & B., XVII, 238.
[40] L. & B., XVII, 202.
[41] TJ to Martha, May 5, 1787 (*Domestic Life,* p. 121).

fountain of Vaucluse twenty miles away, just below Petrarch's reputed home. He remembered the songs of that poet and thought the fountain noble, and here the nightingales serenaded him from every bush and tree.[42] He passed through Nîmes for the second time, having lodgings that were not so good; and at Frontignan he wrote a little dissertation on muscat wine. He made inquiries about commerce at Cette, and here began a designedly leisurely trip along the Languedoc Canal to Toulouse. He had bought at Marseilles a plan of the canal in three sheets and he made full notes as he went along. His carriage being firmly set on a slow-moving bark, he could sit there reflecting and writing when he did not walk along the bank. He made a horseback trip of one day to see the sources of the canal's waters; then he went by land along the Garonne to Bordeaux. He inquired into the wines of the country, remarked on the size and texture of old brick in the ruins of an ancient circus, and did what he could for Thomas Barclay, the consul general, who had got into trouble on account of debt.

At Nantes he looked into a question of a claim against his government; and his trip into Brittany, as far east as L'Orient, was also for purposes of business. Inquiring into the importation of fish oil, he noted imperfections in the provisions of Calonne's letter – which by accident no doubt referred only to whale oil – and on his return to Paris he set about straightening this matter out. He could get little precise information about American vessels, however, and his agricultural observations were disappointing since he found both the soil and the people poor. "The people are mostly in villages," he said; "they eat rye bread, and are ragged. The villages announce a general poverty, as does every other appearance. Women smite on the anvil, and work with the hoe, and cows are yoked to labor." [43]

He found Touraine much richer, but he said little or nothing about its châteaux. He was chiefly interested in inquiring into Voltaire's theory about the spontaneous growth of shells, based on reports from a place near Tours. Apparently he did not actually see the place, being now in too great a hurry, but he talked with an official who had known M. de La Sauvagère, who made the original report, and obtained a copy of the latter's *Dissertation . . . sur la vegetation spontanée des coquilles du château des Places*.[44] The negative conclusions at which Jefferson now arrived probably explain the changes he made in his *Notes on Virginia* after the first printing. At Chanteloup, however, he picked

[42] Cometti, p. 104; TJ to Martha, May 21, 1789 (*Domestic Life*, p. 122).
[43] L. & B., XVII, 229.
[44] L. & B., XVII, 232–235.

up some information from a gardener about the singing of the nightingale, and saw some ingenious mechanical devices.

He had to rush on to Paris, where he caught up with official business and wrote numerous letters occasioned by this trip.

The journey was wholly useless so far as his wrist was concerned, and its official results were slight. What public value there was in it lay in his semiofficial activities, especially those relating to agriculture, and this still seemed considerable to him a dozen years later – after he had had plenty of time to reflect on his entire career in France. When he drew up a list of his own major services in 1800 he did not mention his attempts to negotiate trade treaties and break the tobacco monopoly; he did not refer to the publication of the *Notes on Virginia* or his recommendation of the Maison Carrée to his own Commonwealth and thus, indirectly, of classical forms to the entire United States. But he did speak of the memorable fact that he sent olive trees and upland rice to South Carolina, and just in this connection he said: "The greatest service which can be rendered any country is, to add a useful plant to its culture." [45]

He was not speaking of the wet rice he smuggled out of Lombardy. Though his efforts were appreciated by the polite South Carolinians, this gift was not received by them with delight. Ralph Izard, who had been in Italy, was more than ever convinced of the inferiority of the Italian product after seeing these fresh samples; and, being sure that the culinary difficulties which Jefferson had heard about in Paris were owing to some mismanagement in kitchens, he sent instructions from his own cook. These European seeds would be planted, he said, but at a distance from the existing fields. He did not want to risk mixing the Carolina product with an inferior species, and for this reason hoped that Jefferson would not send any more.[46] The latter, whose mind had already turned to dry rice, managed to secure some that came from Cochin China, only to find that the seeds would not vegetate, having been kept too long. Later still he got some mountain rice from Africa and it was the sending of this that he remembered with such pride, ten years away from France. The planters in South Carolina had done nothing with it, but he understood that it had spread into upper Georgia and was highly prized by the people there. Thus he had rendered genuine service by adding a useful plant.

Of all the plants, however, the one that excited him most was the

[45] List of services, drawn in 1800, in LC, 39161; reprinted without exact date in Ford, VII, 475–477.

[46] Izard to TJ, Nov. 10, 1787 (*Garden Book*, pp. 131–132).

olive tree. Much less known in America than the fig (which he sent to the New World in several varieties), less known than the caper (which he described elaborately), it was the most worthy of being known. "Of all the gifts of heaven to man," he said, "it is next to the most precious, if it be not the most precious."[47] If bread came first, oil was surely second; and, having observed the blessings shed on the poor by this tree, he was eager to establish it in his own country.

His efforts to introduce olive trees into South Carolina and Georgia were spread over a period of several years, and the delays and disappointments were a tax on even his extraordinary patience and persistence.[48] It did not take him long to arouse the interest of the South Carolinians, for he received in 1788 from the agricultural society a deposit to cover the cost of a shipment of young trees. He made arrangements at Marseilles which he thought adequate, and before he left France reported that a parcel of plants had been shipped, but was much mortified when nothing followed, though most of the money was unspent. In 1791, to his great relief, two shipments were made. One consisted of forty young trees for grafts and a box of olives to sow for stocks; the other, sent by way of Bordeaux, contained forty-four trees, most of them very young. Enough of these survived the long sea voyage to be planted – according to instructions sent by the indefatigable Jefferson – and a few of them lived. He had predicted that some of these early attempts would fail, and had recommended that an annual sum be set aside for further shipments. This suggestion was accepted by the South Carolina society, which appropriated fifty guineas a year for three years at least. While he was still secretary of state he commissioned Stephen Cathalan, whom he had met in Marseilles more than five years before, to get the plants, asking that he become "the father of our olive colony," and about 500 were sent altogether.

On the eve of his election as President he was feeling complacent about the olive plants which had been procured at his suggestion and through his unremitting efforts. He understood that the trees were flourishing, though not yet multiplied, and was confident that they would be the germ of future cultivation in South Carolina and Georgia.

[47] TJ to William Drayton, July 30, 1787 (L. & B., VI, 193–204), the fullest letter of agricultural observations; quotation on p. 200.

[48] The story to almost the end of his life can be reconstructed from the letters printed by Betts in the *Garden Book*, including the following: TJ to Drayton, July 17, 1788, and May 7, 1789 (pp. 138, 143); to Ralph Izard, Sept. 18, 1789 (p. 145); to Stephen Cathalan, Jr., Jan. 25, 1791 (p. 160); to Drayton, May 1, 1791 (pp. 163–164); to Stephen Cathalan, Dec. 2, 1792 (pp. 180–181); to James Ronaldson, Jan. 12, 1813 (p. 505); to N. Herbemont, Nov. 3, 1822 (pp. 604–605). See also his list of services in Ford, IV, 477.

Later still, when he was retired and nearly seventy, he was "disheartened by the nonchalance of our southern fellow citizens," fearing that if any of the 500 plants of the olive tree of Aix still existed it was merely as a curiosity in their gardens, since no single orchard of them had been planted. Some hope returned as he moved on toward eighty. Learning that some of the trees were yet alive, he believed that cuttings from them grafted on seedling stocks would soon yield a plentiful supply of trees.

He had never thought that the olive would be extensively cultivated in America, since a suitable climate and soil would be hard to find together, but the net results of his efforts were distressingly slight. He gained much good will, nevertheless. Few of his contemporaries were in a position to view the whole circle of his unremitting activity and many of them failed to grasp his purposes, but it was no accident that before he died he became a member of practically every agricultural society in the United States (along with many in Europe) and that he maintained throughout his political career the support of farmers.

The chief significance of the journey on which Jefferson spent more time than he ever did on any other lay in the contribution which it made to his own education. After his tour was over he wrote his nephew Peter Carr in Virginia that travel made men wiser, but less happy.[49] His own recollections may have been mixed with some vain regrets when he returned to routine business and less enchanting scenes, but his contemporary comments leave no doubt that he had gained great intellectual stimulation and much unalloyed pleasure. Also, he had gathered a store of knowledge which he hoped to apply usefully to his own country. Actually he acquired far more than he ever could put to any use, so insatiable was his appetite. In this respect the journey was typical of his life and perhaps an occasion of unhappiness. But it was thus that he became the best informed and most interesting American of his generation, and if his power among his fellows was partly that of will and very considerably that of faith, it was always to a notable degree the power of knowledge.

He now knew the French land and people in a way that Franklin never did and that no other leading American of the day even approached. Accordingly, his social observations, while obviously carrying no authority, assume a fresh significance, both because of their intrinsic interest and because of their relation to later events at home and abroad. In general he was more confirmed than ever in the con-

[49] TJ to Peter Carr, Aug. 10, 1787 (Ford, IV, 432). This was partly to reconcile Peter to staying in Virginia.

viction – shared no doubt by practically all the Americans who had been in France – that most people could be far happier in their own freer land. However, his specific social comments on the French scene were less severe than some that he had made earlier, when he viewed the countryside with an even fresher eye.

The first and only time that he had followed the Court to Fontainebleau (in the autumn of 1785), he had been shocked by the misery he had observed among the peasants, and had attributed this to the extreme concentration of property in a few hands. He approached the problem in no doctrinaire spirit, being convinced that an equal division of property was impracticable, but he was impressed anew with the importance of ameliorating measures, such as the abolition of entails and primogeniture which he himself had championed in Virginia. Pouring out his mind in a letter to James Madison, he made a suggestion which is fully in accord with the principles of graduated taxation in the twentieth century. "Another means of silently lessening the unequality of property," he said, "is to exempt all from taxation below a certain point, and to tax the higher portions of property in geometrical progression as they rise."[50] He was specially shocked by seeing in France at the same time extensive uncultivated lands and many unemployed poor, and thought it clear that the laws of property had been extended to the point of violating natural right, since "the earth is given as a common stock to man to labor and live on."

By the time he set out on his southern journey he had had some wise and sympathetic comments from his thoughtful little friend in Orange County.[51] While agreeing with him about laws for the subdivision of property, Madison thought that the limited population of the United States had probably played as large a part as political advantages had in producing the relative comfort of the masses. "A certain degree of misery seems inseparable from a high degree of populousness," he said, as though anticipating Malthus. Whether or not Jefferson had now become more accustomed to the sight of misery, he wrote Lafayette, after he had been about six weeks on the road and had gone as far as Nice, that he had found less of it among the people than he had expected, just as he had found the soil of Champagne and Burgundy better than he had thought.[52] He found the people on the first stage of

[50] TJ to Madison, Oct. 28, 1785 (Hunt, II, 247*n.*). In Ford, VII, 33–36, this is improperly addressed to Rev. James Madison.

[51] Madison to TJ, June 19, 1786 (Hunt, II, 246–248).

[52] TJ to Lafayette, Apr. 11, 1787 (L. & B., VI, 106–110). The moderation of Jefferson's comments is emphasized by C. D. Hazen in *Contemporary American Opinion of the French Revolution* (1932), pp. 16–17 – rather too much.

his journey (not in Italy or Brittany) generally well clothed; they were overworked but had plenty of food, vegetable food at least. For their sakes and the sake of the land he thought leases should be longer; and he did not like the congregation of peasants in mean villages or the sight of women working at heavy tasks. But he indulged in no passionate outbursts comparable with his denunciation of slavery in Virginia and of cruelty toward the Indians – partly because it would have been improper if not unjust to apply equally vehement social criticism to an imperfectly understood foreign country as to one's own familiar land. His main object on this trip was not the study of political institutions, and he suggested no drastic economic remedies in the few letters he wrote or in the notes he kept – perhaps because the bright sunshine in which he was traveling kept things from looking wholly black. But he did observe great poverty, not merely in Brittany but also in rich lands with a delicious climate, and he deplored extreme poverty anywhere, without ever equating wealth and happiness. As a realistic observer who had seen much better conditions elsewhere, he drew a depressing though not a desperate social picture, showing himself to be humane without being sentimental, liberal without being doctrinaire. He told Lafayette that he would gain sublime pleasure in finding out how the humble people actually lived in the provinces, and an even sublimer pleasure afterwards when he could apply his knowledge "to the softening of their beds, or the throwing a morsel of meat into their kettle of vegetables." [53] In such a society as this, improvement must be gradual, and it must begin with and proceed from fuller knowledge.

So far as his own country was concerned, however, Jefferson had arrived at firm convictions, not tentative opinions. There were plants to be carried from France to the New World; there were buildings in this old land that richly deserved imitation; there were graces to be acquired here, and he himself was constantly acquiring them; but this social and political system offered nothing for Americans to emulate. Rather than run the risk of contamination, indeed, he preferred that young Americans should not travel here, but should remain at home.

[53] L. & B., VI, 109.

[VIII]

The Jefferson Circle

1787–1788

THE permanent members of the Jefferson family in Paris were his able and devoted secretary William Short, who lived with him like a son, and his daughter Patsy, who was at school at the Abbaye de Panthémont but normally spent Sundays at the Hôtel de Langeac to his immense enjoyment. Patsy was in her fifteenth year when her "dear papa" went on his southern tour, leaving her in the convent with the promise that he would write her once a week. When he had been gone nearly a month she wrote him reproachfully: "Until now you have not kept your word the least in the world."[1] He did better after that but his letters to her now seem unnecessarily mature and excessively didactic, while hers are filled with the brightness and artless charm of youth.

Patsy had inherited her father's height, which was certainly no trifle, and as time went on she looked more and more like him, being not wholly fortunate in this respect. The troubles she was having with Livy – this "ancient Italian" put her out of her wits, she said – suggested that she was unlikely to equal him as a classicist, though she got on very well with Thucydides. A drawing teacher in Philadelphia had given her up, but she was now doing pretty landscapes with her master and drawing flowers all alone, meanwhile beginning to learn some beautiful new tunes. If not a talented girl she was on her way to becoming a cultivated young woman, and obviously she was observant and intelligent. An unusually dutiful daughter, she retained the natural gaiety of youth and manifested a more active sense of humor than her father did. She chattered about *Madame l'Abbesse*, asking if he still wanted her to dine at her table beginning next quarter (as he did), but declined to repeat stories about the Assembly of Notables

[1] Martha to TJ, Mar. 25, 1787 (*Domestic Life*, p. 114).

for fear of taking a trip to the Bastille. She had heard about a gentleman who had recently killed himself, after ten years of marriage, because he thought his wife did not love him, and was afraid that if other husbands did the same Paris would be filled with widows. She was delighted with long letters when she got them but even then objected that the margins were too wide.[2]

This was an era when the habit of parental moralizing was strong, but if Patsy had been less aware of her father's limitless kindness she might have found some of his exhortations rather hard to bear. His standards of industry and resolution were no less appalling because he maintained them himself. In a single letter he said such things as these:

> Of all the cankers of human happiness none corrodes with so silent, yet so baneful an influence, as indolence.
>
> No laborious person was ever yet hysterical.
>
> It is while we are young that the habit of industry is formed. If not then, it never is afterwards. The fortune of our lives, therefore, depends on employing well the short period of youth.
>
> It is a part of the American character to consider nothing as desperate; to surmount every difficulty by resolution and contrivance. In Europe there are shops for every want; its inhabitants, therefore, have no idea that their wants can be supplied otherwise. Remote from all other aid, we are obliged to invent and to execute; to find means within ourselves, and not to lean on others. Consider, therefore, the conquering your Livy as an exercise in the habit of surmounting difficulties . . .[3]

Martha assured him that he might be at ease on the head of hysterics, for she was not that lazy, and she solemnly promised to try to follow his advice with the "most scrupulous exactitude." His later letters were less monitory. He told her – somewhat self-consciously – about climbing the cliffs of the Apennines, about listening to the feathered chorus at Vaucluse, about blissfully sailing on the Canal of Languedoc under cloudless skies. In her woman's sphere, which he always sharply distinguished from that of man, he wanted her to be industrious; he also wanted her to be aware of the incredible interest and richness of life as she went along.

Meanwhile, there were coming events to which she must adjust herself. For one thing, the harpsichord he had ordered from London a year before ought to arrive in Paris about the time he did. He wanted her to practise all her old tunes in order that he might hear her play

[2] For their correspondence during his trip, see *Domestic Life*, pp. 113–123.
[3] In his first letter, Mar. 28, 1787, from Aix (*ibid.*, pp. 115–117).

them immediately on his return; and he wanted her to learn some slow movements of simple melody for the Celestine stop which he had procured with such difficulty. He afterwards wrote Francis Hopkinson that the sound produced by this was between that of the harmonica and the organ heard from a distance.[4] Patsy had her doubts about the arrival of the harpsichord and it turned out that these were entirely warranted. Not until late August did John Trumbull, who became involved in the commission, report that the instrument was really on its way, and not until November did it arrive at Rouen. Jefferson had wanted it to go from there by water, so as to avoid jolting, and it went by cart; but fortunately it arrived, toward the end of the month, in good condition.[5]

There was another and much more exciting prospect: Polly was coming from Virginia, being expected in July. "Then, indeed, shall I be the happiest of mortals," said the elder sister; "united to what I have the dearest in the world, nothing more will be requisite to render my happiness complete." But her father reminded her of sobering responsibilities. "When she arrives she will become a precious charge on your hands," he said. "The difference of your age, and your common loss of a mother, will put that office on you." Patsy must teach her to be good, truthful, and industrious, and never to be angry. The girl thought it vain that she had taken courage with respect to the "ancient Italian" of Livy, but she said she would do the best she could for Polly.[6]

Ever since his first winter in Paris, when he had learned of the death of his youngest daughter in Virginia, Jefferson had been determined to reunite his little family. Polly was six when he and Patsy got to Europe, and he had begun planning her voyage before she was seven, though his plans did not work out till she was nine. His reason told him that the dangers of the voyage were not really great, but he dropped his pen at the thought of them, he said, and he intended to reduce them to the absolute minimum. Hence he limited the months in which she might come to April, May, June, and July — avoiding the winter and the equinoxes — and stipulated that she must cross in a vessel which had made at least one voyage but was not more

[4] TJ to Hopkinson, May 8, 1788 (LC, 6669–6670).

[5] Trumbull to TJ, Aug. 28, 1787 (LC, 5539); TJ to Trumbull, Nov. 13, 1787 (LC, 5895); TJ to Garveys, Nov. 21, 1787 (MHS), announcing arrival. The entire harpsichord episode is described in Shepperson, *Paradise and Ludwell*, ch. XI.

[6] The two letters, both dated April 7, 1787, must have crossed in the mail (*Domestic Life*, pp. 117–118).

than four or five years old. If a colored woman should attend her it should be someone who had already had smallpox. Inevitably the arrangements would be complicated, and rather than run a risk he would wait. He needed all his patience, and not the least of the difficulties was Polly's unwillingness to come.

She could not remember her mother, and her Aunt Eppes, for thus she spoke of her, was more like a mother to her than anyone else on earth. At Eppington there was a houseful of children to play with, and her uncle's plantation was a pleasant place. Her father, though no adept in child psychology, perceived that persuasion was called for. She must come because he and Patsy could not live without her, he wrote, but after a time she could go back to see her aunt and uncle and little cousins. Meanwhile, she could learn to play on the harpsichord, to draw, to dance, to read and talk in French. Such accomplishments did not sound particularly alluring to her. The promise of all the dolls and playthings she wanted was much more to the point, but this was coupled with exhortations which were not reassuring. She must be good and grateful and generous and truthful; she must not go without her bonnet for that would make her ugly and then they would not love her so much. Perhaps she had inherited his tendency to freckle, and unquestionably she was a sensitive and shrinking child. She wrote "dear papa" that she would much like to see him and Sister Patsy but that she was sorry he had sent for her. They must come there, for she could not go to France.[7]

Her aunt and uncle kept hoping her father would countermand his orders since his promises to her seemed to be without effect. He was impelled to explain further to the adults why he was so insistent. She would have advantages in France, undoubtedly, but he was thinking chiefly of something else. He feared that, at her age, continued absence would weaken the tie between her and her father and sister and make them strangers to her throughout life. He was one who set great store by the family tie and his reasoning was entirely sound, though it did not greatly appeal to a little girl who was much more fearful of the weakening of her bond with the people she knew better at Eppington.

Jefferson learned of the stratagems which were finally employed to get his small daughter aboard a ship in a Virginia harbor. Her cousins visited the vessel with her for a day or two, romping with her upon its decks and in its cabins until she began to feel at home; once when she fell asleep the others silently crept away, and when she awakened

[7] For letters, 1785–1786, see *Domestic Life*, pp. 103–108. See also Dumas Malone, "Polly Jefferson and Her Father," *Va. Quart. Rev.*, Jan. 1931, pp. 81–95.

the voyage had begun. This was in the month of May, 1787, and she was on the seas five weeks. As an attendant she had, not an old nurse as had been expected, but a young servant named Sally, sister of James whom Jefferson had brought to Paris, and this girl proved to be of little help. In Captain Andrew Ramsay, however, Polly found a devoted friend. "Her sweet disposition and good nature demanded every attention," he wrote to her father from London after they landed; "and her vexation and the affliction she underwent on leaving her aunt made it necessary to be attentive at first . . . but she soon got over it and got so fond of me that she seldom parts with me without tears – and indeed I am almost the same way with her."[8] As it had been almost impossible to tear her away from her aunt, it was difficult to separate her from Captain Ramsay, who delivered her to Abigail Adams in Grosvenor Square. There she failed to recognize her father from the Mather Brown portrait which was shown her, but soon dried her tears and spent three pleasant weeks with Abigail.

Jefferson, recently back from his own trip and facing an accumulation of three or four months' business, did not feel warranted in going to London for her, though events proved that this would have been the wisest course. He had thought of having her come to France with his friend Madame de Corny, then visiting in England, but did not know just when that lady would return.[9] His solution of the problem was to send Petit, his trusted maître d'hôtel, but the child was afraid of a strange man who spoke an incomprehensible language.

Her father wrote Mrs. Adams: "By this time she will have learned again to love the hand that feeds and comforts her, and have formed an attachment to you. She will think I am made only to tear her from all her affections." He did not underestimate the difficulties, for Polly, having been deceived so often, was clinging tearfully to Abigail. "She is a child of the quickest sensibility, and the maturest understanding that I have ever met with for her years," reported that lady to him. From the other end of the line Jefferson wrote that he could not let Polly stay until she was willing to come, for that would be till Mrs. Adams had ceased to be kind to her, and he could not wait that long.[10]

Petit settled matters by buying tickets on the stage and paying for

[8] Andrew Ramsay to TJ, July 6, 1787 (MHS).

[9] TJ to Madame de Corny, June 30, 1787 (Chinard, *Trois Amitiés*, p. 176). He had given this friend a letter to Mrs. Adams but she had not used it. Abigail reported Polly's arrival to TJ, June 26, 1787 (LC, 5149).

[10] TJ to Mrs. Adams, July 1, 1787 (LC, 5168); Mrs. Adams to TJ, July 6, 1787 (LC, 5217–5218); TJ to Mrs. Adams, July 10, 1787 (LC, 5239). The last letter arrived after Polly's departure.

them without consulting anybody, thus confronting the little girl and her hostess with a *fait accompli,* though one of them would not have expressed it just that way. They parted reluctantly and tearfully. "Her temper, her disposition, her sensibility are all formed to delight," said Abigail, sending daughter to father with a quotation from an old song:

> What she thinks in her heart
> You may read in her eyes
> For having no art
> She needs no disguise.[11]

In the middle of July she arrived in Paris – having got into favor with the ladies and gentlemen on the stage so as to be sometimes on the knee of one, sometimes of another. She had totally forgotten her sister, but her father thought she showed signs of faintly remembering him. After they had renewed acquaintance he put her in the convent with Patsy. Mrs. Adams regretted this, admitting her prejudice against such places, but Jefferson was sure that it was the best school available and reported that she was soon happy there. She visited him once or twice a week at the Hôtel de Langeac, and soon she got a letter from the lady who had been so kind to her in England. "When she received it she flushed, she whitened, she flushed again, and in short was in such a flutter of joy that she could scarcely open it," her father said. The wife of John Adams was more mature in her emotions but she had written: "I never felt so attached to a child in my life on so short an acquaintance." Of all the many memories that bound Abigail to Jefferson, this one proved to be the most enduring.[12]

Polly proceeded with her accomplishments at the convent, but when she was at the Hôtel de Langeac it was Eppington that she most talked about. When she had been months in Paris her face kindled whenever she heard the name of her Aunt Eppes. That amiable lady proceeded to give birth to twins and her brother-in-law congratulated her on this double blessing and her obvious improvement in her trade. Continuing he said:

> . . . Polly is infinitely flattered to find a namesake in one of them. She promises in return to teach them both French. This she begins to speak easily enough, and to read as well as English. She will begin Spanish in a few days, and has lately begun the harpsichord and drawing. She and her sister will be with me to-

[11] Mrs. Adams to TJ, July 10, 1787 (LC, 5240).

[12] TJ to Mrs. Adams, July 16, 1787 (LC, 5270); TJ to Mrs. Adams, Oct. 4, 1787 (LC, 5730); Mrs. Adams to TJ, Sept. 10, 1787 (LC, 5588).

morrow. . . . I will propose to her, at the same time, to write to you. I know she will undertake it at once, as she has done a dozen times. She gets all the apparatus, places herself very formally with pen in hand, and it is not till after this and rummaging her head that she calls out, "Indeed, papa, I do not know what to say; you must help me," and, as I obstinately refuse this, her good resolutions have always proved abortive, and her letters ended before they were begun.[13]

She did not inherit his fluency, and continued to be reluctant to write letters, even to those she loved. Though notably generous he was an exacting father and often a strongly possessive one, but he was never so foolish as to attempt to sever the tie between his little girl and the pleasant white house at Eppington. As things turned out this tie was renewed and strengthened in later years, and, although Polly became devoted to him, she was never her father's daughter in the sense that Patsy was.

The coming of Polly greatly relieved Jefferson's mind and increased his happiness but, like a letter from an old friend, it probably had the immediate effect of increasing his nostalgia. Both of his daughters were in Paris when he wrote Dr. George Gilmer that he wished he could eat some beef and mutton at Pen Park with him and his good old Albemarle neighbors. "I am as happy nowhere else and in no other society," he said, "and all my wishes end, where I hope my days will end, at Monticello. Too many scenes of happiness mingle themselves with all the recollections of my native woods and fields, to suffer them to be supplanted in my affection by any other. I consider myself here as a traveler only, and not a resident." [14]

He could not escape to his own red-clay country but before his letter had time to get there he found a retreat at the hermitage kept by lay-brothers on Mont Calvaire, or Mont Valérien, beyond the Bois de Boulogne above the town of Suresnes. The hermits, who tended vineyards and manufactured stockings, had space for some forty guests. These guests brought their own servants, breakfasted alone, and assembled only for dinner. They could walk but not talk in the gardens, for this was a real hermitage. Beginning in September, 1787, Jefferson withdrew to this quiet and sightly hilltop when business accumulated, denying himself outside contacts until he caught up with his work, and he became a favorite with the brothers. He ordered from their

[13] TJ to Mrs. Eppes, July 12, 1788 (*Domestic Life*, pp. 137–138).
[14] TJ to George Gilmer, Aug. 12, 1787 (Ford, IV, 436). He expressed similar sentiments in a letter of same date to Col. W. M. Cary (LC, 5490).

workshops a dozen pairs of silk stockings for Abigail Adams that winter, vouching for the quality while fearing that she might not like their looks. He took his horse with him to the hermitage and presumably continued his habits of daily exercise. Normally, when at home, he worked all morning at official business, and then rode or walked for a couple of hours in the Bois de Boulogne before dinner, which was at or somewhat before the hour of three.[15]

John Trumbull had a standing invitation to take a bed at the Hôtel de Langeac and resume his position as a member of the family. The Grand Salon opened at the Louvre in late August, 1787, and since this happened only every other year Jefferson hoped that it would lure the young painter to Paris. He sent his artistic friend a list of the treasures, describing David's "Death of Socrates" as the best thing in the exhibition. But Trumbull intended to come when he could do some painting of his own, and he asked when it would be easiest to meet the French officers who had served in the Revolution. He wanted to put Lafayette, Rochambeau, De Grasse, and others in his painting of the surrender at Yorktown. Jefferson thought the period just before or just after the Christmas holidays would be the best time, and it was in December that Trumbull came. Meanwhile, Jefferson asked him to commission Mather Brown to do a portrait of Thomas Paine, who had gone to London after a brief stay in Paris. This was to be of the same size as the one of Jefferson himself which had been left with the Adamses, and he thought Trumbull could bring them both.[16]

Maria Cosway was often mentioned in these letters. She was in Paris more than three months that fall, and it is very likely that she visited the Salon with Thomas Jefferson, though she may have been in a querulous state when she arrived. Annoyed that she had not had more letters from him, she had punished him by replying on a very small sheet of paper to his lyrical account of his trip to her native Italy – lamenting that she was not a castle hanging to a cloud, a stream or a village, a stone on the pavement of Turin or Milan or Genoa.[17] Their reunion in Paris turned out to be rather flat. They did

[15] He took possession of his "apartments" on Sept. 5, 1787, paying for dinner that day, and on Oct. 12 paid for himself and his horse for a period (Account Book). The stocking episode is described in a letter to Mrs. Adams, Feb. 2, 1788 (LC, 6367–6368). His daughter Martha's account in *Domestic Life*, pp. 73–74, has been followed by later writers. For corrections of this and for further valuable details I am indebted to Mr. Howard C. Rice, Jr.

[16] Trumbull to TJ, Aug. 28, 1787 (LC, 5539); TJ to Trumbull, Aug. 30, 1787 (LC, 5549), Oct. 4, 1787 (LC, 5732–5733); Trumbull to TJ, Dec. 7, 1787 (LC, 5988). David's "Death of Socrates" is now in the Metropolitan Museum of Art.

[17] Bullock, p. 71, quoting Mrs. Cosway to TJ, July 9, 1787.

not recapture their first fine careless rapture, and it looked as though neither of them really wanted to.

He saw her the night before she left in early December, then expecting to breakfast with her next morning and to go with her a little way. He was there according to the understanding, only to find that she had gone off at five o'clock, leaving a little note behind her. She could not face the pain of another parting, she said; she left him with "very melancholy ideas"; and she concluded that she could not be useful to him since he had given all his commissions to John Trumbull anyway.[18] When she got back to London, wondering what he had thought of her, she wrote him that she had been very confused and distracted; but at the same time she gave an explanation of the infrequency of their meetings in these recent weeks. This was not the natural one that he was too much engaged with affairs, that he was now too much occupied with other people. "I suspected the reason and would not reproach you since I know your objections to company," she said.[19]

He himself elaborated the same idea. Yes, he had seen too little of her, but it was not his fault, he said, "unless it be a fault to love my friends so dearly as to wish to enjoy their company in the only way it yields enjoyment, that is, *en petit comité*. You make every body love you. You are sought and surrounded therefore by all. Your mere domestic cortege was so numerous, *et si imposante*, that one could not approach you quite at their ease, nor could you so unpremeditately mount into the phaeton and hie away to the Bois de Boulogne, St. Cloud, Marly, St. Germain, etc. Add to this the distance at which you were placed from me. When you come again, you must be nearer, and more extempore." [20]

He could not be one of a court of gallants, dancing attendance on a lady, and if they had not enjoyed such deep intimacy as before, her coquettishness and liking for general adoration was an important reason. Thus things appeared upon the surface, at any rate, and this was a very satisfactory state of affairs for a courteous and punctilious middle-aged gentleman to contemplate. Seemingly the choice between a special and a more general relationship had been made by her. No doubt he had emerged from the infatuation which had once imperiled him, but he had not spurned her. Hence he could remain a sincere friend, more tender than most, without embarrassment. She continued to occupy a unique place within his memory and a favored position

[18] Bullock, p. 83, giving note of Friday night [Dec. 7, 1787?].
[19] Dec. 10, [1787], MHS.
[20] Bullock, p. 85, quoting TJ to Mrs. Cosway, Jan. [14], 1788.

in a select inner circle, but there could be no monopoly of his heart.

Her own realization of this is shown by what she said about her friend Angelica Church, who had come to Paris with John Trumbull soon after Maria's departure and was visiting Madame de Corny. "What do you think of her?" asked Maria. "She calls me her sister. I call her my dearest sister. If I did not love her so much I should fear her rivalship. But no, I give you free permission to love her with all your heart and I shall feel happy if I think you keep me in a little corner of it, when you admit her even to reign queen." [21]

Maria would have denied that she had abdicated, but what her distinguished friend afterwards described wistfully to Trumbull as "our charming coterie in Paris" included Madame de Corny and Mrs. Church as well as Mrs. Cosway.[22] This little society had an artistic flavor, and it soon assumed a more domestic tone, for Angelica brought her daughter Catherine, or Kitty, to Paris and installed her at the Abbaye de Panthémont, where she became great friends with Polly. Madame de Corny, who had no children, vied with the widower Jefferson in doing kindnesses to these girls, and she and he solemnly discussed their school affairs over the teacups. Her husband was a great admirer of things American, and Jefferson heard some congenial political talk in their house on the Chaussée-d'Antin, but he would have liked this beautifully appointed home and gentle hostess anyway.

Her friend Angelica was an American by birth. The daughter of Philip Schuyler and sister-in-law of Alexander Hamilton, she had made a runaway marriage with an Englishman, John Barker Church, who did not stand high in Abigail Adams's opinion but had helped Trumbull greatly in financial matters while the latter had been abroad; and she now made her home at Down Place, where Madame de Corny had visited her. She loved the country, as Jefferson did, and he afterwards accused her of having bitten the Frenchwoman and made her country-mad, besides afflicting her with general Anglomania. Angelica was a small woman, like Maria Cosway, and like Madame de Corny she was delicate in health. She arrived in Paris in December, 1787, under escort of John Trumbull, and returned with him to England about two months later – leaving a trunk behind her which Jefferson had to send.

Trumbull did not bring the portraits that Jefferson wanted, since Mather Brown had not finished the commission, but he made some

[21] Mrs. Cosway to TJ, Dec. 25 [1787] (MHS).
[22] TJ to Trumbull, Jan. 10, 1817 (Chinard, *Trois Amitiés*, p. 170).

pictures of his own at the Hôtel de Langeac. Besides the French officers for the "Surrender of Lord Cornwallis," he painted his host from life for the original small "Declaration of Independence" and thought this one of his best small portraits.[23] Trumbull's "Jefferson," with unpowdered hair and ruddy face, is more vigorous than Mather Brown's, less the courtier, and presumably it is a better likeness. The artist took the picture back to London with him and Maria Cosway asked if she might have a copy of it. "It is a person who hates you that requests this favor," she wrote Jefferson in characteristic hyperbole – being very angry because Trumbull and Angelica had not brought her a letter from him. Trumbull afterwards made two replicas of his little painting – one for Maria and one for her "dearest sister." [24] He thought that Maria wanted to scold hers – which turned out to be more like Jefferson than the other. Angelica said that she had a better likeness in her memory anyway and that she did not mind. Jefferson himself spoke of the matter lightly. "The memorial of me which you have from Trumbull is the most worthless part of me," he wrote to Mrs. Church. "Could he paint my friendship to you, it would be something out of the common line." [25]

There was high quality in it, undoubtedly. "You are capable of feeling the value of this lovely woman," wrote the more talented and temperamental Maria to him when visiting her friend.[26] From England Angelica had replied diffidently to the gallant letter in which he expressed extreme sadness at her departure, but the common tie of daughters served to relieve embarrassment. She sent views of Ireland for Patsy, and in his letters during succeeding months he chattered about the visits of Kitty and Polly for Sunday dinner with him, as he did about the adventures of Monsieur and Madame de Corny in quest of a country house. He thought of Angelica when he rode in the Bois de Boulogne, he said, and when he traveled up the Rhine that spring he had her and Maria with him, one on each hand, thanks

[23] Trumbull to TJ, Dec. 7, 1787 (LC, 5988); Trumbull, *Autobiography*, pp. 150–151; Theodore Sizer, *Works of Col. John Trumbull* (1950), p. 35; Fiske Kimball, in *Procs. Am. Philos. Soc.*, LXXXVIII, 503. The original small "Declaration" is now at Yale. The miniature now owned by Mrs. Edmund Jefferson Burke (Kimball's Fig. 4) was painted in Paris about this time. The head in this is less striking than the one in the "Declaration," but gives the same impression of ruddy health and rugged strength. The replica given Mrs. Church, which is reproduced in this volume, makes Jefferson seem more slender and more fragile. The one made for Mrs. Cosway and regarded at the time as a better likeness has not been located.

[24] Mrs. Cosway to TJ, Mar. 6 [1788] (printed from MHS in Bullock, p. 87); Mrs. Church to TJ, July 21, 1788, printed from LC, 7011 in Bullock, p. 99.

[25] TJ to Mrs. Church, Aug. 17, 1788 (Bixby, p. 32).

[26] Bullock, p. 101.

to an imagination which helped him on cheerily over the world's dull roads.

There was some artificiality in this eighteenth-century gallantry, but his letters to this young countrywoman of his would seem delightful in any age.[27] His stay in France, and his association with charming women, had added lightness and humor to his pen. In their turn these friends were flattered by the attentions of such a learned and distinguished person. Writing him from Down Place, where she and Maria were enjoying the quiet of the country, Angelica said that they often wished Mr. Jefferson were there, "supposing that he would be indulgent to the exertions of two little women to please him, who are extremely vain of the pleasure of being permitted to write him, and very happy to have some share of his favorable opinion." Whether or not Maria showed his letters to everybody, as Lucy Paradise rather maliciously said she did, she undoubtedly took great pride in them.

He liked Maria and Angelica partly because they were so feminine. "The tender breasts of ladies were not formed for political convulsion," he wrote the sister-in-law of Alexander Hamilton; "and the French ladies miscalculate much their own happiness when they wander from the field of their influence into that of politics."[28] The beautiful glass which Madame de Corny sent him was a better symbol of their relationship than the copy of the memoir of Calonne he had previously sent her; and although he discussed the Assembly of Notables with Madame de Tessé, who called him the "apostle of American liberty," his friendship with Lafayette's aunt was grounded in their common love of gardens. At a later time, politics set up a barrier between him and Angelica Church and an even higher one between him and Abigail Adams, but his relationship with fellow Americans was unmarred by political dissension during his stay in France. In Europe he was a friend to all of them, men and women, young and old.

While he was on his southern trip Thomas Paine had arrived from America, laden with letters of introduction to men of science and learning from Benjamin Franklin. Paine could hardly have failed to seek Jefferson out after the latter returned, but he was chiefly interested at this stage in the iron bridge he had designed and he went to London in the fall. It was then that Jefferson commissioned Trumbull

[27] TJ to Mrs. Church, Feb. 17, 1788 (*Mo. Hist. Soc.*, III, 77–78); Mrs. Church to TJ, Mar. 9, 1788 (MHS); TJ to Trumbull, Mar. 27, 1788 (LC, 6546); TJ to Mrs. Church, July 27, Aug. 17, Sept. 21, 1788 (Bixby, pp. 31–35).

[28] Bixby, p. 35.

to get a portrait of him. This action can be attributed to his admiration of the past services of the author of *Common Sense*, irrespective of personal relations, for he was then forming a collection of portraits and busts of public characters. When Paine was back in Paris briefly in midwinter he, Jefferson, and Lafayette discussed the new American Constitution, in what the Marquis described as a convention of their own; but apparently Paine did not see the Virginian again during the latter's stay in France. They had much correspondence about the bridge, and after John Adams left for home Jefferson relied chiefly on Paine for information about political developments in England, but the personal association of the two men was limited in time and appears to have been cordial rather than intimate in nature.[29] It was also while Jefferson was on his southern trip that St. Jean de Crèvecœur had departed for America, leaving two sons in a pension across the street from the Hôtel de Langeac. The Comtesse d'Houdetot practically adopted these boys and the Minister frequently had them for dinner, joining the son of General Nathanael Greene to the company after another year. Joel Barlow brought this lad of twelve to France to be under the special charge of Lafayette, and Jefferson befriended him as a matter of course.[30] These actions brought him unmitigated pleasure such as he could hardly have had from helping Philip Mazzei out of perpetual financial difficulties or from straightening out John Paradise's incredibly tangled affairs.

He was exceedingly fond of children, but was rather too mature for them, and it was with young men that he was at his very best. None of his relationships were more delightful or more revealing than those with young travelers who sought him out and found in him tireless interest and unfailing solicitude. One of the first to feel the sunshine of his benevolence was the son of his old Williamsburg friend Anne Blair: John Banister, Jr., who had come from Virginia to Europe partly on account of his health and stayed mostly in the south of France during the year or two he was abroad. He was in constant correspondence with Jefferson, who gave him much information and received in return affectionate letters containing observations of the temperature and other bits of useful information

[29] Paine arrived in Paris on May 30, 1787, as he wrote Franklin on June 22, 1787 (Foner, II, 1262). TJ wrote Trumbull about the portrait, Oct. 4, 1787 (LC, 5732–5733). The bulk of the correspondence between the two men was in 1788–1789. TJ got the portrait by Jan. 12, 1789. For the discussion of the Constitution, see Gottschalk, *Lafayette between the American Revolution and the French Revolution*, p. 374.

[30] Chinard, *Les Amitiés Américaines de Madame d'Houdetot*, p. 46; Edward Carrington to TJ, May 14, 17, 1788 (LC, 6691–6692, 6717).

that he liked. Young Banister's health did not improve, however, and before he returned home he yielded too much to the allurements of Paris, spending considerably more money than he had intended and getting himself into a most unhappy state of mind. Jefferson helped him out, but there was a sad wastage of all his kindness, for the unfortunate young traveler returned home only to die.[31]

It was during this period that Jefferson began to contribute to the education of his future sons-in-law, as he was still contributing to that of his nephews. He could hardly have anticipated that Jack Eppes would one day marry Cousin Polly, but on request he gave the boy counsel about his studies.[32] His relations with Thomas Mann Randolph, Jr., were of more immediate importance. This son of Tuckahoe, where Jefferson had lived as a boy, was now studying in Edinburgh and wrote from thence, seeking advice from his father's relative and life-long friend. Jefferson, addressing him as "Dear Sir" when he was only eighteen, advised him to remain in Edinburgh long enough to take full advantage of the unequaled opportunities to attend lectures in science, to read history systematically, and then to begin the reading of law in France, since it could be done anywhere and France offered many personal advantages. Coupled with his illuminating comments on books and fields of study were characteristic admonitions about simple diet and regular exercise, especially walking, which were the more appropriate because Randolph had been in bad health. Otherwise, his counselor thought him unusually fortunate. "Nature and fortune have been liberal to you," he said. If the young man would do his own part industriously, his success was sure. Within a few months Randolph reported that his mind had become fixed on "politics" as the subject of his major pursuit and interest, and Jefferson approved, saying that their country had much for newcomers on the stage of public affairs to do.[33] He now advised that Randolph become a member of a family in some little town near Paris as soon as he had laid his scientific foundations in Edinburgh. "You will learn to speak better from women and children in three months than from men in a year," he said. After a couple of years in France and a tour of a few months in that country and Italy, he recommended that a year be spent in Williamsburg under George Wythe. This excellent

[31] TJ to J. Banister, Sr., June 16, 1785 (LC, 2168); TJ to J. Banister, Jr., Oct. 15, 1785 (L. & B., V, 185–188), and July 24, 1786 (LC, 3902); TJ to J. Banister, Sr., Feb. 7, 1787, (LC, 4794); J. Banister, Jr., to TJ from N. Y., Apr. 23, 1787 (MHS); TJ to Mrs. Anne Blair Banister, Aug. 6, 1787 (LC, 5444).

[32] TJ to Jack Eppes, July 28, 1787 (L. & B., VI, 189–190).

[33] TJ to T. M. Randolph, Jr., Aug. 27, 1786, and July 6, 1787 (Ford, IV, 289–295, 403–407); TJ to T. M. Randolph, Sr., Aug. 11, 1787 (LC, 5483–5485).

plan was never carried out, and it seems impossible to verify the family tradition that young Randolph came to Paris in the summer of 1788 and then renewed acquaintance with his cousin Patsy.[34]

This youthful kinsman became one of Jefferson's permanent connections later on. Others came and went, but few failed to carry away memories of his extraordinary kindness. John Brown Cutting, then at the Inner Temple, briefly visited Paris in the autumn of 1787, bearing letters of introduction from John Adams (along with a set of his *Defence of the Constitutions of the United States*) and from William S. Smith; he took letters back to Trumbull and Abigail on his return.[35] He wrote Jefferson many times afterwards, especially after the Adamses had gone, and helped keep him informed of events in England. That same autumn John Rutledge, Jr., of South Carolina, son of the statesman of that name and nephew of Edward Rutledge – both of them friends and correspondents of Jefferson – was in Paris in some financial difficulty. He did not ask for aid in so many words, but the Minister saw that he got an advance, and the grateful young man sent from England news of the trial of Warren Hastings.[36]

Later still, Jefferson met lively young Thomas Lee Shippen of Philadelphia, who was introduced by a letter from his father, Dr. William Shippen, and instructed by the latter to take Jefferson's advice about the way he should spend his time.[37] Then at the Inner Temple, he was a great friend of Cutting's, a nephew of William, Arthur, and Richard Henry Lee, and a relative of Lucy Paradise. He knew the whole history of the elopement of the elder Paradise daughter with the Count Barziza, a Venetian nobleman of doubtful character, in the spring that Jefferson took his southern trip; and in due course he regaled Jefferson and William Short with accounts of a fantastic affair in which high comedy and domestic tragedy were joined.[38] Jefferson's friend John Paradise – gentle, intellectual, and utterly impractical – had strongly opposed the marriage for reasons which now seem good, while the incredible Lucy had abetted it. The eccentric elder pair went to America after it took place, armed with introductions from the tireless American Minister which opened many hearts to them, that is, to John. It was this same young Shippen who had to

[34] The tradition is stated or implied in Randall, I, 558, and *Domestic Life*, p. 172; but it does not fit into Randolph's known itinerary.

[35] Adams to TJ, Sept. 16, 1787 (LC, 5609); Smith to TJ, Sept. 18, 1787 (LC, 5635–5636). The letters on the return were dated Oct. 4.

[36] John Rutledge, Jr., to TJ, Nov. 10, 1787, Jan. 2, 1788, Feb. 18, 1788 (LC, 5885; 6273; 6445–6446).

[37] William Shippen to TJ, Dec. 5, 1787 (LC, 5970).

[38] Fully and admirably described in Shepperson, ch. XII.

write them, in the late fall, that their younger daughter had died in school in London; and by the following summer they were in Paris – on Jefferson's doorstep, so to speak, with their finances and other personal affairs in unutterable confusion.[39] Before this happened, however, Jefferson had lost the Adamses from his intimate European circle, and had made a journey to the Low Countries and up the Rhine.

Toward the end of 1787, at just the same time that he learned of his own re-election as minister for three more years, he got word that John Adams's request for a recall had been granted.[40] Deeply regretting the departure of these friends, whom he looked upon as neighbors, he exchanged compliments with Abigail and raced against time to get for his collection a portrait of John by Mather Brown. A replica of the portrait of Jefferson by this same artist was to remain with John and Abigail, while the original was to come to the Hôtel de Langeac. He finally got both pictures, and Trumbull thought the likeness of Adams the better of the two.[41]

Taking leave of the British Court involved Adams in ceremonies which he found tedious but which he thought must be repeated at The Hague, where he had served formerly and was still accredited. Abigail regretted that her husband must twice make the horrid passage of the Channel, but viewed with entire satisfaction the prospect of going home.[42] She put the matter thus to Jefferson: "Retiring to our own little farm, feeding my poultry and improving my garden has more charms for my fancy, than residing at the Court of Saint James's where I seldom meet with characters as inoffensive as my hens and chickens, or minds so well improved as my garden." Jefferson must have chuckled over this passage – but it was the news that John Adams was going to Holland that caused him to take the road, determined to join his colleague there. Important official business of a financial nature needed to be attended to.[43]

[39] *Ibid.*, ch. XIII.

[40] He was re-elected Oct. 12, 1787 (*J.C.C.*, XXXIII, 665), and was informed in Madison's letter of Oct. 24 (Hunt, V, 37–38), which reached him toward the end of December.

[41] TJ to W. S. Smith, Dec. 31, 1787 (LC, 6087); Smith to TJ, Jan. 16, 1788 (LC, 6312); TJ to Smith, Feb. 2, 1788 (Ford, V, 2–3); Trumbull to TJ, Feb. 22, 1788, and Mar. 6, 1788 (LC, 6460, 6498); TJ to Trumbull, May 18, 1788 (LC, 6718–6720); Trumbull to TJ, May 23, 1788 (LC, 6743); Trumbull to TJ, July 11, 1788 (LC, 41: 6954). On July 2, 1788, he paid £10 for the Adams portrait, the same as for his own (MHS).

[42] Adams to Jay, Feb. 21, 1788 (*Works*, VIII, 480–481); Mrs. Adams to TJ, Feb. 26, 1788 (LC, 6472). He got this on Mar. 2.

[43] TJ to Adams, Mar. 2, 1788 (L. & B., VI, 434). The circumstances are sufficiently explained in his letters of Mar. 13 and Mar. 16, 1788, to Jay (L. & B., VI, 435–439). The official business is described in ch. X, below.

This episode in the dreary financial history of Confederation occasioned Jefferson to reflect much on his country's debts, as we shall see hereafter, but we are now concerned with personal relations and with his journey. Leaving Paris on March 4, 1788, he was away for about seven weeks, approximately a month of his time being spent in the Netherlands and on his way there. Being so anxious to catch Adams, he was tortured by delays on the first leg of the journey. In Rotterdam, on the eve of the Prince's birthday, he saw the most splendid illuminations he had ever seen, but he did not travel to see towns, and found no novelty in corn and pasture lands.[44] He met his colleague at The Hague, fortunately; they went on to Amsterdam together and made financial arrangements; then Adams left him and he stayed on far longer than he had expected to, in order to tie up loose ends. His memoranda show that he went about a good deal, keeping his eyes open, but the little drawings with which he illustrated his notes may imply that, like a schoolboy, he was bored. He left record of drop-leaf tables, joists of houses that were placed diamond-wise, wind sawmills, Dutch wheelbarrows, and the like, but obviously he enjoyed himself much more after he left the city and started southward.

His trip of slightly more than two weeks up the Rhine to Strasbourg, where he appears to have climbed to the top of the cathedral steeple, believing it to be the highest and handsomest in the world, and whence he returned to Paris through Alsace, Lorraine, and Champagne, was the most picturesque and romantic of all his journeys, and he did not attempt to justify it on grounds of utility alone. He had been much impressed by Trumbull's comments on this region, including very enthusiastic ones on the pictures at Düsseldorf, and he gave more time than usual to mere sightseeing. He called that town's gallery "sublime," but he saw no need to describe it; he made fuller notes on the subject of Westphalian ham. He traveled by carriage, following the river as closely as possible and feasting on the scenery, and buying the best available maps in all the important towns. He took note of numerous architectural details and made some little drawings, but, since he did not speak German, he was unable to pick up much information by conversation. Once he went out of his way in the hope of seeing the place where Varus and his Roman legions were cut off by the Germans, near Duysberg, but, finding no person in the village who could understand English, French, Italian, or

[44] TJ to Short, Mar. 10, 1788 (LC, 6508). The whole trip is admirably described in Dumbauld, pp. 110–124. TJ's memorandum of the trip from Amsterdam onward (Mar. 30–Apr. 23) is in L & B., XVII, 244–290.

Latin, he could not ask where to go.[45] He was much struck by the effects of absolutism on the people. "The transition from ease and opulence to extreme poverty is remarkable on crossing the line between the Dutch and Prussian territories," he said. "The soil and climate are the same; the governments alone differ. With the poverty, the fear also of slaves is visible in the faces of the Prussian subjects."[46] He liked the looks of the Germans somewhat better than the Dutch, however, and when passing through the Palatinate he often fancied himself in upper Maryland or Pennsylvania. "I have been continually amused by seeing here the origin of whatever is not English among us," he wrote.[47] He did not find religious tolerance. In Cologne the Protestants, who carried on most of the commerce, were restricted and oppressed by an excessively intolerant Catholic majority. In Frankfort-on-the-Main the reigning religion was Lutheran, and it was equally intolerant of Catholics and Calvinists.

The visit to Frankfort and vicinity was the highest point of the trip in the personal sense, for there Jefferson renewed acquaintance with Baron de Geismar, who had been with the Convention prisoners in Albemarle, and was still in the service of the Landgrave of Hesse, being generally in garrison at Hanau.[48] He made an excursion to this place with the Major, and found other old acquaintances among the soldiers there; and together they visited the vineyards of Hocheim and Rudesheim, whence came the choicest wines. Jefferson got some vines and planted them afterwards in his Paris garden. The Langraviate seemed to him dead under the hand of despotism, practically without sound except that of the fife and drum; and it must have seemed to Geismar, who maintained a surprising spirit of liberalism, that his friend brought a breath of fresh air from the land of freedom. Jefferson, who now had someone who could talk English, picked up some interesting and valuable bits of information besides what he learned about Rhine wines. Among other things he saw (at Bergen) a folding ladder which may have inspired the well-known one he afterwards had at Monticello.

He made further very elaborate notes on wines as he passed through the Champagne country on the last stage of this journey, and one of his agricultural observations anticipated a contribution of his own which was regarded as important in his day. On the road to Nancy, observing the plowmen behind the oxen, he noted the awkwardness of

[45] L. & B., XVII, 253.
[46] *Ibid.*, XVII, 252.
[47] TJ to Short, Apr. 9, 1788 (Dumbauld, p. 121 from LC).
[48] For the earlier association, see *Jefferson the Virginian*, p. 295.

their moldboard, speculated about a better form, and drew rough figures.[49] This was the beginning of the design of his moldboard of least resistance, perfected after he returned to America, for which he gained great acclaim in England and France as well as in the United States.

Back in Paris ten days after his forty-fifth birthday, he extended the benefits of his detailed observations to the circle of his American friends, especially the young men. In the next month Thomas Lee Shippen and John Rutledge, Jr., began a tour which he largely planned. The former described to Jefferson the journey from Paris to The Hague, as he had promised, referring to "the gratitude which your unbounded kindness exacts, and the affection which your virtues have inspired." [50] Soon after this, the older man sent travel notes to them – apologizing for his "little performance" in what Shippen termed "amiable modesty." His plans for them called for a journey up the Rhine, across the Alps into Italy (if they could not go to Vienna), and back through France – thus largely repeating his own itinerary in a different order.[51] The young men followed his advice carefully at almost all points and found it excellent. In Italy, Shippen had to turn back, since his father concluded that he had spent enough money and must return to his legal studies, but before then he began a long letter to Jefferson by saying, "Every stage of my journey has reminded me of you." [52] Jefferson's own experiences had convinced him by now that travel was likely to confirm Americans in their opinion that their own country was superior to all others. Writing the elder Rutledge in South Carolina about his son, he said: "He is likely to be as much improved by his tour as any person can be, and to return home, charged, like a bee, with the honey gathered on it." [53]

He encouraged William Short to join Shippen and Rutledge in the fall – after he had accompanied the Paradises part of the way to Italy and kept an eye on them. He wanted this virtual son of his to see the beauties of Italy, but he also may have wanted him to get away from another sort of beauty for a time. No doubt it was still true that Short found his greatest pleasure in the society of his patron, but he had enjoyed that of the young Duchesse de la Rochefoucauld often enough to excite some comments among his friends. She was much too young for Jefferson's distinguished friend and contemporary the Duke; and

[49] Apr. 18, 1788 (L. & B., XVII, 278–279).
[50] Shippen to TJ, May 29, 1788 (LC, 6771–6772).
[51] *Jour. Sou. Hist.*, XII, 95–106, ed. by Elizabeth Cometti; see ch. VII, note 13.
[52] Shippen to TJ, July 31, 1788, from Strasbourg (LC, 7079).
[53] TJ to Gov. Rutledge, July 12, 1788 (Dumbauld, p. 149, from LC). Similar sentiments were expressed in a letter of May 8, 1788, to Dr. William Shippen.

Short, who seems to have appealed to all the ladies, obviously appealed to her. Up to this point the affair appears to have involved no more than a few sighs and kisses, but it blossomed into a real romance after Jefferson had returned to America, leaving his agreeable secretary behind.[54]

Short set out in September and never did catch up with Shippen, but he joined forces with Rutledge and stayed away from Paris until after the Estates-General had assembled in May, 1789. To Jefferson this was both an inconvenience and a great personal loss, but the Secretary's journey had a vicarious quality and the joys of it were shared. Well briefed by his patron, Short visited the tomb of Virgil, and at Naples he procured a macaroni mold as Jefferson had requested.[55] He, too, became charged like a bee with honey and served as an agent in the cross-fertilization of culture, while his letters breathed an affection such as is rarely displayed even to a father by a son.

[54] G. G. Shackelford, "The Youth and Early Career of William Short" (Master's thesis, Univ. of Va., 1948) is the fullest treatment of him in this period, and is specially valuable for letters cited from the Short Papers (LC). Marie Kimball, "William Short, Jefferson's Only 'Son'" (*N. Amer. Rev.*, vol. 223, pp. 471–486), deals particularly with the romance with the Duchess. This flowered in the years 1790–1792; but after the tragic death of the Duke in 1792, his widow felt that her duty to the Duchesse d'Anville would not permit her to marry Short. The ills which befell this noble family greatly lessened Short's sympathy for the French Revolution.

[55] Short to TJ from Rome, Feb. 11, 1789 (LC, 7971; quoted in Dumbauld, p. 145).

The Rights of Man

[IX]

Considering the American Constitution

1786–1789

THE CHIEF EFFECT of Jefferson's stay in France upon his fundamental political ideas was to confirm him in the ones he held before he went there. Essentially this is true for the whole time that he was abroad, but some distinction can be made between the first and second halves of the period. The year 1787 marked a turning point on both sides of the Atlantic, for in France the Assembly of Notables started a chain of events which led to revolution, and in the United States a new Constitution was framed. Even if Jefferson's political philosophy did not change under the impact of these momentous events it had to be applied or adjusted to them, whereas a much greater degree of philosophical detachment was possible during his first three years abroad.

Before he arrived on the vaunted scene of Europe he had utterly repudiated absolutism in State and Church and had accepted wholeheartedly the doctrine of the natural rights of man. Freedom was his watchword, and to him the most important of all rights – the truly inalienable ones – were the sanctity of the person and the freedom of the mind. Objecting to artificial barriers of all sorts, he had enormous faith in intelligence, and confidence in progress. Regarding government not as an end in itself but as a means to human happiness, and being widely experienced in its actual operations, he was in the best sense an opportunist in practice. At home he was a stanch supporter of representative government who believed in the enlightenment of the people generally and the corresponding enlargement of the electorate. A member of a privileged group by right of birth and inheritance, he opposed special privilege of any sort just as he did artificial barriers; yet, as a reformer, he was a gradualist in temper. In his own country he had been an instigator of armed revolt against what he regarded as political tyranny and his emotions had then been deeply stirred, but what he looked forward to most longingly was the establishment everywhere of the rule of reason.

"The voice of reason is neither seditious nor sanguinary," a French philosopher had said not many years before. "The reforms that it advocates are moderate, and consequently well planned. In becoming enlightened men become milder; they know the price of peace; they learn to tolerate abuses that cannot be destroyed all at once without danger to the state. . . . It is by rectifying opinion, by combating prejudice, and by showing both ruler and people the rewards of equity that reason can hope to cure the evils of the world and firmly establish the reign of liberty."[1] This description of the spirit of enlightened liberalism fitted Jefferson well in this time of peace, but in reality he had little to learn from the *philosophes* in France. In certain respects, he had been in a position to be gentler than many of them were. He had had no such entrenched Old Regime to attack as they had, and even in the bitterest of his fights at home – in behalf of religious freedom – he had pitted himself against nothing that was at all comparable to the Established Church in France. On the other hand, republicanism was to him no mere theory, as it was still to the *philosophes*, since he had actually lived under it.

It is a question whether French thinkers made any appreciable impress upon him during the first half of his stay abroad. His incessant efforts to increase and to promulgate knowledge identify him in spirit with the Encyclopedists; he had much in common with the physiocrats, though he appears more realistic than they; he regarded himself as being in some sense the American representative of the *idéologues* at a later time, after their philosophy had taken form. From all these schools of thought his eager mind got something, but this was predominantly an acquisitive rather than a speculative period for him and he was most immediately and directly affected by his own observations. French government as he saw it at Versailles, French life as he observed it in Paris and Fontainebleau, in Burgundy and Brittany, impressed him more vividly than the words he heard in salons or read in books, and he viewed American government and society with fresh eyes from this new angle. In some ways he became more critical of his countrymen, but he never wholly escaped from nostalgia and the net result of his experiences was to confirm him in his optimism about the future of the American experiment. In the social and political spheres the

[1] D'Holbach, *Système social* (London, 1773), II, 36–37, quoted by J. S. Schapiro in *Condorcet* (1934), p. 58, and in this work by permission of Harcourt, Brace & Co.

main lesson pre-revolutionary France taught him was what Americans should avoid.

When he had been two years in Europe he wrote George Wythe:

> If anybody thinks that kings, nobles, or priests are good conservators of the public happiness, send him here. It is the best school in the universe to cure him of that folly. . . . The omnipotence of their effect cannot be better proved than in this country particularly, where, notwithstanding the finest soil upon earth, the finest climate under heaven, and a people of the most benevolent, the most gay and amiable character of which the human form is susceptible; where such a people, I say, surrounded by so many blessings from nature, are loaded with misery by kings, nobles, and priests, and by them alone.[2]

It was then that he exhorted his old friend in words which are now justly famous: "Preach, my dear Sir, a crusade against ignorance; establish and improve the law for educating the common people."

He still belonged to the gentry of Virginia, whom he loved for their generosity and tolerance, though he was sharply critical of them in other ways. He had long lamented the indolence of his hospitable countrymen, and he now described them privately as clannish, pompous, and aristocratical.[3] He had never liked the form of government they set up in 1776, which was designed to perpetuate the rule of the gentry, but he did not believe that the people in his own Commonwealth or anywhere in America had really experienced oppressions from aristocracy. He himself had congenial friends among the French nobility, but he did not perceive the real evils of a legalized class system (except in the case of Negro slavery) until he began to live abroad. He was not then presented with new theories but confronted with fresh facts.

His fears of the growth of the aristocratic spirit in his own country, which were crystallized and accentuated by his observations abroad, were most clearly and strongly expressed in his comments on the Society of the Cincinnati. Fully aware of the severe criticisms of the organization in liberal European circles, he was somewhat on the defensive in discussing it among the French; and he drew a sharper and more lurid contrast between the two worlds than he might have under less partisan circumstances. There was actually no legalized aristocracy

[2] To Wythe, Aug. 13, 1786 (L. & B., V, 396–397). His opinion of the climate seems to have improved.

[3] To Chastellux, Sept. 2, 1785 (Bixby, pp. 11–13). In this letter he made a highly interesting analysis of the character of Virginians, and of Northerners and Southerners generally.

in America, he told Démeunier, the author of the article on the United States in the *Encyclopédie Méthodique*. There were only private individuals, and officers exercising powers by authority of the laws. Continuing, he said:

> . . . But of distinction by birth or badge they [the Americans] had no more idea than they had of the mode of existence in the moon or planets. . . . A due horror of the evils which flow from these distinctions could be excited in Europe only, where the dignity of man is lost in arbitrary distinctions, where the human species is classed into several stages of degradation, where the many are crushed under the weight of the few, & where the order established can present to the contemplation of a thinking being no other picture than that of God almighty & his angels trampling under foot the hosts of the damned.[4]

He was almost as excited when he wrote Washington several months later. His stay in Europe had convinced him that the Society of the Cincinnati was a real threat to American governments, he said, because it would produce an hereditary aristocracy – not in his lifetime, perhaps, but eventually; it would change the form of American governments from the best to the worst in the world. To know the mass of evil which flowed from this fatal source – hereditary aristocracy – a person must come to France.[5]

He expressed himself vigorously, almost passionately, to George Washington on the subject of hereditary aristocracy at just the time that the tall, sober General and the latter's constant correspondent, thoughtful James Madison, were shaking their heads over domestic disorders in Massachusetts. The uprising of farmers and debtors known to history as Shays's Rebellion, which began in the late summer of 1786 and was put down by force early in 1787, was an important factor in creating the state of mind out of which emerged a new Constitution and stronger federal government. When Jefferson first heard reports of these rural tumults, they caused him genuine embarrassment – partly because the group on which he counted most, the independent farmers, was involved, partly because he had been correcting false reports of American disorders ever since he came abroad. His natural impulse as a diplomatic representative was to explain this one away, because of its ill effects on European opinion; but he soon became more fearful of its effects on opinion at home.

At first his friend John Adams sent him words of reassurance from

[4] Ford, IV, 175.
[5] TJ to Washington, Nov. 14, 1786 (Ford, IV, 328–329).

London. "Don't be alarmed at the late turbulence in New England," wrote this New Englander. "The Massachusetts Assembly had intent to get the better of their debt, laid on a tax, rather heavier than the people could bear. But all will be well, and this commotion will terminate in additional strength to government."[6] Soon after this, Colonel William S. Smith sent him newspaper clippings about the commotions, which had led to no actual fighting as yet, and it is probable that these formed the basis of information for his early judgment of the affair. James Madison failed him as an informant in this matter at the time and seemed rather loath to discuss it with him afterwards. Madison got his first news from Light Horse Harry Lee and, through Washington, from General Knox, and he seems never to have been aware of the real grievances of debtors in Massachusetts. He believed their uprising was designed to bring about an abolition of debts, public and private, and to effect a new distribution of property – just as Washington did – and, like Washington, he recoiled against it. He had not been shocked by Jefferson's recommendation that laws be passed facilitating the wider distribution of property, but he had no sympathy with physical revolt for social and economic ends.[7] As time went on, and the uprising appeared as a real rebellion, John and Abigail Adams also became more perturbed, and in the end Jefferson was practically alone among the national leaders in minimizing the peril of this disturbance.

It might have been said, as afterwards it often was, that in his remote position he was unaware of the actual dangers. But these were exaggerated, partly for political reasons, by persons closer to them, and he had distinct advantages in perspective.[8] His contemporary comments, which inevitably lagged a good many weeks behind the events themselves, could not have been expected to have any immediate influence; but they are significant items in the story of his developing political thought. This episode did much to stimulate his thinking about the basis of political society, and about the alternative forms of government which human experience presented.

At no time did he defend the acts of the rebels in Massachusetts. He was aware of the uneasiness of their minds, because of the stagnation of commerce and the scarcity of money; but on questions of debt and repudiation he was unfailingly conservative, and he did not con-

[6] Adams to TJ, Nov. 30, 1786 (LC, 4475).

[7] Brant, *Madison*, II, 391. See Madison's letters to his father, Nov. 1, 1786, and to Washington, Nov. 8, 1786 (Hunt, II, 277–278, 283).

[8] For the political uses made of this affair, see R. A. East, "The Massachusetts Conservatives in the Critical Period," in R. B. Morris, ed., *Era of the American Revolution* (1939), pp. 349–391.

done the attempts to interfere with the orderly processes of the courts or the other efforts to obtain redress of grievances by threat of force. To him these were "irregular interpositions of the people," they were errors, they were "acts absolutely unjustifiable." But he was specially anxious that the offenders should not be severely punished by their governments. This was not merely because of warm human sympathy; it seemed to him a matter of political wisdom. "The people are the only censors of their governors," he wrote to Edward Carrington, a rather conservative Virginian: "and even their errors will tend to keep these to the true principles of their institution. To punish these errors too severely would be to suppress the only safeguard of the public liberty." [9] A little later, hearing through Abigail Adams that the malcontents had made their submission on condition of pardon, he hoped the government would pardon them. "The spirit of resistance to government is so valuable on certain occasions, that I wish it to be always kept alive," he said. "It will often be exercised when wrong, but better so than not to be exercised at all. I like a little rebellion now and then. It is like a storm in the atmosphere." [10]

In private correspondence with this old friend and some others he resorted to hyperbole. He did not actually *like* rebellion, but he most feared repression, of which he had seen so much abroad; and, as he now said more warmly than hitherto, he was putting his trust in the people. Never before had he sounded so democratic as he did in these private letters about disorders which had deeply disturbed his friends at home. "I am persuaded myself that the good sense of the people will always be found to be the best army," he wrote Edward Carrington. "They may be led astray for a moment, but will soon correct themselves." He did not define his terms, so we cannot be sure just how much he meant by "the people." He certainly meant to include the entire electorate, and his past record showed that he favored the extension, not the restriction, of the franchise. But he had long emphasized the necessity of educating the people generally, and he now strongly stressed the importance of keeping them informed about specific issues. "The basis of our governments being the opinion of the people," he said, "the very first object should be to keep that right; and were it left to me to decide whether we should have a government without newspapers or newspapers without a government, I should not hesitate a moment to prefer the latter. But I should mean that every man should receive those papers and be capable of reading them."

His emphasis on newspapers seems unrealistic in view of the partisan-

[9] TJ to Edward Carrington, Jan. 16, 1787 (Ford, IV, 359).
[10] TJ to Mrs. Adams, Feb. 22, 1787 (Ford, IV, 370).

ship and misrepresentation which he had observed in them since he came abroad, and the gazettes which he had previously read in Williamsburg and Philadelphia seem undeserving of such high praise as agencies of public enlightenment. But he was using them as symbols, and was stating in exaggerated language a fundamental tenet of his faith. The mind of man must be left free, there must be entire liberty of discussion, and both the progress and security of society are contingent on the dissemination of knowledge.

As for happiness, he thought it probably greater among the American Indians than among the great body of the people in Europe, where, under pretense of governing, the population had been divided into two classes, wolves and sheep. If the people in the United States should become inattentive to public affairs, he feared that all officers of government, including himself, would become wolves. "It seems to be the law of our general nature, in spite of individual exceptions," he wrote; "and experience declares that man is the only animal which devours his own kind, for I can apply no milder term to the governments of Europe, and to the general prey of the rich on the poor." [11]

Perhaps the best single statement of the position to which his observations of forms of government had led him is contained in a letter to Madison, whose sentiments on the troubles in Massachusetts he was impatient to learn.[12] He himself was concerned lest "those characters wherein fear predominates over hope" would apprehend too much from these irregularities. Continuing in philosophical vein, he said:

> . . . They may conclude too hastily that nature has formed man insusceptible of any other government but that of force, a conclusion not founded in truth, nor experience. Societies exist under three forms sufficiently distinguishable. 1. Without government, as among our Indians. 2. Under governments wherein the will of every one has a just influence, as is the case in England in a slight degree, and in our states, in a great one. 3. Under governments of force: as is the case in all other monarchies and in most of the other republics. . . . It is a problem, not clear in my mind, that the 1st condition is not the best. But I believe it to be inconsistent with any great degree of population. The second state has a great deal of good in it. The mass of mankind under that enjoys a precious degree of liberty & happiness. It has it's evils too: the principal of which is the turbulence to which it is subject. But weigh this against the oppressions of monarchy, and it becomes nothing. *Malo periculosam libertatem quam quietam servitutem.* Even this evil is productive of good. It prevents the

[11] TJ to Carrington, Jan. 16, 1787 (Ford, IV, 359–360).
[12] TJ to Madison, Jan. 30, 1787 (Ford, IV, 361–363).

> degeneracy of government and nourishes a general attention to the public affairs. . . . Unsuccessful rebellions indeed generally establish the encroachments on the rights of the people which have produced them. An observation of this truth should render honest republican governors so mild in their punishment of rebellions, as not to discourage them too much. It is a medicine necessary for the sound health of government.

The minds of these two friends, both earnest supporters of civil rights and sincere friends of the Union, were now focused on very different dangers. Madison, whose thought was centered on the approaching Federal Convention and a new Constitution, did not regard the disturbances in Massachusetts as a sign of political health. He viewed the rebellion there, even though abortive, as one of the truly alarming symptoms, "which have tainted the faith of the most orthodox republicans, and which challenge from the votaries of liberty every concession in favor of stable Government not infringing fundamental principles, as the only security against an opposite extreme in our present situation." [13]

Jefferson did not let exaggerated fears taint his republican faith, for his observations in Europe had served to quicken it. Certain comments of his on the existing federal government in the United States are in startling contrast with what his friend Madison was saying about the constitutional needs of the hour. Sending information to Démeunier, he said: "The Confederation is a wonderfully perfect instrument, considering the circumstances under which it was formed." [14] He was not merely putting the best face on things American when addressing a European, for he spoke in even stronger language to his own countrymen.

He wrote to one Virginian: "But with all the imperfections of our present government, it is without comparison the best existing or that ever did exist." To another, he said that "with all the defects of our constitutions, whether general or particular, the comparison of our governments with those of Europe, are like a comparison of heaven & hell. England, like the earth, may be allowed to take the intermediate station." His words amounted to a plea for republican government, toward which he was looking back with nostalgia. To still another American he wrote: "If all the evils which can arise among us, from the republican form of government, from this day to the day of judgment, could be put into a scale against what this country suffers

[13] Madison to TJ, Mar. 18, 1787 (Hunt, II, 326). Presumably this was written before Madison got TJ's letter of Jan. 30.

[14] Jan. 24, 1786 (Ford, IV, 141).

from its monarchical form in a week, or England in a month, the latter would preponderate." [15] Yet Madison was so sure of his friend's awareness of the "mortal diseases" of the federal organism that he did not need to point them out to him. Jefferson was a statesman of wide experience, as well as a republican of dauntless faith.

The weakness of government under the Articles of Confederation which his experiences abroad had underlined most strongly was the imperfect control of commerce. Jefferson admitted this to foreigners and spoke of it again and again in letters to his compatriots. He was naturally speaking of foreign commerce and was now giving little thought to trade between the states. Writing to Madison late in 1786 he said: "To make us one nation as to foreign concerns, and keep us distinct in domestic ones, gives the outline of the proper division of power between the general and particular governments." [16] When the time came he did not object to the grant of the right to tax to the federal government, but at this early stage he laid no stress on an increase in its financial powers. When the Federal Convention was still in session, he wrote to another Virginian: "It has been so often said, as to be generally believed, that Congress have no power by the confederation to enforce anything, e.g., contributions of money. It was not necessary to give them that power expressly; they have it by the law of nature. When two parties make a compact, there results to each a power of compelling the other to execute it." [17] This may be regarded as an early and surprising statement of the constitutional doctrine of implied powers; and it is equally surprising that he thought compulsion would be easy and, under the existing Congress, relatively unliable to abuse. As for American public debts, which eventually proved such an embarrassment to him as a diplomatic representative, he believed that they could be paid by the sale of Western lands.

Along with the imperfect provision for control of commerce and lack of unity in foreign matters generally, he objected to the form of the government under the Confederation, favoring a distinct separation of powers between the legislative, executive, and judicial departments. His fear of legislative dominance was of long standing. It was based on his personal experiences as an executive in his own Common-

[15] TJ to Edward Carrington, Aug. 4, 1787 (Ford, IV, 424); to Joseph Jones, Aug. 14, 1787 (Ford, IV, 438); to Benjamin Hawkins, Aug. 4, 1787 (L. & B., VI, 232).

[16] To Madison, Dec. 16, 1786 (Ford, IV, 333). Madison sent him the "first shoot" in his own thoughts of a plan of federal government on Mar. 18 or 19, 1787 (Hunt, II, 324–328), referred to in his autobiography, *W. & M.*, 3 ser. II, 202.

[17] TJ to Edward Carrington, Aug. 4, 1787 (Ford, IV, 424).

wealth, and upon his observations as a legislator in Congress when there was no executive body of any sort, not even a committee. He spoke not merely as a foe of any sort of tyranny but also as an advocate of governmental effectiveness. The lack of such a separation of powers and of a definite executive, as he wrote a fellow Virginian, "has been the source of more evil than we have experienced from any other cause." Continuing, this veteran legislator said:

> Nothing is so embarrassing nor so mischievous in a great assembly as the details of execution. The smallest trifle of that kind occupies as long as the most important act of legislation, and takes the place of everything else.[18]

He approved the calling of the Federal Convention and always expressed the highest opinion of the character and abilities of its members. He could hardly have failed to have confidence in a gathering which Washington and Madison had promoted and which included Franklin, but he gave it even more sweeping commendation. "It is really an assembly of demigods," he wrote John Adams. Yet he also said, that same summer: "I confess I do not go as far in the reforms thought necessary as some of my correspondents in America." [19] He must have been thinking of Madison, who had outlined his own purposes for the Convention to him among the first. These former colaborers for religious freedom and humane laws in Virginia had then begun to disagree.[20]

For the second time in his career Jefferson, who had done such superb service as a legislative draftsman and was so deeply interested in the problem of formulating fundamental law, was denied the opportunity to share personally in the making of a constitution. He had been in Congress when the Assembly of Virginia adopted the constitution of 1776, and now he was in France. Inevitably he would have been a delegate to the convention in Philadelphia if he had been available, and it is interesting to speculate on the influence he might have exerted on those fateful deliberations. His most important actual contribution to the constitutional thinking of this period was made indirectly, through the books he sent Madison from Paris. These enabled that extraordinarily studious statesman to engage in what has been described as "probably the most fruitful piece of scholarly research

[18] *Ibid.* He said much the same thing to Joseph Jones, Aug. 14, 1787 (Ford, IV, 438), and to Madison, Dec. 16, 1786 (Ford, IV, 333).

[19] TJ to Adams, Aug. 30, 1787 (L. & B., VI, 289); to Edward Carrington, Aug. 4, 1787 (Ford, IV, 424).

[20] Madison to TJ, Mar. 19, 1787 (Hunt, II, 326–328).

ever carried out by an American." [21] Knowing the habits and talents of his friend, Jefferson undoubtedly expected him to make good use of the treatises on ancient and modern confederacies which were included in the "literary cargo" he shipped, but it is doubtful if he had an adequate impression of the vast amount of studying and thinking Madison had done on the constitutional problems of the young Republic. The ideas about republican federalism which were evolving in Madison's fertile mind represented a departure from all the confederacies of the past, just as the labors of this little intellectual giant in the Convention resulted in a creative contribution to human government. Jefferson's personal attitude toward these evolving ideas and the result of these labors must be judged from what he said in letters.

Writing in the spring, Madison had outlined his purposes for the Convention under four headings. In the reply which Jefferson wrote after his return from the south of France he passed over two of these in silence, cordially approved one and disapproved another.[22] The friends were in full accord about the desirability of the separation of powers, but Madison's proposal that the federal government be armed with a negative on the state legislatures *in all cases whatsoever* was a new idea to Jefferson and he did not like it. The trouble with this proposal, as he saw it, was that it disregarded the homely but essential principle that the hole and the patch should be commensurate. It proposed to "mend a small hole by covering the whole garment." He doubted if more than one state act out of a hundred concerned the Confederation, and preferred another procedure. He asked: "Would not an appeal from the state judicatures to a federal court in all cases where the act of Confederation controlled the question, be as effectual a remedy, and exactly commensurate to the defect?" Some encroachment of a federal court on the state courts might be expected, but Congress would watch and restrain it to a degree that Congress could not be trusted to restrain itself. This suggestion of a form of judicial review seems inconsistent with later expressions of his regarding the federal judiciary, when John Marshall headed the latter. By way of explanation it may be said that he generally opposed such tyrannies as seemed most menacing at a particular time, and that his deeper consistency lay in his continued advocacy of a balanced government. At this time, the danger of judicial supremacy was exceedingly remote.

[21] Quotation from Douglass Adair's sketch of Madison in *The Lives of Eighteen from Princeton,* ed. by Willard Thorp (Princeton, 1946), p. 150, referring particularly to Madison's notes on the vices of the political system of the United States, and on ancient and modern confederacies (Hunt, II, 361–390). On the books sent by Jefferson, see this volume, ch. VI.

[22] TJ to Madison, June 20, 1787 (Ford, IV, 390–391).

Also, the American government was heavily overbalanced on the side of the states, and neither here nor elsewhere in this period of constitutional discussion did he appear as a notable champion of the latter. The dangers in the new system which impressed him most, when he finally learned just what it was to be, were those relating to the liberty of individuals.

Being at such a distance from the scene, he advanced his own ideas tentatively and, at this stage, vainly. A series of long conversations between him and Madison would have been mutually beneficial. But letters were slow, while events moved rapidly, and during the summer the Convention was shrouded with secrecy. The privacy of the discussions was a wise precaution if the members were really to be free to speak and change their minds, but Jefferson did not like it. He wrote John Adams in London: "I am sorry they began their deliberations by so abominable a precedent as that of tying up the tongues of their members." [23] He was outside this assembly of demigods and these great events, as Adams was; and Madison would not have had time to tell him much about the proceedings, even if he had been free to do so. Eventually the chief mover in this important business wrote him elaborately, even going into lengthy explanation of the negative on state legislation which he had suggested but which Jefferson had greatly disliked and the Convention itself had wisely defeated.[24]

This letter was written more than a month after the Convention ended, and only then did Madison send to his friend in France a copy of the completed Constitution. This is surprising, since he sent copies to other people much earlier.[25] Perhaps he was waiting until he could find time to write at length; perhaps he feared Jefferson's reaction. Jefferson may have suspected that he was not in Madison's full confidence even though he did not say so, and the precise circumstances are not without significance. He got his first copy of the famous document from somebody else; Madison had not fully prepared his mind for it; he began to discuss it with others before he could appropriately do so with the man who knew most about it; and his first impressions of it were about 50 per cent unfavorable. He wrote John Adams, through whose office his first copy came: "I confess there are things in it which stagger all my dispositions to subscribe to what such an Assembly has proposed." [26]

[23] TJ to Adams, Aug. 30, 1787 (L. & B., VI, 289).

[24] Madison to TJ, Oct. 24, 1787 (Hunt, V, 17–41).

[25] For example, he sent one to Edmund Pendleton on Sept. 20, 1787 (Hunt, V, 1).

[26] To Adams, Nov. 13, 1787 (LC, 5904). He had not yet received Adams's letter of Nov. 10 (LC, 5888), in which the latter gave his first impressions and

He made another observation which would have staggered Madison, after all his labors: "I think all the good of this new constitution might have been couched in three or four new articles to be added to the good, old, and venerable fabric, which should have been preserved even as a religious relic." Among the hasty comments to Adams was this: "Their president seems a bad edition of the Polish king." Before long he learned that Adams's impressions were more favorable, but that gentlemen raised a question which was in line with Jefferson's continuing criticism: "What think you of a Declaration of Rights? Should not such a thing have preceded the model?" [27]

His letter to the son-in-law of Adams was more vivid. Tc his devoted young friend Smith he said that he did not yet know whether there were more good things than bad in the new Constitution. He centered his outburst on the provision for a chief magistrate who might continue for life, attributing this directly to the stories of anarchy in America which the British had done so much to spread, and which, wonderful though it was, Americans themselves had come to believe. He now made the most spirited of all his comments on the Shays Rebellion, and spoke of the desirability of occasional rebellion in words so striking that they became indelible. Nothing else shows more clearly how far away from Madison he was in spirit at this stage.

> . . . Yet where does this anarchy exist? Where did it ever exist, except in the single instance of Massachusetts? And can history produce an instance of rebellion so honourably conducted? I say nothing of it's motives. They were founded in ignorance, not wickedness. God forbid that we should ever be 20 years without such a rebellion. The people cannot be all, & always, well informed. The part which is wrong will be discontented in proportion to the importance of the facts they misconceive. If they remain quiet under such misconceptions it is a lethargy, the forerunner of death to the public liberty. We have had 13. states independent 11. years. There has been one rebellion. That comes to one rebellion in a century & a half for each state. What country before ever existed a century & a half without a rebellion? & what country can preserve it's liberties if their rulers are not warned from time to time that their people preserve the

---

said: "I forwarded a few days ago, from Mr. Gerry, a Copy as I suppose of the Result of the Convention." Presumably TJ referred to this in his letter of Nov. 13 to W. S. Smith, where he said: "I do not know whether it is to yourself or Mr. Adams I am to give my thanks for the copy of the new constitution" (Ford, IV, 466). In the course of time he received several other copies but Elbridge Gerry, who got one to him first, was one of the few delegates who declined to sign the finished document.

[27] Adams to TJ, Nov. 10, 1787 (LC, 5888).

> spirit of resistance? Let them take arms. The remedy is to set them right as to facts, pardon & pacify them. What signify a few lives lost in a century or two? The tree of liberty must be refreshed from time to time with the blood of patriots & tyrants. It is it's natural manure. Our Convention has been too much impressed by the insurrection of Massachusetts: and in the spur of the moment they are setting up a kite to keep the henyard in order. I hope in God this article will be rectified before the new constitution is accepted.[28]

Commenting after more than a century on this private letter, the biographer of John Marshall says that "this enraptured enthusiast of popular upheaval [Jefferson] spread his wings and was carried far into crimson skies." The same writer continues: "Thus did contact with a decadent monarchy on the one hand and an enchanting philosophy on the other hand, help to fit him for the leadership of American radicalism." [29] This undiscriminating statement reveals inexact knowledge of the source and nature of Jefferson's political ideas and imperfect perception of his motives in this particular matter. The saying that the tree of liberty must be periodically refreshed by the blood of patriots and tyrants is true enough, either in or out of its context, but what he was really emphasizing was the greater social peace of republican America than despotic Europe; and at this time, as numerous other letters show, the recent event which disturbed him most was the suppression of the Patriots in Holland, following the intervention of the King of Prussia in behalf of the Prince of Orange.[30] His philosophical justification of political revolution in the Declaration of Independence was far more sweeping than anything he was saying here. That was supported in 1776 by the vote of all the states, and to that revolutionary cause the signers had pledged their lives, their fortunes, and their sacred honor. His emotions were now strongly aroused by the trend away from popular liberties and, as he feared, toward despotism in America. But, while wisely refusing to be stampeded, he was as much opposed to the specific objects of the "radicals" in Massachusetts as he had always been, and this letter writer was not essaying the role of rabble-rouser. He did not differ from his major American contemporaries in liking violence more than they did, but he was far more aware than most of them of the everlasting dangers of tyranny and force. Rebellion – occasional rebellion – on the part of men nurtured in self-government seemed to him much the lesser evil.

* * *

[28] TJ to W. S. Smith, Nov. 13, 1787 (Ford, IV, 466–467).

[29] A. J. Beveridge, *Marshall*, I, 303–304.

[30] See below, pp. 184–186.

He had plenty of time to calm down during the month that intervened between his first sight of the Constitution and the receipt of a lengthy and dispassionate letter about it from his friend Madison.[31] Both of these characteristically modest men veiled the importance of the discussion of political fundamentals and constitutional means they were resuming. Madison said that his observations on the Constitution, which actually amounted to almost a score of printed pages, would help fill up a letter if they accomplished no other purpose; and Jefferson said in his reply that, since he had little else to write about, he would add a few words on the same subject – amounting to five pages. The attitude of open-mindedness and mutual respect which they maintained was the best safeguard against the breach which both of them must have feared, and it is to the credit of them both that eventually their differences were largely composed and that, if they did not occupy precisely the same ground, they stood close together as discriminating friends of the Constitution – and also of human liberty.

Had Madison been less patient and more brusque, he might have summed up his attitude to Jefferson as he did a year later to Philip Mazzei:

> You ask me why I agreed to the constitution proposed by the Convention of Philada. I answer because I thought it safe to the liberties of the people, and the best that could be obtained from the jarring interests of States, and the miscellaneous opinions of Politicians; and because experience has proved that the real danger to America & to liberty lies in the defect of *energy* & *stability* in the present establishments of the United States. – Had you been a member of that assembly and been impressed with the truths which our situation discloses, you would have concurred in the necessity which was felt by the other members. In your closet at Paris and with the evils resulting from too much Government all over Europe fully in your view it is natural for you to run into criticisms dictated by an extreme on that side. Perhaps in your situation I should think and feel as you do. In mine I am sure you would think and feel as I do.[32]

In the case of Jefferson, the best procedure was to tell him just what had happened. Long years later Jefferson described his friend's still unpublished notes on the debates as "the ablest work of this kind ever

[31] Madison wrote him Oct. 24, 1787 (Hunt, V, 17–37), and judging from his own reply of Dec. 20, 1797 (Ford, IV, 473–484) he got the letter on Dec. 19 or four or five days earlier.

[32] Madison to Philip Mazzei, Oct. 8, 1788 (Hunt, V, 267–268).

yet executed." [33] Madison did not send these notes across the sea, but he could now unveil the secret deliberations to a considerable degree and help Jefferson see with his own eyes the problems confronting him as he sought to establish a more perfect Union, to create an enduring Republic which was to operate over a larger area than any other republic had ever covered. By general agreement, he said, this could not be based on the principle of a confederation of sovereign states; the government must operate on individuals, hence the change in the principle and proportion of representation. Despite his outburst to John Adams about the good old Articles of Confederation, Jefferson made no attempt to defend the old state principle, and he praised numerous features of the new system on practical grounds. He liked the idea of a government which would not need continually to recur to the state legislatures; he was "captivated" by the compromise between the claims of the large and small states as reflected in the make-up of the two houses of Congress; he was much pleased with the method of voting in Congress by persons and not by states. He liked the grant of power to the federal legislature to levy taxes, and the choice of the larger house by the people directly, because he wanted to preserve inviolate "the fundamental principle that the people are not to be taxed but by representatives chosen immediately by themselves." [34] He saw much "precious improvement" in all of this.

Yet, speaking less tactfully to another than he did to Madison, he said about the same time:

> As to the Constitution I find myself nearly a neutral. There is a great mass of good in it, in a very desirable form: but there is also to me a bitter pill or two.[35]

The pills which continued to be bitter to him were the omission of a bill of rights and the failure to provide for rotation in office, particularly in the case of the President. As to the first, he wrote Madison:

> A bill of rights is what the people are entitled to against every government on earth, general or particular [that is, Federal or state], and what no just government should refuse, or rest on inferences.[36]

His determination that there must be a bill of rights, which was shared by others, like George Mason, who regarded the lack of one as a

[33] TJ to John Adams, Aug. 10, 1815 (Ford, IX, 528).
[34] TJ to Madison, Dec. 20, 1787 (Ford, IV, 475).
[35] TJ to Edward Carrington, Dec. 21, 1787 (Ford, IV, 481).
[36] Ford, IV, 477.

fatal objection to the Constitution, could hardly have failed to impress Madison. The latter afterwards championed what amounted to one, in the first amendments to the Constitution, just as he had championed religious freedom in Virginia. The difference between the two friends at this stage was with respect to the means to be employed in protection of private rights. One of the reasons advanced by Madison for a federal veto on state legislation was the need to prevent capricious and unjust state action against the rights, especially the property rights, of individuals. He frankly stated that "the evils arising from these sources contributed more to that uneasiness which produced the Convention, and prepared the public mind for a general reform" (that is, a new government), than the concern to render the Confederation adequate to its "immediate objects." Jefferson, as we have seen, countenanced no direct invasion of property rights, and he had no doubt that Madison's dominant purpose was to create a just government; but he continued to differ with him both as to the extent of the danger and as to the effectiveness of the remedy. "I own I am not a friend to a very energetic government," he said. "It is always oppressive." [37] It did not even prevent insurrections, as he had seen in Europe; and he reiterated the opinion that unwarranted alarm had been caused by the late rebellion in Massachusetts. Madison spoke at length about the protection of minorities; whereas Jefferson, in his own letter, said: "After all, it is my principle that the will of the majority should always prevail." In its context, this saying meant that if the majority should accept the Constitution in all its parts he would cheerfully concur. But with it he coupled expressions of faith and hope which sharply distinguished him from most of those who were now urging an increase in federal power, and which showed a difference in emphasis between him and Madison. He believed that American governments, state or federal, would retain their virtue as long as society remained chiefly agricultural. He hoped that the education of the common people would be attended to, being convinced "that on their good sense we may rely with the most security for the preservation of a due degree of liberty."

If Madison's faith in the common people, in popular government, and in an agricultural society needed to be renewed, his friend in France was a fit man to renew it; and if Jefferson's mind needed to be recalled to American realities too far away for him to see, Madison was the best of all men to point them out. During the next few months the latter devoted his letters chiefly to a dispassionate account of the struggle for ratification, step by step, letting the events and lists of persons tell their own story and laying no emphasis on his own labors

[37] Ford, IV, 479. The quotation from Madison is from Hunt, V, 27.

and his own zeal. Indeed, he was somewhat less than candid about the latter. Not until after the fight was over did he speak to Jefferson about the *Federalist,* though he had mentioned the essays to Washington eight or nine months earlier when they began to appear in the newspapers. During the winter of 1787–1788 he was not telling Jefferson everything, but he did give him a foretaste of the ideas he incorporated in that political classic, and when Jefferson finally got it he described it as the "best commentary on the principles of government which ever was written." After another year, when there was more time for the discussion of basic questions, Madison returned to the crucial question of liberty and power.[38]

> It has been remarked [he wrote to Jefferson] that there is a tendency in all Governments to an augmentation of power at the expence of liberty. But the remark as usually understood does not appear to me well founded. Power when it has attained a certain degree of energy and independence goes on generally to further degrees. But when below that degree, the direct tendency is to further degrees of relaxation, until the abuses of liberty beget a sudden transition to an undue degree of power. With this explanation the remark may be true; and in the latter sense only is it, in my opinion applicable to the Governments in America. It is a melancholy reflection that liberty should be equally exposed to danger whether the Government have too much or too little power, and that the line which divides these extremes should be so inaccurately defined by experience.[39]

Jefferson's attitude toward the Constitution has great importance because of its relation to his own developing ideas and his later political policies, not because of its influence on the immediate course of events. Had he been on the scene his influence could not have failed to be considerable, but communications lagged so far behind events that the situation itself had changed by the time he could make his position known. Insofar as he exerted any influence on opinion this was probably against the Constitution, since his earliest comments were the least favorable and the fight in America was practically over before anybody there was informed of his final acceptance of the new frame of government. If there was a strain on his relations with Madison during the period it was because these earliest comments, made in private letters to individuals and generally on request, were passed

[38] Madison to Washington, Nov. 18, 1787 (Hunt, V, 54–55); Madison to TJ, Aug. 10, 1788 (Hunt, V, 246); TJ to Madison, Nov. 18, 1788 (Ford, V, 53–54). My attention was called to this delay by Adrienne Koch.

[39] Madison to TJ, Oct. 17, 1788 (Hunt, V, 274).

around. Also, his suggestions about procedure were regarded by Madison as unacceptable, if not actually damaging to the cause of ratification for which he was battling so incessantly.

Not only did Jefferson begin by being shocked and describing himself as almost a neutral. At first he thought that another convention might be necessary after the will of the majority had been revealed. Madison, who always believed that another convention would put them back in the chaos from which they had so painfully emerged, could not face that prospect with any hope. Jefferson's next thought was that the best outcome would be the acceptance of the Constitution by enough states to set the new government going, and rejection by a sufficient number of others to force agreement to its amendment. "Were I in America," he wrote William S. Smith, "I would advocate it warmly till nine should have adopted and then as warmly take the other side to convince the remaining four that they ought not to come into it till the declaration of rights is annexed to it." [40] Among Americans abroad – including Thomas Paine, who discussed the Constitution with him and Lafayette when on a visit to Paris, but not including John Adams – and among "enlightened" Europeans, he had found much agreement with his objections to the perpetual re-eligibility of the President, but letters from home soon convinced him there was no real prospect of changing that article.[41] A sufficient reason for this was the universal confidence in Washington, whom everybody expected to be chosen. Jefferson shared that confidence but he put himself on record with the General in one of the most striking of all his sayings about kings:

> I was much an enemy to monarchy before I came to Europe. I am ten thousand times more so since I have seen what they are. There is scarcely an evil known in these countries which may not be traced to their king as its source, nor a good which is not derived from the small fibres of republicanism among them. I can further say with safety there is not a crowned head in Europe whose talents or merit would entitle him to be elected vestryman by the people of any parish in America.

He was probably thinking of George III and Louis XVI and the reigning King of Prussia, but he himself had respect for the abilities of

[40] TJ to W. S. Smith, Feb. 2, 1788 (Ford, V, 2). He was inclined to speak brashly to Smith, but he said the same to others, including Madison.

[41] Paine to George Clymer from Paris, Dec. 29, 1787 (Foner, *Complete Writings*, II, 1266); Lafayette to Washington, Feb. 4, 188 (Gottschalk, *Letters*, p. 338); Gottschalk, *Lafayette between the American Revolution and French Revolution*, p. 374.

the late Frederick the Great and this was an extreme statement. Washington, in his reply, made no reference to this tirade against kings nor to any danger of monarchy in America, but he did say: "I was ready to have embraced any tolerable compromise that was competent to save us from impending ruin; . . . It is nearly impossible for anybody who has not been on the spot to conceive (from any description) what the delicacy and danger of our situation have been." Jefferson himself had stated that he now regarded the adoption of the Constitution "as necessary for us under our present circumstances," and expressed his willingness to trust the good sense and spirit of his countrymen in the matter of the Presidency.[42]

Before the ratifying convention in his own State of Virginia met in June, 1788, not only had the Constitution gained greatly in his mind; he had also concluded that the best procedure was to adopt it first and amend it afterwards. If the remaining states would follow the noble example of Massachusetts, by ratifying the instrument and proposing amendments at the same time, he did not doubt that they could eventually get a bill of rights.[43] But the trouble was that, not being on the spot, he could not indicate his position to his countrymen in time to help his friend Madison in the Virginia convention. On the contrary, his earlier advice and opinions were actually adduced by Patrick Henry, the chief opponent of ratification and a leader whom Jefferson had long mistrusted. This put Madison in an embarrassing situation.[44]

Eight states had ratified the Constitution by the time the convention met in Richmond, and a ninth (New Hampshire) did so before it adjourned. If the latest counsel that had been received from the distinguished Virginian in France should ever be heeded, surely this was the time and place. He would have been deeply embarrassed had he heard the words of the orator, Patrick Henry: "This illustrious citizen advises you to reject this government till it be amended. . . . At a great distance from us, he remembers and studies our happiness. Living in splendor and dissipation, he thinks yet of bills of rights – thinks of those little, despised things called *maxims*. Let us follow the sage ad-

[42] TJ to Washington, May 2, 1788 (Ford, V, 8); Washington to TJ, Aug. 31, 1788 (Fitzpatrick, XXX, 82–83).

[43] TJ to Edward Carrington, May 27, 1788 (Ford, V, 19–21); to William Carmichael, June 3, 1788 (Ford, V, 23–26).

[44] The Virginia convention ratified the Constitution on June 25, 1788, and adjourned June 27. On July 2, 1788, Madison wrote Edmund Randolph that letters just arrived from Jefferson showed he was "becoming more and more a friend to the new Constitution," and that he had renounced his opinion concerning ratification by nine states and refusal by four (Hunt, V, 235).

vice of this common friend of our happiness."[45] Madison told Jefferson afterwards that Henry and George Mason tried to use the influence of his name against parts of the Constitution which he really approved; and Monroe (who voted against ratification) also thought their conduct improper. But there was no getting away from the advice which this "enlightened and worthy countryman" of theirs had given in private letters that nine states should adopt, and four then reject. Since it was supposed that New Hampshire would ratify the Constitution, there was

The Ninth **PILLAR** *erected !*

"The Ratification of the Conventions of nine States, ſhall be ſufficient for the eſtabliſh-ment of this Conſtitution, between the States ſo ratifying the ſame." *Art.* vii.

INCIPIENT MAGNI PROCEDERE MENSES.

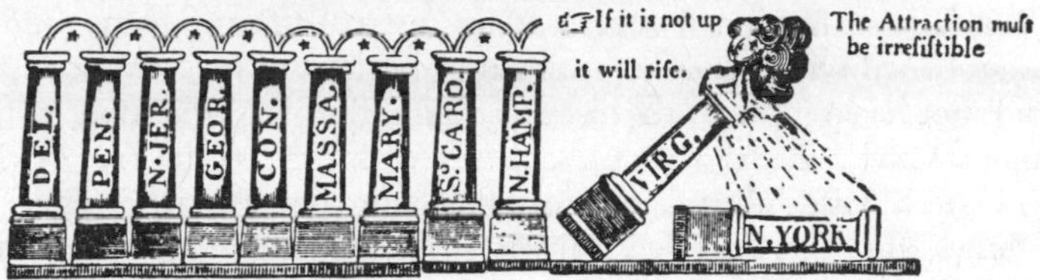

Contemporary Cartoon, from *The History of the Centennial Celebration of the Inauguration of George Washington* (1892) by C. W. Bowen; originally in Boston *Independent Chronicle and Universal Advertiser*, June 26, 1788

no answer to Patrick Henry's question: "Where, then, will four states be found to reject, if we adopt it?"[46]

Monroe reported that Jefferson's opinion, as set forth by the foes of the Constitution, was treated with "great attention and universal respect"; and Madison, referring to him as "an ornament of this state" and "a distinguished character," did the best he could in a difficult situation.[47] He stressed the impropriety of introducing the opinions of men who were not members of the convention, and, understanding Jefferson's temperament so well, he had good reason to suppose that

[45] From Henry's speech of June 9, 1788 (Jonathan Elliot, ed., *Debates . . . on the Adoption of the Federal Constitution* (1836), III, 152–153).

[46] In Henry's speech of June 12, 1788 (Elliot, *Debates,* III, 314); see also Madison to TJ, July 24, 1788 (Hunt, V, 241).

[47] In Madison's speech of June 12, 1788, following Henry (Hunt, V, 175–176). See also Monroe to TJ, July 12, 1788 (S. M. Hamilton, I, 186–187). Use was made of a private letter from TJ to A. Donald, Feb. 7, 1788, and Madison was informed that copies of a letter of TJ's or extracts from it were also handed around at the Maryland convention, with a like purpose of impeding ratification.

the "delicacy of his feelings" would be wounded if he should see in print what was said about him here. He himself was in some measure acquainted with Jefferson's sentiments on the subject, he said. It would not be right for him to unfold them, but at least he must say that he had specifically approved many parts of the Constitution which he was now charged with opposing. He himself believed that if Jefferson were now on the floor he would favor its adoption, and judging from the letters already written, though not yet received, Madison was fully warranted in this belief.

On one of the most difficult questions in this convention, that of the treaty-making power, Madison could have had no doubt of the support of the illustrious citizen whose opinions he thought it improper to unfold. Jefferson had repeatedly expressed his desire to unite the Republic in foreign matters and in control of commerce, and he was so satisfied with the constitutional provisions in these respects that he did not even bother to discuss them. But this question, which became involved in the Virginia debates with that of the free navigation of the Mississippi, was one to which not only Patrick Henry but also James Monroe addressed himself from the side of the opposition, and it is the best single explanation of the preponderant vote of the Kentucky counties against the Constitution. Madison's own record was one of consistent opposition to all attempts to cede away this right of free navigation, and Jefferson himself, at just the same time that he protested against the alarm over the Shays Rebellion, was saying that the threat of closing the Mississippi, through the negotiations of John Jay with the Spanish representative, really filled his mind with fear.[48] Not only did he thus foreshadow an essential feature of his later foreign policy; he strongly emphasized his own determination to preserve the Union, for he believed that the abandonment of the navigation of the great river would result in the separation of the Eastern and Western country. However, he never doubted the wisdom of putting diplomacy in federal hands.

He probably had no particular influence on the convention in his native state beyond that of adding some strength to the movement for amendment; and it is noteworthy that of all those opposed to ratification the only important political supporter of his in the later battles with Hamilton was James Monroe. The lines were not drawn now as they were afterwards, and, despite the closeness of the final vote (89 to 79) there was slight residue of bitterness. As Monroe reported, the event was accompanied with no extraordinary exultation on the part

[48] TJ to Madison, Jan. 30, 1787 (Ford, IV, 363–364).

of the victorious, nor of depression on the side of the defeated. There were no bonfires, though this observer thought that even if there had been, the spirits of all were so elevated that not even the opposition would have cared. It was to General Washington, looming in the background of everybody's mind, that James Monroe gave chief credit for the outcome. "Be assured his influence carried this Government; for my part I have a boundless confidence in him nor have I any reason to believe he will ever furnish occasion for withdrawing it. More is to be apprehended . . . as he advances in age, from the designs of those around him than from any disposition of his own."[49] Jefferson was thinking just that.

As the battle of ratification was being waged and won by others his mood became one of congratulation. To a South Carolinian he wrote: "We can surely boast of having set the world a beautiful example of a government reformed by reason alone without bloodshed." And to Madison, after he had learned of the ninth vote of approval and while he was expecting to hear equally good news from Virginia, he said: "It is a good canvas, on which some strokes only want retouching."[50] He informed Montmorin with satisfaction that the American Constitution had been established, and he reported to Jay that in Europe this was regarded as "a very wise reformation."[51] Meanwhile, since the canvas needed to be retouched somewhat, he proceeded to advise Madison about the provisions which should be included in a bill of rights.

At this stage what Madison most feared was that the demand for alterations would be so great that it would be difficult to maintain the fundamental outlines of the new picture. He believed that at this time the public mind was "neither sufficiently cool nor sufficiently informed" for such a delicate operation as that of amendment, and obviously he wished that the question of alterations had not been raised.[52] Nonetheless, he carefully considered the question of a bill of rights which Jefferson never ceased to press.

Madison's lengthy reply to his friend's suggestions was not only an explanation of his own apparent disregard of a matter which was supremely important to Jefferson; it was also a discussion of the subject in its varying manifestations which made Jefferson's apparent re-

[49] Monroe to TJ, July 12, 1788 (S. M. Hamilton, I, 186).

[50] TJ to Edward Rutledge, July 18, 1788 (Ford, V, 42); to Madison, July 31, 1788 (Ford, V, 45).

[51] He informed Montmorin July 31, 1788 (LC, 7060), and wrote Jay Aug. 3 (*D. C.*, II, 177).

[52] Madison to TJ, Aug. 10, 1788 (Hunt, V, 244). See also Madison to E. Randolph, July 2, 1788 (Hunt, V, 235).

liance on formal guarantees of freedom seem unrealistic.[53] Furthermore, Madison's statement that he had never regarded the lack of a bill of rights in this particular document as a material defect could be accepted at its face value, since he had already proved himself a champion of basic freedoms.

To Jefferson, far away from his native society and observing the perils of monarchical systems only, the most illuminating of his friend's comments must have been those relating to the dangers of democratic majorities.

> . . . Wherever the real power in a Government lies [said Madison], there is the danger of oppression. In our Governments the real power lies in the majority of the Community, and the invasion of private rights is *chiefly* to be apprehended, not from acts of Government contrary to the sense of its constituents, but from acts in which the Government is the mere instrument of the major number of the Constituents. This is a truth of great importance, but not yet sufficiently attended to; and is probably more strongly impressed on my mind by the facts, and reflections suggested by them, than on yours which has contemplated abuses of power arising from a very different quarter. Wherever there is an interest and power to do wrong, wrong will generally be done, and not less readily by a powerful & interested party than by a powerful and interested prince.[54]

Jefferson, who was less fearful of the illiberality and potential tyranny of popular majorities, continued to believe that the most important thing was to "guard the people against the federal government, as they are already guarded against their state governments in most instances." [55] But the friends were never far apart on the larger question. Although Madison regarded bills of right as less essential in popular governments than elsewhere, he thought them useful and favored one in this instance, provided it could be properly defined. There was some difference between him and Jefferson at this stage in regard to definition. Even though there might be some exceptions to general rules, the latter favored the establishment of them even in case of doubt, in order to guard against greater probabilities of evil. Madison, on the other hand, thought that in doubtful cases *absolute* restrictions should be avoided, since later violations were almost in-

[53] Madison to TJ, Oct. 17, 1788 (Hunt, V, 271–275). See also his later discussion of the matter in Congress (Hunt, V, 370–389), and the admirable accounts in Koch, *Jefferson and Madison*, pp. 55–61, and Brant, *Madison*, III, ch. XXI.

[54] Hunt, V, 272.

[55] Ford, V, 47.

evitable. His friend could not have been absent from his mind when he said that his major reason for favoring a bill of rights was that it was anxiously desired by others. Jefferson was not the only one of these. When, in the summer of 1789, Madison introduced amendments in Congress, there were whole groups of dissidents to the Constitution as it stood, whom he was anxious to win over – especially in the still reluctant states of Rhode Island and North Carolina. But there was no other leader whom he was more anxious to attach firmly to the Constitution, and there can be no doubt that Madison quieted his friend's fears.[56]

In later years a common line of partisan attack on Jefferson was that he was in reality a foe to the Constitution. This contention may be dismissed as groundless, though he had a perfect right to oppose it before it was adopted and to criticize it afterwards if he wanted to. His attitude was entirely clear to Madison and Washington, at least, and he has left to posterity a full and candid account of its development.[57] It is wholly incorrect to say, as has been said, that no one knew just how he stood on the fundamental question of the hour when he arrived in Virginia late in 1789, for these leaders did know, and he could not be quoted on both sides except in defiance of chronology.[58] Early in 1789 he wrote to a liberal Englishman: "I did not at first believe that eleven States out of thirteen would have consented to a plan consolidating them as much into one. A change in their dispositions, which had taken place since I left them, had rendered this consolidation necessary, that is to say, had called for a federal government which could walk upon its own legs, without leaning for support on the State legislatures." [59] He raised no objection on particularistic grounds, and he found in these events a new and comforting proof that a well informed people could be trusted to remedy their own government, when the need was manifest. Far from regarding the establishment of a new and stronger government as a *coup d'état*, effected for ulterior economic motives by a governing class in defiance of the popular will, he was specially pleased by the unexpected degree of popular support and with the sanity of the procedure. Uneasy France and despotic Europe should learn another lesson from the intelligent processes of a self-governing society. "The example of changing a constitu-

[56] TJ to Madison, Aug. 28, 1789 (Ford, V, 112–113).

[57] The account in his autobiography (Ford, I, 108–111), written in old age, agrees with his contemporary letters in all essential points, though he did not read the first copy of the Constitution that he received with as "great satisfaction" as he afterwards remembered.

[58] Beveridge's comments in *Marshall*, II, 47–48, reflect the partisan attitude.

[59] TJ to Dr. Richard Price, Jan. 8, 1789 (L. & B., VII, 253).

tion by assembling the wise men of the State, instead of assembling armies," he said a little later, "will be worth as much to the world as the former examples we had given them." And he regarded the Constitution itself, despite the defects which he continued to point out, as "unquestionably the wisest ever yet presented to men."[60]

Thus he wrote to men of varying political complexion, but, in view of earlier private letters which had been passed around and the unauthorized use made of them by Patrick Henry and others, many of Jefferson's compatriots may have been uncertain of his position during the months before he came home. He must have been designated as an "anti-Federalist" by some people, for he wrote a rather elaborate letter because of one report of the sort.[61] His statement of his position in this letter is so colorful that it has lent itself to quotation. It began with an expression of modesty which was in character with the gentleman, and it maintained a balance which may characterize consummate politicians but is unquestionably akin to that of scholars and philosophers:

> . . . My opinion was never worthy enough of notice to merit citing [he said]; but since you ask it I will tell it you. I am not a Federalist, because I never submitted the whole system of my opinions to the creed of any party of men whatever in religion, in philosophy, in politics, or in anything else where I was capable of thinking for myself. Such an addiction is the last degradation of a free and moral agent. If I could not go to heaven but with a party, I would not go there at all. Therefore I protest to you that I am not of the party of federalists. But I am much farther from that of the Antifederalists.

He then traced the development of his attitude to the Constitution, as he did in so many other places, stating that he had always approved the great mass of what was in it, including the "consolidation of the government," but that he still adhered to his two major points of disapproval. One of these he expected would soon be removed, and the other would need to be after Washington had established the new government against the efforts of opposition.

He was of neither party, he said, "nor yet a trimmer between parties." By "parties" he probably meant factional groupings, which he had always steered clear of and which he especially sought to avoid while he was a representative abroad. But the best way to translate his words into modern language is to say that he refused to let his

[60] TJ to David Humphreys, Mar. 18, 1789 (Ford, V, 89).
[61] TJ to Francis Hopkinson, Mar. 13, 1789 (Ford, V, 75–78).

political views be tagged or labeled; he would not let himself be put in any convenient compartment or pigeonhole. No real thinker could ever do that. As to the Constitution and the new government, he sincerely accepted the *fait accompli*, but as a champion of liberty and self-government he intended to maintain his vigilance. The greatest dangers were not immediate but lay ahead.

It was an admirable platform for a philosopher to sit on, and it turned out to be also an excellent political platform. Through force of circumstances, he was freer than most of the leading Americans of the time to heed the voice of popular opinion, and later events showed him to be more disposed than many to do so. Yet he gave no sign of strong personal ambition, and his devoted patriotism may be assumed.

Before he returned to America he gave much thought to the question, whether one generation has the right to bind another, and emerged with the idea that no society has the right to make a perpetual constitution or even a perpetual law. The stimulus came from the discussions then going on in France, and the letter in which he set forth his speculations to Madison was ostensibly directed to the question of public debt, which Madison was considering as a member of Congress. Starting with what he regarded as an axiom of natural law, "that the earth belongs in usufruct to the living," and making elaborate calculations on the life expectancy of such persons as had attained maturity, he arrived at this startling conclusion: "Every constitution, then, and every law, naturally expires at the end of 19 years. If it be enforced longer, it is an act of force and not of right."[62] Madison's perspicuous mind detected flaws in the logic and as a constitution-maker he pointed out grave dangers which would attend periodical revisions of the laws, but he thought the general principle useful and the idea itself a great one. He had long engaged in the practice of correcting the theoretical speculations which emanated from a more daring mind, and was himself immensely stimulated in the process. The most important thing to note here, however, is Jefferson's saying: *The earth belongs always to the living generation.* Believing that, he could be no idolater of any constitution. His genius was not merely that of freedom and reasonableness. It was also the genius of experiment and change.

[62] Ford, V, 121. The letter, written Sept. 6, 1789, but not mailed until Jan. 9, 1790, is in Ford, V, 115–124, with some errors not in the original in the Madison Papers. These have been made known to me by Adrienne Koch, who has a suggestive chapter on this discussion in *Jefferson and Madison*, ch. 4. To this I am much indebted. Madison's reply of Feb. 4, 1790, is in Hunt, V, 437–441*n.* I am unable to do full justice here to this extraordinary exchange of ideas.

[X]

In the Twilight of the Old Regime

1787–1788

THE significance of Jefferson's last two years in France lay less in what he did than in what he saw. As the French domestic crisis developed, from the Assembly of Notables onward, he found it increasingly difficult to attract the attention of the ministers of state to American questions. Toward the end of 1787 he did persuade them to put commercial arrangements with the United States on a firmer basis, as we have seen; and during the next year he negotiated a consular convention yet to be described, which was historically important from the American point of view. But, after a century and a half, his report of the unfolding French drama as contained in his correspondence is more interesting than any account anybody can write of his activities as a mere diplomat. The fact that he regarded himself as a bystander on a colossal scene is one reason why he minimized his own achievements as a minister.

He thought it an important part of his official duty to report such political developments in Europe as might be of interest to his country, and with the passing of time these greatly increased both in number and significance. From his letters to John Jay alone it would be possible to piece out a continuous story of the major events in France which led step by step to revolution, and of the accompanying events on the international scene. He was in a highly favorable position to see history in the making at a time when supremely important history was being made, and he accompanied his informal but careful account of events with thoughtful comments. These reflected his personal philosophy and point of view, and are of special interest now for just that reason, but they were generally penetrating and judicious. If he had had time and inclination he might easily have added to his many titles to distinction that of historian.

He gave no such day-by-day account of the Assembly of Notables in 1787 as he did of the Estates-General in 1789, partly because he left for the south of France soon after attending the opening of the former. The Notables were called, at the instance of Calonne, because of the sad plight of the royal treasury. Jefferson realized that the mere convoking of such a body was an unusual event in the history of France, and that important constitutional questions were likely to come up, but he did not expect this meeting to excite much American attention and thought it wholly unconnected with American interests.[1] After noting the innumerable puns and bons mots the meeting evoked, he wondered how deep the popular interest in it was among the French themselves and if any good would come out of it.[2] Not even he wholly escaped the mania for punning. He said that Lafayette's head was "full of notable things," while the Marquis in his turn told Washington that some wicked people described the members as "not able." Lafayette was next to the youngest member of this aristocratic body.

If Jefferson exercised any influence on the deliberations of these nobles and dignitaries, he did so through the nascent party – sometimes called American – which was represented there and of which his devoted and enthusiastic young friend had already become the symbol. The death of Vergennes, which had grieved Jefferson himself and delayed this meeting, had been a great personal loss to the Marquis. A highly competent judge has said that the exit of the great minister "left Jefferson as Lafayette's chief political adviser in France, and Jefferson was neither so oblique nor so cautious as Vergennes would have been."[3] But the letter which the Virginian wrote his friend on the eve of his own departure for southern France was cautious and moderate enough. In this he pointed, not to the example of the American Republic, but to that of the limited monarchy of England, much as he detested the King who reigned there. "Keeping the good model of your neighboring country before your eyes, you may get on, step by step, towards a good constitution," he said. Far from being alarmed by the financial necessities which had caused this meeting to be called, he thought they provided an opportunity for procuring political improvement. "If every advance is to be purchased by filling the royal coffers with gold, it will be gold well employed," he thought.[4]

[1] See especially his letters to E. Carrington, Jan. 16, 1787 (Ford, IV, 358–359), and Jay, Feb. 23, 1787 (*D. C.*, II, 42–43).

[2] TJ to Abigail Adams (Ford, IV, 370–371).

[3] Gottschalk, *Lafayette between the American and the French Revolution* (1950), p. 286, and chs. XIX, XX.

[4] TJ to Lafayette, Feb. 28, 1787 (L. & B., VI, 101). See Chinard, *Lafayette and Jefferson,* p. 70, for comments on the moderation of this letter.

The great advance already made was the calling of this assembly, and his major concern was that it be continued, that it become more effective in organization, that it be made more genuinely representative. This concern he expressed to Madame de Tessé – writing her from Nîmes, where he claimed to be immersed in antiquities, and probably expecting to get his ideas to Lafayette by this circuitous route. What he wanted was a regular assembly with two elected houses, the Nobility and the Commons, and the obvious prototype was British. "Two Houses, so elected, would contain a mass of wisdom which would make the people happy, and the King great," he predicted. In time they would improve on their English model and create a genuinely rational government, but he now wanted them to move cautiously. "Should they attempt more than the established habits of the people are ripe for, they may lose all, and retard infinitely the ultimate object of their aim," he said.[5] The advice that he offered here set the pattern for all that he gave in France. He advocated gradual reform, and his emphasis was political.

On the other hand, he revealed his awareness of social and economic ills in the observations on the agricultural population which he passed on to Lafayette, and these may have influenced the latter to turn his attention more definitely to the welfare of the people. He recommended that the young nobleman see things with his own eyes, that he ferret the people out of their hovels, look into their kettles, eat their bread, loll on their hard beds. The Marquis could not do that, at this moment, but in the Assembly he did speak of "the sweat, the tears and perhaps the blood of the people," and at a critical time afterwards he was conspicuously willing to renounce privileges which were his by right of birth.[6]

When Jefferson got back to Paris, Calonne had long since fallen, and the Assembly had ended without any agreement on the crucial financial question between the aristocrats and the new chief minister – Loménie de Brienne, whom Jefferson generally referred to as the Archbishop of Toulouse.[7] But he was more impressed by the need of reducing the expenses of the government than that of increasing its

[5] TJ to Madame de Tessé, Mar. 20, 1787 (L. & B., VI, 105).

[6] TJ to Lafayette, Apr. 11, 1787, from Nice (L. & B., VI, 106–110); Gottschalk, pp. 299, 310.

[7] He commented rather noncommittally on the dismissal of Calonne and hopefully on the new ministers to Jay, June 21, 1787, being specially pleased that Malesherbes had been appointed to the Council (*D. C.*, II, 55–57). Despite Lafayette's attack on Calonne, Jefferson was not quite willing to make a scapegoat of the latter at this time, and after a few months he concluded that he was not "the exaggerated scoundrel, which the calculations and the clamors of the public have supposed" (TJ to Madame de Corny, Oct. 18, 1787; L. & B., VI, 342–343).

income, and no consideration of public finance seemed as important to him at the time as the defeat of absolutism and the development of representative government. Accordingly, he was much encouraged by the promises of constitutional reform which had been made by the ministry, especially the establishment of provincial assemblies, and as the summer of 1787 wore on he noted that these reforms had gone on well. That summer, as he wrote to John Adams toward the end of it, had been perhaps the most interesting period ever known in France.

> I think [he said] that in the course of three months, the royal authority has lost, and the rights of the nation gained, as much ground by a revolution of public opinion only as England gained in all her civil wars under the Stuarts.[8]

He knew how these things had happened and approved the results at least. The ministry – acting in good faith, he thought, but expecting to get new supplies of money in return – had promised improvements, and the game had been so played as to secure the improvements to the nation without paying the price. Most conspicuously the game had been played by a judicial body, the Parliament of Paris, which refused to register the edicts for new taxes until forced to do so by the exercise of supreme royal authority. Jefferson's motto was, "Rebellion to tyrants is obedience to God," and on this occasion he was much impressed with the harshness of the King, whom he had previously thought well-intentioned and whom he never thought a bad man, though a weak one and something of a sot. The judges, exiled for a time, were the popular heroes of this drama but Jefferson had no doubt that they derived their strength from public opinion. All tongues were loosed in Paris, if not in all France, he said; never was there more outspoken criticism of any government; there were caricatures and placards everywhere, and nobody had been punished.

A few weeks later he had even more reason to rejoice at the power of public opinion, for the Parliament was brought back and the objectionable taxes were given up.[9] Following the lead of the judicial aristocrats who had defied the Crown, people were saying that the power to tax lay only in the Estates-General, even though that body had not met in more than a century and a half. As one of the authors of the American Revolution, Jefferson never had any doubt that taxation and representation should go together, and he believed that this movement of constitutional reformation could and must go on. In the meantime, however, he could not fail to note the continuing plight of

[8] TJ to Adams, Aug. 30, 1787 (*D. C.*, II, 85).
[9] He reported this to Jay, Sept. 22, 1787 (*D. C.*, II, 90).

the treasury, and, to his considerable chagrin, he saw a reflection of the weakness of the government in its faltering conduct of foreign affairs. In the autumn of 1787 he thought that a general European war was probable, and although his American mind was torn between the various alternatives he was displeased and disillusioned by the way things turned out.

For some months he had been keeping a close watch on the United Netherlands, where the bitter strife between the Patriot party and the supporters of the Stadtholder, the Prince of Orange, developed into an open conflict. His sympathies were with the former group, which was in the ascendant for a time, although he thought that the democrats within it had alienated the moderates by advocating too advanced a program and were losing ground. They were backed by the French, whereas the Stadtholder was supported by the British. The crisis came when the King of Prussia, Frederick William II, ordered his troops into Holland to avenge an alleged insult by Patriot soldiers to his sister the Princess of Orange. To Jefferson the occasion seemed trivial, and the act one of heartless tyranny. He wrote John Jay: "With a pride and egotism planted in the heart of every King, he considers her being stopped in the road as a sufficient cause . . . to spread fire, sword, and desolation over the half of Europe."[10] It was hard to see how war could be avoided, for the French declared that they would interpose if there were a Prussian invasion, and the British countered by saying they would regard this as an act of war. The Prussians invaded Holland, nonetheless, thus assuring the triumph of the Stadtholder over the Patriots, and, after considerable maneuvering behind the scenes, the French backed down.

The English Declaration and the French Counterdeclaration with which this affair concluded seemed to Jefferson false and hypocritical and he found the whole episode deeply disillusioning. He wrote to Jay: "It conveys to us the important lesson that no circumstances of morality, honor, interest, or engagement are sufficient to authorize a secure reliance on any nation, at all times and in all positions."[11] For the submission of the French he did not blame Montmorin, the Foreign Minister, who signed the formal statement while letting it be known that he personally disapproved it, but Brienne, the Chief Minister, who was playing safe. He did not even blame the well-

[10] TJ to Jay, Aug. 6, 1787 (*D. C.*, II, 70). He described the parties and the international alignment in this letter.

[11] TJ to Jay, Nov. 3, 1787 (*D. C.*, II, 104). See also TJ to John Adams, Sept. 28, 1787 (*D. C.*, II, 93–94).

meaning King, except for weakness. Of Louis XVI in this crisis he said: "He hunts one half the day, is drunk the other, and signs whatever he is bid." [12] But, apart from considerations of the responsibility for French inaction, the question arises why Jefferson did not find in the preservation of peace more occasion for rejoicing.

While the storm was rising he had written George Washington: "Upon the whole, I think peace advantageous to us, necessary for Europe, and desirable for humanity." [13] In regard to the probable effects of war on his own country he was having difficulty making up his mind. Though an outcome unfavorable to France would constitute a danger to the United States, he could see certain advantages which would accrue to the American Republic from war if it were a neutral – short-range rather than long-range advantages, however, and material rather than moral gains. Since the question of neutrality was to assume such importance in the future, the attitude he took toward it at this time is of more than momentary interest. The British had sounded him out, asking about the effect of the American treaty with France and the probable American position in case of hostilities. He told William Eden that the United States was obligated to receive in its ports the armed vessels of France, with her prizes, and to refuse admission to the prizes of her enemy. Also, there was a clause by which the United States guaranteed to France her American possessions, and if these possessions were attacked, this clause might force his country into war. The disposition of his government would be to be neutral, however, and he claimed that it would be to the interest of both England and France that she be so, since they would thus be relieved of all anxiety about feeding the West Indian islands. Besides this, the British would avoid all necessity of fighting on the American continent.[14]

Despite these American dispositions, he was obviously uncertain whether or not neutrality could be maintained. Eden told him that the British would assuredly attack French possessions in the New World, and at no time in his entire career was Jefferson more convinced of the enmity of the English to their former colonies, or was he more bitter against them in his own mind. He considered them as "our natural enemies, and as the only nation on earth who wished us ill from the bottom of their souls." John Adams, in England, was calmer about the situation and believed that, for a time at least, the

[12] TJ to Jay, Oct. 8, 1787 (*D. C.*, II, 98).

[13] TJ to Washington, Aug. 14, 1787 (*D. C.*, II, 80). See also TJ to Jay, Oct. 8, 1787 (*D. C.*, II, 97).

[14] TJ to William Carmichael, Dec. 11, 1787 (*D. C.*, II, 117–118).

English would leave the United States and Americans alone, but he was fully aware of future dangers. He wrote Jefferson:

> Whether John Bull has command enough of his passions to see us punctually fulfill our treaties as we must do, without being transported with rage, you, who know him, can tell as well as I. We know this gentleman's hasty temper so well, that I think we may very safely wish for the continuance of peace between France and him, even upon selfish principles; though our commerce and navigation would be greatly promoted by a war, if we can keep out of it.[15]

Jefferson could hardly have found fault, as a patriotic American, with this sensible and forthright statement, and actually there was no clash between the colleagues on the international questions of the hour. Both condemned the conduct of the King of Prussia, both sympathized with the Patriots in Holland, both thought that the French had managed their diplomacy badly, both wondered about the international alignments of the future and what they might bode for the United States. But the final event shocked Jefferson more – perhaps because until now he had been somewhat less realistic about international politics. He had regarded war as practically inevitable because he had supposed that these various courts and ministers meant what they said, and he had got so used to the idea of war that his mind was unprepared for the French backdown.

The worst thing was that the Dutch Patriots had been betrayed, but in this unscrupulous diplomatic game the French had lost face, while the implacable British had gained prestige and power. The financial weakness of the French monarchy was impressed upon him by these events, but he did not think that a sufficient reason for its policy of appeasement. He wrote John Jay: "No nation makes war now-a-days but by the aid of loans; and it is probable that in a war for the liberties of Holland all the treasures of that country would have been at their service. They have now lost the cow which furnishes the milk of war. She will be on the side of their enemies whenever a rupture shall take place; and no arrangement of their finances can countervail this circumstance."[16] If this should turn out to be a truce only, rather than a peace, the French would be weaker when the conflict was resumed, and after this instance of bad faith toward the Dutch he could not have failed to wonder what reliance the American States could place on France, their best friend among the nations. Uncer-

[15] Adams to TJ, Oct. 28, 1787 (*Works*, VIII, 458).
[16] TJ to Jay, Nov. 3, 1787 (*D. C.*, II, 110).

tain as we must be about the policy he would have advocated if he had been a responsible minister of the Crown, and not a mere observer from another land, there is no doubt about what he – and John Adams with him – now recommended for his own country in the light of this precarious situation. "We are, therefore, never safe till our magazines are filled with arms," he wrote John Jay. "The present season of truce or peace should, in my opinion, be improved without a moment's respite to effect this essential object, and no means be omitted by which money may be obtained for the purpose." [17] A minor difference between him and Adams – though perhaps this was an accident of phrase – was that he deferred to the judgment of Congress, while his colleague took this occasion to urge the completion of the Constitution. Jefferson was still more concerned to secure the blessings of liberty and self-government – as in France and Holland – than to create national power anywhere, but this episode shows unmistakably that he was neither an appeaser nor a pacifist, and also that he was learning about the wiles of diplomacy in the best – that is, the worst – of schools.

As the French monarchy staggered on toward bankruptcy, the representative of the United States found himself increasingly embarrassed by his own country's debt, especially its foreign debt. Roughly speaking, somewhat more than two thirds of the latter was owed to the French Crown, and something less than a third had been borrowed in Holland on a French guarantee. By the regular payment of interest on the latter, American credit was maintained in the Dutch money market, but not without recourse to further loans. For some years John Adams had been making financial arrangements in Amsterdam as circumstances required, and he continued to do so after Jefferson arrived. This was a great relief to the Virginia planter, who had no stomach for financial operations of this sort and had trouble enough with his own affairs. He told Madison that money negotiations were the most disagreeable of all forms of business to him and that he was most unfit for them. He did not understand bargaining, he said, nor possess the requisite dexterity, while the New Englander had both experience and skill.[18] It was also a great relief to him that the royal government of France paid no attention to the debt to them, apparently expecting no payments on principal though some were overdue, or even on interest account. The tolerance of the government was all

[17] TJ to Jay, Nov. 3, 1787 (*D. C.*, II, 106). See also Adams to Jay, Nov. 30, 1787 (*Works*, VIII, 462–464).
[18] TJ to Madison, June 20, 1787 (Ford, IV, 393–394).

the more noteworthy in view of the fact that French participation in the struggle against the British was the most important single reason for the plight of the treasury, and to Jefferson this patience was a strong proof of continuing friendliness.

As the financial situation grew more and more critical, however, he became aware that the American debt was creating ill will in France. Under these circumstances a proposal was made to Calonne, at his wit's end to find new sources of revenue, that this debt be transferred to a group of Dutch bankers, who would pay for it a flat sum at less than its face value (twenty million livres for twenty-four) and float a new loan backed by a French guarantee. Without commenting on fiscal details, Jefferson passed the proposal on to Congress, and he continued to approve the general idea while waiting to hear from home. He preferred floating a loan in Holland sufficient to meet the entire French debt but he sounded callous about the Dutch, remarking to John Jay that if any discontents should arise because of the unpunctuality of American payments they would do less harm in Holland than in France. The suggestion was rejected by Congress on the ground that the debt to the Crown of France had been contracted in good faith in the first place, even though nothing had been paid on it, but that the transfer of it to private bankers in Holland would carry a presumable guarantee of prompt payments which, as Congress now knew, probably could not be met. Besides being unjust, the action would be impolitic because a failure in the payment of interest would destroy American credit in the United Netherlands, where other loans might be required.

In the report of the Board of the Treasury, which Congress accepted and Jay eventually transmitted to Jefferson as a formal resolution, there was a note of moral superiority which might well have caused such a sensitive man to smart. The fundamental and fatal weakness in the proposal was the impossibility of giving guarantees at the time. Furthermore, as some delegates in Congress not unnaturally supposed, there was less likelihood of complaints from the French than there would be from the Dutch. It was better to leave well enough alone. But the general idea of a transfer of the debt was approved by as conservative a Virginian as Edward Carrington, while Washington thought it highly worthy of consideration; and John Adams – who had a very low opinion of congressional finance – was willing to consider it as a possibility. The resolution of Congress may have been regarded, at the time, as a mild rebuke to Jefferson, but the political genius of Alexander Hamilton was required to discover signs of financial irresponsibility in his words, five or six years later.

France was still an absolute monarchy, and the plight of the treasury which he deplored was what brought on the Revolution, hence his later critics might have said that his proposal was inconsistent with his own philosophy. But he thought of this matter in terms of political realism, not philosophy. The French had not yet shaken his confidence by failing to support their Dutch allies against Prussian invasion, and his major purpose was to cement friendship with the nation which was most likely to be helpful to the United States.[19]

Besides the large debt to the Crown, the American Republic owed money to French officers who had helped effect independence. Jefferson, who believed that these officers had contributed notably to good will after their return from their overseas adventure, was specially disturbed by this obligation. He mentioned it to Jay repeatedly and told John Adams in the summer of 1787 that it made more noise against the United States than all the other debts put together. Relatively it was a small amount and he thought something should and could be done about it.[20] The pressure had increased as times grew hard in France and the promised American payments fell more and more in arrears. Also, as the troubles of the French treasury had come to be so much talked about, the debt to the Crown itself was more openly referred to. Hard things were said in the Assembly of Notables, although these were toned down in the official record. In the latter it was stated that, although the debt seemed well secured, no early payment of either principal or interest could be expected. A year later Jefferson reported that the French government was now calling for the interest. That is, the item was included in the *compte rendu*, as though a payment were expected by the year 1789. The royal treasury did not get a payment then, but before Jefferson left for home he was able to do something for the officers.[21]

This relatively fortunate outcome was owing to the successful negotiations carried on by him and John Adams in Holland shortly be-

[19] The major references for the episode itself are: TJ to Jay, Sept. 26, 1786 (*D. C.*, I, 813–814); TJ to Jay, Nov. 12, 1786, with memorial from Dutch Co. (*D. C.*, II, 3–8); Resolutions of Congress, Oct. 2, 1787 (*D. C.*, II, 8–10); TJ to John Adams, July 1, 1787 (*D. C.*, II, 64); Adams to TJ, Aug. 25, 1787 (*Works*, VIII, 447); E. Carrington to TJ, Oct. 23, 1787 (LC, 5819); Washington to TJ, Aug. 31, 1788 (Fitzpatrick, XXX, 82). For Hamilton's "tortured" use of TJ's letter of Sept. 26, 1786 to Jay, see note attached to letter of TJ to Washington, Mar. 2, 1793 (Ford, VI, 123–125), and TJ to Madison, March 1793 (Ford, VI, 193), and ch. XXVII, below.

[20] TJ to Jay, Feb. 1, 1787, enclosing a letter from an officer (*D. C.*, II, 27–28, 30–31); TJ to Adams, July 1, 1787 (*D. C.*, II, 64).

[21] TJ to Jay, May 4, 1788, enclosing translated pages from the *compte rendu* (*D. C.*, II, 148, 150–151).

fore the latter left for America in 1788. While his colleague was preparing to depart, a financial crisis arose with which Jefferson himself felt incompetent to cope. The year before that, Adams had arranged with Dutch bankers for a loan of a million guilders, but for various reasons this was only partially subscribed when Jefferson learned that no more money would come from Congress in 1788, that payment of the principal of a small Dutch loan was demanded, and that the bankers claimed that not enough money was available to pay the very considerable interest payments due in June. Incidentally, the expenses of the American establishment in Paris appeared to be wholly unprovided for. The bankers made what he regarded as an impossible proposition: namely, to complete the loan of the year before on condition that an important broker be allowed to deduct the interest on certain certificates of American domestic debt now held by him. Speculation in American paper had begun in Europe, with much greater prospect of profit in the case of the domestic than in that of the foreign debt, if both should be supported by the American government – as, under the leadership of Hamilton, they afterwards were. Jefferson resented this state of affairs, partly because he detested all speculation, and more immediately because arrangements for interest on the foreign debt and the support of his own establishment were endangered. Adams was even more indignant over the proposal of the Dutch bankers, saying that if he were going to remain in Europe he would solicit another loan from another banker before he would submit to it. He felt sorry for his friend, who was now inheriting these vexatious problems, but tried to reassure him by saying that the Amsterdamers were never as bad as they sounded.[22]

Jefferson had written his colleague what he intended as a letter of farewell before he learned that Adams, who had continued all these years to be accredited to the States-General of the United Netherlands, had concluded that he must go to The Hague to present his recall. Then Jefferson as we have seen set out to join him – on the trip which afterwards took him up the Rhine – tortured by fear that he might miss him. "Our affairs in Amsterdam," he wrote, "press on my mind like a mountain." Fortunately, he caught up with Adams, and these old friends collaborated very effectively – for the last time, indeed, in a public matter. Not only did they persuade the bankers in Amsterdam to complete the loan already agreed to, without regard

[22] TJ to Adams, Dec. 12, 1787 (*D. C.*, II, 120–121); TJ to Commissioners of the Treasury (*D. C.*, II, 142–143); Adams to TJ, Feb. 12, 1788 (*Works*, VIII, 473–475). See also, for the loan of 1787, Adams to TJ, Aug. 25, 1787 (*Works*, VIII, 447).

to the claims on domestic interest account which had been advanced. They also provided for the needs of the years 1789 and 1790 by negotiating a new loan subject to the approval of Congress. Thus they gave the new American government time to get started and put its financial house in order. They drew up estimates of expenditure which included provision for the French officers, and Jefferson made arrangements to pay them during the last summer he was in France, though the total amount had been considerably raised by new lists and estimates in the meantime.[23] By that time American credit had become so good in Amsterdam that the bankers told him that any desired money arrangements could be made. Actually, there was competition for American business.

He may have lacked the temperament and training for money negotiations, and John Adams may deserve more praise than he for the accomplishments in Amsterdam, but he was fully aware of the importance of American credit abroad and discussed it with Washington and Madison while the new American Constitution was being ratified. To the future President he said that the English had the best credit because they always paid the interest, while that of France was among the lowest. "Ours stands in hope only," he continued. "They [foreign bankers] consider us as the surest nation on earth for the repayment of the capital; but as the punctual payment of interest is of absolute necessity in their arrangements, we cannot borrow but with difficulty and disadvantage." He predicted, however, that if the new American government should set out on the English plan of never failing to pay interest, the "first degree of credit" would be transferred to it. To Madison he wrote that the first act of the new government should be some provision for the European debts; and before his friend became a member of the new House of Representatives he sent him specific plans. Jefferson recommended that certain import duties on European articles be "sacredly" applied to these purposes, and by beautifully drawn tables he showed how these debts could be entirely liquidated in fifteen or twenty years.

During his last summer in Europe, when the new American government was in operation, he attributed the improvement of American credit in Amsterdam to "the spirited proceedings of the new Congress in the business of revenue"; and before he left for home he could report that the credit of his own country was second to none. What he most feared then was speculation in the American domestic debt

[23] The activities in Holland are best described in TJ's letter to Jay, Mar. 16, 1788 (*D. C.*, II, 134–137), and later developments about the officers in TJ to Jay, Aug. 27, 1789 (*D. C.*, II, 319–320).

in Europe. Furthermore, he was opposed to public debt on principle just as he was to speculation. "I am anxious about everything which may affect our credit," he had written Washington. "My wish would be, to possess it in the highest degree, but to use it little. Were we without credit, we might be crushed by a nation of much inferior resources, but possessing higher credit." The General fully agreed with his fellow Virginian. "I am strongly impressed with the expediency of establishing our National faith beyond imputation, and of having recourse to loans only on critical occasions," said Washington. But, as Jefferson afterwards found out, Alexander Hamilton wanted to go a good deal farther.[24]

After his money negotiations in Amsterdam in the spring of 1788 and his brief trip up the Rhine and back to Paris, Jefferson resumed his role of reporter and commentator. In May he noted that the city was a "furnace of politics." Everybody – man, woman, or child – was politically mad, and the quarreling was really taking all the pleasure out of social life. If he had objected to the frivolous comments on the Assembly of Notables the year before, he now seemed to regret that this society had lost its characteristic gaiety and insouciance.[25] He himself was more serious than he sounded and less a spectator than he affected to be, but it seemed to him that the conflict of the moment had little meaning: "The King and the parliament are quarreling for the oyster," he said. "The shell will be left as heretofore to the people."[26] He was much less familiar than modern historians are with developments in the provinces, where the nobles were so busily exploiting the confused situation and loudly reasserting their ancient privileges, but it became quite clear to him in the summer of 1788 that the present struggle was between "the monarchical and aristocratical parts of the government, for a monopoly of despotism over the people."[27] However, the people would surely be helpless victims if these parties should coalesce.

His own hopes were centered in neither King nor aristocracy,

[24] TJ to Washington, May 2, 1788 (L. & B., VI, 451–454); TJ to Madison, May 3, 1788 (*ibid.*, VI, 455–459); Washington to TJ, Aug. 31, 1788 (Fitzpatrick, XXX, 82); TJ to Madison, Nov. 18, 1788 (Ford, V, 55) with tables (LC, 7518–7526); TJ to Jay, Aug. 27, 1789 (*D. C.*, II, 320); TJ to Jay, Sept. 19, 1789 (*D. C.*, II, 326).

[25] TJ to Madame de Bréhan, May 9, 1788 (Chinard, *Trois Amitiés*, p. 42); to Mrs. William Bingham, May 11, 1788 (Ford, V, 9). Allowance must be made for some indulgence in pleasantries in these social letters.

[26] TJ to Francis Hopkinson, May 8, 1788 (LC, 6670).

[27] TJ to Crèvecœur, Aug. 9, 1788 (L. & B., VII, 113–114). In this letter he made an illuminating comparison between the situations in France and Holland.

whether of the robe or sword, but in the band of "real patriots" who were taking advantage of this conflict to secure gains for the nation as a whole. Toward the end of the summer, after the exigencies of the treasury and the stubbornness of the Parliament of Paris had forced the ministry to concede to the Estates-General the right of taxation and to set a date for the meeting of that long-defunct body (May 1, 1789), Jefferson summed things up realistically but hopefully to his friend Monroe:

> This nation is, at present, under great internal agitation. The authority of the crown on one part, and that of the parliaments on the other are fairly at issue. Good men take part with neither, but have raised an opposition, the object of which is, to obtain a fixed and temperate constitution. There was a moment, when this opposition ran so high, as to endanger an appeal to arms, in which case, perhaps, it would have been crushed. The moderation of government has avoided this, and they are yielding daily, one right after another, to the nation. . . . So that I think it probable, this country will, within two or three years, be in the enjoyment of a tolerably free constitution, and that without its having cost them a drop of blood . . .[28]

He greatly feared the use of force by the Crown, believing that there could be no successful resistance to an army of 200,000 regular troops if the King chose to employ them against his foes. For this reason, he himself favored a "firm but quiet opposition."[29] He regarded the arrest of two of the parliamentary leaders, early in the summer, as an act of high-handed authority, and he did not like some of the royal edicts which followed, but he was more impressed with the moderation than the severity of the government and credited it with some genuine reforms. Brienne had not yet retired, though he was already beaten, when his ministry received from the American apostle of self-government more praise than he could have expected and more than he probably deserved. "I applaud extremely the patriotic proceedings of the present Ministry," wrote Jefferson. "Provincial Assemblies established, the States General called, the right of taxing the nation without their consent abandoned, *corvées* abolished, torture abolished, the criminal code reformed, are facts which will do eternal honor to their administration in history." He could not applaud "their total abandonment of their foreign affairs," which had caused them to lose important allies without gaining any new ones, and he regretted that they had not put on a bolder front, but he was now more

[28] TJ to James Monroe, Aug. 9, 1788 (L. & B., VII, 112–113).
[29] TJ to Jay, May 23, 1788 (*D. C.*, II, 157).

tolerant of them than he had been when they abandoned the Dutch Patriots. Perhaps they were right in concluding that they lacked the financial means to engage in war. "Their justification must depend on this," he concluded, "and their atonement in the eternal good they are doing their country. This makes me completely their friend."[30] He may not have shared the public exultation when Brienne was removed and Necker was called in, for he afterwards thought the latter overrated; and the triumphant return of the parliamentary aristocracy to the seats of power from which they had been temporarily ousted was to him no occasion for rejoicing, for he would have liked to see their privileges curtailed. For his times he probably was juster to the ministry than most, but the only group he really trusted was the little band of "real patriots."

Whether or not this little band could have been properly described as a party in the summer of 1788 is largely a question of definition. Jefferson did not bother to define his own terms, and within a few months he was talking of a very extensive and zealous patriotic party. "This party comprehended all the honesty of the kingdom sufficiently at its leisure to think," he said; "the men of letters, the easy bourgeois, the young nobility, partly from reflection, partly from mode; for those sentiments became a matter of mode, and as such united most of the young women to the party."[31] The close spiritual tie between the leaders of this party and revolutionary America was generally recognized, and it was well symbolized by the intimate friendship between Jefferson and Lafayette, which had suffered no diminution since the Assembly of Notables. Relatively little is known about the organization of the Patriots, but there was an inner group, known as the "Society of the Thirty" or "Committee of the Thirty," which held meetings several times a week at the home of Adrien Duport, leader of the liberal faction among the councillors of the Parliament of Paris, or at the home of Lafayette.[32] Besides liberal lawyers, it contained other liberal noblemen, like Jefferson's friends La Rochefoucauld and Condorcet, and upper bourgeois, with whom he was undoubtedly sympathetic if they advanced ideas of economic freedom. In another summer certain members of the Patriot party in the National Assembly met in his own house in the hope of composing their differences, and his spiritual kinship with these leaders was obvious from the first.

[30] TJ to William Carmichael, Aug. 12, 1788 (*D. C.*, II, 186). See also TJ to Dr. Richard Price, Jan. 8, 1789 (L. & B., VII, 255). His comments on Brienne's removal in his autobiography (Ford, I, 120) were less sympathetic.

[31] TJ to Dr. Richard Price, Jan. 8, 1789 (L. & B., VII, 254).

[32] Albert Mathiez, *French Revolution* (1928), p. 26; Gottschalk, *Lafayette between the American and the French Revolution*, ch. XXV.

For the revolution in opinion which had already forced much salutary reform he gave chief credit to the Patriots, "who were able to keep up the public fermentation at the exact point which borders on resistance, without entering on it."[33] If any of them consulted him privately in the autumn of 1788, he undoubtedly gave them moderate counsel, and he must have talked with them as he did with his correspondents about a possible alliance between the people and the King. By the term "people" he probably meant everybody but the privileged classes, that is, he meant the huge Third Estate of which the most vocal element was bourgeois; and, despite his praise of the ministry for its concessions, he had no real illusions about the Court. It was better disposed toward the people than the nobility and clergy, he believed, but not because of love of them or a sense of justice. The treasury must have money, and, since the people were already squeezed to the last drop, the King had no recourse but to squeeze the privileged orders. To do this he must have the support of the people. The immediate issue in the autumn related to the forms in which, after 175 years, the Estates-General should be convoked, and the Court took the popular side by allowing the Third Estate as large a representation as the other two orders combined. The difficult question remained as to just how votes should be taken when the representatives got there, and Jefferson fully realized that this might cause the assembly to stumble at the threshold; but, apart from this difficulty, he believed that certain important reforms could be obtained without any royal opposition. As stated to John Jay, Madison, and others these were: (1) periodical meeting of the Estates; (2) their exclusive right to taxation; (3) the right of registering laws and proposing amendments to them as now exercised by the Parliaments. The latter would probably oppose their own reduction to mere judicial bodies but they could not succeed against the King and nation.[34]

In his opinion, that was as far as reform ought to go at present. Further governmental reform and civil rights could be gained later. In the light of his own record it may seem surprising that he did not give the first place to guarantees of individual freedom, such as he had insisted should be included in the new American Constitution. He gave the reason to Madison: "The misfortune is that they [the French people] are not yet ripe for the blessings to which they are entitled." He doubted whether the body of the nation, if consulted, would accept a habeas corpus law if offered them by the King. It may also be

[33] TJ to Dr. Richard Price, Jan. 8, 1789 (L. & B., VII, 255).

[34] TJ to Madison, Nov. 18, 1788 (Ford, V, 53–54); TJ to Jay, Nov. 19, 1788 (*D. C.*, II, 232–233).

surprising that one who had denounced monarchy so violently and had such a low opinion of the ability of Louis XVI should have been so anxious to effect and maintain harmony between King and people. To John Jay he said: "It is to be feared that an impatience to rectify every thing at once, which prevails in some minds, may terrify the Court, and lead them to appeal to force, and to depend on that alone." Here he appears as no revolutionary, no visionary, but as a moderate reformer and a political opportunist, ready to employ in the public interest such instruments as were at hand – even a king. Time was to prove Louis XVI too weak an instrument, and the aristocracy, stubbornly defending against the claims of the people the ancient privileges they had reasserted against the King, were to rejoin him and thus make revolution the only recourse of the unprivileged classes. But Jefferson and his friends the Patriots did not need to force that issue yet, and, in the meantime, he had had to attend to some odds and ends and one genuinely important bit of official business.

By the end of the year 1787, it will be recalled, Jefferson had made commercial arrangements with the French authorities which he believed would not be easily upset. These had been incorporated in an *arrêt*, issued with the authority of the entire Council. Though less suspicious by nature than John Jay he soon had reason to agree that the spirit of monopoly and exclusion was still prevalent. Violent objections were raised in French commercial circles, the ministers were alarmed, and he tactfully agreed to give up certain concessions which seemed valueless in order to retain others which seemed important – only to find that something else had got lost in the shuffle and that now he must get that back.[35] He never could relax his vigilance lest concessions already gained at great labor be withdrawn – often by the capricious or irresponsible act of an individual official.

Thus, in the autumn of 1788, he was shocked to learn of an order prohibiting the importation of all whale oils, and believed that an exception in favor of American whale oils had been stricken out at the instance of a single minister. This was not Montmorin, to whom he addressed a letter of remonstrance accompanied by rather elaborate observations of his own on the whale fishery. He thought well enough of these to have them printed and to send copies to John Jay, John Adams, and others, but his primary object was to educate the French, and especially Necker, in a subject of which they were woefully ignorant. The paper is one of many examples of his diligence in informing himself, and it can be read with profit now by anyone interested in

[35] TJ to Jay, Feb. 5, 1788, and May 23, 1788 (*D. C.*, II, 133, 158–159).

the whaling business or the island of Nantucket, but the important point to make here is that his tactful representations were successful. He did not discourage the French from trying to develop their own national fishery, as he had hoped to. He never thought this fishery could succeed, for he regarded French navigation as the "least economical of all in Europe," and whaling called for the most rigorous economy. But he was correct in supposing that the immediate French purpose was to block the English, and he got an explanatory *arrêt* and a letter from the famous Necker excepting American whale oils for the time at least. Before he left France, Jefferson positively gloated over the decline of the northern whale fishery of the English, attributing this to the shutting of French ports against them. In this case he approved of commercial freedom only as far as it favored the United States.[36]

A minor but rather amusing diplomatic episode of this final period was the affair of the Comte de Moustier, who went to the United States late in 1787 as minister, in succession to the Chevalier de la Luzerne, and fell into some trouble. Jefferson commended the new envoy to John Jay and James Madison as a friendly, candid, and unostentatious person; and he described as "goodness itself" the Count's sister-in-law, who went along and aroused considerable comment by so doing. Madame de Bréhan, an artist whom Jefferson may have met through Maria Cosway, viewed the New World through the haze of sentimentality, and although he forewarned her against possible disillusionment, there are marks of eighteenth-century "sensibility" in the rather stilted letters he wrote her, just as there was lack of realism in his original approval of the Count himself. In America, Madame liked Madison, of whom unfortunately she was unable to see much, but she found few people with the candor, simplicity, and goodness of her "dear Mr. Jefferson." In the new land the Count encountered a formality and emphasis on etiquette which he had not expected and of which he complained. Jefferson assured him that disputes over formalities were arbitrary and senseless, wholly without foundation in reason, and wished that etiquette might be dispensed with altogether. This exchange of complaints and reassurances was rather touching, but as

[36] TJ to Jay, Nov. 19, 1788 and Nov. 29, 1788, enclosing copy of *arrêt* of Sept. 28, 1788, TJ's letter of Oct. 23, 1788, to Montmorin, and his Observations on the whale fishery (*D. C.*, II, 233–253); TJ to John Adams, Dec. 5, 1788 (*D. C.*, II, 259–260); TJ to Jay, Jan. 14, 1789, enclosing letter of Jan. 11, 1789, from Necker, and translation of *arrêt* of Dec. 7, 1788, excepting American whale oils, etc. (*D. C.*, II, 266–269); TJ to Jay, Sept. 19, 1789, showing decline in number of ships in English northern fishery (*D. C.*, II, 324); TJ to Necker to the same effect, Sept. 26, 1789 (L. & B., VII, 478).

Jefferson discovered, a major reason why the Count and Madame did not feel at home was that they themselves showed slight skill in social adjustment and were not liked by the Americans. When dining with Hamilton, Moustier refused to partake of the dishes that were served and, on the pretext of a delicate stomach, sent for some that were prepared by his own cuisinier. Madame de Bréhan also disliked the food, found the wines abominable, and complained of the humidity of the climate, but a major trouble was that she did not receive enough attention. She appears to have been a bizarre creature, and although Jefferson thought her fully deserving of Mrs. Jay's friendship and sent her a letter of introduction to Angelica Church, who was visiting the States, the opinion was widespread that her connection with her brother-in-law was improper. "You can easily conceive the influence of such an opinion on the minds and feelings of such a people as ours," said John Jay – probably after he had already heard from his own wife.

After about a year Jay felt compelled to write about the situation, and Gouverneur Morris, who brought the letter to Paris early in 1789 along with one from Madison, added some vivid comments of his own. Madison reported rather more favorably after it was too late, but he now referred to this as a most unlucky appointment. Jefferson had already heard that Moustier's conduct had been politically and morally offensive; and he was convinced that something must be done, if the good feeling between the two countries was to continue. But the situation was so delicate that he resorted again to the invaluable mediation of Lafayette, who impressively presented the case to Montmorin. The net result was that Moustier was given leave to return to France, without the embarrassment of an actual recall, and that Jefferson himself was spared embarrassment by his own departure before the Count and Marchioness arrived in the fall of 1789.[37]

* * *

[37] Jefferson's relations with Moustier and, more particularly, with Madame de Bréhan are described with great understanding by Gilbert Chinard, in *Trois Amitiés Françaises de Jefferson*, ch. 2, where most of the letters relating to the episode are quoted fully or in part. Jay to TJ, Nov. 25, 1788 (from LC) is among these (p. 26). The more important of TJ's letters to Jay are: Feb. 1, 1787 (*D. C.*, II, 27); Oct. 8, 1787 (*D. C.*, II, 98); and Feb. 4, 1789 (*D. C.*, II, 271–273). See also Madison to TJ, Dec. 8, 1788 (Hunt, V, 312–313) and G. Morris, *Diary*, Nov. 25, 1789, telling of the arrival of Moustier and Madame de Bréhan in Paris the day before. Jefferson wrote the latter from Philadelphia, Dec. 3, 1790 (Chinard, pp. 57–58). The French authorities consulted Jefferson about the next appointment. They were already thinking of Colonel Ternant, whom he approved though he had some doubts; but the French had only a *chargé* in the United States when he himself got back, and Ternant did not arrive until after Jefferson had been more than a year Secretary of State.

The crowning achievement of Jefferson as a diplomat in France was his negotiation of a consular convention with that country. The significance of this document was twofold. It fulfilled, to the satisfaction of the French, a provision of the treaty of amity and commerce of 1778; and, at the same time, it parried a serious threat of extraterritoriality, thus serving to protect the independence of the American Republic against the nation which Jefferson continued to regard as her surest friend. John Jay's advice to Congress in this connection has been described as his most important diplomatic service to his country; but Jefferson was the instrument employed to effect ends which both these able and deeply patriotic men recognized as vital.[38]

The danger in the situation arose from a convention which Franklin had negotiated with Vergennes in 1784. This would have been considerably less reciprocal in practice than it was in form, and it granted to French consuls in the United States privileges and powers which were inconsistent with customary American court procedure and incompatible with the dignity of a sovereign state. In a time of fierce international rivalry they constituted a threat against genuine independence and even against national security. Jefferson never thought Franklin as gullible or Vergennes as unscrupulous as the more suspicious Jay did, but when his attention was called to these provisions he agreed without any hesitation that they would not do.

Fortunately, the convention of 1784 had not been accepted by Congress, who had authorized the negotiations a couple of years earlier and had then sent instructions, referred to as the "scheme" of 1782. Jay did not like even this. He believed that the true policy of America militated against such agreements, but since Congress had gone so far he thought they could not wholly withdraw. So the Secretary for Foreign Affairs condemned the convention as being at variance with the scheme, skillfully pointing out the variance, article by article, and showing beyond a shadow of doubt that the honorable Dr. Franklin had departed from his instructions.[39] He submitted all this to the wisdom of Congress, but that body did not hesitate to accept his judgment. Accordingly he sent to Jefferson the various documents, including his own able and elaborate report, and instructed him to propose that the convention be amended so as to correspond perfectly with the scheme, far from unexceptionable as that was, and also that the agreement be limited to eight or ten years' duration. "These papers will possess you fully of the whole business," he wrote. "I am

[38] Jay's services in this connection are admirably described by Bemis, *Secretaries*, I, 252–259.

[39] Analysis, July 4, 1786 (*D. C.*, I, 218–231).

persuaded that it will appear to you, as it does to Congress, to be a delicate one, and to require delicate management."[40]

Jefferson got his instructions while he was still suffering from his injured wrist, though now able to write with the proper hand, and shortly before he set out for the south of France. This trip would offer a sufficient pretext for delay, he thought, in a matter which was too difficult and too delicate to arouse sanguine hopes but for which he wanted a larger grant of powers, nonetheless. Like Jay, he disliked the scheme as well as the convention. Hence he wanted a statement of powers which did not mention the former and thus require him to produce it. Perhaps the French had forgotten it. Jay agreed and sent him a commission couched in general terms, assuring him at the same time that any convention that was no worse than the scheme and was limited in its duration would be ratified by Congress. Meanwhile, Congress had extended the term to twelve years, thus giving him more leeway. Jay also sent him a commission to serve three more years as minister. These and other documents did not reach him until the very end of the year, and there was sufficient reason why he did not enter into this difficult and delicate negotiation until the spring of 1788, but at that time it became his major piece of unfinished business.[41]

It was probably no disadvantage to him that the place of Vergennes was now filled by Montmorin. Jefferson told the Count personally that Congress desired changes in the convention that had been previously negotiated, and described these in general terms in an able and tactful letter.[42] After that, he negotiated chiefly with Rayneval, whom he found reasonable and friendly. The Office of Marine was also involved, since consuls and consulates were under its jurisdiction, and the necessary reference of questions to it at all stages protracted the negotiations. Delay was entirely characteristic of French official procedure but the fundamental difficulty, as Jefferson described it to Jay, was that the extensions of authority in the Convention of 1784 were "so homogeneous with the spirit of this Government that they were prized here."[43]

His own effort was to prevent the extension of immunities, privileges,

[40] Report of Jay and letter to TJ, Aug. 18, 1786 (*D. C.*, I, 232–234; quotation on p. 233).

[41] TJ to Jay, Jan. 9, 1787 (*D. C.*, II, 19–20); report of Jay to Congress, May 10, 1787, with drafts of letters (*D. C.*, II, 22–25); Jay to TJ, Oct. 24, 1787 (*D. C.*, II, 81); TJ to Jay, Nov. 14, 1788, stating that he received his powers on Dec. 19, 1787 (*D. C.*, II, 193).

[42] TJ to Montmorin, June 20, 1788 (*D. C.*, II, 168–173). This gives the best general statement of his position; but see also TJ to Rayneval, Sept. 16, 1788 (L. & B., VII, 142–143).

[43] TJ to Jay, Nov. 14, 1788 (*D. C.*, II, 194).

and powers to consuls, and to restrict these officials to matters of navigation and commerce. He presented the American case strongly but most tactfully. His country managed to get along very well without having consuls in the ports of other countries, he said, but the fact that the French government found them useful was sufficient reason to give them all the functions and facilities which American circumstances would permit. He said to Montmorin: "Instead, therefore, of declining every article which will be useless to us, we accede to every one which will not be inconvenient."[44] He wisely emphasized practicalities, showing that some provisions were unnecessary, that others were actually not in accord with the laws of France, that some – which he himself objected to on much more fundamental grounds – would be unenforceable because they were contrary to American domestic law and custom.

Afterwards, he expressed regret that he had not accomplished more, but said that "more could not be done with good humor." The extent of his own labors and the degree of his success were unmistakably revealed in his elaborate report, in the form of a long letter and annotated documents.[45] He had drafted a fresh "scheme" and submitted it to the French; they had answered it with another; he had replied with a third, and this brought them so close together that they could work out the final convention in a conference. The documents themselves told the story, and Jefferson summed up the principal changes in his letter. It is sufficient to say here that he got the privileges, immunities, and powers of consuls so reduced, and made these officials so amenable to the laws of the land, that only one feature of extraterritoriality remained. French consuls in America were given jurisdiction in civil cases arising there between French subjects, just as American consuls were given this authority in connection with American citizens in France.[46] This he had been unable to remove and it caused him some trouble later on. He got the convention limited to twelve years, however, and he submitted a translation which the French tacitly approved. To Americans the translation was in effect the convention, though the latter was actually signed only in French (August 14, 1788). To a degree which Vergennes would not have liked and which Montmorin probably had not originally intended, this was an agreement between equals.

[44] *D. C.*, II, 173. Since the return of Barclay to the United States, there were no consuls, but only agents.

[45] TJ to Jay, Nov. 14, 1788 (*D. C.*, II, 193–231).

[46] Art. XII of the Convention of Nov. 14, 1788. For comments on this by a modern authority, see Bemis, *Secretaries*, I, 258, and *Diplomatic Hist. of the U. S.* (1936), p. 83.

When John Jay got it, the feeble Congress of the Confederation had flickered out and the new government under the Constitution had not yet started, hence no formal action was possible. But he could write Jefferson: "The alterations in the Consular convention give satisfaction. . . . Your conduct is greatly and deservedly commended." [47] As things very happily turned out, it was the first treaty, except for some with Indian tribes, submitted by the new President to the new Senate. Jay, as Secretary for Foreign Affairs under the former Congress, reported on it by request. He said that the documents as submitted by Jefferson made the comparison between the conventions of 1784 and 1788 so clear that he himself need not make one; that the treaty negotiated by Jefferson was better than either the convention of 1784 or the scheme of 1782; that he expected more inconvenience than help to the country from this convention, but that the circumstances made its acceptance indispensable. He would have preferred no convention at all but obviously this was the best obtainable. By unanimous vote the Senate accepted his sound advice and ratified its first treaty. Through force of circumstances the exchange of ratifications was considerably delayed, but in one respect this was fortunate. When the convention which Jefferson had negotiated with such skill was formally proclaimed, it was attested by him as Secretary of State – the first holder of this office under the Constitution. Not merely may it be regarded as proof of his high technical competence; it was also a clear sign of his determination that the American Republic should fully maintain its sovereignty and independence against the influence and designs of France or any other nation.[48]

[47] Jay to TJ, Mar. 9, 1789 (*D. C.*, II, 259).

[48] Washington presented the Convention to the Senate on June 11, 1789. Jay's report of July 25, 1789, is in *D. C.*, I, 273–275. For the text of the treaty, the translation, and notes about ratifications, proclamation, etc., see Hunter Miller, ed., *Treaties and Other International Acts of the United States of America* (1931), II, 228–244. It was proclaimed Apr. 9, 1790.

[XI]

A Diplomat Awaits His Leave

1788–1789

AFTER he transmitted to America the consular convention he had negotiated, Jefferson, believing that he could do little more for his government in the near future, asked leave of absence for five or six months to go home.[1] One reason that he assigned was the need to attend to his business affairs, after an absence of five years from Monticello and his farms. Another was the desire to take his two daughters back to Virginia and leave them there. He wrote his sister-in-law that their future required that their return be postponed no longer, and that it would have occurred a year sooner if he had not wanted Polly to perfect herself in French.[2] This was the main reason, he said privately, but there could be no possible doubt that his finances required attention. Like his government he was suffering from the embarrassment of foreign debt which could be relieved only by realizing on domestic resources.

During his entire stay in France he relied on his salary, having allocated the profits of his lands to the payment of obligations that had been previously incurred. The largest of these were to two English houses and grew out of the debt with which his dead wife's inheritance had been encumbered. His original efforts to discharge this through the sale of lands were nullified by the depreciation of the currency of Virginia during the American Revolution, and in effect he had to pay it all over again; but, except for demurring against interest during the war years, he fully acknowledged his responsibility.[3] His concern about his financial situation was strongly expressed to Colonel

[1] TJ to Jay, Nov. 19, 1788 (*D. C.*, II, 234–236); to Madison, Nov. 18, 1788 (Ford, V, 54–55).

[2] TJ to Mrs. Francis Eppes, Dec. 15, 1788 (*Domestic Life*, p. 148).

[3] This complicated matter is discussed at some length in my *Jefferson the Virginian*, pp. 441–445. For the state of affairs at the time of his trip to England see TJ to Alex. McCaul, Apr. 19, 1786 (Ford, IV, 204).

Nicholas Lewis, who, along with his brother-in-law Francis Eppes, was managing Jefferson's affairs in his absence. After he had been three years in France he wrote:

> The torment of mind I endure till the moment shall arrive when I shall owe not a shilling on earth is such really as to render life of little value. I cannot decide to sell my lands. I have sold too much of them already, and they are the only sure provision for my children. Nor would I willingly sell the slaves as long as there remains any prospect of paying my debts with their labor.[4]

The profits from his crops proved smaller than he expected and, despite his careful and well-intentioned arrangements, he was able to pay little on his longstanding English debts during his stay in Europe. He thought seriously of renting his farms on his visit to Virginia, and expected to make arrangements for periodical payments with the local representatives of his English creditors.[5]

As we have already seen, he was also in debt for his outfit, which cost considerably more than a year's salary. The half-year's advance he had received at the outset did not cover this necessary expense and he hoped that his government would assume it. He took up the question vigorously with Jay and Madison (then in the Continental Congress) soon after he engaged in public financial operations in Amsterdam, but it was still pending when he left for home a year and a half later. He was afraid that Jay, who seemed strongly disposed toward economy and had not needed much of an outfit when in Europe since he was generally on the road, might not be sympathetic, and there are indications that the Secretary for Foreign Affairs was not wholly so at first. Furthermore, Jefferson was afraid that if the government under which he had incurred these expenses did not settle the claim the new government might think that it had been disallowed. But the old Congress did nothing – partly because of the general disinclination to make any avoidable expenditures and the desire to slide the matter over to the new government, partly because the Congress itself petered out before a committee could report. "Governments so constituted often find it difficult to act nobly," said Jay. The Secretary himself now thought that the government should be charged with Jefferson's extra expenses, despite the lack of warrant under the existing acts, strictly

[4] TJ to Nicholas Lewis, July 29, 1787 (LC, 5345–5346).

[5] Important additional references for this period are TJ to Alex. McCaul of Henderson, McCaul & Co., July 12, 1788 (LC, 6955–6956) and Aug. 3, 1789 (LC, 8602). He wrote J. Dodson, representing the less agreeable house of Farrell & Jones, Jan. 1, 1792 (MHS), that for seven years he had drawn nothing for his own use from the profits of his lands.

construed, because of the reasonableness and propriety of the claim. He said that he would speak to Washington and hoped that the next Congress would be less embarrassed. But it was not until Jefferson himself had been Secretary of State two years, and had established the policy of allowing ministers one year's salary for their outfits, that his own accounts were finally approved.[6]

His request for leave was made in November, though he did not want the leave to begin till spring. He allowed three months for travel, going and returning, two months for his stay at home, and one month's leeway. He hoped to fit the voyages into the interval between the two equinoxes and thus avoid stormy weather. Short could act in his absence, and if anything important should come up he himself would postpone his departure. He knew there were uncertainties in such matters, but, even before he wrote officially to John Jay, he notified the Comte de Langeac that his lease would expire in April.[7] Not until March, 1789, did Jay even write him, and that letter did not reach him until late July. Jay, still acting as foreign secretary, regarded his request as legitimate, but reminded him that there was no Congress to pass on it, nor anybody else with the necessary authority. He promised to submit the request to the new President as soon as he should be in office, and Jefferson himself had written Washington in the meantime.[8] He was constantly expecting his leave from the spring onward, but it did not come till August and he did not return till autumn. His personal life remained unsettled, but he ceased to mind this in the excitement of great events from May onward; and even if he had got his leave earlier he would not have wanted to depart from this engrossing scene.

The winter of 1788–1789 was so cold that Jefferson thought he must be in Siberia rather than Paris. This lover of sunshine exaggerated the rigors of the season, but unquestionably they were great, and there were rare sights on the Seine. Carriages crossed the river on the ice

[6] TJ to Madison, May 25, 1788 (Ford, V, 12–16); TJ to Jay, May 27, 1788 (*D. C.*, II, 160–163); Madison to TJ, Sept. 21, 1788 (Hunt, V, 266), and Oct. 17, 1788 (Hunt, V, 269); Jay to TJ, Nov. 25, 1788 (LC, 7591); *Journals Cont. Cong.*, XXXIV, 447, 494. According to his own note Congress, on July 1, 1790, passed a law, not retroactive, fixing the outfit of a minister as one year's salary, just as he had recommended (LC, 12253–12255). His own account with the U. S., 1784–1789 (LC, 2043–2067), was still unsettled at that date. His account of 1784–1792 (LC, 13215–13229), including one year's salary for his outfit, was sworn to July 9, 1792, and he appears to have been paid about that time.

[7] Oct. 10, 1788 (Account Book).

[8] John Jay to TJ, March 9, 1789 (*D. C.*, II, 259); TJ to Washington, Dec. 4, 1788 (Ford, V, 59).

and it was covered with people from morning till night, skating and sliding. But all was not jollity and winter sport. To a friend in the more fortunate clime of Virginia he wrote: "Great cold carries off men here, as it does cattle with us, and for the same reasons, the want of being housed and fed." As a very old man he remembered that the government kept great fires at the cross streets and that the people gathered round these in crowds to avoid perishing. It took a more cynical American, Gouverneur Morris, to observe that the people lived so close together in their little cabins that they could warm their own air. The continuing difficulty was the lack of food. Jefferson was fully aware that the distress for bread, lasting all summer, was a cause of discontent and increased the difficulties of a government that was already deeply embarrassed.[9]

He loathed cold and, during this very year, had an occasional fire even in the summer. He maintained his health while shivering through the winter, but for more than two months Patsy and Polly were ill – the latter seriously, he said, without describing the malady. They were recovered by February and able to make frequent excursions from the convent to the Hôtel de Langeac to be with their father, who was lonely in the continued absence of William Short, still traveling in the privileged climate of Italy. One Sunday in March, Gouverneur Morris dined with Jefferson *en famille*. Polly's friend Kitty Church had gone to England to join her mother, much improved by her association with the Jeffersons according to Angelica, but the sons of Crèvecœur and General Nathanael Greene were there, along with the author of the Declaration of Independence and the man who had put the finishing touches on the new American Constitution. Gouverneur Morris had come to Paris partly on tobacco business for Robert Morris, whose monopolistic contract with the Farmers-General had not been liked by Jefferson, and this gallant with wooden leg and witty tongue was more a man for the salon or boudoir than a family table, but everything was very friendly in this generous atmosphere.[10]

Jefferson was then expecting hourly his permission to return to America, although Morris, who had arrived early in February with numerous letters, including one of introduction from George Wash-

[9] TJ to Nicholas Lewis, Dec. 16, 1788 (LC, 7717); TJ to Madame de Bréhan, Mar. 14, 1789 (Chinard, *Trois Amitiés*, p. 54); Gouverneur Morris to his brother, Mar. 11, 1789 (*Diary*, I, xliv). TJ mentioned the extreme cold in many other letters, as to F. Hopkinson, Jan. 11, 1789 (LC, 7727), and described it vividly in his autobiography (Ford, I, 122–123). His contemporary record of the temperature, however, does not fully support the memories of old age. (See back of Account Book for 1783–1790, in MHS.)

[10] Mar. 8, 1789 (Morris, *Diary*, I, 8); Angelica Church to TJ, Nov. 19, 1788 (LC, 7567).

ington, must have already told him that he could hardly expect any official action during the virtual interregnum in the American government. Before he got any sort of response from Jay he had written a score of unanswered letters, though he did not write many of them in the spring. "This country being generally engaged in its elections, affords nothing new and worthy of communication," he said.[11] New things had begun to happen when he wrote George Washington again in May, but even then he thought that as a minister he could easily be spared, since there was certain to be no war and the French government was too absorbed in domestic matters to deal with foreign. He was still hoping that he could make his voyage to the States and back during the interval between the equinoxes, and thus avoid shivering at sea in a dreadful winter passage, and he had inquired about vessels in various ports which might be bound for America, in order that he could be ready to sail on a week's notice.[12]

Meanwhile, he had been forced to renew the lease on his house.[13] By now a new wall had been built around Paris by the Farmers General, the Grille de Chaillot had been pulled down, and a new city gate had been installed farther out on the Champs-Élysées. Jefferson did not wholly like the wall, and robbers got into his house three times after the removal of the customs house from his immediate vicinity, causing him to need new silver candlesticks. Previously the customs officials had served in some sense as guards.[14]

Beginning in late April his daughters were regular members of his establishment, for he then removed them from the Abbaye de Panthémont. According to a family tradition the immediate occasion for this action was an impulsive letter to him from Martha, then in her seventeenth year, saying that she desired to become a nun. If his immature daughter did write such a letter it was just the sort of intimate personal record he would have wanted to keep from prying eyes and would have destroyed. The mere existence of the tradition is an argument that there is some degree of truthfulness in the story, but he might easily have withdrawn the girls from the convent at this time for other reasons. He believed that soon they would be going home. Their

[11] TJ to Jay, Mar. 12, 1789 (*D. C.*, II, 276); TJ to Jay, July 19, 1789 (*D. C.*, II, 303). He did not hear from Jay from Feb. 4, 1789, when Morris arrived, till July 28.

[12] TJ to Washington, May 10, 1789 (Ford, V, 95–96); several letters to American agents, Apr. 12, 1789 (LC, 8229–8233).

[13] Account Book, Apr. 14, 1789. He then repaid the banker Grand for a payment made on Apr. 2, to Langeac for the first and last half years of a new lease. In the end he paid rent till July 15, 1790.

[14] TJ to Montmorin, July 8, 1789 (L. & B., VII, 402); TJ to John Trumbull, Aug. 5, 1789 (LC, 8614–8615).

leaving school did not mean that their education was wholly disrupted, for he kept on paying for Spanish lessons for Polly and for harpsichord lessons from the noted Balbastre for them both. Martha now became more expensive in the matter of clothes, but there is no indication that she was launched as a young lady into conventional society in Paris, as has been said. Her father's low opinion of that was one of his important reasons for wanting to take her home.[15]

To Gouverneur Morris, a bachelor who was by no means averse to intrigue with fashionable French ladies, Jefferson was rather too much a family man, seeming to prefer the companionship of his immature daughters in the evening to the company of a man of the world who was engaged also in matters of important private business.[16] Morris was by no means unappreciative of the kindness and hospitality which the Minister showed him that spring, and he noted that Jefferson commanded in France the great respect which was merited by his good sense and good intentions. But there was a certain condescension in some of the judgments he finally arrived at, and this cannot be wholly explained on grounds of later political difference. He said: "The French, who pique themselves on possessing the graces, very readily excuse in others the want of them; and to be an *Étranger* (like Charity) covers a multitude of sins. On the whole therefore I incline to think that an American Minister at this Court gains more than he loses by preserving his originality." [17] In view of Jefferson's cultivation and accomplishments and his unusual amiability, the "graces" which he lacked could only have been social graces in the conventional and artificial sense, and his "originality" must have partly consisted in his disinclination to flit from drawing room to drawing room. Madame de Flahaut, with whom Morris intrigued, had little inkling of the real man from her external view, but William Short, John Paradise, and John Trumbull trusted him implicitly and knew what genius he had for friendship.[18]

His secretary was flooding him with letters, describing the sights

[15] The conventional story is in Randall, I, 538–539, and *Domestic Life*, p. 146. According to this, neither father nor daughter ever mentioned the matter again to each other, though she spoke of it to her own children in later life. His account book shows that TJ paid his account at Panthémont in full on Apr. 20, 1789, and gave money to Patsy for parting gifts there on Apr. 22. Payments for various lessons, clothes, etc., are shown by later items.

[16] On Apr. 3, 1789, he wrote: "Call on Mr. Jefferson and sit an Hour with him which is at least fifty Minutes too long, for his Daughters had left the Room on my Approach and wait only my Departure to return, at least I think so." (*Diary*, I, 29.)

[17] G. Morris to Robt. Morris, July 21, 1789 (*Diary*, I, 159 *n*).

[18] See the comment of Madame de Flahaut to Morris, after seeing Jefferson: "*Cet homme est faux et emporté.*" Entry of Morris, Oct. 12, 1789 (*Diary*, I, 256).

he saw and swearing "unutterable attachment" to him. Short had visited the Paradises at the home of their daughter, the Countess Barziza, at Bergamo not far from Milan, and had left them in a relatively calm state of mind; but the lady afterwards flew into a passion against her hopelessly impractical husband, and the mad pair came back to Paris in the depths of winter. Lucy, obviously adoring Jefferson, was determined on a separation from John, while both were counting on the long-suffering Virginian to straighten out their finances if anybody could. He struggled with these throughout the rest of his stay in France, ably abetted by Dr. Edward Bancroft in London. (It was not known then as it is now that Bancroft, formerly of Massachusetts, was in the secret employ of the British and actually a traitor to his own country. By his patience, kindness, and generosity to the unhappy Paradises he gained a measure of eternal credit, nonetheless.) Jefferson managed to get Lucy back to England at his own expense, while John, who might have been arrested for debt in London, remained in Paris, drinking too much and showing more incompetence than ever. Jefferson, who both liked and pitied him, was offering to take him back to Virginia and give him a home until all his debts were paid, meanwhile advancing money to him which he had expected to apply to his own obligations.[19]

Jefferson informed Short about the Paradises while sending lists of deaths and births in Virginia, recently received from home, and reports of the latest election returns in America – showing at the same time his desire that genuine friends of the new Constitution should be chosen.[20] But there were much more pressing personal questions connected with his projected visit to the States to be discussed with his secretary, who was now in an exceedingly uncertain state of mind about his own future. Would Short stay in France until Jefferson got back? What did he plan to do eventually? The first question was easily answered by Short in the affirmative, for even if he had not preferred to remain a while longer it would have been sufficient that his patron wished it. The long-range question was more difficult, but Jefferson, thinking like a father for his son, concluded that the best course for Short was to return to America after he himself got back to Paris.

He was arguing against his own interest, he said. "For affection and the long habit of your society have rendered it necessary to me. And how much more so will it be when I have parted with my daughters?" The dreariness of the prospect filled him with dismay, for he was a

[19] Full details in Shepperson, *Paradise and Ludwell*, esp. ch. XV.
[20] TJ to Short, Feb. 9, 1789 (LC, 7956–7959; part in Ford, V, 70–72).

deeply sentimental parent and friend, who depended on intimate relationships like these for personal happiness. But he saw no future in Short's continued diplomatic service abroad. The salary would be insufficient to support a wife, and quite obviously he did not want Short to remain as a bachelor in Paris. He strongly recommended marriage on general principles, but at the moment no doubt he was thinking of Short's incipient romance with Rosalie, the young wife of his friend La Rochefoucauld, from which he could foresee no fruit but bitterness. Age was counseling youth, but this champion of an agricultural society was also harping on his old theme after reflecting further on the vain and fleeting pleasures of Paris. After Short had been a little while at home he would realize that the happiness of his own country was "more tranquil, more unmixed, more permanent." . . . What should he do in America? . . . He could serve his country in honorable public station or could return to the bar, where he would soon be without rival, and make money.

Jefferson's statement of the prospects was optimistic on the whole, but Short, while very grateful for it, remained unpersuaded. He could not return to the bar, hating its drudgery as he did, and the public prospect at home did not seem flattering. Hence his only decision was to continue in France for a time and remain undecided. In later years he discussed his affairs with his patron in interminable letters and sought his counsel almost pathetically, but the net result was never what Jefferson hoped for the most cherished of his young friends. Short did stay in the diplomatic service, and, through fault of circumstance rather than lack of merit, in minor positions insufficient to support a wife. He remained in the allurements of Parisian life and saw his romance with Rosalie blossom without gaining from it any permanence of happiness. When he finally did go back to America, much later than Jefferson had recommended, he did make a fortune; but this was not by the drudgery of the law and is quite another story.[21]

Meanwhile Jefferson, still uncertain what Short would finally decide to do but still hoping that he would seek permanent happiness in America, turned his mind to another secretarial possibility. John Trumbull stood next to Short in his affections among his young men and had been carrying out all sorts of commissions for him in England. Some of these were connected with his own projected voyage and some are distinctly interesting in themselves.

For months Trumbull had been trying to get a carriage for him. He

[21] The most important letters about Short's future are TJ to Short, Mar. 24, 1789 (LC, 8165–8168), the source of the quotations; and Short to TJ from Marseilles, Apr. 3, 1789 (LC, 8204–8205).

wanted to take this home with him and leave it for his daughters, getting another for himself on his return, and had sent precise instructions, as usual. Being intended for rough American roads, it should not be so high that it would overturn easily, hence he wanted it to be hung halfway between the old fashion and the new. It finally arrived in February and cost more than a hundred pounds, but he did not take it with him when he sailed.[22]

Commissions for busts and pictures were more in Trumbull's line, though Jefferson also availed himself of the services of Philip Mazzei in this connection. For his historical collection Mazzei got from Florence copies of portraits of Columbus, Americus Vespucius, Cortez, and Magellan that were in the Grand Duke's gallery. But besides a portrait of himself, Jefferson had Trumbull to thank for one of Thomas Paine, which he regarded as a perfect likeness.[23]

His instructions to Trumbull for the procurement of busts and pictures were so numerous that no one can easily keep them straight after a century and a half, and by February he had decided to put all of them off until after he got back from America—with one most interesting exception: he wanted life-sized busts of Bacon, Locke, and Newton copied for him in a picture. He regarded these "as the three greatest men that have ever lived, without any exception, and as having laid the foundation of those superstructures which have been raised in the physical and moral sciences." For this reason he wanted to put them together on one large canvas, and he sent a design showing a possible arrangement of three ovals. Trumbull did not like the idea and recommended three pictures of the same size to be hung together. Jefferson's artistic taste was not impeccable but he was still an ardent disciple of the Enlightenment.[24]

It was in May, 1789—after the Estates-General had assembled and after Trumbull had bought for him a strong traveling trunk covered with black leather—that Jefferson made Trumbull the offer of the secretaryship, contingent on Short's return to America after Jefferson himself came back to France. Lodging and board would go with the position as heretofore, and he believed that the work, consisting mostly of copying papers, would not really interfere with Trumbull's artistic pursuits. This was actually the crux of the matter in the young painter's

[22] The carriage is most fully described in TJ to Trumbull, Aug. 24, 1788 (LC, 7191), and Trumbull to TJ, Sept. 2, 1788 (LC, 7245). The arrival is reported in TJ to Trumbull, Feb. 5, 1789 (LC, 7951).

[23] TJ to Trumbull, Jan. 12, 1789 (LC, 7858).

[24] Trumbull to TJ, Feb. 5, 1789 (LC, 7952); TJ to Trumbull, Feb. 15, 1789 (LC, 7988); Trumbull to TJ, Mar. 10, 1789 (LC, 8064). TJ afterwards showed these pictures to Hamilton (Ford, IX, 296).

mind. If it would be consistent with his "great pursuits" no situation could be so agreeable as one which would place him near Jefferson, under the protection of his advice and example. But he did not agree that Short ought to go home, and all he was sure about in his own case was that he wanted to quit England as soon as possible, since it had become a most unpleasant place for an American. Jefferson encouraged him about the noble art which he professed so eminently, while doubting if his own country was yet rich enough to encourage him as he deserved, and left the secretarial question open. Meanwhile, he told his young friend that as long as he himself remained in any office he preferred the present one. He had recently given the reason to a friend in Philadelphia. "My great wish is to go on in a strict but silent performance of my duty," he said; "to avoid attracting notice and to keep my name out of the newspapers, because I find the pain of a little censure, even when it is unfounded, is more acute than the pleasure of much praise. The attaching circumstance of my present office is that I can do its duties unseen by those for whom they are done." [25]

The duties of that office, as he interpreted them, also involved a continuous exercise of hospitality to Americans who chanced to be in Paris, but this was more a pleasure than an obligation, and he always tried to keep argument and contention away from the board he spread so bountifully. "Mr. Jefferson lives well," said Gouverneur Morris, "keeps a good table and excellent wines which he distributes freely and by his hospitality to his countrymen here possesses very much their good will." On July 4, 1789, he gave a dinner to them which was attended by Morris and the Lafayettes. He had done the same thing the year before; but this was a more memorable occasion, not merely because it preceded the fall of the Bastille by only ten days, but also because it was regarded as a leave-taking party. Morris took this occasion to urge upon the Marquis the importance of preserving some constitutional authority to the nobles, against whom the current was now so strongly setting, and for reasons of his own declined to sign the congratulatory address which was presented to the host that day. But eight Americans – including Joel Barlow, Philip Mazzei, John Paradise, and several men of business – attached their signatures to the paper which the scholarly, liberal, and patriotic, if financially impractical, Paradise must have drawn. Joining the "general voice" of

[25] Quotation from a letter to F. Hopkinson, in which he described his aloofness from American parties, Mar. 13, 1789 (Ford, V, 78). The discussion with Trumbull was carried on chiefly in the following letters: TJ to Trumbull, May 21, 1789 (LC, 8367, 8387); Trumbull to TJ, May 26, 1789 (LC, 8376); TJ to Trumbull, June 1, 1789 (LC, 8384); Trumbull to TJ, June 11, 1789 (*Autobiography*, pp. 157–159); TJ to Trumbull, June 18, 1789 (LC, 8440).

their country and their age, they paid their tribute to "a compatriot so distinguished for his exertions in favour of that country and for the general happiness of mankind," while thanking him for his kindness to every American who had fallen in his way.

There can be little doubt that they were voicing the general opinion, both at home and abroad, and none whatever that Jefferson's letter of thanks was in character. The society of his countrymen had been very dear to him, he said, and he was happy if he had given content in this little family, but he had no claims on his country for any good he had done. Zeal he had had without measure, but who could lack zeal for such a government as theirs. "My little transactions are not made for public detail," he said. "They are best in the shade. The light of the picture is justly occupied by others. To glide unnoticed through a silent execution of duty, is the only avocation which becomes me, and it is the sincere desire of my heart." [26]

The day before the dinner this modest public servant had paid the sculptor Houdon 1000 livres for busts made for him, presumably plaster models. He already had one of John Paul Jones from the same artist, and afterwards at Monticello he had Washington, Franklin, Voltaire, and others. A bust of himself, made by Houdon that year, was probably included.[27] This representation of the Jefferson of the French Revolution is one of the noblest ever made of him. The mouth is firm, the gaze straightforward, the nose finely molded, and the general impression is one of calm, benevolence, and strength. The sculptor caught him in a moment of elevation, as he so easily could have in these last months in France, and translated his serenity of spirit into enduring form.[28]

[26] Morris refers to the dinner, July 4, 1789, in his *Diary*, I, 134; to the address on June 30 (*ibid.*, I, 127–128); to Jefferson's hospitality in his letter to Robert Morris, July 21 (*ibid.*, I, 159*n*). The address itself is printed in Shepperson, *Paradise and Ludwell*, pp. 382–384 (from LC, 8488–8490). Jefferson thanked Paradise for it, July 5, 1789 (LC, 8491).

[27] Account Book, July 3, 1789. See the illuminating discussion by Fiske Kimball in his "Life Portraits of Jefferson and their Replicas," *Procs. Am. Philos. Soc.*, vol. 88, pp. 505–506. Apparently there were several replicas.

[28] The comments here are based on the plaster in the N. Y. Hist. Soc., which is reproduced in this volume by their courtesy, not on the one in the Am. Philosophical Soc., which has had to be repaired. The marble in the Boston Museum of Fine Arts is even more impressive, but Kimball has questioned the history of this somewhat and probably the face is more finely molded than Jefferson's was in life.

XII

Revolution Begins and a Mission Ends

1789

WHEN the Estates-General met in May, 1789, the benevolent and modest man who represented the United States in France viewed the prospects of human liberty and happiness with calm optimism. Early in the year, for the benefit of a kindred spirit in England, Jefferson had summed up the situation as follows:

> Upon the whole, it has appeared to me that the basis of the present struggle is an illumination of the human mind as to the rights of the nation, aided by fortunate incidents; that they can never retrograde, but from the natural progress of things, must press forward to the establishment of a constitution which shall assure to them a good degree of liberty.[1]

As an observant man and an experienced statesman, he clearly perceived difficulties, just as he had noted "fortunate incidents," but he expected natural progress to continue. His faith was not that of a doctrinaire revolutionary, but of an enlightened liberal.

The older man in England, Dr. Richard Price, was equally interested in the progress of civil and religious liberty, and likewise rejoiced in the probability that France would acquire a free constitution of government. He realized that the French were at a disadvantage in having no such body of freeholders and respectable yeomanry as existed in England and America, but, like Jefferson, he saw vast ground for encouragement and hope. "Being now advanced into the evening of life," he said, "it is with particular gratitude I look back and reflect that I have been spared to see the human species improved, religious intolerance almost extinguished, the eyes of the lower ranks of men opened to see their rights, and nations panting for liberty that seemed

[1] TJ to Richard Price, Jan. 8, 1789 (L. & B., VII, 258).

to have lost the idea of it." And he wished that the American who so fully shared his feeling might be long continued "to contribute toward this growing improvement of the world."[2]

This letter was written on the very day that the Estates-General assembled, and it was brought to Jefferson by Dugald Stewart, a young Scottish philosopher of the "common sense" school. The two men were intimately associated during the next few weeks, and the Scotsman sent the American a copy of his first book a few years later. Jefferson, who had condemned the romantic French naturalists for letting their theories and generalizations run beyond their scientific evidence, liked Stewart's way of thinking. Jefferson also believed that philosophy had no meaning unless it was linked with life. The unfolding events in Versailles and Paris constituted for him far more than a colorful drama. Nowhere else except in America had there been such a chance for a philosophical revolution, such an opportunity to apply liberated intelligence to the political organization of a nation. But it was only in personal relations that he could afford to be a sentimentalist, and he viewed this changing scene as no romanticist. He dared believe that ancient barriers to the onward march of the human spirit would be permanently broken down, but he continued to advocate gradualism in political processes, and in a time of intense excitement maintained his balance and exercised his common sense.[3]

He did not report and may not have seen the magnificent assemblage and procession at Versailles on May 4, 1789 — when King and courtiers, nobles, clergy, and commoners, passed through the streets to the Church of Saint-Louis, displaying in their costumes the sharp distinction and disparity between the three orders of the Kingdom; but he witnessed the august ceremony of the opening session of the Estates-General next day. "Had it been enlightened with lamps and chandeliers," he said, "it would have been almost as brilliant as the opera."[4] Unlike Gouverneur Morris, he left no vivid diary; and in his letters to John Jay and other public men he did not waste his time describing pageantry.[5] But he went to Versailles almost every day during the sum-

[2] Price to TJ, May 4, 1789 (LC, 8282–8283), received May 12.

[3] On his associations with Stewart, see TJ to Adams, Mar. 14, 1820 (L. & B., XV, 239–240); TJ to Stewart, Apr. 26, 1824 (*M.H.S.*, 333–334). On their congeniality in philosophy see Koch, *Philosophy of Jefferson*, 48–53. He made a striking statement of his impatience with the "romanticism" of so-called "French philosophers," especially the naturalists, in a letter to John Rutledge, Jr., Sept. 9, 1788 (LC, 7266–7267).

[4] TJ to Crèvecœur, May 20, 1789 (L. & B., VII, 367).

[5] Morris's bright description of the spectacle is in his *Diary*, I, 67–70. TJ offered him the ticket Madame de Tessé had been saving for her favorite William Short, who did not get back from his trip in time, but Morris went independently.

mer, reported events with care, and made illuminating comments on men and issues. He told a story which was fresh to him and to his correspondents, but there is neither space nor need to retell it here. We are chiefly concerned with the attitudes he took and with any personal part he may have played in these momentous events.[6]

The phase of the Revolution of 1789 that was marked by the victory of the Third Estate over the clergy and nobility, late in June, has been called "the bourgeois revolution," in distinction from the aristocratic revolt against the King which preceded it and the popular uprising which followed. It has also been described as a "juridical revolution." [7] Jefferson spoke of the bourgeoisie occasionally that summer, and recognized its leadership; but his own tie with the Patriot party was in the persons of Lafayette and other liberal noblemen, more than in those of lawyers and commercial men in Paris; and when he spoke of "the people," as he often did, he was not thinking narrowly of the economic interests of the bourgeois class. He was far more impressed by the emphasis of this group on progress and the general advancement of humanity, which was so like his own, than by the concern of the bourgeois element to secure power for itself. Hence he would have preferred the term "juridical revolution." To him this was a continuation, in faster tempo, of the constitutional reformation which had already begun. He was much impressed by its orderliness, and his chief fear was that it would proceed too fast and lead to repression and disorder, in the course of which the great gains already made might be lost.

The first major controversy arose over a question of organization, involving the larger question of the distribution of political power. The Third Estate, representing some nineteen twentieths of the population though dominated by the bourgeois, had been allowed as many deputies as the clergy and nobility combined, but this was of no advantage to the popular interest so long as the three estates met separately and thus voted by orders and not by persons. Jefferson's sympathies being with the popular interest, he sided with the Third Estate in this famous struggle, and blamed the impasse on the nobility, as historians have so generally done. The "progress of light and liberty" among the aristocrats had not come up to expectations, he said, and thus a revolution which had gone on hitherto with unexampled quietness, steadiness, and progress now faced a serious check and began to

[6] His contemporary letters are a fuller and more trustworthy source than the account in his autobiography (Ford, I, 125–147), written in old age, even though he reread copies of his more important letters before writing it.

[7] Lefebvre, *Coming of the French Revolution*, esp. p. 89.

wear a fearful appearance.[8] His role was that of a deeply interested observer, and he was nearly always careful of diplomatic proprieties, but he did not hesitate to give private counsel to Lafayette in this situation.

He was very uneasy about his friend, whose political sentiments were so like his own but who, as a deputy of the *noblesse* of Auvergne, was bound by instructions to support the vote by orders. Believing that Lafayette could not continue to sacrifice his principles to the prejudices of the nobility, he was sure that he would ultimately have to go over to the Third Estate, and for the sake of Lafayette's standing with the people Jefferson hoped his young friend would not delay too long. Thus he encouraged the Marquis to follow his conscience and disregard his embarrassing instructions, though he did not really press him to burn them, as he stated in his rather too colorful report to George Washington.[9] In fact he suggested that Lafayette first try to effect a compromise agreement – whereby the privileged classes would be placed together in one House and the unprivileged in another. Jefferson thought this preferable to a "scission." He doubted if a body of 1200 men could be effective, preferred a bicameral legislature anyway, and was still willing for France to follow the model of England with her Lords and Commons. If this conciliatory plan should fail, however, he thought Lafayette would certainly be justified in ditching his instructions.

If he hoped to convince Lafayette that instructions were not laws of conduct he was unsuccessful, for that troubled aristocrat proved to be more scrupulous in this respect than most of the other members of the small liberal minority among the nobles, and did not join the Third Estate until the King himself ordered it some seven weeks later, after a number of other exceedingly important things had happened. Jefferson had declined to advise him further in this matter. On June 12, apparently in response to a direct inquiry, he wrote: "With respect to the utility, or inutility of your minority's joining the Commons, I am unable to form an opinion for myself." [10] This was after a final invitation to the nobles and clergy had been issued by the Third Estate, and the rage of Lafayette's colleagues had made the situation even more critical for him. Jefferson did not care to assume any responsibility, but perhaps there was something more than polite evasion in his statement that he was now uncertain in his own mind.

[8] See especially TJ to Jay, May 9, 1789 (*D. C.*, II, 286–288). I have also drawn directly on TJ to Adams, May 10, 1789 (LC, 8320–8321).

[9] TJ to Lafayette, May 6, 1789 (Ford, V, 91–93); TJ to Washington, May 10, 1789 (Ford, V, 96).

[10] TJ to Lafayette, June 12, 1789 (L. & B., VII, 374).

His moderation and his concern for concord among the warring groups had already been shown in a document which would hardly have been expected from one who had denounced monarchy to his own countrymen and defied George III in the Declaration of Independence. It was a draft of a charter, containing "all the good in which all parties agree." He hoped the King might be induced to bring this forward in his hand at a *séance royale*, and that the representatives of all the orders would be willing to sign it. Then they were all to go home and cool off before reassembling for another meeting.[11]

He was alarmed by the state of affairs — fundamentally because of the danger that force would be used in behalf of the privileged classes, but more immediately because conferences between committees representing the three orders had broken down, though the King wanted them to be renewed. The difficulties in the situation were the subject of a conversation with Lafayette and Rabaut de Saint-Étienne, a deputy of the Third Estate and Protestant champion of religious freedom. This was on June 2, presumably at Versailles, and William Short, now back, was also there. The idea that the King in a royal session should come forward with a document which all could sign appears to have been Jefferson's and he thus described it to Saint-Étienne:

> This charter to contain the five great points which the Resultat of December offered on the part of the King, the abolition of pecuniary privileges offered by the privileged orders, & the adoption of the National debt and a grant of the sum of money asked from the nation. This last will be a cheap price for the preceding articles, and let the same act declare your immediate separation till the next anniversary meeting. You will carry back to your constituents more good than ever was effected before without violence, and you will stop exactly at the point where violence would otherwise begin.[12]

[11] The circumstances of this episode were rather different from those which Jefferson connected with it in the autobiography he wrote in old age, though the spirit in which he acted was well described there. From his later account (Ford, I, 127–130), one would suppose that the date of the "immediate compromise" suggested by him was between June 20–22, and that it was to be announced and accepted at the royal session which actually occurred on June 23. But his "Charter of Rights" was sent to Lafayette and Rabaut de Saint-Étienne on June 3, 1789 (Ford, V, 99–102). It appears to have been connected immediately with the proposal of the King on May 28 that conferences between committees representing the three orders be resumed. Conferences of May 23–27, agreed to by the Third Estate on motion of Saint-Étienne, had proved futile. (See Lefebvre, *The Coming of the French Revolution*, pp. 79–80.) The error of twenty days on TJ's part may be attributed to the imperfect eyesight of an old man, looking at an old document, and to the inaccuracy of his memory after more than thirty years.

[12] TJ to Saint-Étienne, June 3, 1789 (Ford, V, 100).

More specifically, the Charter included provisions for the annual meeting of the Estates-General on November 1, for its control over taxes and appropriations, for legislative power with the consent of the King, along with guarantees of personal liberty and freedom of the press, the renunciation of aristocratic financial privileges, the assumption of the national debt, and a grant of eighty million livres to the King to be raised by loan, taxes being continued as at present to the end of the year. Actually, there was little here that the King did not offer three weeks later. Furthermore, since the question of vote by orders or by persons was left unsettled, along with that of the opening of offices to all classes, this document would not have established equality of rights – even between the two privileged groups and the bourgeoisie. The leaders of the National Assembly could not have agreed to a constitutional monarchy of this sort, and at this time Jefferson appeared more conservative than they.

On the very day that Jefferson sent off his draft of a charter, implying by the act that he retained some hope of concord, Gouverneur Morris noted the discouragement of his fellow American about the Estates-General. "This comes from having too sanguine expectations of a downright republican form of government," he said.[13] The situation became much more critical within the next two weeks and the political differences between these two men became obvious, but Morris stated his own position more accurately than he did that of Jefferson. He wanted the King to intervene in support of the privileged orders, while Jefferson wanted France to move toward the goal of equality before the law, but the foe of entails and primogeniture in Virginia had not yet advocated the annihilation of all distinctions of class in the ancient society of France, much as he disliked them on philosophical and humane grounds.[14] As a statesman he would have preferred to postpone that issue, but when the commoners threw down the gauntlet, there was no possible doubt in his mind that the King should support their political claims against the obstructive aristocrats.

The issue was forced by the announced determination of the Third Estate to proceed to legislate for the country, without the nobles and clergy if these orders would not join them, and the assumption on June 17 of the name "National Assembly." Jefferson listened to most of the debates on that fateful day and reported the critical situation to John Jay.[15] "The fate of the nation depends on the conduct of the

[13] June 3, 1789 (Morris, *Diary*, I, 104).
[14] June 12, 1789 (Morris, *Diary*, I, 113).
[15] TJ to Jay, June 17, 1789 (*D. C.*, II, 291–293).

King and his Ministers," he said. "Were they to side openly with the Commons, the revolution would be completed without a convulsion by the establishment of a constitution totally free, and in which the distinction of Noble and Commoner would be suppressed." But he did not think the event likely. "The King is honest, and wishes the good of his people," he continued; "but the expediency of an hereditary aristocracy is too difficult a question for him. On the contrary, his prejudices, his habits, and his connexions decide him in his heart to support it." If the King should side openly with the nobility, the result would be bankruptcy and probably civil war, but Jefferson thought this issue unlikely, also. The Queen and Princes would hazard it but the Ministry, particularly Necker, would not. Hence he thought it probable that the lower clergy and liberal nobles would join the commoners and proceed to draft a constitution; but he could see no hope for agreement between all groups except possibly in the provision for two houses of the legislature, one of which would be given to the privileged group, as in England.

He would have been more hopeful in this time of dangerously threatening weather if he had had more confidence in Necker as helmsman of the ship of state. In ability he thought the Chief Minister far below his reputation, and in policy wavering and temporizing.[16] In comparison with the Court Junto, however, and with certain high aristocrats among the ministers, he was complimentary to Necker, Montmorin, and Saint-Priest, and continued to think that they exercised the best influence upon the King – whom, until his own dying day, he regarded as a good, honest, and personally unambitious man. "The resolutions of the morning formed under their advice, would be reversed in the evening by the advice of the Queen and Court," he said a generation later. He even said, with the literary exaggeration he sometimes indulged in, that there would have been no revolution had there been no Queen.[17]

What encouraged him most at this stage was the ability and character of the men in the National Assembly. Writing to another experienced legislator, James Madison, he commented on the talents, the firmness, and the moderation of these commoners – most of them lawyers, though he did not call them bourgeois.[18] There were hotheaded members, to be sure, but the most influential ones were "cool,

[16] With his letter of June 17, 1789, to Jay, he sent a sketch of Necker, drawn by an acquaintance who did not like him but which TJ himself thought essentially correct. The best thing said about him was that he was a far less mischievous minister than his predecessors (*D. C.*, II, 294–296).

[17] Autobiography (Ford, I, 122, 140).

[18] TJ to Madison, June 18, 1789 (L. & B., VII, 388–389).

temperate, and sagacious," and he was now willing to say that all their steps had been marked with caution and wisdom. If trouble was brewing, and he thought it was, the major fault lay with the majority group among the nobles, men of very moderate ability on the whole, and now so out of their senses with rage that they had become incapable of debate. Their proceedings had been most injudicious, in his opinion, while he thought the higher clergy wholly guided by self-interest. The lesser clergy were of the people and fundamentally sympathetic with them, but he believed that the bishops and archbishops, jealously guarding their own privileges, had done their best to beguile them from their natural attachment to the Commons.

He had had his baggage ready for a month when the Third Estate constituted itself the National Assembly. After that, things began to happen faster and he made it his business to go to Versailles practically every day. He duly reported the threat of force against the Assembly, leading to the famous Oath of the Tennis Court, that bound the members not to separate, and the royal session of June 23 at Marly. Despite the moderate proposals which he himself had made, the speech and declaration of the King now seemed to him a surrender to the aristocracy against the wishes of Necker and Montmorin at the behest of the Court.[19] The concessions which Louis XVI offered, amounting to the acceptance of the status of a constitutional monarch, along with guarantees of personal freedom and promises of equality in taxation, apparently impressed him no more than they did the members of the Assembly, who had refused to disperse. The bourgeois realized that all this was to fall within the framework of the old system of aristocratic pre-eminence, whereas they were now struggling openly for equality of rights. "Instead of being dismayed with what had passed, they seem to rise in their demands," Jefferson noted, "and some of them to consider the erasing every vestige of a difference of order, as indispensable to the establishment and preservation of a good Constitution."[20] He himself thought, however, there was "more courage than calculation" in the latter project, and despite the philosophical differences between him and Morris he would have agreed with the latter's prophecy to Lafayette that if the Third were now very moderate they would probably succeed, but if violent must fail.[21]

To Jefferson it seemed that the triumph of the National Assembly on June 27 – when at the command of the King the two privileged

[19] TJ to Jay, June 24, 1789, postscript June 25 (*D. C.*, II, 297–301. Morris's comment of June 23 (*Diary*, I, 121), that the nobility had less cause for exultation than they imagined, is illuminating, though he did not have a full report.

[20] *D. C.*, II, 300.

[21] June 23, 1789 (Morris, *Diary*, I, 121).

orders joined that body — was owing to the popular indignation aroused by the royal session and the resulting disaffection of the soldiers. The King and the Court were scared. But in Versailles and Paris the people were now joyous, and the triumph of the Third Estate seemed to be complete. It remained to be seen whether they would leave the nobility anything beyond titles, and he supposed they would not. He wrote John Jay: "This great crisis being now over, I shall not have matter interesting enough to trouble you with as often as I have done lately."[22]

Before he wrote Jay again he had found out that the majority of the aristocrats were quite unwilling to accept this settlement, and had brought irresistible pressure to bear on the irresolute King, who still had some troops at his command, including foreign mercenaries. The resulting threat of royal force, which excited the fears of the Parisians to fever pitch, led to an uprising in the city and ushered the Revolution into a new phase. Three days before Bastille Day, however, the philosophical and optimistic American believed that the Assembly was "in complete and undisputed possession of the sovereignty." He wrote to Thomas Paine in England: "The executive and aristocracy are at their feet; the mass of the nation, the mass of the clergy, and the army are with them; they have prostrated the old government, and are now beginning to build one from the foundation."[23]

In his opinion, the order of the constitutional proceedings announced by the Assembly was admirable. After a declaration of the rights of man, they would set forth the principles of the monarchy, the rights of the nation, the rights of the King, the rights of the citizens — proceeding then to fundamental matters of organization. These seemed to him "the materials of a superb edifice," and he thought they were in skillful hands. His main fear at the moment was that the Assembly was too large to be effective, and that public opinion was not yet ready for the adoption of trial by jury, the only real anchor by which a government could be held to the principles of its constitution.

Meanwhile, he had been unwittingly drawn into a minor controversy which was connected with a major difficulty — the continued scarcity of bread. Before the Bastille fell, the harvest had commenced in the South of France, but in Paris he noted that there was never more than a three days' supply on hand during a period of several weeks. Under these circumstances of acute danger Mirabeau, who was hostile to Necker, stated in the Assembly that Jefferson had made

[22] TJ to Jay, June 29, 1789 (*D. C.*, II, 301–302); quotation, II, 302.
[23] TJ to Paine, July 11, 1789 (L. & B., VII, 405).

an offer to obtain corn and flour from America which Necker had refused. Such was not the case, though Jefferson had written John Jay months before that American corn and flour would have a good sale in France. Informed immediately of Mirabeau's action by Lafayette, he wrote the latter a letter of denial, giving copies to Necker and Montmorin, both of whom he also went to see. Mirabeau presented this letter to the Assembly in a way that was not wholly satisfactory to the Ministry, and caused some embarrassment to Lafayette. He suffered more from the episode than did Jefferson, whose official conduct was open to no attack.[24]

Also, in this period of lull before a storm, Lafayette consulted his friend about a bill of rights. They had talked on this favorite subject months before, and Jefferson's influence on the Marquis in this connection was probably greater than appears in any formal record. In January, Jefferson had written Madison that everybody in Paris was trying his hand at framing a declaration of rights and had sent two drafts, including one by Lafayette.[25] In July, before presenting a declaration to the Assembly, Lafayette sent another draft to Jefferson, and on this the latter made a few annotations.[26] In listing the imprescriptible rights with which every man is born Lafayette had included "property" and "the care of his honor," and these Jefferson wanted to omit, leaving only "the care of his life, the power to dispose of his person and the fruits of his industry, and of all his faculties, the pursuit of happiness and resistance to oppression." [27]

Honor, as he had noted when reading Montesquieu in his young manhood, was the energetic principle of a limited monarchy.[28] He was content that the form of government in France at present should

[24] TJ summarized the affair to Jay, July 19, 1789 (*D. C.*, II, 303–304). The correspondence with Lafayette, July 4–10, 1789, can be most conveniently consulted in Chinard, *Lafayette and Jefferson*, pp. 129–135. For TJ's letter of July 8, 1789, to Necker, see L. & B., VII, 401–402. Lafayette's embarrassment arose from the fact that after Mirabeau gave the contents of the letter, he thought it unnecessary to have a translation of it read afterwards. This annoyed the ministers, but they were authorized by TJ to publish his letter and he reported that it was printed. An English report of the affair was copied in N. Y. *Gazette of the U. S.*, Oct. 3, 1789.

[25] TJ to Madison, Jan. 17, 1789 (Ford, V, 64). Chinard prints Lafayette's draft (from LC, 6250) in *Lafayette and Jefferson*, pp. 136–137; another copy in TJ's handwriting is preserved in the W. C. Rives Collection (Lib. Cong.), along with a list of general principles drawn by somebody else.

[26] LC, 6252–6253, reproduced by Chinard between pp. 136–137, printed and translated pp. 138–140. Chinard also prints letters relating to the subject: Lafayette to TJ, July 4, 1789; TJ to Lafayette, July 6, 1789 (129–131). Apparently TJ returned the draft in person.

[27] Translation that of Chinard, p. 139.

[28] See my *Jefferson the Virginian*, p. 176 and references cited.

be a limited monarchy and raised no objection to Lafayette's reference to the sacredness of the King's person. Also, as the friend of liberal nobles, he still had good reason to value the aristocratic virtues. But the term "honor" at this time and place carried an implication of aristocratic privilege, while the document he was reading was supposed to state the rights of all men. Hence, as he must have thought, it should stick to fundamentals and universals.

His reasons for wanting to omit the word "property," no doubt, were much the same as those that led him to use the expression "pursuit of happiness" instead of it in the Declaration of Independence.[29] He was no more disposed to attack property as an institution now than he was then. The term was used in the Declaration of Rights of his own State, which he had distributed so proudly and which was so highly esteemed by the Patriots at this stage; and, despite his own loss of silver candlesticks by theft, he reported with pride several times that summer that the sanctity of property was generally respected by the excited populace. But he still regarded property, like government, as a means to human happiness — not as an end in itself, not a natural and inalienable right in the same sense as the life and liberty of a person. He wanted to keep first things first.

With respect to the political means which should be employed by society to safeguard the pursuit of individual happiness, his mind was flexible; and nothing was more characteristic of his thinking throughout life than his recognition that changes in institutions are necessary for social progress. His influence on Lafayette was probably reflected in the final article of the latter's draft:

> And whereas the progress of enlightenment, the introduction of abuses and the *rights of succeeding generations* necessitate the revision of all human institutions, constitutional provisions must be made to insure in given cases an extraordinary convocation of the representatives with the sole object to examine and, if necessary, to modify the form of the Government.[30]

This was not so explicit as Jefferson's letter to Madison, written several weeks afterward, in which he denied the right of one generation to bind another and asserted that laws should be renewed or revised every twenty years, but it is far more likely that it represented an earlier stage of his thought on this subject than that Lafayette's ideas stimulated his own later thinking.[31] What he advocated was

[29] On this question, see *Jefferson the Virginian*, pp. 227–228, with notes and references.

[30] Chinard, *Lafayette and Jefferson*, p. 140, italics inserted.

[31] TJ to Madison, Sept. 6, 1789 (Ford, V, 115–124); see p. 179, above, and Adrienne Koch, *Jefferson and Madison*, ch. 4.

not violent upheaval in a moment of turmoil and excitement but reasoned revision, effected periodically in order that government might catch up with social change, and this he thought so important that it could properly be included in a statement of fundamental rights.

It was the universal quality in the movement which the Patriots were conducting that most appealed to him, and he was always more interested in the direction the Revolution was taking than in the immediate forms it assumed. Hence his friend's proposals for a declaration were wholly in his spirit, whether or not he was responsible for all of them or the precise phraseology of any, just as they were in the spirit of the world of philosophy in which his mind was most at home. "Nature has created men free and equal"; distinctions there might be, but these were permissible only so far as they were "founded upon the general good" – such assertions expressed his deepest conviction. The phraseology of the first article of the famous Declaration of the Rights of Man and the Citizen, to which others besides Lafayette contributed, fitted his thinking even better: "Men are born and remain free and equal in rights. Social distinctions may be based only on common utility." He was now far more intolerant of aristocracy than he had been during his life among the genial planters of Virginia, but the equality which he regarded as basic was not that of economic and social condition. It was equality in rights, the equality of all men before the law. As a practical statesman he had doubted – more than the leaders of the Assembly, in fact – that the time was yet ripe to urge it, but he was now speaking, America was speaking – just as a whole philosophical movement was – through the mouth of his intimate young friend Lafayette.

There were clamors which drowned the voice for a time, only to reinforce it afterwards. Between the introduction of a declaration by the Marquis on June 11 and the adoption of the historic Declaration, six weeks of exciting events intervened.

On Sunday, July 12, Jefferson passed in his carriage through the Place Louis XV, now the Place de la Concorde. There he saw German cavalry drawn up and Swiss guards posted behind them, while an angry crowd of people confronted them, on and behind a large pile of stones that had been collected for the building of a bridge. He passed without interruption through the lane, between the mercenary troops of the King and the infuriated people; but in the next moment, the crowd attacked the cavalrymen with stones, forcing their retirement, and he believed that this affair was the signal for universal insurrection.[32] Already panic-stricken because of the assembling of foreign troops, the Parisians had heard that day of the dismissal of Necker and the reconstruction of the Ministry under the leadership of a counter revolutionary, and from this time onward they did their utmost to get hold of arms.

On Tuesday, July 14, the American Minister was visiting at the home of Louis-Dominique Éthis de Corny, where he had so often chatted over the teacups, when that member of the city committee returned from the Bastille. He had gone with a delegation to demand arms of the governor of the historic fortress, and from him Jefferson got the story of events which he told in his letters and, long years later, in his autobiography. How the people got in, after the deputies had retired, he did not claim to know. "Those who pretend to have been of the party, tell so many different stories as to destroy the credit of them all," he said.[33] He knew that they got muskets, and freed what few prisoners there were; that the governor was carried off and that he and the chief officer of the city, supposedly a "traitor," were beheaded. Also he knew that the King went before the Assembly next day and made a speech, which amounted to "a surrender at discretion"; that Lafayette was named commander of the bourgeois militia; that the demolition of the Bastille was begun. He went to see it himself, and afterwards contributed to the widows whose husbands had been slain in the taking of the fortress.[34] He reported the royal confirmation of Bailly, President of the Assembly, as Mayor of Paris; the recall of Necker; the flight of the Princes and other irreconcilables of the Court. Furthermore, he witnessed the coming of the King to Paris with deputies from the Assembly. Dugald Stewart, the young Scottish philosopher, saw the historic procession with him.

The King's carriage was in the center, flanked by the deputies on foot in two ranks. Lafayette was in the lead on horseback, and the bourgeois militia were before and behind, while thousands of citizens armed with muskets, pistols, swords, pikes, scythes, and pruning hooks lined the streets, shouting "*Vive la Nation!*" on the way to the Hôtel de Ville, and "*Vive le Roi et la Nation!*" on the King's return. In Jefferson's opinion, no sovereign had ever made and no people ever received such an *amende honorable.* Tranquillity was now restored in

[32] He mentioned his own presence in the autobiography of his old age (Ford, I, 135), and gave the events in almost identical language without mentioning himself in his letter of July 19, 1789, to Jay (*D. C.*, II, 306).

[33] TJ to Jay, July 19, 1789 (*D. C.*, II, 307). In this letter he gave an extended story of developments since the reunion of the orders and the seeming triumph of the Third Estate on June 27.

[34] Account Book, July 17, July 20, Aug. 21, 1789.

the city and would probably continue unless the lack of bread should disturb the peace, but he could not suppose the paroxysm would be confined to the city. He expected it to spread through the entire country and only hoped that it would be short. His information about provincial developments, however, was and continued to be scanty, and he laid less stress on the revolt of the peasants than modern writers do.

While obviously concerned to correct exaggerated stories of violence in Paris, he reported disorders and popular executions, such as those of the officials of Foulon and Bertier, as soon as he learned of them; and, while never approving them, he apparently regarded them as practically inevitable under existing circumstances. The churches were engaged, he said, in singing "*de profundis*" and Requiems for the "repose of the souls of the brave and valiant citizens who have sealed with their blood the liberty of their nation." [35] He still recognized that the tree of liberty had to be watered with the blood of tyrants and martyrs from time to time. He rejoiced in the flight of the irreconcilables of the Court and undoubtedly wished that the Queen had gone with them. "Seven princes of the house of Bourbon, and seven Ministers, fled into foreign countries, is a wonderful event indeed," he said.[36] He had no doubt of the sincerity of the King in his submission to the popular will, and he rejoiced in the addition of representatives of the popular party to the Ministry, just as he was glad to see Montmorin back; but he continued to have an indifferent opinion of Necker, whose popularity had declined since his return. He was under no illusions, however, about this populace. "Their hatred is stronger than their love," he said.[37]

The degree of his "democracy" that summer, when his interest in the absorbing scene reconciled him to his long wait for his leave of absence, is suggested by his response to an inquiry about juries. Resuming to some extent his functions as minister of information, he sent a list of books on the subject and hastily gave some of his own ideas about popular participation in government:

> We think in America [he said] that it is necessary to introduce the people into every department of government as far as they are capable of exercising it; and that this is the only way to ensure a long continued & honest administration of its powers.[38]

[35] July 19, 1789 (*D. C.*, II, 310).
[36] TJ to William Carmichael, Aug. 9, 1789 (*D. C.*, II, 317).
[37] TJ to Jay, Aug. 5, 1789 (*D. C.*, II, 313).
[38] TJ to "L'Abbé Arnond," July 19, 1789 (Ford, V, 103). This was probably to his old friend L'Abbé Arnoux, whose name he spelled capriciously.

In the judicial sphere they were not qualified to pass on questions of law but could decide questions of fact, and in extreme cases of judicial bias could even intervene in the realm of law. He regarded the administration of justice as the best place for the people to participate personally in government. "The execution of the laws is more important than the making them," he said. His belief that self-government must begin in the local courts was in the Anglo-American tradition, and he seemed to minimize the legislative function at just the time that the Assembly was becoming dominant in France.

His reporting slowed down as the summer wore on, for reasons connected with his pending leave, hence his failure to describe important developments fully does not necessarily imply indifference. It was natural for him to concentrate on the proceedings of the Assembly and the important constitutional discussions which he could follow there. He knew that châteaux continued to burn in the country, though he had hoped that the dramatic renunciation of privileges by nobles and clergy in the Assembly early in August and later actions of that body would serve to tranquilize the country. He regarded these as a corollary of the Declaration of Rights, whose adoption he expected for some weeks before it actually occurred on August 26. Its form could hardly have been wholly pleasing to him – not so much because it included "property" among the natural and imprescriptible rights as because it must have seemed to him equivocal on the subject of religious freedom. He had not ceased to regard liberty of the mind and conscience as the most fundamental of all rights. But this Declaration was both the "death certificate of the Old Regime" and a formulation of ideals to be realized more fully in the future, and he never ceased rejoicing that "the appeal to the rights of man, which had been made in the United States was taken up by France, first of the European nations." [39] It was the sort of promise every country owed its people, and if the feudal system was not completely destroyed by legislative action and agrarian revolt he assumed that eventually it would be.

He was much more anxious for the speedy completion of the constitutional revolution than for the social one. He did not prefer form to substance at this or any other time, but he believed that if a good framework of government were set up the correction of specific economic and social ills would follow, in the course of progress and the light of reason. In our own time it may seem that he laid too little stress on the clash of economic forces, but if he did the fault may be

[39] The judgments are those of the historians Aulard and Lefebvre; the longer quotation is from his autobiography (Ford, I, 147).

attributed to his own predominantly political training and the thought patterns of his slow-moving age. It is not at all surprising that he regarded the making of a constitution as the major piece of unfinished business, and as an experienced legislator he viewed the prospect with some alarm. He regretted the unwieldy size of the Assembly and deplored its tumultuous procedure and the inexperience of its leaders. To Madison he described them as versed in the theory but new in the practice of government, as acquainted with man as they saw him in books and not in the world. He valued their good intentions but blamed them for ineptitude.[40]

Not unnaturally there were those who wanted to avail themselves of the lights of his reason and experience for the good of France. Toward the end of July, the spokesman for a committee appointed to draw up a project for a constitution wrote him a charming letter inviting him to a conference. "There are no foreigners any more in our opinion when the happiness of man is at stake," said the Archbishop of Bordeaux, suggesting a specific time and place when they might see him. But Jefferson begged off on the ground of the pressure of diplomatic business, with an implication of impropriety which he expressed more categorically long years later in his autobiography. He was a diplomat, named to the Chief of the nation, whose powers might be discussed at this meeting, hence there might be criticism of his action. He represented his country with discretion as well as dignity.[41]

By the end of August the situation had changed considerably and perhaps Jefferson thought that he need not be quite so careful of the proprieties. The day after the Assembly adopted the Declaration of the Rights of Man and the Citizen, and cleared the decks for the discussion of the Constitution, he had word that his leave of absence had been granted. The country was becoming calmer, he believed, but acts of violence were always possible and, since no courts would act against them, they were quite unpunishable. France needed a stable government, beyond a doubt, but the issue of the constitutional debates had become uncertain for other reasons than the inexperience of the deputies. The aristocratic party was raising its head and there was a considerable defection from the Patriots, the more conservative of whom had become alarmed by the suppression of privileges, in which many

[40] TJ to Madison, Aug. 28, 1789 (Ford, V, 109). He referred to the unfortunate size of the Assembly in other letters.

[41] Archbishop of Bordeaux to TJ, July 20, 1789; TJ to the Archbishop, July 22 (LC, 8566, 8561; both printed in Chinard, *Lafayette and Jefferson*, pp. 143–145, and discussed, *ibid.*, p. 83). Chinard says TJ's letter is "the only document of importance written entirely in French by Jefferson himself." For the account in the autobiography, see Ford, I, 143–144.

of them were personally interested. The main point at issue, however, was the form of the government and his chief concern was that the two wings of the patriotic or popular party should be brought together. As he described these to John Jay, they were moderate royalists on the one hand, wishing for a Constitution much like that of England; and "republicans" on the other, who (despite the name he gave them) were agreeable to an hereditary executive, but wanted to make him very subordinate to the legislature and to have that legislature consist of a single chamber.[42] The former group favored an absolute royal veto on legislation, and this the latter opposed. Both of them, in his opinion, consisted of honest and well-meaning men, differing only in opinion and both wishing to establish as great a degree of liberty as could be preserved.

He thought Lafayette was attached to both parties, and late in August undoubtedly agreed with him that the factions must be kept together. When Lafayette asked him to have a group of eight for dinner he acceded without protest.[43] Besides the Marquis himself, these included Mounier, the leader of the moderate royalists, and Duport, Barnave, and Alexander Lameth, who were conspicuous on the other side.[44] According to Lafayette, agreement was the only alternative to total dissolution and civil war, and he asked his friend to break every engagement and give them a dinner, since the Marquis's own house was always full. There had been futile conferences at Lafayette's house already, and probably he and the others hoped to gain something from the presence of Jefferson, whom Mounier described as a man "known for his lights and virtues, who had at the same time the experience and the theory of institutions proper for the maintenance of liberty" — adding that he had a favorable judgment of Mounier's own principles.[45]

[42] TJ to Jay, Sept. 19, 1789 (*D. C.*, II, 327–328).

[43] The undated letter of Lafayette to TJ making this request (LC, 8686, tentatively dated Aug. 25) is printed in Chinard, *Lafayette and Jefferson*, p. 145. About the same time he sent TJ a proposed constitution for France (LC, 8685) and TJ wrote about the prospects to Madison on Aug. 28, 1789 (Ford, V, 108–109). TJ then thought the constitution would call for a royal veto and two Houses, one of them to be little more than a council of revision.

[44] The others were Latour-Maubourg, the Marquis de Blacon, and the Comte d'Agoult (Ford, I, 145; Charavay, *Lafayette*, 187).

[45] Mounier, *Exposé de ma Conduite dans l'Assemblee nationale*, p. 40. Besides the conferences at the home of Lafayette and at Jefferson's, Mounier says there was a final meeting at Versailles on Aug. 29, when he refused to sign a *projet de convention*. The story of this affair, as told by various writers, seems based almost wholly on TJ's account in his letter of Sept. 19, 1789 (*D. C.*, II, 328–329) and his autobiography (Ford, I, 144–146) and on Mounier's story, which helps set the date.

In this group the prestige of Jefferson and his country was of the highest. Just about this time he wrote Madison:

> It is impossible to desire better dispositions towards us than prevail in this assembly. Our proceedings have been viewed as a model for them on every occasion; and though in the heat of debate men are generally disposed to contradict every authority urged by their opponents, ours has been treated like that of the bible, open to explanation but not to question.[46]

As Jefferson described this conference long afterwards, he was the silent witness of a discussion comparable with the finest dialogues of antiquity as handed down by Xenophon, Plato, or Cicero. When dinner ended at four the cloth was removed and the wine set on the table in the American manner, and the Patriots began to talk. They continued until ten, and by that hour he must have provided other refreshments. He thought at the time that they had reached a compromise agreement, but the "republican" group had its way in the Assembly, where a suspensive royal veto and a unicameral legislature were approved.

In his old age, his recollection was that the agreement reached at his house saved the Constitution, but the fact is that the opposition of Mounier was borne down in the Assembly. At a later time, also, he was at some pains to meet possible charges of impropriety on his part. He probably did call on Montmorin next day and explain the circumstances, for this action would have been quite in character, and if Montmorin did not then express the hope that Jefferson would continue to assist at such conferences, in order to moderate the warmer spirits and promote wholesome and practicable reformation, he would have been wholly justified in doing so, for it was just that sort of influence that Jefferson would have exerted in these extraordinarily difficult circumstances if any outsider could.

Jefferson remained in Paris for a month after he got his leave of absence on August 26, busily engaged in tying up loose ends of official business and preparing for his own departure. In this interval he did not take the time to sum up the revolutionary developments which he had described almost day by day in his letters, though he did give a last general view to John Jay. Because of his intimacy with Lafayette and his access to the ministry and diplomatic corps, he had been in an extraordinarily favorable position to learn just what was going on, and he reported events in the spirit of a contemporary historian. To a slight but perceptible degree he adjusted his reports

[46] Aug. 28, 1789 (Ford, V, 110).

to the various recipients of them. It was both a virtue and potential weakness of this amiable man with a highly sensitive mind that he perceived the sentiments and attitudes of other people and almost instinctively adjusted himself to them. At the time, however, this was no matter of politics, but rather one of sympathy and manners. He could be stern, and where matters of principle were involved very stubborn, and in the aggregate he seemed strong, not weak, but he hated to hurt anybody's feelings and liked to tell people what they liked to hear. Thus he commented rather more favorably on the course of the Revolution to Dr. Richard Price and Thomas Paine than he did to John Jay or even James Madison. The facts were the same but the nuances were slightly different. He expressed his hopes rather more freely on the one hand, and his fears on the other.

As an enlightened liberal and stanch believer in human progress, he shared the faith of Richard Price that the Revolution would probably be the "commencement of a general reformation in the governments of the world," and when writing this older man on the eve of his departure he stressed the tranquillity which seemed perfectly established in Paris and pretty generally in the whole Kingdom. In the Assembly there was dangerous factionalism, but the mass of the people were united. He showed similar optimism in his parting letter to Thomas Paine, who had been keeping him posted about developments in England. He wrote: "I think there is no possibility now of anything's hindering their final establishment of a good constitution, which will in its principles and merit be about a middle term between that of England and the United States." It will be recalled, however, that he himself would have been content with less, and it may be noted that Paine, earlier in the year, had reported the establishment of very friendly relations with Edmund Burke, whom he afterwards excoriated.[47]

Outside France the lines had not yet been sharply drawn between the friends and foes of the Revolution, and Jefferson himself was at one moment a philosopher of human liberty, rejoicing in the recognition of the rights of man, and at another an objective and realistic statesman, weighing the balance between good and evil in the existing situation. He blended his roles best in his letters to Madison, but these were most notable for his discussion of the American situation and constitutions in general, on the background of his stimulating experiences in France. He attained fullest objectivity in his official letters to Jay,

[47] Richard Price to TJ, Aug. 3, 1789 (LC, 8606–8607); TJ to Price, Sept. 13, 1789 (LC, 8780); TJ to Paine, Sept. 13, 1789 (LC, 8783); Paine to TJ, Jan. 15, 1789 (LC, 7879–7880).

where he spoke for the record as a responsible statesman, and if these letters do not reveal his personal hopes as vividly as those to men like Price and Paine they best represent his measured judgment.[48] To the Secretary for Foreign Affairs he spoke of the slothfulness of the unwieldy Assembly, the impatience of the people, the seeds of dissension sown by the aristocrats, the divisions among the Patriots, the financial plight of the government. He still believed that the party of Patriots would stick together sufficiently to save the situation, basing his hopes chiefly on Lafayette, but he left no possible doubt that the situation was deeply troubled, that civil war was talked of and was entirely possible. The events which might produce it, he thought, were these: (1) the want of bread, which continued amazingly, despite an abundant harvest, and was another proof of governmental incompetence; (2) public bankruptcy, which he had little confidence that Necker could prevent; (3) the flight of the King from Versailles, which was talked about and which would probably be the signal for the massacre of the aristocrats in Paris. He also spoke of the possibility of foreign intervention. On the whole, he did not think it probable as yet that any actual commotion would take place, and none did occur until after he had left Paris.

While Jefferson was waiting for a boat at a Channel port, a mob of Parisian women invaded the palace at Versailles and Lafayette escorted the royal family to the city. These events served to enhance the prestige and power of his trusted friend, but his first impression of them was that they brought the country to the brink of civil war.[49] He had no more news of France for four months, and never again was he a privileged observer of the Revolution.

The sanity of his comments on it while he did observe it firsthand could hardly fail to be recognized even by unfriendly historians. Taine, who certainly did not like or fully understand him, said that of the 1200 statesmen in the National Assembly there was not one who had the sagacity and foresight of Arthur Young, Edmund Burke, and Thomas Jefferson.[50] He was no starry-eyed philosopher who left France in a mood of fatuous complacency, though his faith in the

[48] He came nearest to summing things up in his letter of Sept. 19, 1789, to Jay (*D. C.*, II, 324–330), adding a few recent details on Sept. 30 (*D. C.*, II, 330–332). He wrote Madison at length on Aug. 28, and Sept. 6, 1789 (Ford, V, 107–124), but the latter letter was devoted to the question of whether one generation of men has a right to bind another.

[49] TJ to Madame de Corny, Oct. 14, 1789 (Chinard, *Trois Amitiés*, p. 188).

[50] H. Taine, *Nouveaux Essais de Critique et d'Histoire* (edn. 1909), pp. 211–215. Washington's contemporary comments on the situation reflect more alarm than TJ's but differ from the latter chiefly in degree; see his letter to G. Morris, Oct. 13, 1789 (Fitzpatrick, XXX, 443).

eventual triumph of liberty and enlightenment was undoubtedly quickened by the victories already won. In philosophy and temperament he was more optimistic than John Adams or Edmund Burke; he feared disorder less than George Washington or James Madison; he had no such fears of the turbulence of democracy as Gouverneur Morris or Alexander Hamilton. But he had consistently given counsels of moderation, and when he left Europe he believed that anything might happen.

His reaction to later events, of course, is another story, and quite inseparable from political developments in his own country; but there is nothing in his record as minister to give comfort to advocates of violent revolution in any age. He preferred other means to the ones that had been employed already, and urged more modest immediate objectives. Yet his loyalty to principles which he regarded as universal was so unswerving that he had no thought of surrendering his hopes of this tremendous movement, and he could be expected to set his face like flint against counter revolution, either in France or his own country. As a statesman, he preferred to pursue a course only a a little left of the middle way; and it was for that reason that he seemed relatively conservative in revolutionary France, whereas he appeared as a dangerous radical to many in the United States in a period of conservative reaction. But the glory of his career owes less to the course he steered than to his guiding principles and ultimate objectives. Though the wisdom of his statesmanship may be questioned or forgotten, his devotion to the rights of man, and faith in their ultimate establishment, will surely be remembered as long as anyone on earth believes in equality before the law and the freedom of individuals from all oppression.

The Minister's plans for departure were based on the assumption that he would come back. The day after he got his leave, he wrote Madison, who had sounded him out about his willingness to accept an appointment in America, that whenever he quit his present office he meant to take no other; and Short, who was not only left in charge of American affairs but also of Jefferson's house and very extensive furnishings, bet a beaver hat that he would return. But his two daughters were going home to stay, and they would have a good deal of baggage. This was one of the reasons why he wanted to catch a boat that was sailing straight to Virginia. Also, it was quite obvious that such an acquisitive person would himself have many things to ship. Some of these were for other people. To John Jay he sent two hampers containing samples of the best wines of France, presenting them to him and Washington, that they might decide just what they would like him to get for them in the future. Also, he sent a box of fusils for the war office and two plaster busts of John Paul Jones. He distributed eight busts of the gallant sailor altogether, sending six through the hands of Madison, to whom of course he also sent a box of books. There was another box of books for Dr. Franklin, there was a heavy marble pedestal for the bust of Lafayette which was going to the State of Virginia, and there were his own things, which added up to considerably more than all the rest.[51] To Nathaniel Cutting, an American who was receiving packages for him at Havre, he wrote: "You must be pleased to look on the trouble which the accident of my voyage occasions you like a tempest or whirlwind which heaven in the course of its providence has directed over your fields. Troublesome, but happily transient." [52]

John Trumbull, who was used to his "troublesome" commissions, had found a vessel for him, and he first hoped it would stop at Havre. This was the *Clermont*, a vessel of 230 tons bound for Norfolk. Captain Colley would take the Jefferson party and their baggage, excluding all other passengers, for 120 guineas, and his merchants would agree to his stopping at Cowes on the English side but not at Havre. Jefferson had to acquiesce in the arrangement, though it was less convenient for the baggage and would mean that he would be seasick twice instead of once. Besides Patsy and Polly, he had two servants with him, James and Sally Heming. Petit also went along to manage things, and they set out on September 26.[53]

Jefferson had not said many farewells, partly because he did not like them, partly because he expected to be back. He called on Montmorin, without interesting him much in the matter of getting salt meat from America; and he tried to see Necker, to tell him about the decline in the British whale fishery. He had Lafayette, La Rochefoucauld, and Condorcet for a parting dinner — which was eminently appropriate, since he was so close in spirit to these liberal noblemen — and he invited Gouverneur Morris to be there with them. He was not one to let ideological differences affect personal relationships with a distinguished fellow American, and Morris enjoyed his generous hospitality. But Morris did not see him off, for on September 26 the gay cripple, who was also an astute man of business, got up early and went to Versailles to listen to the discussion of a financial proposal of Necker's, and the next day Madame de Corny told him that

[51] TJ to Jay, Sept. 17, 1789 (LC, 8799–8800); TJ to Madison, Sept. 17, 1789 (LC, 8801); Account Book, Sept. 22, 1789, showing packing expenses paid Petit.

[52] TJ to Nathaniel Cutting, Sept. 17, 1789 (LC, 8803).

[53] Trumbull to TJ, Sept. 11, 1789 (LC, 8820); TJ to Trumbull, Sept. 16 (LC, 8797, 8787); Trumbull to TJ, Sept. 22 (LC, 8842–8843); TJ to Nathaniel Cutting, Sept. 15, 1789 (LC, 8789).

the Virginian had gone. She and William Short shed tears, she said, and Jefferson wrote to her among the first. To most of his friends in Paris, however, he did not write until he was back in America, and then he sent them letters of adieu.[54]

On the road to Havre, the Jefferson party had no accidents except for the breaking of the axletree on the phaeton and a tire on one of the chariot wheels, but when they got there they found that the equinoctial gales, far from subsiding, were raging in the wildest weather the Minister had ever seen. They had to delay ten days, and this gave him a chance to buy a shepherd bitch "big with pups." She produced two puppies on the voyage and all three of the dogs were taken to Monticello, where, some months later, they were joined by others of the breed that were sent from this same place. On October 7, Petit, rewarded for his extraordinary trouble by a handsome tip, returned to Paris; and shortly after midnight the Jeffersons – with slaves, bitch, and baggage – left Havre on the packet *Anna*. They arrived at Cowes after twenty-six hours of "boisterous navigation and mortal sickness," and had to wait there nearly two weeks before boarding the ship for home.[55]

The delay was unwelcome but it provided opportunity for some sight-seeing and shopping. Jefferson wrote few letters, but he learned from English papers that the French King had been brought to Paris. They boarded the *Clermont* at noon on October 22, anchored for a night off Yarmouth, and on the 29th were out of sight of land. John Trumbull sailed for New York the same day that Jefferson did for Norfolk, but their ways as friends had not yet parted. Thomas Paine had asked to be remembered with an overflowing affection to his dear America, both the place and the people – including his old friend Dr. Franklin and beloved General Washington. The movements of the returning Minister himself had not gone unnoticed in the American newspapers, and the good report got around that he had received special consideration at the English customs house by express orders of William Pitt.[56]

Perhaps he bore with him to Virginia a more pleasant memory of English official manners than he had expected, but when he thought

[54] G. Morris, *Diary*, Sept. 17, 26, 27, 1789 (I, 220, 231, 234); Madame de Corny to TJ, Nov. 25, 1789 (Chinard, *Trois Amitiés*, p. 191).

[55] Account Book, Sept. 26–Oct. 22, 1789; TJ to Short from Havre, Oct. 4, 7, 1789 (LC, 8878, 8884); additional information about shepherd dogs in TJ to La Motte, June 27, 1790 (LC, 9506); TJ to Madame de Corny from Cowes, Oct. 14, 1789 (Chinard, *Trois Amitiés*, pp. 188–189).

[56] Trumbull, *Autobiography*, p. 154; Paine to TJ from London, Sept. 15, 1789 (Foner, II, 1295); N. Y. *Gazette of the U. S.*, Nov. 28, 1789, in dispatch from London.

of friendliness to strangers and charm of society his mind ever afterwards turned to France. In his old age he drew also on his memory of the classics for a tribute to the country where he had lived during rich and exciting years, and which he knew better than any other except his own. After the Battle of Salamis, he said, every general voted to himself the first reward of valor and the second to Themistocles. So if any traveler from any nation were asked where he would most like to live, he would name his own country first and then he must inevitably name France.[57] At the end of his own travels he spoke thus for himself; but, as he slipped out of sight of land in late October in his forty-seventh year, his chief thought must have been that he was escaping from the eternal fogs of Europe and returning to the sunshine of his native land.

[57] Ford, I, 148–149.

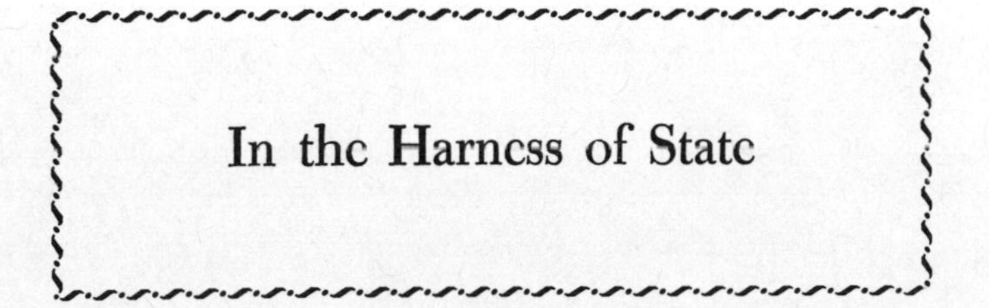

In the Harness of State

[XIII]

The Return of a Virginian

SOME of the American captains detained at Cowes had predicted a nine weeks' passage, but the *Clermont* was only twenty-six days from land to land. After she weighed anchor at Yarmouth she soon got clear of fogs and had favorable winds until she neared the Virginia capes, while Jefferson and his little party, her only passengers, enjoyed the finest of autumn weather. Their seasickness was severe for a time but did not last long, and at the end he congratulated himself that he had crossed the Atlantic twice without running into anything that could be called a storm. He kept a simpler log than on his earlier voyage, he was not studying Spanish now, and he could have had little adult conversation except with Captain Colley, a native of Norfolk and "a bold and judicious seaman." Patsy and Polly occupied much of his time no doubt, and after a while he could observe his new shepherd pups, but he probably spent a good many hours merely reminiscing.[1]

Surely he must have realized that he was leaving the Old World, after more than five years of honorable and devoted service, with an enormously enriched experience. If he had been a novice in diplomacy to begin with, this colleague of Franklin and John Adams who had talked with Vergennes and Montmorin and been snubbed by George III was one no longer. "I feel a degree of familiarity with the duties of my present office," he was soon to write to President Washington, and it was to those duties that he expected shortly to return, little dreaming of the lengthy part he was to play in the conduct of the foreign policy of the United States before he quitted the public stage. Since he anticipated no such career as he afterwards had as secretary of state and president, he could not have been expected to congratulate himself on his magnificent preparation for it, but the historian is in position to congratulate his country.

[1] Account Book, Oct. 23–Nov. 23, 1789; *Domestic Life*, pp. 150–152, giving Martha's story of the voyage; TJ to Short, Nov. 21, 1789 (Ford, V, 132–133).

He himself thought of his international experience as no mere preparation for a particular sort of statecraft. Since it was a part of life he valued it for its own sake, and its significance extended far beyond technical diplomacy. He was more than a technician, more than a statesman as we ordinarily use the term. He was an omnivorous and highly sensitized mind and he had lived in a cockpit of ideas and world seat of culture. It is true that he did not need to go to Europe to get into the current of liberal thought which fertilized the reform movements of his age, for he had already done that before he wrote the Declaration of Independence. But he had found new and highly stimulating friends of light and liberty in the Old World and had become even more conscious of his membership in a noble international brotherhood. In certain respects it was an incongruous company—including as it did Condorcet, La Rochefoucauld, and Lafayette, along with Dr. Richard Price, John Paradise, and Thomas Paine—and he was not in agreement with all its members at all points, but no one was quicker than he to perceive kinship of the spirit. With all his statesmanlike reservations, the revolution in France appeared to him the triumph of enlightened liberalism; and as he read his books afterwards and wrote to his friends he nourished in his own breast the sacred fire. His correspondence lagged in later years as terror increased at home and abroad, as friends of yesterday were engulfed in a revolution that lost its philosophical direction. But his ties with kindred European minds and spirits were never broken, and, both in Europe and America, he became a more conspicuous symbol of enlightened liberalism and the rights of man after the Revolution than he had ever been before. He could not have anticipated this as the *Clermont* sailed homeward, but he must have reflected that a bright chapter had been written in the story of his expanding thoughts and hopes, and have assured himself that the book would not be closed till death.

A bright chapter it was, despite the dark background of European despotism, and he must have thought it also an extraordinarily rich one. Perhaps not even he could completely catalogue his observations and acquisitions in the realms of art and architecture, agriculture and household furniture, science and invention. But he could think of the books and plants and drawings he had sent or was sending home, of the furnishings he had left in the Hôtel de Langeac, of the pictures he had bought or ordered, of the wines he was shipping, of the vineyards and rice fields he had observed in Burgundy and Bordeaux and Lombardy. Many of these things he could take with him. They could go in boxes or be preserved in letters and memoranda. They were his to give or keep for the rest of life. He could even put musical scores in boxes, as actually he did; but until he returned to Europe, such concerts as he had heard in Paris could be only a memory – less real than pictures of the Maison Carrée or the Hôtel de Salm. Only in Europe could the favorite passion of his soul be fully satisfied. More even than Maria Cosway, the music which had delighted him must have seemed like a lovely dream as he listened to the lapping of the waves.

The chief thrills of the voyage came at the very end of it. The coast of the American continent, like that of Europe, was obscured by mists when they neared it and a pilot could not have been seen had one appeared. The bold Captain, running in at a venture without being able to see the Virginia capes, managed to get inside and anchored in Lynhaven Bay, where Jefferson wrote a letter to William Short. Meanwhile, the wind rose, and when they beat up against it they lost their topsails and were almost run down by a brig going before the wind out of port.

The Jeffersons landed at Norfolk about midday on November 23, 1789, and went to Lindsay's Hotel. The Minister promptly reported his arrival to John Jay by letter, but if he did not take his official records ashore with him he nearly lost them. Fire broke out on the vessel before the baggage was unloaded, though their belongings were all saved in the end. Jefferson had much liked the lines of a table on the *Clermont*, and had left with Captain Colley a memorandum to have one made like it for him in London, of the finest mahogany, and shipped to France. He got it in America after a year or so.[2]

He now learned that something important with respect to him as a public man had happened on the very day that he left Paris, though he had been utterly oblivious of it when waiting at Havre and Cowes and while sailing in autumn sunshine on his voyage home. President Washington had nominated him as secretary of state, the Senate had confirmed him, and he was greeted in Norfolk as a high official of the new government and not merely as a diplomat at home on leave.[3] It was three weeks before he got the letter which Washington had written him in October, and well into the new year before he accepted the appointment, but almost at the moment that he stepped on Virginia's soil he was confronted with what amounted to a *fait accompli*. The Mayor, Recorder, and Aldermen of the Borough of Norfolk addressed him two days after his arrival – congratulating him on his safe arrival

[2] TJ to Jay, Nov. 23, 1789 (Ford, V, 134); Memo. for Capt. Colley, Nov. 16, 1789 (MHS).

[3] He was nominated Sept. 25, 1789, and confirmed Sept. 26, along with Edmund Randolph as attorney general. *Journal of the Executive Proceedings of the Senate*, I (1828), 32–33; N. Y. *Gazette of the U. S.*, Sept. 30, 1789.

in his native land, thanking him for his eminent services to the trade of his State, and fervently wishing him happiness and continued success in the important station to which he had been called by a grateful country. His own reply was gracious, patriotic, and noncommittal. "That my country should be served is the first wish of my heart," he said; "I should be doubly happy indeed, were I to render it a service." In times past when he had said "my country" he nearly always meant Virginia, but now he must have been thinking of the Republic as a whole.[4]

Toward the end of the month Jefferson took his little party by ferry across the Roads to Hampton, and then they drove through Williamsburg to Richmond. According to Martha's later story, friends provided horses, but the Master's accounts show that he paid for repairs on the carriages, whether or not they were his own. Nobody reported just how the dogs were transported, but the baggage went by stage to Richmond, where the travelers arrived after about a week, having lingered somewhat at the homes of friends along the way. In the capital city of the Commonwealth, Jefferson received addresses of welcome and congratulation from both houses of the General Assembly, then in session. Here he was described as "late Minister Plenipotentiary," but without direct reference to the secretaryship of state. This occasion was Virginian in flavor, the term "native country" had a more local connotation, and the two committees seem to have waited on him informally. He was back among old political associates and friends.[5]

While he was in Richmond, Jefferson brought himself up to date on the political situation. North Carolina had accepted the new Constitution, but Rhode Island had again rejected it. The amendments Madison had designed to meet the major objections in the Virginia ratifying convention and to provide the protection of individual rights,

[4] He was described as secretary of state in the N. Y. *Gazette of the U. S.*, Dec. 12, 1789, in an extract from a letter from Norfolk dated Nov. 23. The address of the Norfolk officials on Nov. 25 and his reply were printed in the same paper on Dec. 16. As we shall see, he heard from Washington at Eppington and replied on Dec. 15.

[5] The resolutions of the House of Delegates, Dec. 7, 1789, with the names of the committeemen, the report of Henry Lee and TJ's response, were printed from a Virginia paper in the N. Y. *Gazette of the U. S.*, Jan. 2, 1790. The resolutions of the Senate on Dec. 8 were practically identical. Both chairmen reported on Dec. 9. (See *Journal*, for these dates.) Less than a week earlier, the General Assembly had addressed George Washington more elaborately and effusively, but since they were congratulating him on his election as President, and Jefferson merely on his return home, the two situations were hardly comparable. The statement of Beveridge (*Marshall*, II, 57) that the latter was greeted with "polite but coldly formal congratulations" seems gratuitous and unwarranted.

which seemed so necessary to Jefferson and George Mason, had been ratified by the House of Delegates but not yet by the Senate. These seemed sure of adoption and presumably they cut the ground from under the feet of the antifederalists. Jefferson remarked that Patrick Henry, despite his continuing popularity, had been so often in the minority that he had quit the Assembly in disgust, "never more to return, unless an opportunity offers to overturn the new constitution."[6]

He also observed the new capitol for which he had sent a model; and he picked up numerous items of personal information, such as deaths and marriages among the Virginia gentry, which he passed on at the first opportunity to Short in Paris. This opportunity came at Eppington below the James, where his daughters – especially Polly – renewed ties with the Eppes family and he himself received a belated but important letter from the President of the United States. As he had ridden along the rough roads of his beloved Virginia he must have done some thinking about the position in the federal government to which he had been appointed, and about which he must now say something. This he did about the middle of December when he was visiting other relatives of his dead wife, the Skipwiths in Chesterfield County.

He was probably as surprised by the title of the office as by the coupling of his own name with it, for John Jay had been "the Secretary for Foreign Affairs." He soon learned, however, that Congress had put foreign affairs and the whole domestic administration, except for war and finance, into one department, to be headed by a secretary of state. He harbored no real doubts of his ability to handle the foreign business. Since Franklin was too old, John Adams was vice president, and John Jay was now chief justice – though continuing his old offices temporarily – the choice of Jefferson for the conduct of foreign affairs must have seemed little short of inevitable to him, as it did to so many others. But the thought of the additional mass of domestic administration, carrying with it the probability of public criticism and censure, appalled him. So, as he wrote the President, his personal inclination was to remain in the position he was already familiar with. "But," he added, "it is not for an individual to choose his post . . . you are to marshal us as may be best for the public good." Having thus tried to avoid the responsibility of making a difficult decision, he wrote Short that he supposed he would remain as minister. Perhaps

[6] TJ to William Short, Dec. 14, 1789 (Ford, V, 136). The amendments were not finally ratified by Virginia until Feb. 15, 1791, though there was little talk of them in the interim. For Madison's activities in Congress in connection with them, see Brant, *Madison*, III, ch. XXI.

this remark was designed to make his secretary feel better, but Short had already had letters from Jay and Hamilton assuring him that the President's desire could not be resisted. The matter was still unsettled when the Minister on leave received a welcome from his slaves at Monticello and his neighbors in Albemarle which must have reconciled this deeply sensitive man to his inability to return to France.[7]

He got home two days before Christmas. The news of his coming, which he sent ahead in order that the house might be ready, had spread like wildfire through his farms, and the slaves had asked and received a holiday.[8] Their joyful reception of the Master and his daughters constituted a scene like no other that Martha ever witnessed. Accounts differ as to whether the slaves actually unhitched the horses and pulled the carriage up the last ridge of the mountain, but there can be little doubt about what they did when it reached the top. They carried the Master to the house in their arms, some blubbering and some laughing, kissing his hands and feet and the ground beneath him. To their simple minds it seemed that he had come home to stay, and he must have thought it good to be there – though he did not like to be the master of slaves or anyone else; though this wife was dead, and his red lands were wasted.

His neighbors addressed their congratulations to him soon after he got home, upwards of a dozen of them signing a paper: Dr. George Gilmer and Nicholas Lewis, James Monroe – a newcomer there though long a friend, Thomas Garth the steward, three by the name of Nicholas, and half a dozen others. They reminded him that twenty years earlier they had sent him to the House of Burgesses; they believed that his conduct in every stage of public life since then had been as satisfactory to those he served as it had always been to them; and they specially commended him for his strong attachment to the rights of all mankind.

His reply got into the newspapers of the time but since then it has attracted little or no attention. The draft which is preserved in his own papers shows by its many corrections and interlineations how carefully he prepared it, and it remains until this day one of the finest expressions

[7] Washington to TJ, Oct. 13, and Nov. 30, 1789 (Fitzpatrick, XXX, 446–447, 468); TJ to Washington, Dec. 15, 1789 (Ford, V, 140–141); TJ to Short, Dec. 14, 1789 (Ford, V, 139); Short to TJ, Nov. 30, 1789 (LC, 8935). The Department of Foreign Affairs, created by act of Congress June 27, 1789, was superseded by the Department of State, created Sept. 15, 1789. The story of the creation and organization of the department, to which we shall recur in the next chapter, is well told in Gaillard Hunt, *The Department of State* (1914), ch. IV.

[8] *Domestic Life*, p. 152; Randall, I, 552.

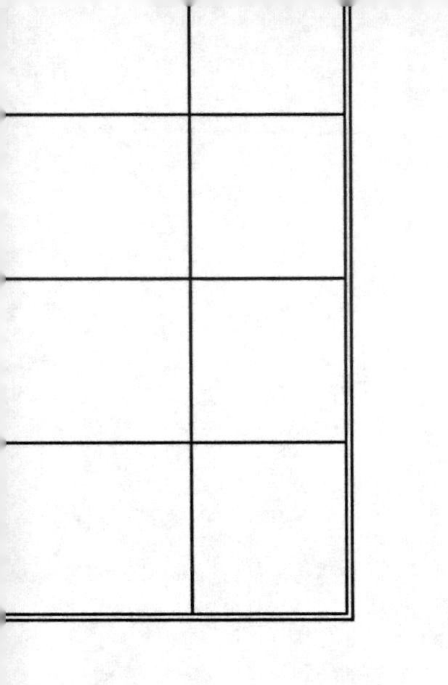

of the thoughts and hopes of a philosophical statesman, of the sentiments of a good neighbor who extended the sunshine of his benevolence to all his countrymen and all the people of the earth. To these old friends, who had assigned him the first public part he ever played and whose affection was the source of his purest happiness, he said:

> . . . We have been fellow-labourers & fellow-sufferers, & heaven has rewarded us with a happy issue from our struggles. It rests now with ourselves to enjoy in peace & concord the blessings of self-government so long denied to mankind: to shew by example the sufficiency of human reason for the care of human affairs and that the will of the majority, the natural law of every society, is the only sure guardian of the rights of man. Perhaps even this may sometimes err but it's errors are honest, solitary & shortlived. Let us then, my dear friends, for ever bow down to the general reason of society. We are safe with that, even in its deviations, for it soon returns again to the right way. These are lessons we have learned together. We have prospered in their practice, and the liberality with which you are pleased to approve my attachment to the general rights of mankind assures me we are still together in these it's kindred sentiments.
>
> Wherever I may be stationed, by the will of my country it will be my delight to see, in the general tide of happiness, that yours too flows on in just place & measure. That it may flow thro all time, gathering strength as it goes, & spreading the happy influence of reason & liberty over the face of the earth, is my fervent prayer to heaven.[9]

In the county of his birth this traveler, just returned from a continent in the first throes of revolution against ancient despotisms, swore allegiance again to the holy cause of freedom, while announcing his undying faith in the sufficiency of human reason and his necessary reliance on the will of the majority. He wrote more famous papers, but never one that better summed up the philosophy by which his feet were guided.

Before he again left his Albemarle neighbors, in this first year of government under the new Constitution, he had to attend to certain important personal matters. He had to make a real decision about the secretaryship of state, for Washington was much too wise to make

[9] The Address of the Citizens and Jefferson's Reply were printed in the N. Y. *Gazette of the U. S.*, Mar. 24, 1790, as from Richmond, Mar. 3. I myself have used the Address and TJ's own draft of his Reply in his papers (LC, 9021–9023), these documents being undated. They have been assigned the date Dec. 24, 1789, but perhaps belong later.

it for him; he soon found out that he had to give away his daughter Martha in marriage; and he must straighten out his financial affairs, whether he returned to France or not.

He talked with James Madison about the secretaryship. While at home from Congress during the Christmas season, this great little architect of the new government, who was closer to George Washington at this stage than any other leader, rode over to Monticello from Orange County to greet and sound out his long-absent friend. Delayed by illness on his way back to New York, Madison wrote Washington early in the new year that Jefferson had no enthusiasm whatever for the domestic business which had been attached to the Department of State and which he supposed would exceed the foreign. Madison himself thought that this would be trifling, that if any man could handle the whole business Jefferson surely could, and that there could be a new division of it if necessary.

These reflections commended themselves to the President and he forthwith repeated them in a characteristically kind letter. "I consider the successful administration of the general Government as an object of almost infinite consequence to the present and future happiness of the citizens of the United States," he said. "I consider the office of Secretary for the Department of State as *very* important on many accounts: and I know of no person, who, in my judgment could better execute the duties of it than yourself." He added the encouraging information that the appointment had given very extensive and very general satisfaction to the public.

It was obviously an admirable appointment, and although Washington said the appointee must make the decision, he left no possible doubt of his own desire. Jefferson was also impressed by the fact that others shared this – more of them, he said, than he expected. Hence he saw no real choice and, in the middle of February, he bowed to the inevitable. The complete sincerity of his frequently expressed preference for his old post in France may be questioned by some, just as he may be charged by some with false modesty, but if he cherished any considerable personal ambition he gave no sign of it even to those most intimate with him. What he did reveal clearly was the conflict of fears within his breast. His sensitiveness to the opinions of others was a major factor in his ultimate political success, but it was also his chief temperamental weakness and a main cause of personal unhappiness. In France, far from the public that he served, he would have been much safer from the public criticism and disapproval that he dreaded; but he would have wounded men whose good opinion he deeply valued if he had rejected this new task, and acceptance seemed the lesser evil.

His fitness for high office was no accident, but there was much that was fortuitous in the precise form that his public service took. He had resolved forever to "bow down to the general reason of society," and he may well have thought that he was doing so by yielding to the polite urging of George Washington, the unanimously elected and deeply revered head of the American Republic.[10]

Madison had written him from New York that "a universal anxiety" was expressed for his acceptance, sending him at the same time a newspaper account of Hamilton's first Report on the Public Credit, just submitted to Congress and not yet fully understood. Jefferson could hardly have realized that this report marked the beginning of a new phase of the administration of George Washington and that a fresh alignment of political forces was to emerge from the conflict over it. On February 11, 1790, in the House of Representatives, Madison opposed the form, though not the essential purpose, of one of Hamilton's major proposals. This event marked the beginning of a breach between the two chief authors of the *Federalist* papers – a breach which was destined to widen; but Jefferson had not had time to hear of it when he wrote his own letter of acceptance three days later. There is no reason to believe that his friend's urging was due to the desire to gain political reinforcement for a pending domestic battle. Madison had merely repeated his former declaration that Jefferson's acceptance of the secretaryship of state would be "more conducive to the general good" and perhaps to the very objects that he had in view in Europe than his return to his former station. It is uncertain whether Jefferson saw Hamilton's full report before he left Monticello on March 1, and even if he did he may have laid it aside for more careful and extended study at a more convenient season.[11] He had his daughter's marriage to her cousin, Thomas Mann Randolph, Jr., on his mind. This took place on February 23. An important motion of Madison's was decisively beaten in the House of Representatives the day before, and Madison spoke on the question of the assumption of state debts the day after, but these facts were still unknown to Jefferson and purely coincidental.

* * *

[10] The most important letters are: Madison to Washington, Jan. 4, 1790 (Fitzpatrick, XXX, 448*n.*); Washington to TJ, Jan. 21, 1790 (*ibid.*, 509–511); Madison to TJ, Jan. 24, 1790 (Hunt, V, 435–436); TJ to Washington, Feb. 14, 1789 (Ford, V, 143). See also TJ to Jay, Feb. 14, 1789 (Ford, V, 143–144); to Short, Mar. 12, 1790 (Ford, V, 147–148); to Lafayette, Apr. 2, 1790 (Ford, V, 151–153).

[11] Madison had promised Jan. 24, 1790 (Hunt, V, 434–435), that he would send the lengthy document "in fractions" but there was no further reference to it in their limited correspondence.

The marriage of Martha Jefferson was an extremely important domestic event, wholly unrelated to public questions. Since the death of her mother, about seven and a half years before, she had been closer to her father's heart than any other person. Polly, nearly six years younger, had been with him much less and was never quite so harmonious with him in spirit. His relations with the Eppes family had remained close despite his long absence, but during his stay in France his ties with his own brothers and sisters, though maintained by occasional letters, had become attenuated. The year before he came home his youngest sister, Anna Scott, the twin of his brother Randolph, had made a late and unimpressive marriage with Hastings Marks, a former neighbor of his with whom he had no particular acquaintance. He had recognized the event and the new relationship by writing them both politely, but, whatever he might say, this circumstance did not touch him closely. Patsy's marriage was quite another matter.[12]

His youngest sister was nearly thirty-three when she finally escaped the old maid's state. Martha was only a few months past seventeen, but early marriage was general in this society and he raised no objection on the score of age. Inbreeding was also common among the Virginia gentry and nobody looked askance at the union of cousins twice or thrice removed. The partner of his daughter's choice, then a little past twenty-one, was the son of Thomas Mann Randolph of Tuckahoe, whom Peter Jefferson had guarded during childhood and Thomas Jefferson had known all his life.[13] Some three weeks before the wedding he wrote the Colonel: "The marriage of your son with my daughter cannot be more pleasing to you than to me. Besides the worth which I discover in him, I am happy that the bond of friendship between us, as old as ourselves, should be drawn closer and closer to the day of our death." [14]

He found "worth" in young Randolph and accepted him without the slightest reservation as a son, but it is a question just how much he had seen of him in recent years. He had corresponded with the student at Edinburgh and given a full measure of advice, but, despite the enduring tradition, it is uncertain whether the young traveler made a visit

[12] TJ to Mrs. Anna Scott Marks, July 12, 1788, and to Hastings Marks, July 12, 1788 (*Domestic Life*, pp. 135–136). His memory must have grown hazy about this marriage, for at some time he entered it in his father's prayer book under the date "October, 1788" and the error is perpetuated in *Jefferson the Virginian*, p. 430.

[13] For an account of the early association, when the Jefferson family lived at Tuckahoe, see *Jefferson the Virginian*, pp. 19–22; and for the precise relationship see the genealogical charts, *ibid.*, pp. 428–429.

[14] TJ to T. M. Randolph, Sr., Feb. 4, 1790 (UVA).

to him in Paris. Hence one wonders just when and how the courtship was conducted. Perhaps the girls stayed for a time at Tuckahoe while their father was greeting old friends in Richmond, and young Randolph must have soon come visiting to Monticello. At all events, he paid his "addresses" to Martha after she returned to Virginia, and her father let her indulge her sentiments freely, scrupulously suppressing his own wishes until hers turned out to be identical. That is what he said, but his daughter could hardly have failed to see that this young man would be highly acceptable to him.[15] Intellectually young Randolph was, or became, a man of parts and his father-in-law found him companionable. Tall and lean and a bold horseman, he was no doubt a dashing figure at this stage, though it soon appeared that he needed much help in the management of his affairs.

As for Martha, later descriptions emphasized the beauty of her character, not her person, and a miniature made in Paris when the bloom of youth was on her is less attractive than her portrait by Sully as a matron. Her rather homely face, as seen by contemporaries in daily life, was brightened by good will and animated by intelligence. She was tall, loosely made, and awkward in movement, but her voice was sweet and her manners were gracious. She had blue eyes and reddish hair, and was best summed up afterwards by the remark that she was a delicate likeness of her father. The similarity was more than physical but while close it was not complete, for she had already revealed a more active sense of humor. Her father had done his best to make her accomplished, but there were other things which concerned him more. He once made some notes on the duties of a wife, and presumably these were for his daughter on the eve of marriage. As read now, his words have an old-fashioned and strongly masculine flavor, and only by contrast do they suggest the salons and boudoirs of Paris. "Sweetness of temper, affection to a husband and attention to his interests, constitute the duties of a wife and form the basis of domestic felicity," he wrote. "The charms of beauty, and the brilliancy of wit,

[15] TJ wrote Randolph a long letter of advice on July 6, 1787 (Ford, IV, 403–407), but had not heard from him when he wrote again on Feb. 28, 1788 (*Va. Mag.*, XLII, 322–323). The tradition, as given in Randall, I, 558, is that Randolph came to Paris in the summer of 1788, but I have found no reference to such a visit; and William H. Gaines, who is preparing a dissertation on him at the University of Virginia, doubts if it was ever made. There is no specific mention of Tuckahoe in TJ's Account Book for the period of his trip from Norfolk to Monticello in late 1789, though he and his daughters may have stayed there during the days he was in Richmond. His fullest statement about the "addresses" of young Randolph to his daughter appears to be in his letter of Apr. 2, 1790, to Madame de Corny (Chinard, *Trois Amitiés*, p. 196).

though they may captivate in the mistress will not long delight in the wife: they will shorten even their own transitory reign if as I have often seen they shine more for the attraction of everybody else than their husbands." Martha had heard him say this sort of thing many times before and did not need to be admonished now. She was quite unspoiled, and time was to show that she fully lived up to his standards for her as a wife and mother.[16]

Colonel Randolph, who had been a widower for a year, offered to convey to his son a tract of 950 acres in Henrico County called Varina, with forty slaves on and belonging to it, and executed the deed promptly on the insistence of the more businesslike Jefferson who promptly matched it, though he wisely made his gift to Martha and her heirs, not to her husband. It consisted of 1000 acres of his Poplar Forest tract in Bedford County and twelve families of slaves, along with some stock. The young couple seemed well provided for.[17]

He saw them wedded on February 23, bore the expense of the license, and paid the clergyman the marriage fee. On March 1 he left them and Polly at Monticello, and during the spring wrote the three of them in turn. His letters were affectionate, solicitous, and monitory; and theirs, when finally they came, were appealingly dependent. Before summer both girls were at Eppington, where Polly remained with her "dear Aunt Eppes," a serious rival of her father in her affections. Meanwhile, young Randolph looked over his farm at Varina, where he and Martha were determined to live despite the inconvenience of the place. He was not well, could not stand the heat, and seemed rather helpless and confused when he unburdened himself to his father-in-law. What the young pair most wanted was to find a place near Monticello, and in the course of time they did. Their financial prospects took a turn for the worse that summer, when Colonel Randolph, who was older than Jefferson, found a much younger lady for a wife and made another marriage settlement. Jefferson, who fully recognized the Colonel's susceptibility, urged his daughter to adjust herself to this confused situation, and he himself entered into negotiations with the elder Randolph in the autumn for the purchase of Edgehill, an admirable

[16] The notes on the duties of a wife are in LC, 41985; see also his letter of Apr. 4, 1790 (*Domestic Life*, p. 180). Among the best of the later descriptions of Martha are those of Margaret Bayard Smith in *First Forty Years of Washington Society* (1906), pp. 34–35, under the date Dec. 26, 1802, and Francis Walker Gilmer in R. B. Davis, *Gilmer* (1939), p. 373, from an even later date. The miniature made in Paris and attributed to Joseph Boze is in the Hugh Campbell Wallace Collection, American Embassy, Paris. It is reproduced in H. C. Rice, *L'Hôtel de Langeac*.

[17] TJ to T. M. Randolph, Sr., Feb. 4, 1790 (UVA); indenture of 1000 acres at Poplar Forest, Feb. 21, 1790 (Edgehill Randolph Papers, UVA). Col. Randolph's deed to his son, mentioned in the indenture, was dated Feb. 15, 1790.

place for Martha and her husband in Albemarle. These dragged on for several years and need not concern us yet.[18]

Jefferson had gained a son but had not lost a daughter. Some years later, when Martha was several times a mother and he was about to return home from the seat of government, she said in the course of a sentimental letter: "The first sensations of my life were affection and respect for you and none others in the course of it have weakened or surpassed that." No *new* ties, she observed, "can weaken the first and best of nature." [19] But she showed toward her husband the loyalty her father had instilled in her, and within the first year of marriage Thomas Mann Randolph, Jr., had accumulated an eternal debt of gratitude to Jefferson. From the beginning the young couple depended on him as on nobody else, and when complications arose he generally managed to straighten things out. But as he set out for Richmond on March 1, 1790, leaving his two daughters and his new son on the mountain, his immediate concern was to tidy up his own tangled finances before proceeding northward to new official duties in New York.

While at home he had not failed to observe that his farms had deteriorated during his long absence from them. He could not give them much personal attention now, and he left Nicholas Lewis in general charge of his local affairs, making a provisional arrangement with Thomas Garth in the event of the death of this friend and neighbor whose health at the time was bad.[20] Perhaps anticipating the sales of more distant holdings which he made later in the year, he rather conservatively estimated his lands as amounting to upwards of 10,000 acres and he now had about 200 slaves. His assets seemed to him sufficient to warrant an advance of money which he sorely needed. Accordingly, he wrote to the bankers in Amsterdam with whom he had conducted official business, inquiring about a personal loan of one or two thousand dollars.[21] Then, in Richmond, he formalized his arrangements

[18] Fees recorded in Account Book, Feb. 23, 28, 1790; family correspondence, Mar. 28–July 17, 1790, in *Domestic Life*, pp. 175–176, 180–188; T. M. Randolph, Jr., to TJ, May 25, 1790 (Edgehill Randolph Papers, UVA). Jefferson carried on negotiations for Edgehill, the original Randolph place in Albemarle, in behalf of his grateful son-in-law in the autumn of 1790, but was not assured of the success of these until the spring of 1792.

[19] Letter received by TJ on July 1, 1798 (MHS).

[20] Mar. 7, 1790 (*Garden Book*, p. 149).

[21] TJ to Nicholas and Jacob Van Staphorst and Hubbard, Feb. 28, 1790 (Ford, V, 144–146). Cash was scarce in Virginia, and the ostensible purpose of this "advance" was the restoration of his lands. The letter seems to have had no immediate results.

with his English creditors. The bulk of his debt, as we have already noted, was attributable directly or indirectly to the burden with which his wife's estate was weighted when he and she got it from her father, John Wayles, and was owed to two chief houses. The total now was more than £7500, and the accumulated interest charges now amounted to more than fifty per cent of the principal. He provided for regular annual payments during the next seven years, thus completing an important part of the personal business which had brought him home, but as he signed his bonds he must have wondered if a thoroughly realistic balance sheet would have shown him to be solvent.[22]

After a week in Richmond, he proceeded to Alexandria, where he received from the Mayor another address of congratulation and made another reply.[23] The thanks which were given him for his services to commerce should really go to the friendly French nation, he said, but he fully agreed with the Mayor about the importance of maintaining a republic in America, being convinced that it was the only form of government which was not openly or secretly at war with the rights of man.

A heavy snow fell on the night of his arrival in Alexandria, whether or not it amounted to the eighteen inches which were reported by this teller of large stories who so hated cold weather. It convinced him that he would have difficulties on the road, so he left his phaeton to be sent by water and went himself by stage, his horses being led by two of his own servants. He had been unable to visit George Mason at Gunston Hall, but in Philadelphia he was visited by Benjamin Rush, and he himself called for the last time on the bedridden and now emaciated Franklin.

Dr. Rush, who had known him in the Continental Congress, found him plain in dress and unchanged in manners, still attached to republican forms of government, still comparing American and European animals to the disadvantage of the latter. Jefferson found Dr. Franklin characteristically cheerful but feared that their animated conversation about the Revolution in France was really beyond the old man's strength. The dean of American diplomacy and chief luminary of philosophy died a month later, and surely the new Secretary of State was his spiritual heir if he left one. But when Jefferson

[22] His specific arrangements with James Lyle – for his debts to Kippen & Co., and Henderson, McCaul & Co. – and with Richard Hanson for his larger debt to Farrell & Jones, are described in his Account Book, Mar. 4, 6, 1790. For the general background, see *Jefferson the Virginian*, pp. 441–445.

[23] Mar. 11, 1790. Address and reply in N. Y. *Gazette of the U. S.*, Mar. 27, 1790; reply in Ford, V, 146–147.

arrived in New York on March 21, two weeks after leaving Richmond, it was his fellow Virginian, George Washington, that he reported to. He did this immediately, even though the day was Sunday, and at that moment a new era in his public life began.[24]

[24] TJ to T. M. Randolph, Jr., Mar. 21, 1790 (Ford, V, 148–149), describing whole journey; Account Book, Mar. 8–21, 1790; Mason to TJ, Mar. 16, 1790 (LC, 9117–9118); TJ to Mason, June 13, 1790 (Rowland, *Mason*, II, 328); Benj. Rush, *Autobiography*, p. 181 (March 17, 1790); TJ to Madame d'Houdetot, Apr. 2, 1790, about Franklin (*Domestic Life*, p. 178); TJ's autobiography (Ford, I, 151–153), giving an account of the visit as remembered in old age; *Diaries of Washington*, IV, 106 (Mar. 21, 1790). Philip Marsh, "The Manuscript Franklin Gave to Jefferson," *Library Bulletin of the Am. Philos. Soc.*, 1946, pp. 45–48, discusses a disputed passage in TJ's autobiography, dealing with Franklin's pre-Revolutionary negotiations with the British.

[XIV]

New York and the Court of George Washington

1790

WHEN Thomas Jefferson ferried across the Hudson and arrived in the temporary capital of the United States, New York was not yet regarded as the metropolis of the country. The first federal census, which they began to take that summer, showed its population to be slightly more than 33,000, and this was greater than that of Philadelphia proper, but the latter city with its contiguous suburbs was the larger center.[1] New York now extended about a mile and a half up the river on the East Side and about a mile on the West Side, and was growing fast. Its trade had recently revived and increased and its port was thriving. But the place was small and plain by European standards, and it could hardly have been impressive to Jefferson, who had recently come from Paris with its half million people and could compare the vast buildings at Versailles with Federal Hall, where George Washington had been inaugurated a year before. Actually, he stayed in New York less than six months (March 21 to September 1) and he appears to have made no comments either for or against the place, except for some characteristic objections to the weather. He found this exceedingly disagreeable in April, when Albemarle County was bursting into bloom, and by June he concluded that there was no spring or fall there. They had ten months of winter and two of summer with some winter days interspersed, he said. He wanted to make a systematic comparison of the temperature with that of his own

[1] The population of Philadelphia was 28,522 without suburbs, and 42,444 with them. The only other cities in the country with more than 10,000 people were Boston, Charleston, and Baltimore. For descriptive details see S. I. Pomerantz, *New York, An American City, 1783–1803* (N. Y., 1938); and T. E. V. Smith, *The City of New York in the Year of Washington's Inauguration* (N. Y., 1889).

region, from readings made at dawn and at 4 P.M., and sought the co-operation of his new son-in-law; but he became discouraged when he could find no spot at his house where a thermometer would be in the shade in both the morning and afternoon.[2] Thus he was unable to demonstrate just how harsh the climate was.

He tried vainly to get a house on "the Broadway," not because of any considerations of sunshine but because he expected his business to center there. Broadway, then badly paved as far as Vesey, was not as important as the streets running off it to the east, especially Wall Street; but the President was living on it, in the pretentious Macomb mansion, which had been newly furnished for him at a cost of ten thousand dollars, and most of the business of the Secretary of State would be with him. The offices of Jefferson's own department, such as they were, were also on Broadway. The house he took was at 57 Maiden Lane. He described it as small and rented it for a year at the rate of £100, expecting to get into it on the first of May; but he did not move in till June and for five or six weeks he was in a lodging- or boardinghouse.[3]

For a time his state was similar to that of most of the representatives and senators, who were also homeless. On his forty-seventh birthday he wrote to an old friend that he had no complaint against anybody, having had more than his share of the confidence of his country, but that any sort of public employment was but "honorable exile from one's family and affairs."[4] Even after he got a house he felt like a transient because of uncertainties about the future residence of the federal government; and the improvements he made were an extravagance, though thoroughly in character. He had a gallery built at the back of the house, and for cabinetwork alone spent more than the amount of a whole year's rent.[5]

After a while he sent back to Virginia one of the servants he had brought with him, Bob, but before moving to Maiden Lane he engaged two others. James, who had been with him in France and appears to have been the cook, purchased the household supplies in the absence of Petit. Jefferson wrote Short that he could not do without his maître d'hôtel, that Petit must be persuaded to come to America,

[2] TJ to T. M. Randolph, Jr., Apr. 18, 1790 (Ford, V, 159); to Mrs. Eppes, June 13, 1790 (*Domestic Life*, p. 184); to Randolph, May 30, 1790 (Ford, V, 171).

[3] The agreement was dated Mar. 29, 1790 (LC, 9149); on June 2 he moved in. A tablet was placed on the building at 57 Maiden Lane in 1929; see excellent editorial, "When Jefferson Lived in New York," in *N. Y. Times*, Apr. 15, 1929.

[4] TJ to Francis Willis, Apr. 13, 1790 (Ford, V, 157).

[5] On the house and the improvements, see Fiske Kimball, *Jefferson, Architect*, p. 150, and Drawing 121. The Account Book mentions payments.

that he really could not set up housekeeping until this invaluable employee had arrived with the furniture. Short was winding up his patron's affairs in Paris, living at the Hôtel de Langeac in the meantime, though Jefferson finally got relieved of the rent of that house by midsummer. The French servants were kept till August 1, when each received a two months' "gratification"; and by September seventy or eighty packages of furniture were at Havre awaiting shipment, though the carriages were not there as yet and some of the horses were not sold till fall. This was exceedingly expensive business and Jefferson did not get his things until another year, being much handicapped in the meantime by the lack of books. His own were divided between France and Monticello and he was distressed to find how few were available in New York. This was not an intellectual center but a mart of commerce.[6]

Abigail Adams informed her sister that the President never rode out without six horses hitched to his carriage, four servants, and two gentlemen before him.[7] The Secretary of State had brought two horses with him, and his phaeton arrived from Alexandria by water after about a month. His position warranted no such style as that adopted by George Washington, but it was largely through force of circumstances that he lived so much more plainly here than he had in Paris, for he followed no cult of republican simplicity when it came to horses and houses. Nor is there good reason to believe that he had lowered his standards of dress, even though William Maclay said his clothes did not fit him.

This senator from the backwoods of Pennsylvania wrote in his diary a description of the Secretary of State,[8] which has been much quoted by historians – not unnaturally since Maclay himself has been termed the original Jeffersonian democrat. But he recognized Jefferson as no chief of his, and since his vivid portraits all tend toward caricature one wonders if this one was true to life. If the Secretary had a rambling, vacant look and spoke unceasingly in a loose and rambling way, he belied his systematic habits and masked his deeply purposeful character. Several items in this familiar description, however, harmonize with those given by others at other times. Jefferson was still slender and loose-jointed, and his posture was rather awkward at times. His face had a sunny aspect, he scattered information every-

[6] TJ to Short, Apr. 6, 1790 (LC, 9198); Short to TJ, Aug. 22 and Sept. 9, 1790 (LC, 9722–9723, 9794–9795); account with Short, 1789–1790 (LC, 12173–12182); various entries in Account Book.

[7] Mrs. Adams to Mrs. Cranch, Aug. 9, 1789 (*New Letters of Abigail Adams*, 1947, p. 20).

[8] *Journal of William Maclay*, May 24, 1790 (1927 edn.), pp. 265–266.

where he went, often using sparkling phrases, and he was persuasive in conference. Maclay observed both stiffness and laxity in his manner, without attempting to resolve the contradiction. Probably he was stiff at first because of shyness, and under sympathetic conditions became relaxed. His clothes may have been too small for him once without always being so, and one need not assume that he habitually sat in a lounging manner, but at first glance he was relatively unimpressive in his person. Unless the rusticity of his nature was quite incurable, he should not have been socially ill at ease in this court after his experiences abroad, but, with all the cultivation of his mind, he was obviously no such figure of a man as George Washington. He did not look like an uncrowned king.

It was during his first few weeks in New York that he participated most actively in social life. He did not blame the many parties he attended for the protracted headache that ensued, but the fact is that he was feasted from table to table, at large set dinners. He always remembered the cordial reception he got from his colleagues and the principal citizens, and Abigail Adams reported to her sister at the time that he added much to the social circle.[9] No doubt he dined at the manor house of Richmond Hill which the Vice President had taken; it stood in what is now Greenwich Village and was then regarded as far out. But it was through the President that he was introduced into the court which centered in that stately figure. He reported to Washington on his first Sunday in New York, just after the General had returned from church; he saw him on Monday, immediately after a sitting which Washington gave John Trumbull, whom Jefferson was glad to see again; he conferred with his Chief on Tuesday, following what Washington called a "full and very respectable levee," and this the new Secretary must have attended. He was at a presidential dinner on Thursday, and, even if he did not go to Mrs. Washington's Friday levee, he had immediate and abundant opportunity to observe firsthand the formalities which had already been deplored as monarchial and were afterwards to be attacked in party warfare.[10]

The miniature tempest over the title of the President which had enlivened the first weeks of the administration had died down by now, though Madison had given Jefferson some report of it at the time and he had responded in just the way that was to be expected. He had learned that his old friend John Adams and his former con-

[9] TJ to Short, Jan. 8, 1825 (Ford, X, 333); Mrs. Adams to Mrs. Cranch, Apr. 3, 1790 (*New Letters*, p. 44).

[10] *Diaries of Washington*, IV, 106, 109 (Mar. 21, 22, 23, 25, 1790).

gressional colleague Richard Henry Lee had espoused the cause of titles with great earnestness in the Senate, over which the former was presiding. The Senate had resolved to designate the chief executive as "His Highness the President of the United States and Protector of Their Liberties," but had been forced to yield to the House of Representatives, where Madison was at work, and call him simply "The President of the United States." Jefferson, who had recently reported the fall of the Bastille and rejoiced in the humbling of a king, thought the proposal of the Senate the most ridiculous thing he ever heard of; and it was then that he repeated Franklin's now-famous characterization of John Adams as always an honest man, often a great one, and sometimes absolutely mad.[11]

While in Virginia, Jefferson must have learned of the uses which the opponents of the government had made of this episode. For a time Patrick Henry's description of the Constitution as squinting towards monarchy was in everybody's mouth and the orator was established among his supporters as a true prophet. The sensitive President was not blamed, but Adams and Lee had been rendered so odious as to lead to the prediction that neither would ever again get a vote in that state.[12] Jefferson was no admirer of Patrick Henry, and when he talked with Dr. Benjamin Rush in Philadelphia he still spoke of Adams respectfully and affectionately as "a great and upright man," but he also deplored the changed attitude of his old colleague to republican forms of government.[13]

In New York he probably picked up further information about the efforts that the Vice President had made, in the supposed secrecy of the Senate, in behalf of titles, forms, and ceremonies. He may even have learned that somebody there had given Adams a title – "Rotundity." His great and good friend had become a comic figure and by his extravagance of speech had disarmed himself as a popular leader. So Jefferson must have thought, but he would have been shocked if he had read the reflections on the Presidency which Adams had sent in the utmost seriousness to George Washington:

> The office, by its legal authority, defined in the constitution, has no equal in the world, excepting those only which are held by crowned heads; nor is the royal authority in all cases to be compared to it. . . . Neither dignity nor authority can be

[11] Madison to TJ, May 23, 1789 (Hunt, V, 369–370*n.*); TJ to Madison, July 29, 1789 (Ford, V, 104). I have reported the matter as Madison did. Minor variations and more vivid details can be seen in Maclay's *Journal*.

[12] Dr. David Stuart to Washington, July 14, 1789 (Fitzpatrick, XXX, 363*n.*); Washington to Stuart, July 26, 1789 (*ibid.*, XXX, 360–363).

[13] Rush, *Autobiography*, p. 181.

> supported in human minds, collected into nations or any great numbers, without a *splendor and majesty* in some degree proportioned to them. . . . If the *state and pomp* essential to this great department are not, in a good degree, preserved, it will be in vain for America to hope for consideration with foreign powers.[14]

Adams recognized that his long residence abroad might have impressed him with views "incompatible with the present temper and feelings" of his fellow citizens. As a political judgment this was clearly an understatement, and similar causes had produced opposite effects in the case of Jefferson, who had been more recently in Europe.

The attitude of the Secretary of State more closely resembled that of Madison than it did that of an acidulous democrat like William Maclay, or an opportunist like Patrick Henry. Fresh from monarchical France, he was more excitable on the subject of titles than the more judicious Madison, but in sober judgment he would have agreed that the chief objection to them was that they were not reconcilable with the nature of the American government and the genius of the American people, and that their effect would be to diminish, not increase, the dignity of the Republic.[15]

Washington needed no title that he did not have already. As Senator Maclay said, it was impossible to add to the respect already entertained for him; and, as many observed, he was far more kingly in his person than most wearers of a crown. Benjamin Franklin, bequeathing to his friend and the friend of mankind, General Washington, his crabtree walking stick with a gold head curiously wrought in the form of the cap of liberty, said: "If it were a sceptre, he has merited it and would become it." [16] Jefferson was inordinately fearful of what sceptres might do to mankind, but his mature judgment was that nature and fortune had never combined more perfectly to make a man great than in the case of Washington.[17] He would not have disputed the comment of Abigail Adams that the President left King George III far behind in social grace, dignity, and ease. He himself said that Washington's person was fine, his stature exactly right, his deportment "easy, erect, and noble," that he was the best horseman of his age and the most

[14] Adams to Washington, May 17, 1789 (*Works,* VIII, 493), italics inserted. He was replying to Washington's inquiries about the line of conduct to be pursued (May 10, 1789; Fitzpatrick, XXX, 319–321). These inquiries were also sent to Jay, Hamilton, and Madison.

[15] Madison, quoted by James Hart, *American Presidency in Action*, p. 37.

[16] Reported by Franklin's executor, May 7, 1790 (Fitzpatrick, XXXI, 43*n.*).

[17] TJ to Dr. Walter Jones, Jan. 2, 1814 (Ford, IX, 449). In this letter he gave one of the best estimates of Washington that has ever been published.

graceful figure that could be seen in any saddle. So impressive a man, with such a background of patriotic achievement, needed no artificial buttressing in a position to which he had been unanimously elected. It was the later opinion of his Secretary of State that Washington, far from being helped by the formalities of these early years, alone made them endurable by his character and personality. In a time of more bitter partisanship than any that had been manifested by the spring of 1790, Jefferson reminded Madison of an observation the latter made to him when he first came to New York – that the satellites and sycophants surrounding Washington "had wound up the ceremonials of the government to a pitch of stateliness which nothing but his personal character could have supported, and which no character after him could ever maintain." [18]

The judgment was fundamentally sound and the prediction was verified, since there has never been another presidential court like that of George Washington, but the existence of this court cannot be wholly attributed to the unwise counsel of satellites and sycophants. The General said he would rather be at Mount Vernon with a friend or two than be attended by all the officers of state and the representatives of every power in Europe; but, besides being a more formal person than Jefferson, he was much more concerned to set precedents of official dignity at the beginning of the government. His conduct was calculated, and the social system he adopted was based to a considerable degree on common sense.

By allotting a specified time each week for the reception of idle and ceremonious visitors Washington hoped to free himself from perpetual interruptions in the conduct of his business.[19] When the Secretary of State, who admired the President so sincerely, attended his first levee on a Tuesday afternoon in March between three and four, he could hardly have done so in a wholly unsympathetic spirit, much as he personally disliked this sort of thing. Gentlemen came as they pleased without invitation, the President bowed to them when they were presented but did not shake hands, the door was closed after a bit and a circle was formed, the President went round it talking briefly with each visitor, then he resumed his position to receive and give the final bows.[20]

[18] TJ to Madison, June 9, 1793 (Ford, VI, 293).

[19] He gave an excellent explanation of his system to David Stuart, June 15, 1790 (Fitzpatrick, XXXI, 53–55).

[20] *Ibid.*, and William Sullivan, *Public Men of the Revolution* (1847), p. 120, quoted by L. D. White in *The Federalists* (1948), p. 109. These precise forms may not have been fully worked out in 1790, but the general character of the levee was the same throughout the administration.

Washington was criticized for the stiffness of his bows, but he thought this could be better attributed to the infirmities of age or the fault of his training than to pride of office. These were solemn affairs, undoubtedly, and if Washington's secretary Tobias Lear was not pompous, his aide David Humphreys, whom Jefferson had befriended in Paris, assuredly was, but it would have taken a more rabid democrat than the Secretary of State to see much harm in this sort of social occasion at this time.

Having no lady to bring to Mrs. Washington's levees on Friday, Jefferson may have escaped these more pretentious affairs, but inevitably he dined at the mansion. The guests were so chosen that his first dinner there was in effect a welcoming party. His fellow Virginian, Attorney General Randolph, was out of town; but his two fellow secretaries, little Alexander Hamilton and huge Henry Knox, were there with their wives, along with the Schuylers, parents of Eliza Hamilton and his friend Angelica Church. The presence of the Jays was entirely appropriate since the former Secretary for Foreign Affairs was his predecessor, if anybody was; Madison and John Page, both members of the House, were his old and intimate friends; and a couple of unnamed senators were thrown in for good measure. If the Secretary of State sat next to Mrs. Washington, as he probably did, he must have liked that plump and amiable lady. The solemn President across the way may have drummed on the table with his knife or spoon between courses, as he did when William Maclay dined there with a senatorial party, but he was probably less bored on this occasion. Jefferson may have exchanged gossip about the Comte de Moustier and Madame de Bréhan with charming Mrs. Jay, who was reputed to have her husband under such firm control; and he must have told Mrs. Schuyler or Mrs. Hamilton how much he regretted missing Angelica Church, who had recently gone back to England. Hamilton himself had a winning social manner, and the Knoxes added weight to the party if nothing else. The Secretary of War weighed some three hundred pounds and his consort did her best to match him. Admittedly they were the largest couple in New York.

Inevitably this was a bountiful dinner, for the presidential couple gave no other kind. Senator Maclay, who was frequently invited to the mansion, described one menu in detail. The soup was followed by roasted and boiled fish; then they had fowls and a variety of meats. For dessert there were pies, puddings, and ice creams; then they had a variety of fruits and nuts. The important business of eating was transacted with solemnity, scarcely a word being said until the cloth had been removed. Then the host arose and drank a toast to every person round the table, and a vast hubbub resulted when everybody imitated him.[21] Jefferson's first dinner was probably not quite so solemn an occasion. The General probably drank his health, and after the ladies withdrew no doubt the men told some stories. The new minister of state could have related some anecdote about Benjamin Franklin or Marie Antoinette that he had picked up in Paris, or given fresh details about the storming of the Bastille, but he could have pleased his host most easily by giving agricultural observations from his southern trip.

Jefferson afterwards said that while he was being feasted in New York he heard shocking monarchical sentiments and had the whole company on his hands when he himself maintained the principles of republicanism.[22] He could not have been thinking of this board, for he knew that George Washington wanted the people to have all the self-government they were competent to exercise. The General had less confidence in "the natural integrity and discretion" of the people than he had, and was thus more cautious about extending the area of self-government, but Jefferson himself was not hasty in this respect, and at no time was it possible for him to think of Washington as any sort of royalist.[23]

No doubt the new American Constitution and the French Revolution were much discussed at other tables in New York, as he recalled, and it would have been surprising if he had not heard extreme talk from some "High Federalists"; but his contemporary letters reflect little disquietude about the situation either in the United States or France at this juncture, and in extreme old age his memory may have played him false about his dates. After he had been harnessed in his new gear ten days he wrote Lafayette with obvious satisfaction that the opposition to the Constitution had almost disappeared, the amendments having brought over most of the objectors. "If the President can be preserved a few years till habits of authority and obedience can be established generally, we have nothing to fear," he said, adding that the little libertine Rhode Island would soon mend her ways and join her sisters. At the same time he wrote the Comtesse d'Houdetot that he found in America "a philosophic revolution, philosophically effected." [24]

[21] The best description is in the entry for Aug. 27, 1789 (Maclay, *Journal*, pp. 134–135).

[22] TJ to Short, Jan. 8, 1825 (Ford, X, 332–333). See Anas (Ford, I, 159–160), also from a very late date.

[23] TJ to John Melish, Jan. 13, 1813 (Ford, IX, 376).

[24] TJ to Lafayette, Apr. 2, 1790 (Ford, V, 152); to Madame d'Houdetot Apr. 2, 1790 (Chinard, *Les Amitiés Américaines de Madame d'Houdetot*, p. 52).

He was much more complacent about the situation in France than he had been when he left there, for things seemed to have settled down; and he did not really become concerned about the outcome of the Revolution until the flight of Louis XVI, more than a year after he himself took over his new office. The King was now in Paris, Lafayette was at the height of his power and prestige, and the National Assembly was engaged in the task of making a constitution. "The change in your government will approximate us to one another," he wrote a duchess.[25] There had been some checks, some horrors, but the way to Heaven had always been strewn with thorns. He had learned that some of his old friends in Paris were not happy in their personal situations. Madame de Corny, who was so grieved by the thought that she would not see him again, had written him that there was grave scarcity of bread and money and that her pretty house was for sale. A darker day had already dawned for her. He expressed the hope that "a revolution so pregnant with the general happiness of the nation" would not in the end injure the interests of persons so friendly to the general good of mankind as Monsieur and Madame de Corny, but it is doubtful if he comforted her very much.[26] He said later that he left France when the Revolution was still in its first and pure stage, but during his first year of absence from that scene he was reminded that the work of destruction had started. "The characteristic difference between your revolution and ours," said Madame d'Houdetot sagaciously, "is that having nothing to destroy, you had nothing to injure." [27]

Jefferson's French friends may have thought that he dismissed too lightly the losses they had suffered even at this early stage, and that he treated them themselves perfunctorily. He wrote a whole sheaf of letters of farewell and some of his expressions of thanks for past services were effusive, but already he appeared deeply absorbed in other affairs than theirs. He had closed one chapter and begun another, and he seemed to be looking at the French as a remote philosopher who was satisfied at the moment with the general prospects of mankind.

Also, he was thinking as a responsible official of his own government. He wrote Lafayette:

> I think, with others, that nations are to be governed according to their own interest; but I am convinced that it is their interest, in the long run, to be grateful, faithful to their engagements

[25] TJ to the Duchesse D'Anville, Apr. 2, 1790 (Ford, V, 154).

[26] Madame de Corny to TJ, Nov. 25, 1789; TJ to Madame de Corny, Apr. 2, 1790 (Chinard, *Trois Amitiés*, pp. 191–196).

[27] Madame d'Houdetot to TJ, Sept. 3, 1790 (Chinard, *Les Amitiés Américaines de Madame d'Houdetot*, pp. 55–56).

> even in the worst of circumstances, and honorable and generous always. If I had not known that the head of our government was in these sentiments, and that his national and private ethics were the same, I would never have been where I am.[28]

With the Marquis as a person he was to maintain cordial friendship, but he had to deal henceforth with France as a nation. His grateful remembrance of her past services to his own country could be no more doubted than could his hopes for her future services to mankind, and he was confident that the President shared his sentiments. In his opinion, his Chief was no more an Angloman than a monarchist, and Washington's own letters show sincere sympathy for the aspirations of the French, and pride in their achievements. A year earlier Washington had written that "the American Revolution, or the peculiar light of the age, seems to have opened the eyes of almost every nation in Europe, and a spirit of equal liberty appears fast to be gaining ground everywhere, which must afford satisfaction to every friend of mankind." This supremely practical man was now expressing some concern lest the advocates of political improvement should make more haste than good speed; but soon he congratulated Lafayette on the favorable aspect of things in France, and before the summer was over he accepted from the hands of his young French friend the key to the Bastille, describing it as "the token of victory gained by liberty over despotism," much as Jefferson would have done.[29]

France herself was important but not central in the Secretary's thought as he turned to his new tasks as an American official. The two nations did appear to be converging in their forms of government, since France had moved definitely toward the left while the United States had shifted toward the right. Just what their respective courses would be in the future he did not know, but he was sufficiently familiar with political navigation to recognize the need for tacking and he had supreme confidence in the American pilot. It was never true that Jefferson, although a professed friend, was in reality the "secret and malignant enemy" of Washington, as was asserted afterwards in the spirit of bitter partisanship.[30] At this time it would have taken a wild imagination even to suggest such an attitude. It was because of his implicit trust in the character and wisdom of the President that the new Secretary of State discounted such wild monarchical talk as he

[28] TJ to Lafayette, Apr. 2, 1790 (Ford, V, 152).

[29] Washington to Crèvecœur, Apr. 10, 1789 (Fitzpatrick, XXX, 281); to Luzerne, Apr. 29, 1790 (*ibid.*, XXXI, 40–41); to Lafayette, June 30, and Aug. 11, 1790 (*ibid.*, XXXI, 44, 85–86).

[30] Examples can be multiplied. This one is from Theodore Dwight, *Character of Jefferson* (1839), pp. 125–126.

heard at first, and the best single clue to his political attitude during this New York period can be found in his loyal devotion to George Washington.

After his first five or six weeks of relative conviviality he was in virtual social retirement almost that many more. Seized on the first of May with one of his periodical headaches, he was confined for about a month. During this month he drafted the most elaborate of his papers of the New York period, his report on weights and measures, and he may have exaggerated his suffering afterwards. At the time he said more about the duration of the headache than its severity, but the conduct of his ordinary business was largely suspended and he probably could not have conferred with Washington even if his Chief had not been dangerously ill in the same month of May. He had already told Lafayette that the General's health was not as firm as it used to be, and there was a day when he was stricken with fear that the ship would lose its sorely needed helmsman.

Washington was taken on May 9 with a bad cold which developed the next day into pneumonia, and within a week his life was despaired of. Jefferson reported that two of the three physicians gave him up, and William Maclay, who went to call, said that tears were in every eye. Fortunately he rallied, and he recovered so rapidly that he could ride out in a carriage less than ten days after his hairbreadth escape, afterwards looking better than he had before. Jefferson wrote Short that the public alarm had passed conception, and that it proved how much depended on this one man's life. Abigail Adams echoed these sentiments in another private letter, shuddering to think how narrow her own escape had been from becoming the First Lady under circumstances which would have imperiled the Union and the permanence of the government. Washington himself remarked that he had undergone more and more severe illness since he had been President than in the thirty previous years together; this was the second severe attack he had had, and he believed that a third would put him to sleep with his fathers. His physicians advised him to take more exercise and apply himself less to business, but, as he wrote Lafayette, he could not escape the conviction that he had to accomplish what he had undertaken, to the best of his abilities, come what might.[31]

[31] Jefferson mentioned Washington's illness in several letters, as in one to Short, May 27, 1790 (Ford, V, 168). Of Washington's own references to it the most interesting are in letters to Lafayette, June 3, 1790 (Fitzpatrick, XXXI, 46; editor's summary *ibid.*, 43*n.*), and Dr. David Stuart, June 15, 1790 (*ibid.*, XXI, 55). Mrs. Adams's vivid comments are in a letter of May 30, 1790, to Mrs. Cranch (*New Letters*, p. 49).

The President was hoping that Congress would recess before the summer was over and that he could then get back to Mount Vernon, and in the meantime he thought himself fortunate in the officials he had managed to gather round him. "I feel myself supported by able co-adjutors, who harmonize extremely well together," he said to Lafayette. Furthermore, he believed that his appointments had given perfect satisfaction to the country. Early in June he took his Secretary of State along on a three days' fishing trip off Sandy Hook. Jefferson went as a harmonious co-adjutor and in some hope of beneficial physical effects. He was not yet relieved of his headache but he hoped he might be, as the result of the seasickness he would probably encounter. He still had it when he got back, but he was now able to attend to ordinary business. By this time he had learned what Washington expected of one of his executive heads, and what his own public business really was. To sum it all up, he was to be an assistant to the President, presumably the most intimate one, and it was the President, not Congress, that he had to please.[32]

[32] The fishing trip was on June 7–9, 1790 (Fitzpatrick, XXXI, 49*n.*); TJ referred to it in his letter of June 6, 1790 to Short (Ford, V, 178).

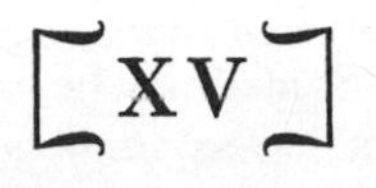

The Functions of the Secretary of State

THE administrative structure that had been created within the new government was simple in form.[1] There were only three executive departments – State, Treasury, and War. The Attorney General, Edmund Randolph, then in Virginia on account of the illness of his wife, was merely the legal adviser of the government and not the only one, for the advice of Jefferson and Hamilton was also asked in legal matters.

The dominant position of the President was the most striking aspect of the developing administrative system. For weeks before the departments were created and the new heads took charge, Washington *was* the executive branch of the federal government, and the result of the congressional debates was to make the department heads removable by him and responsible to him. This outcome was owing to Madison more than to any other congressional leader, and it was entirely agreeable to Jefferson. Long ago he had had his fill of legislative omnipotence, and his disposition to redress the balance of the government was not at all diminished by his own membership in the executive branch. He regarded the transaction of business with foreign nations as altogether an executive matter, and was relieved to learn that he did not have to cater to the whims of Congress.[2] He wanted to perform his own duties out of the public gaze, and hoped he could as an assistant to George Washington.

The department heads were expected to speak only in the President's name and act only with his approval. The way that Washington supervised and controlled their actions is well illustrated by the pro-

[1] For an understanding of the general administrative situation, James Hart, *The American Presidency in Action, 1789* (1948), ch. VII, and L. D. White, *The Federalists: A Study in Administrative History* (1948), chs. II, III, are invaluable.

[2] On his attitude to the executive control of foreign matters, see his opinion of Apr. 24, 1790 (Ford, V, 161–162).

cedure with respect to correspondence. Jefferson described this when he himself was President and was recommending to his own department heads the same procedure.[3] Every day he made up a packet of his correspondence, with drafts of his own letters, and sent it to the President. Washington, who was orderly, industrious, and exacting, though not dictatorial, returned these promptly, generally signifying his approval by saying nothing. Sometimes he made comments or queries, and in certain cases he kept letters until he could hold a conference. At first he generally conferred with his lieutenants singly, asking written opinions from all of them in important matters of general interest and making the decisions himself after these papers had come in. Thus early policies were not the result of group conferences, or what later came to be called cabinet meetings. Washington kept himself fully informed about what was going on in all parts of the Union and in all the departments. As Jefferson put it, he "formed a central point for the different branches," and "preserved an unity of object and action among them" through his own person. He was not so much the captain of a team as the hub of a wheel from which the departmental spokes radiated.

The status of the Secretary of the Treasury was somewhat different from that of his two colleagues, for he was expected to be closer to Congress than they were.[4] The act creating his office provided that he give information to the legislative branch on request, that he digest and prepare plans respecting the revenue and the support of the public credit, that he report to Congress periodically; and it even prescribed the internal structure of his department. Another man than Alexander Hamilton might have resented these provisions as restrictions on his independence as an executive officer, but he accepted them as a challenge and quickly took advantage of his special means of access to the legislature. Such an attitude was quite in accord with his bold and ambitious nature.

In the earliest of his known letters Hamilton wrote to a friend of boyhood: "Ned, my ambition is prevalent, so that I contemn the grovelling condition of a clerk or the like, to which my fortune, etc., condemns me, and would willingly risk my life, though not my character, to exalt my station." [5] His entire career attests the truthfulness of his boyish self-characterization. Unlike the Secretary of State, he had not inherited an assured economic and social position. Born of good stock but out of wedlock in the British West Indies, he had come to New

[3] Circular to the Heads of the Departments, Nov. 6, 1801 (Ford, VIII, 99–101).
[4] The account of the Treasury Department in White, ch. X, is admirable.
[5] Hamilton to Edward Stevens, Nov. 11, 1769 (Lodge, VII, 471–472).

York at fifteen as a promising youth, and he owed his position in the world largely to his own talents and vigor. His alliance with a prominent family through his marriage with Eliza Schuyler should have relieved him from any sense of insecurity in social matters, but at the age of thirty-three he had by no means attained the goal of his vaulting ambition, and in fact he never reached it. Years later, Henry Adams, admitting an aversion to Hamilton, said: "From the first to the last words he wrote, I read always the same Napoleonic kind of adventuredom." [6] The young Secretary did not lust for money, but he did lust for glory and for power.

In that extraordinarily revealing letter of his boyhood, he also said, "I wish there was a war." What he wanted most was military glory, as George Washington must have known, since a famous quarrel between the Commander in Chief and his aide during the Revolution had resulted from that fact. The outward circumstances were that a rebuke of his subordinate by the General, because of a seeming indignity, was followed by a hasty and angry resignation which nothing could persuade Hamilton to withdraw. The inward reality, as he explained it to his father-in-law, was that he intensely disliked the office of an aide, "as having in it a kind of personal dependence," and was determined on a field command where glory might be won.[7] He gained one eventually and distinguished himself in the final operations at Yorktown, leaving no doubt that Lieutenant Colonel Hamilton was a brave and gallant soldier. Yet Washington could not have forgotten the lack of self-control and tendency to overreach himself which his aide had shown, and his later appointment of Hamilton to the secretaryship of the Treasury was a signal example of magnanimity. Also, it was a notable tribute to the character, abilities, and patriotism of the appointee. The fact that Washington trusted Hamilton and depended on him is highly significant.

There were, however, fortuitous elements in the situation. The President, who was so determined that the new government should succeed and grow in strength, knew much more about military affairs than his Secretary of War, and had more definite ideas on the subject of foreign affairs than on fiscal matters. Hence he tended to give much more rein to Hamilton than he ever gave to General Knox, and more than he gave to his trusted Secretary of State. Thus the dynamic young Secretary of the Treasury, who had special access to Congress, was in much better position than either of the other two departmental

[6] Henry Adams to Henry Cabot Lodge, May 15, 1876, in *Letters of Henry Adams, 1858–1891* (ed. by W. C. Ford, 1930), p. 284.

[7] Hamilton to Philip Schuyler, Feb. 18, 1781 (Lodge, VIII, 35–39).

heads to pursue a course of his own devising. He had to gain Washington's approval of his specific legislative proposals, but under the procedure they followed in these early months he did not have to win his colleagues to them, and the maintenance of "unity of object and action" depended on the President himself. Judging from his temperament, Hamilton was likely to be either a dominant or a disturbing factor in this or any other official family.

He had the largest department from the beginning and it was in his domain that the greatest growth was taking place. At the end of 1789 he had thirty-nine on the payroll in his central office and by the end of 1790 he had seventy, so the number was somewhere between these two figures when Jefferson arrived. The Secretary of State found a staff of five in his own department, and one of these was a translator on part time.[8] The field service of the Treasury, which grew by leaps and bounds, was still in its beginnings, and apparently had created no great alarm as yet, but few who knew him could doubt that Hamilton's administrative genius had in it a large element of aggrandizement. "Most of the important measures of every government are connected with the treasury," he said after he had been two and a half years in office. As Jefferson understood the situation, however, Washington thought Hamilton's department, dealing with the single object of revenue, much more limited and much less important than his own, "embracing nearly all the objects of administration." [9]

Rivalry between the two men and their departments might have been expected, but it was not noticeable at the outset, and the President could congratulate himself on the unity of his official family. He saw no need to raise the question of the relative rank of his assistants, but surely he and almost everybody else must have expected Jefferson to stand first. The latter's subordination and responsibility to the Chief Executive were plainly written in the law, hence his office offered fewer opportunities than Hamilton's to carve out an individual career. On the other hand, the supreme importance of the conduct of foreign affairs at this stage in the nation's history was generally recognized, and the Secretary of State "occupied a position of higher dignity than attached to the head of any other department, and a closer relationship to the chief executive." [10]

The additions to the department's original function of conducting

[8] TJ to Charles Bellini, June 13, 1790 (LC, 9387).

[9] Hamilton to E. Carrington, May 26, 1792 (Lodge, VIII, 262); TJ's report of conversation with Washington, Feb. 28, 1792 (Ford, I, 176).

[10] Gaillard Hunt, *The Department of State* (1914), p. 91. An admirable account of the creation and early history of the department is given in this work, chs. III, IV. White, *Federalists*, ch. XI, puts the department in its administrative setting.

foreign affairs under the direction of the President grew out of the recognized need to provide for the safekeeping of the records of the government and the great seal, the handling of federal commissions, and the promulgation of the laws.[11] Considerable dignity was connected with these additional functions, though they were chiefly formal, ceremonial, and clerical. Madison had predicted that they would not be burdensome, but they involved a great deal of paper work. When Jefferson arrived he found two chief clerks: Henry Remsen, Jr., in charge of the foreign office, and Roger Alden in charge of the home office. These young men had been commended to him by John Jay and he kept both of them, though Alden soon resigned. Thereafter, Remsen was the sole chief clerk, until he resigned in 1792 to be succeeded by George Taylor, and the staff as a whole increased in size very little. The total annual expense of Jefferson's establishment, including his own salary of $3500 (he himself used no dollar sign), was about $8,000.[12] His staff did little besides copying, and he did all the important things himself.

The conduct of foreign affairs could be delegated to no clerk, and in its more important aspects it was not even delegated to the Secretary of State, since the President never relaxed his vigilance. Jefferson was the mouthpiece, and an important part of his ordinary activities was the maintenance of contacts with foreign representatives in the United States and with American representatives abroad. There were very few in either category. Since the departure of the Comte de Moustier, France had had no minister plenipotentiary, and the affairs of the Monarchy were in the hands of a chargé, L. W. Otto, until Ternant arrived in the late summer of 1791. Great Britain had no accredited representatives of any grade until the autumn of that year, when George Hammond arrived. In March and April, 1790, Major George Beckwith was in New York, picking up what information he could for the British. In July he returned from Canada and engaged in informal conversations with Hamilton, to which we shall refer later, but Jefferson properly declined to have any official relations with this informal and unaccredited representative, either at that time or during the year and nine months that he remained. The United Netherlands had a minister resident in the person of Franco Petrus van Berkel, and the Spanish Secretary of Legation, José Ignacio de Viar, was acting

[11] The major acts were those of June 27, 1789, and Sept. 15, 1789, to which should be added the supplementary resolution of Sept. 23, 1789, making it the duty of the Secretary to secure copies of the statutes of the states (Hunt, *Department of State*, pp. 67–68, 72–74).

[12] Budget of the department as drawn by him Sept. 16, 1790 (*ibid.*, p. 96).

as chargé. There was no diplomatic corps of any consequence, and Jefferson was faced with no such social requirements as he had been when American minister at the Court of Louis XVI.[13]

In his old post in France was his former secretary, William Short, as chargé d'affaires. But Jefferson thought a regular minister would be appointed from "the veterans of the public stage," of whom Short was not yet one, and warned his young friend against overestimating his personal influence. A year and a half was to pass before the President named Gouverneur Morris. That witty and conservative gentleman was now in England serving as an informal American agent and making some purchases for George Washington on the side. Jefferson assumed the official correspondence with Morris toward the end of the year, but this informal mission antedated his own assumption of office and its negative results served merely to confirm opinions he himself already held.[14] Washington's selection of Thomas Pinckney as minister to Great Britain shortly preceded that of Morris as minister to France, but all this was more than eighteen months after Jefferson himself became secretary of state. Meanwhile, William Carmichael was still in Spain as chargé – proving a most unsatisfactory correspondent – and early in the next year David Humphreys was appointed minister resident to Portugal.[15] There were not many people to communicate with, and such communication as there was was painfully slow. There were consuls to be appointed, now that Jefferson's consular convention with France had been ratified and proclaimed, and during this year sixteen of them were named.

It was part of his business to keep American representatives in other countries informed of the situation and developments at home; and in the course of time he sent regularly to each minister and chargé copies of the laws and legislative journals, along with representative newspapers. His clerks could have attended to such matters, but he kept the letters from abroad in his own current files and answered them himself.[16] A considerable degree of efficiency was to be expected of such an industrious and methodical man as Jefferson, but anyone who knew him might have anticipated that he would not like this routine

[13] Personnel as shown in *Register of the Department of State*, 1874, Part II, "Historical Register."

[14] It will be discussed in this volume, ch. XIX, in connection with Jefferson's report on it.

[15] Feb. 18, 1791 (*A.S.P.F.R.*, I, 128–129).

[16] Memo. of Remsen on the disposition of the papers in the Department of State (early 1792?), in Record Group No. 59, General Records of the Department of State. Reports of Bureau Officers, Vol. 1A, 1790–1834 (National Archives). Another memo. (May, 1790) in the same collection gives some ideas of Remsen about the business of the office.

business, and obviously his position was not one that lent itself to the display of administrative genius if he had had it.

His major official task was the formulation and establishment of a national foreign policy, in relation to the specific problems of his country. Through force of circumstances, however, he was unable to give much attention to the most important of these during the spring of 1790, and what he did in the summer can be more appropriately discussed in a later chapter.[17] At this point, therefore, we shall content ourselves with describing and partly disposing of his domestic tasks.

A considerable amount of business fell to his office because of the fact that, besides issuing commissions of all sorts, he served as the President's medium of communication with the states and such federal officials as did not fall within the jurisdiction of the Departments of War and the Treasury. Thus he wrote governors, and – in the absence of a department of justice – judges and marshals. It is doubtful whether he played any part in connection with the taking of the first census beyond what was involved in his duty of transmitting the law and nominally supervising the printing of the returns.[18] His letters to the governors of the two territories – north and south of the Ohio – were numerous, but most of these were of the routine sort or served merely to communicate the decisions of the Executive. Indian affairs fell within the jurisdiction of the Department of War, while the survey and sale of lands were under the Treasury. Jefferson appears to have advised Washington about territorial matters to some extent. During his first year in office, having considered the journal of the proceedings of the Executive of the Northwest Territory, he informed the President that some of the regulations went beyond the competence of the Executive, and Washington warned Governor St. Clair to be on his guard, perhaps saying less than Jefferson desired. But primarily he was an intermediary in this field, and he gave his thought chiefly to other more important or more pressing matters.[19]

* * *

[17] See ch. XVII, below.

[18] Bureau of the Census, *A Century of Population Growth* (Washington, 1909), pp. 44–45. The letter printed in that work from TJ to the Governor of the Southwest Territory, can be best attributed to his function as the intermediary between the President and the territories. Considerably more authority was given the Department of State in connection with the census of 1800.

[19] TJ to Washington, Dec. 14, 1790 (Ford, V, 260–261); Washington to Gov. Arthur St. Clair, Jan. 2, 1791 (Fitzpatrick, XXXI, 190–191. A survey of *The Territorial Papers of the U. S.*, ed. by C. E. Carter, vols. II, IV (Washington, 1934, 1936) reveals numerous letters, but these are chiefly of a routine nature. TJ was disturbed by certain irregularities in land transactions, and at times rebuked officials for negligence, but in the latter case he may have served only as the President's mouthpiece.

Although responsible to the President rather than Congress, he had to draft reports to that body or one of its branches in response to specific requests, and some of these involved great labor. His report to the House of Representatives on the subject of uniform weights and measures was the first paper of consequence that he drew in the New York period and much the longest. For these reasons, and because of its intrinsic interest, it deserves consideration here.[20]

The request of the House was made several weeks before Jefferson reached New York, but he did not receive it until the middle of April and did not finish his rough draft until a month later. This was his main occupation in the period of his enforced confinement. His headache came on at sunrise and lasted till sunset. Describing the unforgettable circumstances afterwards, he said: "What had been ruminated in the day under a paroxysm of the most excruciating pain, was committed to paper by candlelight, and then the calculations were made." [21] Under these trying conditions he made a mistake which he corrected a few months later. In cubing the new foot measure that he had recommended he made an error amounting to a ten thousandth of a foot in one instance and a millionth in another. It is doubtful whether anybody in the House detected it.

Probably the representatives had not expected as much mathematics and physics as Jefferson regaled them with, in the report he communicated in the summer. He loved these subjects, and, as he wrote David Rittenhouse, would have delighted in this task had it been given him twenty-five years before. But, having been forced for so long a time into very different and much less pleasing lines of thought, he had grown rusty. Furthermore, his books were either at Monticello or in Paris. Hence he asked the foremost American mathematician to go over his paper, and Rittenhouse made certain corrections for which he was most grateful.[22] Some credit for the net result must go to this learned friend, and a little, but not much, to the Bishop of Autun (better known as Talleyrand) who had recently made proposals on the same subject in France. Jefferson had worked out the essentials of his own plan before he heard of these, and the part of it which has

[20] Communicated July 13, 1790, and published by order of the House as *Report of the Secretary of State, on the Subject of Establishing a Uniformity in the Weights, Measures and Coins of the U. S.* (N. Y., 1790). It can be most easily consulted in L. & B., III, 26–59, and is admirably discussed by C. Doris Hellman in "Jefferson's Efforts towards the Decimalization of U. S. Weights and Measures" (*Isis*, vol. XVI, 266–314).

[21] TJ to Thos. Cooper, Oct. 27, 1808 (L. & B., XII, 180).

[22] TJ to Rittenhouse, June 12, 1790 (L. & B., XIX, 73–75), June 14, 20, 1790 (L. & B., VIII, 37–41); Rittenhouse to TJ, June 21, 1790 (LC, 9468); TJ to Rittenhouse, June 26, 1790 (LC, 9505); and other letters.

most abiding interest, his proposed decimalization of weights and measures, was a logical consequence of his earlier successful efforts for a decimal system of coinage. Partly because he touched on coinage in his report, he referred it to Hamilton, who approved it.[23] Washington had started this business by calling to the attention of Congress the importance of establishing uniformity in weights, measures, and the currency. This was part of the process of creating a truly united nation, but Jefferson's specific recommendations were based on standards which he deemed universal.

He thought it necessary to find, in the first place, some measure of invariable length; and he entered into realms of inquiry rarely penetrated by either congressmen or historians. Believing that matter, by its mere extension, furnished nothing invariable, he turned to motion—that is, to the motion of the earth around its axis, which could be measured in days and reduced to seconds. Then he arrived at a pendulum so adjusted in length as to make its vibrations in a second of time, which might itself become a measure of length. Perceiving some uncertainties with respect to the center of the oscillations of such a pendulum, he accepted the proposals of Mr. Leslie, "an ingenious artist of Philadelphia," to substitute for it a uniform cylindrical rod of iron, without a bob, and arrived at the following recommendation:

> Let the standard of measure, then, be a uniform cylindrical rod of iron, of such length as, in latitude 45°, in the level of the ocean, and in a cellar, or other place, the temperature of which does not vary through the year, shall perform its vibrations in small and equal arcs, in one second of mean time.[24]

Originally he had fixed on the latitude of 38°, but when Talleyrand proposed 45°, as a middle term between the equator and the poles, he accepted that, though it was pretty far north for him. He was looking for an internationally acceptable standard, and for just this reason did not approve of the French proposal to base their system on the measurement of a portion of a meridian crossing the 45th parallel within their own territory, which would be inaccessible to others. The issue may seem minute and abstract to laymen, but it illustrates Jefferson's concern for universals.[25]

Before applying the standard he had arrived at, he raised another

[23] *Jefferson the Virginian*, pp. 416–418; TJ to Hamilton, June 12, 1790 (LC, 9375); Hamilton to TJ, June, 1790 (LC, 10195).

[24] L. & B., III, 32.

[25] The relation of his recommendations to contemporary French and English proposals is discussed by Hellman, in *Isis*, XVI, 277–288. I commend this study to anyone who wishes to pursue the abstruse subject further.

question. Did the House of Representatives intend to arrange weights and measures in a decimal ratio, as Congress had done in the case of money? The experiment with respect to the monetary system, for which he himself deserved so much credit, had been approved both at home and abroad, he believed, and only the lack of the actual American coins had prevented the banishment of the pounds, shillings, pence, and farthings which had so long confused the English peoples. He regarded the extension of this decimal system as highly desirable, but feared that the representatives might regard the difficulty of changing the established habits of a people as an insuperable obstacle. Hence he thought it his duty to submit alternative proposals.

The first of these was based on the supposition that the present measures and weights were to be retained but rendered uniform and invariable. He listed the common measures of length and capacity, and showed how these might be brought to "the same invariable standard." Without claiming finality for his figures, he concluded that the standard rod would be 58.723 inches long. Hence he would divide it into 587⅕ equal parts, each of which should be a line; ten of these should be an inch; twelve of these inches should be a foot, and so on. He applied the same standard to measures of capacity, making all of them rectangular. "Cylindrical measures have the advantage of superior strength," he said, "but square ones have the greater advantage of enabling every one who has a rule in his pocket, to verify their contents by measuring them. Moreover, till the circle can be squared, the cylinder cannot be cubed, nor its contents exactly expressed in figures."[26] Thus his pint measure would be 3 inches square and 7½ inches deep. He wanted to get rid of certain sorts of gallon, such as the wine gallon, to fix the gallon to one medium capacity, and to abolish the distinction between wet and dry measure. When stated briefly, his recommendations seem more confusing than they do in his lengthy and luminous report, but they represent an admirable combination of arithmetic and common sense.

In discussing weights, he considered both the Avoirdupois and Troy series. He wished to combine these, retaining the higher denominations of the one (pound and ounce) which were in such general use, and the lower (grain and pennyweight) of the other, after certain minor adjustments between them. These weights must be reduced to some invariable standard, however, and he arrived at this recommendation:

> Let it, then, be established that an ounce is of the weight of a cube of rain water, of one-tenth of a foot; or, rather, that it is

[26] L. & B., III, 41.

the thousandth part of the weight of a cubic foot of rain water, weighed in the standard temperature; that the series of weights of the United States shall consist of pounds, ounces, pennyweights, and grains; whereof

24 grains shall be one pennyweight;
18 pennyweights one ounce;
16 ounces one pound.[27]

With respect to coins, he recommended a tiny increase in the silver content of the dollar in order to link it with the other units, whenever it should be thought proper to extend the decimal ratio to the entire system. Then the dollar, with its alloy, would weigh one ounce precisely, as he showed in the second part of his report.

In this second part he described what he really wanted. He favored a thorough reformation of the whole system, by reducing measures and weights to the decimal ratio already established with respect to coins, and "thus bringing the calculations of the principal affairs of life within the arithmetic of every man who can multiply and divide plain numbers." He recognized, however, that this would require great changes. The unit of measure would remain the same, that is, the rod he had described. He would divide this into five equal parts, each to be called a foot. He continued:

Let the foot be divided into 10 inches;
The inch into 10 lines;
The line into 10 points;
Let 10 feet make a decad;
10 decads one rood;
10 roods a furlong;
10 furlongs a mile.[28]

In an appendix he translated these and other measures into their estimated equivalents. Thus the foot would be somewhat shorter than the English foot, the inch about 1/7 longer, and the mile nearly twice as long.

Among measures of capacity, he wanted to make the cubic foot the unit, calling this a bushel; he would go up and down the scale by tens and use four-sided measures. The smallest of these, the meter, would be a cubic inch. The unit of weight was to be the ounce, and ten ounces were to make a pound. He used old terms whenever they seemed to fit, but had to invent some new ones, and he realized all the time that a shift from the time-honored system, confusing though it was, to a novel one, however rational, would result in considerable temporary incon-

[27] L. & B., III, 47.
[28] L. & B., III, 49.

venience. Hence he favored a gradual transition, suggesting that the new system might be started in the customhouses, then be extended to legal proceedings and all foreign transactions, and finally be introduced to all descriptions of people. If it were postponed too long, however, the difficulties of its reception would increase with the growth of the population.

Though much disturbed by the minor error in calculation which appeared in his report and impelled him to send a postscript to the House of Representatives some months later,[29] he took great pride in the document and sent copies of it to luminaries in Europe as well as America. To William Short he sent a couple for Talleyrand and Condorcet; he asked his son-in-law to transmit two to a learned society in Edinburgh; Sir John Sinclair got one in London and sent a mathematical paper in return. Robert R. Livingston of New York regarded it as "invaluable"; General Philip Schuyler was much interested, which perhaps implies that it was well received in Hamiltonian circles; and President Ezra Stiles of Yale communicated this "philosophical production" to the highest classes of his students and hoped the author would succeed George Washington. Unquestionably this paper added to his deserved fame and, if he had had the choosing, no doubt he would have preferred to be remembered by it rather than by any other paper he drafted as secretary of state. It revealed him as a man of thought and learning, eager for the advancement of human affairs, and the triumph of reason in all fields of man's endeavor. Only one other secretary of state ever prepared such a paper, and, quite appropriately, this was John Quincy Adams. A quarter of a century later the aged Jefferson gave counsel to the son of his old friend about this self-same matter. He was still advocating a universal standard and a decimal system.[30]

It will be assumed, quite correctly, that his efforts were without tangible result. Again and again, action on his proposals was deferred. The nearest they ever came to success was in April, 1792, when a committee of the Senate approved his second and preferred alternative. Nothing else happened while he was in office, and in the meantime the French, by decree, had started what came to be known as the metric system. Their unit of length was to be a minute part of a terrestrial

[29] Dated Jan. 10, 1791, and sent Jan. 17 (L. & B., III, 57–59; LC, 10233).

[30] J. Q. Adams's *Report upon Weights and Measures*, which has been described as a neglected American classic, was published in 1821 (S. F. Bemis, *J. Q. Adams*, 1949, pp. 258–259); TJ wrote him Nov. 1, 1817 (L. & B., XV, 144–149). Of the letters to TJ about his own report the following are of special interest: from Philip Schuyler, Aug. 22, 1790 (LC, 9724); from Ezra Stiles, Aug. 27, 1790 (Bixby, pp. 42–44); from Sir John Sinclair, Dec. 25, 1790 (LC, 10050–10051); from R. R. Livingston, Feb. 20, 1791 (LC, 10575); Rev. James Madison to James Madison, Apr. 10, 1791 (MP, 14:2).

meridian and they were measuring the arc between Dunkirk and Barcelona in order to determine it. Jefferson continued to prefer an oscillating rod or pendulum, and never lost interest in the general subject, though American discussion of it grew less and less as time went on. When writing his autobiography as an old man, he noted that everybody had readily comprehended the odometer he used in traveling which divided the mile into "cents," and concluded that the people would have soon got used to a decimal system of weights and measures.[31] Perhaps nothing short of revolution could have overcome inertia sufficiently to cause such a system to be established, and there was no revolution in America in this decade as there was in France. Thus Jefferson lost a title to fame which he might have cherished more than any of the political honors he gained or the offices he held.

Before he submitted his report on weights and measures, he had made a briefer one, at the request of the House, on a particular proposal to supply the United States with copper coins. He advised that this be declined, since the work was to be done abroad and the implements were to remain the property of the undertaker, and he expressed the opinion that a mint, whenever established, should be established at home.[32] The House then ordered Hamilton to report a plan, which he did at the next session. The eventual result was that a mint was established by law in the spring of 1792, and, somewhat fortuitously, this fell into Jefferson's department.[33] It caused him considerable pain in the end, but the most time-consuming of his domestic duties until his last year in office had to do with patents, which were committed to his care less than three weeks after he arrived in New York. The subject deserves a small section by itself, and in this we shall telescope the calendar.

Under the first patent act (approved April 10, 1790, and entitled "An Act to Promote the Progress of the Useful Arts") he became the first administrator of the American patent system.[34] Ostensibly, the grant-

[31] Ford, I, 75. The legislative history of Jefferson's report is given in detail by Hellman, pp. 297–307. See p. 300 for the committee report in the Senate by Ralph Izard, Apr. 5, 1792.

[32] Communicated Apr. 15, 1790 (L. & B., III, 11–15).

[33] See pp. 432–433, this volume, and White, *Federalists*, pp. 139–143.

[34] The best account is in chs. 6–8 of "Outline of the History of the U. S. Patent Office," *Jour. of the Patent Office Soc.*, Centennial No., vol. XVIII, No. 7 (July, 1936). Ch. 7 of that work, "Operation of the Patent Act of 1790," is a reprint, without references, of an article in that *Journal* (April, 1936) by P. J. Federico, the editor in chief, to whom I am deeply indebted in this connection. See also *Record of the Proceedings in Congress Relating to the First Patent and Copyright Laws,*

ing of patents was entrusted to him, the Secretary of War, and the Attorney General, constituting what he generally called the Board of Arts, but inevitably he was the moving spirit, and his office carried on the routine business. To all who knew this man of limitless scientific curiosity and inventive mind his official connection with the promotion of the useful arts must have seemed eminently appropriate. Washington had connected literature and science in his original recommendation to Congress, but questions of copyright were put in a separate act. Such administration as this involved was assigned to the clerks of the district courts, though the Secretary of State was to receive within six months of publication a copy of any map, chart, or book that was copyrighted. Jefferson's office was not only the first patent office in the United States; it also served as a repository of American publications like the later Library of Congress.[35]

When writing to Madison from France about a bill of rights, Jefferson had wanted to prohibit all monopolies, even limited monopolies, to authors and inventors. Before he left for home, however, he had concluded that the progress of science and the arts would be promoted by securing persons for a time in the exclusive right to their own writings and discoveries.[36] In the course of the years he himself was credited with a number of inventions, but none of these was ever patented. His own ingenuity did not need to be incited by hope of financial reward, but he soon concluded that the legislation of 1790 had a stimulating effect on others. Within three months it had given a "spring to invention" beyond his expectation – though this does not appear to have been high.

The first patent granted through his instrumentality was one to Samuel Hopkins on July 31, 1790, for making pot and pearl ashes, and there were only three that year all told. But he talked with other persons of an inventive turn, such as the builder of the "famous" bridge from Boston to Charlestown, who wanted to patent a pile engine and gave him fascinating information about the impregnation of timbers with codfish oil for their better preservation.[37] After going to such pains to inform himself about the progress of the useful arts abroad, he was now able to keep his finger on the pulse of American discovery; and, now that Franklin was gone, no compatriot of his was so well fitted to fill and enjoy such a position.

As time went on, however, and important diplomatic and political

---

reprinted with revisions from the *Journal*, April and May, 1940, by the Patent Office Society.

[35] The Copyright Act was approved, May 31, 1790 (1 *Statutes at Large*, 124).

[36] TJ to Madison, July 31, 1788, and Aug. 28, 1789 (Ford, V, 47, 113).

[37] TJ to Benjamin Vaughan in London, June 27, 1790 (L. & B., VIII, 50–51).

questions absorbed him, his duties as the first administrator of patents became almost intolerably burdensome. In comparison with later years the actual number of patents, of course, was small. During the life of the first act, fifty-seven were granted, and during Jefferson's incumbency sixty-seven altogether. But there were certainly more than twice that many applications, and the close personal attention of the Secretary of State was necessary if the procedure was not to become meaningless. One can easily imagine what Elihu Root or John Hay or William H. Seward would have thought about this sort of business, and if it was not too much for the more diverse genius of Thomas Jefferson in a far less specialized age it took more time than he could give it.

The procedure was slow and tedious.[38] The Board of Arts met the last Saturday of every month and then read all the applications received since the last meeting. These lay over for another month, but were not acted on then unless suitable specifications, drafts, or models had been submitted. Beginning in July, 1791, the three members read the descriptions separately in their own lodgings, the Attorney General first in order that he might pass on the propriety of the forms. The criticisms and amendments suggested by all three were consolidated by Remsen, the chief clerk of the department, and were considered by the entire group. The question of conflicts with patents already issued could hardly have been important at this early stage, but there were cases of rival claims, as when John Fitch, James Rumsey, and two others applied for steamboat patents. The decision was to give patents to all of them, though the one received by Fitch was broader than the others and there was no necessary duplication.[39]

According to the law, the officials had to decide whether or not the discovery or invention was sufficiently useful and important to deserve a patent, and Jefferson had to assume the major responsibility for their decisions. He ruled out unworkable devices as well as those that were frivolous or amounted only to obvious improvements of things already well known and in common use.

The amount of trouble he took is well illustrated by the case of a man by the name of Isaacs who wanted to patent a process for turning salt water into fresh. He got a cask of seawater, had Isaacs set up the apparatus in his office and called in a couple of distinguished scientists to witness the demonstration – which turned out to be unimpressive.

[38] Undated memorandum by Henry Remsen, Jr., printed in *Jour. of the Patent Office Soc.*, XXV, pp. 603–604; TJ to General Knox, July 22, 1791 (*ibid.*, XIX, 363).

[39] P. J. Federico in *Jour. Patent Office Soc.*, XVIII, 248–251. The decision was reached on Aug. 26, 1791, and apparently did not give complete satisfaction.

Nonetheless, Jefferson thought that attracting attention to the matter would do good, since shipmasters would be reminded that fresh water could be obtained from salt by common distillation.[40]

He and his board slowly established rules and principles, and insofar as these are known they have commended themselves to his more experienced successors in the Patent Office. He believed that patents should be given to particular machines, not to all possible applications or uses of them, that mere change of material or form gave no valid claim, that the exclusive right of an invention must always be considered in terms of social benefit. Probably these principles were clearer in his mind when he thought about the subject long years afterward than in this time of beginnings. One cannot be sure just when he matured the philosophy of patent protection which he set forth in the letters of his old age, but it is this philosophy, more than his mere administration of an office, which most commends him to our own time. He tempered his characteristic individualism with notable social-mindedness and an emphasis on ideas as common property. Thus he wrote:

> . . . If nature has made any one thing less susceptible than all others of exclusive property, it is the action of the thinking power called an idea, which an individual may exclusively possess as long as he keeps it to himself; but the moment it is divulged, it forces itself into the possession of every one, and the receiver cannot dispossess himself of it. Its peculiar character, too, is that no one possesses the less, because every other possesses the whole of it. He who receives an idea from me, receives instruction himself without lessening mine; as he who lights his taper at mine, receives light without darkening me. That ideas should freely spread from one to another over the globe, for the moral and mutual instruction of man, and improvement of his condition, seems to have been peculiarly and benevolently designed by nature. . . . Inventions then cannot, in nature, be a subject of property. Society may give an exclusive right to the profits arising from them, as an encouragement to men to pursue ideas which may produce utility, but this may or may not be done according to the will and convenience of the society, without claim or complaint from anybody.[41]

[40] This was in Philadelphia in March, 1791. He gave a full report of it (L. & B., III, 1–8). See also his letters to James Hutchinson, professor of chemistry at the Univ. of Pa., Mar. 12, 1791 (cited by White, *Federalists*, p. 137), and Caspar Wistar, Mar. 20, 1791 (L. & B., VIII, 151–152).

[41] TJ to Isaac McPherson, Aug. 13, 1813 (L. & B., XIII, 333–334), quoted by P. J. Federico in *Jour. Patent Office Soc.*, XVIII, 241–242. See also TJ to Oliver Evans, Jan. 16, 1814 (L. & B., XIV, 63–67).

As the first administrator of the patent system Jefferson had no doubt of the necessity of social control in such matters, and he sought to deal out justice without partiality or favoritism, but the results were unsatisfactory to him and he was trying to get rid of these duties within a year. More than anything ever imposed upon him, he said, this business cut his time into useless fragments and occasioned poignant mortification. Not having the time to understand and do justice to the applications, he was "oppressed beyond measure" by being obliged to give uninformed opinions on rights that were often valuable and always deemed so by the inventors. Accordingly, he drafted a bill, early in 1791, relieving himself of all except nominal functions, and although this was not passed by Congress, the patent act of Feb. 21, 1793, accomplished a similar purpose. Indeed, this second act went to the opposite extreme from that of 1790, eliminating the examination of the application and making the grant of patents an essentially automatic and clerical matter. Adjudication of disputes was left to the courts, and Jefferson himself believed that a system of jurisprudence would gradually develop in this area. Later still, he concluded that some provision for the preliminary examination of applications was desirable, and it is natural to suppose that his recommendation of changes in the original system was considerably owing to his personal situation. It may be, however, that such procedure as he followed was unnecessary as well as impracticable at that stage. Not until 1836, more than forty years after he ceased administering the patent business and ten years after his death, was the present system instituted. It amounted to a compromise between the rigid examinations he conducted and the opposite extreme of no examinations at all.

When the present Patent Office celebrated its hundredth anniversary, it dedicated a bust of Thomas Jefferson, thus recognizing his title as a pioneer. The first examiner of American patents was undoubtedly the most eminent man who ever assumed that task, and his successors realize better than anybody else how much illumination he cast upon the highly technical problems, infused with social significance, which they have faced through the years.[42]

[42] TJ's draft of a bill to promote the progress of the useful arts is in Ford, V, 278–280. It was introduced Feb. 7, 1791. On his desire to escape from the patent business, see especially TJ to Hugh Williamson, Apr. 1, 1792 (Ford, V, 492). On the act of 1793, see *Outline of the History of the United States Patent Office*, ch. 8. The dedication on Nov. 23, 1936, of the bust, a bronze copy of the Houdon bust in the N. Y. Hist. Soc., is described in *Jour. Patent Office Soc.*, XIX, 71–77 (Jan. 1937); see also pp. 3–4, 11.

[XVI]

Working with Hamilton

1790

THE bitter political conflict which developed during the Presidency of George Washington has often been viewed as a duel, or succession of duels, between Thomas Jefferson and Alexander Hamilton. This oversimplification of a series of complicated situations may be attributed in part to the proneness of almost everybody to personalize political controversies, and, even more, to the general realization that these two men have become symbols of a conflict of ideas which runs through the whole of American national history. No other American statesman has personified national power and the rule of the favored few so well as Hamilton, and no other has glorified self-government and the freedom of the individual to such a degree as Jefferson.

When antagonism is so fundamental, an ultimate personal clash may be regarded as practically inevitable, but no one can fit the events of the first presidential administration into the simple pattern of a political contest between the first Secretary of State and the first Secretary of the Treasury without disregarding other important circumstances and belittling other important men. This is specially true of the New York period, when Madison was the leader of the opposition if anybody was, and there was a surprisingly large area of agreement in policy between Hamilton and Jefferson. In fact, their fight did not start as soon as might have been expected.

Apparently these two historic antagonists had not met before they became colleagues in the spring of 1790. Jefferson, the elder by fourteen years, was the better known, and various later comments lead to the belief that he was highly respected by Hamilton at the outset. It seems unlikely that he himself knew much about the temperament of his associate. Lafayette, who was an innocent party to the break between Washington and Hamilton during the American Revolution, may have told Jefferson something about that revealing episode, but the General himself maintained scrupulous silence on the subject, and the Secretary of State did not have the privilege of reading private letters that are now accessible to any student.[1]

The military reputation of his colleague probably neither impressed nor alarmed him at first, and he may have been slow to realize how much Colonel Hamilton loved command for its own sake, how little he cared for the liberal ideas of the Enlightenment. Once, when the heads of department met at Jefferson's house, after he had received his things from France, Hamilton saw there his portraits of Sir Francis Bacon, Sir Isaac Newton, and John Locke, and asked him who these men were. They were his "trinity of the three greatest men the world had ever produced," Jefferson said, but they meant little or nothing in Hamilton's philosophy. "The greatest man that ever lived," said the Colonel, "was Julius Caesar." [2]

Jefferson afterwards reported this saying, not as an illustration of the differences between him and his famous rival in matters of personal taste and intellectual interest, but as revealing Hamilton's political principles. He was an honest man, but as a statesman he believed in "the necessity of either force or corruption to govern men." This is the conclusion that Jefferson finally arrived at, but it does not represent his judgment at the outset of his career as secretary of state. He knew that Hamilton had collaborated with Madison in writing the *Federalist*, and he approved that work as a whole, even though he was disposed to attribute to Madison what he liked best in it. How much he knew at this stage about the position Hamilton took in the Federal Convention is uncertain. If he had opportunity during his first weeks in New York to go over Madison's notes on the secret proceedings of the Convention, he could hardly have failed to conclude that Hamilton at that time (1787) was practically a monarchist in spirit, that he had no confidence in popular self-government, that he relied on the interest of the moneyed classes to cement the Union and support the government.

Most of his early knowledge of Hamilton's political philosophy, however, he probably gained from conversation with Madison during these first weeks, and of this, unfortunately, there is no record. Judging from Madison's actions, it is a fair supposition that he did not yet

[1] See ch. XV, note 7, this volume.

[2] TJ to Benjamin Rush, Jan. 16, 1811 (Ford, IX, 296). Probably this was in Philadelphia in the spring of 1791. Hamilton compared Jefferson himself to Caesar in 1792, oddly enough.

believe that Hamilton as secretary of the treasury was trying to bring about the sort of national consolidation he had vainly advocated in the Federal Convention; and even if Madison had begun to suspect it he might well have hesitated to tell Jefferson so at first. He had gone to great pains to win over his friend to the sort of federalism, with its checks and balances, which, as he presumed, had prevailed. His dispute with Hamilton until this time had been over means rather than ends, and it had centered in financial questions. Not until another winter was the constitutional issue strongly pressed.

One brilliant writer, who has dramatized this period with extraordinary effectiveness, speaks of the arrival in New York of Jefferson's lumbering stagecoach as "an event of tremendous import." [3] So it appears when historians look backward, but Jefferson did not unsheathe his sword as soon as he stepped off his lumbering stagecoach. On the contrary, he entered with good will into a governmental organization which was already a going concern, devoting himself almost exclusively to his own lagging department at first and showing the utmost loyalty to his Chief, the President.

He had been unwilling to accept any political label while in distant France, but he had definitely repudiated that of "antifederalist," and it may have been a relief to him that the state of the roads had prevented him from visiting George Mason at Gunston Hall on his way northward to assume office. To that true friend of the rights and liberties of mankind, who continued to be fearful of the powers of the new government, he wrote after a time that he approved it in the mass, though desiring amendments beyond those already proposed in order to fix it more surely on a republican basis. He did not specify just what these were, and certainly he was not sighing for the good old days of the Confederation, but probably he was still troubled by the perpetual re-eligibility of the President. "I have great hopes that, pressing forward with constancy to these amendments, they will be obtained before the want of them will do any harm," he said. "To secure the ground we gain, and gain what more we can, is I think the wisest course. I think much has been gained by the late constitution; for the former one was terminating in anarchy, as necessarily consequent to inefficiency." [4] He was in an optimistic and constructive frame of mind, and shared George Washington's deep desire that the new government, and especially its executive branch, should be genu-

[3] Bowers, *Jefferson and Hamilton*, p. 64; see also S. E. Morison, *Harrison Gray Otis* (Boston and New York, 1913), I, 46.

[4] TJ to Mason, June 13, 1790 (Ford, V, 183), replying to a letter of Mar. 16, 1790 (LC, 9117–9118).

inely effective. That was a good reason for co-operating with the Secretary of the Treasury.

He had heard some echoes of the debate on Hamilton's financial proposals while on the road, and could not have failed to observe that opposition was rising in Virginia. After arriving in New York he noted that Congress was principally occupied with the Treasury Report, but he does not seem to have thought much about this while getting his bearings, starting his own department, and recovering from his long spell of headache. The Report had never been submitted to him for official approval, and, according to the procedure of the administration, it need not have been, even if he had been there earlier. By now Hamilton's proposals with respect to the national public debt had survived enough votes to be sure of final passage in essentially the form that he desired. Jefferson was in no position to force the re-opening of that question, and whether he would have wanted to or not can only be judged from the proposals themselves and his general attitude toward public debt and speculation.

The ostensible purpose of the Secretary of the Treasury was to establish the credit of the government by making adequate provision for the public debt which had been inherited from the Revolutionary War and the Confederation. This consisted of both foreign and domestic obligations, and Jefferson had put himself definitely on record while in Europe with respect to the former, especially in letters to Washington and Madison. He had told Madison that the first action of the new government should be some provision for the foreign debts which he and John Adams had found so embarrassing. "The existence of a nation having no credit is always precarious," he said.[5] This question required no arguing, however. The necessity of providing for the foreign debts, at their face value and with accumulated interest, was so generally recognized by the leaders that Hamilton did not bother to discuss the matter in his famous Report, rightly taking consent for granted.

There was more ground for disagreement about the domestic debt, which was much larger and presented special complications because of the variety of its forms and the vicissitudes it had suffered. Disregarding the Continental currency or bills of credit, which in effect he repudiated, Hamilton wanted to redeem the various certificates of indebtedness (for loans, supplies, and services) at their face value with accumulated interest. But these certificates had greatly depre-

[5] TJ to Madison, May 3, 1788 (L. & B., VI, 455). See also TJ to Washington, May 2, 1788 (L. & B., VI, 451–454), and pp. 191–192, this volume.

ciated, most of them had got out of the hands of the original holders, and they were being assiduously bought up by speculators in anticipation of their redemption. Hamilton's proposal was his way of fulfilling what he regarded as a binding contract, but he did not mind creating new wealth by governmental act and seemed quite indifferent to the undeniable speculation.

Madison, the most important critic of this plan, advocated no repudiation, no scaling down of the domestic debt, but had proposed payment to present holders at the current market rate, the balance to go to the original holders, many of them Revolutionary soldiers.[6] He wrote Edmund Pendleton: "I have not been able to persuade myself that the transactions between the United States and those whose services were most instrumental in saving their country, did in fact extinguish the claims of the latter on the justice of the former; or that there must not be something radically wrong in suffering those who rendered a bonafide consideration to lose ⅞ of their dues, and those who have no particular merit towards their country to gain 7 or 8 times as much as they advanced."[7]

His resolution, which was designed to redress the inequity to some degree, was decisively beaten on February 22, "less perhaps from a denial of the justice of the measure, than a supposition of its impracticability," as he believed.[8] In the public debate he was restrained in his comments on speculation. He might have been much less so if he had known that William Duer, Hamilton's assistant, had signed a definite agreement with William Constable, the leading financier of New York, to speculate in the public funds. The profits were to be reinvested in the debts of the States of North and South Carolina, and foreign bankers were to be drawn into this highly profitable business.[9] The Secretary of the Treasury was not personally involved, but he knew the sort of man Duer was, if he did not know the precise operations he would engage in.

Before Jefferson left home Madison wrote him that emissaries were "still exploring the interior and distant parts of the Union in order to take advantage of the ignorance of holders." Had he got to New York six weeks sooner he might have noted the charge in a newspaper that, in anticipation of Hamilton's Report, about forty men in Phila-

[6] Speeches of Feb. 11, 18, 1790 (Hunt, V, 438–458). I have simplified his proposals, making no reference to present holders who were also original holders and thus constituted no problem, nor to intermediate holders, whom he saw no choice but to disregard.

[7] Madison to Edmund Pendleton, Mar. 4, 1790 (Hunt, VI, 6*n.*).

[8] To his father, Feb. 27, 1790 (Hunt, V, 460*n.*).

[9] Brant in *Madison*, III, 302, prints the document.

delphia, forty in New York, thirty in Boston, ten or twelve in Baltimore, and a half dozen in Charleston had acquired the greatest share of the Continental securities. Soon after this, William Maclay, writing without restraint in his Journal, said that "Hamilton, at the head of the speculators, with all the courtiers" comprised the party "actuated by interest," while the opposition were governed by principle.[10] Madison did not say this, even in private letters, but on his way northward Jefferson could have heard some indignant language from Dr. Benjamin Rush, who regarded the bargain obtained by the speculators as little less than highway robbery, and wrote to Madison of the Secretary of the Treasury's "system of injustice and corruption."[11] At a later time the speculation incident to Hamilton's program constituted a distinct count in Jefferson's indictment of it, but he was not talking about that as yet.

If, before he got to New York, he heard the Hamiltonian expression that "a public debt is a public blessing," he could not have failed to be disturbed by that.[12] An excellent clue to his thinking on the general subject can be found in the extraordinary letter to Madison in which he said that "the earth belongs always to the living generation," and applied this principle not only to constitutions and laws but also to the debts of nations.[13] He advanced the theory that, by natural right, debts are binding only during the lifetime of the generation which contracts them. Madison pointed out to him that debts may be incurred for the benefit of the unborn no less than for the living, and that obligations could be rightly inherited along with benefits. By cogent logic he showed that this "theoretical speculation" was less solid than his friend had supposed, though he recognized that it contained a great idea. Jefferson was arguing against the unlimited power of governments to contract binding debts, but, so far as his own country was concerned, he was seeking no escape from existing obligations. He said: "No nation can make a declaration against the validity of long-contracted debts so disinterestedly as we, since we do not owe a shilling which may not be paid with ease, principal and interest, within the time of our own lives."[14] Madison recognized

[10] Madison to TJ, Jan. 24, 1790 (Hunt, V, 435); "An Independent Observer" in *N. Y. Daily Gazette*, Feb. 10, 1790, quoted in *Boston Gazette*, Mar. 1, 1790; Maclay, *Journal*, p. 192 (Feb. 15, 1790).

[11] Rush to Madison, Feb. 27, 1790 (MP, 12:84); Apr. 10, 1790 (MP, 13:6).

[12] *N. Y. Daily Gazette*, Feb. 10, 1790.

[13] TJ to Madison, Sept. 6, 1789 (Ford, V, 115–124); written in Paris but not sent until Jan. 9, 1790. Madison's reply of Feb. 4, 1790, is in Hunt, V, 437–441*n*. For an earlier reference to this correspondence see p. 179, above. See also admirable discussion by Adrienne Koch in *Jefferson and Madison*, ch. 4.

[14] Ford, V, 123.

the real utility of his principle, and hoped that it might always be kept in view "as a salutary restraint on living generations from *unjust* and *unnecessary* burdens on their successors."[15] In matters of debt and property both of these philosophical statesmen were characteristically conservative in practice, and to men of their agricultural background Hamilton, who was deliberately creating fluid capital, was the innovator. In the course of time Jefferson concluded that his colleague's financial policies were extravagant, and imposed unjust and unnecessary burdens on posterity, but at this stage he was not unwilling to give him the benefit of the doubt in his bold effort to establish the credit of the young Republic. This he showed clearly by his co-operation in the matter of assumption.

Hamilton's proposal that the federal government assume the debts of the states was based on the arguments that these had been contracted in a common cause, the war for independence; that a more orderly and efficient provision for them could be made on the basis of a single plan, rather than many plans; and that this action would serve to increase national unity. The federal government was under no contractual obligation to provide for these debts, however, as it was in the case of its own obligations, and did not need to do so in order to establish its own credit; hence the discussion centered to a greater degree on questions of expediency and local interest than it had in the case of the national debt.

The alignment considerably depended on the financial situation of the various states. Massachusetts and South Carolina in particular stood to gain by the measure, because a relatively large part of their Revolutionary debt was still unpaid, while Virginia, which had paid a larger proportion of hers, saw actual disadvantage in it.[16] Except for South Carolina, the Southern states were generally opposed to the measure – a further practical consideration being that much of the paper had fallen into eager Northern hands.

Suspicion of the more commercial and financial states of the North was growing in the agricultural states of the South, especially in

[15] Hunt, V, 441*n.*

[16] In a letter to Edmund Pendleton, Mar. 4, 1790, Madison put the matter thus: "A simple unqualified assumption of the existing debts would bear peculiarly hard upon Virginia. She has paid I believe a greater part of her quotas since the peace than Massts. She suffered far more during the war. It is agreed that she will not be less a Creditor on the final settlement, yet if such an assumption were to take place she would pay towards the discharge of the debts, in the proportion of 1/5 and receive back to her Creditor Citizens 1/7 or 1/8, whilst Massts. would pay not more than 1/7 or 1/8, and receive back not less than 1/5. The case of S. Carola. is a still stronger contrast" (Hunt, VI, 6*n.*)

Virginia. Before Jefferson reached New York, a neighbor and friend of George Washington had written the President about the situation. "A spirit of jealousy which may become dangerous to the Union, towards the Eastern States, seems to be growing fast among us," he said. "It is represented, that the Northern phalanx is so firmly united, as to bear down all opposition, while Virginia is unsupported, even by those whose interests are similar to hers." He had been told that many who had been warm supporters of the new government were changing their sentiments, from "a conviction of the impracticability of Union with States, whose interests are so dissimilar to those of Virginia." Thus, while antifederalism in its old form had seemed dead, some of its old arguments were being revived. About this time, "Lighthorse Harry" Lee wrote Madison that all of Patrick Henry's dark predictions were coming true, and that he would dissolve the Union rather than submit to the rule of "a fixed insolent northern majority."[17]

Washington himself, while urging good temper and mutual forbearance, recognized the reality, even the inevitability, of the clash of interests. He asked his neighbor if it could be expected that either the Southern or Eastern parts of the nation would succeed in all their measures. "Certainly not," he said; "but I will readily grant that more points will be carried by the latter than the former, and for the reason that has been mentioned, namely, that in all great national questions they move in unison whilst the others are divided; but I ask again which is more blameworthy, those who see, and will steadily pursue their interests, or those who cannot see, or seeing will not act wisely?" He specially deplored disunionist talk and saw in the spirit of accommodation the basis of the Constitution, but quite obviously he did not regard opposition to the assumption proposals of his Secretary of the Treasury as disloyalty to the government.[18] Testimony that Virginians were almost unanimously against them continued to pour in. Opinion had been divided on Madison's motion with regard to the national debt. In general, his attitude was approved in the country but not in the towns, where the commercial interests centered. But his personal correspondents reported that practically nobody favored assumption as originally proposed and he undoubtedly increased his local popularity by opposing it.[19] Jefferson's first known comments on the meas-

[17] David Stuart to Washington, Mar. 15, 1790 (Fitzpatrick, XXXI, 28*n.*); Lee to Madison, Apr. 3, 1790 (Hunt, VI, 10*n.*).

[18] Washington to David Stuart, Mar. 28, 1790 (Fitzpatrick, XXXI, 28–30).

[19] Edmund Randolph to Madison, Mar. 2, 10, 1790 (MP, 12:87, 95); Henry Lee to Madison, Mar. 13, 1790 (MP, 12:98); Randolph to Madison, May 20, 1790 (MP, 13:31).

ure were incidental and noncommittal, but showed that he regarded its success as highly doubtful.[20]

It was defeated in the House, in Committee of the Whole, on April 12, the day before his forty-seventh birthday. According to William Maclay's colorful description of the scene, Sedgwick of Massachusetts pronounced a "funeral oration" over it, and then went out of the room; when he returned his face showed the signs of weeping. Others of "Hamilton's gladiators," as Maclay often described them, reddened like scarlet or became deadly white. One man sought to rally "the discomfited and disheartened heroes" by prophesying that the measure would still be adopted, after proper modifications. Then, as Maclay reported: "The Secretary's group pricked up their ears, and Speculation wiped the tear from either eye." [21] Some allowance must always be made for his tendency to caricature, but others were saying the same sort of thing in letters. One report that made its way to Virginia and finally got copied in New York began thus: "Last Monday Mr. Sedgwick delivered a funeral oration on the death of Miss Assumption. Mrs. Speculator was the chief mourner." [22]

Supporters of the measure, however, did not confine themselves to dirges. They raised cries of injured virtue in newspapers and private correspondence. The writer of one letter to the press, referring to Hamilton, hoped that "the Great Necker of America" would be "found proof against the barbed shafts of envy and interested ambition, and eventually triumph over both, in his noble pursuit of the public welfare." [23] Another, writing from Boston, said that the friends of good government, the friends of science, the friends of virtue and honor all lamented that Madison had departed so essentially from his federal principles and that the luster of his character had so declined. "I once thought him a very great, and a very good man," said this New Englander. "I will do so again when his conduct is more open, public spirited, and accommodating. For the present, I suspend my opinion of him." [24] George Cabot, who regarded it as "irrefragable truth" that the national government could not go on without assuming the state debts and was proud of the united support of this measure by New England, could not reconcile Madison's present conduct with his former principles; and Oliver Wolcott, Jr., the Auditor of the Treasury, wrote his father in Connecticut that the Southern states

[20] TJ to T. M. Randolph, Jr., Mar. 28, 1790 (Ford, V, 150).

[21] Maclay, *Journal*, Apr. 12, 1790, pp. 231–232.

[22] Copy of letter of Apr. 14, 1790, finally appearing in N. Y. *Gazette of the U. S.*, June 2, 1790.

[23] AMERICANUS, *in Gazette of the U. S.*, Apr. 24, 1790.

[24] Extract of a letter of Apr. 8, 1790, in *Gazette of the U. S.*, Apr. 17, 1790.

seemed unprepared "for the operation of systematic measures," and that "very many respectable characters entertain political opinions which would be with us thought very whimsical." [25]

The latter observer was not sure that the men who opposed assumption were not as honest as those supporting it, and recognized the real difficulty in adjusting the mutual financial claims of the states. He even admitted the avidity of speculators and regarded the resentment against them as understandable. Though more realistic than most about the disagreement, this supporter of Hamilton could not escape from his sense of the whimsicality of the opposition. "There are men of great abilities and of extensive science," he said; "but they are in some instances prone to indulge their minds in fanciful theories of republican liberty." [26] It is not likely that this methodical son of Connecticut was talking as yet about the Secretary of State, whose illness had removed him from circulation, but he may have been thinking of a very recent action of Congress which was designed to protect soldiers against speculators. Hamilton promptly objected to this and Jefferson soon supported it. This appears to have been the first direct clash between the two colleagues, and the episode, though unimportant in itself, was revealing and symbolical.

The question was that of arrears of pay of soldiers of the Virginia and North Carolina line, amounting to less than fifty thousand dollars according to Hamilton's estimate. Complaints had reached Congress that speculators were buying up the balances due these soldiers. Madison heard that a man from New York by the name of Reynolds, who was in Virginia with a list obtained from a clerk in the Treasury, was getting the soldiers to assign to him for a small consideration all that was due them, without specifying the amount.[27] The resolutions of Congress on May 21, 1790, sought to defeat this sort of fraud. These required payment to the original claimant or his representative in person, or to an attorney who could produce a power attested to by two justices of the peace and specifying the amount.

Hamilton addressed to Washington a strong protest against this action, on the ground that such a regulation, with a retrospective operation, had an unfriendly tendency to the public credit no less than to the security of property. He doubted if assignees would have any

[25] Cabot to Benj. Goodhue, May 5, 1790 (H. C. Lodge, *Life and Letters of George Cabot,* 1878, pp. 36–37); Oliver Wolcott, Jr. to Oliver Wolcott, Sr., Apr. 14, 1790 (Gibbs, I, 46).

[26] To Oliver Wolcott, Sr., May 22, 1790 (Gibbs, I, 47).

[27] Two letters from a man by the name of Wallace, Mar. 25 and Apr. 20, 1790 (MP, 12:109 and 13:11) were probably from the same person, though the signatures are somewhat different.

chance to recover, and, while recognizing that fraud invalidated any contract, believed that only the courts could ascertain it. Thus he threw the burden of proof on the soldiers, though recognizing that something should be done to make legal action easier for them. The action of the legislature he regarded as an "interference," and he thought the relief of a few individuals an insufficient justification for a measure "which breaks in upon those great principles that constitute the foundations of property."[28]

Hamilton urged, with deference and politeness, that the President disapprove the resolutions, believing that his disapprobation would be effective, since the majority for them in the Senate had been small. But, according to his custom when in doubt, Washington got another opinion. Jefferson's differed from Hamilton's in that he regarded as unquestionable the fraud which the Secretary of the Treasury described only as probable, but he joined his colleage in condemnation of retrospective laws.[29] He argued the case solely on grounds of Virginia law – not speaking for that of North Carolina, which he said he knew nothing about. By thus narrowing the ground he took advantage of Hamilton and left him with nothing but generalizations to stand on. The common law of England, adopted in Virginia, permitted no conveyance of a debt not in possession, Jefferson said. Exception was made of bills of exchange, however, by the law merchant, and of promissory notes and bonds by specific statutes. These being the only exceptions, and no provision having been made for the assignment of such debts as the soldiers' arrears of pay, the transactions complained of were already void in law, regardless of the resolutions of Congress. Also, he claimed that the assignments, if unfairly obtained, were void in equity as well as law. Congress, like an individual, should prefer to pay the assignor rather than the assignee, thus putting the burden of proof on the latter and giving "the advantage to the party who has suffered wrong rather than to him who has committed it."

It has been charged that the argument of Jefferson was based on a narrow theory.[30] Even if it should seem an instance of rigid reasoning, it is an example of his desire and ability to find a legal basis for action which he regarded an equitable in fact. He was not unwilling to quibble in behalf of injured and unfortunate individuals. With Hamilton, on the other hand, concern for the sanctity of contracts bordered dangerously on indifference to and condonation of fraud.

Washington followed Jefferson's judgment in this instance, though

[28] His paper, dated May 28, 1790, is in Lodge, II, 142–151.
[29] His opinion, dated June 3, 1790, by the editor, is in Ford, V, 175–178.
[30] Comment of Lodge, II, 143*n.*

we should not lay too much stress on that fact. He was always disposed to approve legislative action when it was possible to do so, and this did not seem a proper occasion for the first presidential veto. Nevertheless, his decision could not have failed to accentuate the sense of frustration from which the Secretary of the Treasury was now suffering.

Madison had predicted that the assumption measure would not be abandoned. "It will be tried in every possible shape by the zeal of its patrons," he had written James Monroe. "The Eastern members talk a strange language on the subject," he continued. "They avow, some of them at least, a determination to oppose all provision for the public debt which does not include this, and intimate danger to the Union from a refusal to assume." Such a coupling of the funding and assumption measures was not necessary, but the "strange language" grew more insistent as Hamilton's prestige appeared to be at stake. Thus the situation seemed to constitute a threat to the establishment of the public credit, for which both Madison and Jefferson were anxious, to the unified government which Washington was trying to set up, and even to the persistence of the Union — since the alignment was so largely geographical. The President, who loathed the sort of quarreling that had been going on in Congress, and the recriminations that were being hurled back and forth, expressed himself moderately on the assumption proposal, saying that "under *proper* restrictions, and after scrutiny into accounts," he thought it would be found just.[31]

Meanwhile, another question in which George Washington had much greater personal interest had been revived. Madison remarked that the seat of government [that is, the location of the federal capital] was again on the carpet. Mixing his figures further, he wrote to Edward Pendleton: "The business of the seat of government is become a labyrinth, for which the votes furnish no clue, and which it is impossible in a letter to explain to you." [32] After a century and a half the bargains and intrigues which gathered round the residence question are still difficult to penetrate, since personal conversations were not often a matter of formal record.

This question had been considerably discussed in Congress during the previous summer, and interest in it was general in that age of slow

[31] Madison to Monroe, Apr. 17, 1790 (Hunt, VI, 13*n.*); Washington to David Stuart, June 15, 1790 (Fitzpatrick, XXXI, 52).

[32] Madison to his father, June 13, 1790 (Hunt, VI, 15*n.*); to Pendleton, June 22, 1790 (Hunt, VI, 17*n.*).

and tedious transportation. Considerations of personal convenience inevitably bulked large in the minds of representatives who were far from home and had to live in boardinghouses, and it was also believed by many that the location of the government was not without influence on public policy. Some thought the financial and commercial atmosphere of New York particularly favorable to Hamilton's policies. and approved or disapproved of this location for just that reason. Sentiments of local pride influenced certain members, and many supposed that definite commercial advantages would accrue to the district where the growing federal government should have its seat. The actual rivalry was necessarily limited to the middle area, from New York to the Potomac. The New Englanders, knowing that their region had no chance to win the coveted honor, naturally preferred New York. The Carolinas and remote Georgia were also out of the competition, but their allegiance was wavering and uncertain. Within the middle region, there was talk of numerous places – New York, the falls of the Delaware, Philadelphia, a site on the Susquehanna, Baltimore, Georgetown or some other place on the Potomac – but in this discussion Congress took a long time without getting anywhere.

The issue was precipitated on the last day of May when the House voted by a large majority to hold the next session in Philadelphia, and it became greatly confused in June by an unexpected vote in favor of Baltimore, which Madison regarded as a maneuver. The leader of the Virginians was much disturbed by the situation, which promised to get no better when the senators from Rhode Island (which ratified the Constitution May 29) should join the Northern group in the closely divided upper house. On June 17 he wrote James Monroe: "The Potomac stands a bad chance, and yet it is not impossible that in the vicissitudes of the business it may turn up in some form or other." Other statements of his seem significant in the light of what soon happened. "The assumption still hangs over us," he continued. "The negative of the measure has benumbed the whole revenue business. I suspect that it will yet be unavoidable to admit the evil in some qualified state. The funding bill is before the Senate, who are making very free with the plan of the Secretary." Less than a week later, he wrote Pendleton: "We are endeavoring to keep the pretensions of the Potomac in view, and to give to all the circumstances that occur a turn favorable to it. If any arrangement should be made that will answer our wishes, it will be the effect of a coincidence of causes as fortuitous as it will be propitious." [33] He had already listed the causes which coincided,

[33] Madison to Monroe, June 17, 1790 (Hunt, VI, 16*n.*); Madison to Pendleton, June 22, 1790 (Hunt, VI, 17*n.*).

and it may be presumed that in the interval of five days between these two letters, the famous residence-assumption "bargain" was arrived at, through the good offices of Thomas Jefferson.

For some days Hamilton had been trying to make a trade. It is said that he met Robert Morris of the Pennsylvania delegation, as though by accident, early one June morning when the latter came to walk on the Battery, and offered the permanent residence at Germantown or the falls of the Delaware (Trenton) in exchange for one vote for assumption in the Senate and five in the House. The presumption was that temporarily the government would remain in New York, and Morris countered by proposing the temporary, and more immediate, residence in Philadelphia as the price. Hamilton's friends would not let him consent to this, and it was then that he turned to the Virginians.[34] In less than a week – on June 20, to be precise – Jefferson described in its essentials the "plan of compromise" which was eventually carried into effect, and the meeting of Hamilton with him and Madison must have occurred by then.[35]

Jefferson had already expressed himself in another private letter as favorable to the compromise of the assumption issue (without mention of the residence question), if the provisions of the measure were changed so as to give credit to the states for past payments, thus removing the unfairness to Virginia. "Great objections lie to this," he said to George Mason, no doubt expecting that stanch supporter of the liberties of states and individuals to disapprove of the whole idea, "but not so great as to an assumption of the unpaid debts only. My duties preventing me from mingling in these questions, I do not pretend to be very competent to their decision. In general I think it necessary to give as well as take in a government like ours."[36] That was what George Washington had been saying all along, and the specific judgment coincided with that of Madison, whose main objection to assumption had always been the unqualified form in which it was originally proposed. The chronology of events makes it impossible, however, to divorce this judgment of Jefferson's from the question of the residence of the government, for the report was already going around that he had suggested an agreement with the Pennsylvanians very much like the one he mentioned to Monroe on June 20, namely, temporary

[34] The story is in Maclay's *Journal*, pp. 284–285 (June 14, 1790), and is well interpreted by Brant (*Madison*, III, 313–314).

[35] TJ to Monroe, June 20, 1790 (Ford, V, 187–189). The conclusion of Irving Brant that this letter was written after the meeting seems a sound one and it may have been written immediately, as he believes. (*Ibid.*, III, 316).

[36] TJ to Mason, June 13, 1790 (Ford, V, 184).

residence for fifteen years at Philadelphia, and permanent residence thereafter at Georgetown.[37]

Though he had already tried to do something about the residence of the government, it was Hamilton, not he, who took the initiative for a settlement of the assumption question. One day, as Jefferson was going to the President's mansion on Broadway, he met Hamilton near the door. His colleague's look was somber, haggard, and dejected, his dress uncouth and neglected.

Standing in the street, Hamilton spoke to him of the necessity of assumption in the general fiscal arrangements and in the preservation of the Union, stressing the attitude of the New England states, who would make the assumption of their war debts "a sine qua non of the continuance of the Union." As for himself, the Secretary was determined to resign if he did not have credit enough to carry through such a measure; and he observed that he and Jefferson should make common cause in supporting one another, since the success of the administration was their joint concern. He suggested, therefore, that Jefferson interest some of his friends in the South, for it was they who provided the strongest opposition. Undoubtedly, Hamilton was thinking of Madison, whom he was more hesitant to approach because of their public differences. Jefferson had tripped him in a legal argument about soldiers' arrears of pay and Hamilton was not the sort of man to forget a setback, but that matter lay within the executive branch of the government and if he had got to the point of threatening resignation he was in a desperate state of mind.[38]

If Hamilton's appeal was not in his customary proud and self-confident manner, Jefferson's response was thoroughly in character with the modest, patriotic, and co-operative public servant he had always been. He did not sum up his colleague's financial system now as he did in his old age, when he said that it had two objects: "1st as a puzzle, to exclude popular understanding and inquiry; 2dly, as a machine for the corruption of the legislature." [39] He did say that he did not yet understand it, meaning that he had gained no such mastery over it as he had over questions of foreign affairs, with which he was immediately concerned. He also said that the assumption proposal had struck him in an unfavorable light, but he was fully aware of the

[37] Maclay, *Journal*, p. 286 (June 15, 1790). Maclay seems a little confused about this, but the coincidence in the figures is striking. The final agreement was for *ten* years at Philadelphia.

[38] I have followed TJ's account of the "bargain" as given in LC, 41531, and printed in Ford, VI, 172–174, and give reasons for this in the second Long Note following the Select Critical Bibliography.

[39] From introduction to the Anas (Ford, I, 160).

dangers of the political situation. Not long after this, he wrote one of his friends in Albemarle that this question had aroused greater animosities than he ever saw take place on any occasion.[40]

Being devoted to the Union, just as Madison was, and knowing the trend of his friend's thinking, it was natural that Jefferson should pass on the olive branch which Hamilton had held out. He had the two men to dinner, being persuaded that "men of sound heads and honest views needed nothing more than explanation and mutual understanding to enable them to unite in some measures which might enable us to get along."[41] He claimed that he merely presided over the discussion from which a settlement emerged. The assumption measure was to be so modified as to remove the gross injustice to Virginia, and, although Madison would not vote for it, he would not be strenuous in his opposition. It would still be a bitter pill to many Southerners, and the removal of the capital to the Potomac was to be the sugar coating. By this means, also, votes were to be gained for assumption. Two Virginia congressmen whose districts lay on the river — Alexander White and Richard Bland Lee — were to be approached. There is nothing in the record to show who was to do the approaching, but Madison could not have been expected to, since he had announced he would continue to oppose assumption. Obviously, Jefferson had to be the agent. He said that Lee made no objection and that White agreed despite his qualms. The votes of Pennsylvanians being needed on the residence measure, Hamilton got them through Robert Morris, with whom he had already treated. "This is the real history of the assumption," said Jefferson; and in simplified form it is. Actually, the residence bill went through first, and the fate of assumption continued to seem precarious until late in the summer, when, combined with the funding measure, it finally became law.[42]

At the time Jefferson regarded the assumption question as one on which honest and able men were equally divided; and, after the inequities of the original measure were removed, he believed that the decision involved no special advantages to either side. The settlement that was finally effected, including the bargain for the location of the capital, seemed to him "least bad" of the various possibilities.[43] As the

[40] TJ to George Gilmer, June 27, 1790 (LC, 9509).

[41] Ford, VI, 173.

[42] On July 1, having concluded that the residence bill would pass, TJ wrote Short to have his baggage sent to Philadelphia instead of New York (LC, 9534); but as late as July 4, 1790, Wolcott thought assumption unlikely at this session (Oliver Wolcott to his father, Gibbs, I, 48).

[43] TJ to David Howell, June 23, 1790 (LC, 9473); TJ to George Gilmer, June 27, 1790 (LC, 9509).

summer wore on, he learned that opposition in Virginia had continued. Monroe doubted if a vote for a Potomac site, to take effect later, would really mean anything, since there would be great difficulty in removing the government from Philadelphia after it once got there, and told him that assumption would create great disgust if adopted under any shape whatever.[44] Jefferson, who never had any doubt that the residence agreement was made in good faith, overcame some of Monroe's qualms on this point. To his friends at home he emphasized the necessity of political compromise. "I saw the first proposition for this assumption with as much aversion as any man," he wrote to one of them. "But the development of circumstances have convinced me that if it is obdurately rejected, something much worse will happen. Considering it therefore as one of the cases in which mutual sacrifice and accommodation is necessary, I shall see it pass with acquiescence."[45] His attitude was much like that of Washington, who believed that the two great questions of providing for the debt and fixing the seat of government had offered real danger of convulsing the government. "I hope they are now settled in as satisfactory a manner as could have been expected," the President said; "and that we have a prospect of enjoying peace abroad, with tranquility at home." The Secretary of State had written a friend in South Carolina: "That question [residence] then will be put to sleep for ten years; and this and the funding business being once out of the way, I hope nothing else may be able to call up local principles."[46] He regarded the success of the compromise as a victory for the cause of union and a harbinger of domestic peace.

The part that he played in it is now well known because of the record he left in his papers, but it does not appear to have been well-known then. In his secret journal, William Maclay, who was displeased with both features of the arrangement, connected Jefferson with the negotiations leading to the acceptance of the Potomac site, but he said more about Hamilton's efforts to make a trade with the Pennsylvania delegation and he thought of Jefferson chiefly as acting in behalf of George Washington. "It is, in fact, the interest of the President of the United States that pushes the Potomac," said this back-

[44] Monroe to TJ, July 3, 1790 (S. M. Hamilton, I, 209–210), July 18, 1790 (*ibid.*, I, 211–214). See also Monroe to Madison, July 25, 1790 (*ibid.*, I, 214–216), and to TJ (*ibid.*, I, 216–217) in which Monroe disapproved of the increased exercise of taxation by the federal government, as compared with the states, which would be an inevitable accompaniment of the measure.

[45] TJ to John Harvie, July 25, 1790 (LC, 9640–9642).

[46] Washington to Marquis de La Luzerne, Aug. 10, 1790 (Fitzpatrick, XXXI, 84); TJ to Edward Rutledge, July 4, 1790 (Ford, V, 197).

country Pennsylvanian. "He, by means of Jefferson, Madison, Carroll, and others, urged the business, and if we [the Pennsylvania delegation] had not closed with these terms, a bargain would have been made for the temporary residence in New York."[47] After he found that the "abominations" of funding and assumption were intimately connected with the deal, Maclay said that the President had become, in the hands of Hamilton, "the dishclout of every dirty speculation," as his name served to wipe blame away and silence all murmuring.[48] The "original Jeffersonian Democrat," though he wrote little about Jefferson and that little in a private journal, anticipated the lines of future conflict in a striking passage. He said: "Fixed, as Congress will be, among men of other minds on the Potomac, a new influence will, in all probability, take place, and the men of New England . . . may become refractory and endeavor to unhinge the Government. For my knowledge of the Eastern character warrants me in drawing this conclusion, that they will cabal against and endeavor to subvert any government which they have not the management of. . . . My consolation for going to the Potomac is, that it may give a preponderance to the agricultural interest. Dire, indeed, will be the contest, but I hope it will prevail."[49] This prophecy was recorded soon after Jefferson had expressed the confident hope that tranquillity would prevail.

Other contemporary commentators, hostile to the settlement, were less clairvoyant than the acidulous Senator from Pennsylvania, but some of them were much more humorous. In certain newspapers it was charged that "Miss Assumption" had given birth to two illegitimate children, "Philadelphia" and "Potowmacus," as the result of the seductive promises of "Mr. Residence."[50] The cry of "corrupt bargain" was raised in a few newspapers, the blame being laid on Hamilton, and Madison's failure to do more against assumption led to some insinuations against him. Jefferson seems to have been overlooked by the few who attacked the settlement and the many who praised it.[51]

He had kept out of public controversy, as he wanted to; and afterwards, when he was drawn into it, there were good reasons why the disputants on both sides should ignore his connection with the settlement if they were aware of it. After party lines had been definitely

[47] *Journal*, p. 304 (June 30, 1790).

[48] *Journal*, p. 319 (July 15, 1790).

[49] *Journal*, pp. 331–332 (July 22, 1790).

[50] *N. Y. Journal*, Aug. 31, 1790; copies in other papers, cited by Donald H. Stewart in his unpublished dissertation "Jeffersonian Journalism" (Columbia Univ., 1950). To this exhaustive study of the opposition press I am deeply indebted.

[51] In his undated memorandum he said that many erroneous conjectures about the history of the assumption had been published, but he did not say just how these involved him (Ford, VI, 174).

drawn, let us say by late 1792, good "republicans" took the line of condemning the financial policy of Hamilton as a whole, hence they would be reluctant to associate Jefferson with it in any way. On the other hand, the line of the Hamiltonians was to give complete credit to the Secretary of the Treasury and to charge the Secretary of State with obstruction from the moment of his arrival on the national scene, hence they would be indisposed to mention his original spirit of cooperation. This episode simply did not fit into the political stereotype of later years. It does fit, however, into the pattern of Jefferson's personality and working political philosophy during the New York period, when he had not perceived the full implications of his colleague's policy and was not yet distrustful of him as a public man.

The development of antagonism between these two statesmen will be traced through successive chapters in this book, hence there is no need to summarize it here. In point of time and importance their differences on foreign policy came first, but something should be said about Jefferson's later judgment of Hamilton's financial policy. In the memorandum on assumption which he drew a few years later for his own satisfaction, and perhaps for the benefit of posterity, he said this about that measure:

> While our Government was still in its most infant state, it enabled Hamilton so to strengthen himself by corrupt services to many that he could afterwards carry his bank scheme, and every measure he proposed in defiance of all opposition; in fact it was a principal ground whereon was reared up that speculative phalanx, in and out of Congress, which has since been able to give laws to change the political complexion of the Government of the United States.[52]

His emphasis was not so much on the Hamiltonian financial system itself as on its political accompaniments and results. He also feared the prostration of agriculture at the feet of commerce and finance, but others voiced the agrarian protest more vigorously and sharply than he did in this period.[53] For the establishment of the public credit he was willing to accept Hamilton's first fiscal measures, though he himself was fundamentally unsympathetic with this bold attempt to create what was to him a relatively unfamiliar form of property and wealth. But when he condemned Hamilton's system he meant something different from that. He was speaking primarily in behalf of freedom.

[52] Ford, VI, 174.

[53] Maclay did, and so did the Virginia resolutions of Dec. 16, 1790, against assumption, which were drawn by Patrick Henry.

Two years after the passage of the funding act (including assumption), he told Washington that Hamilton's system "flowed from principles adverse to liberty," and was "calculated to undermine and demolish the republic, by creating an influence of his department over the members of the legislature." For his own part, he claimed that when he embarked in the government he was determined to meddle not at all with the legislature and as little as possible with the other departments. He now said:

> The first and only instance of variance from the former part of my resolution, I was duped into by the Secretary of the Treasury and made a tool for forwarding his schemes, not then sufficiently understood by me; and of all the errors of my political life, this has occasioned me the deepest regret. It has ever been my purpose to explain this to you, when, from being actors on the scene, we shall have become uninterested spectators only.[54]

When he spoke of Hamilton's "schemes," Jefferson meant his policies, purposes, ambitions, and machinations as a whole, and he himself did not understand these fully in June, 1790. Probably he understood them better by the end of the summer, but he was rather slow in arriving at the conviction that his associate was determined to dominate foreign affairs as well as domestic. The policies of the Secretary of the Treasury must be judged by posterity on their merits, but Jefferson did not exaggerate his colleague's ruthless aggressiveness and lust for power. In this respect Hamilton stands practically without a rival among the great figures in his nation's history. So long as Washington was in office the specter of dictatorship was unreal, but little imagination was required to see a potential dictator in the person of his onetime military aide.

On August 14, 1790, Congress separated. Jefferson reported to his son-in-law that, by mutual sacrifices of opinion, they had reacquired "the harmony which had always distinguished their proceedings, till the two disagreeable subjects of assumption and residence were introduced." He foresaw no other subject "so generative of dissension" that was likely to arise in the future, and, as a friend of the government, he hoped that everything would work well.[55] Harmony had been restored in the legislature, and it had unquestionably been maintained between the Secretary of State and the President. A couple of days before adjournment Jefferson ordered through William Short 40

[54] TJ to Washington, Sept. 9, 1792 (Ford, VI, 102).
[55] TJ to T. M. Randolph, Jr., Aug. 14, 1790 (LC, 9712).

dozen bottles of champagne which Washington desired, and the next day he set out with him on a voyage to Rhode Island.[56] Little Rhody had recently ratified the Constitution and rejoined the Union, and the President wanted to recognize the event.

He was also accompanied by Governor George Clinton of New York, a senator from Rhode Island, and half a dozen others, including Representative William Loughton Smith of South Carolina, an ardent Hamiltonian who afterwards castigated Jefferson but who made no uncomplimentary references to him in the journal he kept on this occasion. The party sailed both ways on the packet *Hancock* and were gone about a week. At Newport they were elegantly entertained in the Representatives' Chamber; at Providence, after being escorted to the Golden Ball Tavern, where they dined, they were entertained at the Courthouse; and in the evening the President, by special invitation of the students, visited Rhode Island College (now Brown University) to see the splendid illumination. The name of the Secretary of State appeared in all accounts, but he was merely standing by. He cared little for sea voyages and even less for ceremonies, but he was a strong supporter of George Washington and the national unity he symbolized. It was fitting that he should be there, and he seemed to be content.[57]

[56] TJ to Short, Aug. 12, 1790 (LC, 9702).

[57] Good contemporary references are: N. Y. *Gazette of the U. S.*, Aug. 18, 21, 22, 28, 1790; and "Journal of William Loughton Smith, 1790," in *Mass. Hist. Soc. Procs.*, LI (1918), pp. 37–38. Smith attacked Jefferson in 1792 in a pamphlet entitled *The Politicks and Views of a Certain Party, Displayed*, and again in 1796. The events of the trip are summed up in Fitzpatrick, XXXI, 93*n.*; and Dumbauld gives an admirable account (pp. 156–158), with further references.

XVII

First Skirmishes over Foreign Policy

THOUGH he was most occupied at first with routine tasks, including many that were domestic in nature, and was temporarily distracted by the controversies over assumption and the residence of the government, Jefferson began to deal with major questions of foreign policy before he left New York. In this connection, differences of opinion between him and the ubiquitous Secretary of the Treasury appeared during the summer, especially toward the end of it, foreshadowing the later antagonism between the two men, but these still lay beneath the surface and did not enter into public disputation.

The chief problems in the field of international relations which the first Secretary of State had inherited, and to which he now gave attention as a policy-making officer, can be briefly summarized:

1. In point of time, the first of the major foreign questions to command the attention of the new government was that of the commercial relations with other countries, especially Great Britain and France. A dispute over it had occurred before either Hamilton or Jefferson was appointed, but the question did not again become acute while they were serving in New York. We raise it here because of its importance in later struggles.

2. The young Republic still faced the necessity of gaining full and genuine control of its own territory. According to the treaty of peace, now seven years old, this territory extended to the British possessions on the north and the Spanish on the south and west, but there were uncertainties about both the northern and southern boundaries and some of these were not removed until after Jefferson had wholly retired from public life. Of more immediate concern were the questions of the navigation of the Mississippi (which constituted the western boundary), the retention of posts in the American Northwest by the British, and the connivance of both the British and the Spanish with the Indians.

3. Finally, there was the question of the position and attitude of the United States in case of European war, especially a general war involving her ally France. This issue, which became acute in 1793, arose in preliminary form in the summer of 1790, during a brief but alarming controversy between Great Britain and Spain which led to significant expressions of opinion on Jefferson's part.

The countries with which the relations of the United States were most important in this era were Great Britain, France, and Spain. In the latter part of Jefferson's secretaryship, and especially his last year, his greatest problems arose from relations with the French. During the first part of it, the greatest difficulties were with the British, although the rivalry between the two great European powers was such that the problems of Anglo-American and Franco-American relations were inseparable. Rightly or not, friendliness toward one country was regarded as hostility toward the other.

As we have seen, Jefferson's liking for the French as a people and for their policy toward the United States as a nation had been manifested before his secretaryship began and before the French Revolution broke out. Toward the British, many supposed him to be unfriendly. His personal experiences during the American Revolution and the rebuffs he suffered in England when visiting John Adams unquestionably tended to create in him such a disposition. "Still as a political man they shall never find any passion in me either for or against them," he wrote during his first year in office. "Whenever their avarice of commerce will let them meet us fairly half way, I should meet them with satisfaction, because it would be for our benefit; but I mistake their character if they do this under present circumstances." [1]

It was in the hope of breaking down the walls of commercial exclusiveness that Jefferson, Adams, and Franklin had tried to negotiate treaties in Europe, based on the principle of commercial reciprocity. Moved by a similar purpose, James Madison, in the first session of the first Congress, proposed discrimination in the tariff and tonnage laws against countries not having commercial treaties with the United States. In later comments on these proposals, writers have given a rather false impression of the policy as a whole by laying greater emphasis on the term "discrimination" than on "reciprocity"; but the effect of such action at the time would have fallen on the British chiefly, since the United States had a commercial treaty with France. Whether or not this was a wise policy is a matter of opinion, but it

[1] TJ to Francis Kinloch, Nov. 26, 1790 (Ford, V, 248–249).

was an old policy, not a new one. In the eyes of its supporters the only real difference in the situation was that the weapon of retaliation would now be really effective, whereas previously it had been little more than an empty threat.[2] It was not used this time, for Madison's proposals were defeated. Provisions favoring American over foreign vessels were incorporated in the new tonnage and tariff laws, and these proved distinctly advantageous to American ships, but no distinction was made between countries having and not having treaties, and in the course of time Jefferson had to consider and answer French protests.

The main reason for the initial defeat of the policy of commercial discrimination, or commercial reciprocity, was fear of interference with the revenue from British imports, which far exceeded the French, and this revenue seemed more and more important after Hamilton's expensive program had unfolded. When the question again came up after the government had moved to Philadelphia, Hamilton's hostility to discrimination was unequivocal. He believed that an "intimate connection" with Great Britain would be advantageous to the United States, and had intimated as much, not only to Washington but also to Major Beckwith, the unaccredited British representative. Jefferson's support of Madison's position might have been anticipated from his own record, but it was not until the winter of 1790–1791, when he began to draft reports on foreign commerce, that he took a public stand on this issue. By that time he had considered other important aspects of the problem of British relations, and was convinced that the threat of commercial discrimination was the most powerful weapon of negotiation that he and his country had.

Even more galling to national pride than the commercial restrictions of the British and their unwillingness to make a commercial treaty were their failure to carry into effect the terms of the treaty of peace (which they sought to justify on grounds of American failure to carry out their own promises about debts and Loyalists) and their disinclination to send a minister to the United States. They had not recognized American independence in the full sense, and by retaining their posts in the Northwest they denied American sovereignty in that region. It was to sound out official British sentiment on all these questions, including a commercial treaty, that Washington had sent Gouverneur Morris to England before Jefferson assumed office. There was only one time when that informal mission offered any promise of good results. This was when a war between Great Britain and Spain seemed to be brew-

[2] Setser, *Commercial Reciprocity Policy of the U. S.*, chs. III, IV.

ing, following the incident at Nootka Sound on Vancouver Island. Momentarily, the British seemed willing to pay a price for American neutrality, even to the surrender of the Northwest posts. To Jefferson, this situation seemed to be one of promise – with respect to Great Britain possibly, and even more with respect to Spain.

The Nootka Sound affair, in the summer of 1790, bore directly or indirectly on most of the important international problems of the United States, and Jefferson's activities in connection with it constituted his first serious attempt to grapple with these. The episode deserves attention here, not because it had any immediate or tangible results, but because of the problems it revealed and the policies it anticipated. The affair directly involved the two countries whose territories bordered the United States, and it threatened to involve France, with whom the young Republic was allied. It underlined the problem of maintaining a balance of power in the New World; it was related to the questions of the free navigation of the Mississippi and the continued retention by the British of the Northwest posts; and it foreshadowed both the difficulties and the opportunities that the United States would face in the event of general European war.

Specifically, the difficulty arose from the seizure by the Spanish of British ships on the faraway Pacific Coast, where the British had attempted to establish a base, and for a time there was a threat of a war between the two powers into which France, Spain's ally, might be drawn. In the end the Spanish, failing to gain French support, backed down completely and yielded to all the British demands. The danger to the United States arose from the possibility of British seizure of Spanish possessions on the North American Continent, and from commitments to France, in case that country should become involved. The first of these dangers bulked larger than the second in the mind of the Secretary of State – not because of sentimental attachment to France or personal antipathy to Great Britain, but because of his conviction that the possession of Louisiana and the Floridas by the British would constitute a grave danger to the security and even to the independence of the United States. Instead of two neighbors, balancing each other, the young Republic would have one; by land and by sea she would be encircled by the forces and possessions of her former master. To avoid this he was willing to go to war ultimately, but he saw no hope of Spanish victory without French support, and he believed that the chance of avoiding the eventualities he dreaded outweighed the dangers of American delay. Meanwhile, he wanted to take full advantage of the bargaining position of the United States.[3]

While the negotiations he set in train proved abortive, the letters he sent to American representatives in Spain, France, and England are highly significant illustrations of his characteristic foreign policy. In the light of later events, the most important letter was the one to William Carmichael in Spain, which was borne by David Humphreys, now sent there on a special mission.[4] The major purpose of this was to secure the navigation of the Mississippi, to which Jefferson claimed the United States had right not merely by treaty, but by nature, since it was indispensable. His statement of the case was little less than ruthless, for he asserted that the free use of the river could and would be gained by force if not attainable by negotiation. He even held out the threat of action in conjunction with the British, embarrassing though he admitted this would be.

What he wanted from the Spanish was the cession of all territory east of the Mississippi; and in return for this, he was willing to guarantee all of her possessions west of that river – which, he said, Americans did not expect to cross for ages. (Fortunately the Spanish did not take him up, on this point.) It now seems that he was offering them too much, but in these early communications he showed himself to be an astute diplomat, anxious to seize the opportunity which a quarrel between European nations afforded to gain advantages for his own country. In case of peace, he said, the American cause would have to be presented more softly and patiently, but he was determined that his objective be attained in the end, at any risk. In order to secure the navigation of the Mississippi – as he showed afterwards even more convincingly than he did now – he was entirely willing to be inconsistent. This is another way of saying that the fixed point in his policy was the American interest, while the means he employed were flexible.

Through William Short in Paris, Jefferson laid plans to secure French support for his representations to Spain. These were contingent on the outbreak of war between England and Spain. France would be drawn into it, he believed, and should want to lessen Spain's enemies, of which the United States would be one unless the navigation of the Mississippi and the means of using and securing it were granted. He

[3] This policy is outlined in the "Heads of Consideration," also approved by Madison, which he submitted to Washington on July 12, 1790 (Ford, V, 199–203).

[4] TJ to Carmichael, Aug. 2, 1790 (Ford, V, 216–218), and "Heads of Consideration on the Navigation of the Mississippi" (Ford, V, 225–231, and dated Aug. 22, 1790). Humphreys remained abroad and was appointed minister resident to Portugal on Feb. 18, 1791.

did not mention the Floridas, but spoke only of the cession of the island of New Orleans, which represented the minimum he would accept.[5]

His willingness to bargain either way for American advantage was revealed by a letter to Gouverneur Morris in England. In case of war he wanted Morris to intimate to the British that the United States could not be indifferent to enterprises against the Floridas and Louisiana, since a due balance of power on the American borders was no less desirable to his country than a balance in Europe was to the British. "We wish to be neutral, and we will be so," he said, "*if they will execute the treaty fairly and attempt no conquests adjoining us.*" Even to the British, this friend of France who was first of all an American was willing to offer neutrality at a price.[6]

Before the Anglo-Spanish difficulty was settled, certain alarming possibilities suggested themselves to George Washington. Supposing Lord Dorchester in Canada should ask permission to move British troops through American territory to the Mississippi, in an attack on New Orleans and the Spanish posts, what should the American answer be? If he should move British troops this way without leave, as seemed more probable, what notice should be taken of this action? The two queries were submitted by the President not only to the three secretaries, but also to John Jay and John Adams, and the replies were not without significance.[7]

Jefferson's was prompt and brief. He again expressed his conviction that the dangers resulting from the addition of Louisiana and the Floridas to the British Empire would justify American entrance into a general war if there were no other way to prevent this, and thus showed himself to be resolute and decisive with respect to long-range policy. On the other hand, he was fully aware of the desirability of neutrality, and wanted to preserve it as long as possible. War is full of chances, he said, and the reasons for entering this one might be removed. Hence he counseled delay and was quite willing to be evasive. In case the British should ask the specific question which Washington had propounded, he would prefer to avoid an answer, but if obliged to answer he would permit the passage of the British troops. He believed

[5] TJ to Short, Aug. 10, 1790, enclosing confidential papers to be submitted to Lafayette in case of war, and then to Montmorin if Lafayette and Short should see fit (Ford, V, 218–221).

[6] TJ to Morris, Aug. 12, 1790 (Ford, V, 224–225). Italics Jefferson's.

[7] For Washington's queries of Aug. 27, 1790, see Fitzpatrick, XXXI, 102–103, and note 80. Jefferson and Jay replied next day, Adams and Knox on Aug. 29, and Hamilton on Sept. 15. See Bemis, *Jay's Treaty*, pp. 71–73, for a summary. Jefferson's reply of Aug. 28, 1790, is in Ford, V, 238–239.

that this passage would constitute no breach of neutrality if allowed the other party also, and saw less immediate danger in consent than in refusal. If passage were refused and the troops passed anyway – as almost certainly they would – the country would be faced with the alternative of swallowing the insult and thus inviting others, or entering the war prematurely. If British troops should pass without asking leave, he would express dissatisfaction and keep the altercation alive until events should decide whether it was better to accept apologies or seize upon the act of aggression as a cause of war. The policy he favored was one of watchful waiting and, under the highly uncertain circumstances, it was realistic.

None of Washington's advisers except John Adams favored a refusal of the hypothetical demand which, as we now know, the British had no intention of making, and not even Adams believed that forceful British action would necessarily involve the potentially strong but unprepared Republic in war. Oddly enough, Hamilton sounded more quixotic than anybody else on that issue, though his predilections for the British were obvious in his reply. Probably Washington did not have to read all of his long and involved opinion, since it arrived much later than any of the others and the supposed dangers had receded by that time.[8] In its prolixity this presents a sharp contrast to Jefferson's brief opinion, and it shows unmistakably Hamilton's difficulties in reconciling his patriotism with his conviction that an "intimate connection" with Great Britain was desirable. After quoting numerous authorities on international law and reviewing the past conduct of Great Britain, Spain, and France, he concluded that there was a right either to refuse passage or consent to it, though the right to consent was less questionable than the right to refuse. Then, after a dozen more pages of pros and cons, he finally reached the position that it was less dangerous to consent than to refuse.

Jefferson had said practically the same thing in a couple of sentences; hence it would appear that the only real difference between the two colleagues on this issue was that the Secretary of State favored a temporary policy of evasion. In the light of the diplomatic practices of that age, Hamilton's reference to this as timid and undignified may be regarded as little more than a debater's trick, but at first glance he appears to have struck a more telling blow against its practicality. Pointing out that there was an American post on the Wabash River, down which presumably the British expedition would go, and that a clash would be likely in the absence of specific instructions to let it

[8] Hamilton to Washington, Sept. 15, 1790 (Lodge, IV, 20–49); Washington to Hamilton, Oct. 3, 1790 (Fitzpatrick, XXXI, 127–128).

pass, he argued that the alternative between consent and refusal must be frankly faced. Probably it would have been, if the British had made a direct request, and Jefferson had made it clear that he favored granting consent if an answer was unavoidable. Furthermore, it would not have been like him to object to Hamilton's suggestion that an explanation should be given to the Spanish. But it is hard to see how any self-respecting government could have sent instructions to an outlying post to let a body of foreign soldiers pass *before* their passage had been requested.

Hamilton's proposals reveal the lengths to which he would go to avoid any sort of clash with his favorite nation among the powers. He could not ignore the dangers which would arise from British seizure of Spanish possessions, but he did all he could to minimize the likelihood of any future collision with Great Britain and to emphasize the differences with Spain. Given his predilections, his aversion to a clash with the British was accentuated by his opinion that the use of force on their part would leave to the United States no recourse except war. His colleagues were not insensitive to the requirements of national honor, but no one of them appears to have been quite so sensitive as he. More than Jefferson, far more than John Adams, he was in this respect a romanticist; and it is no wonder that he finally met his end on the dueling ground.

Behind the scenes, however, Hamilton continued to do things which would have been hard for his contemporaries to reconcile with the purest patriotism, had they been as fully informed of them as we are. Like later actions of the same sort, these can perhaps be explained on the grounds that he was so egotistical that whatever he did seemed right to him, and that his fear of a clash with the British had become an obsession. There is no reason to believe that he sought any private gain from his intrigues with the representatives of a foreign nation, but it is hard not to regard these as underhanded.

Because of the danger of war between Great Britain and Spain, George Beckwith had been sent back to the United States in July, 1790, and he remained in the country twenty-one months after that. Unlike Gouverneur Morris, he bore no proper credentials, hence neither Washington nor Jefferson could receive him. But he was in constant touch with Hamilton, who was "Number Seven" in his dispatches and continued to be regarded by high officials in London and Quebec as the most influential American representative of the British interest. Hamilton's interviews with him were authorized at the outset by Washington, with a view to the extracting of information, but Beckwith's revealing dispatches show indisputably that the British authorities got a fuller report of Hamilton's conversations than the American President did. Also, they got from the Secretary of the Treasury bits of information which Thomas Jefferson would have kept as state secrets.[9]

In the summer of 1790, an American expedition against the Indians, which proved to be ill-fated, was in preparation; and George Washington, late in August, asked the opinion of his Secretary of State as to whether the object of this should be revealed to Lord Dorchester in Canada. Jefferson, who had no doubt whatever that the British were conniving with the Indians, was strongly of the opinion that they should be kept in the dark, else they would defeat the object of the expedition. Also, Lord Dorchester would interpret this information as practically a notification that he could go ahead with the expedition against the Spanish which Washington thought he was planning. Jefferson would have liked to prevent this, even though he did not think his country strong enough to forbid it.[10] He need not have bothered to express an opinion, for in due course General St. Clair informed the British commandant at Detroit that the sole purpose of the expedition was to chastise the savages, and Hamilton had already told Beckwith that. He said that he did this in order to prevent alarm at the posts, and he relied on the Britisher not to speak of the matter in the United States. Beckwith promptly reported it to Dorchester.[11]

Jefferson's instructions respecting negotiations with Spain were subsequently renewed and elaborated. They marked an early phase of proceedings which turned out to be highly successful though not until after he had retired from the secretaryship of state. So far as the British were concerned, his motions in late summer were wholly wasted — as they probably would have been, regardless of Hamilton. He wrote *Finis* to the mission of Gouverneur Morris after the leaves had fallen and he had moved with the government to the banks of the Delaware. Meanwhile, since Congress had recessed and nothing much of a public nature was happening in New York, he went home for a spell, following the example of his illustrious Chief, who had departed for the banks of the Potomac.

[9] On Beckwith and his relations with Hamilton, see Bemis, *Jay's Treaty*, ch. IV and App. I. For interviews during the summer of 1790, see Hamilton to Washington, July 8, 22, 1790 (J. C. Hamilton, IV, 31–35) and Fitzpatrick, XXXI, 102*n*. See also TJ to G. Morris, Aug. 12, 1790 (Ford, V, 224).

[10] Aug. 29, 1790 (Ford, V, 240).

[11] St. Clair gave the information Sept. 19, 1790, and Beckwith's letter to Dorchester was received Sept. 11. (Bemis, *Jay's Treaty*, pp. 74–75.)

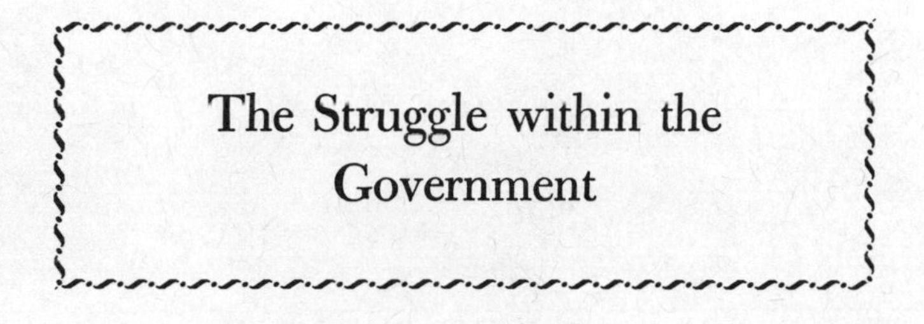

The Struggle within the Government

XVIII

Transition to Philadelphia

ON THE FIRST DAY of September the Secretary of State, leaving his office and personal effects in the capable hands of his chief clerk, took the road to his own red-clay country. Journeys between the seat of government, wherever it was, and Monticello were an old story to a former member of the Continental Congress, and in later years he made the trip often, though it was never again as long as it was this time. His most frequent companion was also his favorite one, James Madison, who went with him as far as Orange County on this occasion.

Riding from New York in Jefferson's phaeton, the two Virginians stayed several days with their old landlady, Mrs. House, after reaching Philadelphia. Proceeding southward, they varied their customary route by going down the Eastern Shore of Maryland and crossing Chesapeake Bay to Annapolis. On this stage of the journey young Thomas Lee Shippen, already attached to Jefferson by kindnesses done him in France, caught up with them. He gained "infinite pleasure" from their charming company but found it expensive, since they traveled well. Also, they took in all the sights there were. At Annapolis, while waiting for their horses to cross in a slower boat, they went to the top of the steeple of the State House to view the prospect. From Georgetown, their next important stop, they rode around the country where the new capital city was to stand, and then went by boat to the Great Falls of the Potomac. Shippen was not with them at Mount Vernon, where they spent a night and the Secretary tipped the servants in his customary handsome way. On September 18 the two travelers arrived at Madison's seat, and on the next day Jefferson was at Monticello. In our own era a motor trip across the North American Continent takes less time than this journey from New York to Albemarle County then took, and no doubt is less fatiguing. Jefferson's return trip, made with the same companion in November, was quicker, since they had to go only to Philadelphia, but almost a third of his recess of three months was spent in travel.[1]

Part of it was spent in rather unpleasant business transactions. While in Virginia, he completed negotiations for the sale of his Cumberland lands south of the James and opposite Elk Island, expecting to apply the proceeds to the old Wayles debt. The price was £1076 and payment was made in bonds ("notes" in our terminology). He wanted to turn these over to his chief English creditors, Farrell & Jones, but their representative was unwilling to accept them, preferring Jefferson's own bonds. Hence this vexatious debt was not speedily liquidated, though it now seemed to be largely provided for.[2]

Another important bit of business was the attempt to secure Edgehill in Albemarle County as a home for Patsy and her husband, and Jefferson made a trip to Tuckahoe on this account. He negotiated for his son-in-law with that young man's father, the elder Thomas Mann Randolph, and this rather unnatural circumstance can be better understood if we recall that his old friend had recently remarried. He thought he had reached an agreement for the sale of Edgehill to young Randolph, but the Colonel afterwards raised the price and stiffened the terms. Jefferson agreed to changes, showing great tact and patience, but he completed no new deal before he went away. The only immediate result was the accumulation of a debt of gratitude to him on the part of his son-in-law.[3]

Meanwhile, the young couple remained at Monticello, where their first child, a daughter, was born in February of the next year. The grandfather, then enmeshed in public affairs in Philadelphia, said that Martha's letter to him about the event brought him greater pleasure than any he had ever before received from her, since he regarded motherhood as the keystone of the arch of domestic happiness. Writing the father about this child, he said: "Happy the man, in the Scripture phrase, who hath his quiver full of them." By this reckoning

[1] The Account Book, Sept. 1–19, 1790, shows the itinerary and expenses of the homeward trip. Brant, *Madison*, III, 318–321, gives details, including quotations from Shippen; and the trip is well described by Dumbauld, p. 159.

[2] Articles of agreement between William Ronald and TJ, Oct. 13, 1790 (MHS); TJ to Richard Hanson, Apr. 5, 1791, and Hanson to TJ, Apr. 30, 1791 (MHS). He tried to use these bonds to settle another debt, but apparently was unsuccessful (TJ to James Lyle, May 11, 1791; MHS). For the general financial situation, see *Jefferson the Virginian*, pp. 442–444.

[3] The story is unfolded in letters in the Edgehill–Randolph Papers (UVA): TJ to Francis Eppes, Oct. 8, 1790; TJ to T. M. Randolph, Sr., Oct. 22, 1790; T. M. Randolph, Jr., to TJ, Nov. 11, 1790. Later letters bearing on the question are: TJ to T. M. Randolph, Jr., Apr. 6, 1791 (LC, 10841–10842); T. M. Randolph, Jr., to TJ, Aug. 22, 1791 (Edgehill–Randolph Papers): TJ to T. M. Randolph, Jr., Mar. 4, 1792 (LC, 12315).

Randolph's life should have been one of unusual felicity, for he begot five sons and seven daughters before he finished. Asked to propose a name for his first grandchild, Jefferson suggested Anne, the name of Randolph's mother, and Anne (or Ann) Cary she was called. Polly, now in her thirteenth year, also remained at Monticello, doing her best to become a scholar, she claimed, but not succeeding very well. Her father gave up the idea of having her join him in Philadelphia in the spring, but her cousin Jack Eppes of Eppington, who was ready to pursue more serious studies under Jefferson's supervision, became a member of the Philadelphia household before summer.[4]

Before leaving New York Jefferson had rented a house in Philadelphia, but, as usual, he wanted extensive alterations. It was at 274 High Street, commonly called Market, on the south side and the fourth house west of Eighth Street, and he liked the location. The President was living on the same street about three blocks away, in the house previously occupied by Robert Morris, and the State House and the home of the American Philosophical Society were in easy reach. His own departmental offices were on the northwest corner of Market and Eighth. Originally he had thought of taking two adjoining houses and using the first floor of both for offices, with living quarters above, but he found himself sharply limited by the amount of rent the government would pay. Not more than £80 a year had ever been allowed as rent for his department. Eventually he himself paid £250 (or $666.67), though he started with a rental of £150. The increase was owing to the alterations and additions, though these were never made according to his full specifications.[5]

The additions, as he finally summed them up, were a bookroom (which he described elaborately in the first instance), a stable, and a garden house. The last of these, which he spoke of last, was to serve as a retreat where he would be unseen and undisturbed even by his own servants, and as eventually built it was so unsuited to his purpose that he used it only as a storeroom. He got some sort of stable soon, though they were still working on it the next summer when his chariot and

[4] Among many family letters, the following may be cited: TJ to Martha, Feb. 9, 1791 (Randall, II, 15); TJ to T. M. Randolph, Jr., Feb. 24 and Mar. 17, 1791 (LC, 10595 and 10718); TJ to Francis Eppes, May 15, 1791 (*Domestic Life*, p. 200).

[5] The fullest account of this complicated business is in Fiske Kimball, *Jefferson, Architect* (1916), pp. 151–154 and drawings, 122–124. The matter is well though more briefly discussed by Dumbauld, pp. 163–166. The most important letters are: TJ to W. T. Franklin, July 16, 1790 (Ford, V, 210–211), and July 25, 1790 (UVA); W. T. Franklin to TJ, Aug. 1, 1790 (LC, 9676); TJ to Thomas Leiper, Aug. 4, 1790, Aug. 24, 1791, Dec. 16, 1792 (all MHS).

sulky finally arrived from Paris – as they were, also, on his bookroom.[6] The internal changes in the house proper need not concern us here, but one feature of his arrangements has specially interested later writers as an innovation in America: the placing of his bed in an alcove or recess.[7] Modern visitors to Monticello can see how he worked out the same sort of idea there, and some of them wonder about the ventilation.

Besides the location, one reason why Jefferson chose this particular house was that he liked the landlord, Thomas Leiper. His claim that he took as good care of a rented house as of his own property was fully warranted, and the cordiality of his relations with Leiper was such that he soon began to avail himself of the latter's services in the marketing of his tobacco. Eventually he agreed to a long lease, providing for relinquishment on three months' notice, and he remained in this place until the spring of 1793. In the end he had some disagreement with Leiper because of the unsatisfactory garden house, and at the very beginning he had reason to be annoyed because of the unreadiness of the main house for occupancy. He was in Philadelphia six weeks before he could move into any part of it. On December 11, he took over the two rooms on the third story, six days later he was able to put his horses and carriages in the stable, and a couple of days after that he got his bedroom, but not until January did he begin to dine at home, and the dining room and front room were not finished even then. Previously he had to take his meals at Mrs. House's.[8]

Meanwhile, a vast quantity of furniture had arrived and this constituted an expense and embarrassment. Two very heavy boxes of books had been shipped from Monticello, along with a musical instrument which seems to have been a spinet, but this was an exceedingly modest shipment compared with the freight that came from France. He paid charges of more than five hundred dollars on the latter before he had any place to put it. Some things he sent to Monticello – a marble pedestal, two chests of drawers, marble tops for these, the driver's seat of a chariot – and after he finished unpacking he expected to send some mattresses, but most of the stuff stayed in his rented house. In the last ten days of the year he paid for the carting of twenty-seven loads of furniture, and he was weeks unpacking it. Upwards of eighty packing cases had been shipped from Havre, fifteen of which were filled with books. It is safe to say that no other American had ever brought from France such a cargo. Soon afterwards he

[6] Henry Remsen, Jr., to TJ, June 16, 1791 (LC, 11183).

[7] Kimball, p. 153; J. T. Scharf and Thompson Westcott, *History of Philadelphia* (1884), I, 462*n.*

[8] Account Book, Dec. 11, 17, 19, 1790; Jan. 8, 11, 20, 1791.

got the tables he had ordered, through Captain Colley, on his voyage home, and he surprised the gallant sailor by paying not only the freight but also a commission.[9]

When this generous-hearted man and lavish buyer finally got his things distributed through Thomas Leiper's large house he must have had an impressive establishment. His need for Petit was now so great that he wrote him urgently, but not until midsummer did his old maître d'hôtel arrive.[10] Before that time he had at least three regular servants, and, whether or not they were technically slaves, he paid them wages. By modern standards these were low, just as Jefferson's own salary of $3500 was. This was payable quarterly and he tried to live within it. Quarter by quarter he analyzed his expenses and ran up his accounts. No carelessness accompanied his fastidious tastes and personal generosity; and if he had not had to allocate his tobacco sales for interest and curtailment on his old debt, he probably could have managed his affairs very nicely. His books and French furniture constituted an extraordinary outlay, but he did not regret the purchase of them and they served to enrich American civilization – particularly his books, which afterwards formed the nucleus of the Library of Congress. Given his position and his tastes, his Philadelphia establishment cannot be properly described as extravagant, but no one can help being impressed by the trouble he took in his effort to perfect it. He may have regarded himself as a temporary exile from his family, but he could hardly have gone to more pains if he had expected to remain in this place indefinitely.

He felt more at home here than in New York, partly because he had been in Philadelphia oftener and longer and was more accustomed to the city, but chiefly because of valued friends here – such as David Rittenhouse, Francis Hopkinson (who died in the spring, unfortunately), Benjamin Rush, Charles Thomson, and other leading lights of the American Philosophical Society. In January, Rittenhouse was elected president of the Society in succession to Franklin, and Jefferson became one of the three vice presidents, not knowing that the mantle of Franklin and Rittenhouse would eventually fall on him.[11] He often had tea with the revered mathematician, who was frail in health and rarely went out, regaling his learned host with items of natural history, such as information about the opossum that had been picked up by young Randolph at Monticello. In the spring he himself

[9] TJ to James Brown, Nov. 4, and Dec. 16, 1790 (MHS); Account Book, Nov. 30, 1790; Dumbauld, p. 163; TJ to Capt. Colley, Feb. 9, 1791 (MHS).

[10] He wrote Petit on Jan. 25, 1791 (LC, 10274), and noted his arrival in his Account Book on July 19, 1791.

[11] He succeeded to the presidency in 1797.

served actively on a committee of the Philosophical Society which was collecting materials on the Hessian fly, and he deeply regretted that his "detestable" official labors left him so little leisure for such fascinating pursuits as the investigation of insect pests. By that time he was longing for the open country life of Monticello; but if he had had to pick an American city to stay in he would have chosen Philadelphia, the scientific center of the country. Here, after he got settled in his house, he could have his committee on the Hessian fly for dinner, and Dr. Benjamin Rush for breakfast, conversing on the more appetizing subject of sugar maples and olive trees.[12] There was less chance for this sort of thing, however, during the winter, when Congress was in session, and he had other associations that were more political.

His friendship with Madison underwent a test toward the beginning of this period, and was all the stronger for having survived it. Early in the new year, after he had partially recovered from his "monstrous bill of freight," he squared his accounts with his recent companion of the road. These were complicated by a most unhappy circumstance. Soon after he got to Monticello he had purchased from Madison a horse, and the creature had quickly died without being paid for. Insisting that the deal was a fair one, and that he would as soon filch the money from his friend's pocket as let him suffer a loss because of this unkind act of Providence, Jefferson paid the stipulated price despite the protests of Madison. In his anxiety he even overpaid his account and had to take a refund.[13] A couple of months later he tried to persuade the little bachelor to leave Mrs. House's and take a bed and plate with him, saying that he had plenty of room and too much solitude and claiming that the proposed arrangement would add nothing to his expense.[14] Madison was unwilling to accept an invitation which he probably thought too generous, but he dined with the Secretary of State very often, rode into the country with him, and, more than anybody else, constituted his link with the congressional group.

Another close friend from Virginia had just joined the first Congress. James Monroe, now a near neighbor in Albemarle, was elected to the Senate in the fall of 1790 to fill an unexpired term. He replaced an even older friend though not now such a close one, John Walker, who had been serving under a temporary appointment, and the aliena-

[12] T. M. Randolph, Jr., to TJ, Apr. 30, 1791 (MHS); TJ to Rittenhouse, May 8, 1791 (LC, 11002); TJ to T. M. Randolph, Jr., May 1, 1791 (Ford, V, 325–326); Rush, *Autobiography*, p. 194 (May 13, 1791).

[13] TJ to Madison, Jan. 10, 12, 1791 (MP, 13:94–95). The amusing and revealing episode is more fully described by Brant in *Madison* III, 321–322.

[14] TJ to Madison, Mar. 13, 1791 (MHS); *Domestic Life*, pp. 197–198, without date.

tion between Jefferson and Walker which had such painful consequences a decade later has been associated with this event. The Secretary of State appears to have exerted no political influence in Monroe's behalf, but with characteristic friendliness he offered to find lodgings for the new Senator and his wife before their arrival. This proffer was not accepted, and Jefferson did not see as much of Monroe as of Madison at this stage, but he retained a high opinion of Monroe's political judgment and was comforted by the thought that he had this ally in the Senate.[15]

In the House of Representatives there was a new member of the Virginia delegation in the person of William Branch Giles, recently elected from a Southside district. The talkative and pugnacious congressman was destined to become an unsparing critic of Hamilton's policies; but that eventuality could hardly have been anticipated by John Marshall, who gave him a cordial letter of introduction to Madison.[16] Giles, a former student of George Wythe's, inevitably met Jefferson, but there is no indication that there was any particular intimacy between the two men at first.

During his first winter in Philadelphia as secretary of state, Jefferson was not specially sociable. Taxed by his official duties, he guarded his precious working hours and was mindful of his health. It was about this time that he fell into the habit of declining all social engagements in the evening.[17] He did not feel natural unless he had companions at dinner, which was generally at three or a little later, but he was hospitable without being convivial, and a considerable degree of solitude was imposed upon him because of the specific nature of his official tasks. These lay within the executive branch of the government but were not predominantly administrative, since his own department was so small. They necessitated little direct contact with members of the legislative branch, though they were much increased by the presence of Congress. That body met on December 6, and for a couple of months thereafter his business was so unremitting that he was forced to apologize for neglecting his correspondence.[18] The business that pressed most heavily upon him was that of drafting reports and opinions. In this period of two months he drew them at the rate of at least one a week.

All of these papers bear the marks of thought and some of them

[15] See *Jefferson the Virginian*, pp. 447–448; Monroe to TJ, Nov. 26, 1790 (S. M. Hamilton, I, 219–220).

[16] Marshall to Madison, Nov. 27, 1790 (MP, 13:73).

[17] TJ to William Thornton, Feb. 14, 1801, saying that he had been in this habit for ten years; Thornton Papers, 3:395 (LC).

[18] TJ to R. R. Livingston, Feb. 4, 1791 (Ford, V, 276), and other letters.

were the fruit of extensive investigation, hence they illustrate his scholarly proclivities no less than his diligence as an official. Through them, primarily, he exerted his influence – on the President, who had requested most of them, and on the legislators, who had requested some and to whom sooner or later others were submitted. He was engaged chiefly in laborious and solitary paper work, not in political chatter or manipulation. He was far less an actor on the public stage than a worker and thinker behind the scenes. He dealt with important questions, however, and many of them were controversial. Those relating to foreign affairs engaged him first and concerned him most, hence we should begin with them.

[XIX]

Foreign Commerce Becomes an Issue

1791

PRESIDENT WASHINGTON was still dealing with his department heads singly, not as a group. At a later time, especially in 1793 when Europe was engulfed in general war, crucial questions were threshed out in ministerial conferences, but he now relied chiefly on written reports and opinions from his assistants. Some of the papers drafted by Jefferson related to matters of domestic administration on which Washington wanted his advice.[1] Others, dealing specifically with foreign questions, were eventually submitted to Congress in some form, even though originally directed to the President; and some were reports to Congress, resulting from the reference of particular questions to the Secretary of State by that body.[2] These questions belonged in Jefferson's department, but some of them impinged on financial policy, and all of them were thus cast into the arena of political debate. Differences of opinion between him and the Secretary of the Treasury on foreign policy, and especially on foreign commerce, that had been previously under cover began to emerge into the open during this legislative session.

Jefferson's differences with Hamilton over domestic financial policy remained incidental until he was drawn into the controversy over the Bank of the United States toward the end of the session. Even then he spoke on the constitutional question only, and the opinion that he drafted for Washington was not seen by Congress. His own policies

[1] For example, the following: (1) Nov. 29, 1790, "Opinion on proceedings to be had under the Residence Act" (L. & B., III, 82–84); (2) Dec. 14, 1790, "Report . . . on the Report of the Secretary of the Government north-west of the Ohio" (L. & B., III, 85–87); (3) Dec. 14, 1790, "Opinion on certain proceedings of the Executive in the North-western territory" (L. & B., III, 88–90).

[2] Two reports of Dec. 28, 1790, relative to the Mediterranean trade and the Algerine prisoners (L. & B., III, 94–111, 112–120) will not be discussed here.

were more directly and openly at issue in connection with foreign matters.

British questions were discussed more extensively in Congress, but we shall consider French relations first.

Early in the session the President submitted to the Senate a report of the Secretary of State on the protests of the French against the United States tonnage laws.[3] It will be recalled that these laws imposed higher charges on foreign than on American vessels, making no exception in the case of the French. The latter took the position that this was in violation of the treaty of amity and commerce between the two nations, but Jefferson was too good a lawyer and too good an American to admit their claim. After careful consideration of the treaty he reported to Washington that the French construction of it was unwarranted, and that, in fact, they did not exempt American vessels from port duties in their own waters. Furthermore, if they should grant such exemption to the United States, they would have to grant it to all others who were on the footing of "most favored nations." On technical grounds, he concluded that they had no case; and he regarded the proposal that the tonnage laws be modified in their favor as impracticable in the form they made it.

He was fully aware, however, of the favors the French had granted to American commerce, having been the American agent in the negotiations, and he detected an implied threat that these might be withdrawn. Specifically, he referred to the admission of whale and fish oils, which he had struggled for as minister and was not disposed to surrender. These particular favors, he noted, were wholly independent of the treaty, and he believed that a relaxation of the tonnage laws might be granted in express consideration of them – *quid pro quo*. This disposition of the matter would put it on such a basis that no other country could demand the same favor without granting an equivalent compensation. Another advantage would be that the American action would be legislative, not by means of a treaty, hence future modifications of the policy would be easy if there were a change in circumstances. He could think of no better way to mollify the French and get around the technical difficulties, and obviously he could not pursue it without the concurrence of Congress.

He wrote George Mason that he was trying "to obtain some little

[3] Specifically, these protests were directed against the acts of July 20, 1789 and July 20, 1790. TJ's report of Jan. 18, 1791, to Washington, following receipt of a protest from Otto, the French chargé, was communicated to the Senate, with annexed papers, Jan. 19, 1791 (Ford, V, 266–273; *A.S.P.F.R.*, I, 109–116; *Exec. Procs. of Senate*, I, 66–71).

distinction for our useful customers, the French," but that there was a "particular interest" opposed to it which he feared would prove too strong.[4] In his report he actually presented several alternatives without specific recommendation. These were: (1) to deny the French demand, on the ground that their interpretation of the treaty was incorrect, and that the exemption proposed by them presented great practical difficulties; (2) to modify the law, if it should seem advantageous to agree to a reciprocal and perpetual exemption from tonnage duties; (3) to modify the law, not as a matter of obligation, but as an act of friendship and in return for specific favors. While he obviously disliked the second of these alternatives and personally preferred the last, he was prepared to accept the first.

Before presenting his report to Washington he consulted not only Madison, who was more inclined to accept the French construction of the treaty than he was, but also Hamilton. As might have been expected, the latter agreed that the exemption from the tonnage laws which the French sought was not claimable as a right under the treaty, but he demurred against granting it on the ground that Jefferson had suggested. "Though there is a collateral consideration," he said, "there is a want of reciprocity in the thing itself." The tendency would be to put French vessels on an equal footing with American in American ports without doing the same thing for American ships in the ports of France. In the existing state of French navigation he thought little immediate harm would ensue, but he feared future developments and did not like this sort of irregularity.[5]

His reasoning was good and Jefferson gave weight to it, but he submitted no substitute proposal, as Jefferson had suggested. He would prefer to negotiate a new treaty with France, he said, by means of which reciprocal advantages might be fixed on a permanent basis.[6] The feasibility of this might have been questioned by Jefferson on the basis of experience, even if he had been sure of the sincerity of his colleague's suggestion. Hamilton revealed a more immediate reason for his attitude when he said that perhaps a new treaty would be less likely to "beget discontents elsewhere." He feared the displeasure of the British, even though he spoke in general terms. "My commercial system," he said, perhaps being unconscious of his own egotism, "turns very much on giving a free course to trade, and cultivating good humor with all the world." That sounded good, but in the common meaning

[4] TJ to Mason, Feb. 4, 1791 (Ford, V, 276).

[5] Hamilton to TJ, Jan. 11, 1791 (Lodge, IV, 52). Otto had pointed out that at least twice as many American vessels entered the ports of France as French vessels entered American ports (Jan. 8, 1791; *Exec. Procs. Senate*, I, 71).

[6] Hamilton to Jefferson, Jan. 13, 1791 (Lodge, IV, 54).

of the term Hamilton was not a free-trader. "I feel a particular reluctance to hazard anything, in the present state of our affairs, which may lead to a commercial warfare with any Power," he added. As the responsible financial officer of the government, he had good reason to feel that way, but, in view of his relations with Beckwith, it is easy to perceive a strong British flavor in his language.

Hamilton doubted the seriousness of the situation with respect to the French. A letter which Jefferson submitted in part to the Senate, a couple of weeks after his report, shed some light on the question. This was from William Short in Paris, who reported that the members of the National Assembly were less interested in American commerce than previously – some supposing that the American attachment to British commerce was too great to be overcome, and others that American trade was a losing business for them. The proposal that American imports and ships be subjected to the same duties as their own in the United States had been rejected, but other unfavorable proposals were pending.[7] On the whole, Short gave the impression that the French were still friendly but regarded themselves as ill treated by their American allies.

The attitude of the Senate toward this matter might have been anticipated from the political complexion of that body, and more particularly from that of the committee to which Jefferson's report was referred. This was dominated by stanch supporters of Hamilton.[8] The general policy of the Hamiltonians was to delay matters as long as they could, and the Senate took no definite action until the very end of the session. Resolutions were then adopted, advising that the answer to the French follow the lines of Jefferson's first alternative. William Maclay, claiming that he was the only person who voted "boldly and decidedly" against the committee's report, said that strong anti-French sentiments were voiced by Oliver Ellsworth and Rufus King in the course of the debate. He himself favored a repeal of the tonnage law on the ground that it conflicted with the treaty, hence he was much more pro-French than anyone could properly have accused Jefferson of being.

The Senate advised that the answer be made "in the most friendly manner." [9] Perhaps this language represented a victory over the ex-

[7] An extract from Short's letter of Oct. 21, 1790, was submitted to the Senate on Feb. 2, 1791 (*A.S.P.F.R.*, I, 120–121).

[8] On Jan. 19, 1791, TJ's report was referred to a committee consisting of Robert Morris, Rufus King, Ralph Izard, Caleb Strong, and Oliver Ellsworth (*Executive Procs.*, I, 72).

[9] Resolutions of Feb. 26, 1791 (*Exec. Procs.*, I, 77). Maclay's comments of that date are in his *Journal*, pp. 390–395.

tremists, and probably Jefferson expected nothing more. He had suffered no open defeat, and at least he was not denied the opportunity to present his interpretation of the treaty to the French authorities in a friendly spirit.

This he did after the session ended. His letter to the French chargé was almost identical with the first part of his own report. "We feel every disposition . . . to make considerable sacrifices where they would result to the sole benefit of your nation," he added, "but where they would excite from other nations corresponding claims, it becomes necessary to proceed with caution."[10] He gave assurances of his own "perfect conviction of the coincidence of our interests," which was more than the Senate resolution had said, and stated that the general subject of navigation would be taken up seriously when Congress met again, having been postponed merely because of the end of the session. He was more optimistic than the circumstances warranted, as later events proved.

The first of Jefferson's papers of this period bearing on British relations was his brief but potent report on the mission of Gouverneur Morris to England. The correspondence of the emissary with the President was referred to the Secretary of State, and from it he drew some basic conclusions: (1) The British had decided not to surrender the posts in any event, and would urge as a pretext alleged obstacles to the collection of their debts, despite the fact that American courts were now open to them. (2) They did not intend to submit their present commercial advantages to the risk which might attend a discussion of them; and they would consider no treaty except one of alliance as well as commerce, thus undermining American obligations to France. (3) There was uncertainty about the prospect of their sending a minister.

As to American policy, he took the position that the initiative with regard to a treaty of commerce and an exchange of ministers must now be taken by the British, since his own government had done all that self-respect allowed; and that American demands for the posts and for indemnification for Negroes taken by the British should not again be made until the United States was in position to enforce them. Thus, for the present, the questions at issue must lie dormant. Also, he recommended that Morris be informed that he had performed his mission satisfactorily and that it was now at an end. The blame for failure Jefferson put squarely on the British, whereas Hamilton – in-

[10] TJ to the French chargé d'affaires, Mar. 29, 1791 (Ford, V, 308–313; quotation from p. 312).

formed by Beckwith that Morris had been too intimate with the French ambassador and with Charles James Fox, the head of the party opposed to the British ministry – was disposed to blame the American representative for the coolness of the British officials. Morris had been considerably less than tactful, but Washington properly suspected Hamilton's suggestion, because of its original source.[11]

Jefferson's view was accepted by Washington and the mission was ended, but not until two months later did the President report the matter to Congress. To the House he then sent a brief letter, and to the Senate he submitted his original instructions to Morris and the pertinent correspondence, along with a covering letter which summed things up.

Jefferson had drafted both of the presidential communications.[12] The tone of the letters was restrained but the purport was entirely clear; and quite obviously there was plenty of anti-British ammunition in these documents. That must have been the main reason why the prudent President was so slow in sending them in. A fire was laid already, and they kindled it.

Jefferson's report on the cod and whale fisheries, which Congress had received about ten days earlier, may likewise be regarded as an anti-British document though it has intrinsic value and interest as a treatise.[13] A representation on the subject from the General Court of Massachusetts had been referred to him by Congress, and this elaborate paper was the result. Jefferson was no sort of fisherman and did not like the water, even though his maternal grandfather had been a sea captain; but he had studied the status and history of the whaling industry with care when in Europe, and had already written extensively about it.[14] He was merely carrying on from the point where he had left off a couple of years before, when seeking and gaining concessions from the French with respect to the importation of American whale and fish oils.

His history of the fisheries will be illuminating even now to most laymen, and his sympathetic presentation of the plight of the New England fishermen should have commended him to them. At best, he

[11] TJ's report of Dec. 15, 1790, is in Ford, V, 261–263. See Hamilton to Washington, Sept. 30, 1790 (J. C. Hamilton, IV, 73); Washington to Hamilton, Oct. 10, 1790 (Fitzpatrick, XXXI, 131–132), TJ to Morris, Dec. 17, 1790 (L. & B., VIII, 115–116).

[12] Feb. 14, 1791. The documents are in *A.S.P.F.R.*, I, 121–127. TJ's drafts of the letters are in Ford, V, 283–284. His report to Washington was not submitted to the Senate.

[13] Feb. 1, 1791. (L. & B., III, 120–144). It was laid before the House, Feb. 4, 1791 (*Annals of Congress*, II, 1754) and ordered sent to the Senate.

[14] *D. C.*, II, 233–253.

thought their business a hard one in both its branches, and so unrewarding that foreigners could not have afforded to engage in it without governmental aid – such as the British had given by bounties of one sort or another. Because of advantages of geography and skill, American fishermen, in his opinion, did not need direct aid from the Treasury, but they did deserve relief from certain taxes which bore heavily upon them (such as customs duties on articles they particularly used); and, most of all, they needed markets. His concern for them was not merely that of a humane man for other human beings. As a patriotic American, he appreciated the importance of seamen, and saw in the fisheries a nursery for them, just as the British did.[15] Setting his discussion on the background of larger commercial considerations, he strongly emphasized the importance of reviving the American carrying trade.

No honest account of such a subject could have helped sounding anti-British, for British fishermen and seamen were the chief rivals of the Americans, and their market was restricted while the French was considerably opened up. The tone of Jefferson's treatise was scholarly, but some of his language was sharp. He said that the British had shown no disposition to arrange any commercial matter on the basis of mutual convenience, and asserted that their regulation "for mounting their navigation on the ruin of ours" could be opposed only by counter-regulations.[16] But he had said equally sharp things while abroad and had been as convinced then as he was now of the natural commercial rivalry between the two English-speaking countries, and the natural friendship between the United States and France. In this paper he brought down to date policies of his own which originated in no personal rivalry with Alexander Hamilton and were wholly unconnected with the French Revolution.

His report had immediate political significance, however, because of the strong anti-British sentiment in Congress, especially in the House. Some of his comments, like the following, were very pertinent:

> If regulations exactly the counterpart of those established against us, would be ineffectual, from a difference of circumstances, other regulations equivalent can give no reasonable ground of any complaint to any nation. Admitting their right of keeping their markets to themselves, ours cannot be denied of keeping our carrying trade to ourselves. And if there be anything unfriendly in this, it was in the first example.[17]

[15] William Maclay objected to the report for just this reason; *Journal*, p. 373 (Feb. 4, 1791).

[16] L. & B., III, 141.

[17] L. & B., III, 142–143.

Hamilton's opposition to legislation of this sort was well-known, not only in Congress but in British official circles. Having been informed before this time that the British had decided to send a minister, he had assured Beckwith that such legislation would fail.[18] He had a card to play which Jefferson did not know about — that is, an announcement of this decision — but he was probably less confident than he sounded, and he could not have relished his colleague's powerful report. Somebody said that from this document one might conceive Jefferson to have been, not a native of the Virginia hill country, but "a regular-bred Boston merchant, who had accumulated a fortune in the traffic in spermaceti," though a merchant of superior information.[19] This sort of approach to current commercial questions, and such proposals as these, were thoroughly unpalatable to the Secretary of the Treasury, who was relying heavily on New England's support of his policies and who, beyond any doubt, was truckling to Old England at this stage — chiefly because he depended on the duties on imported British goods for revenue, but partly because he liked English political institutions.

Jefferson had not only provided considerable ammunition against the British in his report on the cod and whale fisheries; in that document he had also made it clear that he himself favored a retaliatory commercial policy. A serious attempt to adopt such a policy was made in the House of Representatives immediately after Washington informed Congress of the failure of the Morris mission.

His message to the House, which Jefferson drafted, referred merely to the commercial aspects of this mission, stating that one of Morris's purposes had been to inquire whether the British were "disposed to enter into arrangements, by mutual consent, which might fix the commerce between the two nations on principles of reciprocal advantage," but that he himself inferred no disposition on their part to enter into any arrangements "merely commercial." [20] The implication, which was made clear in the longer message to the Senate, was that England would consider nothing short of an offensive and defensive alliance.

In spite of the fact that more anti-British ammunition was furnished the Senate, there was more sentiment for retaliatory legislation in the House. The President's message was referred to a committee, of which Madison was a member, and this committee reported a bill

[18] Bemis, *Jay's Treaty*, p. 81, quoting Beckwith to Grenville, Jan. 23, 1791.

[19] *Public Characters, or Contemporary Biography* (Baltimore, 1803), p. 212. In this American edition of an English work, the sketches of the Americans were presumably written by William Tatham.

[20] Feb. 14, 1791 (Fitzpatrick, XXXI, 214; Ford, V, 283).

which was drawn in imitation of the British navigation laws.[21] In the committee, the margin in favor of this strong measure seems to have been slight; Beckwith picked up the information that it carried by a majority of only one. At the very end of the session it "vanished" from the scene, as Jefferson said. In fact, the report was referred to him with the direction that he report to Congress, at its next session, the nature and extent of the privileges and restrictions of the foreign commerce of the United States, and such measures as he should think proper to be adopted for improvement.[22] This action can be attributed chiefly to the influence brought to bear by Hamilton, who used the prospective appointment of a British minister as an argument for delay.[23] The British decision to send a minister, not yet officially communicated, antedated this particular debate in the House, hence it was not caused by it; but the instructions to Hammond, who arrived in the following autumn, show that the defeat of the movement for anti-British commercial legislation was the chief immediate purpose of his mission. A delaying action in Congress was in perfect accord with the tactical plan of the British, but the defeat of the "discrimination" movement was not yet assured.

Soon after the congressmen went home, Jefferson sent copies of the proposed law to American representatives abroad, hoping that the French, Spanish, and Portuguese might be induced to adopt something like it. In describing it he said: "This act is perfectly innocent as to other nations, is strictly just as to the English, cannot be parried by them, and if adopted by other nations would inevitably defeat their navigation act and reduce their power on the sea within safer limits." To another representative he wrote: "Being founded in universal reciprocity, it is impossible it should excite a single complaint." [24] The purpose of the measure, in his eyes, was to bring Great Britain to a state of reason, instead of contemptuous disregard. In confidential dispatches he talked of forging what would have amounted to a commercial coalition against her, and quite obviously he wanted to apply all possible diplomatic pressure in behalf of what he conceived to be the interests of the United States.

How sanguine he really was about action on the part of other countries is a question. By summer he had even become discouraged about the prospects of American action. At all times, however, he was

[21] *Annals*, II, 1963; Setzer, p. 110; Bemis, *Jay's Treaty*, p. 82.

[22] Feb. 23, 1791 (*Annals*, II, 1969); TJ to Edward Rutledge, Aug. 29, 1791 (Ford, V, 375).

[23] Bemis, *Jay's Treaty*, pp. 80–81; Setzer, p. 110.

[24] TJ to David Humphreys, Mar. 15, 1791; to William Carmichael, Mar. 17, 1791 (Ford, V, 302–303).

convinced that the policy involved in the proposed act was based on just principles, and that strong measures were necessary to wring any sort of commercial concessions from the British. He justified his position on both practical and theoretical grounds.

The theoretical consistency of his position need not be questioned; and if at this stage the application of principles of reciprocity amounted to action against the British, and thus could be described as "discriminatory," the blame can be laid on British policy, whatever the patriotic reasons for that may have been. The wisdom of this particular measure at this time, however, is another question. The argument of Hamilton against it, echoed by his followers, was that it would excite commercial warfare which the young Republic could not yet safely engage in; that it would interfere with the revenue from British imports; that it would upset his financial plans. There was merit in Hamilton's argument, highly colored by his own ambitions and predilections though it was. Yet his fears seem exaggerated, for the actions of the British themselves showed that a retaliatory American policy was what they dreaded most. The threat, at least, of discrimination should not have been surrendered, and foreign policy should not have been made so subservient to a domestic financial policy which was certainly more expensive than it had to be.

Perhaps the measure which Jefferson favored in this instance was too risky, but he was considerably more realistic about British officialdom than Hamilton was. And, in later months, it was exceedingly unfortunate that he was denied the use of his strongest diplomatic weapon, even as a threat, while his colleague the Secretary of the Treasury was playing into British hands.

[XX]

The Bank and the Constitution

1791

WHEN he took up his duties in Philadelphia, Jefferson's attitude toward the financial policies of Hamilton that had already been translated into law was one of acquiescence, and he viewed the economic prospects of the country with considerable satisfaction. He realized that opposition to the assumption of state debts had continued in Virginia, but believed that certain leaders were harping on this subject in order to mask other reasons for disaffection to the government.

In particular he suspected the motives of Patrick Henry, of whom he said: "The measures and tone of the government threaten abortion to some of his speculations; most particularly to that of the Yazoo territory."[1] In his opinion, however, the government was "too well nerved to be overawed by individual opposition." His deep distrust of Henry also serves to explain his apparent indifference to the resolutions of the Virginia House of Delegates, which were drawn by that leader and adopted late in the year (1790). These condemned the assumption of state debts as both injudicious and unconstitutional. Jefferson had never gone that far, and at the time he probably regretted the intemperance of the proceedings.[2]

Meanwhile, Hamilton's vigorous program had passed into its second phase. Jefferson's first comments on his colleague's current proposals

[1] TJ to Gouverneur Morris, Nov. 26, 1790 (Ford, V, 250), not mentioning Henry by name but obviously referring to him. The optimism of this official letter, with respect to the prospects of the government, can be partially attributed to his desire to present things in a favorable light to Americans abroad.

[2] The resolutions of Dec. 16, 1790, can be readily seen in H. S. Commager, *Documents of American History* (1948) I, 155–156. In a letter to Madison, Dec. 24, 1790 (MP, 13:77), Edward Carrington characterized the proceedings as intemperate.

were noncommittal rather than unfavorable. Without revealing any alarm, he reported to his son-in-law that the two most important measures before Congress were for the establishment of a bank and for a tax on ardent spirits, called an excise.[3] Upon its face, his attitude was that of a loyal member of the administration who was absorbed in his own department and not disposed to stray far from it. Not until February, after the pressure of his paper work had relaxed somewhat, did he begin to question his colleague's financial policy. Writing that month to George Mason, whose sincere republicanism he never doubted, he asked: "What is said in our country [Virginia] of the fiscal arrangements now going on?" By this time he was giving more heed to the Southern opposition. "Whether these measures be right or wrong abstractly, more attention should be paid to the general opinion," he said. He was beginning to show traces of resentment at the triumphant march of the Hamiltonian program, and to attribute its success to improper influences, that is, the pressure exerted by the Treasury and interested persons. He was convinced that both the excise and bank bills would pass, as nearly everybody else was. "The only corrective of what is corrupt in our present form of government," he concluded, "will be the augmentation of the numbers in the lower house, so as to get a more agricultural representation, which may put that interest above that of the stock-jobbers."[4] He might have quoted the very words of the Virginia resolutions about assumption, which deplored the erection of a large "monied interest" in an agricultural country and spoke of the prostration of agriculture at the feet of commerce. Soon after this he wrote an old friend in Albemarle: "There are certainly persons in all the departments who are for driving too fast. Government being founded on opinion, the opinion of the public, even when it is wrong, ought to be respected to a certain degree. The prudence of the President is an anchor of safety to us."[5]

His friend Madison, who had accepted the excise tax as a necessary evil, now that the federal government had assumed the debts of the states and had to pay the interest, thought that Hamilton had gone too far in proposing a bank.[6] Madison's arguments had been buried under an avalanche of votes, and the bank bill lay on Washington's desk before the middle of February, but the prudent President was unwilling to sign it until his doubts with respect to its constitutionality had been removed. These had been raised by Madison's speeches in the

[3] TJ to T. M. Randolph, Jr., Jan. 11, 1791 (LC, 10221).
[4] TJ to Mason, Feb. 4, 1791 (Ford, V, 275).
[5] TJ to Nicholas Lewis, Feb. 9, 1791 (Ford, V, 282).
[6] Madison's speeches of Feb. 2 and Feb. 8, 1791, are in Hunt, VI, 19–42.

House of Representatives and were reinforced by an opinion from Attorney General Randolph. Washington next turned to his secretary of state.

There is no reason whatever to suppose that Hamilton had consulted Jefferson before submitting his second Report on the Public Credit, in which he recommended the creation of the Bank of the United States; and the President did not now call on the ranking member of his official family to discuss the proposed institution upon its merits.[7] We are perfectly safe in assuming, however, that if he had had the chance at this time Jefferson would have voted against it. That sort of institution did not fit snugly into the pattern of his thought or experience.

The bank that Hamilton wanted to set up was to be chartered by the federal government and make regular reports to it, but it was to be "under a *private* not a *public* direction – under the guidance of *individual interest*, not of *public policy*."[8] Three fourths of the capital was subscribable in government securities, nevertheless, and the government was to provide one fifth of the total on its own account; hence only a small part of the capital had to be in the form of cash from individuals. The privately administered bank was to be bottomed on the resources and credit of the United States. The funds of the government were to be deposited in it, and its notes, redeemable in specie, were to be legal tender. In return for these great privileges and favors, the bank was expected to aid in the financial operations of the government. One of the practical arguments advanced against it by Madison was that the plan did not represent a good bargain for the public.[9] It could not be doubted, however, that the bank would be a real convenience to the government, and the official who was most concerned with fiscal operations favored it for that reason.

Hamilton's motives went further. He wanted to increase the fluid capital of the country, to improve business facilities, to make credit more available. Hence it is no wonder that his policies were approved by commercial interests generally, as they were by the holders of government paper. His luminous report showed that he had made a careful study of banking, a thing which neither Jefferson nor Madison had been under any necessity of doing. There were only three "public" banks (as distinguished from private bankers or banking firms) then existing in the United States – one each in Boston, New York, and Philadelphia – and none of these was big enough to serve the interests of the entire country.

[7] The report of Dec. 14, 1790, is in Lodge, III, 125–178.
[8] Lodge, III, 162. [9] Hunt, VI, 26.

It seemed to many, however, that Hamilton, while talking in large national terms, was actually favoring a special class and a small one. The bill provided for branch banks, though Hamilton was doubtful about them in the first place. The agricultural districts were without banking facilities, but they were not specially conscious of their need of them, and their doubts with respect to the benefits they would gain from this creation were afterwards borne out by experience.

Jefferson was deeply interested in commerce, despite his greater concern for agriculture, but he viewed financial questions as a conservative. Fearing debt as he did, he was more alarmed than encouraged by the expansion of credit. The sort of wealth which Hamilton's policies were creating seemed unreal to this lover of the land and believer in hard money, and the speculative spirit which they had engendered was objectionable to him on moral grounds. Coupled with these increasing doubts and fears — and more important, probably — was his growing distrust of Hamilton, who seemed to be pressing relentlessly and irresistibly onward in his march toward power. By catering to a relatively small but highly articulate and influential group, he had bound these men to himself by ties of interest and become their champion. In effect he had created a "machine," which would continue to be used in the interest of the favored few. Left to himself, he would change the character of the government.

"Congress may go home," wrote William Maclay. "Mr. Hamilton is all-powerful, and fails in nothing he attempts." [10]

One possible way to stop him was to invoke the Constitution, and Jefferson promptly took the same position as Madison and Randolph when the question was referred to him. The Hamiltonians afterwards emphasized the fact that all three of these men were Virginians, coming from a state which had declared assumption unconstitutional by this time, and where there was great fear lest the establishment of the Bank in Philadelphia would make the removal of the capital to the Potomac difficult. Their constitutional attitude was attributed to local and political considerations. This statement of the matter is itself narrow and partisan and may be discounted on that ground. It is quite obvious, however, that neither Madison nor Jefferson set this constitutional question in a vacuum or was unaware of its economic and political implications in his own state.

The essential arguments of the two men were very similar, and Madison's came first. Whether Jefferson got more from him than he did from Jefferson is a matter of sheer conjecture, but Madison made two points which his friend could not make with the same authority.

[10] *Journal*, Feb. 9, 1791, p. 376.

As he remembered—and he had kept the fullest records—the power to grant charters of incorporation had been rejected in the Federal Convention.[11] Also, recalling the objections that had been raised to the Constitution, and the explanations that had been given in the state conventions ratifying it, he predicted that many people would say that the adoption of the Constitution had been brought about by one set of arguments, while the government was now being conducted under another interpretation.[12] In other words, Hamilton was turning the government into something that neither the people generally, nor Madison himself, had expected it to become.

Regardless of the intrinsic merits or demerits of the Bank, that did seem to be the case; and, more than any other consideration, it seems to explain Madison's attitude.

Since Jefferson had played no direct part in the framing and ratifying of the Constitution, he could speak with no such authority on these subjects; but, by the same token, he was freer than Madison was from embarrassments growing out of past efforts to extend the functions of the federal government. This is one reason, though not the only one, why he went further than his friend in advocating what has come to be known as "strict construction" of the Constitution. It has often been said, since his day, that such limitation of national power as he favored in this instance would have stultified the government in the long run. The force of his argument at the time lay in his contention that the words of the Constitution meant precisely what they said; but the long-range weakness of his doctrine lay in its rigidity. In this dispute, he appears as a legal fundamentalist, and that may seem strange in the light of his unfailing religious liberalism and unwavering confidence in the human mind. He himself, however, would have recognized no parallel between theology and public law. He regarded religion as wholly a private matter, and was thoroughly consistent in distrusting rulers in both Church and State. In both realms, he sought to gain for the ordinary individual a maximum of freedom; and if he now sought to hold the federal government to a strait course and narrow way, he was fully aware that Hamilton, who was contemptuous of ordinary individuals, was in the driver's seat.

The personal and political circumstances go far to explain the lengths to which he carried his argument, and the tone in which he expressed it; but his doctrine of strict construction cannot be detached from the

[11] Hunt, VI, 26. Hamilton claimed, on the other hand, that the circumstances were differently reported by various people, and that no inference whatever could be drawn from the matter. (Feb. 23, 1791; Lodge, III, 196–197.)

[12] Hunt, VI, 35.

larger setting of his general attitude toward public law. He himself was not unwilling to construe Acts of Congress liberally, upon occasion — as indeed he had done recently in the case of the Act establishing the national capital — and as a practising statesman he could not have been expected to be wholly consistent.[13] Even with respect to statute law, however, he tended to be a literalist, and he was characteristically scrupulous about fundamental law as embodied in constitutions. The man who believed that the earth always belongs to the living generation, and who favored the revision of constitutions every twenty years, was certainly no foe to change in the light of experience; but he never felt safe in allowing much leeway to the interpretation of existing law by individual officials — executive, legislative, or judicial. To him laws in general, and constitutions in particular, were shields against tyranny; and he coupled a positive faith in human beings with a predominantly negative attitude toward political agencies and institutions. Hence the position which he took at this time, while explicable in terms of personalities and issues, was by no means incompatible with his characteristic attitude toward government, and especially toward constitutions. To a greater degree than Madison he was consistent with his own past.[14]

In the brief opinion on the Bank which he promptly drew at the request of the President, he made no attempt to summarize his general philosophy but stuck to the bill and the letter of the law.[15] The limitations and extreme rigidity of this paper can be partly attributed to its form, for it is little more than an enlarged outline. Jefferson often submitted skeletonized opinions to Washington, for the President's convenience no doubt, and he is not to be blamed for putting so little flesh on these bones. His argument would have fared better at the bar of history, however, if he had set it on a broader base.

He began by listing the things undertaken by the bill that lay before him: (1) to form the subscribers to the Bank into a corporation — with various powers opposed to the ancient and fundamental laws of the states; (2) to give them what amounted to a monopoly; (3) to give them, in effect, power to make laws paramount to the laws of the states — for such construction of their powers was necessary to protect the institution from the state legislatures. By the tone he used in describing these things he made it obvious that he was opposed to them

[13] For his opinion on proceedings to be had under the Residence Act, Nov. 29, 1790, see Ford, V, 252. In his *History of the U. S.*, IV, 85–86*n.*, Edward Channing calls attention to this, without putting it in its larger setting.

[14] For comments on his attitude, as shown earlier, see *Jefferson the Virginian*, pp. 304–305, 381, and elsewhere.

[15] His opinion, dated Feb. 15, 1791, is in Ford, V, 284–289.

on grounds of policy. The theoretical basis of his argument was the Tenth Amendment to the Constitution, which reserved to the states or the people all powers not delegated to the United States by the Constitution, nor prohibited to the states. Actually, it had not yet been formally adopted, though there was no doubt it would be, and he called it the twelfth amendment. "To take a single step beyond the boundaries thus specially drawn around the powers of Congress," he said, "is to take possession of a boundless field of power, no longer susceptible of any definition." Viewed in the light of his general philosophy, this assertion should be regarded as a protest against the extension of political authority rather than a plea for state authority. He feared unlimited political power of any sort, though he was thinking at the moment of a Congress that was dominated by Hamilton.

Proceeding logically from his sound but narrow premise, he inquired whether the power to incorporate a bank, and to give it such powers, had been delegated to the United States by the Constitution. He could not find this among the powers that were specially enumerated, nor in either of the general phrases. The latter he interpreted literally. In his judgment the "general welfare" clause was a statement of the purpose for which the specific power of laying taxes was to be exercised, not a grant to Congress of a distinct and independent power to do anything it pleased for the supposed good of the Union.[16] The latter interpretation "would reduce the whole instrument to a single phrase." No such universal power was meant to be given Congress. "It was intended to lace them up straitly within the enumerated powers, and those without which, as means, these powers could not be carried into effect."[17] Then he added the item of historic information which Madison had mentioned and which he accepted without question: the power of Congress to incorporate had been considered and rejected by the Convention.

In discussing the "necessary and proper" clause, he denied that means which were merely *convenient* could be regarded as *necessary*.[18] If such a latitude of construction were allowed, this would

[16] For the convenience of the reader we quote from Art. I, Sec. 8 of the Constitution: "The Congress shall have Power To lay and collect Taxes, Duties, Imposts and Excises, to pay the Debts and Provide for the common Defence and general Welfare . . ." Jefferson interpreted this to mean the power to lay taxes, etc., *in order to* pay the debts and provide for the general welfare. The capitalization ("To" in one case and "to" in the other) in the original document perhaps bears out his contention – if one wants to be pedantic. (Farrand, *Records of the Federal Convention*, 1911, II, 655).

[17] Ford, V, 286.

[18] The wording is: "To make all Laws which shall be necessary and proper for carrying into Execution the foregoing Powers, and all other Powers vested by this

"swallow up all the delegated powers." Therefore, the Constitution restrained Congress to "those means without which the grant of power would be nugatory." This assertion was afterwards challenged by Hamilton on the ground that few measures of any government could meet so severe a test.[19]

The restrictions which Jefferson sought to impose would probably have begotten endless uncertainty and embarrassment, as Hamilton soon said; but Jefferson was justified in his contention that large extensions of power should not be made on grounds of minor convenience. This apostle of freedom was inevitably alarmed by the extreme claims of national power which had been made by some supporters of the bank bill in the debates, just as Madison was; and he was trying to find a formula to guard against the dangers he perceived. The insuperable difficulty was that no *unvarying* formula for the proper relations between the nation and the states could be devised.

While insisting on the limitations of congressional authority, Jefferson also recognized limitations on the executive. He regarded the presidential veto as a shield against legislative usurpations, and believed that the reserved rights of the states were invaded in this instance. Nevertheless, in the concluding paragraph of his opinion he said that unless the President's mind was tolerably clear that the bank bill was unauthorized by the Constitution, "a just respect for the wisdom of the legislature would naturally decide the balance in favor of their opinion."[20]

Clearly he thought this a case where Congress had been "misled by error, ambition, or interest"; but he ended his generally dogmatic paper on an undogmatic note.

Washington, who had no confidence in his own judgment in constitutional matters, was much disturbed when he received a second official opinion against the Bank and wasted no time in apprising Hamilton of the situation. He wrote the Secretary of the Treasury bluntly, and sent him the papers of Randolph and Jefferson in order that he might see the arguments he would have to answer.[21] He was seeking further counsel on a grave question, not presiding over a public debate, and it was largely through force of circumstances that Hamilton had the last word.

Constitution in the Government of the United States, or in any Department or Officer thereof." Hamilton said that Jefferson would have inserted "absolutely" before the word "necessary."

[19] Lodge, III, 188.

[20] Ford, V, 289.

[21] Washington to Hamilton, Feb. 16, 1791 (Fitzpatrick, XXXI, 215–216).

While waiting to receive this word, Washington turned to Madison, with whom he had several conversations on the subject; he asked this trusted friend to prepare a veto measure for him in case he should desire to use it. He had vetoed no Congressional Act before this time. Madison drafted a brief paragraph, stating that the power proposed by the bill was not expressly delegated, and did not result from any express power by fair and safe rules of implication. He also drew a slightly longer statement of objections to the measure on its merits, in case the President should desire to use this alone or in addition to the other.[22]

Meanwhile, during this period of suspense, partisans of the bill in New York, the major seat of the rising financial group, indulged in reflections on Washington which Madison thought indecent and actually a reflection on those making them. Writing Jefferson from that city afterwards, he said:

> I have reason to believe that the licentiousness of the tongues of speculators & Tories far exceeded anything that was conceived. The meanest motives were charged on him, and the most insolent menaces held over him, if not in the open streets, under circumstances not less marking the character of the party.[23]

Whether or not Washington knew this – and probably he did not – he was not one to be intimidated. He was suspending his judgment while waiting, somewhat impatiently, to hear from Hamilton.

The Secretary of the Treasury took a full week in drafting his opinion. Jefferson had tossed off a brief, but Hamilton's was a long paper. He generally wrote that kind, and he fully recognized that this was a critical occasion. How magnificently he rose to it, the later constitutional history of his country was to show. His opinion was an extraordinarily skillful defense of his own position and a masterpiece of exposition.[24]

If the gist of Jefferson's argument was that the Constitution meant literally what it said, the task of Hamilton was to show that it meant more than it appeared to. Strict construction as espoused by the Secretary of State would not only defeat the Bank he was trying to set up; he believed that it would also be fatal to "the just and indispensable authority of the United States." He saw no necessity, however, to challenge the premise which Jefferson had drawn from the Tenth Amend-

[22] Feb. 21, 1791 (Hunt, VI, 42–43*n.*). Brant, in *Madison*, III, 330, quotes a memorandum about the conversations. The dates of these are uncertain.

[23] Madison to TJ, May 1, 1791 (Hunt, VI, 48*n.*).

[24] The opinion, in the form of a letter and dated Feb. 23, 1791, is in Lodge, III, 180–225.

ment, being safe in conceding this if he could construe it in his own way. He took his stand on what he regarded as higher ground, and launched his powerful counterattack from there.

Starting with the sovereignty of the United States, he asserted a positive political philosophy, emphasizing what the government *could*, not what it *could not* do, and proclaiming principles of liberal construction which have echoed and re-echoed through the generations. It is fortunate, however, that these can be applied in behalf of more popular interests than Hamilton himself gave thought to, as they have been since his day.

He based his argument on the general proposition that every power vested in any government is, in its nature, sovereign and includes a right to employ all means that are requisite and fairly applicable to the attainment of the ends of such power.

Hamilton could hardly have been expected to know that Jefferson had once approached the same idea from a different angle. Speaking of the old Congress of the Confederation, while in Paris, Jefferson had said that certain powers—such as that of enforcing contributions of money from the states—need not be given expressly, since Congress had them by the law of nature. "When two parties make a compact," he said, "there results to each a power of compelling the other to execute it." [25] At that time he was talking about the execution of laws, not legislation itself, and he spoke more often of limitation of authority than of the extension of it into doubtful fields; but he could not have wholly denied the existence of implicit as well as express powers. At this stage, however, Hamilton was in much better position to twit Madison with inconsistency. In the *Federalist* papers, the latter had written:

> No axiom is more clearly established in law, or in reason, than that wherever the end is required, the means are authorized; wherever a general power to do a thing is given, every particular power for doing it is included.[26]

Perhaps Hamilton was one of the few who knew that it was Madison who had said this, since the papers were anonymous, but no doubt he assumed that Washington was familiar with the general line of Madison's reasoning during the course of the battle for the ratification of the Constitution. It may be claimed that the doctrine of implied powers really originated with Madison. At all events, Hamilton, with consummate skill and probably with deliberate intent, took the words

[25] TJ to Edward Carrington, Aug. 4, 1787 (Ford, IV, 424).
[26] *Federalist* No. 44 (P. L. Ford edn., p. 300).

out of the mouth of one of his present critics when stating his own general position.[27]

Hamilton, in effect, charged the unnamed Madison with repudiating the principle of implied powers. He directly charged Jefferson and Edmund Randolph with overlooking the fundamental principle of sovereignty, and he believed that his own presentation of that principle, and its natural implications, really answered their objections to the constitutionality of the Bank. He thought that he had disposed of them in a few paragraphs. He took plenty of time to answer them specifically, nonetheless. Jefferson's extremely restrictive interpretation of terms, such as "necessary," made him a fair target, and Hamilton scored a number of palpable hits. At the same time he maintained a tone of reasonableness and moderation – which did not accord with his own temperament and philosophy, to be sure, but was well calculated to impress a reasonable man like Washington. "The moment the literal meaning is departed from, there is a chance of error and abuse," he admitted. "And yet an adherence to the letter of its powers would at once arrest the motions of government." [28] He believed that the difficulties resulted inevitably from the division of legislative power between the states and the nation. Some cases would be clearly within the power of the national government, and others outside it; and there would be a third class, about which there would be a great difference of opinion, and concerning which "a reasonable latitude of judgment must be allowed." He sought to create the impression that his critics were unreasonable. It was relatively easy for him to show that Jefferson, in speaking of the "prostration" of fundamental state laws by the proposed incorporation, overstated his case and seemed to favor an unalterable legal system.[29] The Constitution and laws of the United States were the supreme law of the land; and, in Hamilton's opinion, the proposed Bank had a natural relation to the power of collecting taxes, regulating trade, and providing for the common defense. To any reasonable man, he argued, this should be enough.

Perhaps it would have seemed so to almost everybody if he had impressed his contemporaries with his own reasonableness heretofore, and if the Bank had not been his personal creation.

The bill had been presented to Washington on February 14, and Hamilton's lengthy opinion did not reach him until the noon of Wednesday, February 23, two days after Madison outlined a possible veto message.

[27] Brant, *Madison,* III, 331.
[28] Lodge, III, 191.
[29] Lodge, III, 192–193.

According to the constitutional provision it would become a law by the lapse of ten days, and the President inquired of Hamilton with considerable concern just how much more time he had. Hamilton informed him that he had until February 25, since he need not count Sundays or the day he got the bill; and Washington kept it as long as he could.[30] Whether he had time to weigh the arguments as carefully as he would have liked to is a question, and we cannot be sure that he was wholly convinced. He did not have to be, if he followed Jefferson's advice and gave the benefit of doubt to the legislature. At any rate, he did not call on Jefferson for a rebuttal, either because he saw no need for one or because he did not have time enough, and he signed the bill. There seems to be no record that he showed Hamilton's opinion to Jefferson at this or any other time. Nothing in his customary procedure made it necessary that he should.

The debate among the President's advisers had been a strictly private one, conducted in writing, and neither of the now-famous conflicting opinions was made public until many years had passed.[31] It was currently reported that some of the great officers of state had given opinions against the Bank, and the fact that Jefferson had objected to it probably became common knowledge in congressional circles; but Madison's arguments were much better known, and he was still the personal symbol of opposition to Hamilton's policies and doctrines if anybody was.[32] Jefferson had not appeared in public as an advocate of strict construction, and presumably had not heard the other side of the private debate. The only immediate contemporary judgment on it was Washington's, and we cannot be sure just what that was. The judgments that are passed on these two opinions in works of history and biography, therefore, are really the judgments of posterity.[33]

To later commentators it has generally seemed that Hamilton, in his superb opinion, laid the firm philosophical foundation for a genuinely effective national government, armed with powers which later events proved to be indispensable. In this paper he reached the culmination

[30] Washington to Hamilton, Feb. 23, 1791, and the latter's reply (Fitzpatrick, XXXI, 224 and note).

[31] The conflicting arguments are given in John Marshall's *Life of George Washington*, V (1807), 297 and Note III appended to the volume, though the documents themselves are not printed. Marshall saw the two opinions in Washington's papers, and until evidence to the contrary is presented, the best assumption is that their contents had not been considerably divulged before the appearance of his volume.

[32] *Gazette of the U. S.*, May 11, 1791.

[33] The "official" acceptance of Hamilton's position certainly cannot be dated earlier than 1819, when Marshall incorporated his arguments in his decision in the case of *McCulloch* vs. *Maryland*. Jefferson himself seems never to have withdrawn from his own position: that the Bank was unconstitutional.

of his positive, constructive, and creative genius. John Marshall drew on it heavily in another century, and it has been quoted as a classic by advocates of governmental effectiveness and national power in every generation since. It should be obvious, however, that the constitutional philosophy to which Hamilton gave enduring literary form was natural doctrine for one in his position at that time, and that contemporary distrust of his position inevitably accompanied distrust of him as a man and leader. No acceptable explanation can be given for the shift in Madison's constitutional emphasis – which he himself could hardly have explained on intellectual grounds – except his growing conviction that national power, when in the hands of Hamilton and his partisans, was liable to grave abuse. To Jefferson it seemed, no doubt, that the Secretary of the Treasury was interpreting and would continue to interpret the Constitution as he liked.

These events had not served to diminish his own distrust of rulers, but later developments showed that there was more merit in the specific measure Hamilton was championing than Jefferson could see. The first Bank of the United States was more serviceable to merchants and manufacturers than to small farmers, but, considered as a financial institution, it was wisely administered and justified its creation by its record. Jefferson's own secretary of the treasury found it exceedingly useful in the next decade. Throughout its life, its personnel was largely confined to what came to be known as the Federalist party, and it was chargeable with political ineptitude, but in this decade it evinced no subserviency to its creator.[34] Jefferson's fears of this particular corporation, though not unnatural, now seem extreme.

His fears of Hamilton, and of the consolidation of government and power which his brilliant colleague symbolized, seem much more justifiable. Partisan writers continued to explain his attitude toward the Bank and the Constitution on personal and narrowly political grounds. More than twenty years later Timothy Pickering, dipping his pen in vitriol, wrote that envy and hatred of his rival still rankled in Jefferson's breast, that he had never forgotten his signal defeat, and that if he could prevent the rechartering of the Bank he would regard himself as finally victorious.[35] If the Secretary of State did not feel bitter about the Secretary of the Treasury by the spring of 1791 he had plenty of reason to, but until this time Jefferson had acted much more like a sentinel of freedom than an ambitious politician.

[34] See the admirable article by J. O. Wettereau, "New Light on the First Bank of the U. S.," *Pa. Mag. of History*, July, 1937, pp. 263–285.

[35] Pickering to Judge Richard Peters, Jan. 30, 1811, quoted by Charles Warren in *The Supreme Court in U. S. History* (1922), I, 504*n*.

It now appears, however, that the doctrine of strict construction which he had advanced would have been an imperfect shield against what he conceived to be potential despotism. Fixed fortifications are no sure defense against a mobile adversary who will agree to no unvarying rules of warfare. Perhaps this was not yet entirely clear to Jefferson, but he was beginning to realize that if Hamiltonianism was to be combatted effectively, more aggressive tactics would have to be employed by somebody, and other weapons than constitutional arguments must be used.

[XXI]

Storm over the Rights of Man

1791

THE final session of the first Congress ended on March 3, 1791, much to the relief of the first Secretary of State. This period of three months had been laborious for him, and he had considerable reason for discouragement at the end. The movement for commercial discrimination against the British had been checked, the bank bill had been signed, Hamilton was triumphant, and if Jefferson had suffered no conspicuous public defeat he was unquestionably discomfited. Less than a week before the session ended he offered the clerkship for foreign languages in his department to Philip Freneau, poet and stanch republican, whom Madison was encouraging to set up a newspaper in Philadelphia. Freneau promptly declined the modest offer, however, and nothing came of it until late summer. Jefferson's personal political activity at this stage can be easily overemphasized, but this proposal was a straw that showed how the wind was blowing.[1]

After Congress adjourned he began to catch up on his private correspondence, and he enlarged it somewhat as occasion offered. Political implications can be read into some of his letters by those who have the benefit of hindsight, for he inquired about public opinion in other states than his own and let it be known that "republicanism" needed reinforcement in Congress. Except when writing old friends, however, he guarded his expressions, and if he had any thought of organizing the opposition to Hamilton's policies he was not doing very much about it.[2]

[1] TJ to Freneau, Feb. 28, 1791 (LC, 10617); Freneau to TJ, Mar. 5, 1791 (LC, 10650). Later developments are discussed in ch. XXV.

[2] His correspondence with Harry Innes of Kentucky, which Innes initiated, probably fits best into the political category, but it was also concerned with natural history and there were official reasons why TJ needed to be informed of Western opinion. See TJ to Innes, Mar. 7, 13, 1791 (Ford, V, 294–295, 299–301). Innes, whom TJ already knew, replied to the former letter May 30, 1791 (LC, 16864) and was flattered by TJ's readiness to enter into correspondence.

He was predominantly occupied with matters falling within the executive sphere, such as the planning of the new national capital, which we shall discuss in the next chapter; and during Washington's absence of some weeks in the spring, on a Southern tour, he regarded himself as specially obligated to keep the President informed of happenings. Washington asked that the department heads meet for conference in certain contingencies, calling in the Vice President if he should be in town. Informing Washington of one meeting of the sort, Jefferson also reported and concerned himself with a vacancy which had arisen in Hamilton's department. This action was afterwards objected to by the Secretary of the Treasury, who gave the impression that Jefferson had provoked an incident in the administrative sphere. The vacancy occurred on April 16, through the not-unexpected death of Nicholas Everleigh of South Carolina, Comptroller of the Treasury. Writing the President next day, Jefferson transmitted an application from Tench Coxe, then Assistant Secretary of the Treasury, along with a blank commission from the supply that he kept on hand. The haste of this action can be explained on the ground that he expected the letter to reach Washington in Charleston, and wanted to reduce the inevitable delay. How he came by the application is another question, and it looked as though Coxe was going over Hamilton's head, in connivance with Jefferson.

If Coxe reported the circumstances correctly to the Secretary of State, Hamilton had already discussed the situation freely with his subordinate. At the time Oliver Wolcott, Jr., held the office of auditor, and it was he who eventually got that of comptroller. In a letter to Jefferson, Coxe described the situation thus:

> . . . There appear to be circumstances, which originated at the time of Mr. Wolcott's appointment to his present office, that operate to restrain the Secretary of the Treasury from moving in favor of any other person, & this information he gave me unasked. He entertains an opinion also, that the relation between the offices of the Comptroller and Auditor creates a kind of pretension in the latter to succeed the former. He however added in a very kind and flattering way his opinion, that he should see as many public advantages from the appointment of myself as any other person, and that he would by no means advise my declining to apply to the President.

This part of Coxe's letter was sent to Washington by Jefferson, and it seemed to him to provide a sufficient explanation of his own action. As all commissions passed through his hands, no doubt many applications did, and the assumption was that the President followed his own judgment in important appointments. Jefferson did not recommend Coxe, and he took the liberty of suggesting a man from South Carolina, in case Washington should think it desirable to appoint a successor to Everleigh from the same state.[3]

In the part of Coxe's letter which Jefferson properly retained, because of its personal character, the Assistant Secretary of the Treasury gave signs that he was cultivating Jefferson's favor. Also, he allowed him some discretion in the matter of the application. This was to be forwarded unless Jefferson, in conference with Madison, should decide otherwise. The Secretary of State saw no reason why he should wait to consult Madison, since he was troubled by no doubts, but he went beyond the requirements of politeness in expressing to Coxe the hope that his application would be successful. Perhaps he was not unwilling to do a certain amount of flirting with one of Hamilton's aides. On the other hand, it was in his character to err on the side of personal compliment, and Coxe was making himself helpful by providing him with statistical information. The uses which Jefferson hoped to make of this might have been regarded by the Secretary of the Treasury as anti-British, but the plan for an American manufacturing establishment which Coxe had just submitted to the Secretary of State, while agreeable to the latter no doubt because of its patriotic emphasis, was much more in line with Hamilton's ideas of industrial development. Hence no important difference of opinion between Hamilton and Coxe would naturally have been supposed.[4]

By an odd accident of circumstance, Washington did not get Jefferson's letter and its enclosures until he was back at Mount Vernon two months later. Hamilton had been no more prompt in writing but was more successful in getting his letter through. He specifically recommended Wolcott, about whom he had already spoken to the President, and Washington had decided to appoint Wolcott before he got Coxe's application. Hamilton said he had information that other candidates would be brought to the President's attention by "weighty advocates," but said nothing about impropriety, and if he regarded this as a minor test of strength he probably had little doubt

[3] TJ to Washington, Apr. 17, 1791 (Ford, V, 322), enclosing two pages of letter of Tench Coxe to TJ, Apr. 16, 1791 (JP from National Archives). I have not discovered Coxe's letter of application to Washington.

[4] Coxe to TJ, Apr. 16, 1791, part of letter retained; TJ to Coxe, Apr. 17, 1791; Coxe to TJ, Apr. 20, 1791 (all by courtesy of JP). For comments on the plan for a manufacturing establishment, see J. S. Davis, *Essays in the Earlier History of American Corporations* (Cambridge, 1917), I, 351–355.

that he would win it.[5] Also, he could exploit it and did so to some extent. A few weeks later, Madison, learning that complaints about Jefferson's "interference" were in circulation, expressed surprise that so serious a face should have been put on the matter in view of the particular circumstances. He had been informed of the application of Coxe at the latter's express request, but nobody else was supposed to know about it except Hamilton. Jefferson concluded that his colleague had given out the story in garbled form, and questioned the propriety of his revealing confidential matters of administration.[6]

As a rule, Jefferson was more scrupulous about proprieties than Hamilton. In this instance, he would have done well to check Tench Coxe's story with the latter's superior and tell Hamilton that he was forwarding the application as a routine act. Also, he might have guarded his complimentary expressions in his private letter to Coxe. Conventions with respect to appointments were not firmly established by this time, however; and, in the light of the known circumstances, the chief significance of this episode behind the administrative scene seems to lie in the clues to character and personality which it provides.[7]

Another episode of this period, involving John Adams and Thomas Paine, received wide publicity. From the political point of view the chief result of the affair was that the Secretary of State, who much preferred to keep out of sight, was thrown on the public stage as a supporter of the principles of the French Revolution. It is also of interest as revealing certain apparent contradictions in Jefferson's mind and conduct.

Early in the year 1791, the first part of Paine's now-famous work, *The Rights of Man*, had been published in England. It was a direct reply to Edmund Burke's equally famous *Reflections on the Revolution in France*, which had appeared a few weeks earlier. As the dedication to George Washington showed, Paine coupled the French Revolution with the American. In the summer he sent fifty copies of his pamphlet for Washington and his friends, boasting of the run the work was having in England and Ireland. It is possible to attribute Wash-

[5] Hamilton to Washington, Apr. 17, 1791 (J. C. Hamilton, V, 467–469); Washington to Hamilton, June 13, 1791 (Fitzpatrick, XXXI, 293; Washington to TJ, June 17, 1791, making no mention of Coxe (Fitzpatrick, XXXI, 298).

[6] TJ to Madison, July 27, 1791 (Ford, V, 358–359); Madison to TJ, July 31, 1791 (MP, 14:39).

[7] It seems to me that L. D. White, in *The Federalists*, pp. 224–225, overemphasizes this episode, and accepts without question the partisan interpretation (See J. C. Hamilton, *History of the Republic*, IV, 513–514).

ington's delay in acknowledging it to his desire to brush Paine off, but he did not publicly repudiate this author, and in consistency the Father of the Republic would not have been warranted in so doing.[8] Paine also attacked the English constitution, but not to the same extent as in the second part of the work, published a year later, which led to charges of sedition against him in England and his flight from that country before he could be tried. The first part was primarily though not wholly a defense of the French Revolution to date, and the American controversy that was excited by it was over ideas rather than specific public issues. The controversy between Paine and Burke symbolized the clash between the idea of revolution and the reaction against it among English-speaking peoples; but the counter-revolutionary movement gained momentum in the United States later than in England, and American sentiment was overwhelmingly sympathetic with the Revolution in France when Paine's pamphlet appeared in an American edition, as its reception clearly showed.

This was in May, 1791, and Jefferson was appropriately if unwittingly associated with the event. It will be recalled that he had given counsels of moderation to Lafayette and other leaders while in France. In policy he was a gradualist rather than an immediatist, provided that the goals he thought desirable were definitely recognized, and in spirit he was much closer to the liberal French nobles than to Paine. Events had moved faster in France than he had expected, but nothing that had happened there as yet had aroused his serious fears of violence. A few weeks later he was genuinely disturbed by news of the flight and recapture of the King, probably fearing foreign intervention on his behalf, and he then wrote to a distinguished Englishman: "It would be unfortunate were it in the power of any one man to defeat the issue of so beautiful a revolution."[9] When he first saw Paine's pamphlet he unquestionably thought it a defense of a beautiful revolution — one that had attained glorious ends with a minimum of disorder. He had supposed the revolution safe, but it had been vigorously attacked from the English angle.

Summing things up long years later, he said: "The appeal to the rights of man, which had been made in the United States, was taken up by France, first of the European nations."[10] Like Paine, he connected the two revolutions, and he believed that their fortunes were interrelated, if not inseparable. The firm establishment of the French

[8] Paine to Washington, July 21, 1791 (P. S. Foner, *Complete Writings of Thomas Paine* (1945), II, 1318–1320); Washington to Paine, May 6, 1792, acknowledging also the gift of 12 copies of the latter's new work (Fitzpatrick, XXXII, 38–39).

[9] TJ to Sir John Sinclair, Aug. 24, 1791 (LC, 11440).

[10] In his autobiography (Ford, I, 147).

government would be followed, in his opinion, by the spread of liberty all over Europe, and a setback there would have the opposite effect. Furthermore, he now considered the success of that government as necessary to support the American government, and to "prevent it from falling back to that kind of halfway house, the English constitution." [11] When in France, he had urged Lafayette and the Patriots to look toward this halfway house, since they were not yet ready for the degree of self-government that had been attained in America; but American movement in the English direction would amount to retrogression. By the spring of 1791 he was saying privately that important leaders in his own country believed that the English constitution contained all that was "perfect in human institutions," and he called this group a "sect." He was convinced, however, that the great mass of the people, and the President, were untainted by these "heresies"; and on this conviction he built his hope that the labors of the patriots had not been in vain, and that the American experiment would still prove that men can be governed by reason, rather than force and fear. His foreign policies had grown out of his observations and experiences in the pre-Revolutionary period, hence they were not ideological in their basis, but the Anglo-French rivalry had now manifested itself as a battle of sentiments and ideas. Hence the controversy between Burke and Paine had symbolic significance for him, and the latter's pamphlet would have appealed to him if he had read nothing but its title.

If he had actually read Burke's *Reflections* by now he had not done so as a dispassionate thinker in a cloister. Writing an English friend about this time he said: "To judge from what we see published, we must believe that the spirit of toryism has gained nearly the whole of the nation: that the whig principles are utterly extinguished except in the breasts of certain descriptions of dissenters." [12] The change in the "principles" of the British appalled him and he spoke of the "rottenness" of Burke's mind. He believed that Paine's answer would bring England herself to reason if it were read there, and he even spoke of "revolution" as the logical result. He was more in character, however, when he predicted that the same things would be said in milder language, that they would make their way among the people, and that England would reform at last. Meanwhile, Paine's pamphlet would be a refreshing shower to American republicans, who were still in overwhelming preponderance, although a few notable men had "apostatized from the true faith." It is a striking fact that Jefferson, an apostle of enlightenment and intellectual liberty, described the rising political

[11] TJ to George Mason, Feb. 4, 1791 (Ford, V, 274–275).
[12] TJ to Benjamin Vaughan, May 11, 1791 (Ford, V, 333).

controversy in religious terms and identified himself with orthodoxy. This was no mere matter of the mind with him. His feelings were aroused, and, as his actions at the time of the Declaration of Independence had showed, his passionate devotion to what he regarded as a vital and sacred cause could turn the scholar and thinker into a partisan. He was definitely partisan in this instance – on the side of the rights of man, against all tyrants, real, potential, or imagined.

He claimed, however, that the circumstances of his public commendation of Paine's work were largely accidental. A copy of the English edition belonging to John Beckley, clerk of the House of Representatives, was loaned to Madison, who loaned it in turn to Jefferson. Before the latter had finished reading it Beckley asked him to send it on, as soon as he had finished, to one Jonathan B. Smith – who was unknown to him and whose brother was going to reprint it. With it Jefferson sent a note of explanation which he brightened with an expression of approval of the work, and the enterprising printer used part of this in the preface of the Philadelphia edition without asking his permission. The main purpose of the printer was to promote sales, no doubt; but he introduced the quotation by comments on Jefferson himself which served to give that retiring gentleman a considerable degree of political advertisement. Not only did the partially quoted note do justice to the writings of Paine; the printer said that it also reflected honor on the Secretary of State, "by directing the mind to a contemplation of that Republican firmness and Democratic simplicity which endear their possessor to every friend of the Rights of Man." These words of commendation gained no such currency as the direct quotation from Jefferson which they introduced, but to some people they seemed to point to collusion between him and the printer and to make his own explanations of the episode sound insincere.

His comments on the pamphlet followed:

> I am extremely pleased to find it will be reprinted here, and that something is at length to be publickly said against the political heresies which have sprung up among us.
>
> I have no doubt our citizens will rally a second time round the standard of Common Sense.

This was early in the month of May, and these words were soon quoted in most of the newspapers of the country.[13] Before they were

[13] Ford, V, 354*n.*; also M. D. Conway, *Life of Thomas Paine* (1892), I, 291–292. TJ said he kept no copy of his letter, but he paraphrased his comments in several contemporary letters much to the same effect. They were quoted in Philadelphia, *Gazette of the U. S.*, May 14, 1791; and J. Q. Adams is authority for the statement that they appeared in most of the newspapers (*Writings*, ed. by W. C. Ford, I (1913), 67).

widely circulated their author had explained to Washington and Madison just how they got out.[14] Jefferson said that these were his true sentiments but that he had not expected to be quoted. He frankly admitted that he was thinking of John Adams's *Discourses on Davila*, which, over a period of many months, ran in one of the Philadelphia papers without being replied to, but claimed that he had not intended to attack his old friend in public, and there is insufficient reason to believe he did.

The uses of controversy in building up a popular reputation began to be revealed at this precise point in his national career, but ever since his governorship of Virginia his dread of controversy had been little short of an obsession, and he had shown far greater desire for the good opinion of informed persons than for general popularity. So far as the larger public was concerned, he hoped to avoid dislike, which was exceedingly unpleasant to his sensitive nature, but what he most wanted was to be left alone. He noted that Hamilton and Beckwith were "open-mouthed" against him, since his approval of Paine might give offense to the British Court. He did not mind that, since the same charge could be brought against Burke and John Adams with respect to the French, but he did mind hurting the feelings of Adams, whom he preferred to Hamilton on political grounds, and whom he liked as a human being, probably, far better than he did Paine.

He wrote to Washington:

> . . . I am afraid the indiscretion of a printer has committed me with my friend Mr. Adams, for whom, as one of the most honest & disinterested men alive, I have a cordial esteem, increased by long concurrence in opinion in the days of his republicanism; and even since his apostacy to hereditary monarchy & nobility, though we differ, we differ as friends should do. . . . I certainly never made a secret of my being anti-monarchical, & anti-aristocratical; but I am sincerely mortified to be thus brought forward on the public stage, where to remain, to advance or to retire, will be equally against my love of silence and quiet, & my abhorrence of dispute.[15]

The sincerity of this statement is no more open to question than his abhorrence of personal dispute is. The role he had been trying to play was that of a disinterested public servant, and he viewed that of political gladiator with repugnance. Furthermore, he had long made a fine art, almost a fetish, of friendship. On the other hand, he found

[14] TJ to Washington, May 8, 1791 (Ford, V, 329); to Madison, May 9, 1791 (Ford, V, 331–332).

[15] Ford, V, 329.

it practically impossible not to express himself in some way when a battle of sentiments and ideas was raging. His commendation of Paine's work may thus be regarded as a spontaneous outburst rather than a studied act. His characterization of the doctrines of his old friend Adams does more credit to his own zeal for human rights than justice to Adams's political philosophy; and one wonders if he had read the *Discourses on Davila* extensively and carefully. Probably not, for he was a busy man and the work was so long and dull that hardly anybody read it. But it moved in the wrong direction and that was enough for him; it seemed to reinforce the enemies of human rights and he wanted it to be challenged. It is possible to explain his actions, as his political enemies did a few months later, on the ground that he was trying to build himself up at Adams's expense; but, in the light of his previous career, it is easier to take his own word that he hoped his personal part would escape wide notice.

At just this time, early in the month of May, he was arranging for a holiday trip up the Hudson with Madison, who had already gone to New York. The fact that some of the Hamiltonians scented politics in this is a sign that they were aware of his growing political prominence, though his actions require no political interpretation. Taking advantage of an interval of quiet in the public business, he hoped, by exercising his mind less and his body more, to rid himself of the headache which had been troubling him. Madison, who said his own objects were health, recreation, and curiosity, was indifferent to details of the itinerary and left these largely in his friend's hands. Allowing himself a month, Jefferson planned to go as far as Lake George and to return through the heart of New England. He described the route to his daughter Polly in order that she might trace it on the map, afterwards extending it to take in Long Island. Besides building up his health, he wanted to make scientific observations. He had hoped that David Rittenhouse would accompany them, but the mathematician decided not to go, being unable to find a proper horse. Jefferson called a meeting of the gentlemen of the committee on the Hessian fly in the hall of the Philosophical Society shortly before he left. He was particularly anxious to get their report, since his projected journey would carry him through regions (New York and Long Island) where this pest had been raging. Even on a pleasure trip he wanted to be useful.[16]

[16] TJ to Maria, May 8, 1791 (Ford, V, 328); to Madison, May 9, 1791 (Ford, V, 330–331); to Dr. B. S. Barton, May 12, 1791 (*More Books: The Bulletin of the N. Y. Public Library for April 1943*, pp. 156–157); to Washington, May 15, 1791 (Ford, V, 335); Madison to TJ, May 12, 1791 (Hunt, VI, 51*n.*).

Leaving Jack Eppes in Philadelphia, he set out on May 17, accompanied by at least one servant, and recorded in his account book that day that he heard the season's first whippoorwill. He was back at the seat of government one month and two days later, after a journey of 920 miles. He kept a careful record of stages and distances, marking a considerable number of the inns as good, bad, or middling; he made notes of his observations of scenery, vegetation, and industries; and he passed on some of his most vivid impressions in letters. One of these, to Polly, he wrote on a piece of birchbark while sailing on Lake George. This he described as the most beautiful body of water he had ever seen. It did not represent the northernmost point of his journey, for he and Madison sailed for about twenty-five miles into Lake Champlain, which he found much less pleasant. He wrote Washington about a disagreeable incident which had occurred near one of the British posts and which he had inquired into.[17] There was no crisis at the moment, and the report itself is chiefly significant in showing that as an official he continued to be alert. In the course of the journey, he and Madison also manifested their patriotism by visiting historic military sites and scenes, such as Stillwater, Saratoga, Crown Point, Ticonderoga, and the battlefield at Bennington. This was one way that they gratified their curiosity. Also, they amused themselves to some extent in sport.[18]

Since Jefferson has left so few records of his sporting activities, it is worth noting that his party shot three red squirrels, that they fished for speckled trout, salmon trout, and bass in Lake George, and even that they killed two rattlesnakes (of a "sutty dark color and obscurely checkered") on its borders. He wrote a full description of a nailery he saw on his way northward, and probably profited by this in later years when he established one of his own, but his most extended description was of Lake George and the "botanical objects" which so delighted him. In particular he noted those that were rare or unknown in Virginia: the sugar maple, white pine, silver fir, pitch pine, spruce pine, juniper, and a new kind of azalea. He described the juniper as "a shrub with decumbent stems about 8 f. long, with single leaves all round the stem, and berries used for infusing gin"; and he regarded the rose-

[17] TJ to Washington, June 5, 1791 (Ford, V, 339).

[18] The best sources for the trip are Jefferson's Account Book, May 17–June 19, 1791, with the record of the stages and distances he made on June 20; the manuscript notes, chiefly botanical, in LC, 11910 ff., of which I have been provided a transcript through the kindness of JP; and his family correspondence in Ford, V, 337–338, 340–342, and *Domestic Life*, pp. 201–205. See also *Garden Book*, pp. 166–170, and the admirable and thoroughly annotated account in Dumbauld, pp. 172–177.

colored azalea, with its large flowers and strong fragrance, as the richest shrub he had ever seen. The almost undecipherable notes on the Hessian fly which are preserved in his papers may reflect some of the observations of this trip, but in general he saw nature in a more pleasant form. The heat surprised him somewhat, and on the whole he preferred the seasons of Virginia, but this brief journey was memorable. In the last year of his life he wrote about it to his granddaughter, who virtually repeated more than half of his itinerary on her wedding trip to Boston.[19]

After fishing on Lake George and sailing on Lake Champlain, he and Madison returned to Saratoga, crossed to Bennington, went through the Berkshires to Pittsfield, and then to Northampton; they proceeded down the Connecticut, crossed Long Island Sound, followed the northern coast of Long Island to Brooklyn, and then crossed to New York. On their way they visited a nurseryman in Flushing, Long Island, and Jefferson left with him a large order for trees and shrubs, including all the sugar maples that were available. He got sixty of the latter in the fall, and had them planted at Monticello. His enthusiasm for them almost rivaled that for olive trees, but his maple orchard did not turn out well. Jefferson, who had almost forgotten his headache and soon shook it off entirely, left Madison in New York thinking him in better health than he had ever seen him.

In all respects this was a successful journey. There were some comments on it in the papers of the time, and a couple of items from Albany are of interest. One of these said that the Secretary of State was accompanied by "the Charles Fox of America, the celebrated Madison," thus implying that Jefferson's companion was regarded as the leader of the opposition in Congress. Another expressed regret that the stay of these visitors was so short that the principal citizens were unable to pay them the respectful attention that was due their distinguished merit, and noted that while the President was exploring one extremity of the empire, these "enlightened patriots" were doing the same in the other.[20]

For suspicions of ulterior motives we are indebted to Hamilton and his intimates. George Beckwith wrote to England that he believed the trip was for the purpose of agitating an anti-British policy and that he himself frustrated the objects of the Virginians by a tour of his own.[21]

[19] Ellen W. Coolidge to TJ, Aug. 1, 1825; TJ to Ellen W. Coolidge, Aug. 27, 1825 (*M.H.S.*, pp. 349–350, 353).

[20] Philadelphia *Gazette of the U. S.*, June 8, 1791, item of May 30 from Albany; Philadelphia *General Advertiser*, June 29, 1791, item of June 21 from Burlington, citing Albany paper.

[21] Bemis, *Jay's Treaty*, p. 83, citing Beckwith to Grenville, June 14, 1791.

About the same time an ardent supporter of Hamilton in New York wrote him as follows:

> . . . There was every appearance of a passionate courtship between the Chancellor [Livingston], Burr, Jeffersen & Madison when the two latter were in town. Delenda est Carthago I suppose is the maxim adopted with respect to you. They had better be quiet, for if they succeed they will tumble the fabric of the government in ruins to the ground. Upon this subject, however, I cannot say that I have the smallest uneasiness. You are too well seated in the hearts of the citizens of the northern & middle states to be hunted down by them.[22]

On the strength of this report, Hamilton's son, writing in the middle of the next century, asserted that "after frequent interviews with Chancellor Livingston and Burr, they made a visit to Clinton under the pretext of a botanical excursion to Albany, thence extended their journey to Vermont; and, having sown a few tares in Connecticut, returned to the seat of government." From this source the story of a predominantly political trip, on which the organization of the opposition to Hamilton was effected, came into the current of American historical writing.[23] It is possible that the travelers saw Burr and Livingston in New York and Clinton in Albany, even though their stay in the latter place was very short and they seem to have left no record of these meetings in their own papers. Furthermore, Madison had plenty of time for talk in New York before Jefferson joined him and after they separated. But there were many things in their minds which were not dreamed of in the philosophy of Hamilton and his inner circle, where political considerations seem to have drowned and obscured all others. In the fall, another supporter of Hamilton reported to him that at a large dinner of Connecticut officials ridicule was heaped on the tour of Jefferson and Madison, "in which they scouted silently through the country, shunning the gentry, communing with and pitying the Shayites, and quarreling with the eatables; nothing good enough for them. . . . They are supremely contemned by the Gentlemen of Connecticut, which state I found on a review right as to national matters."[24] The gentlemen of Connecticut may have been wholly right from the Ham-

[22] Robert Troup to Hamilton, June 15, 1791 (Hamilton Papers, vol. XI).

[23] Quotation from J. C. Hamilton, *History of the Republic*, IV (1859), 506. The use of the story by later historians is well illustrated by the following wisecrack from S. E. Morison and H. S. Commager, *Growth of the American Republic*, I (1942), 343: "On a 'botanizing excursion' that led Jefferson and Madison up the Hudson in the summer of 1791, they undoubtedly found occasion to study *Clintonia borealis* and other hardy perennials in Ulster County and the neighborhood of Albany."

[24] N. Hazard to Hamilton, Nov. 25, 1791 (Hamilton Papers, 13:1724).

iltonian point of view, but they had a very incomplete understanding of these two gentlemen of Virginia. They thought of Jefferson, especially, as more political than he thought himself and played no small part in creating a legend. Meanwhile, other events had served to the same effect.

Not until his return to Philadelphia did the Secretary of State become aware that his commendation of Paine's pamphlet and condemnation of John Adams's "heresies" had provoked a little storm. His earlier account of the circumstances to Washington shows that he had anticipated this possibility, but when the storm actually broke in the newspapers he was disposed to minimize his own responsibility for it. He then threw himself unnecessarily into toils of private explantation from which it is difficult to extricate him wholly. At the same time he began to emerge as a popular public figure, and the episode as a whole served to promote the political ideas he favored.

The controversy was certainly inflamed, and he himself insisted that it was really started, by a spirited criticism of Paine, which constituted a defense of Adams, in a series of letters to a Boston paper, beginning in June and signed PUBLICOLA. When Jefferson learned of these he accepted the common judgment that they were the work of the Vice President himself. He wrote Madison with obvious concern that Adams was "very indecently attacked" in two of the Philadelphia papers because of them. Madison, who was less appreciative of Adams, believed that the latter's attack on Paine, which he himself had not yet seen, would draw attention to his "obnoxious principles more than anything else he had published." [25] Somewhat later, Madison reported that the papers of PUBLICOLA were probably "manufactured" by John Quincy Adams, out of materials furnished by his father, and observed that there was much less of clumsiness and heaviness of style than in the latter's writings. Young John Quincy, then in his twenty-fourth year, was indeed the author, and was acting on his own – yet when the work was afterwards reprinted in Great Britain it was attributed to John. The Vice President's contemporaries were loath to accept his denials.[26]

Madison also reported from New York that the doctrines themselves

[25] TJ seems to have learned of PUBLICOLA from Madison's letter of June 23, 1791, from New York (Hunt, VI, 51–52*n.*), to which he replied June 28 (Ford, V, 345–347). See also Madison to TJ, June 27, 1791, and July 13, 1791 (Hunt, VI, 53*n.*, 56*n.*).

[26] J. Q. Adams, *Writings*, I, 65–110, with an extensive editorial note. The "Letters of PUBLICOLA," eleven in number, appeared in the Boston *Columbian Centinel*, June 8–July 27, 1791, and according to a contemporary note were "reprinted in all the most respectable papers to the southward" (I, 94*n.*). C. F. Adams commented on them in his edn. of J. Q. Adams's *Memoirs*, I (1874), 25–26.

were exceedingly unpopular, even in New England; and Jefferson, noting that a host of writers had arisen in defense of Paine, concluded that in the Philadelphia district at least the spirit of republicanism was sound. He believed that PUBLICOLA was censuring him, along with the author of *The Rights of Man*, admitting privately that he deserved it, since he professed the same principles as Paine. He wanted his friends to know, however, that he was not one of the "anti-publicolas," hiding behind a pseudonym; he was not BRUTUS or AGRICOLA or PHILODEMUS.[27]

He did not champion Paine in public after his first inadvertent act, but he had no thought of abandoning him. At this very juncture he advocated his appointment to the office of Postmaster General, which Samuel Osgood was resigning, though it is uncertain just how far his representations went. No doubt he agreed with Edmund Randolph that this seemed to be "a fair opportunity for a declaration of certain sentiments," but practical objections could easily be urged against the appointment of a man from overseas, regardless of his political philosophy, and the post went to Timothy Pickering, who afterwards proved to be one of the bitterest of the High Federalists. According to the later Hamiltonian interpretation, Jefferson and Paine, who were in "full, dangerous confidence," were thus prevented from disseminating insurrectionary opinions throughout the United States. The Secretary of State did not mention this matter when he wrote to the author of *The Rights of Man* in midsummer, though he did tell him that the doctrine of King, Lords, and Commons had been checked by the pamphlet, and the people confirmed in "their good old faith." Edmund Randolph, also a landed gentleman from Virginia, took the same position – saying that the crest of aristocracy had fallen since the standard of republicanism had been raised.[28] This talk sounds paradoxical from a member of the gentry, but the spirit of the Enlightenment was still strong in that state, and the old landed aristocracy seemed more loyal to the theory of republicanism than the relatively new group of commercial and financial elite whom Hamilton's policies had so greatly strengthened.

While Jefferson rejoiced that the popularity of republican principles had been demonstrated in this war of pamphlets, and let it be known to a few intimates that he continued to reprobate the doctrines of

[27] TJ to Monroe, July 10, 1791 (Ford, V, 351–353); see also Monroe to TJ, July 25, 1791 (S. M. Hamilton, I, 225–226).

[28] TJ to Madison, July 10, 1791 (Ford, V, 351); Randolph to Madison, July 21, 1791, quoted in M. D. Conway, *Omitted Chapters of History Disclosed in the Life and Papers of Edmund Randolph* (1888), pp. 188–189; J. C. Hamilton, *History of the Republic,* IV, 515; TJ to Paine, July 29, 1791 (Ford, V, 367).

John Adams, he took no satisfaction in the personal discomfiture of his old friend, and, as time went on, he became fearful lest Adams should think that he had joined in the public attack upon him. The distinction between public and private actions which Jefferson drew so sharply is often blurred by writers who disregard the original privacy of letters that are now a matter of public record because of the historic prominence of the men who wrote them. This distinction accorded with his strict views of official propriety and seemed to permit the continuance of personal friendship, despite differences about political doctrines and public questions. To him public conflict between friends was improper as well as painful, and at this juncture he began to be alarmed lest he be thought false to his own high code. It is doubtful if many public men, then or at any other time, would have had such qualms. Others besides him have found it hard to remain gentlemen in public life, but few conspicuous American statesmen have been so sensitive and fine-grained as he. It was to his credit as a gentleman that he brought himself, after much hesitation, to write a letter to John Adams – though he hereby showed himself to be rather ingenuous. This was in midsummer and the pamphlet warfare was still raging.[29]

Saying that truth between candid minds can do no harm, he wrote as candid a letter as could have been expected. He explained the circumstances of the publication of Paine's work as he had to Washington, Madison, and Monroe with only one important difference. He did not bluntly say that he was thinking specifically of Adams's writings when he spoke of "political heresies." This omission on the part of a polite and friendly man is understandable, however, and he was frank enough in recognizing his doctrinal disagreement with Adams. "That you and I differ in our ideas as to the best form of government is well known to us, both," he said; "but we have differed as friends should do, respecting the purity of each other's motives, and confining our differences of opinion to private conversation." He told Madison that he often called Adams a heretic. What disturbed him most was that their names had been "thrown on the public stage as public antagonists," and he solemnly assured the Vice President that he had written no anonymous pamphlet against him.

He attributed the public controversy primarily to PUBLICOLA, and his references to that author now seem untactful. By this time he had reason to identify him with John Quincy Adams, whom he had taken to concerts in Paris, but probably he still believed that the father had had a hand in this business, and he may have been saying indirectly

[29] TJ to Adams, July 17, 1791 (Ford, V, 353–356).

that the Adamses themselves were more to blame for airing the antagonism than he was. The papers were still appearing, and this may have been his way of suggesting that they should stop, though they did not censure him as strongly as he may have supposed when he first heard about them. There were relatively few direct references to him and, though pointed, these were unfailingly polite. Young John Quincy had twitted him about the expression "political heresies," wondering if Paine's work should be considered "the canonical book of political scripture," but had sought to avoid all appearance of disrespect toward this holder of high office whose learning he always admired so greatly. Jefferson himself could hardly have challenged the description of him that was given in the first paper: "He is a friend to free inquiry upon every subject, and he will not be displeased to see the sentiments which he has made his own by a public adoption, canvassed with as much freedom as is consistent with the reverence due to his character." [30]

Both of the Adamses appreciated Jefferson's character more than Hamilton ever did, and John accepted his explanation in good spirit, giving full credit to his story of the publication of his note.[31] The Vice President could not dismiss the whole matter lightly, however, for he believed that the printer, by his misconduct, had sowed the seeds of more evil than he could ever atone for. Jefferson's words had been industriously circulated and had been generally considered as a direct and open attack on him. He denied that he was PUBLICOLA or had assisted him, but his language was somewhat equivocal since he did not reveal the identity of that writer. Like Jefferson he was telling the truth, but not quite the whole truth. He fell back on a natural line of defense and tried to show, by specific instances, that much damage had been done before PUBLICOLA began to write. Thus he declined to accept his friend's contention about the main cause of the trouble, and this was partly because he sought to shield his son.[32]

An equally challenging and even more interesting passage in Adams's letter, which is considerably longer than Jefferson's, relates to their alleged differences about government and the popular misconception of his own ideas.

> You observe [he said], "that you and I differ in our ideas of the best form of government, is well known to us both." But, my dear Sir, you will give me leave to say that I do not know this. I know not what your idea is of the best form of government.

[30] J. Q. Adams, *Writings*, I, 69.

[31] Adams to TJ, July 29, 1791 (*Works*, VIII, 506–509).

[32] His exact words were as follows: "I neither wrote nor corrected PUBLICOLA. The writer, in the composition of his pieces, followed his own judgment, information, and discretion, without any assistance from me." (*Works*, VIII, 507.)

> You and I have never had a serious conversation together, that I can recollect, concerning the nature of government. The very transient hints that have ever passed between us have been jocular and superficial, without ever coming to an explanation. If you suppose that I have, or ever had, a design or desire of attempting to introduce a government of King, Lords, and Commons, or in other words, an hereditary executive, or an hereditary senate, either into the government of the United States or that of any individual State, you are wholly mistaken. There is not such a thought expressed or intimated in any public writing or private letter, and I may safely challenge all mankind to produce such a passage, and quote the chapter and verse. . . .
>
> Upon this occasion I will venture to say, that my unpolished writings . . . have not been read by great numbers. Of the few who have taken the pains to read them, some have misunderstood them, and others have wilfully misrepresented them, and these misunderstandings and misrepresentations have been made the pretence for overwhelming me with floods and whirlwinds of tempestuous abuse, unexampled in the history of this country.[33]

Adams's besetting vanity had caused him to exaggerate the abuse of him, and he ignored the fact that there was ground for it in the tone of his writings, if not in his precise recommendations, but there was considerable justification for his complaint that he had been misunderstood. There was a real difference of opinion between him and Jefferson, for he was much more skeptical about popular government, and he should have sensed this, even in jocular conversation, but he was right in thinking that it had been over-emphasized. He did not blame Jefferson directly for the misrepresentations of him, however, and he ended his letter on a note of affectionate confidence.

> It was high time that you and I should come to an explanation with each other [he said]. The friendship that has subsisted for fifteen years without the smallest interruption, and, until this occasion without the slightest suspicion, ever has been and still is dear to my heart. . . . Your motives for writing to me I have not a doubt were the most pure and the most friendly; and I have no suspicion that you will not receive this explanation from me in the same friendly light.

Jefferson did receive it in a friendly spirit, and he seems to have brooded somewhat over the plight of Adams during the next few weeks. Despite the latter's formal disclaimer, he continued to place him in the party favoring English forms, along with Hamilton, Jay, Knox, and many of the Cincinnati, but he regarded the Vice President

[33] *Works,* VIII, 507–508.

as the most honest of the party and regretted that he was suffering from his imprudence while others were holding their tongues and gaining ground. About the middle of the month he had a conversation with Hamilton, which seemed important enough to deserve recording. The sum and substance of this was that, while dubious of the present government and believing that it would probably be expedient for it to go into the British form, Hamilton had found republicanism more successful than he expected it to be and wanted to give the experiment a fair chance. He should have been complacent because of the strength of his personal position, if for no other reason. He blamed Adams for disturbing the present order by his writings, though convinced of the purity of his motives.[34] Jefferson himself had never had any doubts on that point, and after a bit he decided to put another patch on his strained friendship with the most honest leader of the aristocratic party, who claimed to be more republican than he sounded. Upon the face of the record it now seems that this was unnecessary. Having written a sufficiently candid letter and received an affectionate and sufficiently candid reply, he should have left well enough alone. He protested entirely too much in his second letter.[35]

The only point in this was to argue further about the occasion of the newspaper controversy, from which Adams had suffered so grievously both in his feelings and popular reputation. After going into certain particulars, in which he implied that he was somewhat less critical of Adams in the first place than his contemporary letters show that he actually was, he said:

> . . . But you will perceive from all this, my dear Sir, that my note contributed nothing to the production of these disagreeable pieces. As long as Paine's pamphlet stood on its own feet & on my note, it was unnoticed. As soon as Publicola attacked Paine, swarms appeared in his defence. To Publicola then & not in the least degree to my note, this whole contest is to be ascribed and all its consequences.

Standing by itself, this may be regarded as merely an overstatement of a not-unreasonable hypothesis, but in his effort to escape blame for an "execrable paragraph" in the Connecticut papers, which appeared before PUBLICOLA began to write, he went a good deal further.

> . . . Indeed it was impossible that my note should occasion your name to be brought into question; for so far from naming you, I had not even in view any writing which I might suppose to be

[34] Aug. 13, 1791. Notes of conversation. (Ford, I, 168–169.)
[35] TJ to Adams, Aug. 30, 1791 (Ford, V, 380–383).

yours, and the opinions I alluded to were principally those I had heard in common conversation from a sect aiming at the subversion of the present government to bring in their favorite form of a king, lords & commons.[36]

He may have based his charges of political heresy more on hearsay than on the careful examination of any particular work, and the *Discourses on Davila* had been published anonymously, but in view of the specific mention of that work in his private letters to Washington and Madison his statement involves a contradiction which cannot be wholly explained away.[37]

John Adams had not seen those letters to Washington and Madison, and if he continued to be suspicious his state of mind must be explained on other grounds. His descendants did see them, since the private letters of eminent men eventually become accessible to the public if they are preserved. In the middle of the next century, Charles Francis Adams, grandson of John and the editor of his works, seeing no possible escape from this particular contradiction, commented thus on the character of Jefferson:

"More ardent in his imagination than his affections, he did not always speak exactly as he felt towards either friends or enemies. As a consequence, he has left hanging over a part of his public life a vapor of duplicity, or, to say the least, of indirection, the presence of which is generally felt more than it is seen."[38]

According to John Quincy Adams, a "double-dealing character" was often imputed to Jefferson in his lifetime and was sometimes exposed — as he thinks it eventually was in the case of this "most insidious attack" on John Adams, with which were coupled "never-ceasing professions of respect and affection for his person and character."[39]

The incident does not deserve the emphasis the later Adamses gave it, and they did not understand Jefferson's temperament as well as their famous ancestor did. Unlike John Adams, Jefferson was not of a testy temper; in social intercourse this Virginia gentleman always tried to

[36] Ford, V, 382.

[37] Randall's treatment of the episode, which I refrained from reading while arriving at my own interpretation, is characteristically full and illuminating. His explanation of this statement, however, seems labored and I find it unconvincing. (II, 2–10, and especially 9*n*.)

[38] From his "Life of John Adams," in the latter's *Works*, I, 616; see also p. 619. A more extended quotation would show that he admired many things in Jefferson and saw a contradiction, not merely in this particular statement and episode, but in his career and character as a whole.

[39] *Memoirs*, VIII, 272 (Jan. 12, 1831). It should be noted that this was a record in his diary, not a public statement. It is not cited here as representing J. Q. Adams's full and final judgment, but because of its connection with the episode in question.

keep things pleasant on the surface; and an important reason why Adams always loved him, as he said he did, was that he was amiable. The boldness of his mind was sheathed in a scabbard of politeness, and he was conciliatory in minor matters. It would have been surprising if such a man did not occasionally cross the dim line between courtesy and deception. It is hard to see what personal political gain he could have expected from conciliating the Vice President, though he unquestionably thought him less dangerous than Hamilton, and, after his own original outburst, he suffered a revulsion of feeling when Adams seemed to be discredited. The contradiction in his concluding letter can be easily reduced to human terms. In reporting his own thoughts somewhat differently, after the passage of two or three months, from the way that he had reported them before, he deceived either himself or his correspondent, but even under the worse construction his purpose was to salve the wounded feelings of a friend.

[XXII]

Starting the Federal City

JEFFERSON'S association with the beginnings of the new capital on the Potomac, which he and Washington generally called "the Federal City," was more intimate than that of any other high official of the government except the President himself. It has seemed best to group in one section the activities he entered into in this connection while he was the Secretary of State. One reason for describing them at this point is that the most crucial problems in this matter arose in the years of 1791 and 1792. The relations between Washington and Jefferson in this period cannot be fully understood without some reference to their close co-operation in this undertaking. It was dear to their hearts for local reasons, though both of them believed that they were creating a new bond of national unity.

According to the Residence Act of 1790, the federal government was to be seated beside the Potomac after ten years, but the precise location of the capital within a range of some eighty miles was to be determined by the President, and its development was left to his direction. Many people in Maryland and Virginia feared, as many in Philadelphia hoped, that the project would never be carried out. Except for Washington's prestige, persistence, and wisdom, it might not have been; but Jefferson, generally abetted by Madison, was the President's trusted helper at every stage and made distinctive contributions to the final result.[1]

The choice of the site just above the Eastern Branch of the Potomac was Washington's, but his two fellow Virginians fully concurred in it. The Act limited the size of the federal territory to ten miles square,

[1] For the whole story of the planning during this period see W. B. Bryan, *Hist. of the National Capital*, I (1914), chs. II–VIII. The important documents relating to TJ's part in it have been conveniently assembled in *Thomas Jefferson and the National Capital* (1946), ed. by Saul K. Padover (hereafter referred to as Padover).

and authorized the acquisition of lands on the eastern side of the river for the use of the government. When called upon by Washington to interpret the Act, Jefferson held that the district could comprehend the opposite shore; and as the boundaries were originally drawn, it was a square or diamond which the Potomac roughly divided in half. Washington and Jefferson were glad to include lands from their own State of Virginia.

Toward the end of the year 1790, Jefferson drew for the President an important memorandum on proceedings.[2] He interpreted the Act liberally, and favored the full exercise of the executive authority and control in this early stage. One vague expression in the law, empowering the acquisition of "such quantity of land as the President shall deem proper for the United States," might have been given a limited application to public grounds and building sites, but he interpreted it as extending to lands sufficient for a town. He had no doubt that this was the wish of Congress, but he also wanted to seize an unusual opportunity to lay out a town on an ordered plan. He himself suggested that the streets be at right angles, as in Philadelphia, and that they should be wide. He was not disposed to imitate that city by requiring the houses to be built at a given distance from the street, believing that this produced "a disgusting monotony," but he favored a limitation on the height of buildings such as he had observed in Paris. In the light of the city plan which L'Enfant drew a few months later, his proposals seem modest. One reason may have been that he was thinking of a town rather than a city, and another almost certainly was his consciousness of practical limitations. When he suggested that 1500 acres would be enough, he probably thought no more could be readily acquired. He believed that the commissioners whom Washington was to appoint should have some taste in architecture, but even more important was his insistence that they be subject to the President's direction in all things, and that he approve the plan for the public buildings. Beside him would be the Secretary of State, who was intensely interested and widely experienced in matters of architecture.

The value of the counsel which his versatile assistant could give him about plans and buildings was obvious to Washington, but Jefferson made himself most helpful at first by describing, one by one, the steps which should be taken to carry the Act into effect. Like his Chief, he believed that if this opportunity to establish the seat of government on the Potomac were not seized now it would be forever lost. No appropriation had been made by Congress, and any attempt to get

[2] Nov. 29, 1790 (Ford, V, 252–253; Padover, pp. 30–33). The latter part of the document, as given by Padover, seems to belong later (see pp. 69–70).

one at this stage would have been perilous, since it might easily have provoked a debate on the whole residence question. It was much safer to let sleeping dogs lie. A grant of $120,000 for public buildings had been voted by the General Assembly of Virginia, and Maryland was expected to make a grant, as it soon did to the amount of $72,000. Money from these sources became available, but at the outset Jefferson thought it unwise to rely on it. Hence he outlined plans for receiving gifts of land and selling part of them. Washington himself never lost sight of practical necessities, but he was rather more disposed than Jefferson to do things on a large scale.

Early in 1791 the President issued a proclamation, which Jefferson had drawn, defining the boundaries of the district, and he appointed three Commissioners with whom Jefferson assumed official correspondence.[3] The Secretary of State was consulted repeatedly about the boundaries, which were extended after the first proclamation, but he appears to have exercised no special influence on the choice of the first Commissioners: Thomas Johnson (who was inactive at first), David Stuart, and Daniel Carroll of Rock Creek. Whether or not he suggested that Andrew Ellicott be sent to survey and map the district, he gave the Major those instructions.[4]

He also gave instructions to Major Pierre Charles L'Enfant in March. Months before the passage of the Residence Act, that brilliant French engineer had written the President, asking, in effect, that he be permitted to make the plan of the new capital city, and leaving no doubt of his conviction that this should be drawn on a sufficient scale to allow for the future greatness of the country.[5] Jefferson supposed that the task of L'Enfant was to pick sites for the public buildings, and the latter afterwards claimed that his authority to make the grand plan of the city and put it in operation came straight from Washington, who visited the scene that spring. The name of Major "Longfort" got into the local newspaper in March, 1791, and he then seemed to be a man of genius. Not for some months did he appear to be also a man of extreme temper.[6]

L'Enfant's past services, as an officer in the Continental Army, the

[3] The first proclamation and TJ's first letters to the commissioners were dated Jan. 24, 1791 (Fitzpatrick, XXXI, 202–204; Padover, pp. 38–39).

[4] TJ to Andrew Ellicott, Feb. 2, 1791 (Padover, pp. 40–41).

[5] L'Enfant to Washington, Sept. 11, 1789, in Elizabeth S. Kite's useful collection of documents, *L'Enfant and Washington* (1929), p. 34 (hereafter referred to as Kite).

[6] TJ to L'Enfant, March 1791 (Padover, pp. 42–43); L'Enfant to TJ, Mar. 10 and 11, 1791 (*ibid.*, pp. 44–45).

designer of the eagle which members of the Society of the Cincinnati wore, and the architect of Federal Hall, where the first President was inaugurated, were amply sufficient to commend him to Washington.[7] His instructions from Jefferson were that he begin at the Eastern Branch and proceed upwards, "laying down the hills, valleys, morasses, and waters." The engineer soon concluded that the rising ground to the eastward, toward Carrollsburg, offered better sites for public buildings than the lowlands near Georgetown. He was specially impressed with Jenkins Hill (now Capitol Hill) which, as he soon said, was like a pedestal awaiting its monument. At the time, however, the landholders in that neighborhood seemed unco-operative. Assuming that the lands toward Georgetown were more likely to be available, the Secretary of State himself drew a rough sketch of a city plan that was accommodated to them. Washington brought this with him toward the end of March, along with a memorandum from Jefferson outlining the objects which might merit his attention when he conferred with the Commissioners and the landholders.[8]

Washington succeeded in reconciling the conflicting interests of Georgetown and Carrollsburg, and secured from the proprietors the promise to cede to the United States, under specified conditions, all the land from Rock Creek along the river to the Eastern Branch to a breadth of about a mile and a half, the whole tract comprising between three and five thousand acres, which was considerably more than Jefferson had thought necessary. When this was laid off each proprietor was to retain every other lot and be paid at a stipulated price for such lands as were used for public purposes, except for streets. When Washington informed him of this, Jefferson described the acquisition as "noble." He had recently reported that a bill for buildings for the federal government in Philadelphia had passed one house of the Pennsylvania legislature and been defeated by a close vote in the other. He believed that the "spirited proceedings" at Georgetown would prevent the revival of this, and Washington used the information locally as an argument for continued zeal. The President now felt warranted in issuing another proclamation, which Jefferson had already drawn.[9]

[7] See the admirable article on L'Enfant by Fiske Kimball in the *D.A.B.*, and the Introduction to Kite by J. J. Jusserand.

[8] TJ's memorandum or opinion, dated Mar. 11, 1791, is in Padover, pp. 47–50; and his rough sketch is reproduced, *ibid.*, opp. p. 28. His letter of Mar. 17, 1791, is in Padover, p. 51.

[9] The proclamation, dated Mar. 30, 1791, which Washington sent TJ next day for the annexing of his signature and the seal, and his letter are in Fitzpatrick, XXXI, 254–258, and Padover, pp. 52–55. For TJ's letter to him, Apr. 10, 1791, see Padover, pp. 60–61.

From this, however, Washington omitted a paragraph in which Jefferson had described the lands near Georgetown as the site of the public buildings, saying that the whole situation had been changed by the enlarged agreement and that the precise location of the public buildings could and should wait on the survey of the entire ground. There is no reason whatever to suppose that Jefferson regretted this decision. The time had come for an enlarged and more daring plan. Washington directed L'Enfant to make one, and Jefferson was pleased that the planning had been left in such good hands. His own rough sketch, drawn on a modest scale, was now outmoded. Washington turned it over to L'Enfant, but doubted if the latter would gain any material advantage from it.[10] Actually, some of its features did survive in the later plan. The relation between the President's House and the Capitol was much the same, though the distance was greatly expanded; the public walks he had allowed for reappeared elsewhere; and L'Enfant was unable to escape wholly from the rectangular arrangement, although it seems that he wanted to at first.[11]

His immediate reaction to Jefferson's ideas appears to have been unfavorable. Speaking of the grand plan for the whole city which he had in mind, he said, in a rather patronizing tone:

> In endeavoring to effect this, it is not the regular assemblage of houses laid out in squares and forming streets all parallel and uniform that it is so necessary, for such a plan could only do on a level plain where no surrounding object being interesting it becomes indifferent which way the opening of the streets may be directed. . . .
>
> Such regular plans indeed, however answerable they may appear upon paper or seducing as they may be on the first aspect to the eyes of some people must even when applyed upon the ground the best calculated to admit of it become at last tiresome and insipid and it never could be in its origin but a mean continuance of some cool imagination wanting a sense of the real grand and truly beautiful only to be met with where nature contributes with art and diversifies the objects.[12]

In comparison with L'Enfant, Jefferson may have had a cool architectural imagination, and his distaste for cities may have been suffi-

[10] Washington to L'Enfant, Apr. 4, 1791 (Fitzpatrick, XXXI, 270–271).

[11] On the subject generally, see Fiske Kimball, *Jefferson, Architect*, pp. 47–51.

[12] Kite, pp. 47–48, from an undated note. Unless this was written long enough after Apr. 4 to allow for the receipt of Washington's letter, L'Enfant could not have been referring directly to Jefferson's rough sketch. The latter's ideas, however, had been presented to Washington in other forms and could easily have been communicated.

cient to deter him from even attempting a large-scale plan. L'Enfant intended to be original, but he asked Jefferson for such city plans as could be procured, and the Secretary sent him a dozen that he had collected during his travels in Europe and greatly prized. His comments to Washington implied that he still preferred a rectangular arrangement of streets, and he told L'Enfant that very liberal provision should be made for the public grounds. He pressed no particular ideas of his about the location of the public buildings, but let it be known that he had definite preferences with respect to their form.

> Whenever it is proposed to prepare for the Capitol, [Jefferson said] I should prefer the adoption of some one of the models of antiquity, which have had the approbation of thousands of years, and for the President's House I should prefer the celebrated fronts of modern buildings, which have already received the approbation of all good judges. Such are the Galerie du Louvre, the Gardes meubles, and two fronts of the Hotel de Salm.

He wrote Washington that he had the plates of a dozen or two of the handsomest private buildings in Europe, and that if these were engraved and distributed gratis among the inhabitants of Georgetown, they might decide the taste of the new town. In the meantime he showed every disposition to allow L'Enfant a free hand.[13]

Washington gave L'Enfant's sketch his approval, subject to certain changes, after he got back from his Southern trip toward the end of June, 1791; and Jefferson did not see the plan until the end of August, when L'Enfant brought it to Philadelphia. This was shortly before he began a trip to Monticello which included a stop at Georgetown to meet with the Commissioners, and he left the impression in that place that he was well pleased with the plan.[14] L'Enfant imposed radiating avenues upon a pattern of rectangular streets, and Jefferson afterwards observed that the angular buildings at the beginning of the avenues might be offensive to the eye if not well managed by the use of bow windows, semicircular porticos, and other fancies; but he must have seen that the planner had effected an arrangement which combined convenience of communication with pleasing prospects.[15] It was a brilliant plan, though it probably seemed grandiose to many

[13] L'Enfant to TJ, Apr. 4, 1791; TJ to L'Enfant, Apr. 10, 1791; TJ to Washington, Apr. 10, 1791 (Padover, pp. 56–61).

[14] Andrew Ellicott to L'Enfant, Sept. 12, 1791 (Kite, pp. 73–74).

[15] TJ to the Commissioners, Mar. 8, 1792 (L. & B., XIX, 90).

people at the time, and the Secretary of State worked harmoniously with his Chief in trying to carry it into effect.

Certain differences of opinion about procedure soon appeared. L'Enfant opposed the early sale of lots, hoped that the major features of his plan could be developed simultaneously, and favored the procuring of a large loan. There was nothing cool about *his* imagination. Washington and Jefferson, on the other hand, were chiefly concerned to set operations going quickly in order to squelch the hopes of the Pennsylvanians about keeping the capital in Philadelphia, and they were optimistic about the returns from sales.[16] For these reasons, a sale of lots had been set for October 17, 1791, and the President decided that an immediate meeting of the Commissioners was necessary on that account.[17]

Jefferson and Madison attended this on their way home in September, and the Commissioners then decided to name the new city "Washington" and the new federal territory "Columbia."[18] The Secretary of State presented certain queries which had been drawn in the conference with Washington; and the Commissioners concurred unanimously at every point with what had already been thought best in Philadelphia.[19] So far as procedure was concerned, the most important conclusions were: that it would be inadvisable to postpone the sale of lots; that the practicability of a loan at this stage was doubtful; and that work on the public buildings should be begun that fall, at least to the extent of digging earth for brick. Certain building restrictions are of particular interest as reflecting Jefferson's ideas. There were to be no wooden houses in the town; and, while liberty would be permitted with respect to the distance of houses from the street, limits as to height were set.

The first auction of lots in October was honored by the presence of the President, the Secretary of State, and Congressman James Madison, but the weather was bad, no copies of the map of the city were available, though the engraver was supposed to be at work, and the sales were relatively small. Nevertheless, Washington gave a favorable report in his message to Congress, stating that the sales already made gave promise that there would be ample funds for the necessary pub-

[16] The assertion in Kite, pp. 72–73, that TJ's views were "wholly opposed" to those of L'Enfant seems much too strong.

[17] TJ to the Commissioners, Aug. 28, 1791 (Padover, pp. 65–66); Washington to TJ, Aug. 29, 1791 (Fitzpatrick, XXXI, 349–350, 351–352).

[18] Notes on Commissioners' meeting of Sept. 8, 1791; Commissioners to L'Enfant, Sept. 9, 1791 (Padover, pp. 70–75).

[19] TJ to Washington, Sept. 8, 1791 (Padover, p. 68).

lic buildings.[20] By this time he believed that the Eastern members were so reconciled to the residence measure that attempts to repeal it, if any had been contemplated, could be defeated. He saw a continuing danger, however, that "side blows" would be aimed against the project, and believed that unfavorable rumors would discourage the sale of lots.[21] He and Jefferson were talking about another sale, and inquiring anxiously about the engraving of the map, when L'Enfant created a first-class disturbance and brought the smoldering controversy between him and the Commissioners to a burning issue.

Toward the end of November the Commissioners informed the President that the Major L'Enfant, without their authority, had proceeded to demolish a house belonging to a prominent landholder in the district, Daniel Carroll of Duddington, nephew of the Commissioner of the same name.[22]

Several weeks before this, Jefferson had suggested that L'Enfant would have to be subjected to the Commissioners, and Washington had been shocked into action when he learned that the engineer had refused them the use of his map (not yet engraved) in connection with the sale of lots. The patient President, who regarded L'Enfant as the best qualified man in the country for projecting public works and carrying them into effect, was generally disposed to humor the feelings of this man of talent, but he had not expected such "perverseness." After the map episode, through his secretary, Tobias Lear, he gave L'Enfant to understand that he must look to the Commissioners for directions in the future.[23]

Washington was also informed of the dispute between L'Enfant and Daniel Carroll of Duddington a few days before it reached its climax, and the whole matter could have been accommodated if the disputants had received his wise advice in time and had heeded it.[24] The difficulty arose because a house being built by Carroll, and actually started before L'Enfant's plan was drawn, partially blocked an important projected street.[25] Carroll was one of the largest landholders

[20] In his third annual message, Oct. 25, 1791 (Fitzpatrick, XXXI, 500).

[21] Washington to David Stuart, Nov. 20, 1791 (*ibid.*, XXXI, 422–423).

[22] Commissioners Stuart and Carroll to Washington, Nov. 25, 1791 (Padover, pp. 78–79).

[23] TJ to Washington, Nov. 6, 1791 (Padover, p. 76); Washington to Stuart, Nov. 20, 1791 (Fitzpatrick, XXXI, 419–423).

[24] Washington to Daniel Carroll of Duddington, Nov. 28, 1791, replying to a letter of Nov. 21; Washington to L'Enfant, Nov. 28, 1791 (Fitzpatrick, XXXI, 429–431). He had not yet received the letter of Nov. 25 from the commissioners.

[25] New Jersey Avenue, S.E. Elisabeth S. Kite (p. 80), after studying the map, said that the house occupied an eminence which L'Enfant had chosen as one of his focal points, hence had to be moved entirely. In the contemporary cor-

in the eastern district and a good deal of a troublemaker on his own account. Jefferson said that he had acted imprudently and intemperately, though not illegally; and Washington took the position that he could not reasonably object to the removal of his house if it stood in the way of the city plan. In his later attempt to justify himself, L'Enfant claimed that he was barred from appealing to the Commissioners, since there were only two of them actually in service and Daniel Carroll of Rock Creek had said that he would take his kinsman's side. There were other allegations of favoritism on the part of the Commissioners, and some other people thought that L'Enfant's troubles were in considerable part due to his zeal for the public interest. Carroll had procured an injunction against him, though it turned out that this had not been served. When Washington turned over all the papers in this vexatious case to his Secretary of State he expressed a strong desire to retain L'Enfant's services. Continuing, he said: "At the same time *he must know* there is a line beyond which he will not be suffered to go. Whether it is zeal, an impetuous temper, or other motives that lead him into such blameable conduct, I will not take upon me to decide; but be it what it will, it must be checked; or we shall have no commissioners." [26]

In conference with Madison, Jefferson drafted a letter to L'Enfant and one to the Commissioners for the President. The former might seem too severe, he said, but L'Enfant had given the "go-by" to the sentiments of the President as conveyed by Lear, and showed that he would not heed correction unless it was pointed. The letter as Washington sent it contained a stern admonition:

> In future I must strictly enjoin you to touch no man's property without his consent, or the previous order of the Commissioners. I wished you to be employed in the arrangements of the Federal City: I still wish it: but only on condition that you can conduct yourself in subordination to the authority of the Commissioners (to whom by law the business is entrusted, and who stands [*sic*] between you and the President of the United States), to the laws of the land, and to the rights of its citizens.[27]

By inserting the parenthesis Washington made the assertion of the Commissioners' authority even stronger than Jefferson did, but in

respondence, however, the fact that the house protruded into a proposed street was what was talked about.

[26] Washington to TJ, Nov. 30, 1791 (Fitzpatrick, XXXI, 432).

[27] TJ to Washington, Dec. 1, 1791 (LC, 11709); draft of letter to L'Enfant (LC, 11710); draft of letter to Commissioners (LC, 11711). The latter, as sent, is printed in Fitzpatrick, XXXI, 432–433; but the text of the one to L'Enfant, as printed (*ibid.*, 434–435), contains a misplaced line. Washington's insertion consisted of the parenthesis.

two paragraphs that he added he reduced the severity of the letter somewhat by pointing out the necessity of L'Enfant's acting under the direction of these men, by stressing their reasonableness, and by urging harmony.

The Commissioners were conciliatory. They soon wrote Jefferson that Carroll did not think it worth while to have the injunction served. Despite their instructions that he desist from the work of demolition, L'Enfant had continued it; but they believed that matters could be adjusted between him and Carroll, who had reason to suppose that he would be compensated. Washington was pleased that things had worked out so well, but not at all pleased by a lengthy letter from L'Enfant, who showed no signs of contrition or accommodation. In this he claimed that he had as much right to pull down a house as a tree.[28]

Washington turned it over to Jefferson for an opinion and the latter demolished it on strict legal grounds. He thought it would be unwise for the President to draw any line of demarcation between the engineer and the Commissioners, as the former wished, since this would lead to endless chicanery and contention. "I am thoroughly persuaded that, to render him useful, his temper must be subdued," Jefferson said, "and that the only means of preventing his giving constant trouble to the President is to submit him to the unlimited control of the commissioners; we know the discretion and forbearance with which they will exercise it." This judgment was accepted as unescapable by Washington, who incorporated it, without reference to L'Enfant's temper, in a letter which he undoubtedly hoped would be final. Being painfully aware of the difficulty of replacing L'Enfant, he suggested to the Commissioners that they give him general and ample powers, for defined objects, until convinced that he would abuse them; but he left no doubt that the engineer's powers and instructions were to flow from them.[29]

L'Enfant probably assumed that he had won a victory in this dispute, but in the case of another house, belonging to another man, he showed commendable moderation and no incident resulted.[30] A serious difficulty between him and the Commissioners soon arose, however, in connection with plans for the winter's work. This came to a head,

[28] Commissioners to TJ, Dec. 8, 1791 (Padover, pp. 81–82), L'Enfant to Washington, Dec. 7, 1791 (Kite, pp. 89–91), answering Washington's of Nov. 28.

[29] Opinion of Dec. 11, 1791 (Padover, pp. 82–86, esp. p. 86); Washington to L'Enfant, Dec. 13, 1791 (Fitzpatrick, XXXI, 442–444); Washington to the Commissioners, Dec. 18, 1791 (Fitzpatrick, XXXI, 445–448), containing an admirable summary and notably just appraisal of the entire controversy.

[30] L'Enfant to Commissioners, Dec. 22, 1791 (Kite, pp. 101–102).

actually, after L'Enfant himself had left the District for Philadelphia, to do something about the engraving of his plan and to work out further projects. The elaborate report to Washington, which he drew in Philadelphia, went far beyond a single season.[31] This showed the vividness and sweep of his creative imagination and made the Commissioners seem dull and timid by comparison. During the year 1792 he wanted to employ more than 1000 workmen and spend more than 300,000 dollars, estimating that the grants from Virginia and Maryland and a loan of a million dollars would be roughly sufficient for four years at this rate. He was willing to cut the costs approximately in half during the first year, but even in his reduced estimate he allowed for practically the same total expense in four years. He reiterated his opposition to the early sale of lots, which not only the Commissioners but Washington and Jefferson had favored. There was some ground for his position, but he had already aroused fears that the enterprise would be bankrupted before it was really started.

These long-range recommendations showed his continued disposition to go over the heads of the Commissioners, but the specific issue grew out of a conflict of authority in the District itself. L'Enfant had left instructions about the employment of the workmen – some seventy-five in number – which his assistant, Isaac Roberdeau, tried to carry out. This was at just the time that the Commissioners had decided that, because of financial considerations and the coming of winter weather, all work should be suspended until spring. The net result was that the men, including Roberdeau, were discharged, and that he, having defied the Commissioners, was arrested for trespass. Washington was now convinced that L'Enfant's subordination to them would have to be established if chaos were to be avoided. He was getting worn out with this business. He expressed the fervent wish that it could be brought to a conclusion, though he supposed an agreeable one was not to be expected. There was sharp dissension in the District, for a considerable number of the residents supported L'Enfant. Finding that one of these, George Walker, was in town, the President had Jefferson interview him, and Walker served as a sort of intermediary for some time afterwards.[32]

The Secretary of State had no escape from this vexatious business. Washington passed on to him the letters and other papers that kept

[31] In the form of a letter to Washington, with attached estimate, and presented on Jan. 17, 1792 (Kite, pp. 110–132).

[32] The local situation is described in a letter of the Commissioners to Washington, Jan. 9, 1792, and in letters from Roberdeau to L'Enfant, Jan. 2 and 7 (Kite, pp. 104–108). See also Washington to TJ, Jan. 15, 18, Feb. 7, 9, 1792 (Fitzpatrick, XXXI, 459, 462, 476, 477).

coming in, summoned him to repeated conferences – generally asking that Madison also come along – and relied on him to bear the main burden of correspondence. The President approved the action of the Commissioners in dismissing the workmen as a necessary exercise of authority. "It is certainly wise to take a view of the work to be done, the funds for carrying it on, and to employ the best instruments," he wrote. "Major L'Enfant might be an useful one if he could be brought to reduce himself within those limits which your own responsibility obliges you to prescribe to him. At present he does not appear to be in that temper."[33] Jefferson undoubtedly agreed with this judgment, and he was speaking for Washington when he wrote to L'Enfant, about a month later, and laid down the law.[34]

The gist of his letter was in this sentence: "I am charged by the President to say that your continuance would be desirable to him; and at the same time to add that the law requires it should be in subordination to the Commissioners." L'Enfant's opposition to them and his determination "no longer to act in subjection to their will and caprice" was owing to his devotion to the work itself, he claimed, and he faced the issue without blinking. He replied: "If therefore the law absolutely requires without any equivocation that my continuance shall depend upon an appointment from the commissioners, I cannot nor would I upon any consideration submit myself to it."[35]

The extraordinarily patient President made one last effort to overcome L'Enfant's suspicions of the Commissioners. He sent his secretary to see him, but L'Enfant brushed Tobias Lear off, saying "that he had already heard enough of this matter."[36] That finished the brilliant Frenchman with Washington, who felt that he had been insulted. The brief note which Jefferson wrote next day contained these words: "I am instructed by the President to inform you that notwithstanding the desire he has entertained to preserve your agency in the business the condition upon which it is to be done is inadmissible, and your services must be at an end."[37]

Washington believed that he had done everything within his power,

[33] Washington to the Commissioners, Jan. 17, 1792 (Fitzpatrick, XXXI, 461–462). On Jan. 15, Jefferson wrote him that his own conference with L'Enfant was put off until the next day (Padover, p. 88).

[34] Washington to TJ, Feb. 22, 1792, 7 A.M. (Fitzpatrick, XXXI, 482–483); TJ to L'Enfant, Feb. 22, 1792 (Padover, pp. 93–94). Washington had a draft of this by Feb. 15. See also L'Enfant to Washington, Feb. 6, 1792 (Kite, p. 133).

[35] L'Enfant to TJ, Feb. 26, 1792 (Kite, pp. 145–150 esp. p. 150).

[36] Washington to TJ, 4 o'clock, Feb. 26, 1792 (Fitzpatrick, XXXI, 486–487); Washington to TJ, Mar. 14, 1792 (*ibid.*, XXXII, 3–4).

[37] TJ to L'Enfant, Feb. 27, 1792 (LC, 12287 and Padover, p. 100). According to Fitzpatrick, XXXI, 487*n.*, a draft in the writing of Hamilton is also in LC.

compatible with the law, to accommodate himself to L'Enfant's wishes – except to change the Commissioners. This he could not do on grounds of propriety, justice, or policy.[38]

By this time they undoubtedly needed bolstering. Jefferson told Thomas Johnson, who was now assuming his duties as one of them, that not only L'Enfant but also certain residents held them in sovereign contempt. Explaining matters to one of the latter, he said: "I think you have seen enough of his [L'Enfant's] temper to satisfy yourself that he never could have acted under any control, not even that of the President himself: and on the whole I am persuaded the enterprise will advance more surely under a more temperate direction; under one that shall proceed as fast but no faster than it can pay." [39] That seemed a sensible prediction, but he still had to use his powers of explanation and persuasion on the large group of landholders who espoused L'Enfant's cause.[40]

He convinced these gentlemen of the inevitability of the President's action, but the controversy had served to discredit the whole enterprise and had slowed things up. Jefferson did all in his power to calm troubled minds and set things going again, but it is difficult to distinguish his own ideas and recommendations from those of the President for whom he spoke. The suggestions that both L'Enfant and Daniel Carroll of Duddington be generously treated and that proceedings against Roberdeau be dropped could have emanated from either man, though Washington appears to have made and Jefferson to have transmitted them.[41] Presumably it is Washington who should be credited with the decision to abide fully by L'Enfant's plan, regardless of the desire of the Commissioners to make some alterations in it, though there is every reason to believe that Jefferson fully supported him.[42] At no time during his term of office did Jefferson show any inclination to keep this from being Washington's particular undertaking, but no important decision appears to have been made against his advice.

A large part of Jefferson's extensive correspondence with the Commissioners during this year and the next one dealt with minor matters of routine. His suggestion that skilled workmen be imported from

[38] Washington to L'Enfant, Feb. 28, 1792 (Fitzpatrick, XXXI, 488–489).

[39] TJ to George Walker, Mar. 1, 1792 (Padover, p. 101); see also TJ to Thomas Johnson, Feb. 29, 1792 (*ibid.*, p. 100).

[40] The correspondence with these in March, 1792, through George Walker, and between them and L'Enfant, is conveniently assembled in Kite, pp. 167–181.

[41] L'Enfant declined the offer of 500 guineas and a lot, though some years later he successfully presented a claim to Congress. Carroll accepted compensation.

[42] TJ to Commissioners, Apr. 20, 1792 (Padover, pp. 137–138).

Europe was characteristic, but nothing came of it. Indirectly he was responsible for the use of the Indian name Anacostia for the Eastern Branch, though Andrew Ellicott, whom he stimulated to make the inquiry, actually ascertained it. Early in the next year this surveyor, of whom Jefferson had a high opinion, got into a serious quarrel with the Commissioners and was removed. Rumors ran round that Jefferson was supporting him, and the Secretary of State took the precaution of sending to Washington copies of all his letters to him, in order to show that if he had tried to compose the differences he had done no more than the President wanted him to do.[43]

If the Federal City became a graveyard of reputations by unhappy accident, the monumental quality eventually attained by its architecture was intended – and by no one more than by Jefferson. His ideas about the form of the Capitol and President's House had been given to L'Enfant, who was expected to design these first public buildings but never got around to them. No doubt they were also communicated to Washington and the Commissioners, and it may be assumed that no plan sharply at variance with his general ideas could have been adopted. The idea of holding competitions and offering premiums was his, and after L'Enfant's removal he urged that the Commissioners advertise immediately for plans for these two major buildings. Besides correcting a draft of an advertisement for a plan of the Capitol, he himself made one for a plan of the President's House, offering a premium of $500 or a medal of that value for the most approved plan, and submitting with it a memorandum of the precise requirements.[44]

It was perhaps because of his fear that good designs would be few that he made two of his own, submitting the more modest of these anonymously. In the more pretentious one he tried to combine the "celebrated fronts" he had so greatly admired in France and had mentioned specifically to L'Enfant – the Hôtel de Salm, the Garde-meuble, and the Louvre – but, recognizing the impracticability of this, he abandoned it. The other design was modeled chiefly on Palladio's Villa Rotunda. It had a dome and porticos and was thus in the grand manner, but it also had alcove bedrooms and stairs like those in his own Paris house.[45]

Washington first saw James Hoban's plan on a visit to the District in July, 1792. What he may have thought of Jefferson's anonymous

[43] Ellicott to TJ, Jan. 9, 12, 1793 (Padover, pp. 167–169); TJ to Ellicott, Jan. 15, 1793 (*ibid.*, pp. 169–170): TJ to Washington, Mar. 4, 1793 (*ibid.*, pp. 175–176).

[44] TJ to Commissioners, Mar. 6, 1792 (Padover, pp. 104–106; Kimball, *Jefferson, Architect*, pp. 154–155).

[45] Kimball, pp. 52–53 and Figures 125, 126, 131.

design is a matter of sheer speculation, but he liked the sample of work that Hoban exhibited and the choice of this plan may be regarded as his.[46] Apparently Jefferson had not seen it, but the design was one that he might have been expected to approve. The cornerstone of the building was laid next fall, but it was still unfinished when he moved into it early in the next century. Although it was only a big box, its proportions were good, and from it the simple and stately White House of later times could grow.

His connection with the beginnings of the Capitol was more intimate. A number of plans were submitted and these were generally unsatisfactory. Stephen Hallet, a French architect living in Philadelphia, proved a serious contender, however, and he availed himself of Jefferson's suggestions. The Secretary of State first commended the temple form which he himself had employed in the Capitol of Virginia, and when Hallet abandoned this because of his inability to adapt it to the scale of the proposed building he suggested a spherical model, of which he regarded the Pantheon in Rome as the most perfect example and the Pantheon in Paris as the one most adaptable to this situation. He translated this idea into a sketch of his own which has been described on high authority as "one of the most suggestive, as well as one of the freest in technique, of all his drawings."[47] Hallet's second plan called for a central dome with wings, and by means of it he started a style in American capitols, even though his own design was unsuccessful. Dr. William Thornton, an amateur who had entered vigorously into the competition, picked up this idea and applied it more impressively. His original design has not been preserved, but the President liked it so much that its acceptance was a foregone conclusion. It was submitted in Philadelphia and Jefferson reported to the Commissioners that it had so captivated the eyes and judgment of all as to leave no doubt that they would prefer it when they saw it. He himself described it as "simple, noble, beautiful, excellently distributed, and moderate in size."[48] It was duly awarded the prize, though Hallet was given the same financial reward because of his disappointment, his needs, and his general architectural services.

Employed to draw working plans and supervise the construction, Hallet soon made an unfavorable report on Thornton's design — on

[46] Washington to David Stuart, July 9, 1792 (Fitzpatrick, XXXII, 85–86); Washington to the Commissioners, July 23, 1792 (*ibid.*, p. 94). TJ heard about Hoban in a letter of July 5 from the Commissioners (Padover, p. 152), and the award was made July 17.

[47] Kimball, *Jefferson, Architect*, p. 55, and Figure 132; see also TJ's own account of the Virginia Capitol in L. & B., XVII, 353.

[48] TJ to Commissioners, Feb. 1, 1793 (Padover, p. 171).

grounds of practicality, time, and expense. Washington got this report in the summer of 1793, when on one of his many visits home, and forthwith instructed Hallet and James Hoban, then employed on the President's House, to attend a conference with Jefferson, Thornton, and others in Philadelphia. The Secretary of State was to preside over this and recommend what should be done. Washington thought it most unfortunate that the investigation of the practicality and cost of Thornton's plan had not preceded the adoption of it, and attributed the hasty decision to the desire to gratify the impatient public, particularly the Carrollsburg interest. For himself he said: "I do not hesitate to confess I was governed by the beauty of the exterior and the distribution of the apartments, declaring then, as I do now, that I had no knowledge in the rules or principles of architecture, and was equally unable to count the cost." He insisted on speedy and decisive action of some sort. "The case is important," he said. "A plan must be adopted; and good, or bad, it must be entered upon." He put the matter squarely up to Jefferson, who had plenty of other public troubles at this juncture.[49]

Jefferson called together Dr. Thornton, a builder named Carstairs whom Thornton selected as a competent judge, Hallet, and Hoban, and made a judicious but decisive report.[50] The sum and substance of this was that the objections raised to Thornton's plan were valid, but that these could be remedied by alterations. In fact, they had already been made by Hallet in a plan drawn by him, which "preserved the most valuable features of the original and rendered them susceptible of execution," and was regarded as "Dr. Thornton's plan reduced into practicable form."

The persons who were consulted agreed that the "reformed" plan was a work of great merit, but objected to the removal of the portico on the eastern front, which seemed necessary to Hallet in order to correct a major defect, the want of light and air. They believed that the proposed recess in the east front would have an extreme ill effect, and wanted the portico restored, suggesting other changes to this purpose. A merit of the "reformed" plan was that it was expected to cost about half as much as the original one. Jefferson secured some estimates of costs in Philadelphia and these were transmitted in due course for the benefit of the Commissioners. Washington approved the report in its entirety after he got back to Philadelphia. He agreed that the restoration of the portico on the east front was desirable, but saw

[49] Washington to TJ, June 30, 1793 (Fitzpatrick, XXXII, 510–512); Washington to James Hoban and Stephen Hallet, July 1, 1793 (*ibid.*, XXXIII, 1–2).
[50] TJ to Washington, July 17, 1793 (Padover, pp. 184–186).

no reason why work could not be begun immediately on the foundation of the other parts of the building according to Hallet's version of the plan. The question of the unpleasant recess could be considered later.[51] Thus the matter was settled, to the apparent satisfaction of those most intimately concerned, though some important questions were postponed and some uncertainty remained as to whether the plan was now Hallet's or Thornton's.

In later years Jefferson had plenty of troubles about the Capitol, which was far from finished when he was inaugurated President. He was not there when the cornerstone was laid by Washington, after considerable ceremony, on September 18, 1793. His presence would have been eminently appropriate, but it is doubtful if his absence caused him any chagrin, since he disliked all sorts of ceremonies and still regarded the Federal City as George Washington's special preserve. His interest in it constituted a strong personal bond between him and the President during almost the whole of his secretaryship. This was specially true at just the time when divisive tendencies were gaining momentum in the federal government and dangerously threatening, if not actually destroying, the unity of the official family.

[51] Washington to Commissioners, July 25, 1793 (Fitzpatrick, XXXIII, 29–30); TJ to Commissioners, Aug. 15, 1793 (Padover, pp. 186–187); Washington to Commissioners, Aug. 29, 1793 (Fitzpatrick, XXXIII, 74).

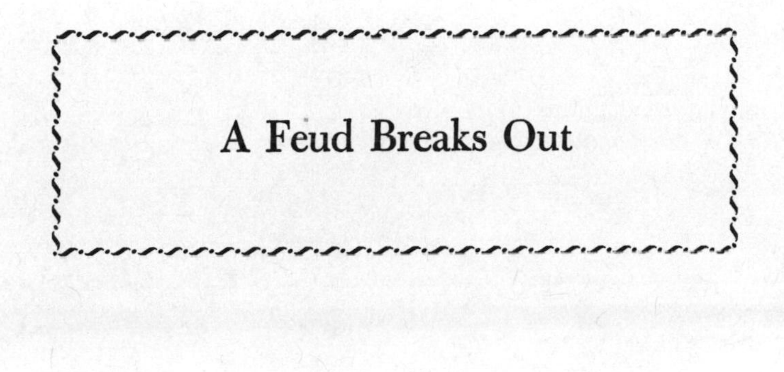

A Feud Breaks Out

[XXIII]

New Actors on the Diplomatic Stage

1791–1792

ON personal grounds, Jefferson's second winter in Philadelphia as Secretary of State should have been more pleasant than his first. His domestic establishment was now in good running order. While he was on his northern trip with Madison his house had been painted, and by fall he had so much stable room that he could offer some of it to James Monroe, even though his own chariot and sulky had arrived from France in the summer, along with a shipment of wines from Champagne and Bordeaux. A much more important arrival was that of his old maître d'hôtel, Petit. This led to certain changes in his domestic staff, but his mind was at ease about his household when he went home for a month in September.[1]

On his way down, as we have noted, he had a first and harmonious meeting with the District Commissioners in Georgetown. At the start of this long trip he attached an odometer to his phaeton. Until this failed him at the very end, he estimated his distances by means of it, assuming that the wheels made exactly 360 revolutions in a mile. The measurement he made at Monticello showed him, however, that they made 354.95 revolutions, hence he adjusted his figures by adding one mile at the end of every seventy-one.[2]

On his trip back he brought Polly with him, though the girl actually traveled with Mrs. Washington from Mount Vernon onwards, her father being involved in the auction of lots in the new Federal City between times. The officials arrived in Philadelphia in time for the opening of Congress on October 24, though the President got his dates

[1] Henry Remsen, Jr., to TJ, June 16, 1791 (LC, 11183–11184); TJ to Monroe, July 10, 1791 (Ford, V, 351); Account Book, July 19, 1791, noting Petit's arrival; *ibid.*, Sept 2, 1791, showing domestic changes; directions to Remsen, Sept. 2, 1791 (LC, 11506).

[2] Account Book, Sept. 2–12, 1791.

mixed and had to follow a less leisurely course than he had expected. Learning by chance from his secretary that the appointed day was not the last Monday in October but the fourth, he said he had no more idea of this than he had of its being Doomsday. He was afraid that he would not have time to prepare his address if the members were punctual, but with the assistance of his department heads and Madison he got it ready and delivered it on the 25th. Meanwhile, Polly became immersed in her new acquaintances, her father said, being specially happy with Mrs. Washington's granddaughter, Nellie Custis, then twelve and a few months her junior, and being "particularly attended" by the President's wife herself. Before long he placed the girl in school with Mrs. Pine, but she spent holidays with him at home, and her cousin Jack Eppes, who was now nineteen, lived there. Jefferson did not have enough members of his own clan near him to satisfy him as a family man, but in this respect his situation in Philadelphia had improved, and his personal relations with Washington, whom he was assisting so loyally in the affairs of the District of Columbia, left nothing to be desired.[3]

Some financial clouds hung over him that fall and winter and these grew darker in the spring. His expenses were increased by Polly's board and schooling (for it had cost little to maintain her at Monticello) and they must have been by Petit's presence, though he regarded the Frenchman as a careful manager. Presumably he was still living within his salary, but before he left Monticello he had been sued or threatened with suit by the agent of his chief British creditor, who had refused to accept the bonds he had received for Jefferson's Cumberland lands. Jefferson, having received less than he expected from his crops and being unable to realize immediately on his sale of lands in a region where cash was scarce and everybody was in debt, had fallen behind with his payments to the house of Farrell & Jones. Under these circumstances he brought suit on his own account against the two tenants of his Elkhill plantation whom he had long indulged. They had paid him no rent for six years and still owed him a considerable sum for the slaves attached to this plantation whom they had purchased from him.[4] Early in the new year he decided to sell Elkhill, and he began negotiations to that effect in the spring. These were ultimately successful but long protracted. Before Christmas he had managed to make a substantial payment to Farrell & Jones, only to

[3] Account Book, Oct. 12–22, 1791; Washington to Lear, Oct. 14, 1791 (Fitzpatrick, XXXI, 387) and other letters of the same date; TJ to T. M. Randolph, Jr., Oct. 25, 1791 (LC, 11557).

[4] TJ to Col. Robert Lewis, Oct. 5, 1791 (MHS). Lewis's son Robert and Captain S. Woodson were the tenants.

receive a complaining letter in reply. This mortified him deeply, for he had been scrupulous about this inherited debt. In the end he largely satisfied this creditor, but we shall drop the unpleasant matter now, as he himself had to, under the unceasing pressure of affairs of state.[5]

Even in the story of his public life these circumstances have significance. His horror of public debt was related to his own sufferings from private; and his experiences with relentless British creditors in Virginia imparted some emotional coloration to his negotiations with the British Minister, even though his own skirts were clean. Furthermore, his weariness with public life, which he kept talking about to intimates, and the definite purpose to retire from office which he soon made known to Washington, were not unconnected with the desire to straighten out the tangles in his own affairs.

Despite the troubles of the Federal City which we have described, and the growing political conflict over domestic issues which we shall speak of hereafter, Jefferson devoted himself to foreign affairs at this stage of his secretaryship to a much greater degree than he had previously been able to do. The most important reason for this was that the British had at length established full diplomatic relations with the United States by sending George Hammond as minister. Anglo-American questions were Jefferson's predominant concern from the opening of Congress till summer, especially in the spring, though the issues he raised with Spain were of comparable importance and stirred him just as much. French problems did not greatly occupy him, though they continued to loom in the background. A new minister had come from that Court, which had been represented for months by a mere chargé, and an American minister was named to Jefferson's old place. At the same time Washington made appointments to London and The Hague. The American foreign establishment, though still tiny, was beginning to look like something, and the diplomatic corps in Philadelphia, while not yet impressive, was taking form.

The new French Minister, Jean Baptiste Ternant, who arrived in August, had been officially though rather informally received by Washington and Jefferson before they left Philadelphia for Virginia. Ternant, now a little past fifty, had served as an officer in the American Revolution and was cordially commended by Lafayette. "He in a great measure belongs to both countries," the Marquis said; and Washington, who remembered him, accepted the characterization. Ternant on his own part believed that his reception augured well. He noted no special

[5] It is summed up sufficiently in a letter from TJ to Mr. Dobson (or Dodson), Jan. 1, 1792, replying to one of Dec. 18, 1791 (MHS).

cordiality on the part of Jefferson, however, and the Secretary of State maintained strict proprieties in his intercourse with him at all times.[6]

Apparently the only question he raised before Jefferson went home was that of American payments on account to France in depreciated *assignats*. With the concurrence of Hamilton, whose suggestions about phraseology he accepted entirely, Jefferson assured Ternant that the United States had no expectation of taking any advantage of France by paying her in depreciated currency.[7] After his departure a more important matter came up. A delegation arrived from the French colony of St. Domingo, seeking help against the Negro insurrection in that island, and Ternant referred their requests to Hamilton and Knox, who promptly made money and arms available. Washington confirmed these actions as soon as they were reported to him, and in a letter to Ternant he testified to the disposition of the United States to render every aid in their power to their good friends and allies the French, in order that the latter might quell this alarming revolt. Some differences arose between Ternant and the commissioners from St. Domingo, who were inclined to go over his head, and Jefferson did what he could to maintain proper procedure after he got back. In the light of later controversy, however, it is more significant that the other executive officers, not he, provided aid to the French in the first place, and that Hamilton established friendly personal relations with Ternant at the very start.[8]

The Secretary of the Treasury, who was never one to let the grass grow under his feet, had held a four-hour conversation with the Frenchman – who spoke English fluently – while Jefferson and Washington were still out of town.[9] Commercial relations with France were not on as firm a footing now as they had been when Jefferson left that country, and, before Ternant arrived, Jefferson had protested strongly against a recent action of the French Assembly imposing heavier charges on tobacco brought in American ships than French and

[6] Ternant was received Aug. 12, 1791, and described his reception to Montmorin, who was still the French Minister of Foreign Affairs, Aug. 13. See *Correspondence of the French Ministers to the U. S., 1791–1797*, ed. by Frederick J. Turner. (*Annual Report Am. Hist. Asso. for the Year 1903*, Vol. II, 1904, pp. 43–45.) This work will be referred to hereafter as *C.F.M.* See also Lafayette to Washington, June 16, 1791 (*Letters of Lafayette and Washington*, p. 356), and Washington to Lafayette, Sept. 10, 1791 (Fitzpatrick, XXXI, 363).

[7] TJ to Ternant Sept. 1, 1791. (Ford, V, 383–384, with footnote showing Hamilton's suggestions.)

[8] Ternant to Montmorin, Sept. 28, 1791 (*C.F.M.*, pp. 45–51); Washington to Ternant, Sept. 24, 1791 (Fitzpatrick, XXXI, 375–376 and note); TJ to Short, Nov. 24, 1791 (Ford, V, 394–397).

[9] Ternant reported this to Montmorin, Oct. 9, 1791 (*C.F.M.*, pp. 57–60).

striking against the carrying trade.[10] The matters at issue between the two countries were fully understood by him, and the propriety of Hamilton's entering into a deliberate discussion of them in his absence was doubtful, even though commerce was involved.

Hamilton took this occasion to say that all the disputed questions could be settled in a new treaty of commerce and that he himself strongly favored this. The wary Frenchman did not reveal his own instructions on this point (which Hamilton was seeking to ascertain), contenting himself with the observation that a scrupulous observance of the existing treaties by the United States was a necessary preliminary to the negotiation of a new one.

Ternant believed that the indifference he showed with respect to the expected arrival of a British minister surprised the Secretary of the Treasury. Hamilton's discussion of future negotiations with the British, which naturally would be conducted by the Secretary of State, was indiscreet and presumptuous under the best interpretation of it, and deliberately deceptive at the worst. He assured Ternant that the United States would regard the full admission of American shipping to the British West Indies as a necessary condition of a new treaty of commerce; and that the expected British proposal that a treaty of alliance be coupled with one of commerce would be rejected.[11] He was as correct in this as anyone can be in prophecy, for his colleague Jefferson had firmly taken the same position, but his strong protestations of attachment to France are hard to reconcile with other words and actions. According to Ternant, he and Hamilton parted as great friends, and he expected other interviews of this sort in the future, believing that Washington desired them, though there is no reason to suppose he did.

By contrast, when Ternant saw Washington and Jefferson again, he found them disappointingly uncommunicative about official matters. He was even more surprised that the President's message to Congress contained no reference to the report on commerce which Jefferson had been instructed to prepare for this session, following the heated discussion in the last Congress about a navigation act like that of Great Britain and actually directed against that country. The delay in submitting Jefferson's report he attributed in part to the pending negotiations with the new British Minister. Hamilton had discussed these with him freely but he continued to wonder what their real purpose was.

[10] TJ to Short, July 28, 1791 (Ford, V, 362–363).

[11] On Oct. 6, 1791, Hamilton quoted to Washington a paragraph from a letter just received from England, reporting the unfavorable disposition of the Ministry (J. C. Hamilton, IV, 177). He may have been pessimistic about the British at the moment.

The Secretary of State had affected an extreme official reserve, he said, though he hoped to see more signs of confidence in himself and attachment to France in the future.[12] Jefferson did not submit a full report on commerce until the very end of his own term, and he never revealed much to the Frenchman about the negotiations with the British representative, but Ternant was right in assuming that the arrival of the latter had appreciably altered the political and diplomatic situation.

George Hammond, the first British Minister Plenipotentiary to the United States, then twenty-eight years old, reached Philadelphia several days before Congress opened but waited three weeks before presenting his credentials. Jefferson had won his point that the British must make the first step in establishing full diplomatic relations, but their envoy bided his time until he had tangible proof that an American minister to his country would be appointed. He learned from Jefferson that the mission to England had been offered to an unnamed gentleman – afterwards revealed as Thomas Pinckney of South Carolina – and he was formally presented to the President by the Secretary of State on November 11. He had called on Jefferson the week after his arrival, only to find him out, and Jefferson had no greater success when he tried to return the compliment. Ternant, who made no ceremonial visits except to officials with whom it was his duty to deal, reported somewhat tartly that the young Britisher visited everybody, especially the Senators, before his official reception; and we now know that he had been specifically instructed to cultivate influential people. Among these, of course, was Hamilton. Whether or not he looked up the Secretary of the Treasury at once, his first long and confidential conversation with him fully confirmed his previous judgment of that gentleman's "just and liberal way of thinking." [13] He never had any doubt that Hamilton still belonged to the "party of the English interest."

Jefferson, playing the part of a wary diplomat, sparred with the overconfident young Britisher at first. The issues between the two countries which could now be the subject of negotiation fell into two groups: those connected with the alleged failure on both sides to carry the treaty of peace into effect, and those relating to commerce. Jefferson wanted to defer consideration of the latter and concentrate on the effort to get the British out of the Northwest posts. This seemed

[12] Ternant to Montmorin, Oct. 27, 1791 (*C.F.M.*, p. 67). See also his letter of Oct. 24. (*ibid.*, pp. 60–62).

[13] Hammond to Grenville, Dec. 19, 1791, quoted in *Instructions to the British Ministers to the U. S., 1791–1812*, ed. by Bernard Mayo (*Ann. Report of the A.H.A. . . . 1936*, Vol. III, 1941, pp. 24–25*n.*). This work is referred to hereafter as *I.B.M.*

all the more important because the Americans were engaged in warfare with the Indians at this very moment and he was convinced that the British were abetting the savages. Behind the scenes, however, he had to contend with Hamilton, who wanted him to press commercial negotiations with both the British and the French, though he himself believed these would be unavailing in both cases.

The Secretary of the Treasury now let it be known that he had conversed with Ternant. The French National Assembly had resolved that a new treaty of commerce with the United States be negotiated, and Jefferson favored negotiations to this purpose, but he thought that the initiative should come from France and he found out that Ternant had no specific instructions on the subject. Hamilton urged, nonetheless, that he work out proposals with Ternant and that these be presented to France for acceptance or refusal. Astute diplomat that he was, Jefferson objected to this, believing that a volunteer proposal would be binding on the United States but not on France. It would show the American hand before the French cards were down, though he did not use just that figure. Washington thought the experiment worth trying, however, and Jefferson drew up a brief plan of a treaty. The substance of this was that the citizens, ships, and products of either country were to be received and treated in the other just as though they belonged there, the only exception being in the matter of tariff duties, which were to remain as they were, provided they did not exceed a certain percentage.[14]

Hamilton objected to this startlingly simple plan on the ground that some existing American duties would bear raising. If Jefferson's private memorandum, made some weeks later, can be relied on, his colleague worked out a schedule, making advances of from 25 to 50 per cent with respect to the French. Jefferson put the matter thus: "So they were to give us the privileges of native subjects, and we, as a compensation, were to make them pay higher duties." [15] He suspected a trap. Hamilton, who had got Washington to agree that informal negotiations might be entered into with Ternant, despite the fact that the latter had no instructions, suggested that the same thing be done with Hammond. This seemed reasonable to Washington, but Jefferson, believing that Hamilton was merely making a pretext out of a French treaty which he would have defeated anyway, insisted that nothing

[14] TJ to Short, Nov. 24, 1791 (Ford, V, 394); "Clauses for Treaty of Commerce with France (November, 1791) and "Questions to be Considered of," Nov. 26, 1791 (Ford, V, 397–400); Note in Anas, dated 1791 and committed to writing Mar. 11, 1792 (Ford, I, 185–186).

[15] Ford, I, 185; Washington's letter of Dec. 9, 1791, to TJ shows the approximate date (Fitzpatrick, XXXI, 442).

be done about a commercial treaty with either nation at this stage. This episode serves to explain why Ternant got so little out of the Secretary of State, though he had had fair words from the Secretary of the Treasury. Also, it sheds light on Jefferson's efforts to find out just how far Hammond's instructions went.

Toward the end of November he asked the Britisher in suave language two searching questions: Was he authorized to give the explanations of his Court regarding the nonexecution of the seventh article of the treaty, calling for removal of all British forces from all parts of the United States, with all convenient speed but without carrying away any Negroes or other property? Was he instructed to conclude or negotiate commercial arrangements? Hammond's reply to the first of these came straight from his private instructions: the nonexecution of the seventh article was owing to American noncompliance with Articles IV, V, and VI (dealing with lawful impediments to the recovery of debts, and the confiscation of Loyalist property). His answer to the second was not so clearcut, and led to further questions and answers, but the net result was just what Jefferson had expected. He finally smoked out of Hammond the admission that he was not authorized to conclude any definitive commercial arrangement, though he could *discuss* one in his general plenipotentiary character.[16] In fact, the British Minister had been specifically instructed that on no account was he to conclude anything without previous and express directions from England.[17]

The principles he was at liberty to discuss were embodied in a confidential report of a committee of the Privy Council on American trade, which had been made early in the year. The main conclusion of this was that the existing state of this commerce was most satisfactory from the British point of view, so long as there was no discriminatory legislation.[18] The main British policy, therefore, was to seek pledges against the revival of the discriminatory movement, and to grant no concessions of any importance – least of all in the admission of American shipping into the West Indies. Jefferson knew about this report and at least its tendency, and may even have procured an abstract of it by now.[19] Hence he rightly assumed that commercial negotiations with Hammond would have been entirely futile. Hamilton could have been expected to connive with the latter in his efforts to check the dis-

[16] The correspondence, Nov. 29–Dec. 14, 1791, is in *A.S.P.F.R.*, I, 188–189.

[17] Grenville to Hammond, Sept. 1, 1791, in *I.B.M.*, p. 18. For his full instructions, admirably annotated, see pp. 2–19.

[18] This is well discussed by Bemis, *Jay's Treaty*, pp. 84–85.

[19] Phineas Bond to Grenville, Oct. 8, 1791 (*I.B.M.*, p. 6*n.*) An abstract of it was found in TJ's papers and printed a century later.

criminatory measures which Jefferson unquestionably would have recommended as the only effective weapon against the British if he had presented a report of his own to Congress.

The question of the nonexecution of the treaty remained, and Jefferson addressed himself to this about the time that news of the disastrous defeat of General St. Clair by the Indians was received in Philadelphia.[20] He had already got from the Secretary of War a list of the eight posts still held by the British within the territory of the United States when, in the middle of December, he suggested to Hammond that they simplify their discussions by specifying acts in contravention of the treaty. He set the example by specifying British failure to withdraw from the posts and the carrying away of American slaves and other property, appending supporting documents. He also mentioned the dispute about the boundary growing from the application of the name St. Croix to two different rivers.[21] The matter of the posts came first, and the situation in the Northwest had become even more dangerous than he supposed, for the hopes of the British for a new boundary settlement were revived and this soon took the form of an Indian barrier project. Jefferson issued a challenge and Hammond accepted it. The latter asked for time to collect his materials, however, and his answer did not come till March.[22] The Secretary of State believed that he was stalling, but in the meantime he himself could do something to set the diplomatic house in order.

Jefferson did not know Thomas Pinckney, and the idea of appointing him as minister to London seems to have originated with Washington, who recognized him as a fine gentleman with an admirable military reputation in the Revolution and was glad to give this choice post to a South Carolinian. Also, knowing that Pinckney had gone to school in England and lived there a good many years in his youth, the President believed that he would be acceptable to the British, as he was. Hammond described him as belonging to the "party of the British interest," though actually he did not to the same extent as Hamilton and John Jay. Jefferson approved the appointment of Pinckney to a high diplomatic position, but for some reason preferred that he be sent to France. The nomination did not go to the Senate until nearly the

[20] St. Clair's defeat of Nov. 4, 1791, was known to TJ by or before Dec. 8, when he got a letter telling him about it. (From Augustine Davis, Dec. 1, 1791; LC, 11712.) It was reported to Grenville by Hammond, Dec. 10, 1791 (*I.B.M.*, p. 25*n.*) and to Congress by Washington, Dec. 12 (Fitzpatrick, XXXI, 442).

[21] TJ to Hammond, Dec. 15, 1791 (*A.S.P.F.R.*, I, 190–193).

[22] Hammond to TJ, Dec. 19, 1791 (*A.S.P.F.R.*, I, 193). His reply of Mar. 5, 1792, will be referred to later.

end of the year, and confirmation was delayed, for reasons which reflected in no way on Pinckney. Speed was no consideration, for Jefferson did not expect anybody to cross the Atlantic until after the spring equinox and thought it just as well for the new envoy to wait until the negotiations with Hammond had proceeded further. Pinckney did not sail until June and these had come to a dead end by then.[23]

The appointment of a minister to France had been long delayed, and William Short, still there as chargé, was making no effort to conceal from Jefferson his desire to receive it. He had already made himself useful to Hamilton in connection with fiscal operations in Europe, and Jefferson was doing what he could for him, though he realized that Short's youth and relative obscurity would operate against him and never held out too much hope. He assumed all along that Washington would follow his own judgment. "To overdo a thing with him is to undo it," he wrote Short, and we may presume that he did not press his personal opinions upon the President.[24] There is certainly no reason to believe that he recommended the man on whom Washington's choice fell. Gouverneur Morris himself had previously said that would be impossible.[25] Morris was still abroad, engaged in financial schemes which were better understood by William Duer than by Thomas Jefferson, though the latter afterwards described Morris's employment in Europe as that of a "news vender of back lands and certificates." [26]

In the absence of direct evidence, it would be unfair to say that the influence of the group of international speculators to which Hamilton's former assistant Duer belonged was responsible for the interest of the Secretary of the Treasury in this appointment, but Morris afterwards thanked Hamilton for his exertions to effect it and spoke of him as "patronizing" it. At the same time he solicited a confidential correspondence, of which obviously the Secretary of State was not to be apprised.[27] Washington himself may have thought first of Morris,

[23] The draft of TJ's letter of invitation to Pinckney was dated Nov. 6, 1791 (LC, 11579). Approved by Washington, on Nov. 9, except that the designation was to be England, not France, it was sent on that date (Fitzpatrick, XXXI, 413). In his famous letter of 1800 against John Adams (J. C. Hamilton, VII, 700) Hamilton said the choice of Pinckney was attributed to Washington at the time, and denied an English agency. S. F. Bemis, "The London Mission of Thomas Pinckney" (*AHR*, XXVIII, 228–247), is an authoritative account with abundant references.

[24] TJ to Short, Mar. 3, 1791 (Ford, V, 296).

[25] Jan. 20 and 23, 1791 (*Diary*, II, 101, 106).

[26] TJ to Archibald Stuart, Mar. 14, 1792 (Ford, V, 454). On the connection of Morris with Duer's schemes, see J. S. Davis, *Essays in the Earlier History of American Corporations*, I, 169–172, and elsewhere.

[27] Morris to Hamilton, Mar. 21, 1792 (*Diary*, II, 389). Hamilton accepted the "challenge" on June 22, 1792 (*ibid.*, II, 389–390).

whose conduct in England he and Jefferson had approved, while Hamilton was critical of it. At all events, the President nominated him, taking care of Short at the same time by appointing him minister resident to The Hague. This particular conjunction of circumstances may have made it embarrassing for Jefferson to oppose Morris's nomination. Presumably he believed that his hands were tied, and, while he had doubts about Morris all along, these were accentuated by reports of the debate in the Senate and by later word from France.

The three nominations were submitted to the Senate shortly before Christmas and the discussion of them continued for several weeks, off and on, before they were approved.[28] As Jefferson described the events privately to Short, the nomination of Morris was extremely unpopular, and those whose personal objections to him "overweighed their deference to the President" joined with another small party which opposed all foreign appointments and tried to "put down the whole system." [29] The question whether it was desirable to appoint ministers plenipotentiary to reside permanently at foreign courts was indeed raised in the Senate, and Jefferson was prepared to go to great lengths to maintain the system and uphold executive prerogatives in connection with it. He drafted for Washington a paper, asserting that, under the Constitution, the President was the sole competent judge with respect to the grade and destination of foreign ministers, the powers of the Senate being limited to giving or withholding their consent to the persons nominated. By this he did not mean to deny to the two branches of Congress the right to review the entire diplomatic establishment periodically, but fortunately this brusque paper was not used.

The matter was referred to a committee of the Senate, under the chairmanship of Caleb Strong of Massachusetts, and the Secretary of State was summoned by them to conference. By his clear and tactful explanations of the diplomatic situation he saved the establishment, though the vote on the ministry to The Hague was actually a tie, which was broken by the Vice President. The nomination of Pinckney was approved without a record vote, but that of Morris was sharply contested, carrying by sixteen to eleven. Among the Nays were such stalwart conservatives as Caleb Strong and George Cabot of Massachusetts, so the alignment was not precisely the same as in later party struggles, but among them also were the two Virginia senators, Richard Henry Lee and James Monroe. The arguments of the latter were of the sort which would most appeal to Jefferson. Besides having un-

[28] Submitted Dec. 22, 1791. Pinckney and Morris were confirmed Jan. 12, 1792, and Short on Jan. 16 (*Senate Executive Jour.*, I, 92, 96–98).

[29] TJ to Short, Jan. 28, 1792 (Ford, V, 434).

conciliatory manners and an indiscreet character, Morris was a "monarchy man," said Monroe, and he went to Europe "to sell lands and certificates." It is worthy of note that of the two New York senators, Aaron Burr opposed both the mission to France and the appointment of Morris, while Rufus King, who was intimate with Hamilton and the financial group, supported the latter. Morris thanked him, along with Hamilton, for "effecting" his appointment, and also invited confidential correspondence with him. It is much more likely at this stage that King's attitude reflected Hamilton's than that Monroe's was colored by that of Jefferson, for the latter's deference to the President had outweighed his personal objections to the appointment.[30]

The nomination of Short was confirmed by an even narrower margin, but the opposition in this case was to the mission rather than to the man.[31] Jefferson had to explain this to his young friend, and in the meantime Short had been appointed, with William Carmichael, to a special and temporary mission to Spain, which called for elaborate instructions. Before issuing these, however, the Secretary of State had to launch Morris with as many precautions as possible. The most serious danger was that he would make himself offensive to the French. Short had sent an alarming report before the nomination, when Morris sought to give the impression that it was his for the asking, though Short did not think his words to that effect had made any particular impression. "But his aristocratical principles – his contempt of the French revolution and of the French nation expressed in all societies without reserve – and his dogmatising manner and assumed superiority has exposed him generally to ill will and often to ridicule. For some time he was a favorite among the aristocratic party, but even that is now worn off." [32] Jefferson had ample reason to give counsel in his official letter to the new Minister Plenipotentiary. With respect to the French government, he said, it was well to avoid the expression of private opinions which might offend any party. Should expressions be unavoidable, these would naturally be in conformity with the sentiments of the great mass of Americans, "who having first, in modern times, taken the ground of Government founded on the will of the

[30] Abstracts of the speeches of Roger Sherman, Monroe, and Burr against Morris are in King, *Life and Correspondence of Rufus King* (1894), I, 419–421, and are followed by the letters of Morris to King, Apr. 6, 1792, and King to Morris, Sept. 1, 1792 (421–423, 424–426). TJ's draft of a message for Washington, replying to the pending Senate resolution of Dec. 29 or 30, 1791 (*Senate Exec. Journal*, I, 93) is in Ford, V, 415; and his account of the conference with the committee, dated Jan. 4, 1792, is in Ford, I, 170–173.

[31] Jan. 16, 1792 (*Senate Exec. Jour.*, I, 97–98). The vote was 15 to 11 and both Monroe and Lee were against him.

[32] Short to TJ, Oct. 6, 1791 (LC, 10949); received Dec. 20.

people, cannot but be delighted on seeing so distinguished and so esteemed a Nation arrive on the same ground, and plant their standard by our side."[33]

The person who really read a lecture to Morris, however, was the President. He drafted a letter, which he sent to Jefferson for comments, and the Secretary suggested softening its expressions somewhat, "lest they should be too much felt," though his advice did not have much effect on Washington. The President told Morris with devastating frankness just what had been said in the Senate about his faults of manner and conduct and his hostility to the Revolution, and urged him to silence his critics by discretion.[34] Morris received these admonitions with good grace, when they finally reached him in the spring of 1792, and the supposition in high circles was that he would be more circumspect.[35] Jefferson was postponing such issues as there were between the United States and France at this stage, but he was beginning to be disturbed by the attitude of Washington toward the French Revolution and he tended to blame Morris for this. An episode which occurred in March may be cited by way of illustration.

Communication was so slow in those days that it was not until February that Ternant transmitted to the President a letter from the King, addressed to the United States and written in the previous September, in which he announced his acceptance of the new French Constitution. Washington submitted it to the Senate and House of Representatives for their information and the latter body passed a resolution which occasioned the President some embarrassment. Part of this resolution, which was passed with only two dissenting votes, expressed satisfaction with the action of the King and asked the President in his reply to express the "sincere participation" of the House "in the interests of the French nation, on this great and important event." The other part, which was agreed to by a vote of more than two to one, could be interpreted as an expression of approval of this French Constitution, as designed to promote the happiness of the people.[36] Washington's qualms arose from his apprehension that the legislature was invading the executive sphere, and from his reluctance

[33] TJ to Morris, Jan. 23, 1792 (Ford, V, 428).

[34] Washington to Morris, Jan. 28, 1792, with letter to TJ covering draft (Fitzpatrick, XXXI, 467–470); letter as edited by TJ (LC, 12153). Fitzpatrick's notes show the suggested changes.

[35] He first learned of his confirmation on Mar. 20, 1792, and wrote Washington next day, but the official letters did not reach him until Apr. 6. He wrote both TJ and Washington that day (*Diary*, II, 390, 399–400, 402–404).

[36] Washington transmitted the letter on Mar. 5, 1792, and the resolution was adopted Mar. 10 (*A.S.P.F.R.*, I, 133; *Annals of Cong.*, 2 Cong., 1 & 2 sess., pp. 100, 456–457).

to express a judgment on the French Constitution itself. In his own letter to the King of France, which Jefferson had drafted, the question of approbation had been scrupulously avoided. Jefferson also reassured him by saying that if this expression of the sentiment of the House was an invasion of executive prerogatives it was so faint a one that a public partial to the French Revolution could hardly be persuaded that it was objectionable.[37] At the same time he noted that Washington lacked confidence in the outcome of the French Revolution, though he still wanted it to succeed. "The fact is," Jefferson said, "that Gouverneur Morris, a high flying monarchy-man, . . . has kept the President's mind constantly poisoned with his forebodings." The tone of Morris's letters to Washington before he learned of his own appointment was unquestionably cynical and pessimistic. In one of them he had said that every day proved more clearly that the new Constitution was "good for nothing."[38]

It seemed to the French Minister at this time that the Revolution in his country was becoming an issue in American domestic politics. In his opinion the new Constitution of France provided for a greater degree of popular participation in the government in that country than in the United States, and for that reason many representatives, nearly all the senators, the President himself, and the chief executive officers feared any commendation of it. This would give to the "anti-federalist party an influence dangerous to public tranquility."[39] Ternant did not identify the Secretary of State with the latter party, thus testifying indirectly to Jefferson's circumspection. The lines were being formed, however. Among those who had manifested approval of the French Constitution were his friends Madison and Page, along with William Branch Giles and Nathaniel W. Macon; while such stalwart supporters of Hamilton as Fisher Ames, Theodore Sedgwick, and William Loughton Smith were ranged on the other side. Furthermore, he had no doubt that the friends of the French Revolution were in a large majority in the country as a whole, as they were in the more popular branch of Congress.

In terms of his own career the political implications were remote, for he had determined to retire from public life after another year. He informed William Short of his decision late in January in order that his young friend might govern himself accordingly. The information was strictly confidential and at this time had been given nobody

[37] Note of Mar. 12, 1792 (Ford, I, 187–189).

[38] Morris to Washington, Dec. 27, 1791 (*Diary*, II, 332–333). TJ's comment is in Ford, I, 188.

[39] Ternant to Lessart, Mar. 13, 1792 (*C.F.M.*, p. 95).

else but the President and Madison. Judging from the debate in the Senate, he doubted if Congress would support a representative at The Hague after a year and this was one reason why he was glad that Short was ordered on a special mission to Spain. The young diplomat might hope to distinguish himself there while his patron was still in office. Jefferson hoped that his former secretary would regard that mission as the most important of his life, and would meditate on it night and day. It grew directly from his own thoughts and labors, and he regarded it as supremely important to the interests of his country.[40]

[40] TJ to Short, Jan. 28, Mar. 18, 1792 (Ford, V, 435, 458–460).

[XXIV]

An American Champion Meets Disappointments

1792

FUNDAMENTAL in Jefferson's diplomatic policy was the determination that American commerce should flow down the Mississippi to the sea without fear of hindrance by any foreign power. The means that he employed to this end while Secretary of State and afterwards as President varied with circumstances, but his purpose never changed. The nation that held the mouth of the great river was regarded by him as a natural enemy of his own country, and it was also, to a greater degree than any other, the object of his cajolery and threats. He was never so fearful of Spanish possession of New Orleans and lower Louisiana as he had been, briefly, of British control, and was afterwards of French – because he perceived that the power of Spain was lessening, and believed that time would play into American hands. His immediate concern, therefore, was to secure a settlement of the questions of the southern boundary and the navigation of the mighty stream; and his willingness to play one country against another in order to do this had been clearly revealed in his actions during the Nootka Sound controversy, when for a time there was threat of war between Spain and Great Britain. That crisis ended before he could take advantage of it, but in the following year his alert mind seized upon an old Spanish incident which he had lately learned of, and he began to exploit this with skill, zeal, and daring. The uses he made of it show what a shrewd diplomat he was, and how bellicose he could be.

In the spring of 1791 he wrote these words to a resident of Kentucky: "The nail will be driven as far as it will go peaceably, and further the moment that circumstances become favorable." [1] Soon after this he informed William Carmichael, the chargé in Madrid, of the

[1] TJ to Harry Innes, Mar. 7, 1791 (Ford, V, 295).

flagrant case which had provided him with the opportunity he had been looking for. It was that of Joseph St. Marie, an American citizen, whose clerk and goods had been seized four years before by Spanish soldiers, acting under orders to seize all property on both sides of the Mississippi below the mouth of the Ohio. The offending officer claimed to have authority and instructions from the Governor of New Orleans, and the latter claimed in turn to have orders from the Spanish Court. Jefferson requested representations to the latter, looking toward the punishment of the offender and the indemnification of the injured American. More important still, he instructed Carmichael to urge upon the Court the necessity of a speedy acknowledgment of the American right to navigate the Mississippi, in order to avoid accidents which might make parleying impossible. After mentioning the "impatience" of the Westerners, he said: "Should any spark kindle these dispositions of our borderers into a flame, we are involved beyond recall by the eternal principles of justice to our citizens, which we will never abandon. In such an event, Spain cannot possibly gain, what may she not lose?" [2]

Not content with instructions to Carmichael, whom he regarded as lazy, he sent a copy of this letter and accompanying documents to Short in Paris, asking him to communicate them to Montmorin and seek his "efficacious interference." He wanted Lafayette to be informed as well, and again he used blustering language.[3] Lafayette and Montmorin, impressed by all this, recommended forcible American action, but Montmorin served a better purpose by transmitting the papers to Spain, where they created a great stir in official circles. Fearing revolution and distrusting the French at this stage, the Spanish Court decided to negotiate. By the autumn of 1791 Jefferson had learned that the Court was disposed to yield the navigation of the Mississippi and to enter into a treaty. Out of these circumstances, so skillfully exploited at an opportune time, arose his recommendation that another American representative in Europe be joined with Carmichael in Madrid on a special mission. His report to the President on negotiations with Spain was sent to the Senate along with the nominations of Carmichael and Short as commissioners, and these were approved after the latter had been confirmed as minister to The Hague.[4]

[2] TJ to Carmichael, Mar. 12, 1791 (Ford, V, 297–298).

[3] TJ to Short, Mar. 12, 1791 (Ford, V, 299–300). An admirable account of all this is given by S. F. Bemis in *Pinckney's Treaty* (1926), pp. 176–184.

[4] TJ's report, dated Dec. 22, 1791, was transmitted to the Senate by Washington on Jan. 11, 1792, and Carmichael and Short were confirmed on Jan. 24 (*Senate Executive Journal*, I, 95, 99). Ford prints the report (V, 407–408) from this source. It is also in *A.S.P.F.R.*, I, 251–252.

In his representations to the Spanish Jefferson often sounded like a swashbuckler, but at home he was scrupulously proper in his procedure as an official. Learning that the Court wanted the negotiations extended to commercial matters, he drafted another report, giving a detailed description of the sort of commercial treaty he thought practicable and desirable. Washington submitted this to the Senate and that body promptly consented to an extension of the powers of the commissioners and agreed in advance to ratify a treaty conforming to Jefferson's recommendations.[5] In all respects this was a model performance. The Secretary of State had submitted to the Secretary of the Treasury a draft of his full instructions to Carmichael and Short. His colleague suggested several minor alterations and he accepted nearly all of them. His final paper, presented to the President on March 18 in the form of a report, was approved by Washington, hence his instructions unquestionably expressed the official policy of the government. The same cannot be said of the famous financial proposals of Hamilton, who had followed no comparable procedure.[6]

A commercial treaty with Spain was a secondary and incidental matter in Jefferson's eyes, but he put much thought and labor on that subject, as he did also on a convention with the Spanish provinces for the return of fugitives from justice.[7] He wanted a full settlement if he could get one, and his specific proposals demonstrated his high technical competence. He did not regard Spain as yet ripe for an equal exchange on the basis of the privileges of native citizens, such as he wanted to offer France. He proposed that the treaty with them be on the basis of the most favored nation, and be modeled on the existing commercial treaty with France, certain articles being omitted or modified.

His major concern was to effect a settlement of the questions of the southern boundary and the navigation of the Mississippi, each of which

[5] TJ's report was submitted to the Senate, Mar. 7, 1792, and advice and consent were given on Mar. 16 (*Senate Exec. Jour.*, I, 106–110, 115); see also *A.S.P.F.R.*, I, 133–135. Ford prints the draft submitted to Washington (V, 441–449), but his notes on it are misleading. He describes it as a preliminary copy of the paper submitted in the form of a report on Mar. 18 (Ford, V, 460–481). Actually it dealt with commerce and, after minor changes, became the concluding and least important section of the final report, which dealt also with the questions of the southern boundary and the navigation of the Mississippi.

[6] Hamilton's notes with TJ's answers (Ford, V, 442–445*n.*) are understandable only if connected with TJ's full report of Mar. 18, 1792 (Ford, V, 460–481). For another text of the latter, see *A.S.P.F.R.*, I, 252–257. It was transmitted to Congress, with other papers relating to negotiations with Spain, on Dec. 16, 1793.

[7] Report and project of a convention, dated Mar. 22, 1792 (Ford, V, 481–487). The latter was sent to the two commissioners Apr. 24, 1792 (*A.S.P.F.R.*, I, 257–258).

he regarded as a *sine qua non* condition of the settlement as a whole. In his mind these constituted the real Spanish question. The importance he attached to this has sometimes been attributed to political motives, but there is certainly no need to assume that his representations were owing to his ambition for further and greater political preferment.[8] His interest in the Spanish question had antedated his secretaryship of state and his conflict with Hamilton, just as the similar interest of James Monroe and James Madison did. It was, in effect, the Western question; and he believed that the maintenance of the Union depended on a successful solution of it. In a sense, it was a sectional question, since most of the Western settlers had come from Southern states, and it bore directly on the advancement of the agricultural interest, as compared with the commercial interest that centered in the East. But in the fullest sense it was also national, and in this connection John Jay, who had been willing to barter the navigation of the Mississippi for Eastern commercial advantage, and Alexander Hamilton, who catered to small and relatively localized economic groups despite his nationalistic language, can be more correctly described as "sectionalists" than can Thomas Jefferson. In the large meaning of the term rather than the narrow, his motives were political. He did not try to settle this question because he hoped to be President, nor primarily because he was a Virginian, but because he was a fervidly patriotic American and sensed the vast future importance of the West.

The document he drew in this instance was not directed to the voters, nor even to the Senators, though they saw the commercial and least important part of it and had already approved his major purposes. It was addressed to the President and consisted of instructions and arguments for two relatively obscure American emissaries to a foreign court. It is not one of Jefferson's noblest papers, since it contains a large element of special pleading. In it the scholar was turned advocate. The Secretary of State made out the best case he could for the American contentions. Legally and philosophically he may have been on shaky ground, but his patriotism was unquestionable.

As to the Southern boundary, he regarded the American claim to the thirty-first parallel as incontestable, though modern American scholars have often thought otherwise. He based his argument on the pre-revolutionary boundaries of Georgia as set by the English King, and the treaty with Great Britain at the end of the war, ceding her territories to the thirty-first parallel. He disregarded the fact that Great Britain did not then hold either East or West Florida. The Spanish,

[8] S. F. Bemis, in *American Secretaries of State,* II, 45–46, citing Ford, V, 460–461*n.*

who did hold them, claimed that the latter province extended to the mouth of the Yazoo River, drawing the line as the British themselves had done during practically the whole of the time they held it.[9]

His argument supporting the American contention about the free navigation of the Mississippi was also weakened by its reliance on British treaties, but he believed that American "right" was built on broader and firmer ground, namely, the law of nature and nations. In appealing to the law of nature, as "written in the heart of man," he displayed deep emotion without showing much precision in the use of terms. The sentiment "that the ocean is free to all men, and their rivers to all their inhabitants," he regarded as practically universal. Continuing, he said: "When their rivers enter the limits of another society, if the right of the upper inhabitants to descend the stream is in any case obstructed, it is an act of force by a stronger society against a weaker, condemned by the judgment of mankind."[10] He cited the late case of Antwerp and the Scheldt and suggested that the members of the mission examine carefully what was written on that occasion. The sentiment in favor of the upper inhabitants was all the stronger because of the vast extent of habitable American territory on the Mississippi and its tributaries, compared with the smaller and much less habitable territory of the Spanish at the mouth of the river. The passage of the Western products down the stream which was their only outlet was of no injury to the Spanish, and would in fact enrich them. Thus he concluded: "The real interests then of all the inhabitants, upper and lower, concur in fact with their rights."

He based his argument at last on the solid ground of interest, which was absolutely vital on the American side, and admitted that rights, though real, were imperfect until recognized by the Spanish. He cited numerous authorities on international law, but the little drawing of the winding channel of the Mississippi which he inserted is more arresting. By means of this he showed that the river must be free through its whole breadth in order to be really navigable, just as it must be free throughout its entire length in order to meet American necessities. He appeared in this paper as an advocate of liberal rather than strict construction of treaties. Hamilton may have been surprised and no doubt was pleased to read the following: "It is a principle that the right to a thing gives a right to the means without which it could not be used, that is to say, that the means follow their end."[11] He was not talking about the American Constitution, to be sure, but

[9] Bemis, *Pinckney's Treaty*, pp. 48–50; *American Secretaries of State*, II, 47–48.
[10] *A.S.P.F.R.*, I, 253.
[11] *Ibid.*, I, 254.

he was using the language of common sense when he spoke of incidental riparian rights and the necessity for an *entrêpot* toward the mouth of the river. He really wanted New Orleans and later events proved that he could not rest content until he got it, but he now recommended a landing place below that city and even suggested a precise spot. He had made a careful study of maps as well as recondite treatises and was determined that vital American interests should be provided for.

Under modern conditions of communication and transportation his patriotic *tour de force* might have proved successful. He had skillfully seized upon a favorable opportunity and had marshaled arguments which might have been effective at a time when the Spanish feared an American *rapprochement* with Great Britain and were aware of the increasing number and restlessness of the "men of the western waters." But time was the essence of the problem. Jefferson told Short that the mission must be completed before his own retirement and a possible change in the administration.[12] He expected Short to reach Madrid in May, but his own letters were so delayed that his young friend reproached him for not writing oftener and showing more signs of friendship. Short did not leave Paris until May 15, 1792, and then he went to The Hague. It was not until February 1, 1793, that he got to Madrid, and by that time the whole international scene had so changed that the Spanish were in no mood for negotiation. Hence the American mission kicked its heels for months in the antechambers of the Court. Toward the very end of his secretaryship, Jefferson sought to press matters by protesting against the Spanish Indian policy in the Southwest, in the light of recent developments, but his efforts were in vain. The settlement of the Spanish question along the lines that he had laid down was postponed until he himself was out of the government, and the credit for it went to another Secretary of State and another emissary.[13] William Short suffered more frustration than Jefferson, for in the course of time the latter was able to take up the Western question again and to contribute dramatically to its ultimate solution, by acquiring Louisiana. He was a major architect of American expansion beyond a doubt, but as Secretary of State he was baffled in his heroic efforts to serve the "men of the western waters." He was defeated in this instance by circumstances – not by his colleague Hamilton.

* * *

[12] TJ to Short, Mar. 18, 1792 (Ford, V, 458–460).

[13] The circumstances leading to the Treaty of San Lorenzo in 1795 are fully and admirably described by Bemis in *Pinckney's Treaty*.

The negotiations with Hammond, which were resumed about the time that instructions were being drawn for the commissioners to Spain, were another matter. By forcing Hammond to admit that he had no authority to negotiate a treaty of commerce, Jefferson had narrowed the discussion to the infractions of the treaty of peace. He had opened the debate in December, but Hammond took more than three months to reply, alleging that the necessity of collecting materials had occasioned the delay.[14] Possibly this was true, though procrastination was the approved method of his mission. Phineas Bond, the British consul in Philadelphia, had industriously collected documents for him, and Hammond was greatly pleased with his paper. He wrote home: "I flatter myself . . . that this statement will be found . . . to contain a body of proof so complete and substantial as to preclude the possibility of cavil and contradiction on the part of this government."[15] He was much too self-satisfied, and greatly underestimated his opponent. He set out to prove American violations of the fourth, fifth, and sixth articles of the treaty, by which the United States had agreed that creditors should meet no lawful impediment to the recovery of debts previously contracted, that Congress should recommend to the states that provisions be made for the restitution of the confiscated property of British subjects and Loyalists, and that no future confiscations should be made or prosecutions commenced against persons of these descriptions. He had collected, by title at least, about a hundred legislative acts and cases, which he listed in five appendices. He supposed that these fully supported the arguments he advanced in the text, though actually they were not tied closely with them, and he asserted that the King had suspended full execution of Article VII because of previous American infractions of the treaty, thus emphasizing the order of events and laying himself open to disproof and contradiction.

Jefferson's reply to Hammond's statement was the greatest paper he drew as Secretary of State in the opinion of competent authority, but the diplomatic duel which the two men engaged in has also been described as an unpleasant and wholly futile "game of recrimination."[16]

[14] TJ to Hammond, Dec. 15, 1791 (*A.S.P.F.R.*, I, 190); Hammond to TJ, Mar. 5, 1792 (*ibid.*, I, 193–198) with appendices, pp. 198–200.

[15] Hammond to Grenville, Mar. 6, 1792 (*I.B.M.*, p. 27*n.*).

[16] The former opinion, to which I adhere, is that of Bemis (*American Secretaries of State*, II, 44–45), who has described the debate more fully than any other writer in *Jay's Treaty*, ch. V. The latter judgment is that of A. L. Burt, in *The U. S., Great Britain, and British North America* (1940), p. 121, who gives the impression that this "strenuous controversy" was going on at just the time that Hammond, out of regard for American sensibilities, was holding back on British proposals to couple the execution of Article VII of the treaty with the establish-

Obviously, each man was trying to excuse his own country by accusing the other, and it is possible to argue that there was no causal relationship between one set of violations and the other. But Hammond claimed that there was such a relationship, and if Jefferson as an official was disposed to minimize the failings of his countrymen, he was personally aware of their difficulties as debtors. Furthermore, nothing that they had done, and certainly no action of the federal government, seemed to him remotely comparable with the retention of the posts by the British. The sinister implications of British policy were borne home forcefully that spring by the situation with respect to the Indians, who had disastrously defeated General St. Clair and who had received gifts of arms if not encouragement from British sources.[17] It would have been strange indeed if Jefferson had not tried to get the British to surrender the posts in any way he could. Realizing that more than argument was needed, he had wanted to use the weapon of commercial discrimination. He held up his recommendation of that, however, recognizing the weight of Hamilton's contention that it might endanger the negotiations with Hammond, and agreeing that the possession of the posts was much the most important issue.[18]

He was aware that the Britisher was in close and regular communication with his colleague, and shy of Jefferson himself. About this time he got the report of a comment from Hammond on this point. It was made to a Senator friendly to Jefferson, who had sounded out the envoy. The latter said: "The Secretary of the Treasury is more a man of the world than Jefferson and I like his manners better, and can speak more freely to him. Jefferson is in the Virginia interest and that of the French. And it is his fault that we are at a distance. He prefers writing to conversing and thus it is that we are apart." [19] Probably he did prefer writing, partly because he was better at it, partly because he liked to put things definitely on record. At all events, he saw in Hammond's statement of the British case something that needed answering and that he could answer.

He took great pains about it, collecting materials from many quar-

---

ment of an Indian barrier state. Actually, these proposals, communicated to Hammond in a letter of Mar. 17, 1792, from Grenville (*I.B.M.*, pp. 25–27), had not yet reached him when he presented his paper to Jefferson and the latter had no reason to suspect forbearance on his part when, not unnaturally, he answered it.

[17] See TJ's report of a consultation of the President and department heads, Mar. 9, 1792 (Ford, I, 179–183).

[18] Note in Anas, Mar. 11, 1792 (Ford, I, 186–187).

[19] Report of a conversation between Gen. [Philemon] Dickinson [Senator from New Jersey] and Hammond, transmitted to TJ by Benj. Hawkins, about Mar. 26, 1792 (LC, 12575–12576). According to Dickinson, Hammond said he had "full and ample powers."

ters, especially the Southern states, which had been particularly complained of, and examining the legislative acts and legal cases with care. Unlike Hammond, he did not content himself with drawing up a list.[20] The materials on which he based his letter to Hammond may still be seen in his papers. These consist of outlines, rough notes, beautiful tables showing state acts on the questions of debt, and numerous other documents.[21] A close examination of them would tax the industry and patience of any scholar, and they attest the extraordinary thoroughness of his procedure.

He was equally careful about the paper he drafted from these materials. He submitted it to Madison, who made some corrections, then to Attorney General Randolph, and then to Hamilton. The Secretary of the Treasury was of the opinion that much strong ground had been taken and strongly maintained, but expressed some doubts. Certain suggestions of his, including the omission of one considerable section, were accepted by Jefferson. His most important objection, however, was not acceptable. This related to the degree of justification of certain states with respect to the debts, Hamilton favoring extenuation rather than vindication. Jefferson referred the conflict of opinion on this point, and another of less importance, to Washington, along with the document as a whole. The President approved it just as it stood, particularly the article on debts. Thus the paper, prepared from extensive materials and submitted to his chief colleagues in advance, had full official sanction and, with only one exception of any importance, appeared to have Hamilton's full approval.[22]

The starting point of Jefferson's argument was the end of the war. He set this at the date April 11, 1783, when Congress received an official copy of the provisional articles of peace from Franklin. Accepting the good advice of Hamilton, he omitted a long and fervid passage which had been inspired by Hammond's extended reference to legislative actions against Loyalists and in behalf of debtors during the

[20] As an example of his procedure, his letter of inquiry of Apr. 11, 1792, to Southern senators and representatives may be mentioned (LC, 12660–12661). In this he reported the allegation of Hammond that in some of the Southern states there had been no single instance of recovery of a British debt in their courts.

[21] LC, 16750ff.; also 453, 574, 1136.

[22] The draft which TJ submitted to Hamilton is in Ford, VI, 7–69, with Hamilton's notes and TJ's comments on them. As transmitted to Hammond on May 29, 1792, with 60 appendices, it is in *A.S.P.F.R.*, I, 201–237. The draft was ready before the middle of May, but submission to Madison, Randolph, and Hamilton delayed it. See TJ to Washington, May 16, 1792 (Ford, V, 514); TJ to Madison, June 1, 1792 (Ford, VI, 69). Hamilton's notes are in Lodge, IV, 60–64; and TJ's comments on them, wrongly dated, are in J. C. Hamilton, IV, 144–145.

Revolution. Originally he had described in considerable detail the legislative warfare which, he claimed, Parliament began and had waged against entire towns and provinces without discrimination of persons, but he wisely decided to omit this detailed countercharge and content himself with a general statement. He disposed of Hammond's numerous complaints about American actions *during* the war much more effectively by dismissing them as irrelevant. The acts previous to the chosen date which he thus got rid of comprised about half of those that Hammond had listed. Jefferson extracted and assembled the titles and neatly deposited them in an appendix. Hamilton had demurred against this wholesale elimination, but all he really suggested was that the date be set back a little.[23] The difference was merely one of detail, and he did not contest his colleague's major assumption that this was a discussion of alleged infractions of the peace treaty, not of the conduct or issues of the war.

Having skillfully narrowed the field and cleared the ground, Jefferson took up the question of the treatment of the Loyalists. The right to seize enemy property in time of war seemed to him undeniable, but the American government had made certain promises in the treaty of peace about the restitution of confiscated property and had been accused of not keeping them. The gist of his argument on this point was that Congress had *recommended* to the various state legislatures that they take action, which was all Congress had promised to do, all it could do, all that the British negotiators and Ministry and Parliament understood that they would do. He cited and quoted documents to prove his case, stated precisely what Congress had done, and described one by one the state acts which Hammond had listed in this connection. The states were free to pass these acts, he said, regardless of the recommendation of Congress. They had also been objected to as infractions of the article in the treaty which forbade future confiscations, but Hammond had been careless in this matter. Jefferson pointed out that none of them related to an estate that had not been confiscated during the war, and he believed that "there was not a single confiscation made in any one of the United States, after notification of the treaty." On the whole, he concluded that more states had complied with the recommendations of Congress and in greater degree than was generally expected.[24]

Having disposed of the Loyalist question in masterly fashion, he

[23] Hamilton's second objection (Ford, VI, 8*n*.), one of the two which TJ did not yield to.

[24] The Loyalist question is treated in Sections 4–25 of his letter, and in the recapitulation in Sect. 56. Quotation from Sect. 23.

turned to the more difficult question of the debts. In order to put American proceedings "on their true grounds," he took a view of British proceedings which seemed to justify them. Here he availed himself of the opportunity which Hammond had presented when he had unwisely claimed that British failure to carry Article VII into effect was owing to the *previous* infraction of the treaty by the Americans. Jefferson did not miss this chance to discuss the retention of the posts and the removal of American slave property, though the latter was relatively unimportant. By careful study of dates and documents and shrewd inference he reached conclusions which are in close accord with the findings of modern scholars who have had access to British records. The slaves were carried away after the terms of the treaty were plainly known and in clear defiance of it. The action, which the British commander of the time admitted, was palliated on moral grounds, but Americans were deprived of cultivators of the soil, the produce of which was to pay the debts. He was far more damning on the subject of the posts, most of which could have been given up without delay. But, far from their being evacuated "with all convenient speed," according to the treaty, no order with respect to them had been received. Thus he rightly concluded that no order had ever been *given* and that none had ever been *intended*. In this case, therefore, British infraction dated from the signature of the treaty, or at least from April, 1783, when the order for evacuating New York was given. This infraction with respect to the posts was highly injurious, he said, "by depriving us of our fur trade, profitable in itself, and valuable as a means of remittance for paying the debts"; and "by intercepting our friendly and neighborly intercourse with the Indian nations, and consequently keeping us in constant, expensive, and barbarous war with them." [25]

From the facts known to him Jefferson shrewdly surmised and correctly concluded that "the treaty was violated in England, before it was known in America, and in America [by the British] as soon as it was known, and that too, in points so essential, as that, without them, it would never have been concluded." [26]

The weakest point in his argument lay in his attempt to establish a causal connection between British infraction of the treaty, which is incontestable, and later American actions with respect to the debts. Given the economic circumstances, some of these actions would probably have been taken anyway, and Hamilton preferred to palliate

[25] Quotation from recapitulation in Sect. 56. See also more extended treatment in Sects. 26–28.

[26] Sect. 28.

rather than justify them. Jefferson's own comments in private letters show that he had scant respect for any person who did not make every possible provision for his debts, as he himself had done, but he was undoubtedly correct in saying that British policy had had real effect on the American mind. He was not content, however, with a reference to psychology; he found sanction in law. "On the breach of any article of a treaty by the one party," he said, "the other has its election to declare it dissolved in all its articles, or to compensate itself by withholding execution of equivalent articles; or to waive notice of the breach altogether." [27] He mentioned some specific American protests, and described in detail the actions of various states with respect to the debts. Anyone who may wish to investigate this complicated subject will find in his letter a rich and convenient source. He regarded these actions, on the whole, as moderate and did not believe that these states could be charged with doing wrong in retarding in this mild degree the execution of parts of the treaty, as an equivalent to what the British had previously refused to fulfill. His presentation of the legal and moral case did not quite convince Hamilton, but it satisfied George Washington, as it had James Madison, and he let it stand.[28]

His treatment of the debt question itself was elaborately detailed, but it need not long detain us. He found that four states had modified the recovery of debts by indulging their citizens in various ways, most of the measures being moderate and of short duration. He showed that Congress had asked a formal repeal of every act of that nature, while pointing out that this requirement was really unnecessary, since treaties controlled the laws of the states and the courts were open. His treatment of the question of interest specially impressed Hamilton. He argued that this was not covered by the provisions of the treaty but was a matter for the courts. These had generally decided against it, for the period of the war at least, and their reasons seemed cogent, but there was room for honest difference of opinion on this point, and the ground for withholding execution of the treaty on this account was entirely insufficient.[29]

In this powerful state paper Jefferson took full advantage of the strong American case and Hammond's weak presentation of that of the British. It is hard to see how he could have failed to receive a favorable verdict from any intelligent and reasonably impartial jury,

[27] Sect. 29.

[28] Hamilton's 3rd objection and TJ's reply (Ford, VI, 8–9*n.*); TJ to Madison, June 1, 1792 (Ford, VI, 69).

[29] See especially the recapitulation in Sect. 36.

and in this case he can appear with confidence at the bar of history, but his magnificent presentation of his country's cause was wholly unproductive of results at the time. In Jefferson's last month as Secretary of State, Washington communicated this paper to Congress, along with other important ones dealing with relations with France and Great Britain, but at the moment it was merely delivered to Hammond.[30] The young Englishman acknowledged it promptly enough but made no attempt to answer it. The matter in it was so various and extensive that he could not be expected to do that immediately, he said, frankly admitting that reference to his own country was necessary. Furthermore, the difference between him and Jefferson in the statement of "positive facts" was so great, that he must recur to his own sources for corroborating testimony.[31] After receiving this acknowledgment, Jefferson sought Hammond out, had him for dinner alone, and tried to talk things over in a friendly way. Washington did not have very high hopes of this conference, and actually it accomplished nothing except to verify Jefferson's impressions about Hammond's instructions and to raise new fears — with regard to British designs to redraw the northwestern boundary, so as to give them access to the Mississippi.[32] The French Minister noted that month that private interviews between the Secretary of State and Hammond had been very frequent of late, but found himself quite unable to find out what was going on. Jefferson "enveloped himself in commonplaces" and was much more reserved than Ternant thought fitting. The latter even got the impression that the prospects of a commercial treaty between the United States and Great Britain were more hopeful, thus showing that the Secretary of State was exceedingly wary and discreet in dealing with the representative of allied France.[33]

The conduct of the Secretary of the Treasury toward Hammond was very different, as the latter's communications with his own home office showed. Sending Jefferson's letter to Grenville, Hammond described it as an acrimonious paper, full of irrelevant matter and unjustifiable insinuations. He had not said that in his conference with Jefferson, who gained some impression that Hammond was glad that the British Ministry would now be fully informed of the American

[30] Submitted to Congress in a message dated Dec. 5, 1793 (*A.S.P.F.R.*, I, 141–142).

[31] Hammond to TJ, June 2, 1792 (*ibid.*, I, 237).

[32] Washington to TJ, June 2, 1792 (Fitzpatrick, XXXII, 51); TJ's Notes of conversation, June 3, 1792 (Ford, I, 193–198); TJ to Madison, June 4, 1792 (Ford, VI, 71–72).

[33] Ternant to Minister of Foreign Affairs, June 15, 1792 (*C.F.M.*, p. 129); Ternant to Dumourier, June 20. 1792 (*C.F.M.*, p. 133).

position. The idea that the British had committed the first infraction of the treaty would be a new one to them, he said. Obviously he was startled by the force of Jefferson's counterattack, and under these circumstances it was a comfort to him to talk freely with Hamilton about this "extraordinary performance." He reported confidentially to his home government that Hamilton lamented the "intemperate violence" of his colleague, and assured him that Jefferson's letter by no means met his own approbation or truly represented the views of the administration. He claimed that Washington had not read it, but had merely taken it at Jefferson's word.[34] In view of the fact that Hamilton himself had read the paper and approved most of it, and that his objections had been presented to Washington and overruled, his remarks to Hammond constitute an "extraordinary performance" if anything that happened in high official circles in the United States ever did. If either Washington or Jefferson had known about them there would have been a memorable scene.

Phineas Bond went to England with Jefferson's letter, and during the summer he was given the task of examining it and reporting on it in detail. While his work was pending, the British withheld a reply, and they kept on withholding it. A year after Hammond's acknowledgment, Jefferson inquired of him why there had been no answer, and he made a similar inquiry five months later, when he was nearing the end of his own term of office.[35]

One reason why the British pigeonholed his magnificent paper was that the state of the world changed greatly in the months after they got it, and new problems pushed old ones into the background. Another reason must have been that the assurances of Hamilton, as relayed by Hammond, convinced them that they could safely ignore it. One would have to search far in American history to find a more flagrant example of interference by one high officer of the government with the policy of another which was clearly official policy, and the attempt to defeat it by secret intrigue with the representative of another country. By the summer of 1792 Jefferson did not yet realize that his negotiations were futile, though he had an inkling. He did not fully know, though he suspected, why his greatest labors were in vain.

[34] Hammond to Grenville, June 8, 1792 (Bemis, *Jay's Treaty*, pp. 106–107; *I.B.M.*, p. 30*n.*).

[35] Bond's observations on TJ's paper, dated Oct. 12, 1792, are in *A.H.A. Report . . . 1897* (1898), pp. 500–523. TJ wrote Hammond June 19 and Nov. 13, 1793 (*A.S.P.F.R.*, I, 238).

[XXV]

The Beginnings of Party Struggle

1791–1792

HAMILTON'S intrigue with George Hammond need not be explained in terms of current domestic controversy, since it marked the culmination of efforts to circumvent the foreign policy of his colleague which began during Jefferson's first year in office. Nevertheless, the conflicts between the two men on both the foreign and domestic fronts came to a climax almost simultaneously, and this cannot be regarded as a mere coincidence. The most notable political development of the winter and spring of 1792 was the rise of what Hamilton contemptuously termed a "faction," and he was soon blaming Jefferson for it. The first number of the *National Gazette*, edited by Philip Freneau whom some of the Hamiltonians called a "poetaster," had appeared on October 31, 1791, the week after the opening of Congress. Historians have generally described this as an opposition paper, and have frequently said that its establishment marked the beginning of a party.[1]

Before inquiring into Jefferson's personal relations with the enterprise, we should point out that the terms "party" and "opposition," which are so commonly employed in this connection, are misnomers if used in the full modern sense. Jefferson himself had long been talking about "republican" principles, and within a few months of the appearance of the *National Gazette* he was speaking of the "republican party." His failure to capitalize the adjective may perhaps be attributed to his penchant for the lower case, but he was certainly not referring to a formal organization. The expression "republican interest" was more commonly used, at first, by those who identified themselves with it; and this better reflects the actualities of the early situation, partly

[1] See, for example, J. B. McMaster, *History of the People of the United States*, II (1885), 49.

because of its very vagueness. Jefferson resented Hamilton's designation of the republican group as a "faction" because of the connotation of pettiness. He tended to divide political men into two major groups, describing them as "tories" and "whigs," or "monarchists" and "republicans." But the battles of this time were between rival groups rather than rival organizations, and there was great emphasis on ideas and policies, as the case has been more often in the beginnings than in the maturity of American parties.

The use of the term "opposition," in its modern sense, also tends to create a false impression of this situation. The federal administration had unity only in that it centered in the person of George Washington. Until this time there were few policies, if indeed there were any, which had been worked out by him and all his ministers in conference, and which could thus be said to represent a common judgment.[2] Furthermore, the President scrupulously kept himself aloof from Congress and can hardly be said to have had a legislative policy beyond that of maintaining executive prerogatives. What "opposition" there was to the "government" was not directed against Washington, except in exceedingly small degree; nor was it to the Constitution, except in rare cases. Some people continued to sputter against the forms and ceremonies of which John Adams had become the unhappy symbol, and these continued to provide talking points; but the main objection was to the policies that had been initiated and carried through by Hamilton, and to the ideas he represented. His followers always tried to identify the government with him, but he was considerably less than the government even at the height of his prestige and power. Furthermore, he was not warranted at this stage in interpreting the growing desire to check him as a threat to overthrow the financial structure he had set up.

Washington expected no unanimity of opinion among his counselors, but he assumed that they would acquiesce in what had been done with his sanction in both the domestic and foreign fields, or at least not attack it openly. Jefferson, who was intensely loyal to the President and still stood in some awe of him, was fully conscious of this assumption and had tried to live up to it. He had expressed his growing disapproval of Hamilton's "system" in some private letters, as the record shows, and in private conversation with friends, as he admitted. How far he went in talk it is impossible to say. From his temperament and

[2] Particular reference is made here to the situation in the autumn of 1791. Conferences became more frequent as time went on, but these were generally occasioned by conditions of national danger. For example, the administration as a whole considered difficulties arising from the Indian war and, later, the war in Europe.

manners he could have been expected to be discreet and proper. Furthermore, his political friends were chiefly Virginians and so did not need to be argued into an anti-Hamiltonian position. None of them excelled Jefferson if any of them equaled him in zeal for human rights, but there were those who disapproved of the financial policies sooner than he did and were more ardent than he in championing the particular interests of their state.

From the assumption question onward, the trend of opinion among the political leaders of Virginia had been strongly against Hamilton on both practical and ideological grounds, and there were very few of them who went with him all the way.[3] Patrick Henry, who had been an antifederalist in the older meaning of the term, was the bellwether of the opposition to Hamilton's program at first, but, besides Madison, staunch supporters of his in the ratification fight, like Pendleton and Wythe and George and Wilson Cary Nicholas, identified themselves with the "republican interest" before long; and earlier antifederalists like George Mason and Monroe restored amicable relations with Madison, who had become fearful of Hamilton's brand of nationalism. In the summer of 1791, after he had received a copy of Paine's *Rights of Man* from Jefferson, Monroe wrote him: "Upon political subjects we perfectly agree, and particularly in the reprobation of all measures that may be calculated to elevate the government above the people, or to place it in any respect without its natural boundary. . . . The bulk of the people are for democracy, and if they are well informed the risk of such [undemocratic] enterprises will infallibly follow."[4] Monroe set the highest value on the older man's friendship, but this Virginian movement was anti-Hamiltonian rather than pro-Jeffersonian.

Both before and after his trip to Lake George with the Secretary of State, Madison was in New York, reading the political horoscope and talking with individuals. The later designation of him by the Hamiltonians as "General," and of Jefferson as "Generalissimo," does not reflect the actualities of their relationship at this juncture.[5] Madison was a sincere defender of human rights, as his record clearly showed, but he was less fervid in this respect than Jefferson and no

[3] Two unpublished doctoral dissertations have been most helpful in this connection: David K. McCarrell, "The Formation of the Jeffersonian Party in Virginia" (Duke University, 1937); and Harry Ammon, "The Republican Party in Virginia, 1789 to 1824" (Univ. of Va., 1948).

[4] Monroe to TJ, June 17, 1791 (S. M. Hamilton, I, 223-224).

[5] Their relations are well described by Brant in *Madison*, III, ch. XXVII, though, in my opinion, he gives a less favorable impression of TJ's prudence than the facts warrant, chiefly because he does not put it in its full official setting.

doubt he was warmed by the greater ardor of his friend. On the other hand, there is no more reason to suppose that Jefferson dictated either Madison's political strategy or his tactics than that Madison dictated Jefferson's. If anybody "organized" the "opposition" at this stage it was Madison, and it was certainly he who did most to induce his old Princeton friend Freneau to set up a newspaper in Philadelphia. His efforts were far from secret to Jefferson, but, for a variety of reasons, the Secretary of State made a special point of keeping his skirts clean, and there is good reason to believe that his own negotiations with the journalist were carefully confined to official matters.

Philip Freneau, whom Madison had vied with but not equaled as a writer of satirical verse when they were fellow students at Princeton, was a seafaring man who had served and suffered during the American Revolution and come to be known as the poet of that struggle.[6] He was connected with the *Daily Advertiser* while the government was in New York, and Jefferson had then been asked if there was any place for him in the Department of State. There was none, but Freneau, who married about this time, was in financial difficulties and his friends interested themselves in his behalf after the government moved to Philadelphia. At the suggestion of "Light-Horse Harry" Lee, who had also known and liked him in college, Madison again called him to Jefferson's attention. There was then a vacancy, since the translator of the Department, John Pintard, who was also connected with the *Daily Advertiser*, had declined to move to the new capital and that sort of place was hard to fill. Jefferson promptly offered it to Freneau by letter, apologizing for the small salary of 250 dollars but saying that the work was so slight that it would not interfere with other occupation at the seat of government.[7] This was on the last day of February, 1791, the week before the adjournment of Congress.

The presumption must have been that the other and more remunerative work would be on some newspaper, since Freneau could hardly have been expected to support himself by writing poetry, and the establishment of a new paper in Philadelphia must have been suggested by Madison or Lee to Freneau by then. Jefferson's later state-

[6] Because of the controversial nature of the Freneau episode, the literature on it is extensive. The most important general treatments are Lewis Leary, *That Rascal Freneau* (1941), an admirable biography and literary study, and an older but still useful work, S. E. Forman, *The Political Activities of Philip Freneau* (1902). Philip Marsh has written numerous helpful articles on the subject, and reference will be made to some of these hereafter.

[7] TJ to Freneau, Feb. 28, 1791 (LC, 10617).

ment to Washington, that he could not remember whether this possibility was mentioned to him personally at this time or soon afterwards, sounds equivocal, and even if literally true it was unnecessary since he admitted that he liked the idea from the moment that he did first hear of it. This may be cited as another case where his excessive regard for official proprieties and extreme sensitivity in the face of possible criticism caused him to protest more than the circumstances required. At all events, Freneau promptly declined the offer of the translator's post on the ground of previous commitments, and the report soon got out that the "Pindar of America," who had just prepared for the press another volume of his writings, expected to set up a paper in his home town in New Jersey. Madison saw him in New York, however, and by May was seeking him out to dissuade him from burying his talents in rural obscurity, arguing that Philadelphia offered him superior opportunities.[8]

Madison afterwards said that his primary motive in advising Freneau was to advance the latter's interests, but in private he admitted that he had another motive, in which he actually took pride. He hoped that an independent and popular paper, edited by a man of genius and a friend of the Constitution, would serve as an antidote to the monarchical and aristocratic doctrines then being circulated.[9] He was as confident of his old friend's journalistic abilities as he was of his character and political principles. He wrote Jefferson from New York that Freneau was without a rival in the whole catalogue of American printers. He also thought him well fitted for the minor post of translator in the Department of State, which was still open, and expected him to see and talk with Jefferson about it on a visit to Philadelphia, but Freneau changed his mind about going, much to Jefferson's regret. Apparently the Secretary had played no direct part in the attempt to persuade Freneau to set up his paper at the seat of government, and he may have mentioned it only to his son-in-law, but he now identified himself with it in spirit.[10]

Philadelphia did not then lack papers that were "republican" in their principles. Jefferson regarded John Fenno's *Gazette of the United States,* which enjoyed the patronage of the Treasury, as "a paper of pure Toryism, disseminating the doctrines of monarchy, aristocracy, and the exclusion of the influence of the people." Among the other

[8] TJ to Washington, Sept. 9, 1792 (Ford, VI, 106–108); Freneau to TJ, Mar. 5, 1791 (LC, 10650); *Gazette of the U. S.* (Philadelphia), Apr. 27, 1791; Madison to TJ, May 1, 1791 (Hunt, VI, 46–47*n.*).

[9] Madison to Edmund Randolph, Sept 13, 1792 (Hunt, VI, 117*n.*).

[10] TJ to Madison, May 9, 1791 (Ford, V, 330); TJ to T. M. Randolph, Jr., May 15, 1791 (Ford, V, 336–337).

papers, however, were *Dunlap's American Daily Advertiser*, in which many communications favorable to the republican cause afterwards appeared, and the *General Advertiser* (later the *Aurora*), edited by Benjamin Franklin Bache, grandson of Poor Richard, whose political principles Jefferson liked. Both of these papers, however, were dailies and included advertising, and, under existing law and custom, they did not circulate readily through the ordinary mails. What he wanted was a "whig vehicle of intelligence," to be a rival to Fenno's semi-weekly edition for the country. He was thinking in national terms, except possibly for Virginia, and he also wanted to increase the scope of the intelligence, being specially anxious to make the materials from the foreign papers, which came to his office, available in translation. Freneau, who would combine the functions of translator and printer, promised to be a more effective dispenser of foreign news than Fenno or Bache.[11]

When Jefferson went to New York soon after the middle of May to join Madison, he met Freneau at the breakfast table in Mrs. Elsworth's boarding house, but apparently he did not talk with him at that time except in public.[12] In the middle of the summer, after he had returned to Philadelphia, he learned from Madison that Freneau had given up the idea of a paper in that place, for reasons Madison himself was unable to determine, "unless those who know his talents and hate his political principles should have practiced some artifice for the purpose." Jefferson's comments on this unwelcome turn of events showed what he himself would have been willing to do to help Freneau. "I should have given him the perusal of all my letters of foreign intelligence and all foreign newspapers; the publication of all proclamations and other public notices within my department, and the printing of the laws, which added to his salary would have been a considerable aid." [13] The shop connected with Freneau's paper got a considerable share of Jefferson's departmental printing after he finally came to Philadelphia, but it was not through Jefferson's agency that the journalist solved his fundamental financial problem.[14]

[11] He discussed this matter at some length in his letter of Sept. 9, 1792, to Washington. (Ford, VI, 106.)

[12] Ford, VI, 107; Account Book, May 20, 21, 1791.

[13] TJ to Madison, July 21, 1791 (LC, 11314), replying to Madison's letter of July 10 (Hunt, VI, 55).

[14] During 1791–1792 Andrew Brown, publisher of the *Federal Gazette*, got some of this printing, and Hamilton claimed that Brown was increasingly hostile to him for just that reason (Hamilton to Carrington, May 26, 1792, in Lodge, VIII, 253). On Dec. 6, 1791, Brown wrote TJ and thanked him for his patronage (MHS). For a partisan statement of what Freneau's office got, see the communication by CANDOR, in *Gazette of the U. S.*, Aug. 18, 1792. This probably meant little to Freneau personally.

The crucial question was answered in August when Francis Childs, publisher of the *Daily Advertiser*, and his partner John Swaine assumed the expense and risk of the undertaking. Freneau was relieved of financial responsibility but he did not barter away his personal independence. Madison made a highly significant comment on the arrangement in a letter to Jefferson: "In the conduct and title of the paper it will be altogether his own." The tone of the paper that Childs was conducting in New York was agreeable to Hamilton, but the tone of this one was to be set, not by Childs or Madison or Jefferson, but by Freneau himself. He wanted to show Jefferson a copy of the prospectus before printing it, and presumably he did. As advertised in advance in other papers, the *National Gazette* was to be a "Periodical Miscellany of News, Politics, History, and Polite Literature." Because of its editor's reputation it might have been expected to be more literary than its competitors, and its republicanism was assured by his political principles. Events proved that Philip Freneau, besides being the most gifted journalist of his day and a man of notably independent character, was a more extreme republican than Thomas Jefferson, who was generally willing to make some concessions to the exigencies of circumstance, and never ceased to recognize the responsibilities of high office.[15]

Financial arrangements having been completed, Madison gave what aid he could to Childs in the solicitation of subscriptions, a matter in which Lee, Jefferson, and others co-operated at one time or another. The most important immediate act of the Secretary of State, however, was the formal appointment of Freneau as clerk for foreign languages in mid-August. The new translator took the oath immediately, but he returned to New York, where he made a last contribution to the *Daily Advertiser* in September and his wife gave birth to a daughter. A few days before the first number of the *National Gazette* appeared, news of his appointment as "interpreter of the French language" got into the papers, though apparently it was little noticed. From his own account the total returns from his work as translator were trivial. His duties extended to all languages, and when they were beyond his powers he was supposed to procure translations from others and pay for them. Obviously, neither he nor his paper was supported by his public pay, and apparently he was charged with no leakage of state

[15] Madison to TJ, July 24, 1791, quoted by Philip Marsh in "Philip Freneau and James Madison, 1791–1793" (*Procs. N. J. Hist. Soc.*, Oct. 1947); Freneau to TJ, Aug. 4, 1791 (LC, 11396); account of financial arrangement and advertisements in Leary, pp. 191–192, with refs.; comment of Hamilton on Childs as "a very cunning fellow," who was a Federalist in N. Y., and, by proxy, an Antifederalist in Philadelphia (Hamilton to Rufus King, July 25, 1792, in Lodge, VIII, 272).

secrets. The character and patriotism of Freneau, like that of his rather remote and excessively discreet patron Jefferson, can withstand close scrutiny. He took his political principles very seriously, however, and his zeal for republicanism as he understood it eventually led him into some indiscretion.[16]

One stanza in the poetical address to his public which he printed in his first issue shows clearly where his sympathies lay in the world conflict of ideas.

> The King of the French, and the Queen of the North
> At the head of the play for the season we find:
> From the spark that we kindled a flame has gone forth
> To expand thro' the world and enlighten mankind:
> With a code of new doctrines the Universe rings,
> And *Thomas* is preaching strange sermons to kings.

The "Thomas" he was referring to was Paine, not Jefferson, but he interpreted the relations between the American and French Revolutions just as the Secretary of State did. So did most of his countrymen for that matter, hence he was voicing popular doctrines which had not yet been effectively challenged. From the beginning, the tone of Freneau's paper offered a contrast to the "royal gibberish" of John Fenno, and his "poetical address" also revealed his lightness of touch, gaiety of spirit, and desire to please. The last paragraph summed up his purposes.

> Thus launch'd as we are on the Ocean of News,
> In hopes that your pleasure our pains will repay,
> All honest endeavors the author will use
> To furnish a feast for the grave and the gay;
> At least he'll essay such a track to pursue
> That the world shall approve . . . and his news shall be true.[17]

He continued to tickle the palates of his readers with light verse and gained subscribers because he produced a good paper. Being a semiweekly, it lent itself to wider circulation than a daily. Jefferson, send-

[16] TJ noted the appointment of Freneau as clerk for foreign languages on Aug. 16, 1791, and he took the oath the next day (LC, 11423). Leary appears to have accepted Freneau's later account ("To the Citizens of South Carolina," reprinted from Charleston *City Gazette* of Jan. 5, 1801, in *Aurora*, Aug. 14, 1802), and believes that he did not take the oath till late September or October (p. 192). The appointment was noted in *Gazette of the U. S.*, Oct. 29, 1791, and, according to Leary, in the *Daily Advertiser*, Oct. 24. Freneau's account of his duties and remuneration is from *National Gazette*, Oct. 20, 1792.

[17] *National Gazette*, Oct. 31, 1791, p. 4. For an account of poems published by Freneau in the first weeks, see Leary, p. 198. Most of them had already been contributed to the *Daily Advertiser* and were merely reprinted.

ing it to his son-in-law, said that in two papers it would contain as much good matter as Bache's in six. Besides making accessible to Freneau the foreign journals in his own office, he had David Rittenhouse furnish him with meteorological observations once a week. Before the end of the year, Madison wrote Lee that the paper had justified the expectations of Freneau's friends and merited the "diffusive circulation" they had tried to get for it.[18] By that time he himself was sending unsigned contributions to it, and he continued to do so with considerable regularity till spring. The first of these dealt with population and emigration, in partial anticipation of Malthus. Others related to governmental questions and showed more definitely the trend of Madison's own republicanism, but they maintained a tone of mild detachment and, except for the last of the series, they could not be regarded as sharply controversial.[19] Another college friend of Freneau's, Hugh Brackenridge, also contributed, but there is no indication that Jefferson did, at this or any other time. Communications from persons who had political ideas similar to his own were undoubtedly welcomed by Freneau, but they also got into other papers, and at the end of his first six months he claimed that he had shown no partiality to parties or opinions.[20] So far as communications were concerned, this may have been true of his paper and others, but by spring some of the most severe attacks on Hamilton in his columns were coming from his own witty and fearless pen. He was most to be dreaded because of his ability and indomitable independence, and if his was the most influential republican paper, the main reason was that it was the best one.

The session of Congress which began shortly before Freneau set up the *National Gazette* was marked by the presentation of the third of Hamilton's great reports, the one on manufacturing, which was designed to initiate the third phase of his financial policy.[21] During the summer the stock of the Bank of the United States, against which Jefferson had vainly argued on constitutional grounds, had been heavily oversubscribed, though Jefferson reported with apparent satisfaction that very little of it had been taken in his State of Virginia. He expressed no regret that the Virginians had thus failed to gain a proportionate share of the speculative profits which followed, and

[18] TJ to T. M. Randolph, Jr., Nov. 20, 27, 1791 (LC, 11656, 11695); Madison to Henry Lee, Dec. 18, 1791 (Hunt, VI, 69*n.*).

[19] Madison's contributions from Nov. 21, 1791 to Apr. 2, 1792, are in Hunt, VI, 43–105. Brant summarizes them, III, 346–347.

[20] Leary, p. 203.

[21] The Report on Manufactures was communicated to the House on Dec. 5, 1791 (Lodge, III, 294–416).

he viewed with alarm the "delirium of speculation" in the financial centers. The speculation centered in bank scrip, that is, certificates for initial part-payments on bank stock, hence the terms that were bandied about at the time – "scrippomony," "scripomania," "scripophobia." Bank scrip was quoted at advances of from 100 to 300 per cent before there was a reaction. Some allowance must be made for the perplexity and concern of an inveterate countryman like Jefferson in such a situation, but we are not dependent on him alone for accounts of this madness. Other people said that there was no historic parallel except those provided by Law's Mississippi scheme and the South Sea Bubble.[22] The frenzy had calmed considerably by fall, though scrip remained very high; and federal securities, while adversely affected for a time during the summer, had increased enormously in value during the two years Hamilton had been in office. His policies had vastly enhanced the wealth and importance of a rising moneyed group, and this group strongly supported him.[23]

While recognizing that economic conditions in general were good, Jefferson strongly objected to what he regarded as financial trickery and gambling. He said little about financial issues as such that winter, however, until he began to talk confidentially with George Washington about the causes of popular discontent, as currently expressed in newspapers. He was absorbed in the affairs of his own department, and the framework of his thought was political rather than economic anyway. Some of the representatives from Virginia, like John Page and William Branch Giles, could be aptly described as localists at this stage. Jefferson was no more a localist in spirit than Madison, but he shared his friend's anxiety about maintaining poise and balance in government. His continued invocation of the Constitution was to be expected. Writing to a fellow Virginian, who had asked what should be done about a new frame of state government, he said:

> I wish to preserve the line drawn by the federal constitution between the general & particular governments as it stands at present, and to take every prudent means of preventing either from stepping over it. Tho' the experiment has not yet had a long enough course to shew us from which quarter encroachments are most to be feared, yet it is easy to foresee from the nature of things that the encroachments of the state governments will tend to an excess of liberty which will correct itself (as in the late in-

[22] An authoritative account is given by J. S. Davis, *Essays in the Earlier History of American Corporations* (1917), I, 202–212. See also TJ to Pendleton, July 24, 1791 (Ford, V, 357–358); TJ to Edward Rutledge, Aug. 25, 1791 (Ford, V, 375–377, where it is wrongly dated Aug. 29).

[23] Davis, I, 195.

stance) while those of the general government will tend to monarchy, which will fortify itself from day to day, instead of working its own cure, as all experience shews. I would rather be exposed to the inconveniences attending too much liberty than those attending too small a degree of it. Then it is important to strengthen the state governments: and as this cannot be done by any change in the federal constitution, (for the preservation of that is all we need contend for,) it must be done by the states themselves, erecting such barriers at the constitutional line as cannot be surmounted either by themselves or by the general government. The only barrier in their power is a wise government. A weak one will lose ground in every contest.

He then recommended specific changes in the government of Virginia, looking toward strengthening the executive and dignifying the judiciary.[24] He still objected to legislative omnipotence.

The author of the *Notes on Virginia* was certainly not one to minimize the claims of agriculture, as compared with industry; and Hamilton's elaborate argument for manufacturing was directed against such ideas as his, no doubt, whether or not the Secretary of the Treasury had this work definitely in mind.[25] Jefferson's preference for agriculture, however, and his distaste for manufacturing, were based on moral and political grounds more than economic; and it is noteworthy that such objections to Hamilton's famous Report as he voiced at the time were those of a constitutionalist rather than an agrarian. In this he may have been following the lead of Madison, who was appalled by Hamilton's sweeping assertions regarding the "welfare clause," in connection with his recommendation of bounties to manufacturers. As Hamilton interpreted the phrase, the power to pronounce upon the objects which concern the general welfare was left to the discretion of Congress and unquestionably extended to whatever concerned "the general interests of learning, of agriculture, of manufacturing, and of commerce." This went considerably beyond his earlier claims. Writing Henry Lee, now Governor of Virginia, Madison said: "The federal government has been hitherto limited to the specified powers, by the greatest champions for latitude in expounding those powers. If not only the *means*, but the *objects* are unlimited, the parchment had better be thrown into the fire at once." [26] Jefferson said much the

[24] TJ to Archibald Stuart, Dec. 23, 1791 (Ford, V, 409–410). See also TJ to James Sullivan of Massachusetts, July 31, 1791 (Ford, V, 369).

[25] There was some tendency to minimize the differences between them on this point at this time (*Gazette of U. S.*, Jan. 28, 1792).

[26] Madison to Lee, Jan. 1, 1792 (Hunt, VI, 81*n.*). The passage in Hamilton's Report he was referring to is in Lodge, III, 371–372. See also Madison to Pendleton, Feb. 21, 1792 (Hunt, VI, 95*n.*).

same thing to Washington a little later, declaring that this was "a very different question from that of the bank, which was thought an incident to an enumerated power." [27]

Fortunately for their peace of mind, the Report on Manufactures was shelved, and in the meantime Hamilton had set up the Society for Establishing Useful Manufactures in Paterson, New Jersey. This private corporation was destined to have a checkered history, and associated with him in it was William Duer, whose failure in the spring pricked the bubble of speculation and gave the critics of his financial policies their first real day in court. If Jefferson had any thought of gaining political benefit from this he could not have expected to do so soon, for he had already announced to Washington his determination to retire from office. He had said this in January and again in February, while troubles did not begin to crowd upon Hamilton till March.

Jefferson's desire to retire from office was not at all surprising in view of his temperament and situation. His qualifications for his present post were unusual, yet it had never suited him as well as the one he had held in France. Its duties were miscellaneous and the work was arduous and confining. He was restive under the burden of incessant paper work which seemed to have no appreciable results and he found the political atmosphere increasingly unpleasant. Early in the new year he wrote his elder daughter that his thoughts of the scenes through which they had passed together alleviated the "toils and inquietudes" of his situation and made him want, more than ever, to exchange "labor, envy, and malice for ease, domestic occupation, and domestic love and society." Incurably a home and family man, he was suffering acutely from nostalgia. He wrote his son-in-law in February that he had not seen the face of the earth for months; the temperature had been above freezing only two mornings in seven weeks and was at 16° that very day. At the beginning of the spring he wrote Martha that the coming year would be the longest in his life, and the last of such hateful labors; after that they would sow their cabbages together. He had made up his mind some weeks before. The end of a presidential term would be a convenient end for his term. That gave him till March, 1793, and the only real question was whether or not he could last that long.[28]

He left a memorandum of a long conversation with Washington at

[27] Memo. of conversation of Feb. 29, 1792 (Ford, I, 177).

[28] TJ to Martha, Jan. 15, 1792 (Ford, V, 422); TJ to T. M. Randolph, Jr., Feb. 20, 1792 (LC, 12248); TJ to Martha, Mar. 22, 1792 (Ford, V, 487–488). He had reached his decision by the earliest of these dates.

the end of February about his retirement. Oddly enough, it started in a discussion of a possible addition to his official responsibilities.[29] The President had recently signed a bill which put the Post Office on a more permanent basis, and Jefferson was to discuss with him a proposal to double the speed of the post riders from fifty miles a day to a hundred. In view of the delays he himself had suffered in getting mail from Monticello, he had personal reason to be concerned with this matter; and the Act itself, which among other things made newspapers mailable, was one that this apostle of enlightenment would have been naturally interested in. The earlier Postmaster General, predecessor to Timothy Pickering, had been annexed to Hamilton's department, being regarded as a revenue officer. According to the new law, however, the purpose of the Post Office was much more broadly defined and its revenues were made merely incidental to its services. Jefferson conceived, therefore, that it now belonged in the Department of State.

In this private conversation he gave Washington another reason for such allocation, to wit, that the Treasury "possessed already such an influence as to swallow up the whole Executive powers, and that even the future Presidents (not supported by the weight of character which himself possessed) would not be able to make head against this department." [30] Probably he had never before spoken so bluntly to the President about his colleague, but he claimed that his interest was not personal. Even if he were "supposed to have any appetite for power," he would not remain in office long enough to gratify it appreciably, and he believed there was justification for his proposal on public grounds.

Washington had to leave to attend one of his levees, and when the conversation was resumed next day after they left the breakfast table he merely asked that Jefferson commit his ideas to writing. This the latter did only to the extent of making suggestions about increasing the speed of the post riders.[31] His more important verbal proposal was never agreed to, since Washington preferred to let well enough alone. When he finally got around to telling Jefferson this, he showed that the latter's comments on the aggrandisement of the Treasury had not been wholly vain. The main reason why the President assigned the newly established mint to the Department of State was that he did not want to multiply further the duties of the Treasury. The mint was established by law that spring and David Rittenhouse was ap-

[29] The memo. of the conversation which began on Feb. 28, 1792, and continued next morning is in Ford, I, 174–178. The account of the circumstances as given by White in *The Federalists*, pp. 226–227, is excellent, but the interpretation is precisely what Hamilton himself would have given.

[30] Ford, I, 174. [31] Ford, V, 435–436.

pointed director at Jefferson's suggestion, though it did not clearly pass into his jurisdiction until fall. It did not do well and really should have been assigned to the Treasury, as the Post Office should have been to the Department of State. Hamilton himself recognized this eventually and advocated a swap, but this was some time after Jefferson had carried out the resolution to retire which he discussed at such length with Washington after breakfast on the last day of February, 1792.[32]

Jefferson seemed to take it for granted at this time that Washington would be unwilling to serve another term, and was relieved by the thought that his own continuance beyond this one could not be urged on grounds of personal loyalty. If Washington had not yet made a direct statement to him, he had doubtless learned of the President's determination from Madison, to whom it seems to have been revealed several weeks earlier. In these personal matters he and Madison were on a more intimate footing with Washington than Hamilton was.

Jefferson's reference to his own purposes, which he coupled with Washington's, opened the floodgates of talk; and if he had had the slightest doubt beforehand he was now convinced that the public business was exceedingly irksome to the President and that his desire for tranquility had become "an irresistible passion." But Washington believed in continuity in government and feared that if the great officers went out with him the shock on the public mind might be dangerous. In the face of such protestations, Jefferson felt impelled to justify his own decision, but he assured Washington of one thing: neither of his brethren in the administration had shown the slightest disposition to retire. On the contrary, Hamilton was presenting fiscal plans which would require years for completion. It was then that Washington expressed the conviction that the Secretary of State, because of the scope of his duties, was a much more important officer than the Secretary of the Treasury, who had only to do with revenue. Deeply disturbed by the symptoms of dissatisfaction that had lately appeared (in the newspapers, especially), Washington wondered how far these might go in the case of "too great a change in the administration." Jefferson seized upon the unusual opportunity to state the reason for these discontents. In his opinion, they arose from a single source – the "system" which had been set up by the Secretary of the Treasury.

[32] For an account of the mint in this period, see White, pp. 139–143, 227. It was established by law in April, 1792, and the best date for its assignment to Jefferson's department is that of Washington's letter to him, Oct. 20, 1792 (Fitzpatrick, XXXII, 187). Hamilton's suggestion of a swap was made Jan. 31, 1795, on the eve of his own retirement, in a letter to Washington (J. C. Hamilton, V, 70–72).

The indictment of the policies of his colleague which he wrote down next day out of his memory of this conversation went beyond anything he had previously written on that subject. If he wanted to speak his mind freely about Hamilton in private, he picked the proper auditor in George Washington, especially since the executive procedure had offered him little or no opportunity to discuss the domestic policies which he opposed. He did not refer here to foreign questions and did not have time to elaborate his objections to anything, but he left no doubt whatever that he intensely disliked the speculative accompaniments of Hamilton's financial policy, and its "corrupting" effects on the legislature, and greatly feared the Hamiltonian construction of the Constitution. This bit of recorded conversation should not be cited as a statement of fact, and it is not even a full expression of opinion. On the other hand, one cannot dispose of it by labeling it as partisan and throwing it out the window, for what he was championing was public morality and what he feared was the aggrandisement of power. His partisanship had been manifested only in private thus far, and the public attack on Hamilton's "system" that spring was not due to Jefferson's representations to George Washington. Financial developments provided the immediate occasion for it.

Until this time it could have been said, as it was in the United States in the 1920's, that prosperity had tended to absorb all issues. The prosperity of the country under the new government was undeniable. Jefferson referred to it repeatedly in letters to Americans abroad, and it extended to the Southern agricultural states sufficiently to take the edge off the early opposition of Southern leaders to Hamilton's financial policies and make this seem rather academic. Elsewhere the disposition to credit the prosperity to these policies was general, and the successive spurts in the security market were regarded in the commercial and financial centers as indisputable proof of their wisdom and success. The trend of the market was upward until the high point was reached in January, 1792, but there was a definite break in March, prices fell sharply thereafter, and then there was a panic which was not quieted till fall. Though a novel experience then, it was a "typical stock market and financial panic." It was largely confined to a few centers, especially New York, and mercantile failures were few.[33] There was poetic justice in the fact that the greatest losses occurred among the speculators, and Jefferson was entitled to say, "I told you so." There was poetic justice also in the damage that these events did to the

[33] Davis, *Essays in the Earlier History of American Corporations*, I, 307. For the panic as a whole, see pp. 278–315.

exaggerated reputation of Hamilton, who now became a victim of the tendency to overstress the importance of the security market after having been its beneficiary. His situation was the more embarrassing because the most conspicuous failure at this point was that of William Duer, who was for some months the Assistant Secretary of the Treasury. His personal intimacy with Hamilton was notorious.

The appointment of Duer had been unwise in the first place, though he had served as secretary to the old Treasury Board and was regarded as a skilled financier, besides having important connections.[34] His actions lent color to the charge that certain speculators availed themselves of advance information of governmental policy, and it is hard to escape the conclusion that some of them did so through him. Hamilton seemed surprisingly indifferent to these dangers, but undoubtedly he was relieved when Duer resigned. This fantastic operator was engaged in so many farflung enterprises that no one could keep up with them, but a major activity of his after leaving the Treasury was speculation in federal securities. He formed a partnership with Alexander Macomb at the end of 1791 for that avowed purpose. He was a bull on the market, as Hamilton himself was for public reasons, and the decline in securities found him overextended. On March 9, 1792, he was forced to suspend payment, and within a few days fate played an ironical trick when the Treasury itself pushed him further down the road to ruin. Through Oliver Wolcott, the government instituted action against him because of funds still unaccounted for by him as secretary of the old Board of the Treasury, the precise sum being 240,000 dollars. The circumstances are confused, but the Department appears to have carried this unsettled account entirely too long, possibly because of Duer's personal relations with Hamilton, and Wolcott seems to have acted because reports of the state of Duer's affairs showed him that he now had to. At this stage, the conduct of Wolcott and Hamilton as public officials was irreproachable. The Secretary refused to intervene and such counsel as he gave his old friend was wise and moderate. The net result of Duer's calamities was that he went to jail – which was really fortunate for him since he was there protected from mob violence – and that the suit against him was pending throughout the rest of his life. It was dropped about the time of his death in 1799 and the wonder is that the affair did not continue to be a scandal.[35]

[34] The best sketch of Duer's career is in Davis, I, 111–338.

[35] For the whole story, see Davis, I, 289–297, 313, 316ff. Among other prominent bankrupts in 1792 was his partner Macomb.

The week before Duer went to jail Jefferson wrote his son-in-law:

> Here the *unmonied farmer*, as he is termed, his cattle & crops are no more thought of than if they did not feed us. Scrip & stock are food & raiment here. Duer, the king of the alley, is under a sort of check. The stocksellers say he will rise again. The stock-buyers count him out, and the credit & fate of the nation seem to hang on the desperate throws & plunges of gambling scoundrels.

A month later, writing his former clerk, now in New York, he said that the bursting of the bubble of speculation was inevitable, that the public debt was and must be regarded as solid and sacred, but that "all that stuff called scrip, of whatever description, was folly or roguery." He believed that his countrymen would be happy if they would return to the "plain unsophisticated common sense" from which they should never have been decoyed, and spoke of the "criminality of this paper system." In matters of high finance he himself was unsophisticated and he accepted without question exaggerated reports of the extent of this calamity. He believed that most of the newspapers were keeping pretty quiet about speculation, Freneau's being a conspicuous exception; and his judgment may be presumed to have been correct with respect to Philadelphia, even if he was not fully informed about the situation elsewhere.[36]

It was just at this time that the criticisms of the Secretary of the Treasury and his policies in that paper increased both in number and severity. The communications signed BRUTUS, which began in the middle of March, marked the full assumption by the *National Gazette* of its role as the spokesman and medium of the republican interest.[37] These constituted an arraignment of Hamilton's financial measures as a whole. Freneau himself, in an editorial, had already blamed these for the rise of speculation, and he and his correspondents pressed the attack all along the line during the next few weeks. Jefferson's cordial approval of many of these editorials and communications may be assumed – especially of one that Madison wrote. This was published on April 2, and sought to answer the question, *Who are the real friends of the Union?* [38] They were *not* those who increased the public debt unnecessarily and pampered the spirit of speculation, nor

[36] TJ to T. M. Randolph, Jr., Mar. 16, 1792 (Ford, V, 455); TJ to Henry Remsen, Jr., Apr. 14, 1792 (LC, 12699–12700; Ford, V, 507–508, wrongly addressed to Francis Eppes); TJ to Randolph, Apr. 19, 1792 (Ford, V, 509–510).

[37] The BRUTUS papers began Mar. 15, 1792, and the sixth and last of them appeared Apr. 9. The papers of CAIUS, which began Jan. 16, were reprinted from the *American Daily Advertiser*.

[38] Hunt, VI, 104–105.

those who sought, by means of "arbitrary interpretations and insidious precedents," to pervert a limited government into one of unlimited discretion, nor those who held monarchical and aristocratic principles. They *were* the friends of liberty and popular authority and supporters of the republican policy of "opposition to a spirit of usurpation and monarchy."

In the light of the later history of the country, the reference to monarchy which Madison made here and which Jefferson undoubtedly applauded may seem forced and even demagogic, but the American Republic then occupied a lonely position in a world of kingdoms and the danger of the concentration of government in the hands of a small and unrepresentative group which might become self-perpetuating was real. It was hard to think of Washington as a potential monarch or chief oligarch but easy to think of Hamilton as either, and it was against him that this simple statement of issues and principles was directed. The emphasis was on opposition to his policies, not on specific alternatives to them, and it was natural to suppose that this appeal would be popular at a time when circumstances had served to discredit him.

The make-up of Congress had not changed, however, and Hamilton's influence was still in the ascendant in that body. He said rather boastfully that Madison was practically lost (*perdu*) during most of the session. Toward the end of it, however, there were signs that his own grip was loosening somewhat, and he attributed to Madison certain moves which he rightly interpreted as hostile to himself and his "administration." One of these was the attempt to prevent direct reference of questions and requests to heads of executive departments. Jefferson had drawn papers at the request of Congress, but most of his reports were made to the President and those that were submitted to Congress (generally to the Senate) were transmitted by Washington as a rule. Because of the form of the act creating his office, Hamilton's relations with the legislative body had always been closer and more direct, and his great reports had been made in response to specific congressional requests. Even now it is uncertain just what Washington's original connection with them was, though his general approval of their recommendations has been assumed.

It seemed to many of those who opposed Hamilton's "system" that his intimate relations with Congress constituted a major element in his political strength and even enabled him to dispense with the President. Also, they seemed to mark a departure from the doctrine of separation of powers.

The occasion for both an attack on Hamilton's position and an assertion of his distinctiveness was provided by a resolution, introduced early in the year, asking that the President direct the Secretary of the Treasury to provide information respecting the additional revenue required to increase the military establishment. In the House, a motion to strike out the name of the President and thus address the resolution to the Secretary himself was made and carried. The matter was not finally decided until March, however, and the outcome was uncertain for a time. Hamilton said that Madison knew he would have resigned if the close vote had gone the other way, and Jefferson interpreted the episode as a sign that the Treasury influence was tottering.[39]

Hamilton may have been warranted in regarding the vote as one of confidence, whoever was responsible for forcing the issue. It can also be argued that the special relationship between the Treasury and Congress was desirable in that it overcame some of the practical disadvantages of the sharp separation of the executive and legislative branches. On the other hand, this special relationship could be conscientiously objected to, and there was no impropriety in raising the question why the Secretary of the Treasury should enjoy a degree of independence of the President which was not accorded his fellows. Jefferson, whose freedom of action in foreign affairs was so sharply limited, would certainly have been warranted in raising it in some way, even if the Secretary of the Treasury had been another and less aggressive person. Also, it was like him to want to reduce Hamilton's special privileges rather than to increase his own, for this constitutional purist preferred making his reports to Washington.

Had Hamilton had access to Jefferson's private records, no doubt he would have concluded that his colleague was responsible for this particular move against him; and such may have been the case, though there is no way of knowing who had the idea first and it would be difficult to prove that the Secretary of State had departed from the strait path of official propriety. The general question of references by the legislature to department heads was discussed in his own house after dinner by certain congressmen who were afterwards involved in this fight, and, as a department head, he could not have been blamed for entering into a discussion which affected him directly.[40] Whether this astute man dropped a specific suggestion or this excessively proper man refrained from making one, and let somebody else do it, is an unanswerable question.

[39] Final vote on Mar. 8, 1792 (*Annals of Cong.*, 2 Cong., 1 & 2 sess., pp. 437–452); Hamilton's comments in letter to Edward Carrington, May 26, 1792 (Lodge, VIII, 254). For TJ's memo. dated Mar. 10, see Ford, I, 178–179.

[40] Among those who dined with him on Jan. 2, 1792, was Thomas Fitzsimons of Pa., whose part in later events he referred to in his memo. of Mar. 10 (Ford, I, 178–179).

The relations between Congress and the executive departments again came up for discussion when the House of Representatives appointed a committee to inquire into the causes of the failure of the St. Clair expedition, and sought certain papers from the Department of War. The difficulties arising from the St. Clair debate had already occasioned consultations between the President and his Secretaries which may be regarded as early meetings of the cabinet, though nobody used that term.[41]

The congressional inquiry served to discredit William Duer further, for that ubiquitous financier had been the "contractor" of the expedition and was charged with "gross and various mismanagements and neglects" in the matter of supplies.[42] The outcome was embarrassing to Hamilton, though the Secretary of War was more directly blameable. The immediate question, however, was one of procedure and propriety and as such Jefferson regarded it as important.

The department heads and the Attorney General, meeting with the President, agreed that the House had a right to request papers and that the President should communicate them, unless in his opinion their disclosure would injure the public. That is, he should exercise discretion. Except for Hamilton, who made some qualifications of his own, they also agreed that congressional requests should be addressed to the President, not the individual department heads. Hamilton observed that the act constituting his department had made it subject to Congress in some points, but that he did not feel obliged to produce all the papers the legislators might call for, since they might demand "secrets of a very mischievous nature." Jefferson was certainly not disposed to tell Congress everything, but he believed that his colleague feared an inquiry into the part that members of the government had played in stock speculation. He concluded that Hamilton wanted "to place himself subject to the House when the Executive should propose what he did not like, and subject to the Executive when the House should propose anything disagreeable." If this was not a fair judgment it was not an unnatural one in view of Jefferson's belief that Hamilton interpreted the Constitution and the law to suit his own purposes. Whether he did or not, the record leaves no doubt that the Secretary of State was far more scrupulous.[43]

His constitutional scruples were manifested in still another connection that spring. The struggle over the apportionment of representa-

[41] See, e.g., TJ's memo. on the consultation of Mar. 9, 1792 (Ford, I, 179–183).
[42] Discussion in Davis, I, 261–262, with references.
[43] See TJ's memo. on the consultations of Mar. 31 and Apr. 2, 1792 (Ford, I, 189–190). This personal account is colored by his feelings, no doubt, but there are abundant indications of the attitudes of the two men in other records.

tives, after the results of the first census became available, was in many respects a sectional struggle.[44] In terms of the conflict between the two leading members of Washington's official family, however, it is most noteworthy because the President, following the representations of the Secretary of State and disregarding those of the Secretary of the Treasury, vetoed an Act of Congress for the first time, and did this on grounds of unconstitutionality.

The apportionment bill which was laid on Washington's desk late in March had passed the two houses of Congress by the narrowest of margins, and the President had many doubts about it. He kept it to the last day, as he had the Bank bill, and he got formal opinions on it from Jefferson, Hamilton, Randolph, and Knox, and at least an informal one from Madison. The Constitution stated that the number of representatives should not exceed one for every 30,000, and the size of the lower house had been determined by dividing the total population of the country by that number. The Constitution also required that representatives should be apportioned among the states according to their respective numbers. The bill specified how many representatives each state should have without setting forth any principle, and Jefferson, who subjected it to closer examination than any of his colleagues, concluded that a different ratio had been used with respect to some states than others. The results seemed to him tolerably just, but he objected to the apportionment on the ground that it was arbitrary, and that the Fathers had anticipated the use of a uniform ratio or common divisor. Perhaps they had, though one wonders how he could have been so sure of their intentions. He himself recognized that this mathematical process created problems in the form of fractions, for congressmen could not be divided into parts. In his opinion the simple and sensible procedure would be to disregard the fractions, which would shift around from decade to decade in such a way as to balance occasional irregularities. Time proved that he was not as good a prophet as he thought, for the "method of rejected fractions" which he recommended and which Congress actually followed during the next forty years, though undeniably simple, turned out to be so inequitable that it was abandoned.[45] In trying to avoid the dangers which he believed "the scramble for the fractionary members" would invariably lead to, he proposed a cure which was in some respects worse than the

[44] The geographical basis of the struggle is emphasized, perhaps too much, by McMaster in his *History*, II, 53–57.

[45] For critical comments, see the excellent article of Zechariah Chafee, Jr., "Congressional Reapportionment," in *Harvard Law Rev.* XLII (1929), 1021–1023.

disease. On the other hand, his fears that Congress would play tricks with apportionment, if not constrained by considerations of principle, were in no sense exaggerated. Also, he was fully aware that this particular bill was disadvantageous to Virginia and may have disliked it for just that reason.

There were further objections to it on constitutional grounds, however. Many claimed that the provision that the number of representatives shall not exceed one for every 30,000 extended to the states individually (except that each state must have at least one representative), as well as to the country as a whole. If this interpretation was correct, and he believed it the natural one, the bill was clearly unconstitutional, for in eight states there was to be one congressman for every 27,770 people. He believed that this bill should be vetoed even if it were regarded as an "inconvenient exposition" of the language of the Constitution. Indeed, he recommended this action on grounds which in the large sense were political. He thought it high time that the presidential veto should be used, in order to give assurance that the President was guarding the Constitution. Thus the tendency of the state legislatures to throw up barriers of their own against Congress would be checked. Also, he believed that the application of any single ratio would be intelligible and therefore acceptable to the people, whereas the complex operations of this bill could not be understood and would not be approved.

The alignment within the official family was just what would have been expected. Randolph thought the bill unconstitutional, though his position was somewhat more equivocal than Jefferson's; and Knox and Hamilton wanted Washington to sign it, though neither of them discussed it at much length. Perhaps we may assume that Hamilton did not regard the matter as of supreme importance. Washington agreed with Jefferson that the bill was contrary to the general understanding of the Constitution, but he was disturbed by the geographical alignment and feared that he might be accused of taking the Southern side. While recognizing the delicacy of this position, Jefferson and his fellow Virginians stood their ground and had their way. Madison and Randolph were summoned and, being assured of their concurrence, Washington signed the brief veto message which the Secretary of State had drawn. Congress failed to override it and passed a bill which was not open to objections on the same grounds. Jefferson believed that the first presidential veto was greeted with satisfaction, as a sign that the President was on guard, but the latter's fears of sectional conflict and possible disunion lingered in his mind. This was one of the reasons for his concluding that Washington must be persuaded to remain in the scene of conflict from which he himself expected to escape. The greater the dissension the more the President was needed, and dissension became more acute and much more personal in the late spring and summer.[46]

[46] For TJ's opinion of Apr. 4, 1792, on the bill apportioning representation and his draft of the veto message, dated Apr. 5, see Ford, V, 493–501. For the opinions of Hamilton, Randolph, and Knox, and TJ's recapitulation, see Hamilton's *Works*, J. C. Hamilton edn., IV, 206–215. Hamilton had not seen the text of the bill. For the final conference with Washington, in which Randolph and Madison joined TJ, see his memo. of Apr. 6, 1792 (Ford, I, 192). Congress voted to apportion at the rate of one representative to 33,000.

[XXVI]

The Causes of Discontent

1792

AS he reviewed his conduct afterwards, the Secretary of the Treasury was impressed with the great patience he had shown toward Jefferson during their first two years as fellow members of the official family.[1] It is hard to think of Hamilton in the role of silent sufferer, and it is a fair supposition that until the spring of 1792, when his public position was weakened by unhappy financial developments, he was confident of his ability to defeat or circumvent the Secretary of State whenever there was an important issue between them. It may also be assumed that he talked to his own friends about the "machinations" of his colleague without much restraint. Nevertheless, his claim that on one occasion he had been instrumental in preventing "a very systematic and severe attack" on Jefferson must have had real foundation. This was in the autumn of 1791, when two or three of his supporters wanted to punish the Secretary of State for his "indiscreet and light" letter to the printer about Paine's *Rights of Man*, which had resulted in the "persecution" of the Vice President.[2]

The person most exercised against Jefferson in this connection seems to have been Jonathan Trumbull of Connecticut, Speaker of the federal House of Representatives and brother of Jefferson's friend the painter. On the other hand, Oliver Wolcott, Jr., from the same state, whose position in the Treasury kept him very close to Hamilton, counseled delay. Like Hamilton he regarded this ideological dispute as trivial and he believed that a continuance of it would really injure Adams, whether or not he fully appreciated the political dangers of building up Jefferson further as a friend of the rights of man.[3] If

[1] Hamilton to Washington, Sept. 9, 1792 (Lodge, VI, 385–386).

[2] Lodge, VI, 386.

[3] N. Hazard to Hamilton, Nov. 25, 1791 (Hamilton Papers, 13:1724). See also Oliver Wolcott, Jr., to his father, Oct. 14, 1791 (Gibbs, I, 69).

Hamilton exerted his personal influence to prevent this proposed attack, as he may well have done, he showed more political astuteness than he did later on. He was not particularly concerned to safeguard the reputation of John Adams, but there was nothing to be gained by advertising Jefferson further as an advocate of principles which were popular.

The Secretary of State, most of whose official activities were out of sight and whose private actions were so discreet, was not very vulnerable to direct attack. In the midst of the congressional session he described himself to his daughter as a spectator of the heats and tumults of conflicting parties, and he had been relatively immune till then.[4] He was soon subjected to criticism in a pamphlet, however, and this deeply grieved his recent chief clerk, Henry Remsen, Jr., who sent him a copy of it. Following the death of his father, Remsen had returned to New York, and his resignation had forced upon Jefferson an unwelcome choice between two members of his little staff for promotion to the vacant place. He had finally decided to elevate George Taylor rather than Jacob Blackwell, because the former had a family while the latter was unmarried. The letter of explanation that he wrote Blackwell provides an admirable example of the courtesy and consideration which marked the administration of his office, just as the correspondence between him and Remsen reveals the affection which had characterized their relations. In him there was no suggestion of the bureaucrat.[5]

Remsen thought that the Secretary of State whom he had served so loyally was spoken of with great indecency in this pamphlet.[6] It dealt with the three executive departments and their heads, praising the Secretary of the Treasury while sharply criticizing the two others and condemning Washington indirectly for appointing them. It was signed MASSACHUSETTENSIS and did not sound like Hamilton. The tone of the pamphlet and the *nom de plume* suggest a New England author who approved of Hamilton but followed his own line with respect to other leaders.

This author described Jefferson's department as unimportant, since

[4] TJ to Martha, Mar. 22, 1792 (Ford, V, 487–488).

[5] TJ to Jacob Blackwell, Apr. 1, 1792 (Ford, V, 490–491); Remsen to TJ, Apr. 11, 1792, sending a copy of the pamphlet (LC, 12663).

[6] Judging from the comments on it in the correspondence, this seems to have been a pamphlet of 32 pp., entitled *Strictures and Observations upon the Three Executive Departments* . . . , by MASSACHUSETTENSIS (1792). Remsen had heard that Fisher Ames wrote it, though Rufus King denied this. TJ said it was written and printed in Philadelphia and that the author could not be mistaken, but did not say who he was.

the United States was not supposed to meddle in European politics. MASSACHUSETTENSIS continued:

> The Atlantic was, however, traversed to bring from thence a man, *fresh from the fountain of intrigue*, to fill the unimportant post of secretary for foreign affairs. The man at length arrives, and no sooner does he enter upon the functions of office, than a secretary of state is converted into the tool of a party. Instead of the open manliness of a mind at large, we find him become the willing instrument to raise up one European power, at the expence of another.[7]

There was no reference here to the French Revolution, which had not deeply colored discussions of foreign policy as yet, but there was the contention that Jefferson was conducting his office as a party man and was subservient to France. This charge afterwards crystallized into party dogma, and in Hamilton's hands it assumed a stronger hue and sharper flavor. If it can be proved or denied, it must be from the record. Anybody who could have looked over Jefferson's shoulder while he was writing his reply to Hammond about this time might have accused him of being anti-British, but if he was pro-French, Ternant does not appear to have noticed it.

The writer admitted that Jefferson had been greatly respected as long as he stayed at home and devoted himself to natural history. "To those scenes and walks of life," said MASSACHUSETTENSIS, "every American must wish his speedy retreat; and there to spend the remainder of his days, in ease and quiet." [8] Jefferson was the one American who most approved of that idea. He wrote Remsen that fortunately he would not have to endure much obloquy, since it had begun so late, and that he himself wished his retirement a thousand times more ardently than anybody else did.[9] His former chief clerk ascribed the attack to party spirit and assured him that he had the approbation of all good and honest men, but what the Secretary of State was really sighing for was home and private life. The day before his forty-ninth birthday, when he knew that spring was creeping softly over his own hillsides, he wrote a neighbor in Albemarle: "I am never a day without wishing myself with you, and more and more as the fine sunshine comes on, which seems made for all the world but me." [10]

[7] *Ibid.*, p. 9.
[8] *Ibid.*, p. 15.
[9] TJ to Henry Remsen, Jr., Apr. 14, 1792 (LC, 12699–12700). This letter is printed in Ford, V, 506–508, where it is wrongly addressed to Francis Eppes. Remsen's reply of Apr. 23, 1792, is in LC, 12727–12728.
[10] TJ to Nicholas Lewis, Apr. 12, 1792 (Ford, V, 504).

Life in Philadelphia offered some compensations, and compliments on his scientific standing were not always left-handed. After April had passed into May, Dr. Benjamin S. Barton, reading a paper before the American Philosophical Society, announced that the plant previously called *Podophyllum diphyllum* would hereafter be known as *Jeffersonia* – not in tribute to the Secretary of State in his political capacity but in respectful recognition of his unusual attainments in natural history.[11] This was gratifying beyond a doubt, but at the moment the recipient of the honor was largely debarred from botanical pursuits, and *Jeffersonia diphylla* remained on paper a long time before reaching a flower bed at Monticello.

Meanwhile, party warfare was being waged to some extent in jingles. An unnamed bard sent the following ironical bit of verse to the *National Gazette:*

Public exigencies pressing –
Public debt's a public blessing!
But *secure*, there nothing worse is:
Public debts are public curses!

Whereupon Freneau rejoined:

Public debts are public curses
In soldiers' hands! then nothing worse is!
In speculators' hands increasing,
Public debt's a public blessing! [12]

To George Washington, however, this was no joking business, and he could hardly wait to get away from the scene of squabbling. The same feelings were welling up within him as within the Secretary of State, and before he took advantage of the recess of Congress to make a quick trip to Mount Vernon he called in Madison to discuss personal plans. By now he had told not only Jefferson but also Hamilton and Knox and Edmund Randolph that he intended to stay at home after his four years were up, and he believed that the commencement of the next congressional session would be a good time to tell everybody. He wanted counsel, however, and the fact that he sought it from Madison is clear proof that this major spokesman of the republican party in Congress had retained his full confidence.

Madison's sober report of their conversation is a moving and reveal-

[11] This was on May 18, 1792; see *Garden Book,* pp. 172–173 and Plate XI, showing Barton's drawing.
[12] *National Gazette,* May 3, 1792.

ing document.[13] Disclosing his state of mind freely, Washington said that he could not believe that he himself was now necessary to the successful administration of the government. Indeed, he insisted that he had found himself deficient in many of the essential qualifications of his office – primarily because of "his inexperience in the forms of public business, his unfitness to judge of legal questions, and questions arising out of the Constitution." Furthermore, his health was more infirm than it used to be and he feared his faculties were failing. Finally, "the fatigues and disagreeableness of his situation were in fact scarcely tolerable to him"; and he was more inclined "to go to his farm, take his spade in his hand, and work for his bread" than to remain in it. What distressed him most was that the spirit of party was dividing men within the government, and discontents were arising among the people outside of it.

Madison's calm and judicious comments could hardly have failed to be encouraging. He said there was no doubt whatever that, with the aid of counsel, Washington's judgment must have been as good as that of anyone else who might have been in his place, and that in many cases it had certainly been more so. He assured him that in conciliating and uniting all groups his services had been absolutely essential, and took the position that the rising spirit of party was an argument for his remaining in office, not leaving it. Madison himself believed that the dangers of parties were not as great as some people thought, and was convinced that "the conciliating influence of a temperate and wise administration" might be expected, before another term had run out, to give such tone and firmness to the government as would secure it against danger from either extreme.

Continuing his argument in favor of another term, he discussed possible successors to the first President and pointed out difficulties and objections in the case of all of them. The name of the Secretary of the Treasury was not on the brief list he drew. Madison did not mention him any more than he did himself. The option evidently lay between a few men, he said, and he named Adams, Jay, and Jefferson.

He ruled out his best political friend almost immediately. In Madison's thoroughly informed opinion, Jefferson's "extreme repugnance to public life and anxiety to exchange it for his farm and his philosophy" made the gaining of his consent seem almost impossible. Besides, there were strong local prejudices against him in the Northern states, and

[13] Madison's long memo. of the conversation of May 5, 1792, and briefer notes on that of May 9, are in Hunt, VI, 106–110*n*. Letters and memos. (Feb. 19–Oct. 20, 1792) dealing with Washington's proposed retirement have been assembled in convenient and impressive form in V. H. Paltsits, *Washington's Farewell Address* (N. Y. Pub. Lib., 1935), pp. 211–237.

the Pennsylvanians would particularly object because of the question of the location of the seat of government. Washington stood with his Secretary of State on that point, as of course Madison knew, but he also knew that Pennsylvanians and other Northerners would accept in Washington what they would not in Jefferson. As for the Vice President, Adams's "monarchical principles" and his recent conduct with respect to the representation bill had produced such dislike among republicans everywhere, and Southerners in particular, that Madison thought him quite out of the question. He may have been thinking of Jefferson when he said that it would not be possible for those who had a high opinion of Adams's private character and were willing to trust him in public office despite his principles "to make head against the torrent." He regarded John Jay as no more acceptable. Some people thought his political principles as obnoxious as those of Adams, and there were special objections to him because of his attitude toward the debts to the British and his past negotiations with respect to the navigation of the Mississippi. In other words, Washington was the only man who could command the support of the entire country.

Madison saw the President again before the latter left for his short visit to Mount Vernon, but observed no relaxation in his determination to retire. Soon after that, Washington wrote him about a valedictory address, telling him just what matters should be dealt with in it, and asking him to submit a draft of one in the fall. Thus the groundwork for the famous Farewell Address was laid, though the draft lay four years dormant. Washington said that only one consideration would cause him to change his mind about retiring: the conviction that his withdrawal would involve the country in serious disputes respecting the Presidency. He did not believe that any real evidence on this point could be obtained before election, but he got some from his Secretary of State very shortly.[14]

Jefferson was aware of the general state of the President's mind when he wrote him at Mount Vernon with the ostensible purpose of persuading him to accept re-election.[15] He had an ulterior motive. He wanted to set forth more fully the causes of public discontent which he had hitherto been able to describe only in part, and his representations amounted to a brief against the Treasury "system," though

[14] Washington to Madison, May 20, 1792 (Fitzpatrick, XXXII, 45–49). Madison met Washington on the road on May 25 and was then handed this letter (Hunt, VI, 110–111*n.*).

[15] TJ to Washington, May 23, 1792 (Ford, VI, 1–6). This did not reach Washington until after he had returned to Philadelphia.

actually he did not mention Hamilton's name. He did not present these views as his own, nor did he assert that they were wholly correct. He sought to convince Washington that the discontent was great, and, viewing the causes of it in the mass, he gave to each "the form, real or imaginary," under which it had been presented. Thus he excused himself in advance for possible exaggeration and tried to impart to his strong language a flavor of impersonality.

Despite its form, this statement has commonly been regarded by historians as a personal indictment of the domestic policies of his colleague, and in general this interpretation is warranted, but Jefferson may have picked up some of the financial particulars from his fellow Virginians or Freneau's paper and transmitted them on hearsay. Washington himself afterwards associated the charges as a whole with George Mason, among others, intimating that this neighbor and former friend of his was unfriendly to the government.[16] He did not thus describe the Secretary of State, and would not have been his own judicious self if he had, in view of Jefferson's intense personal loyalty to him and incessant labors for the government. He also knew, as Hamilton did not, that Jefferson was determined to retire from office, hence he had no reason whatever to doubt that the appeal for his own continuance was disinterested.

The tone of it might be objected to today as being too self-depreciatory on the one hand and too deferential on the other, but Jefferson often spoke of himself like that, and he knew that Washington had grown accustomed to the language of adulation. It is more noteworthy that he wholly dissociated the President from the causes of public discontent, thus attributing to him a freedom from responsibility for the financial policies of the government which Washington himself was too just a man to claim. He was not far from the truth, however, in believing that the public blamed Hamilton almost entirely for what it did not like, just as he did himself. Until this time the nearest Jefferson had ever come to being a monarchist was in his persistent belief that Washington could do no wrong.

The objections to the financial policies which he stated in this important letter numbered twenty-one, as Washington afterwards cited them to Hamilton. Roughly half of these dealt with finances as such, while the remainder dealt with political consequences and implications. Jefferson was more at home with political than fiscal questions and the latter group of objections probably coincided more closely with his personal convictions than the former. The criticism of the provisions

[16] Washington to Hamilton, July 29, 1792 (Fitzpatrick, XXXII, 95).

for debt which is of greatest interest, now, was that this was unnecessarily large and resulted in a needless burden of taxation. In his predominantly agricultural mind there was little or no sympathy with Hamilton's purpose to create fluid capital, and his moral indignation against "paper speculation" must be viewed in the light of his own lifelong abstention from speculative activity of any sort. To such later financiers and stockbrokers as may have read his words, no doubt they sounded quaintly old-fashioned, and to a major architect of a bourgeois civilization like Hamilton they were anachronistic even then, but their sincerity is beyond question.

In his mind the political consequences of the prevailing policies were more objectionable than the economic, and it was when he turned to these that his language became most vehement. When he spoke of the corruption of the legislature, he meant that holders of securities in Congress were the personal beneficiaries of their own legislative actions, and that Hamilton's successive measures could never have been carried through without their support. He spelled out these charges more fully afterwards than he did on this occasion and he actually compiled lists of "paper-men" in Congress.[17] The natural tendency among patriotic historians, especially such as have written in the Federalist tradition, has been to attribute his charges to partisanship and to minimize or deny them for that reason. Others, however, have found factual support for his contentions, and have even wondered how he acquired such precise information. The crux of the matter seems to be, not the fact that security-holders were numerous in Congress (which seems indubitable) but the interpretation of that fact in the light of what actually happened. The votes did not follow the lines of personal interest all the time, and the opposition as well as the support of Hamilton's policies tended to follow the lines of group or local economic interest. In the last analysis, completely disinterested representation was not possible or even desirable, and to that extent Jefferson's moral indignation was extreme.[18] On the other hand, it should not be regarded as spurious or quixotic. Hamilton had deliberately catered to a relatively small group and had caused this to wax strong on the food he fed it. Also, while attaching influential individuals and groups to the government, he was attaching them to himself and creating an instrument of power which he had shown little disposition to wield in behalf of the unmoneyed and inarticulate.

[17] See especially his memo. of a conversation with Washington, July 10, 1792 (Ford, I, 200), and his list of Mar. 23, 1793 (Ford, I, 223).

[18] These are essentially the conclusions of C. A. Beard, *Economic Origins of Jeffersonian Democracy* (1915), ch. VI, esp. pp. 194–195.

At last, Jefferson objected to Hamilton most for what he seemed to be doing to the government and the human spirit. The ultimate object as Jefferson saw it was to prepare the way for a change from republicanism to a monarchy, and, couched in this language, the fear may now sound fantastic. But arbitrary power changes its garb from age to age, and Jefferson's main reason for opposing his colleague's "system" was that he perceived in it a serious threat to human freedom. He did not hope or even want Hamilton's financial structure to be immediately or wholly overturned, for he believed such action would be contrary to right and public faith. He was no repudiationist. But he placed his hopes in the approaching elections and believed that the new Congress could undo some things (he did not say just which) and check others. He wanted to stop Hamilton and change the trend of the government.

He was no more a disunionist than he had ever been. His strongest plea to Washington was grounded on their common concern to preserve the Union and their common recognition of the dangers resulting from a geographical alignment in political controversy. On sectional questions, Washington stood so straight that he leaned backwards. Jefferson never did that, and at this juncture he was prone to emphasize Southern sacrifices to Northern interest and opinion. Quite clearly he believed that these should not and could not continue, but the immediate answer to the danger of disunion was the continuance in office of the President, who was above sections as well as parties.

> The confidence of the whole union is centred in you [he said]. Your being at the helm, will be more than an answer to every argument which can be used to alarm & lead the people in any quarter into violence or secession. North & South will hang together, if they have you to hang on.[19]

Jefferson had no exaggerated opinion of the importance of his own public services, but he regarded George Washington as indispensable. This was one point on which he and Hamilton were in complete agreement.

It was several weeks before he could talk with the President about these questions, and that conversation was only partially reassuring.[20] Though he was more anxious than ever to retire, Washington stated that if he were convinced there would be real danger in it of course he would conquer his longing. As to the existing causes of uneasiness,

[19] Ford, VI, 5.
[20] Memo. of conversation of July 10, 1792 (Ford, I, 198–201).

however, he believed that the "suspicions against a particular party" had been carried much too far – and this patient man showed clear signs of impatience at this point. There might be *desires* to change the form of government into a monarchy, but he did not believe there were *designs* to do it, and he was confident of the steady republicanism of the main body of the people in all parts of the country. Jefferson himself was confident of this, just as he was of Washington's own position, but he was far more sensitive than the President to ideological trends, just as Washington was much more disturbed about tendencies toward disorder. The President, unlike Hamilton, did not crave power, but throughout this controversy he stood like a rock as a symbol of Order and Union, and he was disturbed by certain criticisms which seemed to Jefferson a sign of political health and vitality. He disliked some of the pieces which had been appearing in Freneau's paper, believing that they were inciting rebellion against such measures as the excise law and by tending toward anarchy were endangering the Union. Furthermore, he was quite unwilling to dissociate himself from the measures which had been attacked, saying that "if they thought there were measures pursued contrary to his sentiment, they must conceive him too careless to attend to them or too stupid to understand them." He had signed many acts of which he had not wholly approved, but never one which he had not approved in general.

Jefferson supplemented and reinforced his own previous statement of objections to the financial system, but does not appear to have strengthened the case perceptibly in Washington's mind. The President was silent on the subject of corruption, by which Jefferson really meant improper influences on the legislature, and he manifested a strong disposition to support the policies of the Treasury as a whole. He could hardly have done otherwise in the face of public criticism without reflecting seriously on his own administration. He was not yet ready to admit that a chasm had opened within his official family, and for the present he kept to himself the allegations that had been made by his Secretary of State.

Jefferson had eased his own mind no doubt, and he was partially reassured about Washington's continuance in office, but he concluded that further argument with the President on the subject of the Treasury was futile. As a member of the government he had said all he could, and in view of Washington's temperament he probably had said too much. His representations had been made in private on what he regarded as public grounds. He had not mentioned Hamilton's interference in foreign affairs, which was his greatest personal grievance against his aggressive colleague. He had set forth the causes of public, not private, discontent.[21]

Hamilton's assumption of more offensive tactics against Madison and Jefferson cannot be attributed in the first instance to the critical comments on the Treasury "system" that the latter made to Washington, since the President had not received these when Hamilton showed, by an extraordinary letter, that he was resolved to wage private war against them in their own country.

This letter was addressed to Edward Carrington, who had been appointed United States Marshal for Virginia at Madison's suggestion but had had relations with Hamilton in connection with the excise law and was supposed by the latter to be sympathetic.[22] He must have been, if he read the *whole* of Hamilton's communication. While it is not as long as the official letter about infractions of the peace treaty which Jefferson delivered to George Hammond, about this time, it would fill most of this chapter if reprinted here. It marked the beginnings of a definite attempt to build up organized support for the Treasury in Virginia, and, incidentally, made available a vast supply of political ammunition.

Other actions of the indefatigable Secretary about this time pointed in the same direction. For example, he cultivated John Marshall, hoping that that lanky and conservative gentleman might be induced to run for Congress from the Richmond district.[23] As the head of the Treasury he need not have been greatly disturbed by the form the opposition had assumed in Virginia. James Monroe was now saying that, while republican principles were clearly in the ascendant in the state, there seemed to be no particular financial measure which could be opposed with wisdom and safety. The people did not like the excise, but who could suggest any other effective tax which they would like better? [24] In other words, Hamilton's move was not warranted on the ground that his financial measures were seriously threatened from this quarter. The political wisdom of his action may be questioned, and actually he never gained much of a personal following in Virginia; but the historic significance of his letter to Carrington does not lie in its local results.

[21] He did not bring foreign affairs and his own department into the discussion until his letter of Sept. 9, 1792, to Washington (Ford, VI, 102–104).

[22] Hamilton to Carrington, May 26, 1792 (Lodge, VIII, 248–265); Brant, *Madison*, III, 351.

[23] TJ to Madison, June 29, 1792 (Ford, VI, 95).

[24] See especially Monroe to Madison, June 27, 1792 (S. M. Hamilton, I, 235–236); see also Monroe to TJ, July 17, 1792 (*ibid.*, I, 238–239).

He gave here his own interpretation of the causes of opposition to him, and his own characterization of the two men whom he designated as the leaders of it. He considerably disclosed the strategy of his offensive defense and, unwittingly, he revealed himself.

During the last session of Congress, the Secretary said, he had arrived at the following conviction:

> . . . That Mr. Madison, cooperating with Mr. Jefferson, is at the head of a faction decidedly hostile to me and my administration; and actuated by views, in my judgment, subversive of the principles of good government and dangerous to the Union, peace, and happiness of the country.[25]

The latter part of this statement, a value judgment, became an essential element in Hamiltonian dogmatics; but, since many republicans were disposed to make a reverse application of it with comparable dogmatism, it need not greatly concern us here. The relative dangers of the republican and Hamiltonian attitudes and policies will have to be weighed by every student and reader for himself, in the light of all the evidence available to him. There are implications here, however, which no one can miss. Opposition to Hamilton and his policies was coupled with "subversion," and opposition itself was described in personal terms. Partisan loyalties and antipathies have often been expressed with great extravagance, but there was an exceptional degree of arrogance in Hamiltonianism. Proneness to personalize is also a very common political phenomenon, but here is an early and extreme example of it.

Hamilton was entirely realistic in his conclusion that there was a faction or party *decidedly* hostile to him and his administration of the Treasury, which in the minds of some would have amounted to the administration of the whole government if he could have had his way. He was correct in regarding Madison as the head of that group in Congress, and he did not overestimate the degree of Jefferson's sympathy with his friend's efforts to shake the grip of Hamilton's hand on the government. As to the extent of Jefferson's own *activities* against him, however, he indulged in a good deal of exaggeration. Most of the particular matters that Hamilton mentioned in this letter have already been referred to in this narrative in their proper setting of time. The charge that Jefferson had brought Freneau to Philadelphia and that the latter's paper was under his patronage was now made specifically, though only in private as yet. Also, when claiming that Jefferson questioned the expediency of funding the debt at all, which

[25] Lodge, VIII, 251.

was certainly untrue in the sense that Hamilton meant it, he completely ignored his colleague's co-operation with him during their early months together, when his whole financial policy was on the verge of defeat. His memory was conveniently short, and he was wholly oblivious of the possibility that the opinions of honest and patriotic men can change with circumstances.

Hamilton's statements of fact were glaringly inaccurate in many cases, but he erred most in his ascription of motives. Finding in Madison's conduct a more uniform and persistent opposition than he could resolve into a sincere difference of opinion, he finally concluded that his true character was the reverse of the "simple, fair, candid one" that he had assumed; that he had been embittered by successive defeats at Hamilton's hands; and that the still incredible changes in his position must be considerably attributed to the influence of Jefferson. Unfortunately for this argument, however, the facts seem to show that the reverse was true with respect to important financial questions.

His interpretation of Jefferson was a tissue of errors and misconceptions which hardly seems worth unraveling at this point, especially since he said so many of the same things in print a little later. His explanation of the grounds of his colleague's opposition to him was personal and narrowly political. He attributed to Jefferson disappointment at not having as important a part in the government as he had counted on, which at best was a half-truth; he thought perhaps he had expected to be in charge of finances, which was an absurd suggestion; and he charged him with an ardent desire to be President, a thing which his intimates would have denied emphatically. He finally summed Jefferson up as "a man of profound ambition and violent passions." [26] Hamilton must have been looking in the glass.

His anger against Jefferson already surpassed that against Madison. His own intimation that he resented the opposition of the former more because it was less open can hardly be regarded as a sufficient explanation, in view of his detestation of any sort of opposition and his own recourse to indirect methods whenever he could not accomplish his purposes by direct ones. He may have been particularly annoyed with his colleague, however, because of the difficulty of getting at him and grappling with him. The distinctive combination, which Jefferson had effected, of scrupulous propriety and politeness on one hand, and fervid devotion to abstract principles on the other, may have been peculiarly irritating to a man of Hamilton's aggressiveness, impatience, and lack of subtlety. Men sometimes hate those opponents most whom they find most incomprehensible.

[26] Lodge, VIII, 265.

Hamilton was uttering a half-truth when he wrote Carrington that the only enemy that republicanism had to fear in the United States was the spirit of faction and anarchy.

> If I were disposed to promote monarchy and overthrow State governments, I would mount the hobby-horse of popularity [he said], I would cry out "usurpation," "danger to liberty," etc., etc.; I would endeavor to prostrate the national government, raise a ferment, and then "ride in the whirlwind, and direct the storm." [27]

He did not believe that Madison would do that, but he strongly implied that Jefferson might, thus translating the philosophic lover of liberty and light into a self-seeking demagogue.

There were depths of character and motivation which Hamilton had not sounded. Also, there were far deeper causes of popular discontent than he perceived upon the surface.

[27] Lodge, VIII, 264.

XXVII

Hamilton *vs.* Jefferson

DURING the summer of this election year Jefferson was only a bystander on the scene of domestic politics. There is no reason to doubt that he adhered to his long-standing policy of not intermeddling in local contests, even in his own County.[1] Hamilton imposed no sharp limitation on his activities in any quarter, but he was most deeply concerned, early in the season, with the gubernatorial election in his own State of New York, where he had induced John Jay to oppose the perennial and hitherto unbeatable Governor, George Clinton, and with certain republican maneuvers respecting the vice presidency. The plot thickened, as he wrote John Adams whom he did not admire excessively, and "something very like a serious design to subvert the government" disclosed itself.[2] Jefferson believed that Hamilton and his partisans were the people who really had subversive designs, but he played no part in republican policy in this particular matter except to disapprove of it.

The facts behind the rhetoric were that the republicans in New York, whom the Jayites described as "the antis" and who were certainly anti-Hamiltonian, lined up with Clinton, and that republican leaders elsewhere were talking of supporting him afterwards for the vice presidency against Adams. Clinton's repute as a former opponent of the Constitution gave the Hamiltonians a strong handle against him to begin with, and the issue of the election gave them another. Thanks to the action of the canvassers, who rejected the returns from three counties on the ground of irregularities (including one county in

[1] TJ to Charles Clay, Sept. 11, 1792 (Ford, VI, 110–111), replying to a letter of Aug. 8 (LC, 13301).

[2] Hamilton to Adams, June 25, 1792, in the latter's *Works*, VIII, 514.

which Jay's majority seemed overwhelming), Clinton was elected, but the moral victory was Jay's.[3]

Jefferson's private comments on this situation were in his real character, though not in the one Hamilton assigned him. Writing Madison, he said that it did not seem possible to defend Clinton as a "just or disinterested man" if he did not decline the office, and he apprehended that the cause of republicanism would suffer if its votaries supported him. Their only gain would be to draw over the antifederalists, who were not sufficiently numerous to be worth the effort. To Monroe he wrote that it was dishonorable for Clinton to retain the office when a majority were probably against him. Jefferson noted that the charges of fraud in the election had silenced all the clamor in New York about the bankruptcies. This was good news for Hamilton, as he clearly saw, and amounted to the loss of an effective issue by the critics of the Treasury. It was no fault of Jefferson's that he was toasted along with the President in a celebration of Clinton's election in New York in midsummer, and the plans of the Virginians to support the Governor for the vice presidency were pursued without his concurrence.[4]

The burden of official business lightened considerably during the summer. Jefferson, having done all he could with the British Minister, found time to catch up on his scientific correspondence and to draw up certain agricultural notes at Washington's request.[5] His interest in farming constituted a tie with the President which Hamilton did not have, and the two Virginians had a stronger impulse to leave the city for the country. In the middle of July, Jefferson took advantage of the relaxed situation to go home, as the President had already done. About a month later, writing David Rittenhouse about a scientific instrument, Jefferson said: "I am here indulging in reverie and rural occupations, scarcely permitting anything to occupy my mind seriously. When I count the days I still have to remain here, I wish I could see at their end only the pleasure of meeting you again, and keep behind the curtain the table piled with papers, and the eternal sound of the door bell." For a variety of personal reasons, including

[3] On the election, see Frank Monaghan, *John Jay*, pp. 333–340, and E. W. Spaulding, *His Excellency George Clinton* (1938), pp. 202–205.

[4] TJ to Madison, June 21, 1792 (Ford, VI, 89–91); TJ to Monroe, June 23, 1792 (Ford, VI, 93–94); Brant, *Madison*, III, 359; Monroe to TJ, July 17, 1792 (S. M. Hamilton, I, 237–238); *Gazette of the U. S.*, July 25, 1792, describing the celebrations.

[5] Notes on Arthur Young's letter about American agriculture, June 18, 1792 (Ford, VI, 81–87). We shall refer to agricultural matters in the next volume of this work.

illness in the family, he did not get back to the seat of government until October.[6]

Meanwhile, Hamilton remained in Philadelphia. The Secretary of the Treasury should be credited with a high degree of official diligence, no doubt, but the main impression one gains from the records is that he was exceedingly active in political matters while his colleague was in virtual retirement.

At a time when Jefferson was doing little more in politics than receive information from close personal friends like Madison and Monroe, Hamilton was corresponding with political leaders in various parts of the country, encouraging his supporters and condemning his critics. Furthermore, he became a prolific pamphleteer and addressed himself to the larger public. Following the custom of the time, he wrote under one pseudonym or another, hence his attacks on his foes, while direct and violent, cannot be described as open. Jefferson, before he left for home, concluded that his colleague was the author of a communication to Fenno's paper in which all the complaints against the excise and the Bank were attributed to a "faction," of which Freneau's paper was the organ.[7] This was a real storm signal, for Hamilton made a furious attack on the editor and the supposed sponsor of the *National Gazette* a month later.

It may be that he first planned to defend his policies and attack Jefferson and Madison without mentioning their names. Certain papers that he wrote but did not publish bear out this impression.[8] In one of these he drew a recognizable caricature of Jefferson, while describing one class of "opponents" of the government:

> . . . A sect of political doctors; a kind of Popes in government; standards of political orthodoxy, who brand with heresy all opinions but their own; men of sublimated imaginations and weak judgments; pretenders to profound knowledge, yet ignorant of the most useful of all sciences — the science of human nature; men who dignify themselves with the appellation of philosophers, yet are destitute of the first elements of true philosophy; lovers of paradoxes; men who maintain expressly that

[6] As his Account Book shows, he left Philadelphia on July 13, 1792, and returned on Oct. 5. He wrote Rittenhouse on Aug. 12 (LC, 13305).

[7] *Gazette of the U. S.*, June 27, 1792; TJ to Madison, June 29, 1792 (Ford, VI, 95).

[8] This suggestion is made by Brant in *Madison*, III, 360, and the papers are in Lodge, II, 285–305, where they are tentatively dated 1791, though obviously in error.

> religion is not necessary to society, and very nearly that government itself is a nuisance; that priests and clergymen of all descriptions are worse than useless.[9]

Why he decided to attack Jefferson by name in conjunction with Freneau, largely disregarding Madison, and why he did it just when he did, is a question which naturally arises. Presumably the criticisms in the newspapers incited him to action and determined the direction of his first onslaught. Those in the *National Gazette* may have been no more severe after Congress recessed than they had been before, and some of the contributions were actually directed against Jefferson,[10] but there were criticisms in July which must have been peculiarly exasperating to Hamilton. On July 4, for example, Freneau printed on the front page an unsigned article giving "rules for changing a limited republican government into an unlimited hereditary one," the most important of these being to increase the national debt and establish a bank. Also, as an example of the tone of the editorial paragraphs, there was a stinging reference to the "corrupt speculation and avaricious jobbing" which had polluted the government. The disinterestedness and magnanimity of Washington were mentioned by way of contrast, and there was a remark about lopping off rotten branches. A less impatient man than Hamilton would have resented this sort of language in public print; and if he had not concluded that his loyal defender, Fenno, could not handle Freneau, he certainly should have by this time. At all events, Hamilton, late in the month, attempted to kill two birds with one stone. He hoped to destroy the influence of both Freneau and Jefferson by asserting that one man attacked the government because the other paid him.

On July 25, when the President was at Mount Vernon and the Secretary of State at Monticello, the following letter, signed "T.L.," appeared in John Fenno's paper:

> The Editor of the "National Gazette" receives a salary from government.
>
> *Quere* — Whether the salary is paid him for *translations;* or for *publications*, the design of which is to villify those to whom the voice of the people has committed the administration of our public affairs — to oppose the measures of government, and, by false insinuations, to disturb the public peace?
>
> In common life it is thought ungrateful for a man to bite the

[9] Lodge, II, 288–289.

[10] A letter to Friend Thomas, signed Ephraim Stedfast, in the issue of May 28, 1792, poked some fun at Jefferson.

hand that puts food in his mouth; but if the man is hired to do it, the case is altered.[11]

Freneau reprinted the letter immediately, saying that it was beneath reply while making a counterattack on Fenno. Describing himself as the editor of a free newspaper and terming his rival a "vile sycophant," he asserted that Fenno received far larger emoluments from the government (through public printing) than he did. He inserted in his own paper a mock "want ad" from an officeseeker who offered to take the translator's place, if vacated, agreeing to accept extraordinarily low wages and surrender his soul, body, and conscience to the absolute disposal of the government. In the same issue he challenged Fenno, who was a heavy fellow and deserved to be called Pomposo, in a characteristic bit of doggerel.[12]

Since the day we attempted the Nation's Gazette
Pomposo's dull printer does nothing but fret;
Now preaching
And screeching,
Then nibbling
And scribbling,
Remarking
And barking,
Repining
And whining,
And still in a pet
From morning till night with the Nation's Gazette. . . .

One National Paper, you think, is enough
To flatter and lie, to pallaver and puff;
To preach up in favour of monarchs and titles,
And garters and ribbons, to prey on our vitals:
Who knows but our Congress will give it in fee
And make Mr. Fenno the grand patentee!
Then take to your scrapers
Other national papers –
No rogue shall go snacks,
And the Newspaper-Tax
Shall be puff'd to the skies
As a measure most wise –
So a spaniel, when master is angry and kicks it,
Sneaks up to his shoe, and submissively licks it.

[11] *Gazette of the U. S.*, July 25, 1792. This is in Lodge, VI, 313. See also Hamilton to R. King, July 25, 1792 (Lodge, VIII, 272) intimating his desire that this line of attack be pursued elsewhere.
[12] All in *National Gazette*, July 28, 1792.

Fenno was stunned by this sally and met it feebly,[13] but Hamilton returned to the attack, stating emphatically that Freneau was "the faithful and devoted servant of the head of a party."[14] This reiterated charge needled Freneau, who was no hireling though undeniably a partisan, and he soon appeared before the Mayor of Philadelphia and took an oath, which was duly published. He swore that Jefferson had entered into no negotiation with him for the establishment of his paper, that he established it by his own voluntary act, that the Secretary of State had never sought to influence it in any way and had never written anything for it.[15]

Hamilton had to admit that the statement might be literally true so far as the actual negotiations went, but he now took occasion to say that a "particular friend" of Jefferson's had served as intermediary. About the same time he made further inquiries about Madison's negotiations, writing the man who had first informed him of them and practising some deception on his own part. He said that the attack on Freneau had been made by a friend of his on the basis of information he himself had passed on, and that this friend had asked him to secure authentication of it.[16] He was also confusing the situation by contributing to the papers simultaneously under two different pseudonyms.

Hamilton dismissed as absurd the claim of Freneau that no line of the *National Gazette* had been written or dictated by Jefferson, saying that the editor could not possibly be sure of the authorship of all the communications. In the absolute sense this was true, and he may have found it difficult to believe that Jefferson had not contributed something since he himself assuredly would have done so in a similar situation. It may be suggested, also, that his unwillingness to acknowledge Freneau's independence was owing to his inability to recognize a free man when he saw one. The propriety of Freneau's having any sort of place in the Department of State is another matter, and Jefferson unwittingly did a disservice to the freedom of the press by giving him one and rendering him suspect.

[13] *National Gazette*, Aug. 1, 1792. There were further charges and countercharges about printing contracts. The strong piece of CANDOR, in *Gazette of the U.S.*, Aug. 28, 1792, replying to "G," in *National Gazette*, Aug. 15, may have been by Hamilton (Marsh in *N.-Y. Hist. Soc. Quart.*, XXXII, 292).

[14] *Gazette of the U. S.*, Aug. 4, 1792 (Lodge, VI, 315), communication signed AN AMERICAN.

[15] *Gazette of the U. S.*, Aug. 8, 1792. It can be conveniently seen in Leary, p. 212.

[16] Hamilton to Elias Boudinot, Aug. 13, 1792 (Lodge, VIII, 279). His comments on Freneau's affidavit are in *Gazette of the U. S.*, Aug. 11, 1792.

Having reason to believe that the sensational charge that Freneau was the paid tool of Jefferson would be taken up by others, as in fact it was, Hamilton might have contented himself with making it and reiterating it after it had been denied. But he kept on firing at his colleague throughout the rest of the year, and the original accusation may thus be regarded as merely the first shot in a long campaign. His half-dozen communications signed T.L. and AN AMERICAN and appearing in July and August constituted the first phase of an offensive.[17] The editor continued to be a target throughout this phase, but a public character of much greater importance had become the main one long before it ended.

From the beginning Hamilton probably intended to assert that there was an identity of political purpose between Jefferson and Freneau and to castigate them simultaneously on this ground. He did just that in one of his early communications, though not the first one.[18] He claimed that there was no need to show that the *National Gazette* was virulently hostile to the government, since any intelligent reader could see that for himself, and said that its reflection of the views of its patron might be assumed. To make sure of Jefferson's damnation, however, he gave some gratuitous information about that gentleman's attitude toward the Constitution and the financial policies of the government. His assertions were not made without qualification, but the implications were false, namely, that Jefferson was hostile to the Constitution and honorable provisions for the public debt. Hamilton expressly said that the trend of his tenets was toward disunion, disorder, and discredit. This was the picture of his colleague that he sought from this time forward to impress on the public mind, and he skillfully blended fact and fancy to achieve the desired effect. But he was either unaware of the power of suggestion or indifferent to it when he designated Jefferson as the head of a party and intimated that he might become the toast of political clubs and the theme of popular acclaim.

Besides being politically unwise, this magnification of his colleague's leadership appears to have gone beyond anything Hamilton had previously said, even in private. He may not have intended to go that far when he first attacked Freneau, but in the meantime he had received from Washington the letter in which the twenty-one objections to his

[17] Besides the T.L. piece of July 25, 1792, Lodge prints three communications from AN AMERICAN, which appeared Aug. 4, 11, and 18 (VI, 314–327). All these were in the *Gazette of the U. S.*, which also printed two others from T.L. on Aug. 1 and 11.

[18] Writing as AN AMERICAN, Aug. 4, 1792.

system were presented.[19] The President did not mention the name of the Secretary of State in connection with them, but they were stated in his language. Hamilton was thoroughly familiar with that, and he had undoubtedly heard from his colleague's mouth some of these same ideas; hence he probably attributed this document in its entirety to Jefferson, and recognized it as a major threat and challenge. Accordingly, he intensified his anonymous public attacks, which were now counterattacks in reality, and made them more direct. He defended himself brilliantly before George Washington at the same time; then he paused briefly in his campaign while the President was vainly trying to arrange an armistice.

Hamilton's reply to the twenty-one objections was characteristically elaborate, being eight times as long as the letter he was answering.[20] He wrote it in considerable heat, as he admitted. "I acknowledge that I cannot be entirely patient under charges which impeach the integrity of my public motives or conduct," he said, believing that he merited these "*in no degree.*"

As he had been masterful in advocating specific financial policies, he was always masterful in defending them, and his critics never had much success when they argued with him on fiscal matters. His defense of his financial system itself appears to have fully satisfied George Washington, but Jefferson did not see it and it need not concern us here. Hamilton had to admit that there had been some ill effects from paper speculation, but he pointed again to the benefits resulting from the increase of fluid capital. Washington himself had noted that most people regarded the country as prosperous, and he had right to believe that the confidence that had been lost as a result of the stock-market panic was being steadily regained.

Hamilton's denial of the claim that the funding of the debt had furnished means for corrupting the legislature was marred by the violence of his language. He did not content himself with a statement that the charges were extravagant and that motives should not be impugned because of the mere fact that legislators owned securities. In behalf of the accused representatives he bitterly denounced their "defamers," charging the latter with holding narrow and depraved ideas and describing their charges as false and malignant. He called no names, but he probably was thinking of Jefferson when he said:

[19] Hamilton got Washington's letter of July 29 on Aug. 3 (J. C. Hamilton, IV, 237).

[20] Hamilton to Washington, Aug. 18, 1792 (Lodge, II, 236–279), replying to Washington's letter of July 29 (Fitzpatrick, XXXII, 95–100) Hamilton repeated the objections, thus enlarging his own letter to that extent.

"Your principles of liberty are principles of licentiousness. You sacrifice everything that is venerable and substantial in society to the vain reveries of a false and new-fangled philosophy." [21] If Washington was ever disposed to take Jefferson at Hamilton's valuation, that time had certainly not yet come. On the other hand, he was quite prepared to believe that some of the current criticisms of the policies of the Treasury had emanated from enemies of the government. This was a good line of argument with him, therefore, so long as it did not involve direct attack on men whom he trusted. Hamilton had pursued it in his earlier plea to the President to stand for re-election, when he emphasized the danger that the government might fall into the hands of its foes, covering his partisanship with a veil of patriotism which was not quite so transparent.[22]

Hamilton saw no danger whatever that monarchy might arise from the present trends of the government and contended that the "true artificers of monarchy" were those who resisted the establishment of public order.[23] There was a time when Madison had said much the same thing, but Hamilton had particular persons in mind. The description he gave here fitted Aaron Burr better than anybody else, but he talked about mounting "the hobby-horse of popularity," and referred to Catiline and Caesar in much the same way that he did later when writing about Jefferson. Also, he indignantly denied that he himself had advocated monarchy in the Federal Convention.

Certain comments of his on the sectional alignment in politics and the dangers of disunion were revealing. "In the South," he said, "it is supposed that more government than is expedient is desired by the North. In the North, it is believed that the prejudices of the South are incompatible with the necessary degree of government, and with the attainment of the essential ends of national union." [24] Like all the other responsible leaders, he wanted to prevent a schism, but as a Northern leader he was not disposed to make concessions. If the conflict had been between "*great* and substantial national objects on the one hand, and theoretical prejudices on the other," he did not believe that in any case the North should have yielded. He may not have been conscious of the self-righteousness in his attitude, but it was there.

Washington undoubtedly agreed with him that prosperity extended to the country as a whole, and the President took little stock in the-

[21] Lodge, II, 264.
[22] Hamilton to Washington, July 30, 1792 (J. C. Hamilton, IV, 235–237).
[23] Answering Objection 14 (Lodge, II, 267–270).
[24] Lodge, II, 273.

oretical prejudices of any sort, hence he tended to regard the political controversy of the time as unnecessary if not positively dangerous. What he abhorred most, however, was personal controversy, and by now it was clear to him that Hamilton and Jefferson were engaged in that. Regarding them both as invaluable, he did not weigh them in the scales, and he was undisposed to enter into the merits of either case. What he tried to do was to pour oil on the troubled waters. He wrote his two Secretaries about the same time, and addressed them in essentially the same language.[25] He emphasized the dangers that the government and Union faced from real enemies, and the necessity of avoiding internal dissensions until both should be firmly established. His language was moving, almost eloquent. He spoke of the goodly fabric they were erecting, of the danger of losing "the fairest prospect of happiness and prosperity that ever was presented to man" – sounding much like Lincoln two generations later.

So far as Jefferson was concerned, the specific injunctions which were implied in Washington's exceedingly polite phrases were that he be more tolerant of philosophical differences, that there be no pulling the other way after measures had been decided on. Washington addressed Hamilton at somewhat greater length, and mentioned "temper" and newspapers as he did not to Jefferson, but he probably regarded his pleas for greater charity and forbearance as interchangeable. He believed that these two Secretaries were "men of abilities, zealous patriots, and having the same *general* objects in view," and that common sense required the steering of a middle course. He did not realize or would not admit that they were incompatible in temperament and irreconcilable in philosophy.

By coincidence they replied to him on the same day in September. Jefferson's letter, written at Monticello, was the longer, though he never caught up with Hamilton in wordage.[26] He described the policy of not intermeddling with the legislature and other departments which he had tried to follow, acknowledging no real deviation from it except in the part he had played in the assumption fight, which he now so deeply regretted; and he completely denied that he had ever intrigued with members of the legislature to defeat Hamilton's plans. He frankly admitted, however, that in his private conversations he had utterly disapproved of the system of the Secretary of the Treasury, and gave the fundamental reason for abhorring it: "His system flowed from

[25] Washington to TJ, Aug. 23, 1792 (Fitzpatrick, XXXII, 130–131); to Hamilton, Aug. 26, 1792 (*ibid.*, XXXII, 132–134). The earlier date of the letter to TJ has no significance, since the occasion was provided by official business.

[26] TJ to Washington, Sept. 9, 1792 (Ford, VI, 101–109).

principles adverse to liberty, and was calculated to undermine and demolish the republic, by creating an influence of his department over the members of the legislature."[27] He elaborated upon the specific objections that he had previously made – dismaying Washington, no doubt – and he now told the President as he never had before what he really thought about Hamilton's interference with *his* policies and *his* department. He asserted that Hamilton, by "cabals" with the legislature and other methods, had caused his own foreign policy to be largely adopted, instead of what Jefferson favored and had supposed that Washington preferred. The Secretary of State had then been expected to carry out this policy, whether he liked it or not, and he called the President to witness how sincerely he had done it. He referred also to Hamilton's self-assumed conferences with the British and French representatives. He did not fully realize what had been going on, but he knew enough to claim, and claim rightly, that Hamilton had done far more interfering than he had, and had done it first.

He gave a lengthy account of his connection with Freneau which may be regarded as a sufficient answer to Hamilton's charges, even if it be granted that his concern for Washington's good opinion caused him to protest his innocence somewhat more than the facts warranted and the circumstances required.[28] If his defense of the propriety of giving a minor place to Freneau was not quite convincing, he used the *tu quoque* argument effectively, making some very pointed remarks about Hamilton's large distribution of patronage.

Of more immediate importance was his reference to his own retirement at the end of the first presidential term. This he made with a tone of finality. Until the time of his release, he said, he had no intention of intermeddling with the legislature or of getting involved in newspaper contests, though he might write something in defense of himself over his own name afterwards. His comments on Hamilton in this connection were perhaps the bitterest he ever made on him: "I will not suffer my retirement to be clouded by the slanders of a man whose history, from the moment at which history can stoop to notice him, is a tissue of machinations against the liberty of the country which has not only received and given him bread, but heaped its honors on his head."[29] Jefferson was not the man of extreme ambitions and violent passions whom Hamilton had described to Carrington, but until this time no American public man had ever inspired in him such detestation as the Secretary of the Treasury had.

Washington had not succeeded in soothing him, but neither had

[27] Ford, VI, 102. [28] See pp. 423–424, above. [29] Ford, VI, 109.

Jefferson's words alienated the President. The Secretary of State spent the night at Mount Vernon on his way back to Philadelphia a few weeks later, and they went over the old ground without getting anywhere.[30] He continued to urge Washington to remain in office, however; and his host's last words to him were an exhortation not to decide too positively on his own retirement. Washington knew how hard it would be to replace him. "I believe the views of both of you are pure and well meant," the President wrote a little later, adding that he had a great and sincere esteem and regard for both. This unusually patient man refused to take sides in a personal quarrel and continued to hope that he could patch up a truce, thus showing that he was also a man of extraordinary optimism.[31]

He could not have been pleased with Hamilton's response to his peacemaking efforts.[32] Not knowing Jefferson's purposes, the Secretary of the Treasury suggested that if no accommodation could be effected perhaps they should both get out, but that was not what Washington wanted and Hamilton could count on the President's unwillingness to let him go. He now admitted that he had had some part in the "retaliations" which had lately fallen on certain public characters, but said that he was unable to recede from his course *for the present*. He regarded himself as "the deeply injured party" in the dispute. It was at this time that he spoke of having been so long a silent sufferer, and declared that he had met with uniform opposition from Jefferson from the moment of the latter's arrival in New York. He attributed his present attitude to his conviction that a definite party, bent on undoing the funding system and subverting the government, was in existence. He was trying to resist this "torrent," and to "draw aside the veil from the principal actors," believing that events would prove that he had done rightly. At a *later* time, he would be glad to consider a plan to reunite the members of the administration, he said – probably meaning that he would proceed with his campaign until after the elections.

That is what he did, at all events. More than a dozen communications to the newspapers after Washington's intervention have been identified as Hamilton's. By means of these he sought to tear the veil from one who had previously been distinguished as "the quiet, modest, retiring philosopher," and as the "plain, simple, unambitious republican," and to show him in his true colors as "the intriguing incendiary, the aspiring, turbulent competitor," who deserved comparison with

[30] Memo. of Oct. 1, 1792 (Ford, I, 202–205).
[31] Washington to TJ, Oct. 18, 1792 (Fitzpatrick, XXXII, 186).
[32] Hamilton to Washington, Sept. 9, 1792 (Lodge, VI, 384–387).

Caesar and Catiline.[33] As things turned out, however, the Secretary of the Treasury was not wholly successful.

The war that was waged in the newspapers was by no means one-sided, for defenders of the Secretary of State appeared along with fresh assailants. That was probably one of the reasons why Hamilton concluded that he could not stop. He was not challenged by Jefferson himself, for that astute man did not permit himself to notice unsigned articles. As he wrote in September to Edmund Randolph, who offered his services, he had long since resolved never to write in public without subscribing his name and had no intention of engaging an anonymous adversary. Furthermore, even if newspaper squabbling between two public ministers had not seemed indecent to him, he regarded the President's admonitions as a virtual injunction not to engage in it. He did not say that his sensibility was more delicate than Hamilton's, but he did say this: "Every fact alleged under the signature of 'an American' as to myself is false, and can be proved so; and perhaps will be one day. But for the present, lying and scribbling must be free to those mean enough to deal in them, and in the dark." [34]

Madison regarded the attack as an "extraordinary maneuver of calumny," but believed that it would serve Jefferson and the public if it should lead to an investigation of his character and public opinions.[35] That is precisely what it did lead to, though this investigation took the form of a newspaper debate between unnamed champions in which the rules of evidence were not always honored. Edmund Randolph, Monroe, and Madison himself appear to have participated in it, and Hamilton measured swords with them week after week throughout the fall. In this series of duels he gave vent to the loudest war cries, but his opponents seem to have repulsed his charges.

After ringing the changes on Jefferson's connection with the *National Gazette*, he directed his attention to his colleague's original criticisms of the Constitution. He seems to have been only vaguely informed about these and he was promptly asked to prove his contentions. The challenger, who called himself ARISTIDES, was probably Edmund Randolph, who had been a member of the Virginia ratifying convention.[36] Describing Jefferson's "calumniator" as a "cowardly

[33] See especially the CATULLUS piece of Sept. 29, 1792 (Lodge, VI, 353–354).

[34] TJ to Edmund Randolph, Sept. 17, 1792 (Ford, VI, 112), replying to a letter of Aug. 26 (LC, 13340).

[35] Madison to Edmund Randolph, Sept. 13, 1792 (Hunt, VI, 117*n.*).

[36] The first paper of ARISTIDES appeared in the *Gazette of the U. S.*, Sept 8, 1792. It is partly quoted by Philip M. Marsh in *Pa. Mag. of Hist. and Biog.*, July, 1948, pp. 247–248, in a well-documented article entitled "Randolph and Hamilton."

assassin" who struck in the dark, he suggested that "a certain head of department" was the real author or instigator of this virulent attack. This obvious reference to Hamilton was too much for Fenno, who cautioned ARISTIDES about personal strictures and threatened not to publish anything further from him unless he revealed himself. Calling attention to the glaring inconsistency and unblushing partisanship of this position, ARISTIDES sent his second and last communication to Freneau.[37]

Before that time, Hamilton had returned to the fray as AMICUS, CATULLUS, and SCOURGE. He addressed himself particularly to ARISTIDES and sank to his lowest controversial depths under the two last disguises.[38] First he had AMICUS defend the Secretary of the Treasury against the current charge that he had expressed monarchical sentiments in the Federal Convention, and it was fortunate for him that the records of that body were not accessible. Some of his language at the time sounded unrepublican, whether or not it can be properly described as monarchical, and he might have been confronted with embarrassing quotations. His renewed attack on Jefferson's comments on the Constitution while in France was much riskier, since he certainly had not seen all of the letters of his colleague on the subject, and may not have seen any when he launched his first charge. But they were not produced immediately and he created a diversion in the meantime by developing an offensive along another line.

Out of the records of the old Board of the Treasury, of which William Duer had been secretary, or the proceedings of the old Congress, he dug up the proposal of 1786 that the American debt to France be transferred to a private Dutch company. Jefferson had transmitted this, under circumstances which Hamilton did not describe; and had commended it, with qualifications he did not bother to mention. Tearing from its context a sentence in which Jefferson had suggested that if there should be discontent about unpunctual payments, it might be better to transfer this from a Court of whose good will the United States had so much need to the breasts of a private company, he sought to create the impression that his colleague showed a lack

[37] *National Gazette*, Sept. 26, 1792.

[38] All these papers were in Fenno's *Gazette of the U. S.* He wrote as AMICUS on Sept. 11, 1792 (Lodge, VI, 327–330), as CATULLUS on Sept. 15, 19, 29, and Oct. 17 (Lodge, VI, 330–365). A copy of the paper of SCOURGE (Sept. 22), in Hamilton's handwriting, was discovered by Philip M. Marsh in the Hamilton Papers, and has been reprinted in considerable part in his pamphlet, *Monroe's Defense of Jefferson and Freneau against Hamilton* (Oxford, Ohio, 1948), pp. 19–21. See also his article, "Hamilton's Neglected Essays," in *N.-Y. Hist. Soc. Quart.*, XXXII, 280–300.

of "moral feeling" in this financial matter.[39] Jefferson's friends soon claimed that the quotation was mutilated, as it was to some extent so as to make a worse impression, but a more important objection was that it was an extract which inadequately represented the total situation. Jefferson himself afterwards sent Washington a full document.[40] Hamilton's procedure can be condemned on even more fundamental grounds. The episode was irrelevant and the implications he drew from it were utterly unwarranted. It had no connection with any current question of public debt and Jefferson's total record made charges of financial irresponsibility preposterous. For his own political purposes Hamilton had tortured his words so as to give an entirely false impression. Perhaps the Secretary of the Treasury believed that anything was fair in politics, as in love and war, and his critics were often unfair to him, but it would be difficult to find among the national leaders of that time anybody that matched him in artful misrepresentation. Before he got through with this campaign he entered into other episodes of his colleague's past, including the controversy in which Paine and John Adams figured; but this charge about the debt to France was probably the hardest one to meet before an uninformed public.[41]

His printed comments on Jefferson's character may perhaps be regarded as misconceptions rather than deliberate misrepresentations, but in making them he descended to the level of the most irresponsible journalists of the era. Toward the end of September, when the Secretary of State was returning from Monticello by way of Madison's Montpelier and Washington's Mount Vernon, CATULLUS had this to say about him:

> How long it is since that gentleman's real character may have been *divined*, or whether this is only the *first time* that the *secret* has been disclosed, I am not sufficiently acquainted with the history of his political life to determine; but there is always a "*first time*" when characters studious of artful disguises are unveiled; when the visor of stoicism is plucked from the brow of the epicurean; when the plain garb of Quaker simplicity is stripped from the concealed voluptuary; when Caesar *coyly refusing* the

[39] He did this in CATULLUS II, on Sept. 19, 1792 (Lodge, VI, 343–345). The letter referred to was from TJ to Jay, Sept. 26, 1786 (*D. C.*, I, 813–814), and the episode is described in its proper setting in ch. X of this work, p. 188.

[40] Enclosure in his letter of Oct. 17, 1792 (Ford, VI, 123–125*n.*). Ford's comment that neither Hamilton's quotation nor TJ's fuller extract followed the original text exactly is unwarranted so far as TJ is concerned. I have noted no variations except in capitalization, punctuation, and italics.

[41] Note the comment of John Beckley in a letter of Sept. 2, 1792, to Madison, quoted by Philip M. Marsh in *Pa. Mag. of Hist. and Biog.*, January, 1948, p. 58.

proferred diadem, is seen to be Caesar rejecting the trappings but grasping the substance of imperial domination. . . .

It has been pertinently remarked by a judicious writer, that *Caesar*, who *overturned* the republic, was the Whig, Cato, who *died* for it, the Tory of Rome: such, at least was the common cant of political harangues, the insidious tale of hypocritical demagogues.[42]

If Hamilton was recklessly abusive as CATULLUS he showed his worst taste when he wrote as SCOURGE.[43] In trying to poke fun at Jefferson, however, he unwittingly supported the latter's repeated claim that he had expressed his abhorrence of Hamilton's political principles only in private to his own friends. Replying to the assertion of ARISTIDES that he had done this with "manly freedom," SCOURGE said:

. . . How far he may declare his sentiments on this subject with *manly freedom* among his own party, is best known to them; but certain it is, that in other societies he is distinguished for a very different mode of procedure; cautious and shy, wrapped up in impenetrable silence and mystery, he reserves his *abhorrence* for the arcana of a certain snug sanctuary, where seated on his pivot-chair, and involved in all the obscurity of political mystery and deception . . . he compounds and, with the aid of his active tools, circulates his poison thro' the medium of the *National Gazette*.

The pivot-chair seemed to fascinate SCOURGE, who found in it an explanation of Jefferson's shifting position on the Constitution.

. . . In short, his opinion appears to have been as versatile as his chair, and as in schools, applications to the breech are said to have a wonderful effect on the head, by driving up learning, so there appears to be such a wonderful connexion between the seat and the head of this great politician, . . . that we may say with the American poet —

But should his Honor raise Bum-fiddle,
The Charm would break off in the middle.

SCOURGE casually compared Jefferson's proposed amendments to the Constitution with the wild schemes he was said to have recommended to a set of raw politicians in Paris, from which most of the calamities of France had resulted. His main theme, however, was that Jefferson feared Hamilton and wanted to ruin his rival:

[42] Sept. 29, 1792 (Lodge, VI, 354–355).
[43] Marsh, *Monroe's Defense*, pp. 19–21, from *Gazette of the U. S.*, Sept. 22, 1792.

> . . . To this end were all his means to be directed – on the one hand, a monstrous affectation of pure republicanism, primitive simplicity, and extraordinary zeal for the public good – on the other hand, to cry down the funding system, the bank, the excise law, as emanations from the Secretary of the Treasury, to make these measures odious to the people, and then attribute them all to Mr. Hamilton's machinations.

Before he got through, however, SCOURGE went back to events that occurred long before the Secretary of the Treasury assumed office. He referred ironically to Jefferson's eminent services in Virginia at the time of Tarleton's raid, thus striking him below the belt.

An anonymous pamphlet which appeared about this time closely followed the line that Hamilton had laid down. This was entitled, *The Politicks and Views of a Certain Party, Displayed*, and the author has been identified as William Loughton Smith, a representative from South Carolina and partisan of Hamilton's who wrote just like him.[44] The general argument was that everybody was pleased with the proceedings of the government until Jefferson arrived from France, and that the attacks on Hamilton were the products of a *system*, "established to promote *private* and *party* purposes and not the public good," the chief one being the overthrow of Hamilton as the main obstacle in Jefferson's path to the presidency. Madison was dubbed "General," and Jefferson "Generalissimo," as though the two had always stood in that relative position. According to this writer, however, the Generalissimo had little with which to oppose the splendid abilities of Hamilton:

> . . . Had an inquisitive mind in those days sought for evidence of his Abilities as a Statesman, he would have been referred to the confusions in France, the offspring of certain political dogmas fostered by the American Minister, and to certain theoretical principles fit only for Utopia: As a Warrior, to his Exploits at *Montecelli;* as a Philosopher, to his discovery of the inferiority of Blacks to Whites, because they are more unsavory and secrete more by the kidnies; as a Mathematician, to his whirligig Chair.[45]

[44] The pamphlet, dated 1792, appeared before Oct. 31, when it was commented on in the Philadelphia *General Advertiser*. William Smith, as the author was then known, acknowledged it afterwards. The account of him in *S. C. Hist. & Gen. Mag.*, IV, 252–256, and abundant contemporary references, show his political intimacy with Hamilton. TJ recorded an anecdote about him on Mar. 11, 1792 (Ford, I, 184), suggesting his hostility to trial by jury. Madison, who was severely attacked in the pamphlet, commented on it to Pendleton, Nov. 16, 1792 (MP, 15:96).

[45] *Politicks and Views*, pp. 28–29.

Realizing his inferiority, he sought to exalt himself and depress his rival by means of stratagem and maneuver, finesse and deception.

> . . . The first object would be promoted by decorating himself in the modest garb of pure Republicanism; the second by endeavoring to persuade his fellow citizens that they were miserable, and that the Secretary of the Treasury was the author of their misery. In the prosecution of the first part of the system, it was necessary to resort to all those little pitiful tricks which must render the inventor of them contemptible in the eyes of discerning citizens. A ridiculous affectation of simplicity, stiling himself in the public papers and on invitation cards, plain Thomas, and similar frivolities, a pretended outcry against Monarchy and Aristocracy may have had a momentary effect with the few ignorant and unsuspecting, but have long ago excited the derision of the many, who know that under the assumed cloak of humility lurks the most ambitious spirit, the most overweening pride and hauteur, and that the *externals* of pure Democracy afford but a flimsy veil to the *internal* evidences of aristocratic splendor, sensuality and Epicureanism.[46]

There is some biographical value in this exaggerated partisan portrait because of certain clues it offers about Jefferson's manners. The most important thing to note, however, is that a picture of him as a scheming and self-serving politician was definitely emerging through the deliberate design of Hamilton and his intimates.

Whatever may be said of the language of republican editors in an era of reckless and irresponsible journalism, the defense of the Secretary of State at the hands of his personal friends was pitched on a higher plane of argument and manners than the one that Hamilton had descended to. The identity of the author of the second paper signed ARISTIDES is more uncertain than that of the author of the first, and he may not have been Edmund Randolph.[47] His defense of Jefferson was strong, and he called attention to the similarity of style between the writings of AN AMERICAN, CATULLUS, and SCOURGE and strongly intimated that this trio constituted one and the same person.

The main reply to Hamilton, however, appeared in six parts and was the work of Monroe, in collaboration with Madison. They began it without consulting Jefferson, and there is no indication that he wrote

[46] *Ibid.*, pp. 29–30.

[47] *National Gazette*, Sept. 26, 1792; summarized and quoted by Marsh in *Pa. Mag. of Hist.*, July, 1948, pp. 250–251.

any part of it except the letters that they quoted; but to all practical purposes it was official.[48]

Monroe got from Madison a batch of Jefferson's letters from France and printed extracts containing successive comments on the new Constitution. To anybody but a rabid partisan these were a sufficient answer to Hamilton's charges and showed how unfounded the latter had been. He himself questioned the authenticity of the extracts at first and never quite conceded it, but his virtual abandonment of the constitutional line of attack amounted to an admission that he had been worsted.[49] The answer to the charges about the *National Gazette*, which was largely written by Madison, did not meet all the issues squarely, but the comments of an old friend on Freneau's character and independence must carry weight with anyone seeking to pass fair judgment on these events.[50] Hamilton was now leaving Freneau to others, and his duel with Jefferson's VINDICATOR in its last phase was fought over the irrelevant question of the transfer of the French debt.[51] The line of defense was that the proposal was not immoral in itself, that it had been inadequately described, and that there had been deliberate misquotation. CATULLUS was challenged to produce a full document and also to reveal his identity, in which case VINDICATOR offered to unmask himself. Hamilton did neither, and he had to admit a degree of misquotation. He wasted much valuable time carrying on an argument which never should have been started, and by December

[48] It appeared originally in *American Daily Advertiser*, beginning Sept. 22, 1792, and ending Dec. 31, and was reprinted in both the *National Gazette* and the *Gazette of the U. S.* The various papers have been collected by Philip Marsh and printed by him under the title, "The Vindication of Mr. Jefferson," in his pamphlet, *Monroe's Defense of Jefferson* (1948). See also Brant, *Madison*, III, 362–363. TJ wrote Washington on Oct. 17 (Ford, VI, 123) that when he arrived in Philadelphia on Oct. 5, a number of his letters had been printed though no word had been said to him about them. This agrees with the statement in the first publication and may be presumed to be correct as of that date. By the time he wrote Washington, however, he must have known who the authors were, hence his statement, while literally true, gives a false impression about the series as a whole. Madison wrote him on Oct. 9 about a "packet" which had been in his hands and which seems to have contained a later article (MP, 15:88), but he was perfectly capable of not looking into it and he could hardly have been so foolish as to deliver it personally to the printer. Throughout this business he probably maintained an attitude of strict correctness, though he really need not have been so careful, either in act or word.

[49] The extracts were printed and discussed in Nos. I, II of the "Vindication," appearing Sept. 22, 26, and Oct. 10, 1792. CATULLUS replied in *Gazette of the U. S.*, Oct. 17. The recipient of the letters, Madison, was described as a "particular friend."

[50] No. III, Oct. 20, 1792.

[51] "Vindication," Nos. IV–VI, Nov. 8, Dec. 3, 31, 1792; CATULLUS on Nov. 24, Dec. 22, 1792, in Lodge, VI, 370–382.

he must have grown tired of it, since he let his adversaries have the final say. His own last words were to accuse them of artifice and indecency, while Monroe indulged at the last in irony. He expressed the wish that CATULLUS "would exhibit himself to the public view, that we might behold in him a living monument of that immaculate purity, to which he pretends, and which ought to distinguish so bold and arrogant a censor of others."

Monroe was now informed of Hamilton's illicit affair with Mrs. Reynolds, as Jefferson was, and he may have been thinking of it. Since Hamilton, by revealing it, had fully cleared himself of charges reflecting on his public honor, Monroe had agreed to treat this as a confidential private matter. The later exploitation of it by less scrupulous men was not his fault, and perhaps he should not have thought of it now, since it was irrevelant. Yet his words were fitting. By making unwarranted attacks on the public conduct of others in a self-righteous spirit Hamilton had invited retribution.[52]

By this time the public must have grown weary of this controversy. Early in November, Jefferson wrote his son-in-law:

> . . . They [the monocrats] have kept up the ball with respect to myself till they begin to be tired of it themselves. Their chief object was to influence the election of this state [Pennsylvania), by persuading them there was a league against the government, and as it was necessary to designate a head to the league, they did me that honour. This indulged at the same time the personal enmity of a particular gentleman, who has written & written under all sorts of shapes & signatures without much advancing the cause of his part. Tho' I have no reason to be dissatisfied with the impression made, yet I have too many sources of happiness at home, and of the tranquil kind which are alone happiness to me, not to wish for my release.[53]

He was entitled to chuckle over one of the papers that had been aimed at him. Writing as METELLUS, Hamilton had prescribed an admirable code of propriety for members of the administration, and he was undoubtedly speaking of Jefferson when he said:

> Let him not cling to the honor or emolument of an office, whichever it may be that attracts him, and content himself with

[52] TJ made a bare note of the Reynolds affair, Dec. 17, 1792 (Ford, I, 212). This came up again in 1796 and 1797, as we shall see in the next volume of this work. The person who revealed it appears to have been John Beckley. (See Philip Marsh, in *Pa. Mag. of Hist. and Biog.*, Jan. 1948, p. 64.)

[53] TJ to T. M. Randolph, Jr., Nov. 2, 1792 (Ford, VI, 128).

> defending the injured rights of the people by obscure or indirect means. Let him renounce a situation which is a clog upon his patriotism.[54]

Many of Jefferson's friends believed that the main purpose of Hamilton's campaign was to run him out of the government, and for just that reason they soon began to urge him to stay in it. The Secretary of the Treasury had really been working against his own purposes. By making unwarranted personal attacks he had incited an able and spirited defense, and by saying that Jefferson was the idol of his votaries he had helped to make him that. A votary of his own had asserted that the public must choose between the two Secretaries. George Washington did not think so, but pressing that issue had one inevitable result: it established Jefferson in the public mind as the leader of the opposition to the policies and principles that were identified with Hamilton.

[54] Oct. 24, 1792 (Lodge, VI, 369).

[XXVIII]

An Election and Its Promise

1792

THE national election of 1792 was in reality a series of local contests, and the party spirit which marked it was chiefly displayed in the selection of state legislators and members of the lower house of Congress. This was inevitable in view of the political structure and the unique public position of George Washington. The state legislatures not only elected the Senators but also the electors who chose the President and Vice President, hence the real campaigning was on the local level. The electoral system lent itself to interstate intrigue and there was some with respect to the second executive office, but there was no need of any in Washington's case. All the important leaders regarded him as indispensable and everybody who knew about his desire to retire did his utmost to dissuade him.

When Madison sent the President the valedictory address he had drafted for him early in the summer, he suggested that the middle of September would be a good time to release it if he persisted in his purpose, as Madison sincerely hoped he would not. Besides Jefferson and Hamilton, Edmund Randolph brought strong pressure to bear on Washington during his respite from official duties.[1] The Constitution was still in a state of probation, the Attorney General said, and only Washington could give stability to the public deliberations. If a civil war should arise he could not stay at home, and it would be much easier to disperse the factions which were "rushing to this catastrophe" than to subdue them after they had appeared in arms. "It is the fixed opinion of the world," Randolph said, "that you surrender nothing incomplete." From other sources Washington was reassured about the general public attitude toward him personally and the pros-

[1] Randolph's letter of Aug. 5, 1792, is printed in part in Paltsits *Washington's Farewell Address*, pp. 234–235.

pect that he would receive another unanimous vote. From what he heard he had abundant reason to conclude that the criticisms of the government had not been aimed at him, and he understood the personal attitudes of the men whom Hamilton had designated as the leaders of the opposition party. The conception of a President who was above partisan wrangles still dominated the minds of Jefferson and Madison, and their loyalty to Washington was beyond dispute.

These representations and considerations might have been amply sufficient to deter the President from declining re-election, but the argument for his continuance was reinforced from another quarter before the middle of September. To his fears of the disruption of the government by partisan and sectional dispute were added new fears occasioned by threats of actual resistance to the government in the frontier region of Pennsylvania. This incipient revolt, which developed some months later into the Whiskey Rebellion, was directed against another of Hamilton's policies. The men of the backcountry bitterly resented the excise tax on whiskey, which would have been unnecessary but for the assumption measure and the resulting interest charges, and they loathed the revenue men who were trying to collect it. Late in August a conference of the protestors was held in Pittsburg, and at this a remonstrance to Congress and strong resolutions against the excise officers were adopted. Committees of correspondence were even set up, and the whole affair was reminiscent of the actions of the Patriots against British taxation before the American Revolution. There was a considerable difference in the temper of the times, however, and this was not a case of taxation without representation. Albert Gallatin afterwards had occasion to regret that he had signed these resolutions.[2]

Washington had no sympathy whatever with attempts to obstruct the operation of laws that had been passed under full constitutional authority, and regarded the proceedings as dangerous to the very existence of the federal government. Hence he drew a strong proclamation while still at Mount Vernon and sent it to the Secretary of State at Monticello for his signature. Jefferson suggested one minor alteration which Washington accepted. He wanted to leave out a phrase implying that this particular law was necessary and thus make the language more general without weakening its force. The omission was significant because he did not wholly like the law, but nevertheless he gave no countenance to resistance. "I am sincerely sorry to learn that such proceedings have taken place," he said; "and I hope the proclama-

[2] For the circumstances, see L. D. Baldwin, *Whiskey Rebels* (Philadelphia, Univ. of Pa. Press, 1939), pp. 85–86.

tion will lead the persons concerned into a regular line of application which may end either in an amendment of the law, if it needs it, or in their conviction that it is right."[3]

Things quieted down somewhat in western Pennsylvania during the next year, and when trouble afterwards arose Hamilton made the most of it, but the episode is mentioned here because of the effect it must have had on the mind of Washington. The time for him to retire from command was not when trouble threatened. He did not issue his valedictory, and by October, if not earlier, most leaders were confident he would not. He would stay in office a while longer – perhaps two years more, as Hamilton had suggested during the summer. That possibility may have made the Vice President's office seem more important to Hamilton, but at all events it was the only elective executive post that remained in any doubt and he interested himself actively in it, somewhat to the chagrin of John Adams.

Making a virtue of necessity, Hamilton was supporting the incumbent, and it now appears that he was exaggerating the possibility of his defeat. He viewed the political scene as a commander and offered Adams some gratuitous advice. Learning with pain that the Vice President did not plan to reach Philadelphia until late in the approaching session of Congress, and fearing that this would give a handle to misrepresentation, he urged him in the name of all his friends to lose no time in getting there. However indifferent Adams might be to the outcome of the election, Hamilton hoped he was not indifferent to the cause of good government, that is, his election over George Clinton, and assured him that his early presence would accord with the "firmness and elevation" of his character, and his disposition "to meet all events, whether auspicious or otherwise, on the ground where station and duty" called him. Adams had a right to regard the letter as presumptuous and he did not answer it. Even if he thought of himself as belonging to a party, he was not disposed to recognize Hamilton as the seat of authority in it; and he thought he was entitled to the office on grounds of his long and honorable service, just as Jefferson did.[4]

Hamilton interpreted the opposition to Adams as part of the effort of "factious men to introduce everywhere, and in every department, persons unfriendly to the measures, if not the constitution, of the national government." Before Congress assembled, he noted that

[3] The proclamation, bearing its original date of Sept. 15, 1792, but amended according to TJ's suggestion of Sept. 18 (Ford, VI, 113–114), is in Fitzpatrick, XXXII, 150–151.

[4] Hamilton to Adams, Sept. 9, 1792, in the latter's *Works,* VIII, 514–515.

the undercover campaign for the vice presidency was threatening to take a new direction. As an alternative to George Clinton, a man of "narrow and perverse politics," who had been "invariably the enemy of national principles," Aaron Burr – who had supplanted Hamilton's father-in-law General Philip Schuyler as Senator from New York – was being talked about. The Secretary of the Treasury had not yet fully made up his mind about Burr, he said, but he expressed his doubts about the young Senator's personal character and attributed to him no political principles whatever except to mount, by any means, to all the honors he could attain. From his vantage point in Philadelphia he sent warnings to South as well as North against these two New Yorkers, coupling them with another warning which was much less justifiable, namely, that the real plan might be to divide the votes of the Northern and Middle states and let Jefferson in by the votes of the South. Addressing General Charles Cotesworth Pinckney of South Carolina, who was corresponding pleasantly with Jefferson about this time on the subject of olive trees, he wrote:

> I will not scruple to say to you, in confidence, that this also would be a serious misfortune to the government. That gentleman whom I once *very much esteemed*, but who does not permit me to retain that sentiment for him, is certainly a man of sublimated and paradoxical imagination, entertaining and propagating opinions inconsistent with dignified and orderly government.

As a self-appointed commander he was mobilizing his forces on the whole field of battle, and his strategy was to define the issue as one between the administration and its opponents. It was never that clear-cut, but his critics played into his hands by supporting Clinton, who could easily be designated as an antifederalist. The republican leaders in Virginia appear to have been driven to this course by what they regarded as political necessity, for they would not support Burr, and could not support Jefferson under the existing circumstances.[5]

The proposal that Burr be backed instead of Clinton, who was reported to be relatively indifferent to the office, came from New Yorkers and was distinctly embarrassing to Monroe and Madison. Their main reason for objecting to this, and certainly the one they could most safely talk about, was that Burr was young and unproved. They could not justify the rejection of an old public servant like

[5] Hamilton to C. C. Pinckney, Oct. 10, 1792, and to John Steele, Congressman from N. C., Oct. 15, 1792 (Lodge, VIII, 286–290). See also Oliver Wolcott, Jr., to his father, Oct. 8, 1792 (Gibbs, I, 80).

Adams for a man like that, and they regarded the movement for Burr as "highly injudicious and improper." On the other hand, they did not want to risk offending their newly-won Northern allies and recognized that they must proceed with discretion. Presumably they were tactful, for they managed to stop the Burr boom and maintain the alliance.[6] They would undoubtedly have preferred to support Jefferson, but, besides his own objections, there were other insuperable obstacles – which Hamilton should have perceived. The Constitution required that one of the two votes each elector cast be for a person outside his own state, hence no Virginian could vote for both Washington and Jefferson. Furthermore, the dread of jealousy on the part of other states would make it unwise to urge him upon the electors elsewhere. He did get four votes from Kentucky, but the electors of both Virginia and New York gave their second vote for Clinton.

Jefferson himself remained entirely aloof from the conflict and probably continued to prefer Adams. If he did not actually urge anybody to support his old friend, who was intensely unpopular in Virginia, he gave him a good name whenever he had a favorable opportunity. One of the Virginia electors wrote him that the character he had given Adams as a man of wisdom and honesty had made him reluctant to vote against the Vice President, but that there was a unanimous desire in the delegation to remove him. While the outcome was still somewhat uncertain, Jefferson reported the situation to the American Minister in England as follows: "The occasion of electing a Vice President has been seized upon as a proper one for expressing the public sense on the doctrines of the monocrats. There will be a strong vote against Mr. Adams, but the strength of his personal worth and his services will, I think, prevail over the demerit of his political creed." This statement reflects his own attitude. He thought that the author of the *Discourses on Davila* deserved a rebuke, but was glad that his utterly honest and staunchly patriotic friend was re-elected.[7]

The real struggle for power occurred in the congressional elections, and these best reflected the conflict of opinion. Jefferson played no public part in defining issues, but Madison did, and certain simple

[6] Their attitudes toward the Burr complication are sufficiently indicated in the following letters: Monroe to Madison, Oct. 9, 1792 (S. M. Hamilton, I, 242–245, giving letter of John Nicholson to Madison, Oct. 3, 1792, in a footnote); Madison to Monroe, Oct. 11, 1792 (MP, 15:9).

[7] Archibald Stuart to TJ, Dec. 6, 1792; in "Glimpses of the Past: Correspondence of Thomas Jefferson, 1788–1926," *Missouri Historical Society* III (Apr.–June, 1936), p. 80; TJ to Thomas Pinckney, Dec. 3, 1792 (Ford, VI, 144).

statements of his, published anonymously in Freneau's newspaper, amounted to a party platform. Writing in September, Madison briefly sketched the history of American parties, and in effect dismissed the charge of "antifederalism" as irrelevant, since the term belonged in an era which ended with the regular establishment of the federal government under the new Constitution.[8] The present division of parties arose afterwards, he said, and he regarded it as a natural division, just as Jefferson did. On the one hand were those who favored the interests of the few rather than the many, and who hoped that, by means of the turn they gave the administration, the government itself would be narrowed into fewer hands and be approximated to an hereditary form. There was no reference here to specific measures, but there was clear reference to the trend of administration in the hands of Hamilton. The other division consisted of those who believed in the doctrine that men are capable of governing themselves, who hated hereditary power "as an insult to the reason and an outrage to the rights of man," and who were offended by measures not tending to preserve republican government. These were the "republicans," while others were the "antis." He did not call them "democrats," for that word was still thought to imply mob rule, but he was talking confidently of a people's party. Nothing was said here about financial questions as such, nothing about foreign policy. Madison sought to reduce the conflict to its essence, and the definition that he arrived at reflects the influence of Jefferson upon him. Jefferson's political genius lay in his ability to sense fundamental issues in the maze of complexities, and in this case the two friends thought as one.

The results of the congressional elections were generally known before the electoral vote was cast, and these were distinctly gratifying to the republicans. Since nobody wore an official party label, party gains and losses could not be tabulated with mathematical precision, but Jefferson noted with satisfaction that republicans had been elected in nine of the eleven districts of Pennsylvania, and said that the vote of that state generally turned the balance in the House of Representatives. He hoped for a time that Fisher Ames, "the colossus of the monocrats and paper men," might be defeated in Massachusetts, and rejoiced that Freneau's paper was now getting into that state under the patronage of John Hancock and Sam Adams. He believed that the body of the people were republican in sentiment practically everywhere, and had no doubt that the Third Congress would be less amenable to Hamilton's leadership than the Second had been. The

[8] "A Candid State of Parties," in *National Gazette*, Sept. 26, 1792 (Hunt, VI, 106–119).

Second Congress would remain in office until March, however, and as the members were returning to Philadelphia he wrote his son-in-law: "The less they do, and the more they leave to their successors, the better in my opinion." He did not have much hope that these particular men would be affected by the expression of public sentiment in the election, but he looked with calm confidence toward the more distant future.[9]

He revealed his optimism not merely to his son-in-law at home but also to representative Americans abroad when informing them of the domestic situation. In a private letter to Thomas Pinckney in England, early in the session, he summed things up as follows:

> . . . The elections for Congress have produced a decided majority in favor of the republican interest. They complain, you know, that the influence and patronage of the Executive is to become so great as to govern the Legislature. They endeavored a few days ago to take away one means of influence by condemning references to the heads of department. They failed by a majority of five votes. They were more successful in their endeavor to prevent the introduction of a new means of influence, that of admitting the heads of department to deliberate occasionally in the House in explanation of their measures. The proposition for their admission was rejected by a pretty general vote. *I think we may consider the tide of this government as now at the fullest, and that it will, from the commencement of the next session of Congress, retire and subside into the true principles of the Constitution.* An alarm has been endeavored to be sounded as if the republican interest was indisposed to the payment of the public debt. Besides the general object of the calumny, it was meant to answer the special one of electioneering. Its falsehood was so notorious that it produced little effect. They endeavored with as little success to conjure up the ghost of antifederalism, and have it believed that this and republicanism were the same, and that both were Jacobinism. But those who felt themselves republicans and federalists too, were little moved by this artifice; so that the result of the election has been promising.[10]

The heart of this passage lies in the sentence we have italicized, and this reveals Jefferson, not as an antifederalist, but as one who regarded the "true principles of the Constitution" as a protection against the encroachments of power from any direction. Consolidation had gone far enough, and he now believed that it would go no farther. Thus

[9] See especially his letters to T. M. Randolph, Jr., Nov. 2, 16, 1792 (Ford, VI, 128, 134).

[10] TJ to Thomas Pinckney, Dec. 3, 1792 (Ford, VI, 143–144). Italics mine.

the prospect pleased him as a constitutional republican who supremely distrusted Hamilton.

He was in a cheerful frame of mind as he proceeded with his own plans to retire from the government in March along with the Second Congress. By September the report of his approaching retirement had got out in Virginia and he himself confirmed it in occasional private letters. Writing one of his countrymen who regretted it, and from whom he was offering to buy a horse, he said — as he had so many times before — that he had never participated in public life from personal choice. "The times heretofore made it a duty to sacrifice one's wishes to a common cause," he continued. "The duty no longer exists, and I determined therefore some time ago to retire with the close of the Congress about to sit. It will be no loss to the public, and a great relief to me. The difficulty is no longer to find candidates for the offices, but offices for the candidates." [11]

He made a point of informing his official correspondents abroad about his personal intentions. In November he instructed the chief American representatives in Europe to address their official communications hereafter to the Secretary of State, not to him personally, since he might be at Monticello when their next letters came. About the same time he took up his plans for work at Monticello. He expected to make extensive alterations and hoped to begin digging a cellar in April. In December he informed Thomas Leiper that at the end of three months he would give up his lease, and he was now trying to get a new manager for his farm.[12] He sold some of his furniture that would not suit Monticello and started packing the rest early in the new year, little suspecting what another year had in store for him, for his party, for his country, and for the world.

Before leaving him in this state of blissful ignorance, we shall briefly anticipate the circumstances and events which combined to delay his return to Albemarle, and some of which decisively affected his whole later history. For one thing, his political friends pressed him not to leave the government just after he had been attacked, even though he had been so well defended. There was no official reason why he should go, for the President was only too glad for him to stay, and he reluctantly considered the possibility of remaining until summer.[13] Long

[11] TJ to Col. John Syme, Sept. 17, 1792 (LC, 13382), replying to a letter of Sept. 2 (MHS). See also TJ to Archibald Stuart, Sept. 9, 1792 (Ford, VI, 110).

[12] TJ to Stephen Willis, Nov. 12, 1792 (MHS), largely in *Garden Book*, p. 173; TJ to Thomas Leiper, Dec. 9, 1792 (MHS); TJ to Samuel Biddle, Dec. 12, 1792 (*Garden Book*, pp. 182–184).

[13] TJ to Martha, Jan. 26, 1793 (Ford, VI, 163–165).

before summer the official pressure became irresistible, for the world situation took several turns for the worse and his services seemed indispensable. The net result was that he remained through the entire year of 1793, facing the most arduous tasks of his secretaryship because of the general European war, which also had profound effects on the domestic political situation.

War had broken out on the Continent some months before, and by the summer of 1792 had practically paralyzed his own diplomatic activities. The struggle between revolutionary France and Austria and Prussia had aroused considerable interest in the United States, but not until Great Britain was drawn into the maelstrom in the new year did American interests become involved directly. The French King had been deposed in the late summer of 1792, and the Republic had been established early in the autumn, but news of these events was slow in reaching America and Louis XVI had not yet been executed. Developments abroad had entered into the American elections to only a slight degree. Some apprehension that zeal for liberty might be carried too far in America, as it already had in France, was expressed in Hamiltonian circles in connection with the threat of revolt in Pennsylvania, and there was some attempt to stigmatize the republicans as "Jacobins," but the issues of the campaign were still predominantly domestic. Political conflict was not yet highly colored by the emotions which the turmoil in Europe had created, though a close observer might have anticipated that it soon would be.

Late in the year, Hamilton's chief assistant in the Treasury wrote:

> We are waiting impatiently for news from France. Our Jacobins are indecisive while the fate of their brethren is in suspense. By a strange kind of reasoning, some suppose that the liberties of America depend on the right of cutting throats in France. . . . It is strange that we cannot be contented with our lot, which is certainly a good one, but must raise disquiets out of the quarrels of other nations.[14]

From this time forward, opposition to the policies and principles of Hamilton was associated by his partisans with the revolutionary spirit, and conservatives who were far from subservient to him rallied round him as a guardian of public order. On the other hand, Jefferson rejoiced with his republican fellows in French military victories, and believed at this time that the name of "Jacobins" could be assumed by them with pride.[15] On the first day of the new year the first of a series

[14] Oliver Wolcott, Jr., to Frederick Wolcott, Dec. 15, 1792 (Gibbs, I, 84–85).
[15] TJ to J. F. Mercer, Dec. 19, 1792 (Ford, VI, 147).

of popular demonstrations, following the declaration of the French Republic, was held in Philadelphia, and for a good many months the actions and successes of the French were an immense stimulus to republican zeal.[16] In American politics the French Revolution proved to be a two-edged sword, but at last the course of events enabled the conservatives to wield it more effectively than the liberals.

At the end of 1792, when the Secretary of State believed that he was nearing the close of his official life, he was actually entering upon a fresh phase of his country's history and his own service. His entire public life from this time on, with relatively brief intermissions, was to be cast on the background of world war. Foreign policy immediately assumed enhanced importance, and the events of the next year attested the wisdom of Washington in retaining both Jefferson and Hamilton in his official family, for between them a policy of genuine neutrality was hammered out. In a sense the duel between them was resumed on the foreign front, but it is a more significant fact that, in an hour of national emergency, the President was finally able to effect what might be called a truce.

The eternal feud did not lie in the foreign field, however, except as developments there related to the cause of human rights, and Jefferson was henceforth at a disadvantage on the home scene because of the vast confusion which foreign events engendered. He could not forget that the appeal to the rights of man, which he himself had made in the Declaration of Independence, had been taken up by the French first among the European peoples, but it was now obscured by the conflict of national interests and discredited by excesses. He had already observed among the leaders in his own country a reaction against the doctrines of the American Revolution, but he believed that this was checked by the congressional elections, and he had no doubt that the civilized world was moving in the direction he himself had pointed. The most striking difference between the phase of history which was passing and the one that was coming was that the cause which was dearest to his heart was now thrown on the defensive. Throughout the rest of this decade, he struggled against the current of counter-revolution in his own country, and gained both obloquy and fame as a consequence.

He could not have anticipated all this when he was looking forward so joyously to retirement and was viewing the domestic political prospect so confidently, and it was fortunate that he did not know what tests awaited him. Whatever the future might hold, he could look back on the past with satisfaction, for he had been far more than

[16] Scharf & Westcott, *Hist. of Philadelphia,* I, 472.

a devoted public servant and staunch supporter of the Union. He had kept the faith which he regarded as distinctively American while hoping it would become universal. He had never ceased to believe that men by right are free in their minds and persons, and that human society should guide its steps by the light of reason.

Acknowledgments

TO a very considerable extent the acknowledgments of help rendered and kindnesses shown me in connection with this book must duplicate those made in my earlier volume, *Jefferson the Virginian*, and for that reason I shall speak briefly here. I refer to specific individuals and institutions at various places in the notes and bibliography in such a way as to show my gratitude. No doubt there have been inadvertent omissions, but I trust that all of the acknowledgments added together will seem sufficient.

Nearly all of the research on this period of Jefferson's career that was not done in my own study, and much of the basic research on the period immediately following it (not yet written up), was done during the life of a grant from the Rockefeller Foundation. This grant also enabled me to free more of my time for writing. Hence I again express my sincere thanks to that great and generous Foundation and particularly to David H. Stevens, whose continuing interest in my task showed him to be not only a man of sympathetic understanding but also a man of unusual patience.

I am indebted to the Council for Research in the Social Sciences at Columbia University, and especially its former chairman, Professor Robert M. Haig, for grants for expenses over a period of several years. Various officials at Columbia co-operated in providing favorable working conditions, and a personal word of appreciation should go to my colleague in history, Dean John A. Krout.

In this volume I have availed myself of research work done in Paris years ago on a Sterling Senior Fellowship from Yale University. I hope the present and former officials of the University, especially President Emeritus Charles Seymour, will share my gratification that some crumbs of the bread they once cast upon the waters have at length returned.

As will appear from the reference to manuscript collections in the Bibliography, my major indebtedness is to the Library of Congress, the Alderman Library of the University of Virginia, and the Massachusetts Historical Society. In these repositories and institutions essentially the same people helped me with this volume as with its predecessor, and I will not repeat the long list here. Nor do I need to recur to the continuing kindness of the Editors in the Jefferson Office at Princeton, since my consciousness and appreciation of it may be assumed from the references to them in the Bibliography and elsewhere.

In the interim between volumes I have incurred a deep obligation to Howard C. Rice, Jr., head of the Department of Special Collections in the same Library. Besides providing valuable information in his own writings and furnishing some admirable illustrations, he has done me an extraordinary kindness by reading all the chapters in this book dealing with Jefferson's life in France and by making helpful comments on them.

Julian P. Boyd performed a similar service with respect to the chapter dealing with Jefferson's attitude toward the Constitution.

I want to say a special word of thanks to the following individuals, who do not fit into any of the groups already mentioned:

Edwin M. Betts of the University of Virginia, for suggestions growing out of his unrivaled knowledge of Jefferson's horticultural and agricultural interests, and for the privilege of looking at his edition of the Farm Book in advance of publication.

Mrs. Helen Duprey Bullock of Washington, for suggestions throughout the course of my work, especially with reference to Jefferson's personal life and musical interests.

Edward Dumbauld of Uniontown, Pennsylvania, for comments growing out of his extensive knowledge of Jefferson's legal activities and supplementing his admirable book about Jefferson's travels.

P. J. Federico of the United States Patent Office, for providing extensive printed materials on Jefferson's connection with patents and giving me the benefit of his expert counsel on this difficult technical subject.

Adrienne Koch of Washington, for continued suggestions, especially with respect to Jefferson's thought and his relations with Madison.

Philip Marsh, for sending me copies of many useful pamphlets and articles of his, dealing chiefly with the Freneau episode.

Theodore Sizer of Yale University, for valuable information about Trumbull's portraits and comments on art subjects.

Carleton Sprague Smith of New York, for information regarding Jefferson's interests and activities in the realm of music which I hope I can use more extensively in the future than I have been able to as yet.

E. Millicent Sowerby, for the privilege of looking at the materials she has collected at the Library of Congress respecting Jefferson's books, which I have been unable to utilize as fully as I had intended to.

Mrs. Marjorie M. Keith, for valuable research assistance in the Library of Congress, especially in newspapers.

John B. Stabler, for valuable aid in connection with bibliography and newspapers.

Mary W. Strickland, for devoted services as part-time secretary and the copyist of the first half of this volume.

Lucille Ogden, for copying the second half with unusual accuracy under circumstances of great pressure.

Finally, I wish to thank Douglas Southall Freeman again for his abiding interest in this undertaking and for further suggestions arising from his notable historical craftsmanship; I want to express my continued gratitude to my wise and patient publishers, Little, Brown and Company; and I must apologize again to my wife for taking myself out of this world so long in order to live in that of Jefferson and Washington and for proceeding more in the tempo of their age than in that of my own.

List of Symbols and Short Titles[1] Most Frequently Used in Footnotes

Account Book	Jefferson's informal account books, in various repositories. Cited by date only.
Adams, *Works*	*Works of John Adams*, ed. by C. F. Adams.
Annals	*Annals of Congress.*
A.H.R.	*American Historical Review.*
A.S.P.F.R.	*American State Papers, Foreign Relations*, ed. by Lowrie and Clark. References here to Vol. I (1833).
Bixby	*Thomas Jefferson Correspondence Printed from the Originals in the Collections of William K. Bixby.*
C.F.M.	"Correspondence of the French Ministers to the U. S., 1791–1797," *Ann. Report A.H.A. 1903*, Vol. II.
D.A.B.	*Dictionary of American Biography.*
D. C.	*Diplomatic Correspondence of the U. S., 1783–1789* (3 vols., 1837).
Domestic Life	*Domestic Life of Thomas Jefferson*, by Sarah N. Randolph.
Dumbauld	*Thomas Jefferson: American Tourist*, by Edward Dumbauld.
Fitzpatrick	*Writings of George Washington*, ed. by J. C. Fitzpatrick.
Ford	*Writings of Thomas Jefferson*, ed. by P. L. Ford (10 vols.).
Garden Book	*Thomas Jefferson's Garden Book*, annotated by E. M. Betts.
Gibbs	*Memoirs of the Administrations of Washington and John Adams*, ed. from the Papers of Oliver Wolcott by George Gibbs.

[1] Repositories are designated by Roman capitals run together, the names of editors and authors are in Roman type, and the abbreviated titles of printed works are in italics. Further details about these works, and about others frequently used but more easily identified from the references in the notes, are in the Select Critical Bibliography which follows. To avoid excess of italics in the lists, long titles are printed there in Roman.

HEH	Henry E. Huntington Library. Unless otherwise indicated, references are to the Jefferson manuscripts.
J. C. Hamilton	*Works of Alexander Hamilton*, ed. by J. C. Hamilton.
S. M. Hamilton	*Writings of James Monroe*, ed. by S. M. Hamilton.
Hunt	*Writings of James Madison*, ed. by Gaillard Hunt.
I.B.M.	"Instructions to the British Ministers to the U. S., 1791–1812," *Ann. Report A.H.A. 1936*, Vol. III.
J.P.	*Papers of Thomas Jefferson*, ed. by Julian P. Boyd (Princeton, 1950–).
JP	Jefferson Office in Princeton University Library and files for the Boyd edn.
L. & B.	*Writings of Thomas Jefferson*, ed. by Lipscomb & Bergh.
LC	Library of Congress. Unless otherwise indicated the references are to the Jefferson Papers there.
Lodge	*Works of Alexander Hamilton*, ed. by H. C. Lodge (10 vols.)
MHS	Massachusetts Historical Society. Unless otherwise indicated the references are to the Jefferson Papers in the Coolidge Collection.
MP	Papers of James Madison, Library of Congress.
Papers, MHS	*Jefferson Papers, Collections Massachusetts Historical Society*, 7 ser., I.
Randall	*Life of Thomas Jefferson*, by H. S. Randall.
UVA	Alderman Library, University of Virginia. Unless otherwise indicated the references are to the Jefferson manuscripts.
VSL	Virginia State Library.
Va. Mag.	*Virginia Magazine of History and Biography.*
W. & M.	*William and Mary Quarterly Historical Magazine.*

Select Critical Bibliography

A. *Manuscripts*

IN the first volume of this work I gave an account of the most important collections of Jefferson's papers bearing on the period of his life (1743–1784) covered by that volume. There is no need to repeat here the descriptive comments on those collections, and the information about the manuscript sources which is being made available in the successive volumes of *The Papers of Thomas Jefferson* (ed. by Julian P. Boyd at Princeton) will relieve future biographers of the necessity of describing either the collections or the manuscripts in detail. The published volumes of that work have not yet reached the years that are covered in this book (1784–1792), but I have again been privileged to check my own findings with the extensive files in Princeton.

The procedure of the biographer is necessarily selective, and in all periods of Jefferson's life except the first he is faced with an extreme embarrassment of riches. For the purposes of the present volume I have drawn most heavily on the collections in the Library of Congress (LC), the Massachusetts Historical Society (MHS), and the University of Virginia (UVA). The papers in the former repository that bear on the period are chiefly in Volumes 12–79, and are at least six times as numerous as those I went through while preparing *Jefferson the Virginian.* These papers are cited here by dates and by the folio numbers that are stamped on the documents. I have not cited the volume numbers, since there is no necessary permanence about the physical arrangement of this imperfectly arranged collection. The papers in the Massachusetts Historical Society and the University of Virginia are cited here by date only. As the notes will show, materials have been drawn from other collections of Jefferson manuscripts, but for this volume these three have been much the most important. I have not yet had occasion to draw extensively on the Missouri Historical Society, and such items as I have got from the National Archives in Washington have generally come through my friends in the Jefferson Office at Princeton.

* * *

The Account Books have continued to be invaluable. Since I cite these only by date, I should say here that the originals for this period are located as follows:

1784–1790 Massachusetts Historical Society
1791–1792 New York Public Library

I have been privileged to see in manuscript form the edition of the Farm Book which has been annotated by Edwin M. Betts, but this bears more on the next phase of Jefferson's life than on this one.

Of the manuscript papers of Jefferson's contemporaries, the most useful are those of James Madison, especially Volumes XII–XV in the Library of Congress (designated as MP). These are cited by the volume and folio numbers stamped on the documents. The Hamilton Papers in the same repository (for the years 1789–1792) have been rewarding, but not to the same degree. As the notes will show, various items have been found in other collections, such as those of William Short (Library of Congress), but in general it has seemed sufficient to rely on the printed writings of Jefferson's contemporaries. These comprise an enormous body of materials which, to the best of my knowledge, have never been fully exploited by any of his biographers.

B. *Jefferson's Published Writings*

All other printed collections are being superseded by the following work as its successive volumes appear:

The Papers of Thomas Jefferson. Julian P. Boyd, ed., Lyman H. Butterfield and Mina R. Bryan, asso. eds. (Princeton, Princeton University Press, 1950–).

Only three of the fifty-odd volumes that are projected have been published at this writing, and it will be some time before that edition reaches the period covered by this book. As I stated in the previous volume of this work, the chronological form of citation to which I have adhered will make reference to the great Princeton edition easy. Meanwhile, besides giving dates for all the sources cited, I am continuing to refer to existing printed collections by volume and page for the convenience of readers. I have cited printed sources wherever possible, for the same reason, and, as in my earlier volume, I have drawn chiefly on the two following collections:

The Writings of Thomas Jefferson. Paul Leicester Ford, ed. (10 vols., New York, G. P. Putnam's Sons, 1892–1899). The slight bias of the editor against Jefferson appears as the controversy with Hamilton develops, and he falls into some errors in dating documents, but this is the best of the older collections and is cited by preference.

The Writings of Thomas Jefferson. A. A. Lipscomb and A. E. Bergh, eds. (20 vols., Thomas Jefferson Memorial Asso., 1903). Larger but much less reliable than Ford.

The following smaller collections contain valuable materials:

The Jefferson Papers. Collections Massachusetts Historical Society, 7 ser., I (Boston, 1900).

Thomas Jefferson Correspondence. Printed from the Originals in the Collections of William K. Bixby. With notes by W. C. Ford (Boston, 1916).

Some Jefferson Correspondence, 1775–1787. W. C. Ford, ed. (reprinted from *New-England Historical and Genealogical Register*, 1901–1902). Letters to Jefferson, and more valuable for the previous period than this one.

The Letters of Lafayette and Jefferson. Introduction and notes by Gilbert Chinard (Baltimore, The Johns Hopkins Press, 1929).

Trois Amitiés Françaises de Jefferson, by Gilbert Chinard (Paris, 1927). Correspondence with Madame de Brehan, Madame de Tessé, and Madame de Corny.

Jefferson et les Idéologues, by Gilbert Chinard (Baltimore, The Johns Hopkins Press, 1925). Correspondence with Destutt de Tracy, Cabanis, J.-B. Say, and Auguste Comte, and more important for a later period than this one.

Glimpses of the Past. Correspondence of Thomas Jefferson, 1788–1826, Missouri Historical Society, Vol. III, April–June 1936, Nos. 4–6, pp. 77–133 (St. Louis, 1936). Chiefly valuable for a later period.

Thomas Jefferson and the National Capitol. Saul K. Padover, ed. (Washington, Government Printing Office, 1946). A convenient collection of notes and correspondence from various publications and repositories.

In this period, Henry S. Randall's *Life of Thomas Jefferson* (3 vols., New York, 1858) continues to serve to some extent as a source book, because of the letters and documents contained in it, as does Sarah N. Randolph's *Domestic Life* (New York, Harper and Bros., 1871) to a lesser degree.

Jefferson's own gardening activities were at a minimum during this period, but *Thomas Jefferson's Garden Book*, annotated by Edwin M. Betts (Philadelphia, American Philosophical Society, 1944), continues to be of great value because of the letters it contains.

Anyone desiring full and precise details regarding the literary history of Jefferson's only real book can consult with profit *A Further Check-list of the Separate Editions of Jefferson's Notes on the State of Vir-*

ginia, by Coolie Verner (Bibliographical Society of the University of Virginia, Charlottesville, 1950). When discussing the contents of the famous work I have cited the text in Ford, III, 68–295, for convenience of reference, but I am appending to this Bibliography a note on the publishing history of the English edition of 1787, which was too long to use in the body of this book, and I give below a list of the editions in this period:

Notes on the State of Virginia; Written in the Year 1781, Somewhat Corrected and Enlarged in the Winter of 1782, for the Use of a Foreigner of Distinction, in Answer to Certain Queries Proposed by Him . . . MDCCLXXXII. (Private printing in Paris, actually completed in May 1785.)

Observations sur la Virginie, par M. J. . . . Traduites de l'Anglois. (Paris, chez Barrois, l'aîné, 1786.) The translation by Morellet, actually printed in 1787.

Notes on the State of Virginia. Written by Thomas Jefferson. (London, printed for John Stockdale, 1787.) The most important edition. See Long Note following this Bibliography.

Notes on the State of Virginia. Written by Thomas Jefferson. (Philadelphia, 1788.) The first known American edition. Set from a pirated copy of the Stockdale edition. The next known American edition was in 1794.

While he was secretary of state, Jefferson began to make the memoranda which have come to be known as the "Anas." These have been treated as a distinct unit in editions of his collected writings (as in Ford, I, 154–339), on the ground that they do not lend themselves to chronological arrangement, and have even been published separately: *The Complete Anas of Thomas Jefferson*, F. B. Sawvel, ed. (New York, Round Table Press, 1903). In my opinion, such treatment is unfortunate if not actually unwarranted, since the memoranda were originally bound with Jefferson's official opinions as secretary of state, from which they have since been separated, and they give a false impression when made to stand alone. Furthermore, as private memoranda these entries lend themselves admirably to chronological arrangement. Without entering here into the question of Jefferson's own purposes with respect to these in his last years, I will merely say that I have utilized them for just what they were at the time he made them, that is, as private notes which reflected the mood of the moment rather than mature judgments. As such, I regard some of them as important, especially his records of conversations. The introduction to the "Anas," however, is of late date and lacks the value of a contemporary document. As the Long Note on Jefferson's account of the residence-assumption "bargain" (following this Bibliography) will show, records closer to the events themselves have been used whenever available.

C. *Official and Semiofficial Collections*

Diplomatic Correspondence of the United States, 1783–1789 (3 vols., Washington, 1837). Invaluable for the French period (referred to as *D. C.*).

American State Papers. Class I. Foreign Relations, ed. by Walter Lowrie and Matthew St. Clair Clarke. Only Vol. I (Washington, 1832) relates to this period (referred to as *A.S.P.F.R.*).

"Correspondence of the French Ministers to the United States, 1791–1797," ed. by Frederick J. Turner (referred to as *C.F.M.*), in Annual Report of the American Historical Association, 1903, Vol. II (1904).

"Instructions to the British Ministers to the United States, 1791–1812," ed. by Bernard Mayo (*I.B.M.*), in Annual Report of the American Historical Association, 1936, Vol. III (1941).

Treaties and Other International Acts of the United States of America, ed. by Hunter Miller, Vol. II, 1776–1818 (Washington, Government Printing Office, 1931).

Secret Journals of the Acts and Proceedings of Congress (4 vols., Boston, 1821), covering the years 1775–1788.

Journal of the Executive Proceedings of the Senate of the United States, Vol. I, 1789–1805 (Washington, 1828).

Debates and Proceedings in the Congress of the United States, Vols. I–III, 1789–1793 (1834). Better known as Annals of Congress.

Territorial Papers of the United States, ed. by Clarence E. Carter (4 vols., Washington, 1934–1936).

D. *Contemporary Writings*

1. CORRESPONDENCE AND DIARIES

ADAMS, ABIGAIL. Letters of Mrs. Adams, the Wife of John Adams, ed. by C. F. Adams (4th edn., Boston, 1848).

——. New Letters of Abigail Adams, 1788–1801, ed. by Stewart Mitchell (Boston, Houghton Mifflin Co., 1947).

ADAMS, JOHN. Works, ed. by C. F. Adams. 10 vols. (Boston, 1856).

ADAMS, JOHN QUINCY. Memoirs, ed. by C. F. Adams. Vol. I (Philadelphia, 1874).

——. Writings, ed. by W. C. Ford. 7 vols. (New York, Macmillan, 1913–1917).

ADAMS, MISS. See Smith, Abigail Adams.

AMES, FISHER. Works, with a Selection from His Speeches and Correspondence, ed. by Seth Ames. 2 vols. (Boston, 1854).

BURNETT, E. C., ed. Letters of Members of the Continental Congress. 8 vols. (Washington, Carnegie Institution, 1921–1936). Of less value in this period of Jefferson's life than in the previous one.

GIBBS, GEORGE. See Wolcott, Oliver.

HAMILTON, ALEXANDER. Works, ed. by John C. Hamilton. 7 vols. (New York, 1850–1851). Supplemented but not superseded by the Lodge edn.

——. Works, ed. by Henry Cabot Lodge. 9 vols. (New York, 1885–1886). Indispensable but badly arranged and edited in an extremely partisan spirit.

HOUDETOT, MADAME DE. Les Amitiés Américaines de Madame d'Houdetot, by Gilbert Chinard (Paris, 1923).

JAY, JOHN. Correspondence and Public Papers, ed. by Henry P. Johnston. 4 vols. (1890–1892).

KING, RUFUS. Life and Correspondence, ed. by Charles R. King. Vol. I, 1755–1794 (New York, 1894). One of the best sources for the opinions of Hamilton's partisans.

LAFAYETTE, MARQUIS DE. Letters of Lafayette and Washington, ed. by Louis Gottschalk (privately printed, New York, 1944).

——. Mémoires, Correspondance et Manuscrits du Général Lafayette. 6 vols. (London, 1837).

LA ROCHEFOUCAULD, DUC DE. La Correspondance du Duc de La Rochefoucauld d'Enville et de George Louis Le Sage (Paris, Leclerc, 1918).

L'ENFANT, PIERRE CHARLES. L'Enfant and Washington, 1791–1792, Published and Unpublished Documents Now Brought Together for the First Time, by Elizabeth S. Kite (Baltimore, The Johns Hopkins Press, 1929).

MACLAY, WILLIAM. The Journal of William Maclay, United States Senator from Pennsylvania, 1789–1791, introduction by Charles A. Beard (New York, Albert & Charles Boni, 1927). This vivid diary reflects the first strong hostility to Hamilton.

MADISON, JAMES. Writings, ed. by Gaillard Hunt. 9 vols. (New York, 1900–1910). Inconveniently arranged and considerably less than complete, but indispensable.

MONROE, JAMES. Writings, ed. by S. M. Hamilton. 7 vols. (New York, 1898–1903).

MORRIS, GOUVERNEUR. A Diary of the French Revolution, ed. by Beatrix Cary Davenport. 2 vols. (Boston, Houghton Mifflin Co., 1939).

PAINE, THOMAS. Complete Writings, collected and ed. by Philip S. Foner. 2 vols. (New York Citadel Press, 1945).

——. Writings, ed. by Moncure D. Conway. Vols. II, III (New York, 1894).

RUSH, BENJAMIN. The Autobiography of Benjamin Rush, ed. by George W. Corner (Princeton, Princeton University Press for American Philosophical Society, 1948). "Travels through Life" and "Commonplace Books."

SMITH, ABIGAIL ADAMS. Journal and Correspondence of Miss Adams, Daughter of John Adams, ed. by Her Daughter (New York, 1841).

SMITH, WILLIAM LOUGHTON. Journal of William Loughton Smith, 1790–1791, ed. by Albert Matthews (Cambridge, University Press, 1917), from Proceedings of the Massachusetts Historical Society (also in the published *Proceedings*, LI, 1918, pp. 20–88). Journal of the trip of Washington and his party to Rhode Island.

WASHINGTON, GEORGE. Diaries, ed. by J. C. Fitzpatrick. Vol. IV, 1789–1799 (Boston and New York, Houghton Mifflin Co., 1925).

———. Washington's Farewell Address, ed. by Victor H. Paltsits (New York, New York Public Library, 1935). Valuable for this volume because of the documents bearing on Washington's proposed retirement in 1792.

———. Writings, ed. by J. C. Fitzpatrick. 39 vols. (Washington, Government Printing Office, 1931–1941). This period is covered by Vols. XXVII–XXXII, and these have been indispensable to this study.

WOLCOTT, OLIVER. Memoirs of the Administrations of Washington and John Adams, ed. from the Papers of Oliver Wolcott by George Gibbs. 2 vols. (New York, 1846). Because of the letters, comparable with King as a source of Hamiltonian opinion.

2. TRAVELS AND REMINISCENCES

CHASTELLUX, MARQUIS DE. Voyages . . . dans l'Amérique Septentrionale dans les années 1780, 1781 et 1782. 2 vols. (Paris, 1786).

GRIMM, BARON DE. Historical and Literary Memoirs and Anecdotes, Selected from the Correspondence of Baron de Grimm . . . between the Years 1770 and 1790. Vol. II (London, 1814, trans. from the French).

MAZZEI, PHILIP. Memoirs of the Life and Peregrinations of the Florentine Philip Mazzei, 1730–1816, trans. by Howard R. Marraro (New York, Columbia University Press, 1942).

MORELLET, ANDRÉ. Mémoires de L'Abbé Morellet. 2 vols. (Paris, 1821).

TRUMBULL, JOHN. Autobiography, Reminiscences and Letters (New York, 1841).

E. *Newspapers, Periodicals, and Contemporary Pamphlets*

Newspapers are of very slight importance in a study of the career of Jefferson until after he became secretary of state, and of no great importance until 1791. During the period that he was in France, American affairs were discussed less in gazettes than in literary journals. As the notes show, two of the latter proved to have some value:

L'Année Litteraire (Paris).

Mercure de France (Paris), of which Charles J. Panoucke had the *privilège*.

In a dissertation on Jeffersonian journalism (listed among secondary works) which I had a small share in directing and was privileged to read, Donald H. Stewart has made abundantly clear the importance of newspapers in the development of Jefferson's party. Even in terms of the party, however, the important period did not begin until the fall of 1791, and the great time of newspaper controversy was from 1792 onward. During Jefferson's secretaryship, the following papers have seemed most important, as representing conflicting opinions:

[New York] Gazette of the United States (Apr. 15, 1789–Oct. 13, 1790), published by John Fenno.

[Philadelphia] Gazette of the United States, published at the new seat of the government by the same John Fenno, beginning in the fall of 1790. This was regarded by the critics of Hamilton as subservient to him.

[Philadelphia] National Gazette, established by Philip Freneau, Oct. 31, 1791, and described at length in the text.

[Philadelphia] General Advertiser, published by Benjamin F. Bache. Not so important through 1792 as it became later as the *Aurora.*

Newspapers copied one another freely in this period, hence important news items and communications kept reappearing. The controversial tracts generally appeared in newspapers first, but the two following, which are of considerable importance with respect to Jefferson, were used by me in pamphlet form:

Strictures and Observations upon the Three Executive Departments (1792), by Massachusettensis.

The Politics and Views of a Certain Party, Displayed (1792), now known to have been written by William Loughton Smith.

As the notes show, many of the communications of important public men to the newspapers can now be seen in their published writings. This is not always the case, however, and I am particularly indebted to:

Philip M. Marsh, ed., Monroe's Defense of Jefferson and Freneau against Hamilton (Oxford, Ohio, 1948), containing extracts from Hamilton's attacks, and "The Vindication of Mr. Jefferson."

F. *Secondary Works and Articles*[1]

AMMON, HARRY. The Republican Party in Virginia, 1789 to 1824 (Doctoral dissertation, University of Virginia, 1948).

BEMIS, SAMUEL FLAGG. "John Jay," and "Thomas Jefferson," in *American Secretaries of State and their Diplomacy*, ed. by S. F. Bemis, vols. I, II (New York, Knopf, 1927).

——. Jay's Treaty. A Study in Commerce and Diplomacy (New York, Macmillan, 1924).

[1] This very select list contains the titles of indispensable works and others to which I am specially indebted.

BEMIS, SAMUEL FLAGG. Pinckney's Treaty. A Study of America's Advantage from Europe's Distress (Baltimore, The Johns Hopkins Press, 1926).

BEVERIDGE, ALBERT J. The Life of John Marshall. 4 vols. (Boston, Houghton Mifflin, 1916–1919.) Requires considerable correction with respect to Jefferson.

BOORSTIN, DANIEL J. The Lost World of Thomas Jefferson (New York, Holt, 1948).

BOWERS, CLAUDE G. Jefferson and Hamilton (Boston and New York, Houghton Mifflin, 1925).

BRANT, IRVING. James Madison [II]: The Nationalist. 1780–1787. (Indianapolis and New York, Bobbs-Merrill, 1948.)

——. James Madison [III]: Father of the Constitution. 1787–1800. (1950.)

BROWNE, CHARLES A. Thomas Jefferson and the Scientific Trends of His Time (Chronica Botanica Co., Waltham, Mass., Nov. 1943).

BRYAN, WILHEMUS B. A History of the National Capital, I, 1790–1814 (New York, Macmillan, 1914).

BULLOCK, HELEN DUPREY. My Head and My Heart: A Little Chronicle of Thomas Jefferson and Maria Cosway (New York, Putnam's, 1945). Contains a number of previously unpublished letters.

BURT, A. L. The United States, Great Britain, and British North America (New Haven, Yale University Press, 1940).

CHARAVAY, ETIENNE. Le Général La Fayette, 1757–1835. Notice Biographique. (Paris, 1898).

CHINARD, GILBERT. Honest John Adams (Boston, Little, Brown, 1933).

——. Thomas Jefferson, The Apostle of Americanism (Boston, Little, Brown, 1939).

COMETTI, ELIZABETH, ed. "Mr. Jefferson Prepares an Itinerary," *Journal of Southern History*, XII, 89–106 (February, 1946). Travel notes for John Rutledge, Jr., and Thomas Lee Shippen.

CONWAY, MONCURE D. Omitted Chapters of History Disclosed in the Life and Papers of Edmund Randolph (New York and London, Putnam's, 1888).

CRÈVECŒUR, ST. JEAN. Lettres d'un Cultivateur Américain. 3 vols. (Paris, 1787.)

DAVIS, JOSEPH S. Essays in the Earlier History of American Corporations. (Harvard Economic Studies, Vol. XVI.) 2 vols. (Cambridge, Harvard University Press, 1917.) Invaluable for the financial operations of the 1790's.

DUMBAULD, EDWARD. Thomas Jefferson: American Tourist (Norman, University of Oklahoma Press, 1946). An admirable account of Jefferson's travels.

DUNBAR, LOUISE B. A Study of "Monarchical" Tendencies in the United States, from 1776 to 1801. (University of Illinois Studies in the Social Sciences, X, 1922, 1–164.)

EAST, ROBERT A. "The Massachusetts Conservatives in the Critical Era," in Richard B. Morris, ed., *The Era of the American Revolution*, pp. 349–391. (New York, Columbia University Press, 1939.)

FAŸ, BERNARD. The Revolutionary Spirit in France and America (New York, Harcourt, Brace, 1927).

FORMAN, SAMUEL E. The Political Activities of Philip Freneau. (The Johns Hopkins Studies in Historical and Political Science, Series XX, Nos. 9–10; Baltimore, The Johns Hopkins Press, 1902.)

GARLICK, RICHARD CECIL, JR. Philip Mazzei, Friend of Jefferson. (The Johns Hopkins Studies in Romance Literatures and Languages, extra vol. VII; Baltimore, The Johns Hopkins Press, 1933.)

GOTTSCHALK, LOUIS. Lafayette and the Close of the American Revolution (Chicago, University of Chicago Press, 1942).

——. Lafayette between the American and the French Revolution (Chicago, University of Chicago Press, 1950).

GRAHAM, GERALD S. Sea Power and British North America, 1783–1820 (Cambridge, Harvard University Press, 1941).

HAMILTON, JOHN C. History of the Republic . . . as Traced in the Writings of Alexander Hamilton and His Contemporaries, Vols. IV, V (New York, 1859–1860). Amounts to an official history and is the actual source of many continuing traditions about the Hamilton-Jefferson controversy.

HART, JAMES. The American Presidency in Action, 1789 (New York, Macmillan, 1948).

HELLMAN, C. DORIS. "Jefferson's Efforts towards the Decimalization of the United States Weights and Measures," *Isis*, Vol. XVI (November, 1931), pp. 266–314.

HUMPHREYS, FRANCIS L. Life and Times of David Humphreys. 2 vols. (New York, Putnam's, 1917.)

HUNT, GAILLARD. The Department of State of the United States (New Haven, Yale University Press, 1914).

IRWIN, RAY W. Diplomatic Relations of the United States and the Barbary Powers (Chapel Hill, University of North Carolina Press, 1931).

KIMBALL, FISKE. "The Life Portraits of Jefferson and Their Replicas," Proceedings American Philosophical Society, Vol. 88, No. 6 (December, 1944), pp. 497–534.

——, Thomas Jefferson, Architect (Boston, 1916).

KIMBALL, MARIE. The Furnishings of Monticello (1940).

——. Jefferson: The Scene of Europe, 1784 to 1789 (New York, Coward-McCann, 1950).

KOCH, ADRIENNE. Jefferson and Madison: The Great Collaboration (New York, Knopf, 1950).

LEARY, LEWIS. That Rascal Freneau: A Study in Literary Failure (New Brunswick, Rutgers University Press, 1941).

LEFEBVRE, GEORGES. The Coming of the French Revolution, trans. by R. R. Palmer (Princeton, Princeton University Press, 1947).

McCARRELL, DAVID K. The Formation of the Jeffersonian Party in Virginia (doctoral dissertation, Duke University, 1937).

MARSH, PHILIP M. "John Beckley, Mystery Man of the Early Jeffersonians," in *Pennsylvania Magazine of History and Biography*, January, 1948.

——. "Randolph and Hamilton," in *Pennsylvania Magazine of History and Biography*, July, 1948.

——, "Jefferson and Freneau," in *American Scholar*, Vol. XVI, No. 2 (Spring, 1947). Other valuable articles of his dealing with the Freneau episode are cited in the footnotes.

MONAGHAN, FRANK. John Jay, Defender of Liberty (New York and Indianapolis, Bobbs-Merrill, 1935).

RICE, HOWARD C. L'Hôtel de Langeac, Jefferson's Paris Residence, 1785–1789 (Paris and Monticello, 1947).

ROWLAND, KATE MASON. The Life of George Mason. 2 vols. (New York and London, 1892.)

SCHACHNER, NATHAN. Alexander Hamilton (New York, Appleton-Century, 1946).

SCHAPIRO, J. SALWYN. Condorcet and the Rise of Liberalism (New York, Harcourt, Brace, 1934).

SETSER, VERNON G. The Commercial Reciprocity Policy of the United States, 1774–1829 (Philadelphia, University of Pennsylvania Press, 1937).

SHEPPERSON, ARCHIBALD BOLLING. John Paradise and Lucy Ludwell of London and Williamsburg (Richmond, Dietz Press, 1942).

STEWART, DONALD H. Jefferson Journalism, 1790–1801 (doctoral dissertation, Columbia University, 1950).

VAN DOREN, CARL. Benjamin Franklin (New York, Viking Press, 1945).

WHITE, LEONARD D. The Federalists: A Study in Administrative History. (New York, Macmillan.) An exceedingly valuable study from a fresh point of view.

WOOLERY, WILLIAM K. The Relation of Thomas Jefferson to American Foreign Policy (The Johns Hopkins University Studies in Historical and Political Science, XLV, No. 2, 1927).

Long Note on the English Edition of *Notes on the State of Virginia*

SINCE all other editions of the *Notes* in Jefferson's lifetime were based on the English edition of 1787, the publishing history of this is of special interest. On Aug. 8, 1786, John Stockdale, a well-known printer, publisher, and bookseller whom Jefferson had undoubtedly met when he was in London and from whom he was regularly ordering books, wrote him that he was thinking of printing the *Notes,* which were highly spoken of in England except for the parts relating to that country (MHS). Since only a very few copies of the private printing had gone to England the question is just what persons Stockdale had heard talking. He may have been speaking for himself chiefly, but presumably he referred to the matter again. Writing him on Feb. 1, 1787 [1] Jefferson said Stockdale had two or three times proposed the printing of the *Notes.* By that time the author had decided to let the original appear, since a translation was coming out; he had corrected a copy and made some additions; and he had had a map engraved which he thought more valuable than the book. If Stockdale would like to print the work he would send him the corrected copy and, later on, the plate of the map. Having gone to the expense of the latter, he expected to be paid for it at the rate of a shilling for each map that Stockdale might use.

Stockdale replied on Feb. 13, 1787 that he would print 500 copies.[2] On Feb. 27, Jefferson wrote that he was sending the corrected copy by tomorrow's diligence and urged the most careful proofreading, especially of the tables, in order that there should be perfect accuracy.[3] He himself was having the plate for the map corrected. In an earlier letter to W. S. Smith [4] he said that he had found 172 errors in two thirds of it and expected about 250 in the whole; and Short, in whose hands he left the matter when he went into the south of France, wrote of going over corrections and spoke of 63 errors.[5] Writing Stockdale, Jefferson described the map as "very particular, made on the best

[1] Ford, III, 76–77.
[2] *Papers, MHS,* p. 25.
[3] Ford, III, 77.
[4] Jan. 15, 1787 (LC, 4705–4706).
[5] Short to TJ, Nov. 12, 1787 (LC, 4897–4898).

materials which exist" and being of a very convenient size. He thought it would make the book sell, and recommended that 400 copies be printed for the American market, 200 to go to Richmond and 200 to Philadelphia. In the preface, which he dated Feb. 27, 1787, he was modest about the work itself. "The subjects are all treated imperfectly; some scarcely touched upon," he said. Some of the imperfections could be justly attributed to the time and circumstances under which the work was first done, he thought, but most of them to the want of talents and information in the writer. But he now offered them to the public – for the first time, actually – and permitted the work to appear openly over his own name.

Stockdale printed his entire edition in three weeks, according to Jefferson, but because of the dilatoriness and negligence of the French printer (Barrois) to whom the plate had been sent for the printing of maps for Jefferson and Morellet, he did not get the plate until July, after Jefferson had returned from the south of France.[6] The latter had bound copies in August, 1787. Stockdale thought the delay detrimental to sales, since the book business was not good in the summer, and he sought a reduction in the charge for the use of the plate on the claim that it was worn; he was sending copies of the "advertisement" (preface) to seventy or eighty papers in England and Scotland at a cost of more than thirty pounds, which he hoped the sale would repay. Before he could ship his 400 copies to America, he was disturbed further by the report that the work had been printed in Philadelphia.[7] Jefferson doubted this report, which afterwards was proved to be erroneous, although a pirated edition, inferior to Stockdale's and without a map, did appear there in 1788.

The Stockdale edition contained, besides the map, appendices including the notes of Charles Thomson which Jefferson prized so highly, his own draft of a constitution for Virginia, and the Virginia act establishing religious freedom. Years later he prepared and published an appendix on the Logan affair, and he left corrections of the text which were utilized in the edition of 1853, long after his own death, but the text of all later editions in his lifetime followed that of Stockdale.

[6] TJ to Morellet, July 2, 1787, in Ford, III, 77–78; Stockdale to TJ, July 10, 1787 in *Papers, MHS,* p. 26.

[7] To TJ, Aug. 3, 1787 (*Papers, MHS,* p. 29).

Long Note on Jefferson's Accounts of the Residence-Assumption "Bargain"[1]

I KNOW of no account of the "bargain" that is contemporaneous with the events themselves in the papers of Jefferson, Madison, or Hamilton, though some such document may one day be found. Nor does the affair seem to be referred to in any of the contemporary letters of these men, all of whom kept their counsel well. The story as customarily told in biographies and works of history is based on Jefferson's later accounts of it. Writers have often had recourse to the extended story he told in a sort of introduction to the "Anas,"[2] which he himself dated Feb. 4, 1818. This was nearly twenty-eight years after the events and he was almost seventy-five years old. It reflects the strong resentment he still felt at the injustice that had been done him in John Marshall's *Life of Washington*, and is exceedingly bitter toward Hamilton. Its extravagant phrases lend themselves to quotation because of their vividness, and they have kept reappearing in books of history. This account is hard to reconcile with contemporary letters, however, and a more credible story is available. Unfortunately, this is undated,[3] but internal evidence leads to the opinion that it was certainly written after the establishment of the Bank of the United States in 1791, presumably before Jefferson's own presidency, and probably while Hamilton was at the height of his influence in the Washington administration. Jefferson may have written it about the time he left that administration, that is, late in 1793 or early in 1794. At all events, it should probably be dated within a few years of the events described, and it seems the best available source of information about his own part in the transaction. He was generally an accurate reporter when he did not wait too long to make his records, and I see no reason why he should not be trusted in this instance.

[1] If this note had been inserted in the body of this work, as it would have been but for its length, it would have been Note 38, ch. XVI.

[2] Ford I, 154–168, esp. pp. 162–164.

[3] LC, 41531, printed in Ford, VI, 172–174, with the conjectural date of February, 1793.

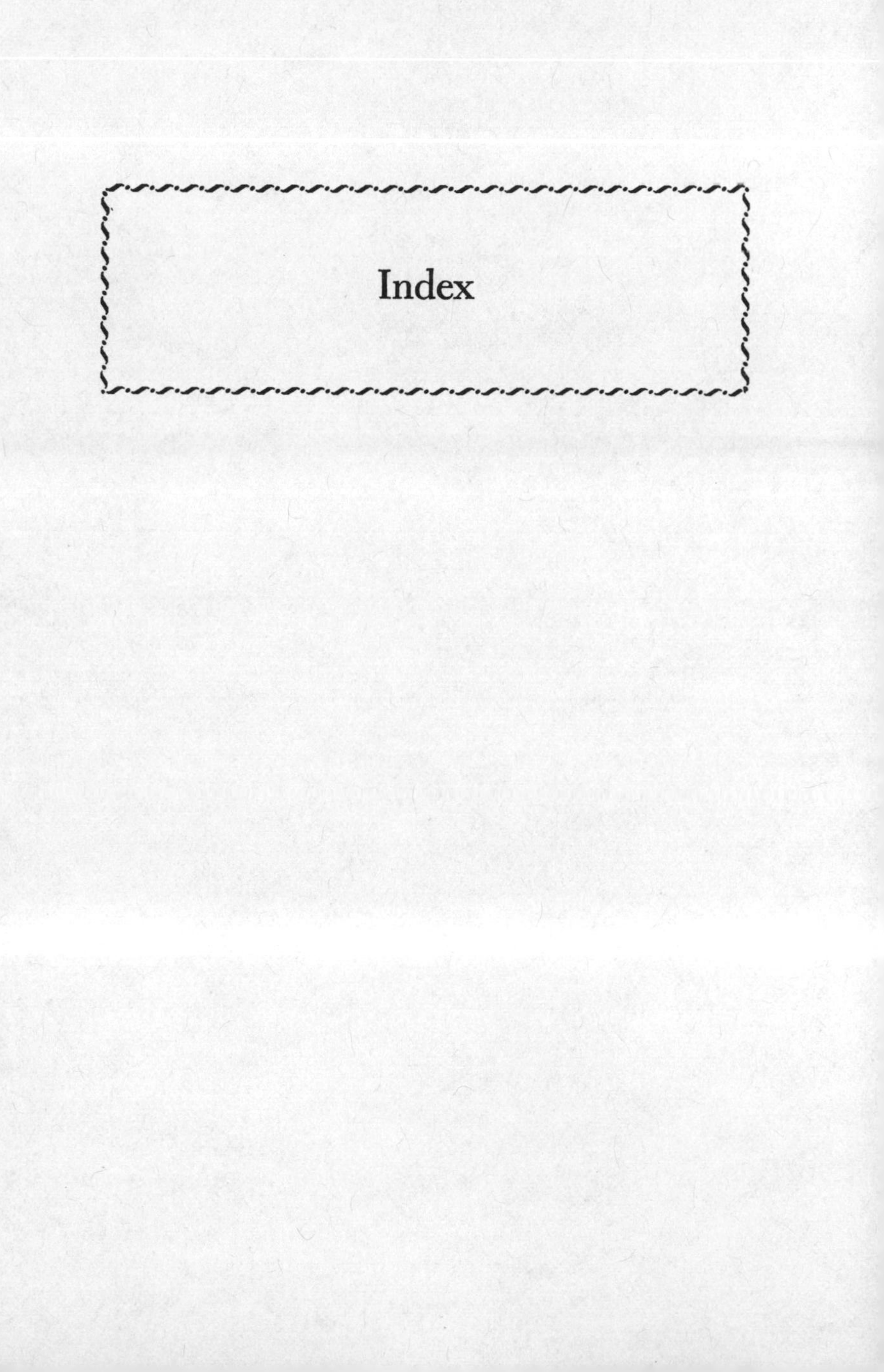

Index

Index

Public Career